THE VAGABOND VALISE

First English Edition
Translation by Rupert Bottenberg
Production assistance by Noah van Nostrand

Printed by IMAGO in China

Library and Archives Canada Cataloguing in Publication

Siris
[Vogue la valise. English]
The vagabond valise / Siris ; Rupert Bottenberg, translator.

Translation of: Vogue la valise.
ISBN 978-1-77262-027-6 (softcover)

1. Comics (Graphic works). I. Bottenberg, Rupert, translator
II. Title. III. Title: Vogue la valise. English.

PN6734.V624S5713 2018 741.5'971 C2018-902979-X

Part of the BDANG Imprint from Conundrum Press
Conundrum Press
Wolfville, Nova Scotia, Canada
www.conundrumpress.com

Conundrum Press acknowledges the financial assistance of the Canada Council for the Arts, the Government of Canada, and the Nova Scotia Creative Industries Fund toward this publication. We acknowledge the financial support of the Government of Canada through the National Translation Program for Book Publishing, an initiative of the Roadmap for Canada's Official Languages 2013-2018: Education, Immigration, Communities, for our translation activities.

Canada Council for the Arts Conseil des Arts du Canada NOVA SCOTIA Canada

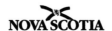

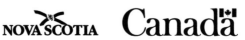

THE VAGABOND VALISE

SIRIS

CHAPTER 1

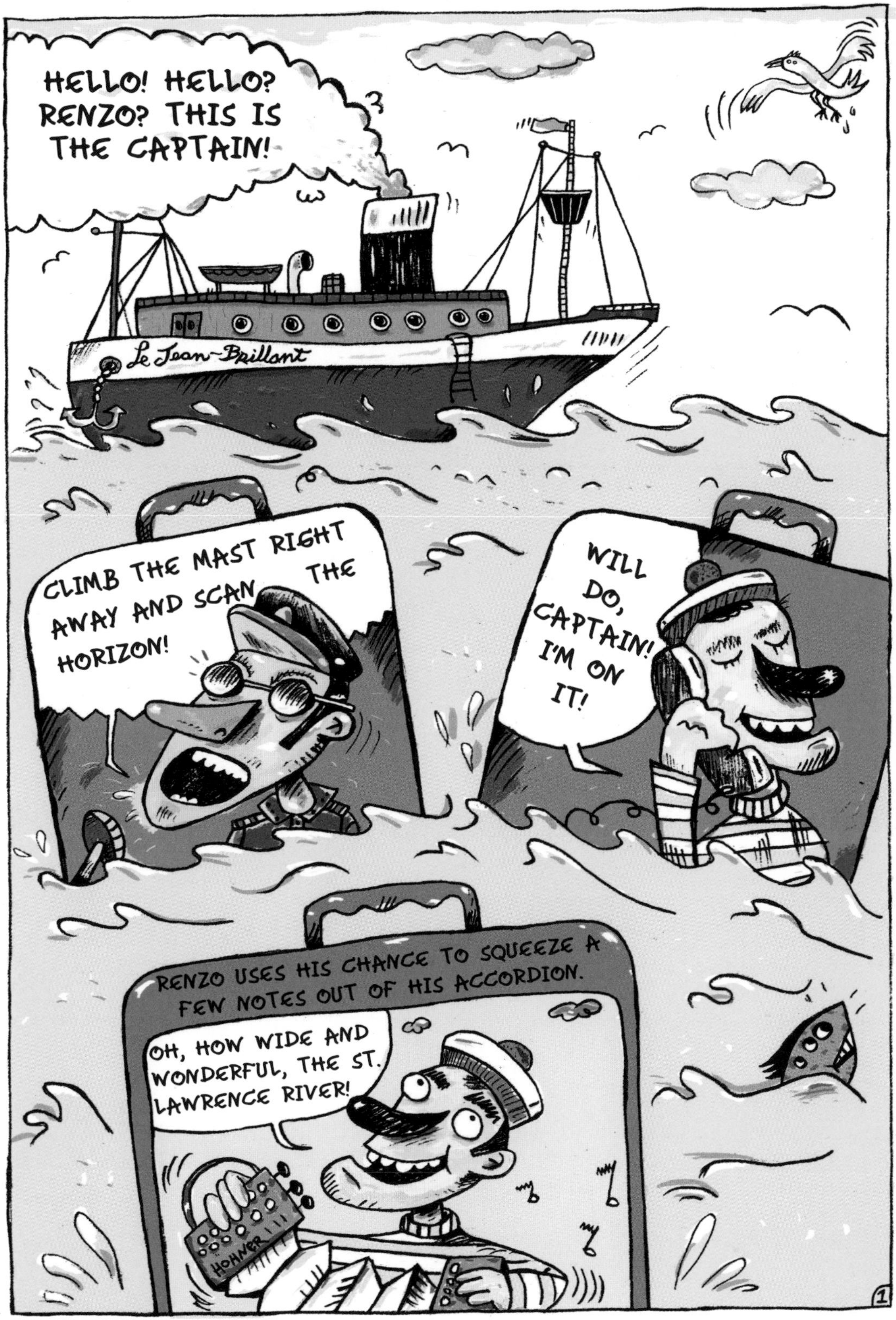
HELLO! HELLO? RENZO? THIS IS THE CAPTAIN!
Le Jean-Brillant
CLIMB THE MAST RIGHT AWAY AND SCAN THE HORIZON!
WILL DO, CAPTAIN! I'M ON IT!
RENZO USES HIS CHANCE TO SQUEEZE A FEW NOTES OUT OF HIS ACCORDION.
OH, HOW WIDE AND WONDERFUL, THE ST. LAWRENCE RIVER!
HOHNER
1

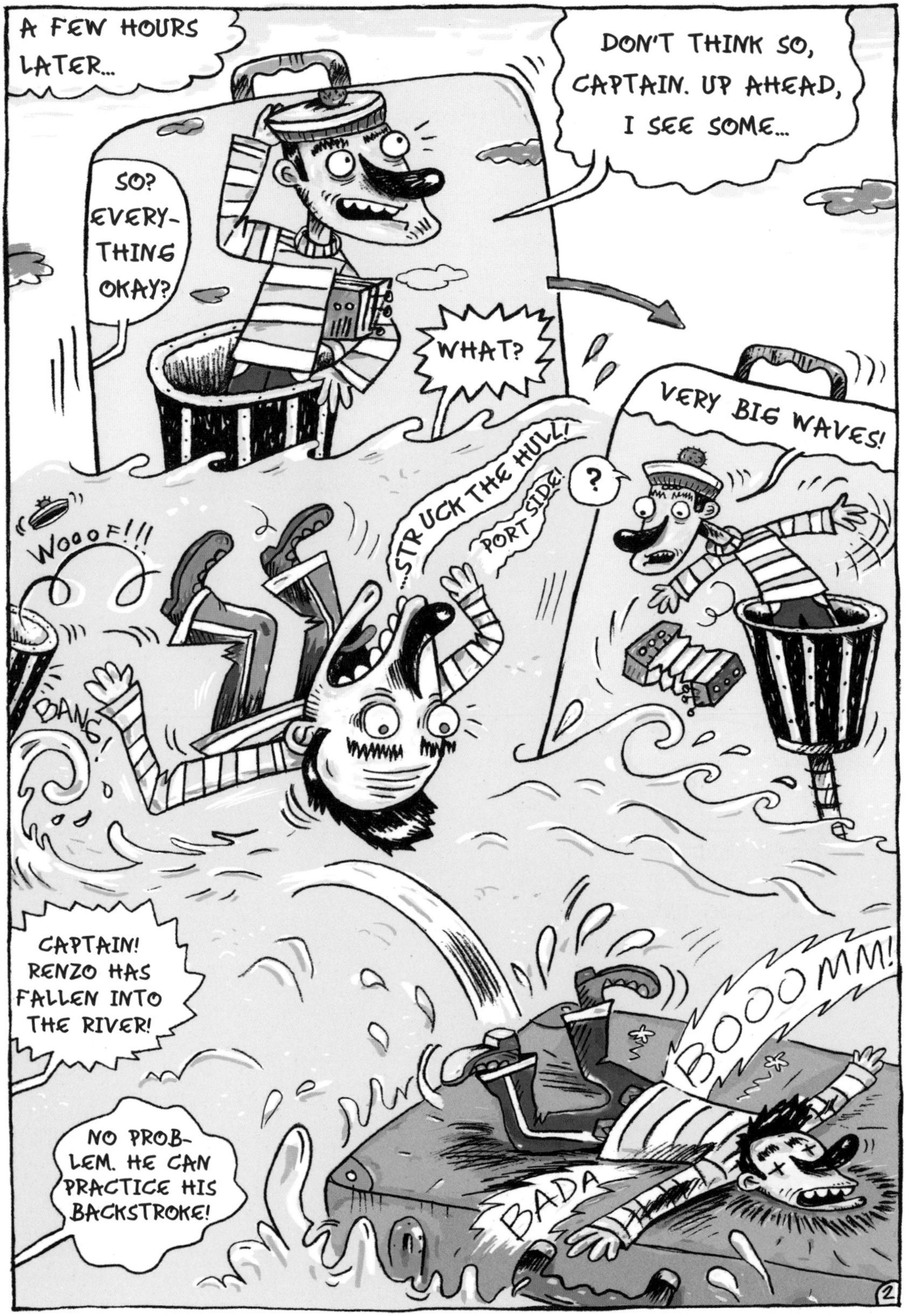
A FEW HOURS LATER...
SO? EVERY-THING OKAY?
DON'T THINK SO, CAPTAIN. UP AHEAD, I SEE SOME...
WHAT?
VERY BIG WAVES!
?
WOOOF!!!
...STRUCK THE HULL!
PORT SIDE!
BANG!
CAPTAIN! RENZO HAS FALLEN INTO THE RIVER!
NO PROB-LEM. HE CAN PRACTICE HIS BACKSTROKE!
BADA
BOOOOMM!
2

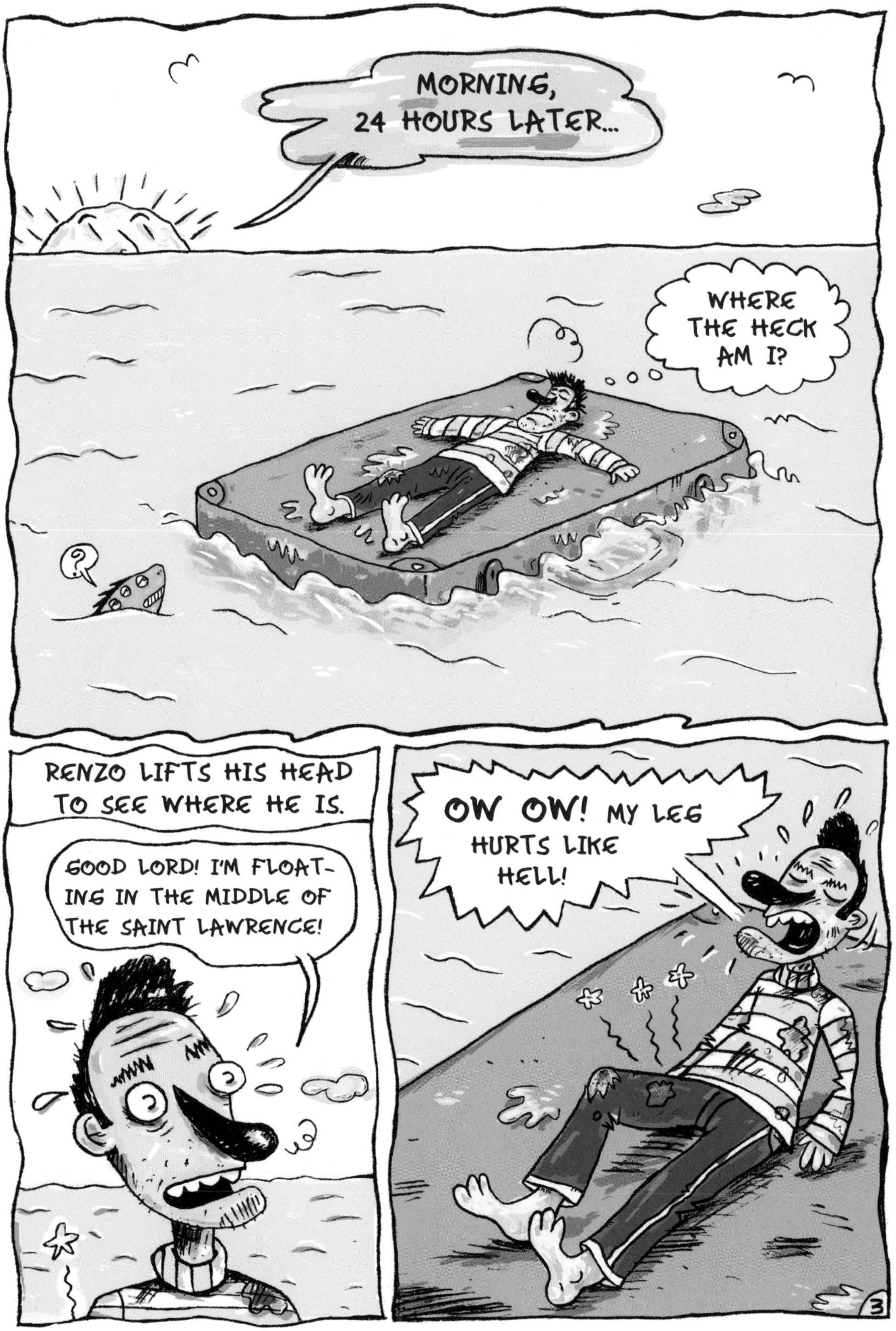
MORNING, 24 HOURS LATER...
WHERE THE HECK AM I?
RENZO LIFTS HIS HEAD TO SEE WHERE HE IS.
GOOD LORD! I'M FLOATING IN THE MIDDLE OF THE SAINT LAWRENCE!
OW OW! MY LEG HURTS LIKE HELL!
3

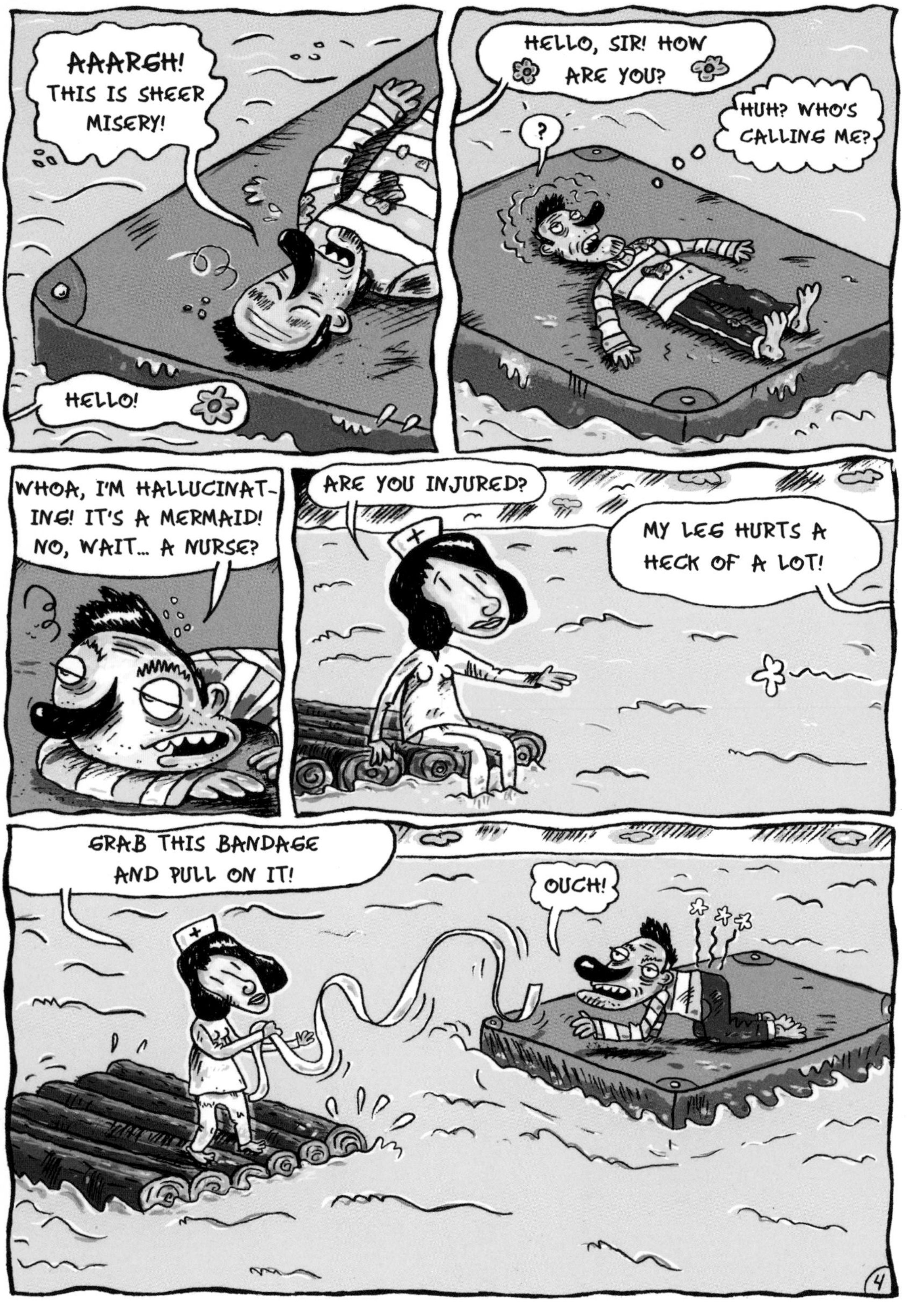
AAARGH! THIS IS SHEER MISERY!
HELLO!
HELLO, SIR! HOW ARE YOU?
?
HUH? WHO'S CALLING ME?
WHOA, I'M HALLUCINAT-ING! IT'S A MERMAID! NO, WAIT... A NURSE?
ARE YOU INJURED?
MY LEG HURTS A HECK OF A LOT!
GRAB THIS BANDAGE AND PULL ON IT!
OUCH!
4

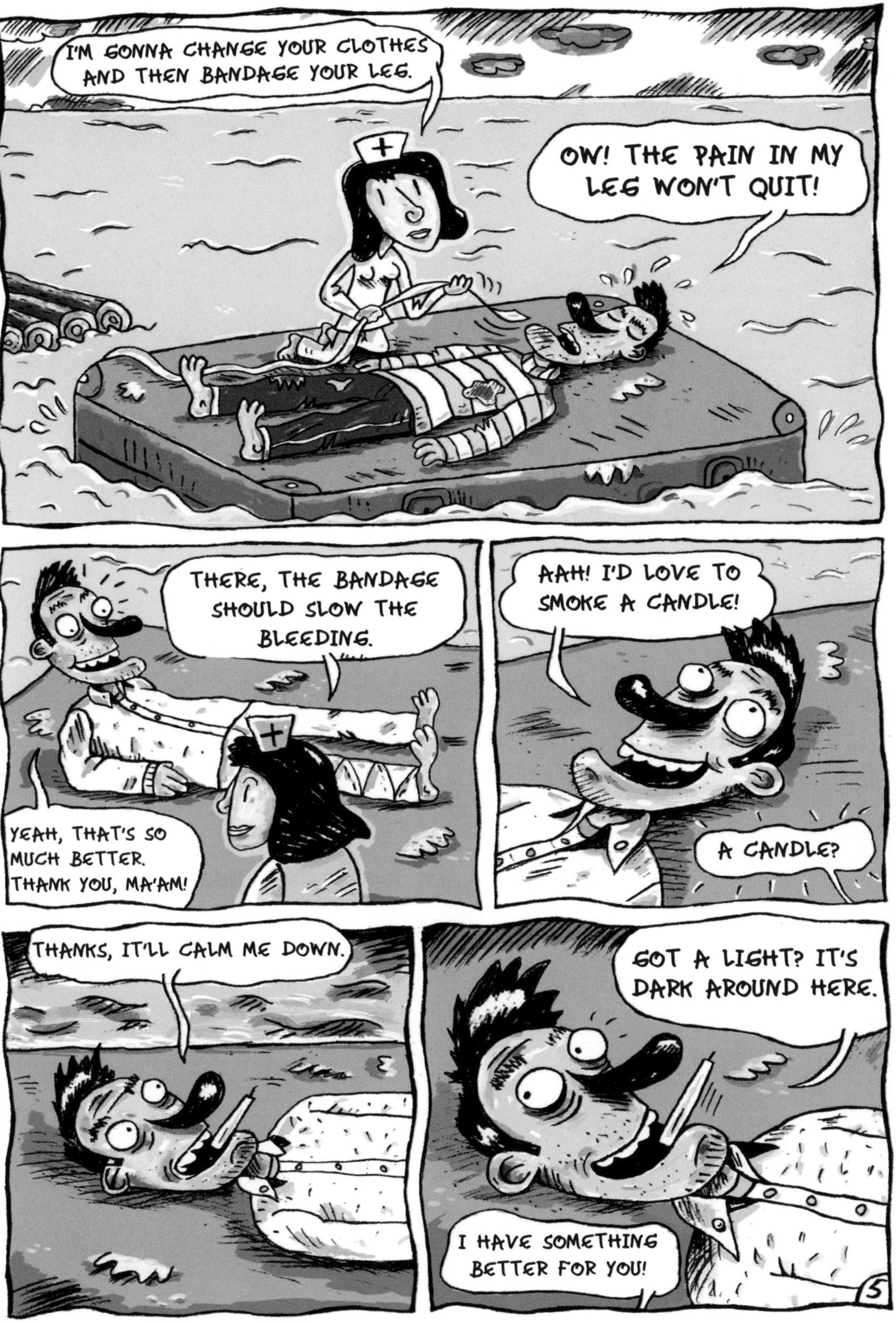
I'M GONNA CHANGE YOUR CLOTHES AND THEN BANDAGE YOUR LEG.
OW! THE PAIN IN MY LEG WON'T QUIT!
THERE, THE BANDAGE SHOULD SLOW THE BLEEDING.
YEAH, THAT'S SO MUCH BETTER. THANK YOU, MA'AM!
AAH! I'D LOVE TO SMOKE A CANDLE!
A CANDLE?
THANKS, IT'LL CALM ME DOWN.
GOT A LIGHT? IT'S DARK AROUND HERE.
I HAVE SOMETHING BETTER FOR YOU!
5

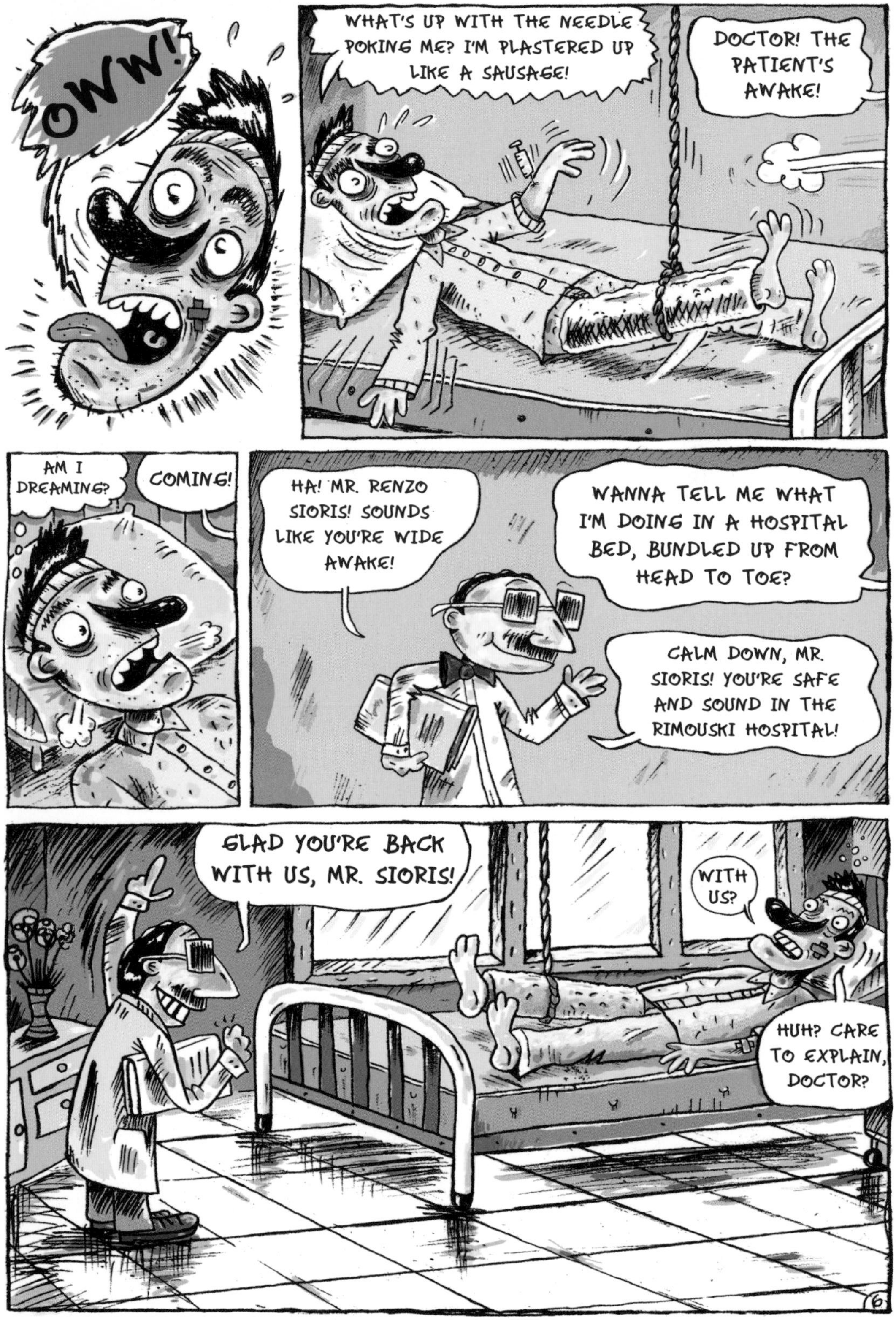
OWW!
WHAT'S UP WITH THE NEEDLE POKING ME? I'M PLASTERED UP LIKE A SAUSAGE!
DOCTOR! THE PATIENT'S AWAKE!
AM I DREAMING?
COMING!
HA! MR. RENZO SIORIS! SOUNDS LIKE YOU'RE WIDE AWAKE!
WANNA TELL ME WHAT I'M DOING IN A HOSPITAL BED, BUNDLED UP FROM HEAD TO TOE?
CALM DOWN, MR. SIORIS! YOU'RE SAFE AND SOUND IN THE RIMOUSKI HOSPITAL!
GLAD YOU'RE BACK WITH US, MR. SIORIS!
WITH US?
HUH? CARE TO EXPLAIN, DOCTOR?
6

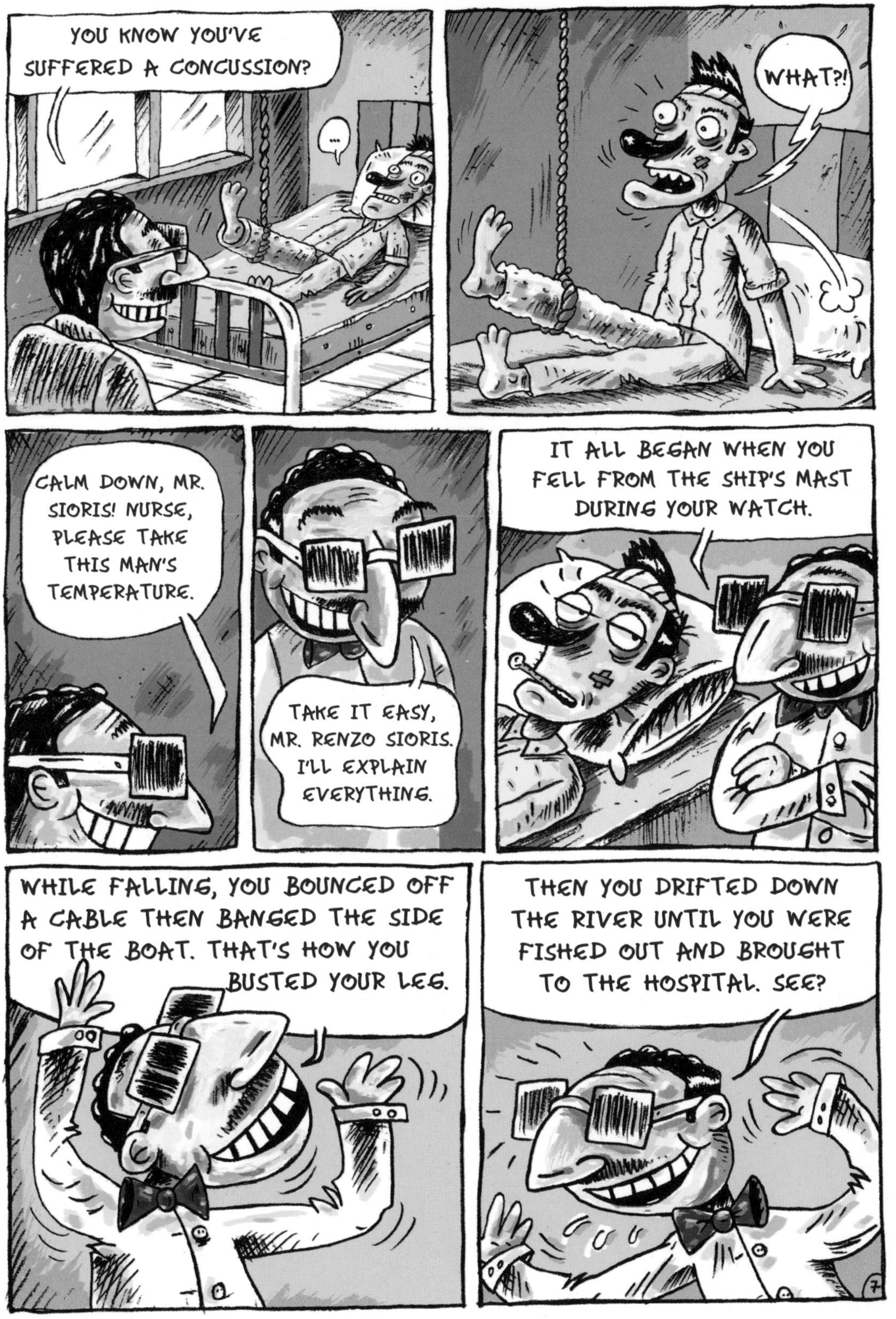
YOU KNOW YOU'VE SUFFERED A CONCUSSION?
...
WHAT?!
CALM DOWN, MR. SIORIS! NURSE, PLEASE TAKE THIS MAN'S TEMPERATURE.
TAKE IT EASY, MR. RENZO SIORIS. I'LL EXPLAIN EVERYTHING.
IT ALL BEGAN WHEN YOU FELL FROM THE SHIP'S MAST DURING YOUR WATCH.
WHILE FALLING, YOU BOUNCED OFF A CABLE THEN BANGED THE SIDE OF THE BOAT. THAT'S HOW YOU BUSTED YOUR LEG.
THEN YOU DRIFTED DOWN THE RIVER UNTIL YOU WERE FISHED OUT AND BROUGHT TO THE HOSPITAL. SEE?
7

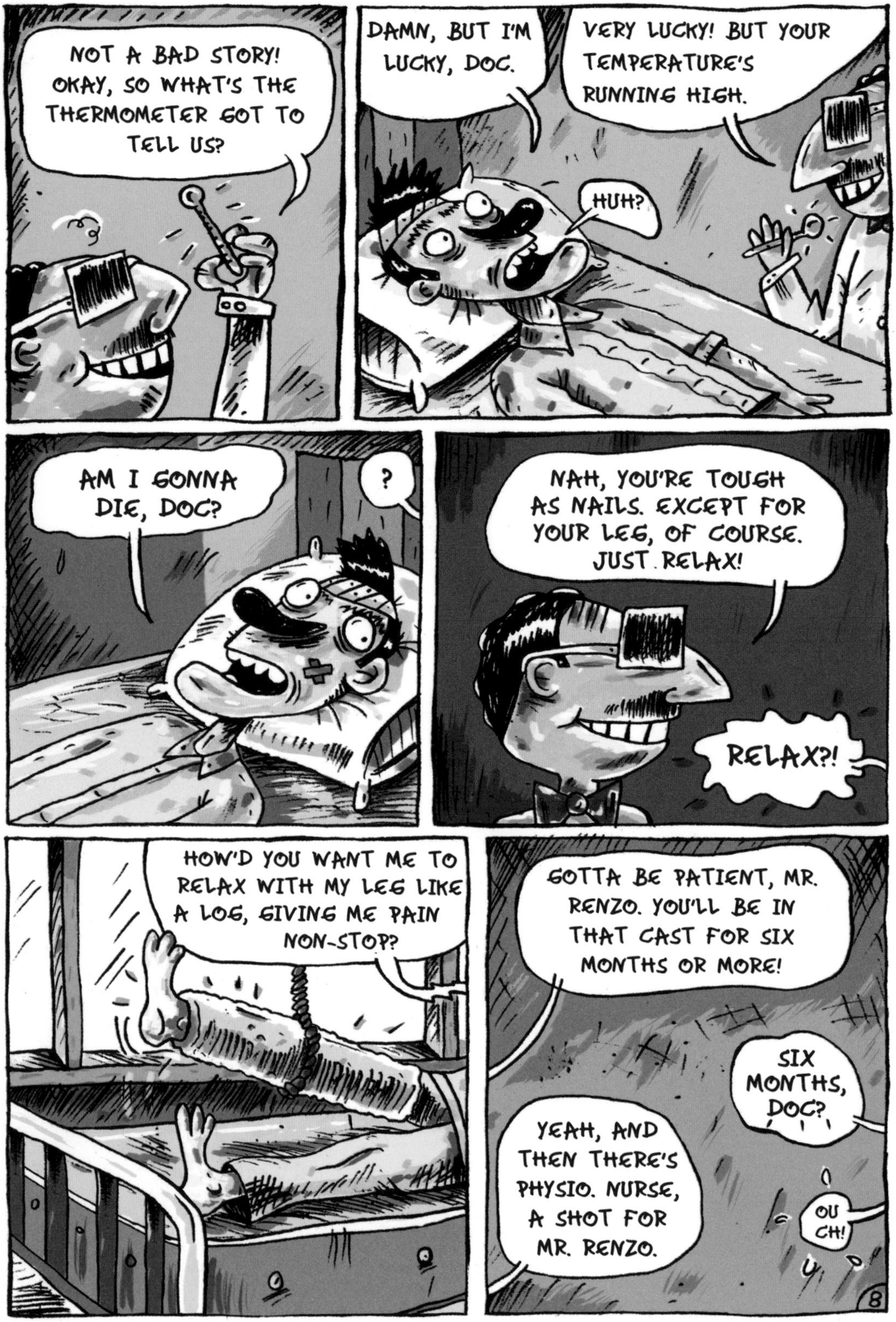
NOT A BAD STORY! OKAY, SO WHAT'S THE THERMOMETER GOT TO TELL US?
DAMN, BUT I'M LUCKY, DOC.
VERY LUCKY! BUT YOUR TEMPERATURE'S RUNNING HIGH.
HUH?
AM I GONNA DIE, DOC?
?
NAH, YOU'RE TOUGH AS NAILS. EXCEPT FOR YOUR LEG, OF COURSE. JUST RELAX!
RELAX?!
HOW'D YOU WANT ME TO RELAX WITH MY LEG LIKE A LOG, GIVING ME PAIN NON-STOP?
GOTTA BE PATIENT, MR. RENZO. YOU'LL BE IN THAT CAST FOR SIX MONTHS OR MORE!
SIX MONTHS, DOC?
YEAH, AND THEN THERE'S PHYSIO. NURSE, A SHOT FOR MR. RENZO.
OU CH!
8

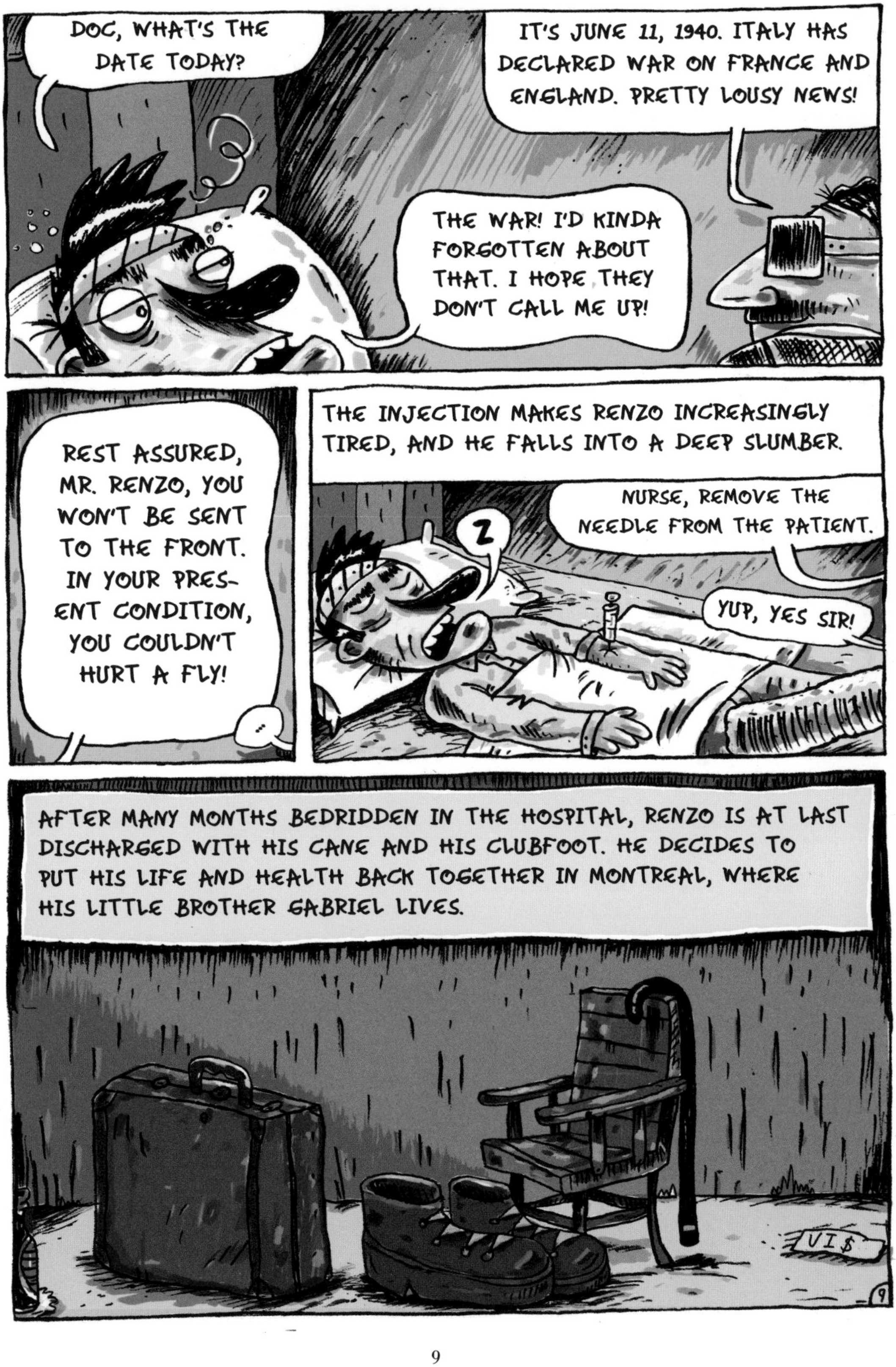
DOC, WHAT'S THE DATE TODAY?
IT'S JUNE 11, 1940. ITALY HAS DECLARED WAR ON FRANCE AND ENGLAND. PRETTY LOUSY NEWS!
THE WAR! I'D KINDA FORGOTTEN ABOUT THAT. I HOPE THEY DON'T CALL ME UP!
REST ASSURED, MR. RENZO, YOU WON'T BE SENT TO THE FRONT. IN YOUR PRES-ENT CONDITION, YOU COULDN'T HURT A FLY!
THE INJECTION MAKES RENZO INCREASINGLY TIRED, AND HE FALLS INTO A DEEP SLUMBER.
Z
NURSE, REMOVE THE NEEDLE FROM THE PATIENT.
YUP, YES SIR!
AFTER MANY MONTHS BEDRIDDEN IN THE HOSPITAL, RENZO IS AT LAST DISCHARGED WITH HIS CANE AND HIS CLUBFOOT. HE DECIDES TO PUT HIS LIFE AND HEALTH BACK TOGETHER IN MONTREAL, WHERE HIS LITTLE BROTHER GABRIEL LIVES.
VI$
9

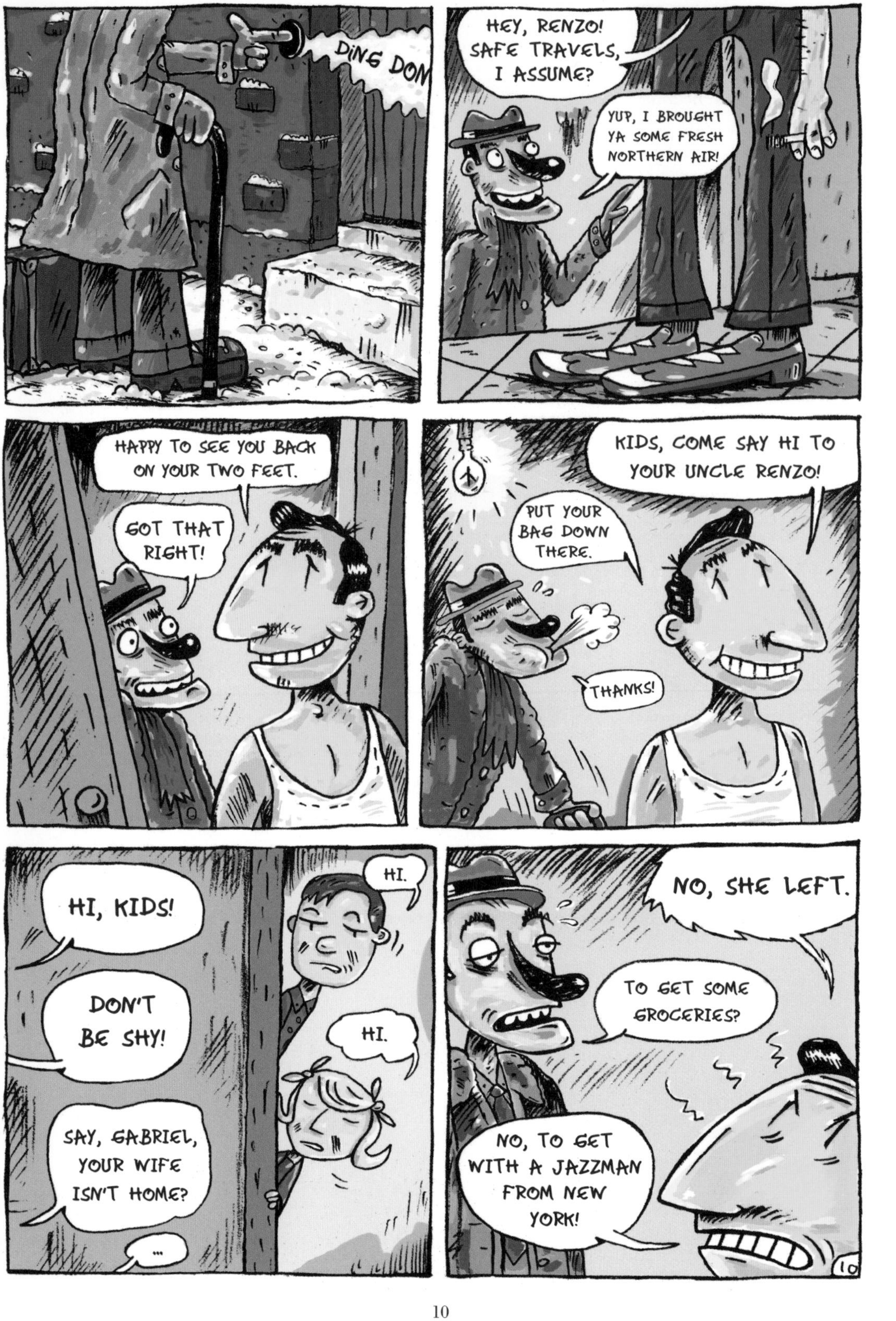
DING DONG
HEY, RENZO! SAFE TRAVELS, I ASSUME?
YUP, I BROUGHT YA SOME FRESH NORTHERN AIR!
HAPPY TO SEE YOU BACK ON YOUR TWO FEET.
GOT THAT RIGHT!
KIDS, COME SAY HI TO YOUR UNCLE RENZO!
PUT YOUR BAG DOWN THERE.
THANKS!
HI, KIDS!
HI.
DON'T BE SHY!
HI.
SAY, GABRIEL, YOUR WIFE ISN'T HOME?
...
NO, SHE LEFT.
TO GET SOME GROCERIES?
NO, TO GET WITH A JAZZMAN FROM NEW YORK!
10

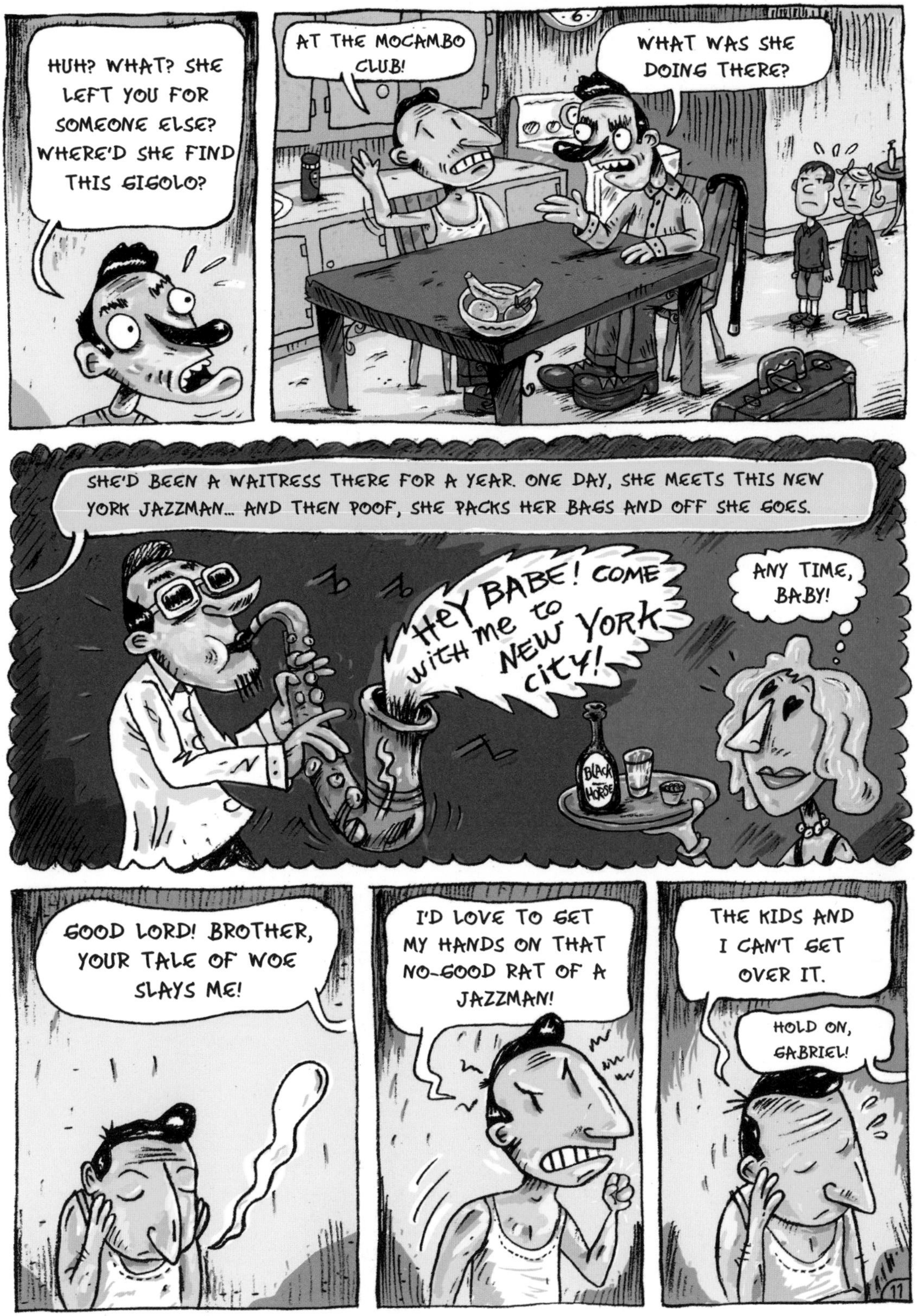
HUH? WHAT? SHE LEFT YOU FOR SOMEONE ELSE? WHERE'D SHE FIND THIS GIGOLO?
AT THE MOCAMBO CLUB!
WHAT WAS SHE DOING THERE?
SHE'D BEEN A WAITRESS THERE FOR A YEAR. ONE DAY, SHE MEETS THIS NEW YORK JAZZMAN... AND THEN POOF, SHE PACKS HER BAGS AND OFF SHE GOES.
HEY BABE! COME with me to NEW YORK city!
ANY TIME, BABY!
BLACK HORSE
GOOD LORD! BROTHER, YOUR TALE OF WOE SLAYS ME!
I'D LOVE TO GET MY HANDS ON THAT NO-GOOD RAT OF A JAZZMAN!
THE KIDS AND I CAN'T GET OVER IT.
HOLD ON, GABRIEL!
11

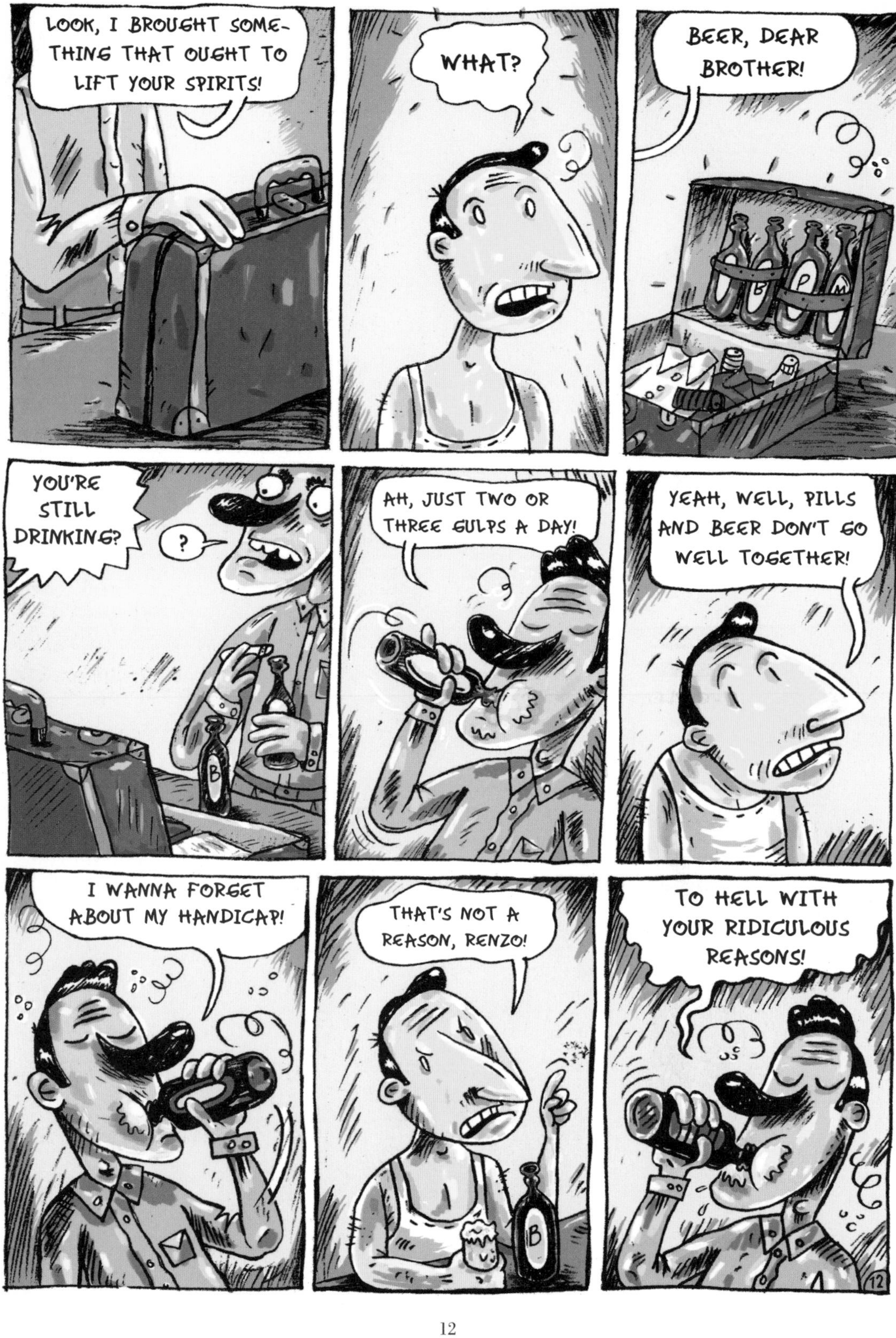

LOOK, I BROUGHT SOME-THING THAT OUGHT TO LIFT YOUR SPIRITS!
WHAT?
BEER, DEAR BROTHER!
YOU'RE STILL DRINKING?
?
AH, JUST TWO OR THREE GULPS A DAY!
YEAH, WELL, PILLS AND BEER DON'T GO WELL TOGETHER!
I WANNA FORGET ABOUT MY HANDICAP!
THAT'S NOT A REASON, RENZO!
TO HELL WITH YOUR RIDICULOUS REASONS!
12

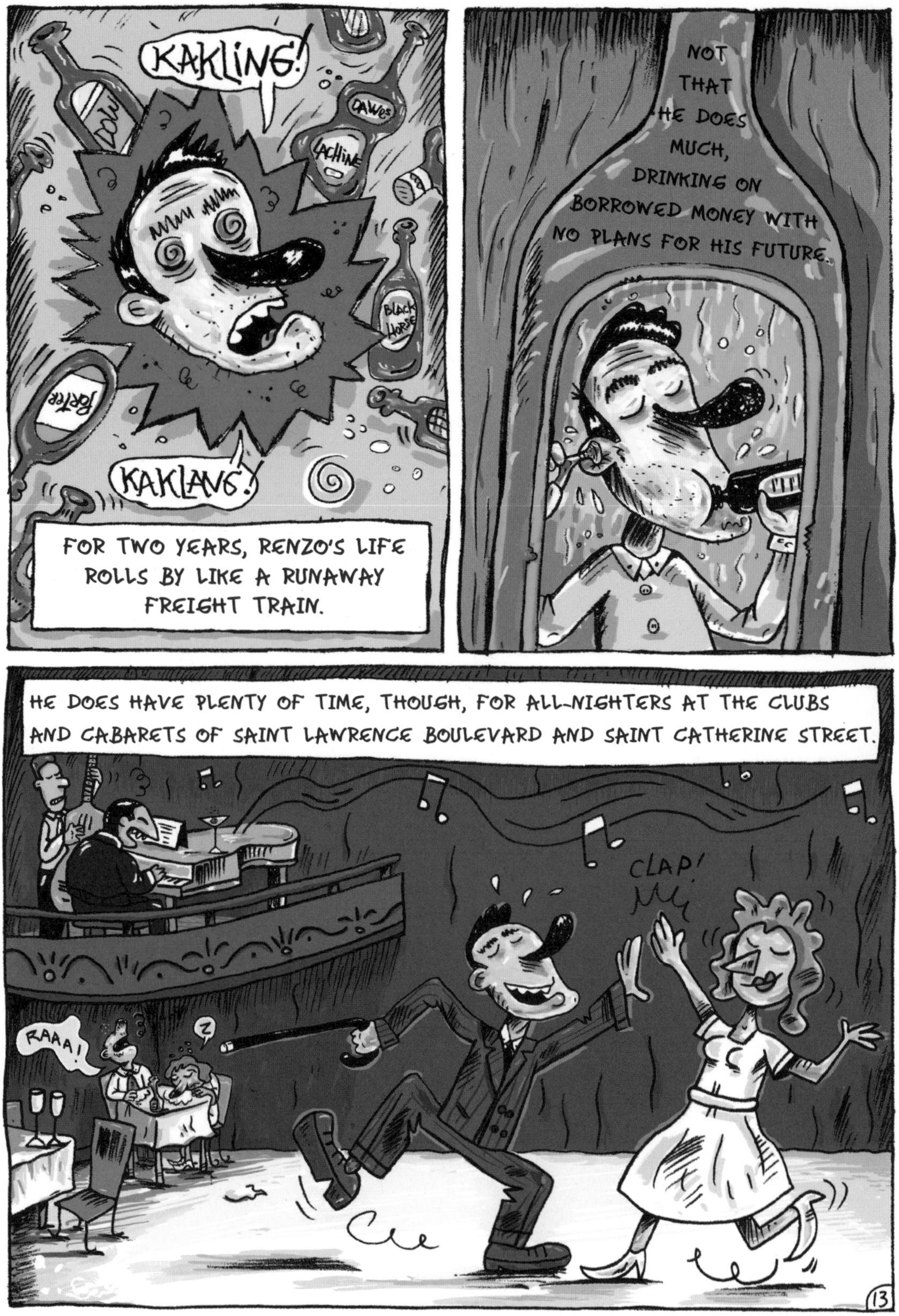
KAKLING!
DOW
DAWES
LACHINE
BLACK HORSE
PORTER
KAKLANG!
FOR TWO YEARS, RENZO'S LIFE ROLLS BY LIKE A RUNAWAY FREIGHT TRAIN.
NOT THAT HE DOES MUCH, DRINKING ON BORROWED MONEY WITH NO PLANS FOR HIS FUTURE.
HE DOES HAVE PLENTY OF TIME, THOUGH, FOR ALL-NIGHTERS AT THE CLUBS AND CABARETS OF SAINT LAWRENCE BOULEVARD AND SAINT CATHERINE STREET.
CLAP!
RAAA!
Z
13

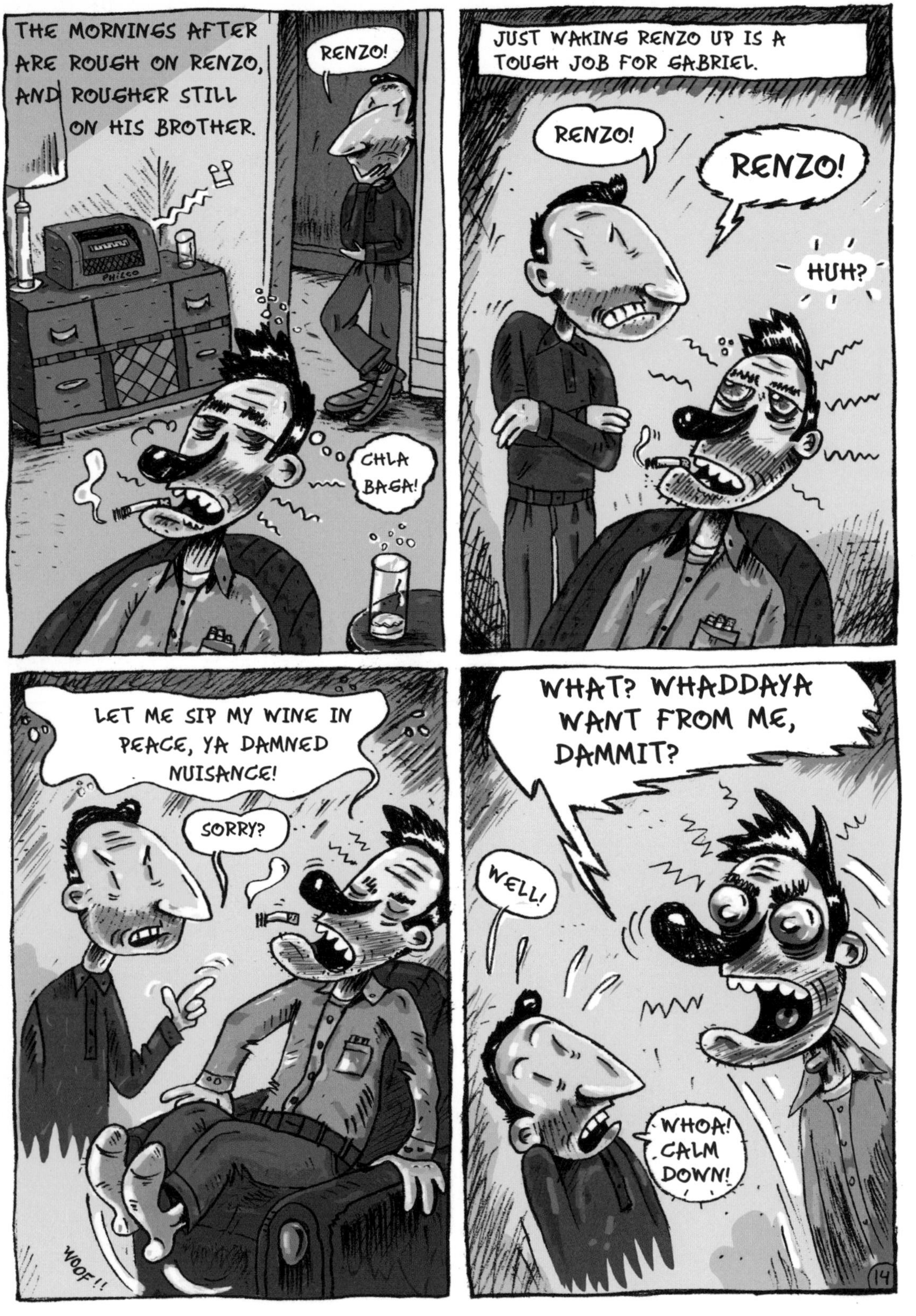
THE MORNINGS AFTER ARE ROUGH ON RENZO, AND ROUGHER STILL ON HIS BROTHER.
RENZO!
PHILCO
CHLA BAGA!
JUST WAKING RENZO UP IS A TOUGH JOB FOR GABRIEL.
RENZO!
RENZO!
HUH?
LET ME SIP MY WINE IN PEACE, YA DAMNED NUISANCE!
SORRY?
WOOF!!
WHAT? WHADDAYA WANT FROM ME, DAMMIT?
WELL!
WHOA! CALM DOWN!
14

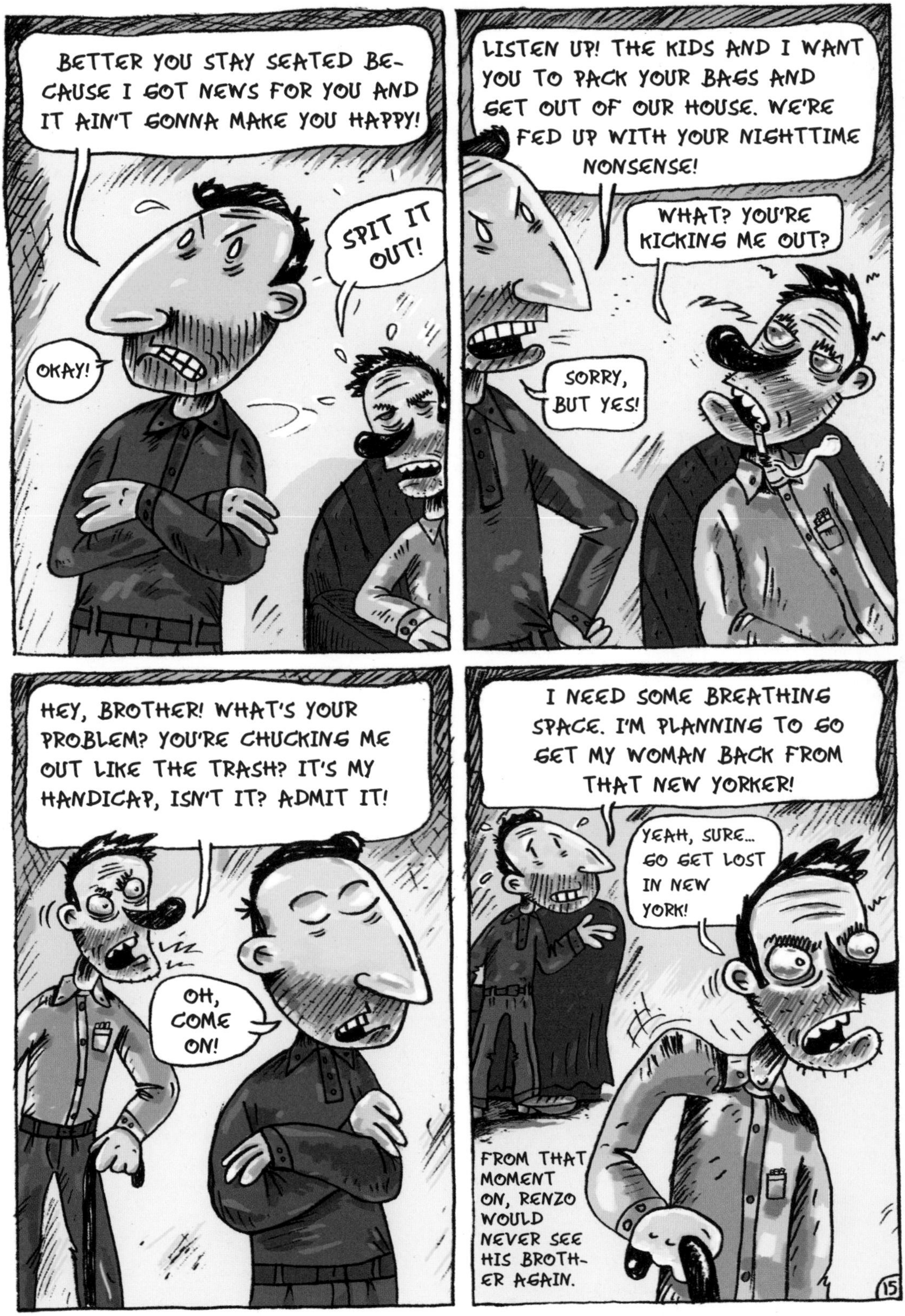
BETTER YOU STAY SEATED BE-CAUSE I GOT NEWS FOR YOU AND IT AIN'T GONNA MAKE YOU HAPPY!
SPIT IT OUT!
OKAY!
LISTEN UP! THE KIDS AND I WANT YOU TO PACK YOUR BAGS AND GET OUT OF OUR HOUSE. WE'RE FED UP WITH YOUR NIGHTTIME NONSENSE!
WHAT? YOU'RE KICKING ME OUT?
SORRY, BUT YES!
HEY, BROTHER! WHAT'S YOUR PROBLEM? YOU'RE CHUCKING ME OUT LIKE THE TRASH? IT'S MY HANDICAP, ISN'T IT? ADMIT IT!
OH, COME ON!
I NEED SOME BREATHING SPACE. I'M PLANNING TO GO GET MY WOMAN BACK FROM THAT NEW YORKER!
YEAH, SURE... GO GET LOST IN NEW YORK!
FROM THAT MOMENT ON, RENZO WOULD NEVER SEE HIS BROTH-ER AGAIN.
15

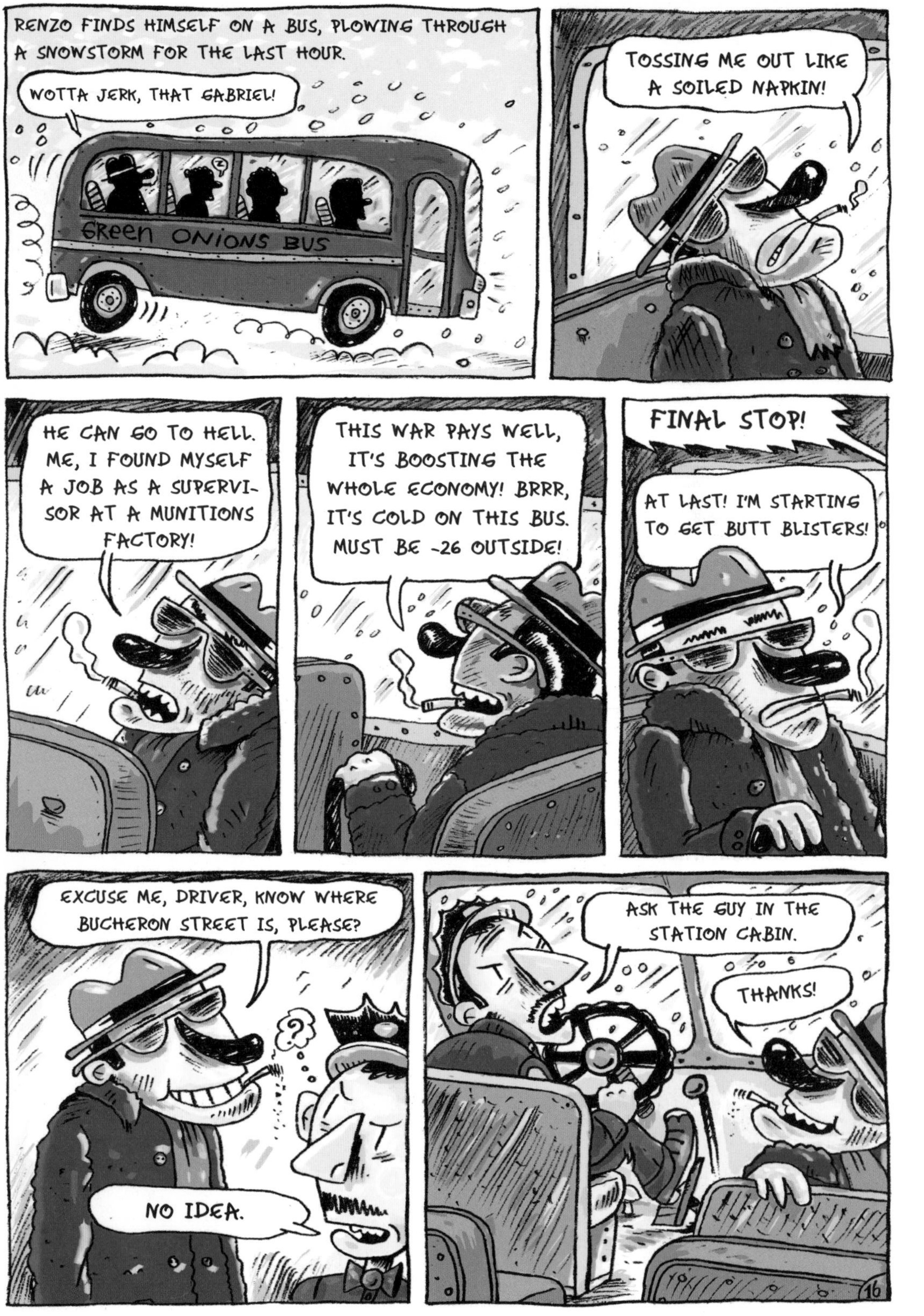

RENZO FINDS HIMSELF ON A BUS, PLOWING THROUGH A SNOWSTORM FOR THE LAST HOUR.
WOTTA JERK, THAT GABRIEL!
GReeN ONIONS BUS
TOSSING ME OUT LIKE A SOILED NAPKIN!
HE CAN GO TO HELL. ME, I FOUND MYSELF A JOB AS A SUPERVI-SOR AT A MUNITIONS FACTORY!
THIS WAR PAYS WELL, IT'S BOOSTING THE WHOLE ECONOMY! BRRR, IT'S COLD ON THIS BUS. MUST BE -26 OUTSIDE!
FINAL STOP!
AT LAST! I'M STARTING TO GET BUTT BLISTERS!
EXCUSE ME, DRIVER, KNOW WHERE BUCHERON STREET IS, PLEASE?
?
NO IDEA.
ASK THE GUY IN THE STATION CABIN.
THANKS!
16

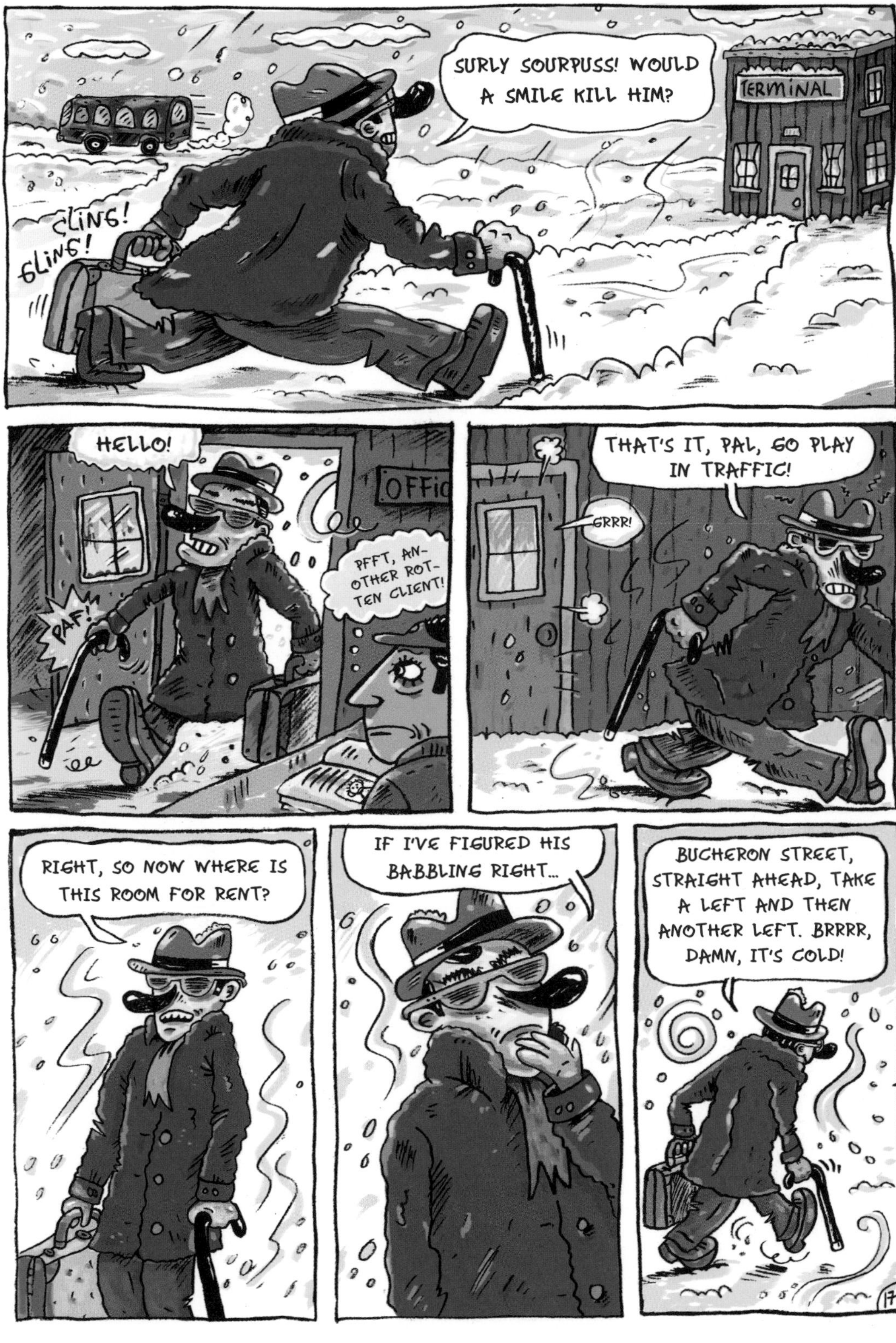

SURLY SOURPUSS! WOULD A SMILE KILL HIM?
TERMINAL
CLING! CLING!
HELLO!
OFFIC
PAF!
PFFT, ANOTHER ROTTEN CLIENT!
THAT'S IT, PAL, GO PLAY IN TRAFFIC!
GRRR!
RIGHT, SO NOW WHERE IS THIS ROOM FOR RENT?
IF I'VE FIGURED HIS BABBLING RIGHT...
BUCHERON STREET, STRAIGHT AHEAD, TAKE A LEFT AND THEN ANOTHER LEFT. BRRRR, DAMN, IT'S COLD!
17

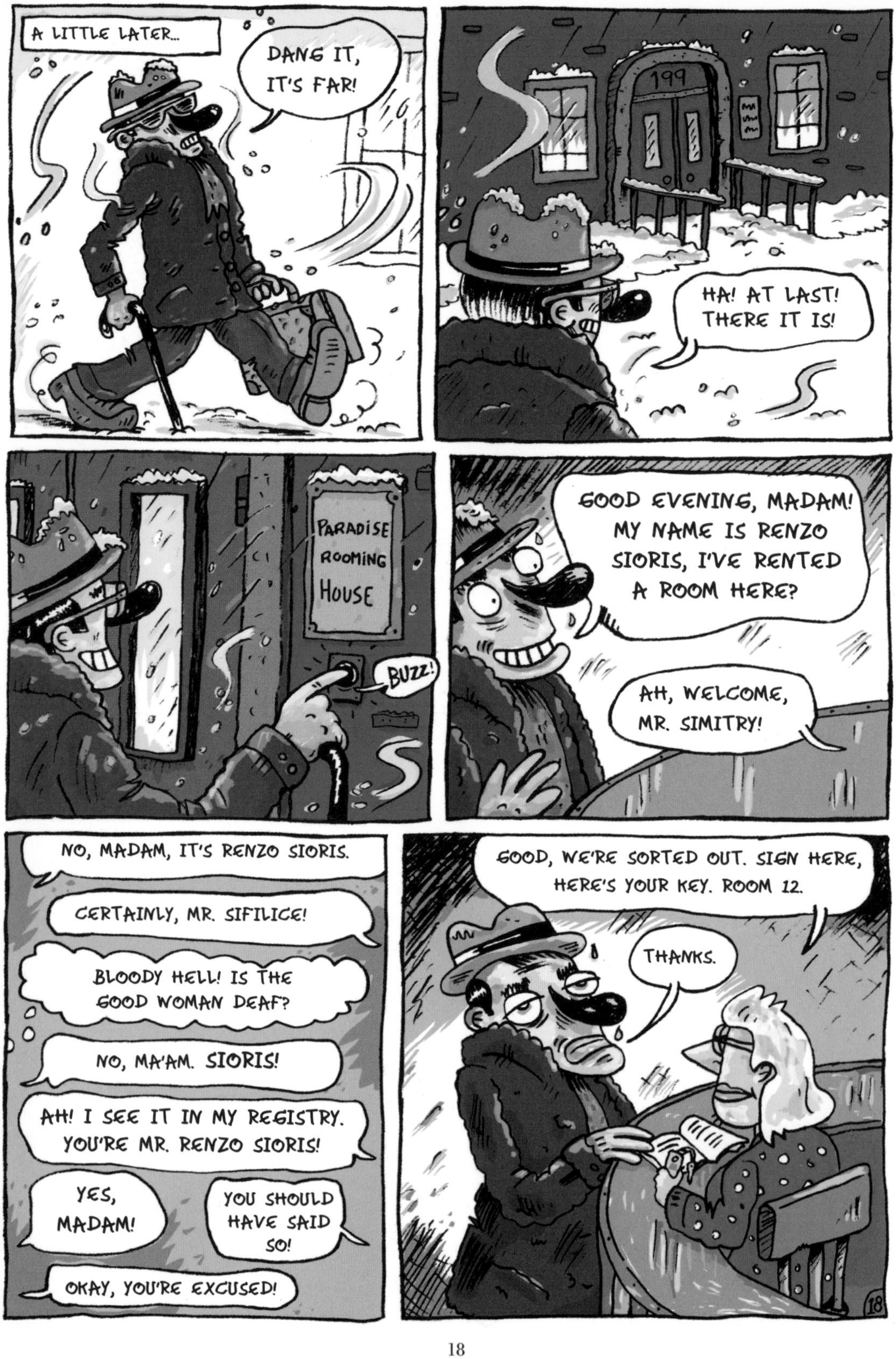
A LITTLE LATER...
DANG IT, IT'S FAR!
199
HA! AT LAST! THERE IT IS!
PARADISE ROOMING HOUSE
BUZZ!
GOOD EVENING, MADAM! MY NAME IS RENZO SIORIS, I'VE RENTED A ROOM HERE?
AH, WELCOME, MR. SIMITRY!
NO, MADAM, IT'S RENZO SIORIS.
CERTAINLY, MR. SIFILICE!
BLOODY HELL! IS THE GOOD WOMAN DEAF?
NO, MA'AM. SIORIS!
AH! I SEE IT IN MY REGISTRY. YOU'RE MR. RENZO SIORIS!
YES, MADAM!
YOU SHOULD HAVE SAID SO!
OKAY, YOU'RE EXCUSED!
GOOD, WE'RE SORTED OUT. SIGN HERE, HERE'S YOUR KEY. ROOM 12.
THANKS.
18

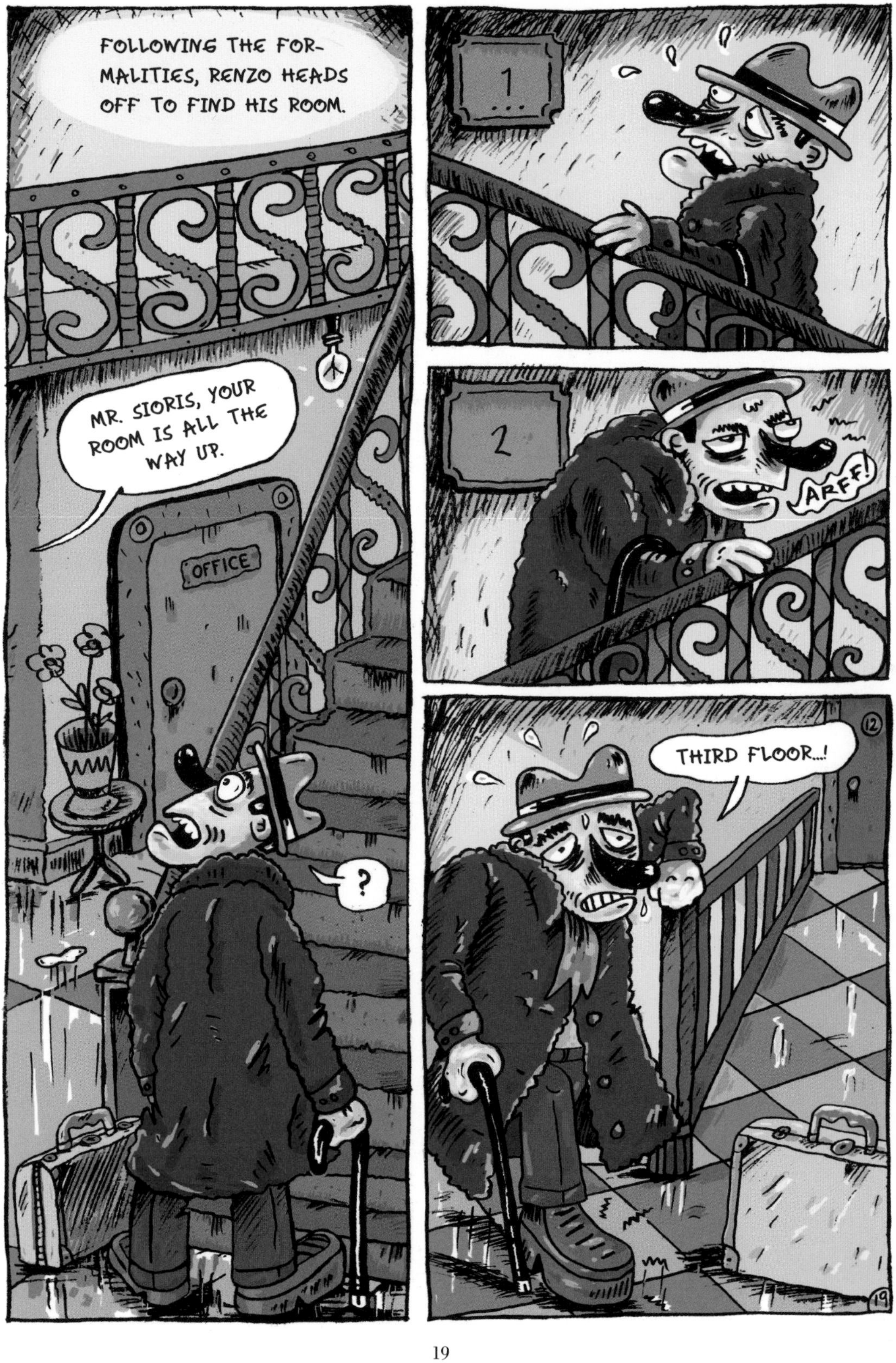
FOLLOWING THE FOR-MALITIES, RENZO HEADS OFF TO FIND HIS ROOM.
MR. SIORIS, YOUR ROOM IS ALL THE WAY UP.
OFFICE
?
1
2
ARFF!
THIRD FLOOR...!
12
19

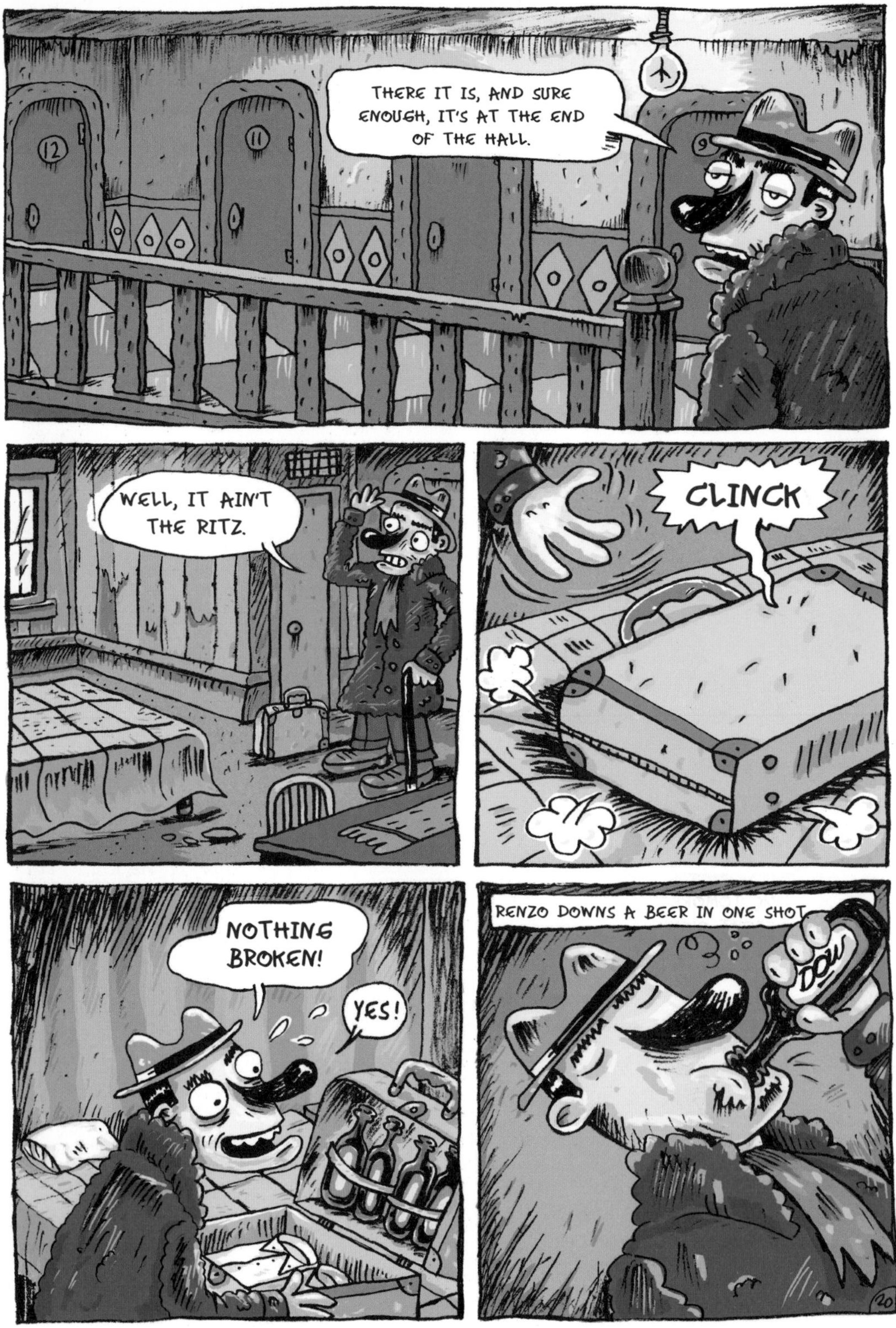
THERE IT IS, AND SURE ENOUGH, IT'S AT THE END OF THE HALL.
WELL, IT AIN'T THE RITZ.
CLINCK
NOTHING BROKEN!
YES!
RENZO DOWNS A BEER IN ONE SHOT
DOW

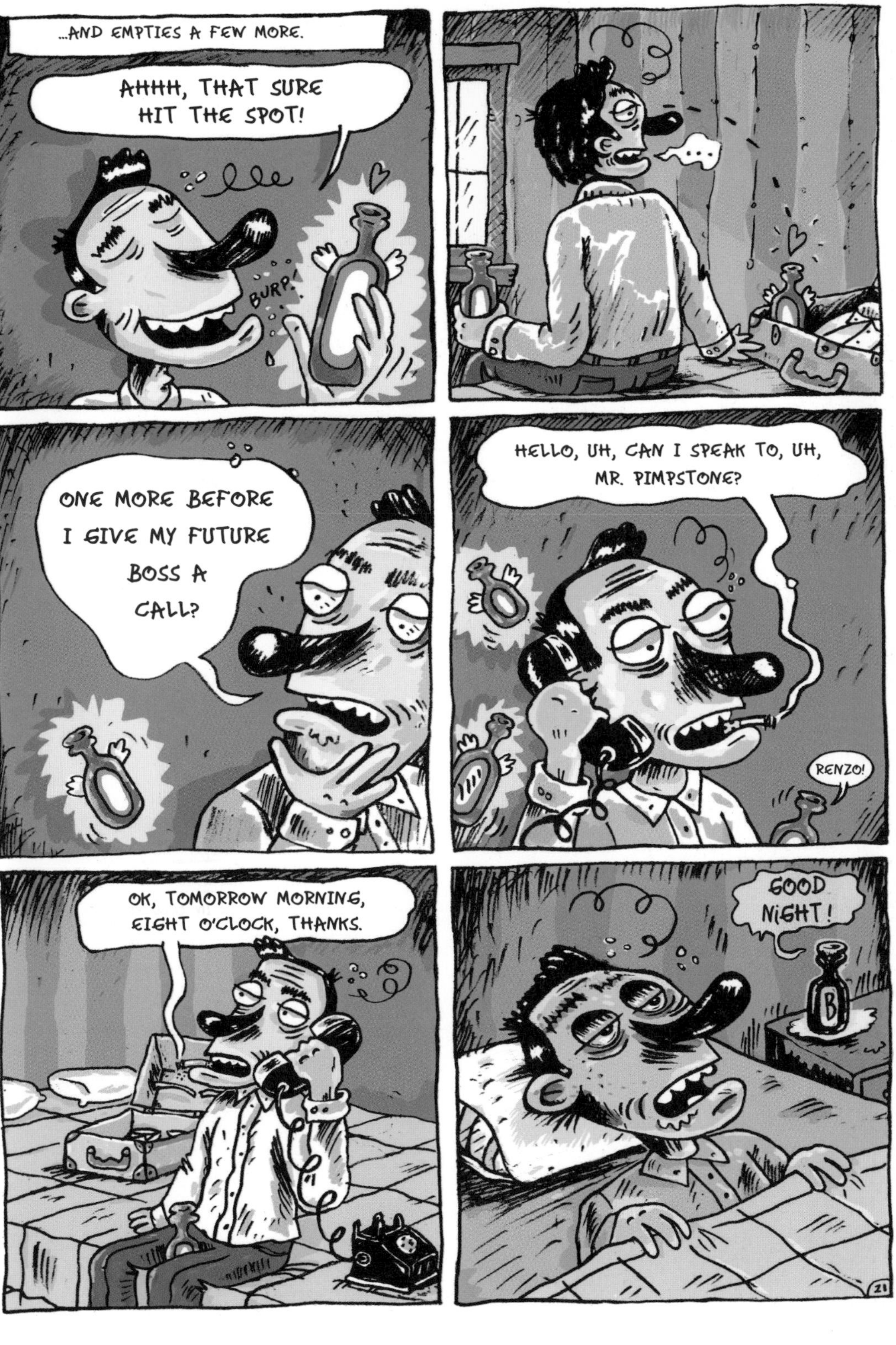
...AND EMPTIES A FEW MORE.
AHHH, THAT SURE HIT THE SPOT!
BURP!
ONE MORE BEFORE I GIVE MY FUTURE BOSS A CALL?
HELLO, UH, CAN I SPEAK TO, UH, MR. PIMPSTONE?
RENZO!
OK, TOMORROW MORNING, EIGHT O'CLOCK, THANKS.
GOOD NIGHT!
B

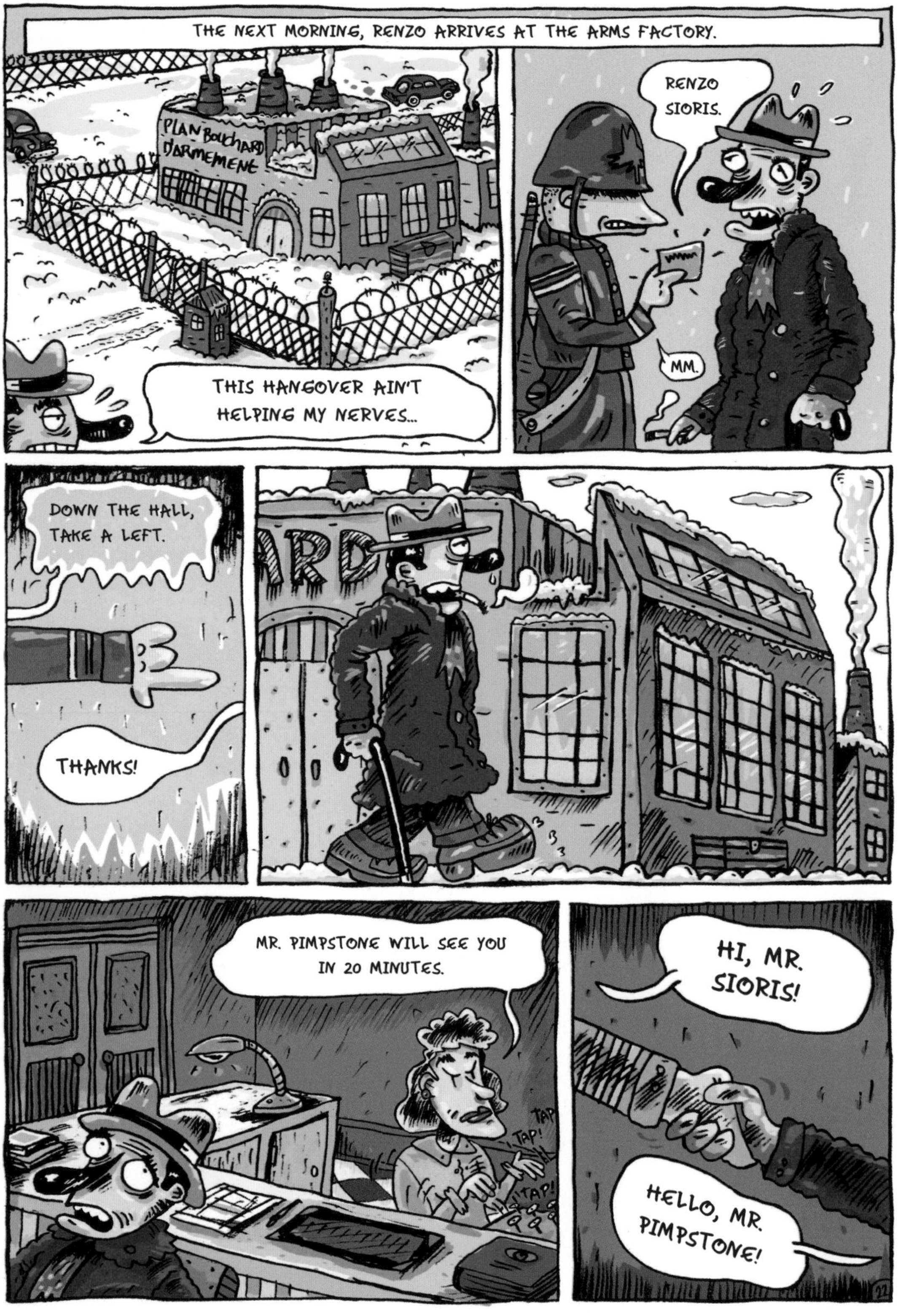
THE NEXT MORNING, RENZO ARRIVES AT THE ARMS FACTORY.
PLAN Bouchard D'ARMEMENT
THIS HANGOVER AIN'T HELPING MY NERVES...
RENZO SIORIS.
MM.
DOWN THE HALL, TAKE A LEFT.
THANKS!
ARD
MR. PIMPSTONE WILL SEE YOU IN 20 MINUTES.
TAP
TAP!
TAP!
HI, MR. SIORIS!
HELLO, MR. PIMPSTONE!

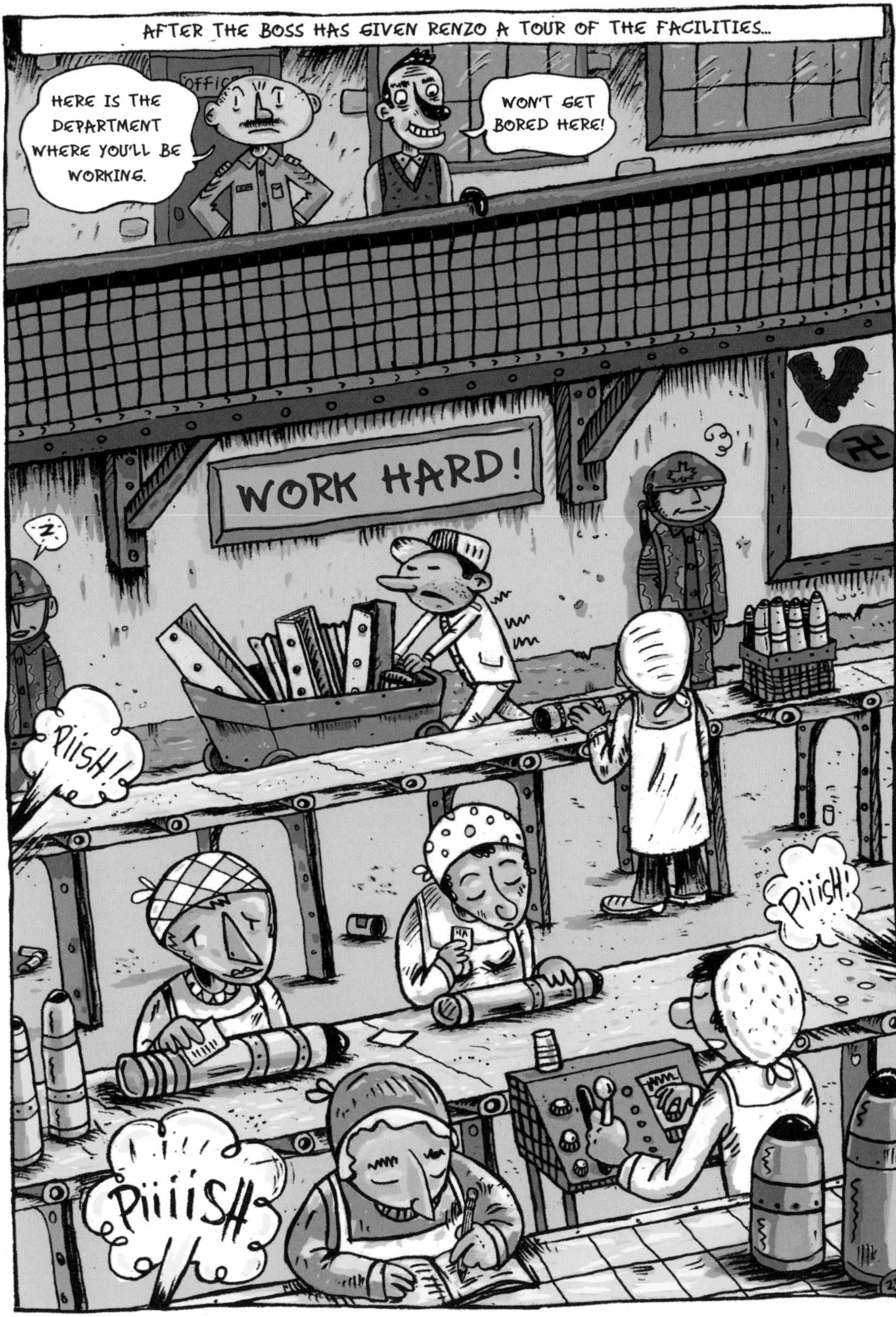
AFTER THE BOSS HAS GIVEN RENZO A TOUR OF THE FACILITIES...
HERE IS THE DEPARTMENT WHERE YOU'LL BE WORKING.
WON'T GET BORED HERE!
WORK HARD!
Z
PIISH!
PIIISH!
PIIISH

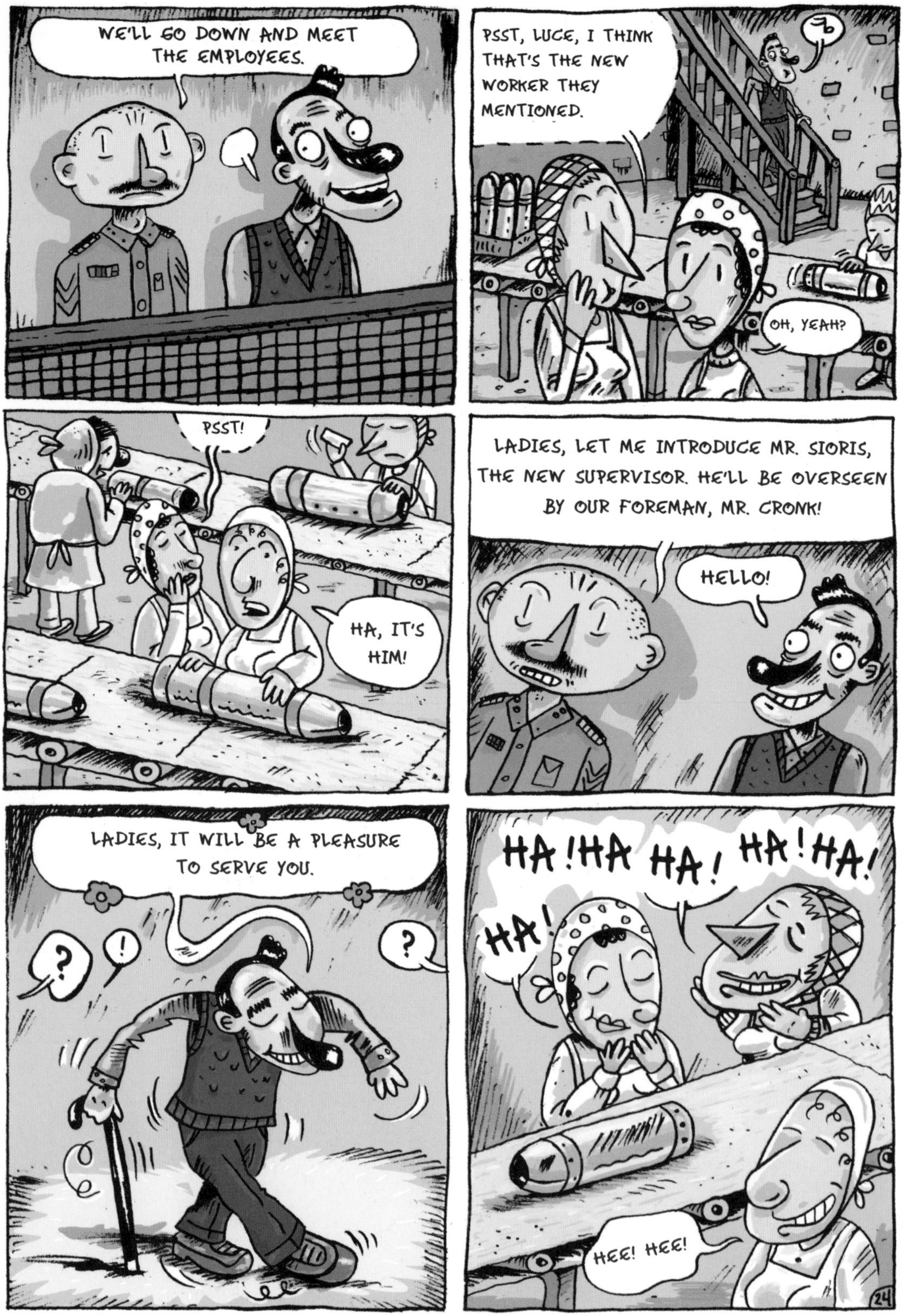
WE'LL GO DOWN AND MEET THE EMPLOYEES.
PSST, LUCE, I THINK THAT'S THE NEW WORKER THEY MENTIONED.
OH, YEAH?
PSST!
HA, IT'S HIM!
LADIES, LET ME INTRODUCE MR. SIORIS, THE NEW SUPERVISOR. HE'LL BE OVERSEEN BY OUR FOREMAN, MR. CRONK!
HELLO!
LADIES, IT WILL BE A PLEASURE TO SERVE YOU.
?
!
?
HA!HA HA! HA!HA!
HA!
HEE! HEE!
24

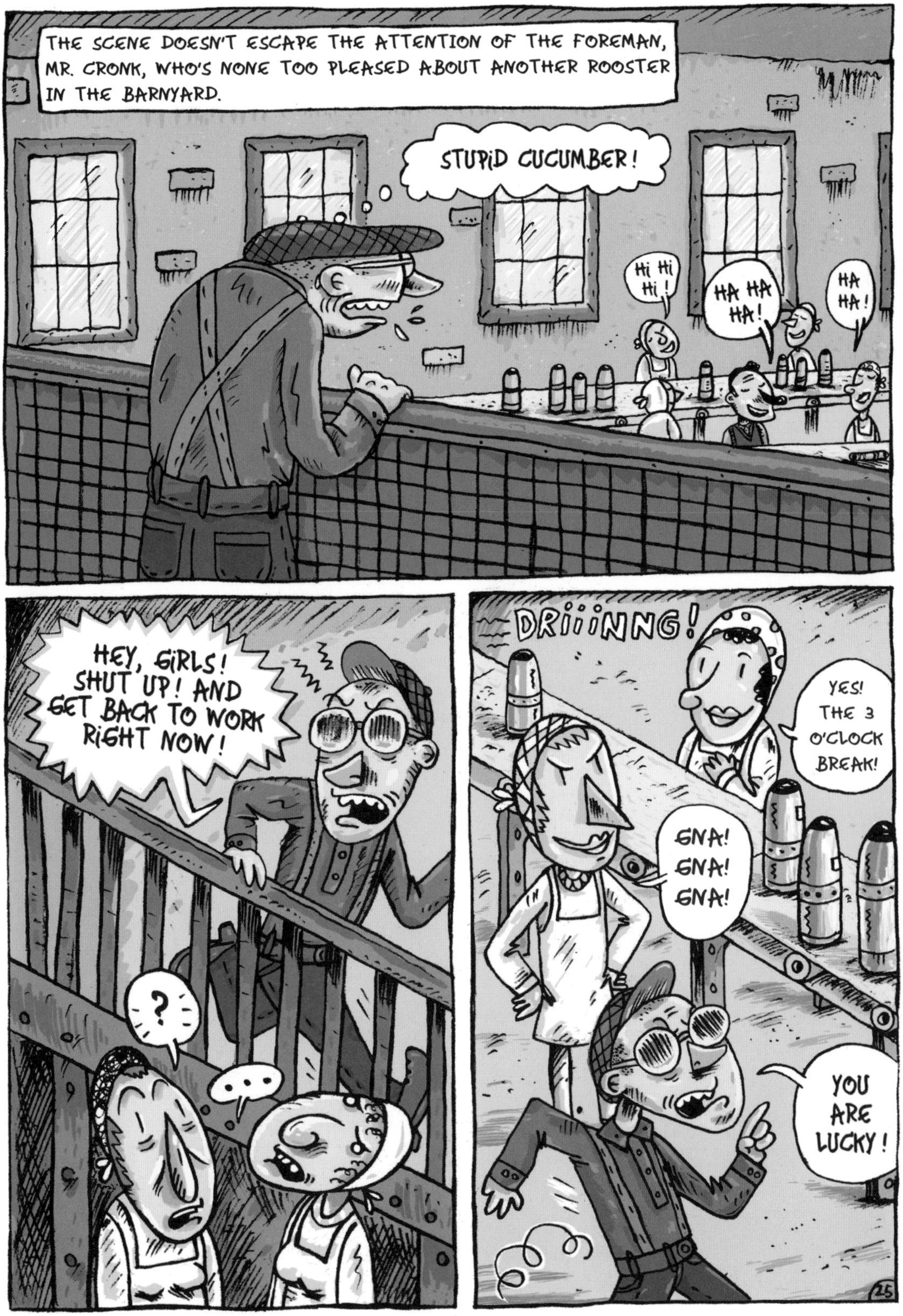
THE SCENE DOESN'T ESCAPE THE ATTENTION OF THE FOREMAN, MR. CRONK, WHO'S NONE TOO PLEASED ABOUT ANOTHER ROOSTER IN THE BARNYARD.
STUPID CUCUMBER!
Hi Hi Hi!
HA HA HA!
HA HA!
HEY, GIRLS! SHUT UP! AND GET BACK TO WORK RIGHT NOW!
?
...
DRIiiNNG!
YES! THE 3 O'CLOCK BREAK!
GNA! GNA! GNA!
YOU ARE LUCKY!
25

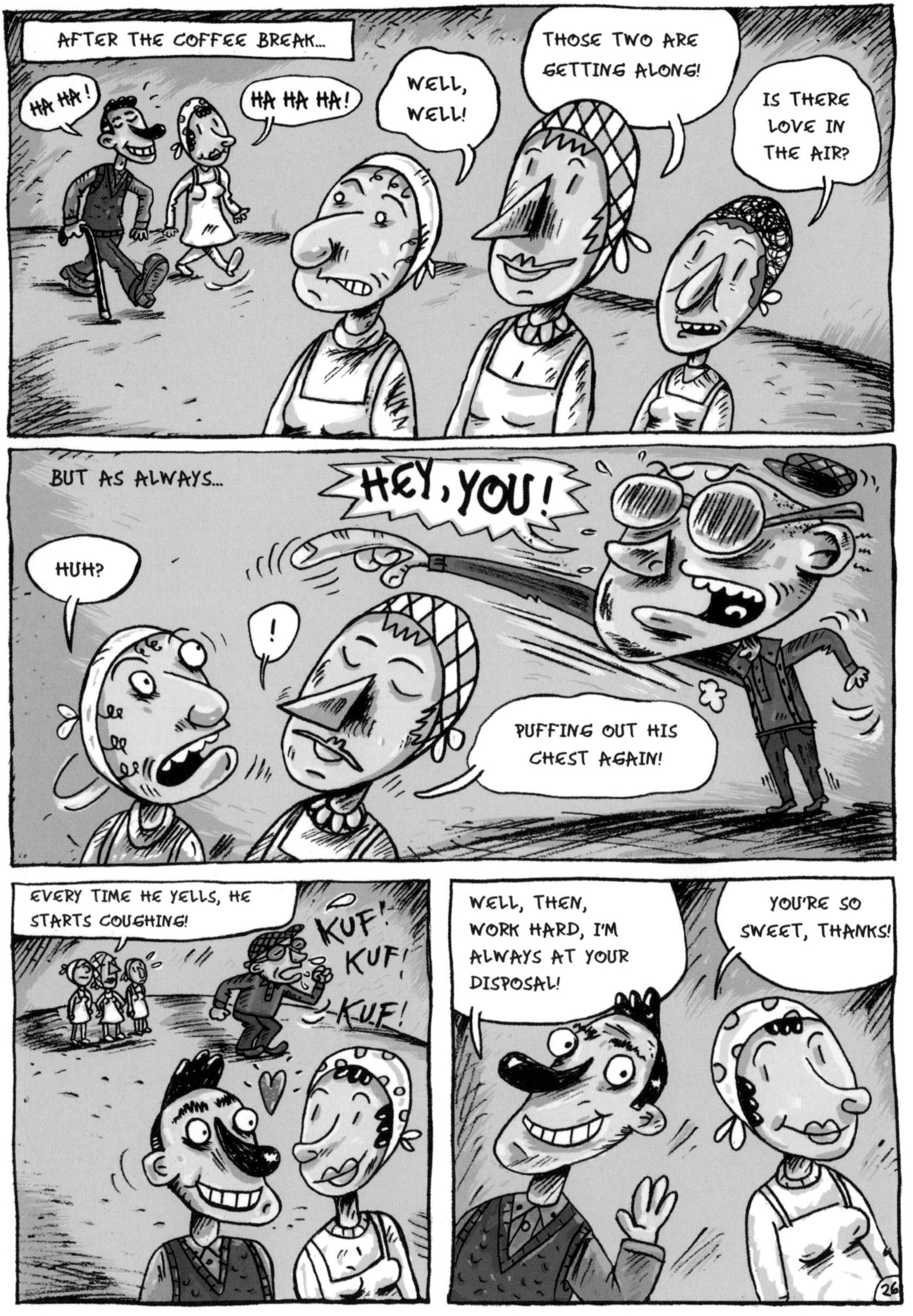
AFTER THE COFFEE BREAK...
HA HA!
HA HA HA!
WELL, WELL!
THOSE TWO ARE GETTING ALONG!
IS THERE LOVE IN THE AIR?
BUT AS ALWAYS...
HEY, YOU!
HUH?
!
PUFFING OUT HIS CHEST AGAIN!
EVERY TIME HE YELLS, HE STARTS COUGHING!
KUF! KUF! KUF!
WELL, THEN, WORK HARD, I'M ALWAYS AT YOUR DISPOSAL!
YOU'RE SO SWEET, THANKS!
26

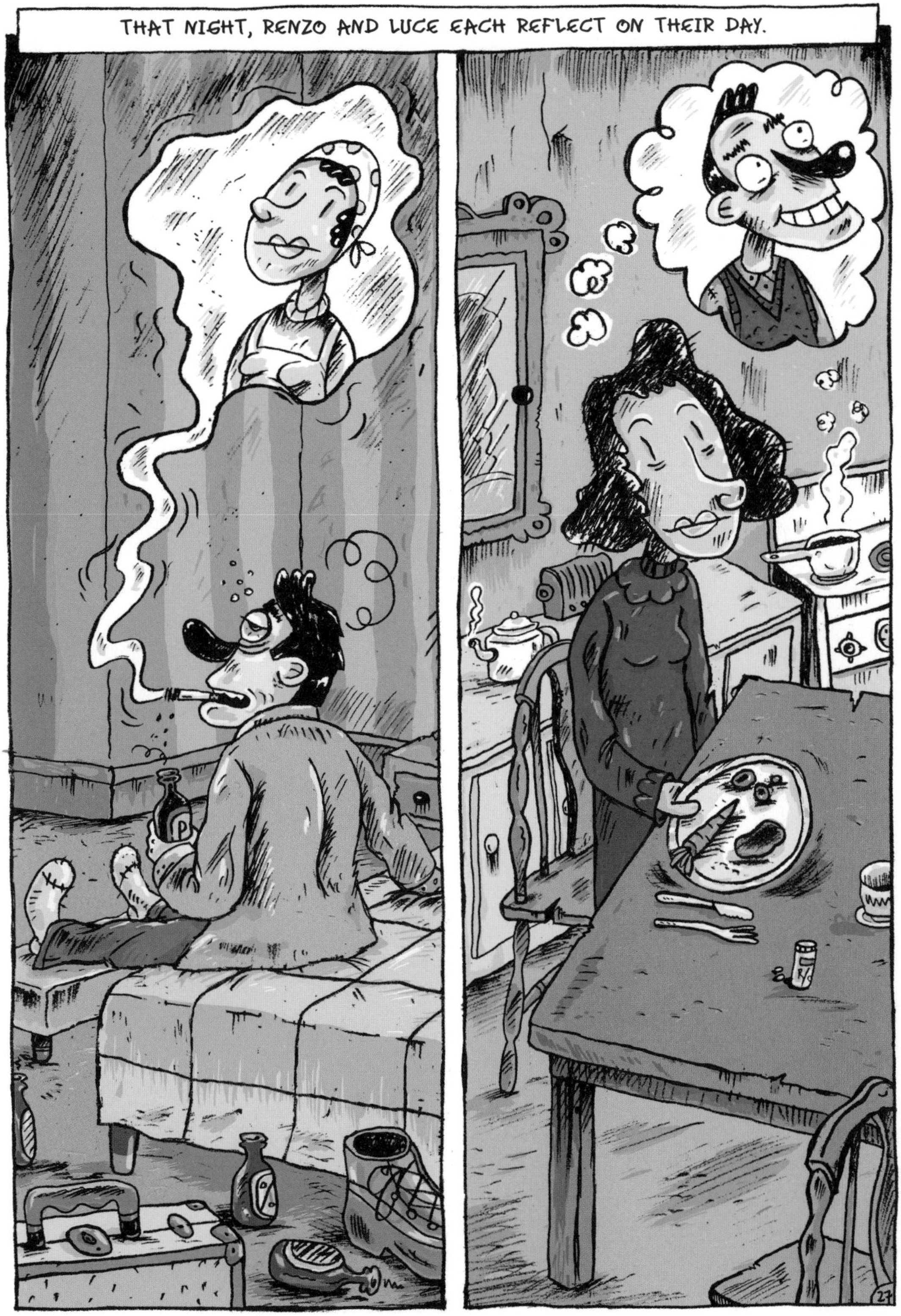
THAT NIGHT, RENZO AND LUCE EACH REFLECT ON THEIR DAY.

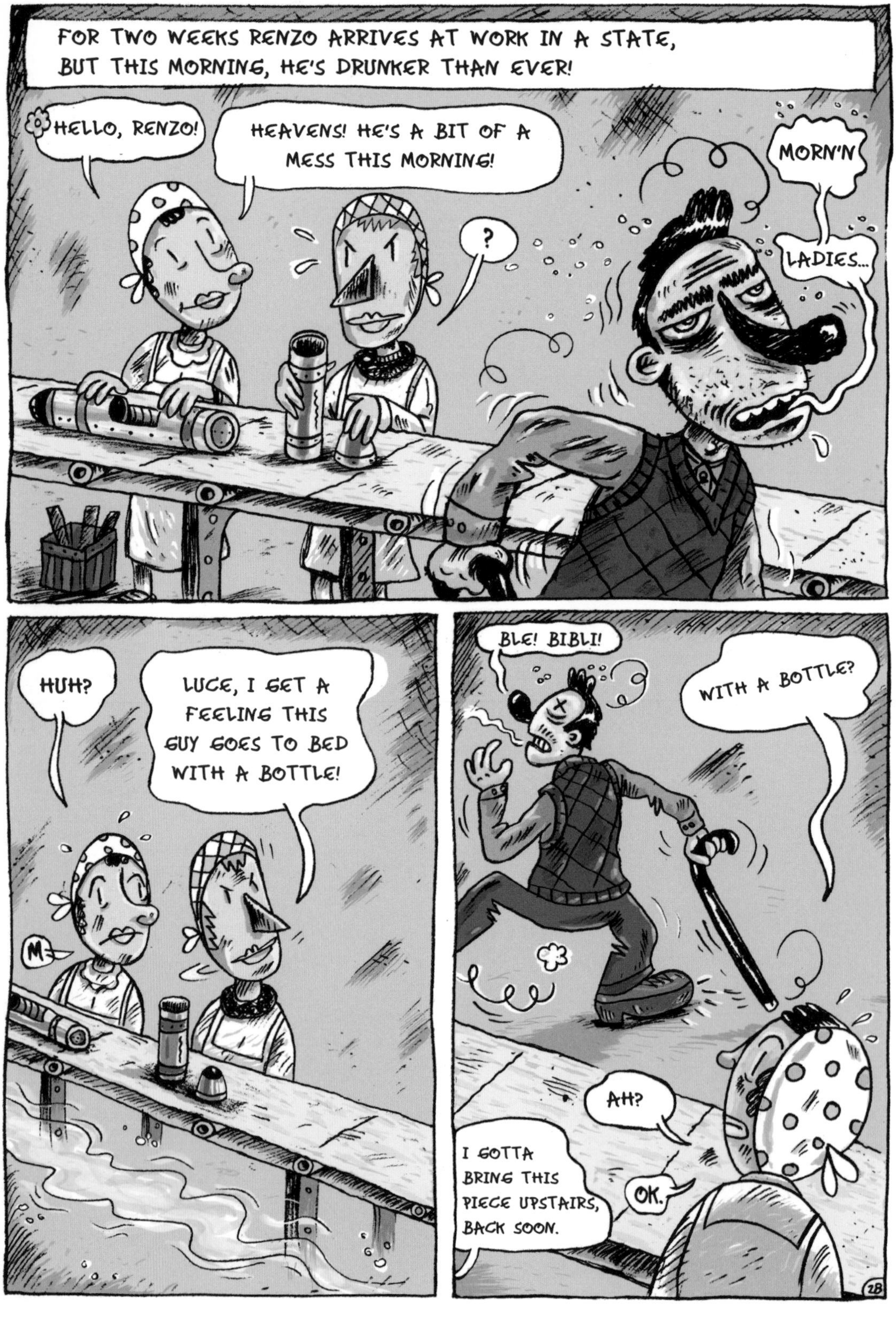
FOR TWO WEEKS RENZO ARRIVES AT WORK IN A STATE, BUT THIS MORNING, HE'S DRUNKER THAN EVER!
HELLO, RENZO!
HEAVENS! HE'S A BIT OF A MESS THIS MORNING!
?
MORN'N
LADIES...
HUH?
LUCE, I GET A FEELING THIS GUY GOES TO BED WITH A BOTTLE!
M
BLE! BIBLI!
WITH A BOTTLE?
AH?
I GOTTA BRING THIS PIECE UPSTAIRS, BACK SOON.
OK.
28

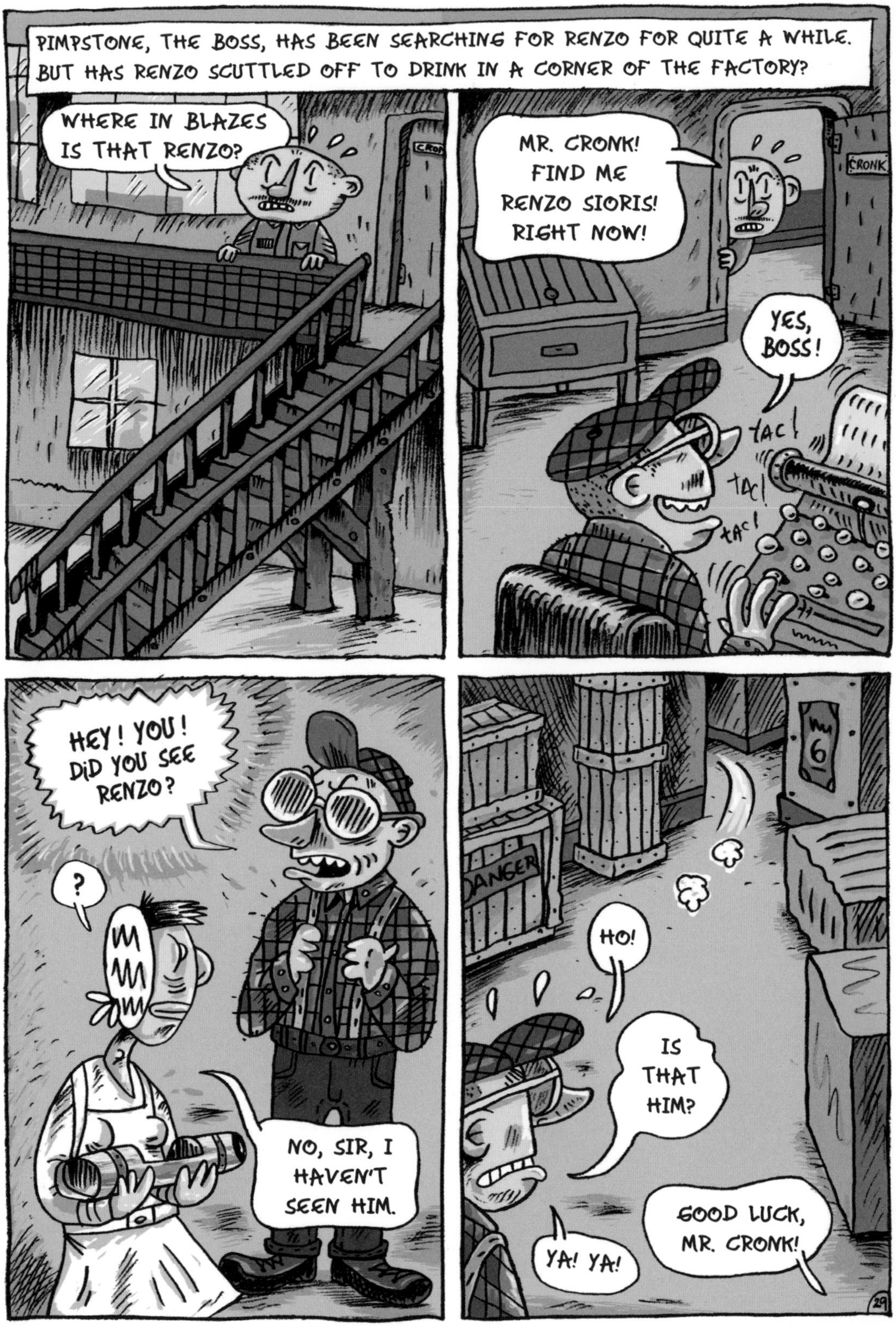
PIMPSTONE, THE BOSS, HAS BEEN SEARCHING FOR RENZO FOR QUITE A WHILE. BUT HAS RENZO SCUTTLED OFF TO DRINK IN A CORNER OF THE FACTORY?
WHERE IN BLAZES IS THAT RENZO?
MR. CRONK! FIND ME RENZO SIORIS! RIGHT NOW!
CRONK
YES, BOSS!
TAC!
TAC!
TAC!
HEY! YOU! DID YOU SEE RENZO?
?
NO, SIR, I HAVEN'T SEEN HIM.
6
DANGER
HO!
IS THAT HIM?
YA! YA!
GOOD LUCK, MR. CRONK!
29

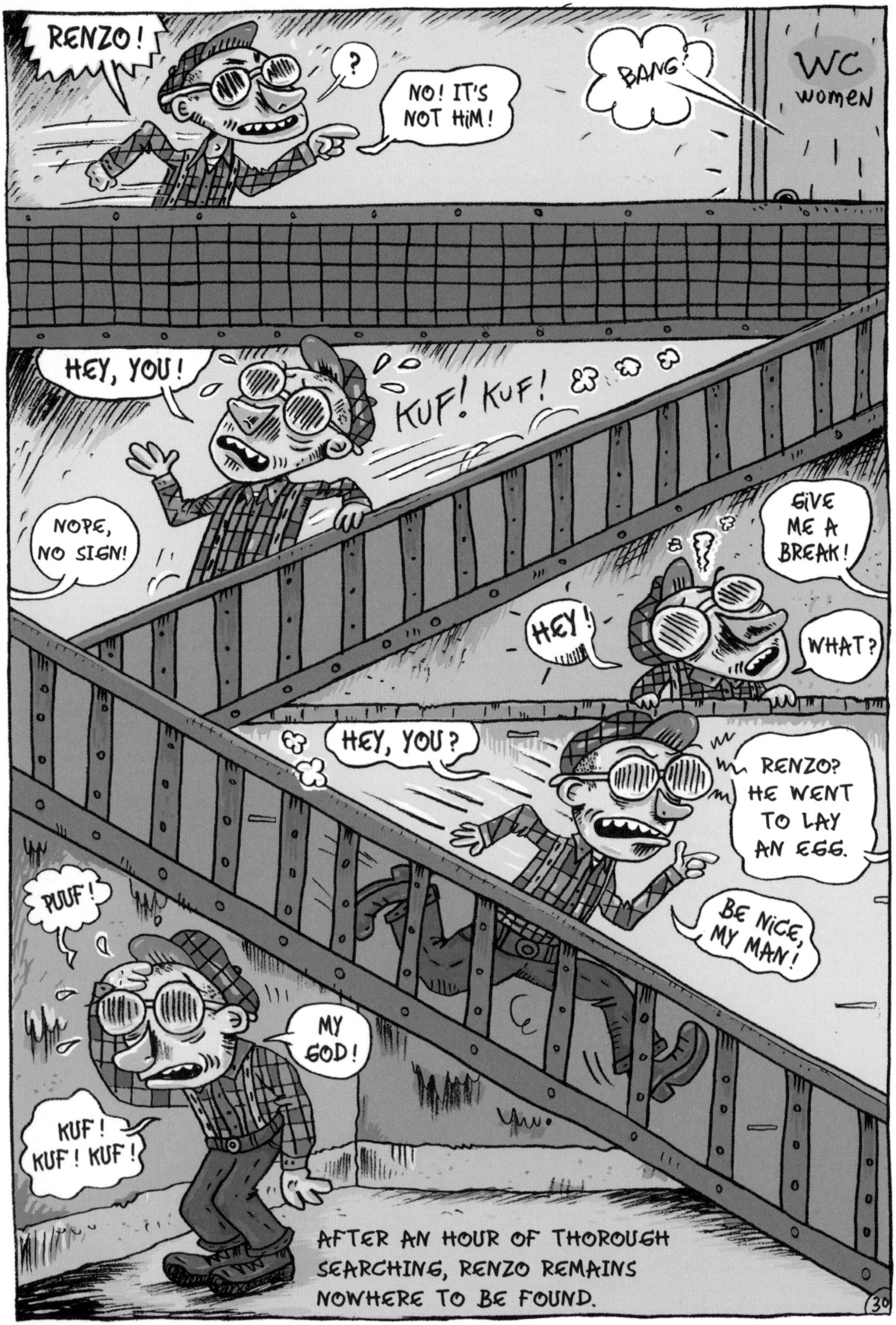

RENZO!
?
NO! IT'S NOT HIM!
BANG!
WC women
HEY, YOU!
KUF! KUF!
NOPE, NO SIGN!
GIVE ME A BREAK!
HEY!
WHAT?
HEY, YOU?
RENZO? HE WENT TO LAY AN EGG.
BE NICE, MY MAN!
PUUF!
MY GOD!
KUF! KUF! KUF!
AFTER AN HOUR OF THOROUGH SEARCHING, RENZO REMAINS NOWHERE TO BE FOUND.
30

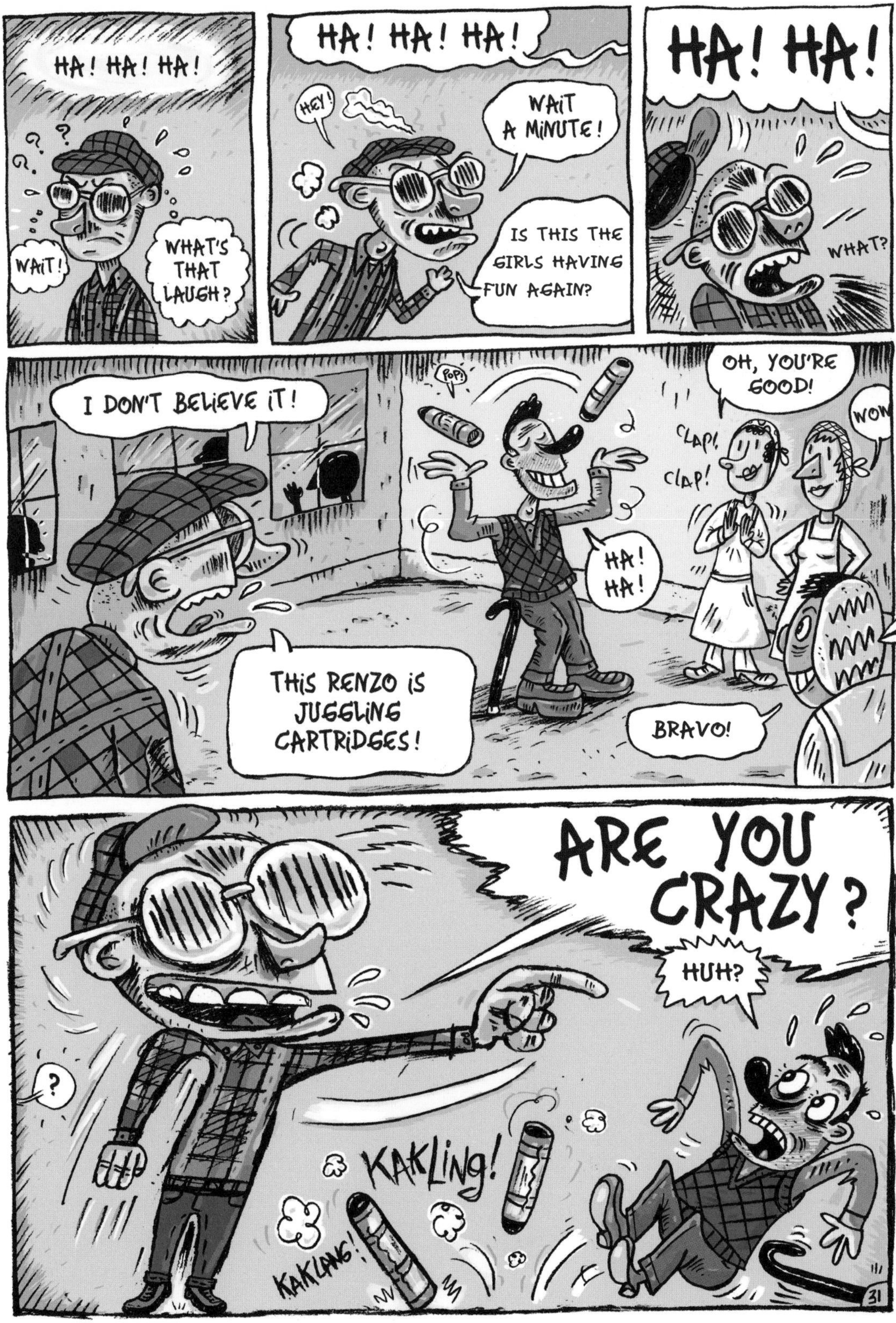
HA! HA! HA!
WAIT!
WHAT'S THAT LAUGH?
HA! HA! HA!
HEY!
WAIT A MINUTE!
IS THIS THE GIRLS HAVING FUN AGAIN?
HA! HA!
WHAT?
I DON'T BELIEVE IT!
THIS RENZO IS JUGGLING CARTRIDGES!
POP!
HA! HA!
OH, YOU'RE GOOD!
CLAP! CLAP!
WOW
BRAVO!
ARE YOU CRAZY?
HUH?
?
KAKLING!
KAKLANG!
31

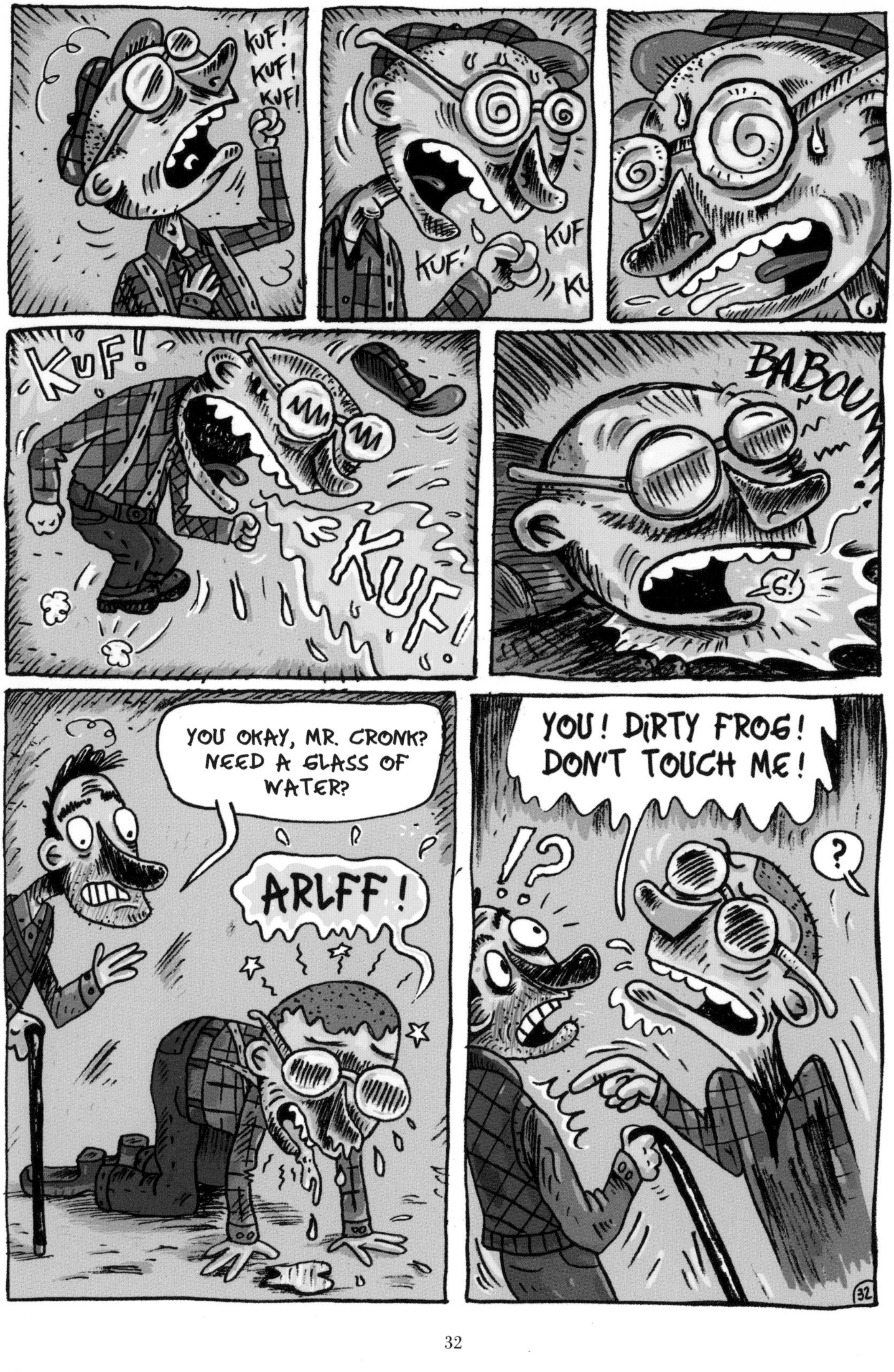
KUF! KUF! KUF!
KUF! KUF! KU
KUF!
KUF!
BABOUM
G!
YOU OKAY, MR. CRONK? NEED A GLASS OF WATER?
ARLFF!
YOU! DIRTY FROG! DON'T TOUCH ME!
!?
?
32

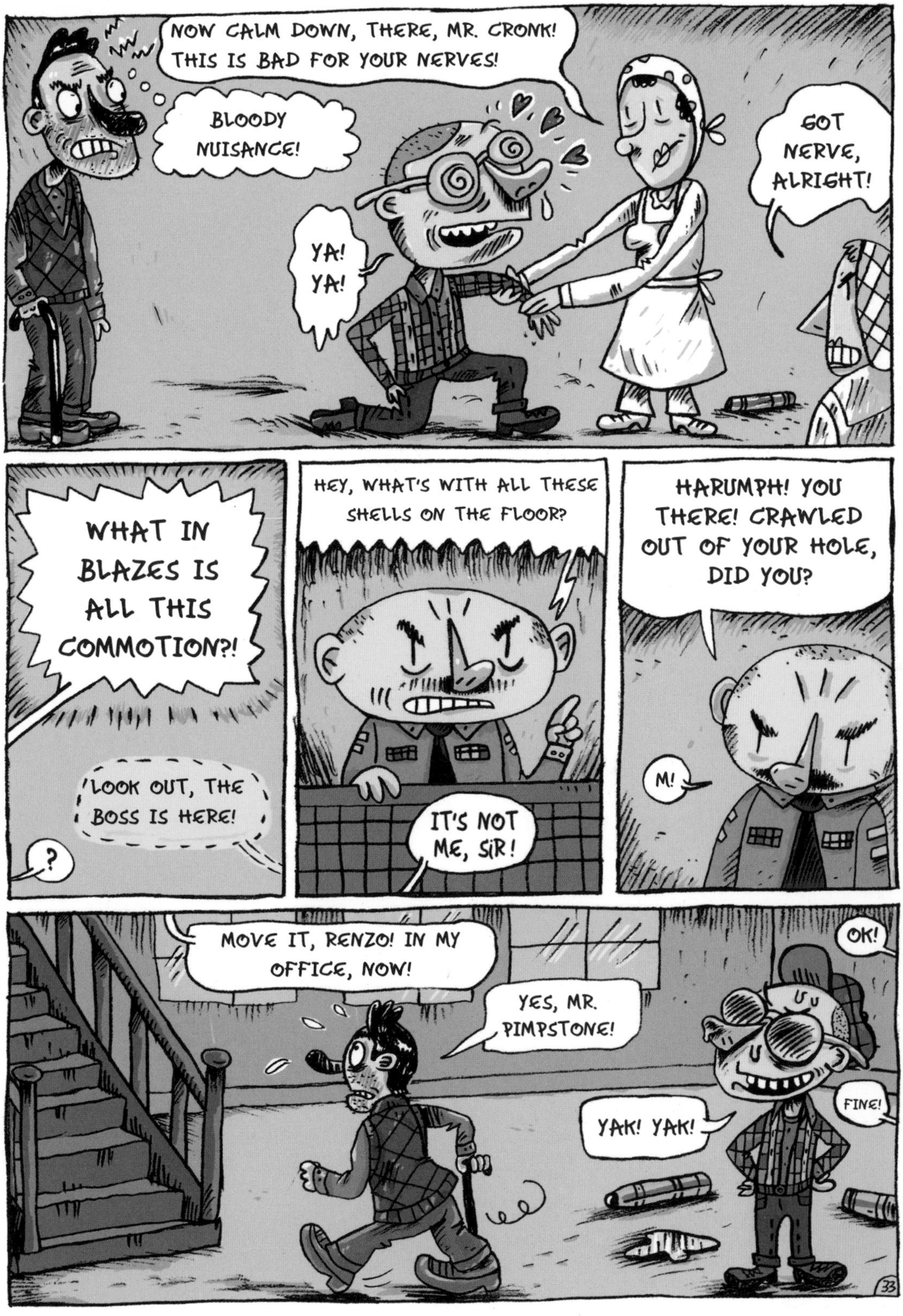
NOW CALM DOWN, THERE, MR. CRONK! THIS IS BAD FOR YOUR NERVES!
BLOODY NUISANCE!
YA! YA!
GOT NERVE, ALRIGHT!
WHAT IN BLAZES IS ALL THIS COMMOTION?!
LOOK OUT, THE BOSS IS HERE!
?
HEY, WHAT'S WITH ALL THESE SHELLS ON THE FLOOR?
IT'S NOT ME, SIR!
HARUMPH! YOU THERE! CRAWLED OUT OF YOUR HOLE, DID YOU?
M!
MOVE IT, RENZO! IN MY OFFICE, NOW!
OK!
YES, MR. PIMPSTONE!
YAK! YAK!
FINE!
33

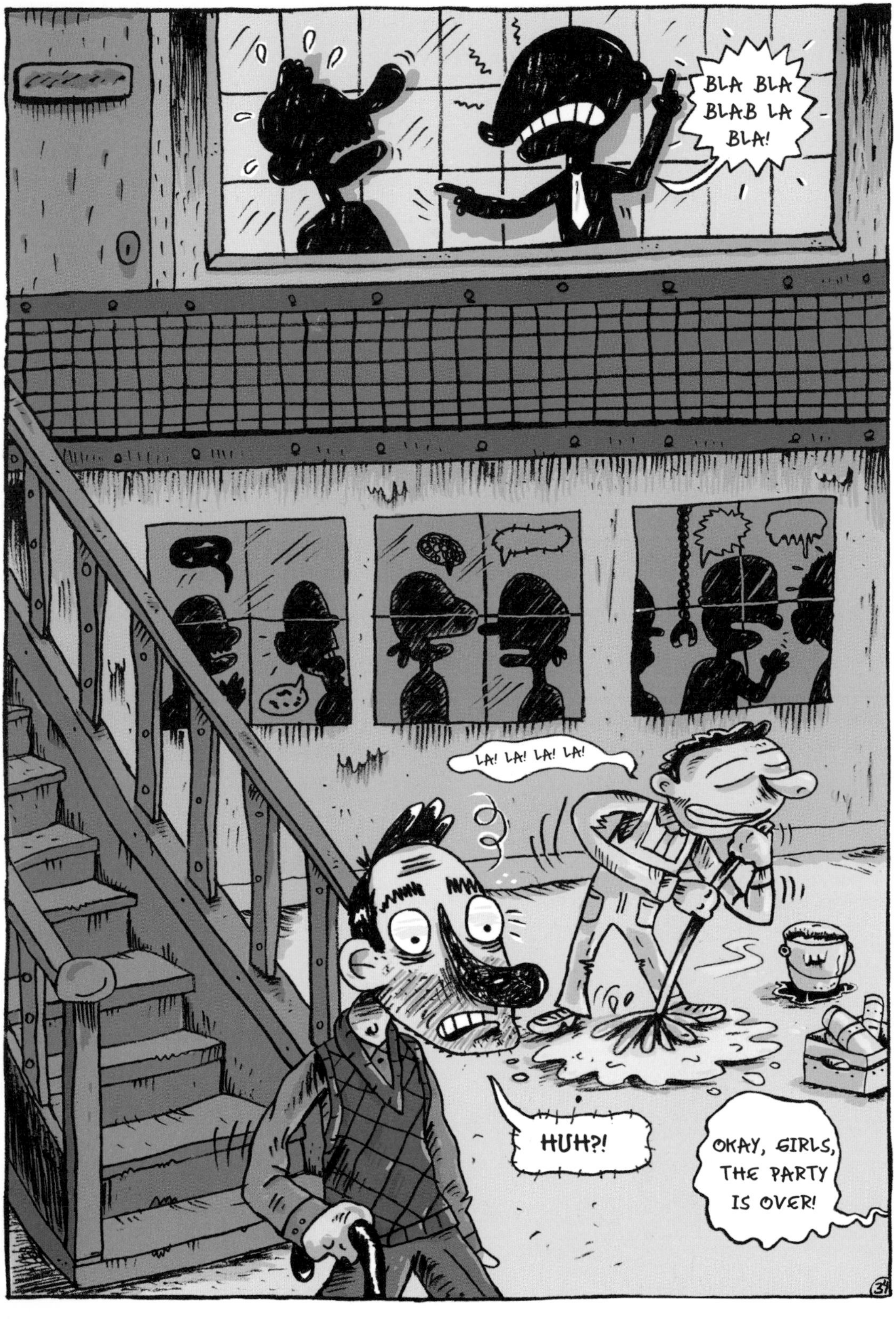
BLA BLA BLAB LA BLA!
LA! LA! LA! LA!
HUH?!
OKAY, GIRLS, THE PARTY IS OVER!

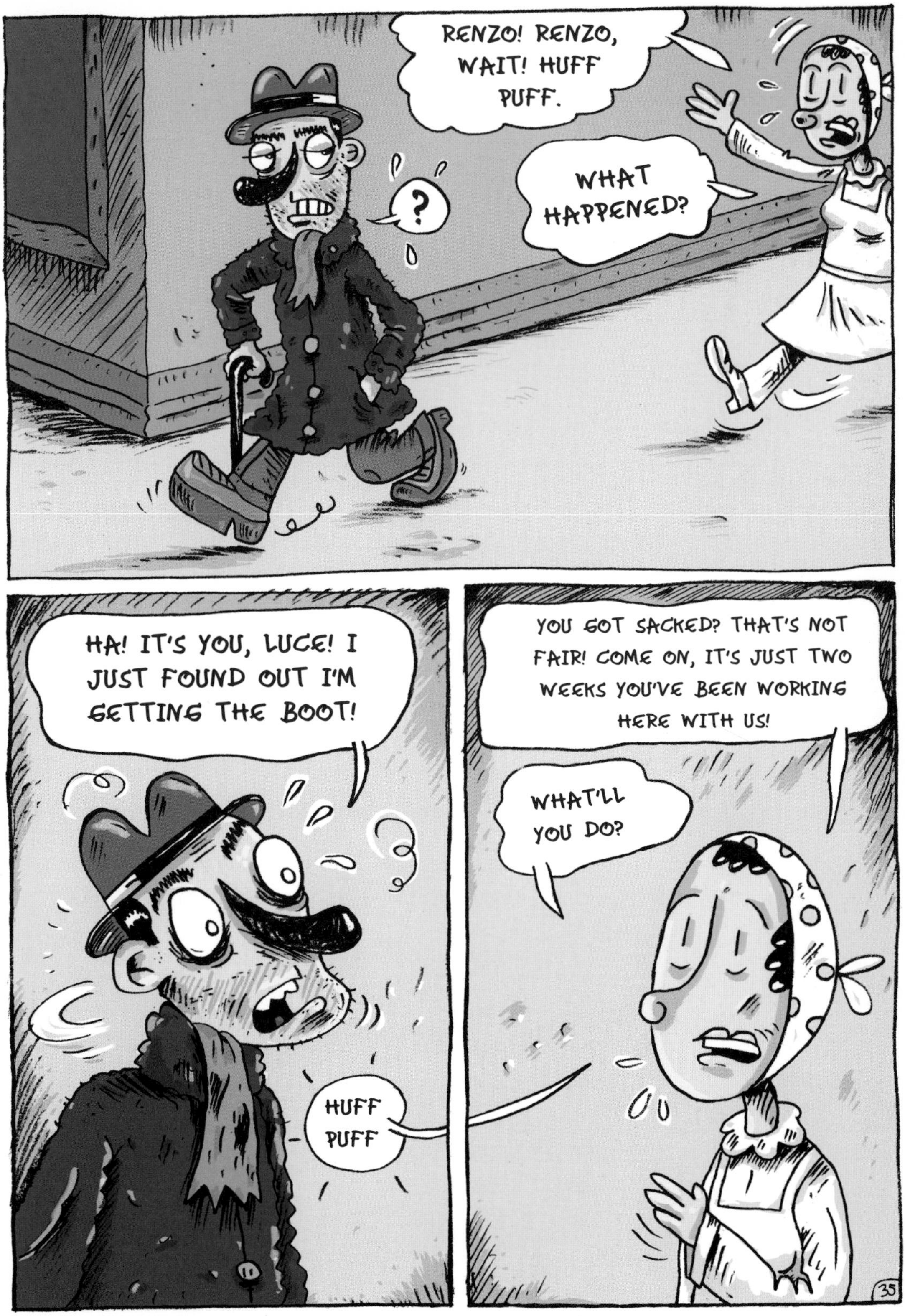
RENZO! RENZO, WAIT! HUFF PUFF.
?
WHAT HAPPENED?
HA! IT'S YOU, LUCE! I JUST FOUND OUT I'M GETTING THE BOOT!
HUFF PUFF
YOU GOT SACKED? THAT'S NOT FAIR! COME ON, IT'S JUST TWO WEEKS YOU'VE BEEN WORKING HERE WITH US!
WHAT'LL YOU DO?
35

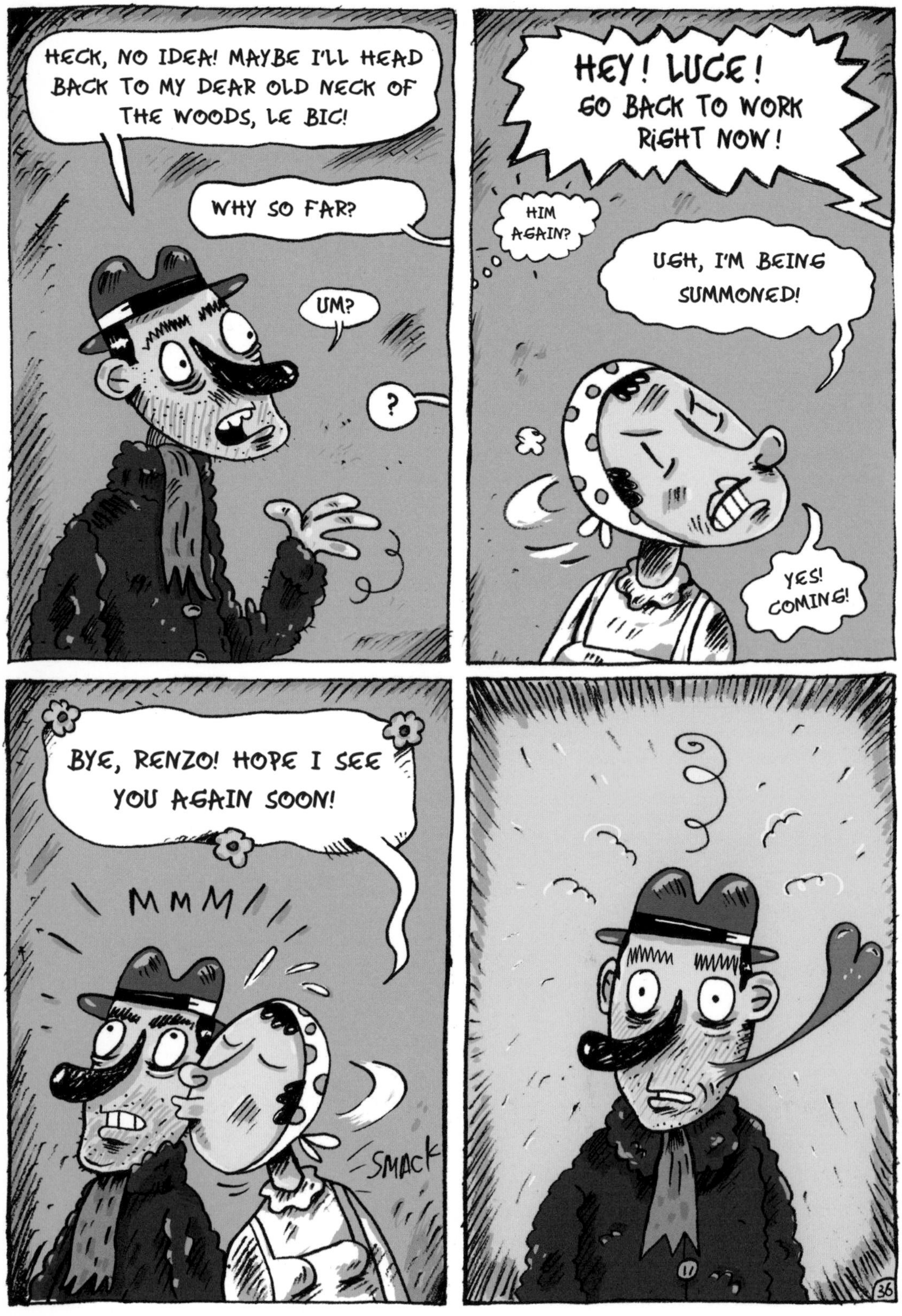
HECK, NO IDEA! MAYBE I'LL HEAD BACK TO MY DEAR OLD NECK OF THE WOODS, LE BIC!
WHY SO FAR?
UM?
?
HEY! LUCE! GO BACK TO WORK RIGHT NOW!
HIM AGAIN?
UGH, I'M BEING SUMMONED!
YES! COMING!
BYE, RENZO! HOPE I SEE YOU AGAIN SOON!
MMM
SMACK
36

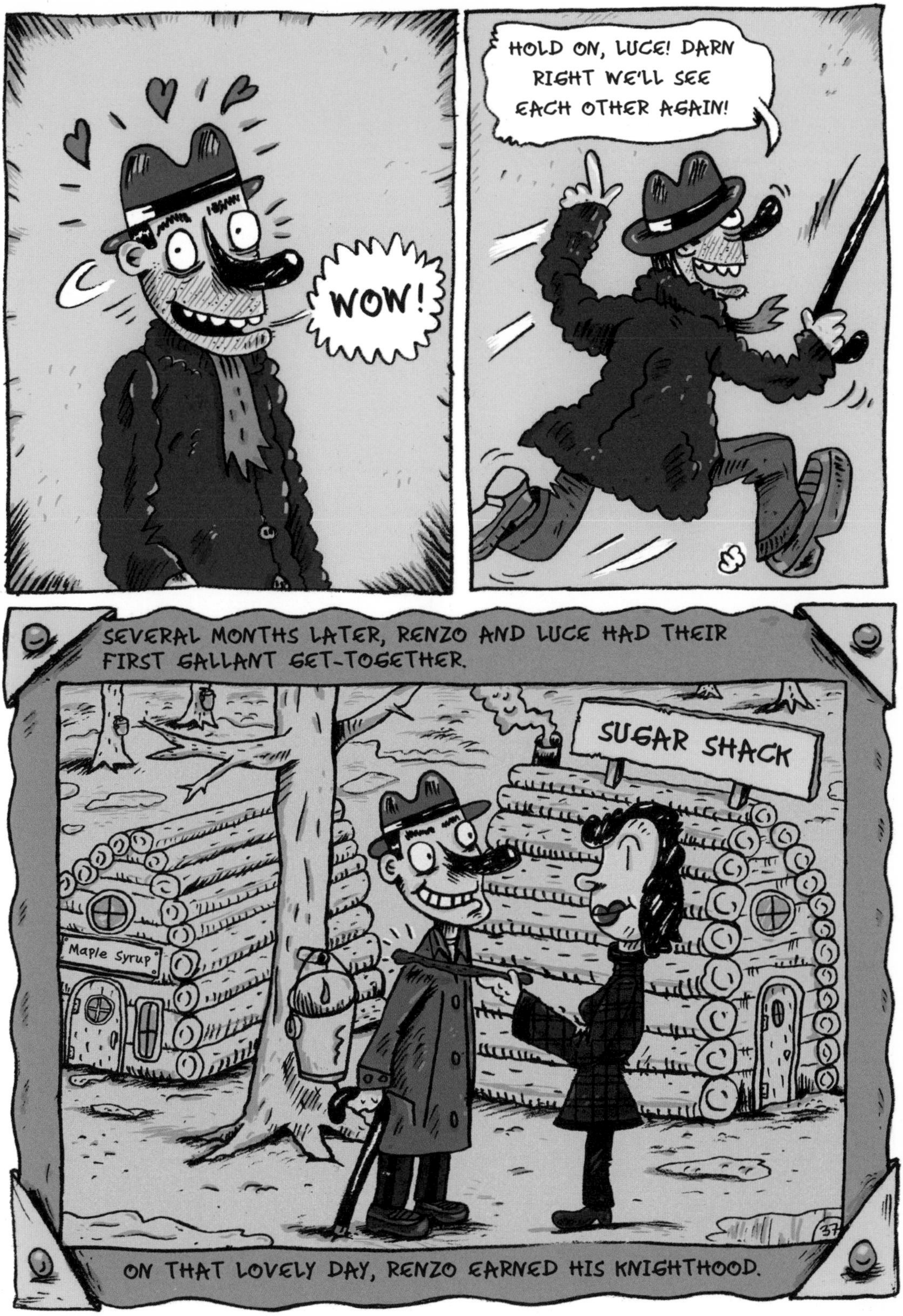
WOW!
HOLD ON, LUCE! DARN RIGHT WE'LL SEE EACH OTHER AGAIN!
SEVERAL MONTHS LATER, RENZO AND LUCE HAD THEIR FIRST GALLANT GET-TOGETHER.
SUGAR SHACK
Maple Syrup
37
ON THAT LOVELY DAY, RENZO EARNED HIS KNIGHTHOOD.

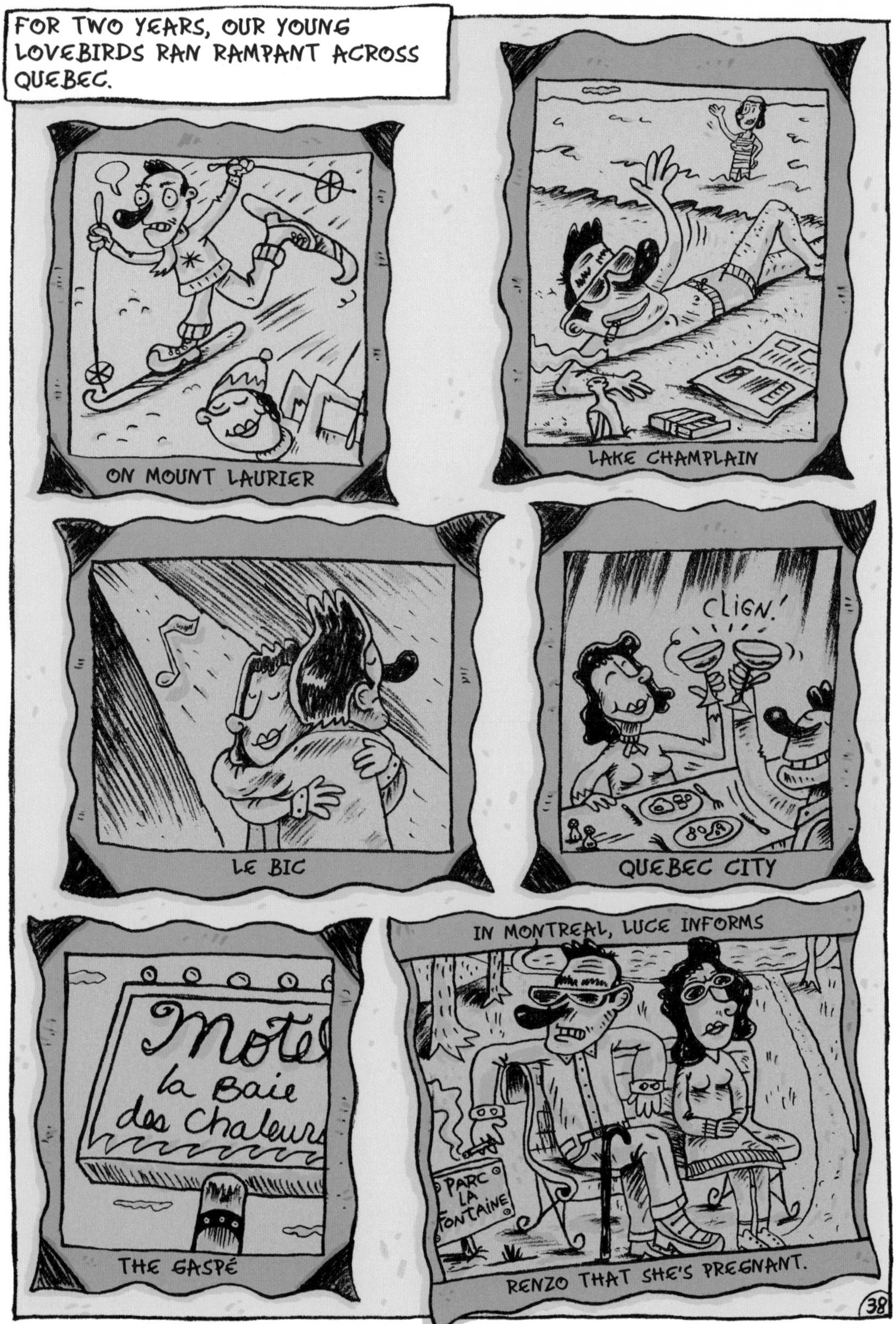
FOR TWO YEARS, OUR YOUNG LOVEBIRDS RAN RAMPANT ACROSS QUEBEC.
ON MOUNT LAURIER
LAKE CHAMPLAIN
LE BIC
CLIGN!
QUEBEC CITY
Motel la Baie des Chaleurs
THE GASPÉ
IN MONTREAL, LUCE INFORMS
PARC LA FONTAINE
RENZO THAT SHE'S PREGNANT.
38

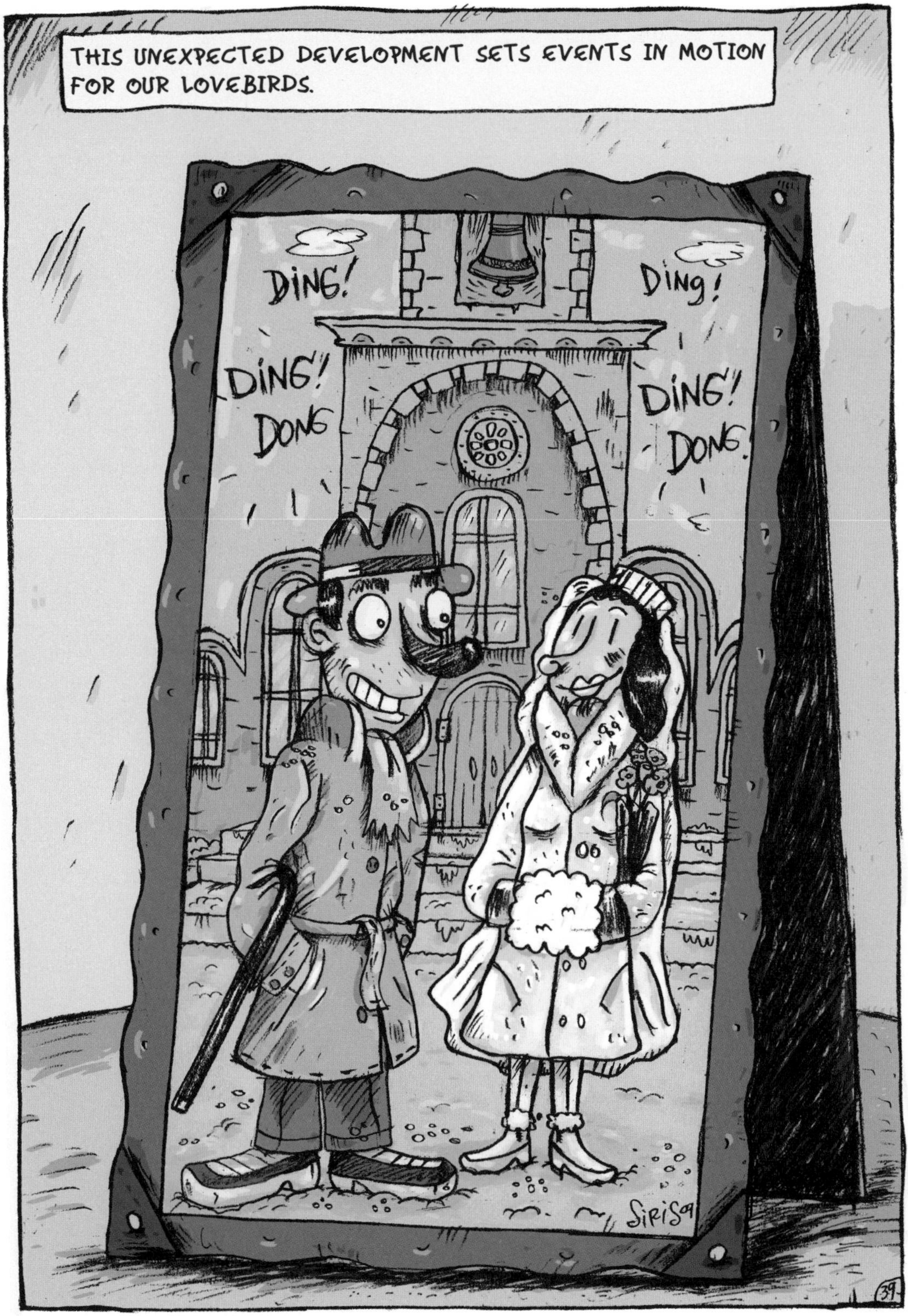
THIS UNEXPECTED DEVELOPMENT SETS EVENTS IN MOTION FOR OUR LOVEBIRDS.
DING!
Ding!
DING! DONG
DING! DONG

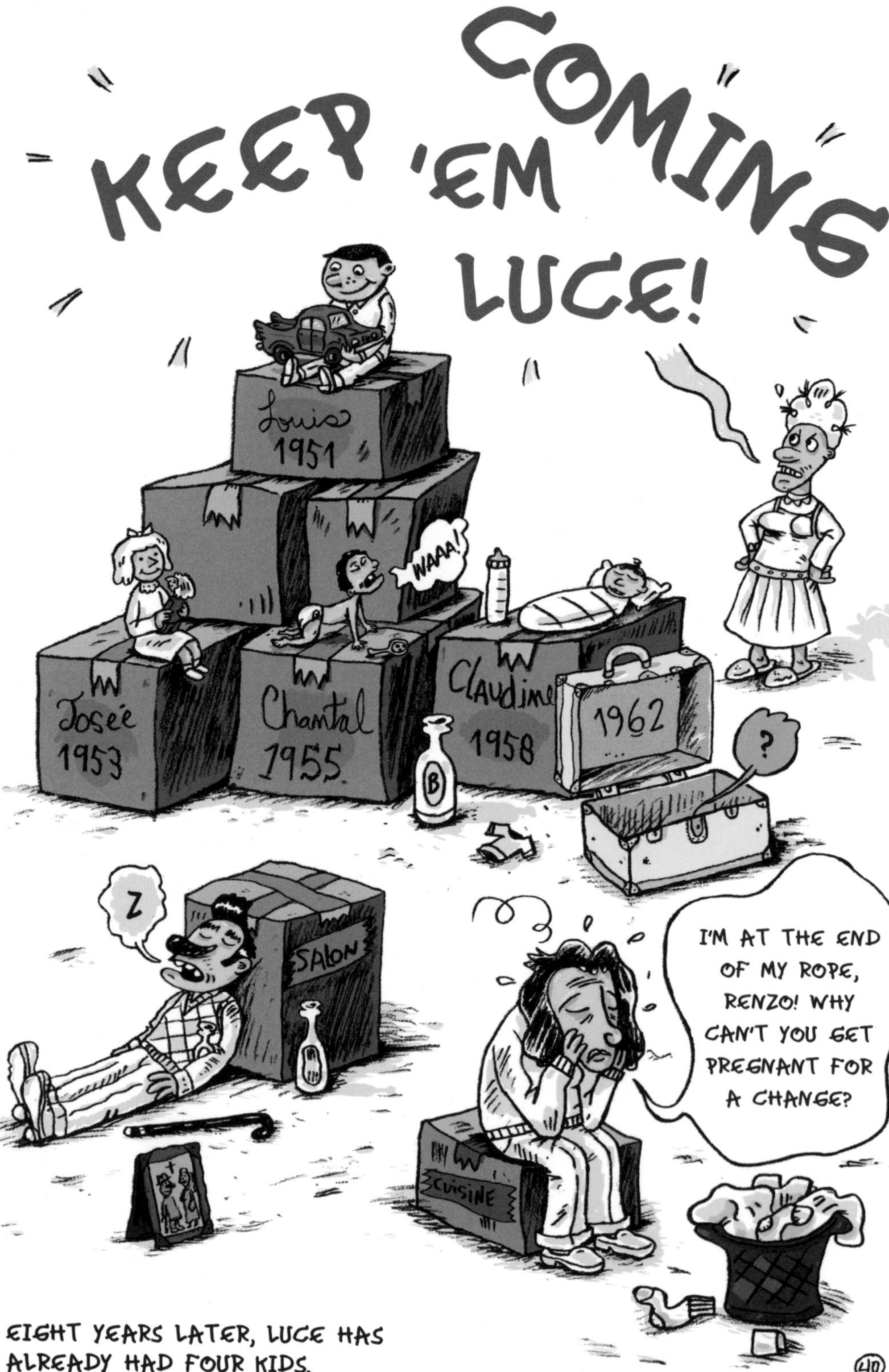
KEEP 'EM COMING LUCE!
Louis 1951
Josée 1953
Chantal 1955
Claudine 1958
1962
WAAA!
?
B
Z
SALON
CUISINE
I'M AT THE END OF MY ROPE, RENZO! WHY CAN'T YOU GET PREGNANT FOR A CHANGE?
EIGHT YEARS LATER, LUCE HAS ALREADY HAD FOUR KIDS.
40

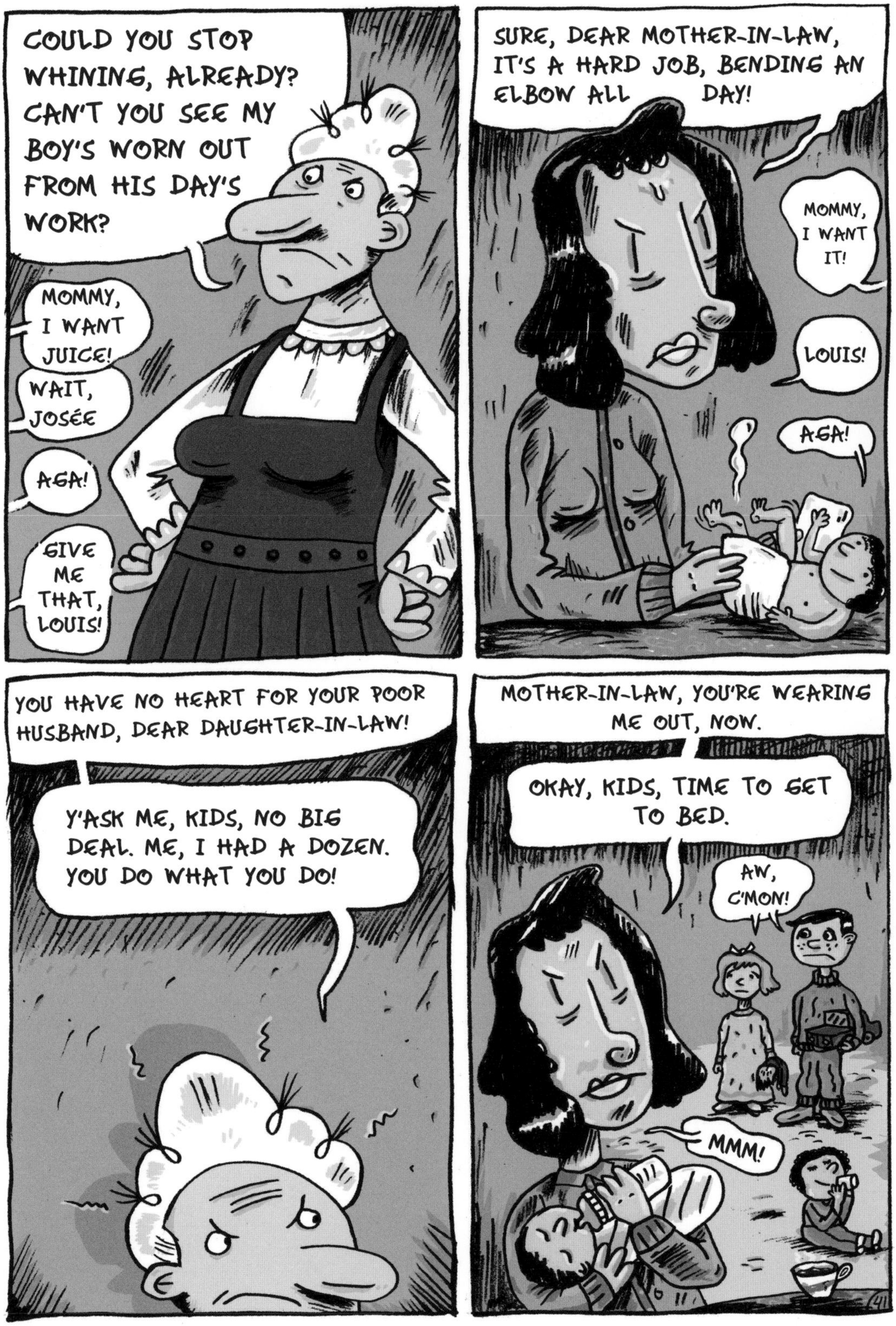
COULD YOU STOP WHINING, ALREADY? CAN'T YOU SEE MY BOY'S WORN OUT FROM HIS DAY'S WORK?
MOMMY, I WANT JUICE!
WAIT, JOSÉE
AGA!
GIVE ME THAT, LOUIS!
SURE, DEAR MOTHER-IN-LAW, IT'S A HARD JOB, BENDING AN ELBOW ALL DAY!
MOMMY, I WANT IT!
LOUIS!
AGA!
YOU HAVE NO HEART FOR YOUR POOR HUSBAND, DEAR DAUGHTER-IN-LAW!
Y'ASK ME, KIDS, NO BIG DEAL. ME, I HAD A DOZEN. YOU DO WHAT YOU DO!
MOTHER-IN-LAW, YOU'RE WEARING ME OUT, NOW.
OKAY, KIDS, TIME TO GET TO BED.
AW, C'MON!
MMM!

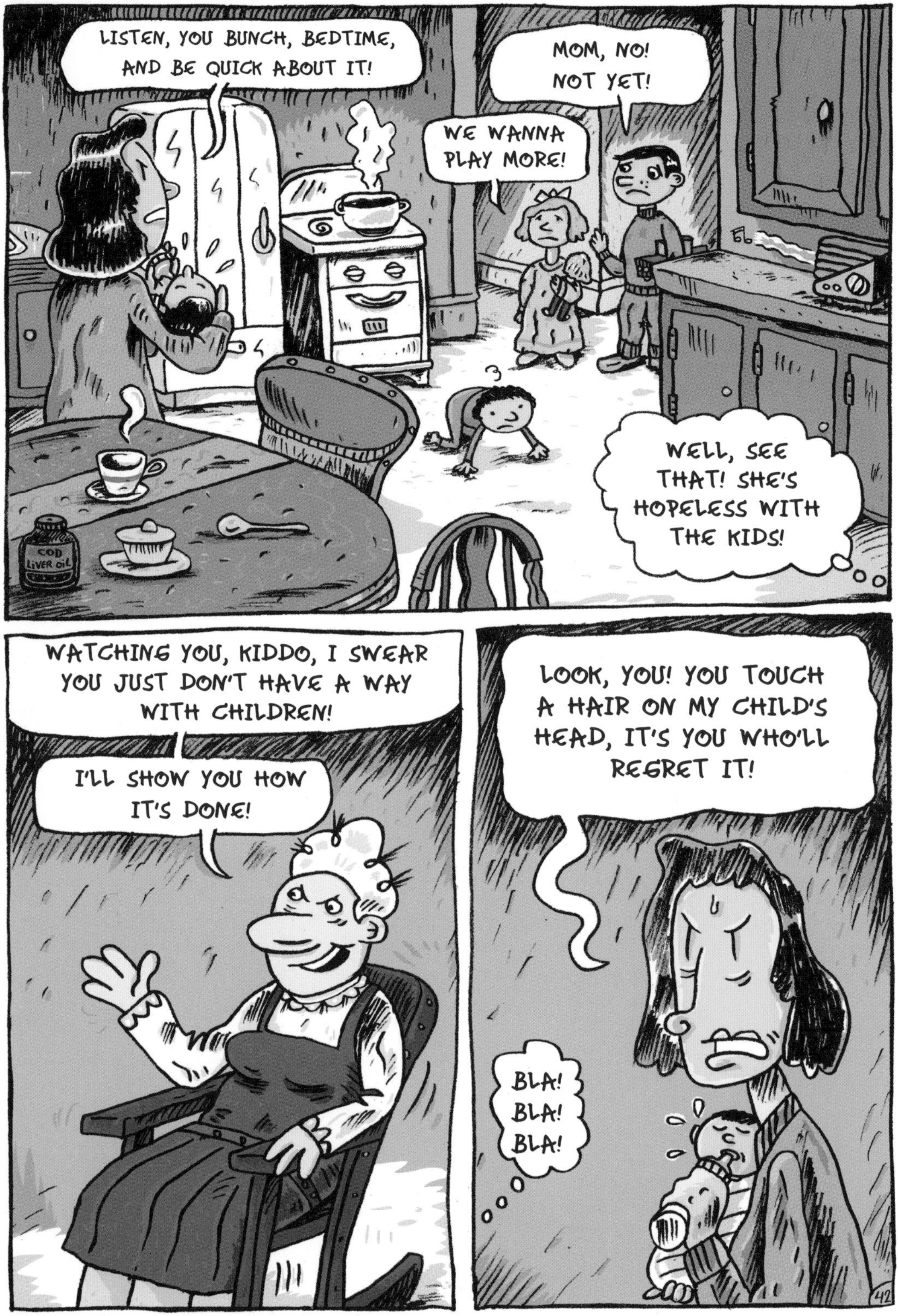
LISTEN, YOU BUNCH, BEDTIME, AND BE QUICK ABOUT IT!
MOM, NO! NOT YET!
WE WANNA PLAY MORE!
COD LIVER OIL
WELL, SEE THAT! SHE'S HOPELESS WITH THE KIDS!
WATCHING YOU, KIDDO, I SWEAR YOU JUST DON'T HAVE A WAY WITH CHILDREN!
I'LL SHOW YOU HOW IT'S DONE!
LOOK, YOU! YOU TOUCH A HAIR ON MY CHILD'S HEAD, IT'S YOU WHO'LL REGRET IT!
BLA! BLA! BLA!

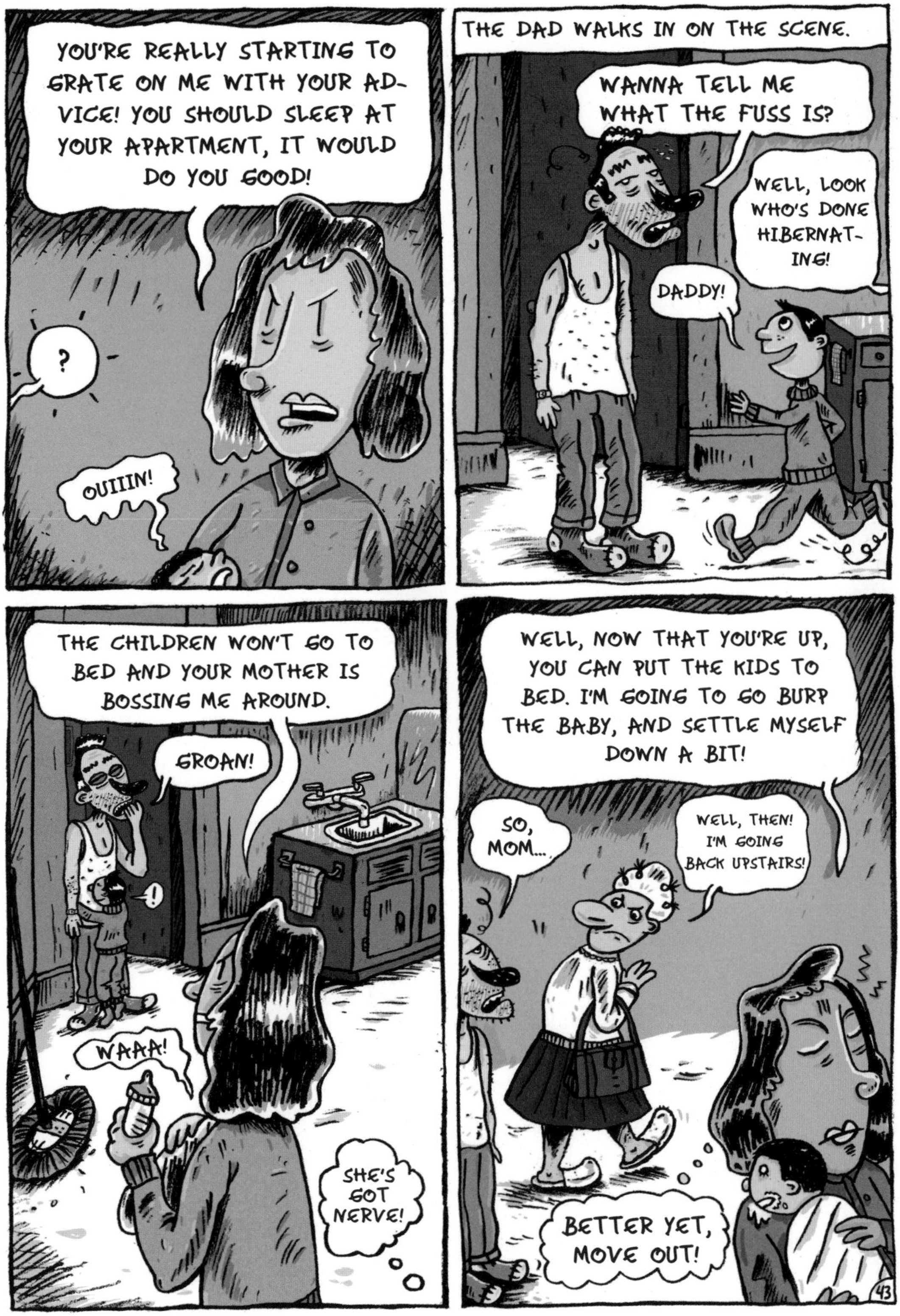
YOU'RE REALLY STARTING TO GRATE ON ME WITH YOUR ADVICE! YOU SHOULD SLEEP AT YOUR APARTMENT, IT WOULD DO YOU GOOD!
?
OUIIIN!
THE DAD WALKS IN ON THE SCENE.
WANNA TELL ME WHAT THE FUSS IS?
WELL, LOOK WHO'S DONE HIBERNATING!
DADDY!
THE CHILDREN WON'T GO TO BED AND YOUR MOTHER IS BOSSING ME AROUND.
GROAN!
!
WAAA!
SHE'S GOT NERVE!
WELL, NOW THAT YOU'RE UP, YOU CAN PUT THE KIDS TO BED. I'M GOING TO GO BURP THE BABY, AND SETTLE MYSELF DOWN A BIT!
SO, MOM...
WELL, THEN! I'M GOING BACK UPSTAIRS!
BETTER YET, MOVE OUT!
43

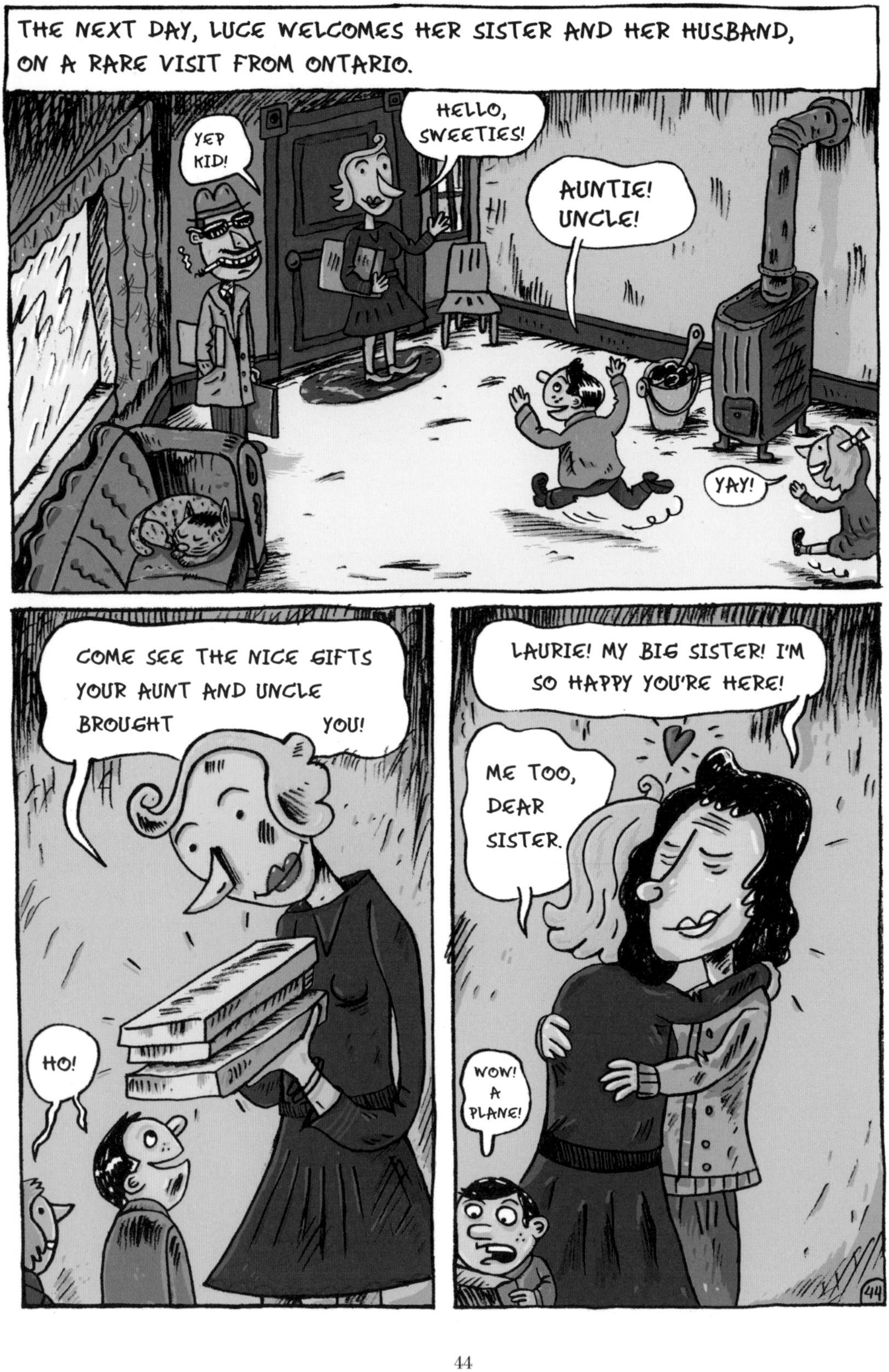
THE NEXT DAY, LUCE WELCOMES HER SISTER AND HER HUSBAND, ON A RARE VISIT FROM ONTARIO.
YEP KID!
HELLO, SWEETIES!
AUNTIE! UNCLE!
YAY!
COME SEE THE NICE GIFTS YOUR AUNT AND UNCLE BROUGHT YOU!
HO!
LAURIE! MY BIG SISTER! I'M SO HAPPY YOU'RE HERE!
ME TOO, DEAR SISTER.
WOW! A PLANE!
44

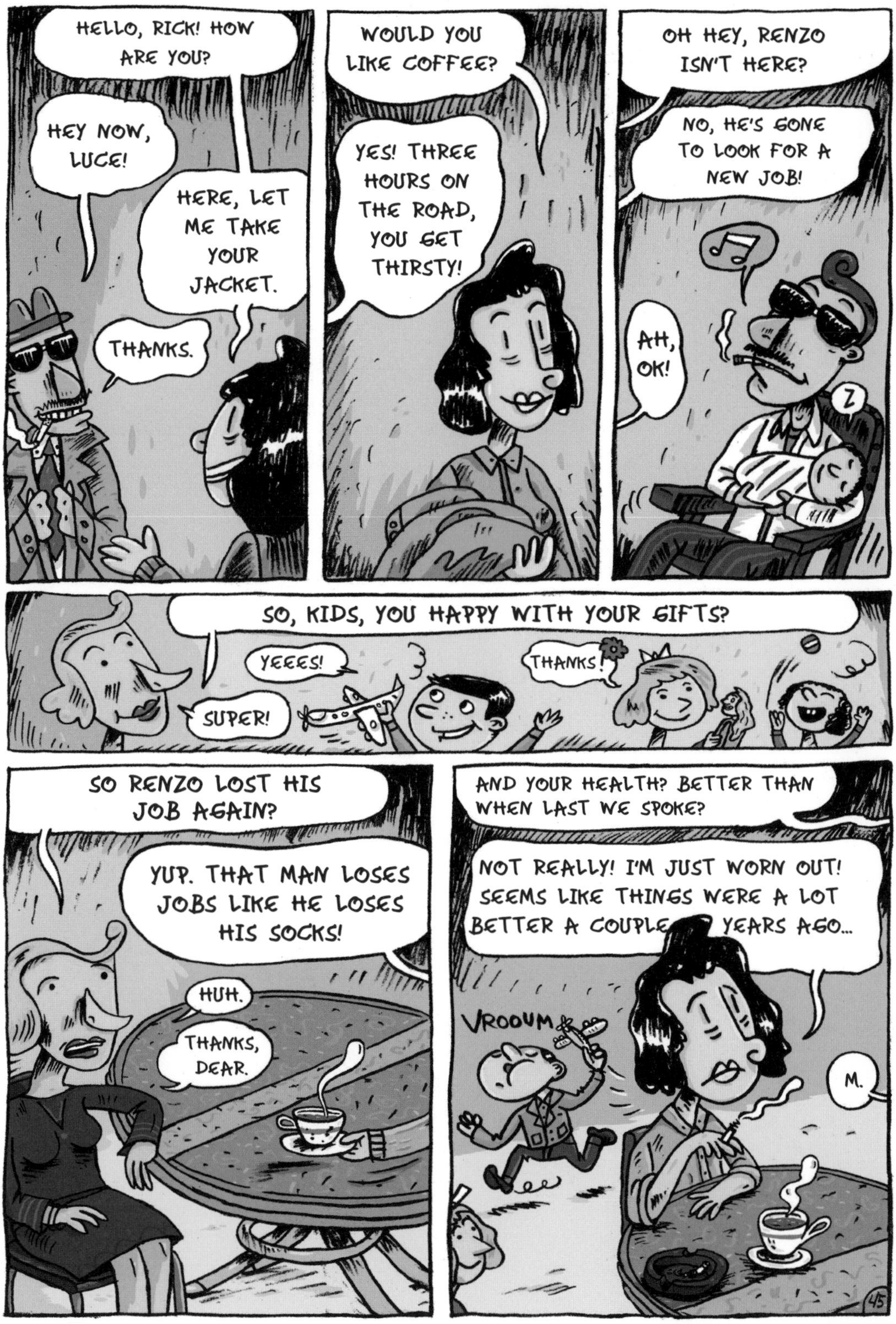
HELLO, RICK! HOW ARE YOU?
HEY NOW, LUCE!
HERE, LET ME TAKE YOUR JACKET.
THANKS.
WOULD YOU LIKE COFFEE?
YES! THREE HOURS ON THE ROAD, YOU GET THIRSTY!
OH HEY, RENZO ISN'T HERE?
NO, HE'S GONE TO LOOK FOR A NEW JOB!
AH, OK!
Z
SO, KIDS, YOU HAPPY WITH YOUR GIFTS?
YEEES!
SUPER!
THANKS!
SO RENZO LOST HIS JOB AGAIN?
YUP. THAT MAN LOSES JOBS LIKE HE LOSES HIS SOCKS!
HUH.
THANKS, DEAR.
AND YOUR HEALTH? BETTER THAN WHEN LAST WE SPOKE?
NOT REALLY! I'M JUST WORN OUT! SEEMS LIKE THINGS WERE A LOT BETTER A COUPLE YEARS AGO...
VROOUM
M.
45

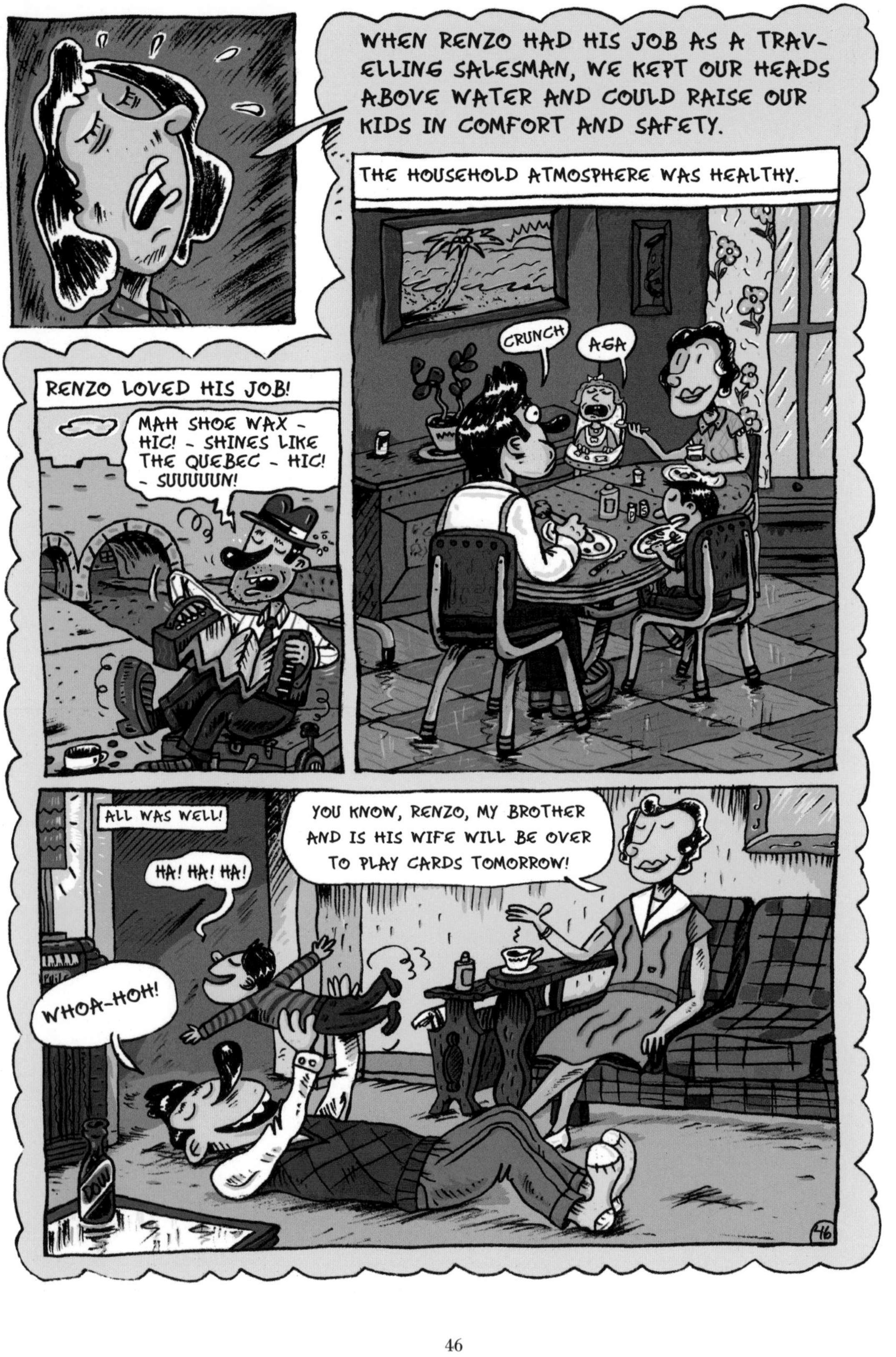
WHEN RENZO HAD HIS JOB AS A TRAVELLING SALESMAN, WE KEPT OUR HEADS ABOVE WATER AND COULD RAISE OUR KIDS IN COMFORT AND SAFETY.
THE HOUSEHOLD ATMOSPHERE WAS HEALTHY.
CRUNCH
AGA
RENZO LOVED HIS JOB!
MAH SHOE WAX - HIC! - SHINES LIKE THE QUEBEC - HIC! - SUUUUUN!
ALL WAS WELL!
HA! HA! HA!
WHOA-HOH!
YOU KNOW, RENZO, MY BROTHER AND IS HIS WIFE WILL BE OVER TO PLAY CARDS TOMORROW!
46

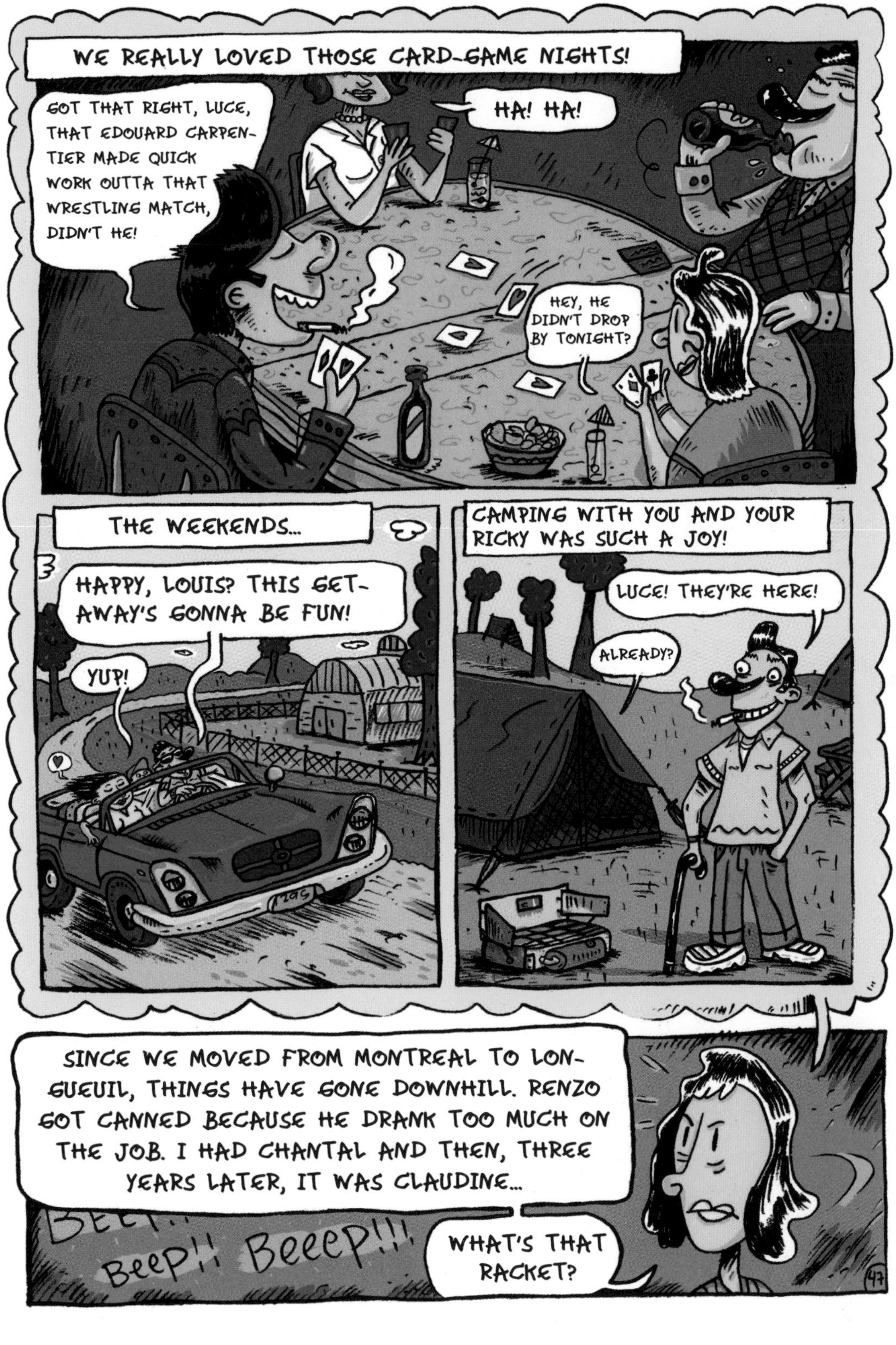
WE REALLY LOVED THOSE CARD-GAME NIGHTS!
GOT THAT RIGHT, LUCE, THAT EDOUARD CARPEN-TIER MADE QUICK WORK OUTTA THAT WRESTLING MATCH, DIDN'T HE!
HA! HA!
HEY, HE DIDN'T DROP BY TONIGHT?
THE WEEKENDS...
HAPPY, LOUIS? THIS GET-AWAY'S GONNA BE FUN!
YUP!
CAMPING WITH YOU AND YOUR RICKY WAS SUCH A JOY!
LUCE! THEY'RE HERE!
ALREADY?
SINCE WE MOVED FROM MONTREAL TO LON-GUEUIL, THINGS HAVE GONE DOWNHILL. RENZO GOT CANNED BECAUSE HE DRANK TOO MUCH ON THE JOB. I HAD CHANTAL AND THEN, THREE YEARS LATER, IT WAS CLAUDINE...
Beep!! Beeep!!!
WHAT'S THAT RACKET?
47

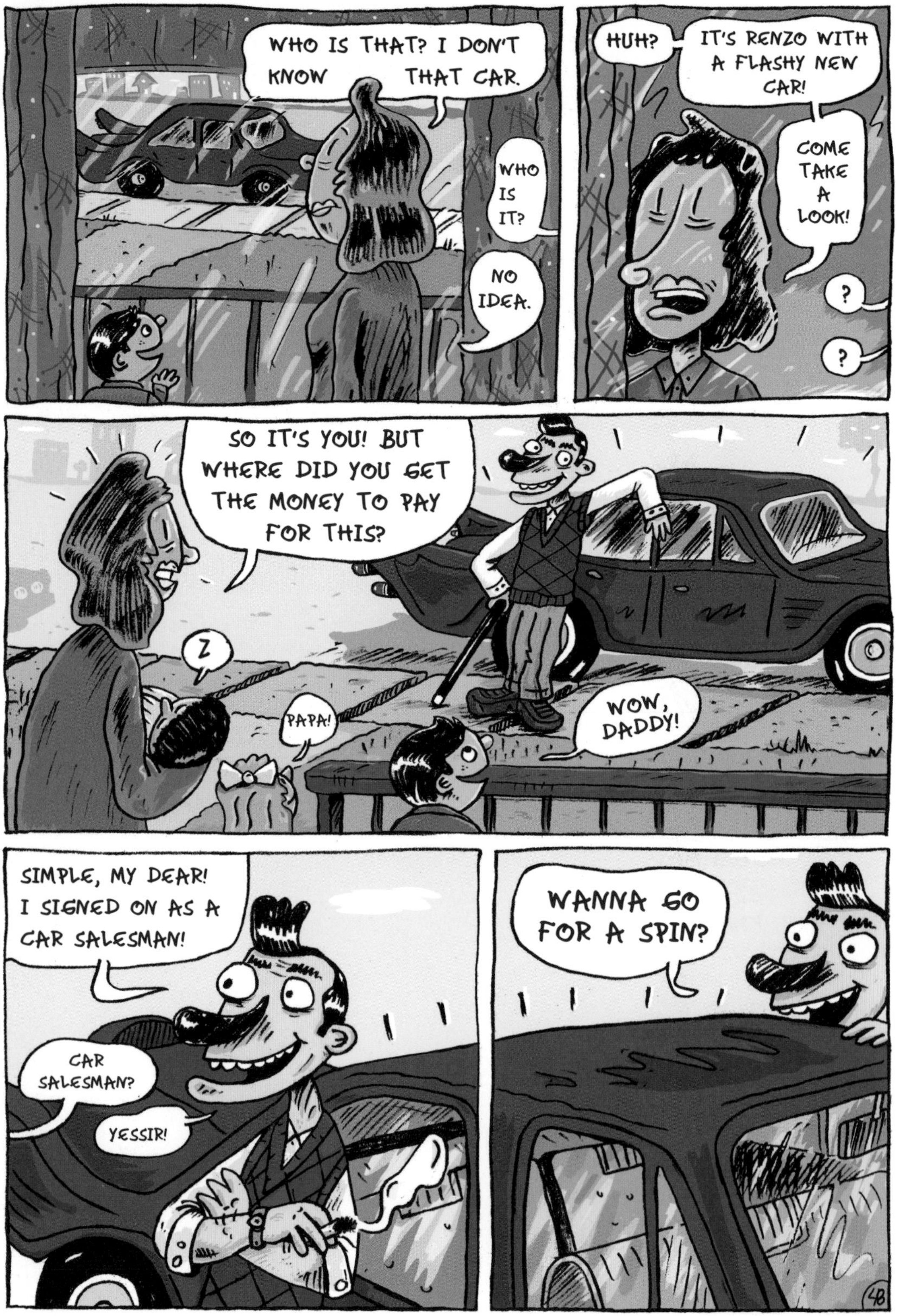
WHO IS THAT? I DON'T KNOW THAT CAR.
WHO IS IT?
NO IDEA.
HUH?
IT'S RENZO WITH A FLASHY NEW CAR!
COME TAKE A LOOK!
?
?
SO IT'S YOU! BUT WHERE DID YOU GET THE MONEY TO PAY FOR THIS?
Z
PAPA!
WOW, DADDY!
SIMPLE, MY DEAR! I SIGNED ON AS A CAR SALESMAN!
CAR SALESMAN?
YESSIR!
WANNA GO FOR A SPIN?
48

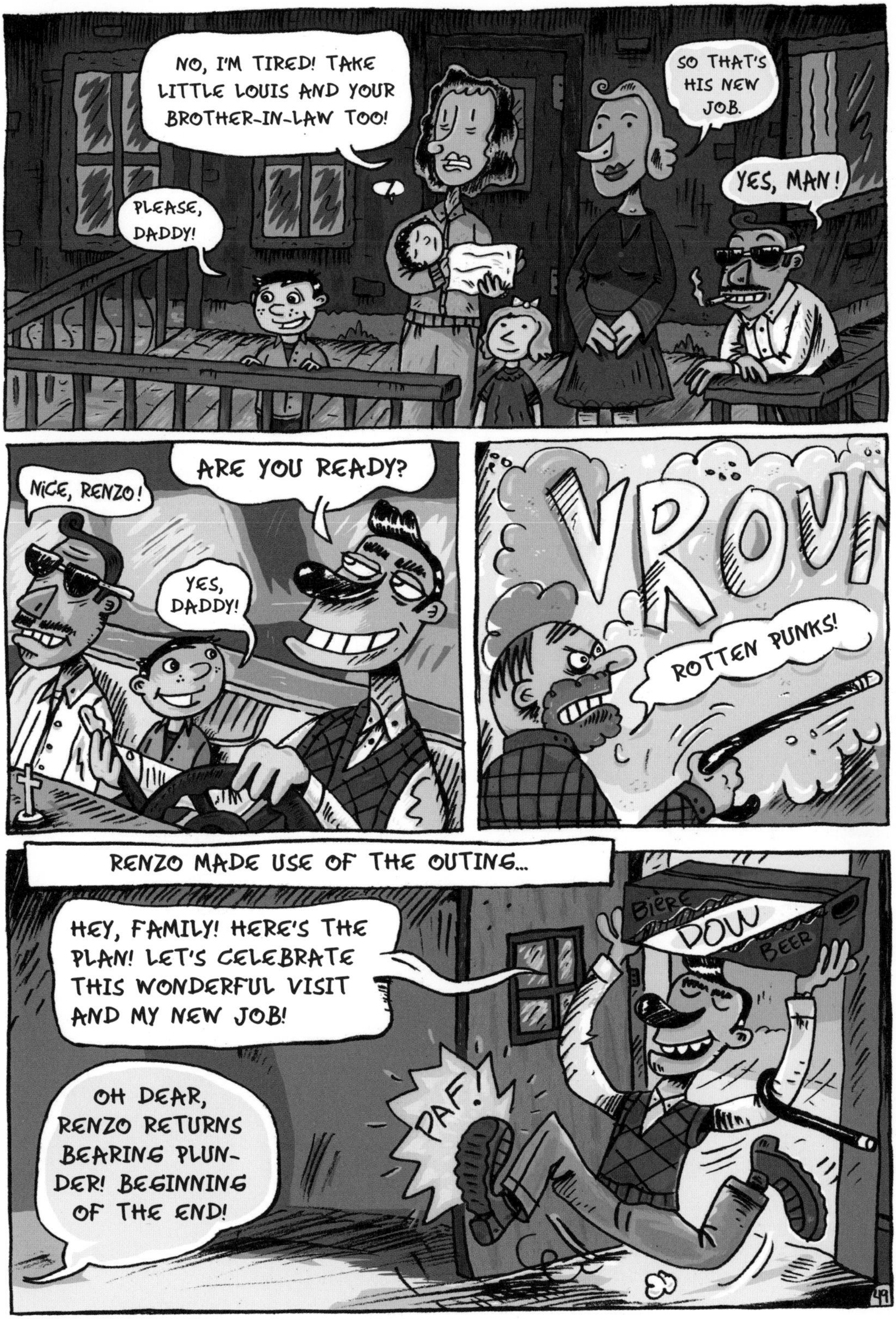
NO, I'M TIRED! TAKE LITTLE LOUIS AND YOUR BROTHER-IN-LAW TOO!
SO THAT'S HIS NEW JOB.
PLEASE, DADDY!
YES, MAN!
NICE, RENZO!
ARE YOU READY?
YES, DADDY!
VROUM
ROTTEN PUNKS!
RENZO MADE USE OF THE OUTING...
HEY, FAMILY! HERE'S THE PLAN! LET'S CELEBRATE THIS WONDERFUL VISIT AND MY NEW JOB!
BIERE
DOW
BEER
OH DEAR, RENZO RETURNS BEARING PLUNDER! BEGINNING OF THE END!
PAF!
49

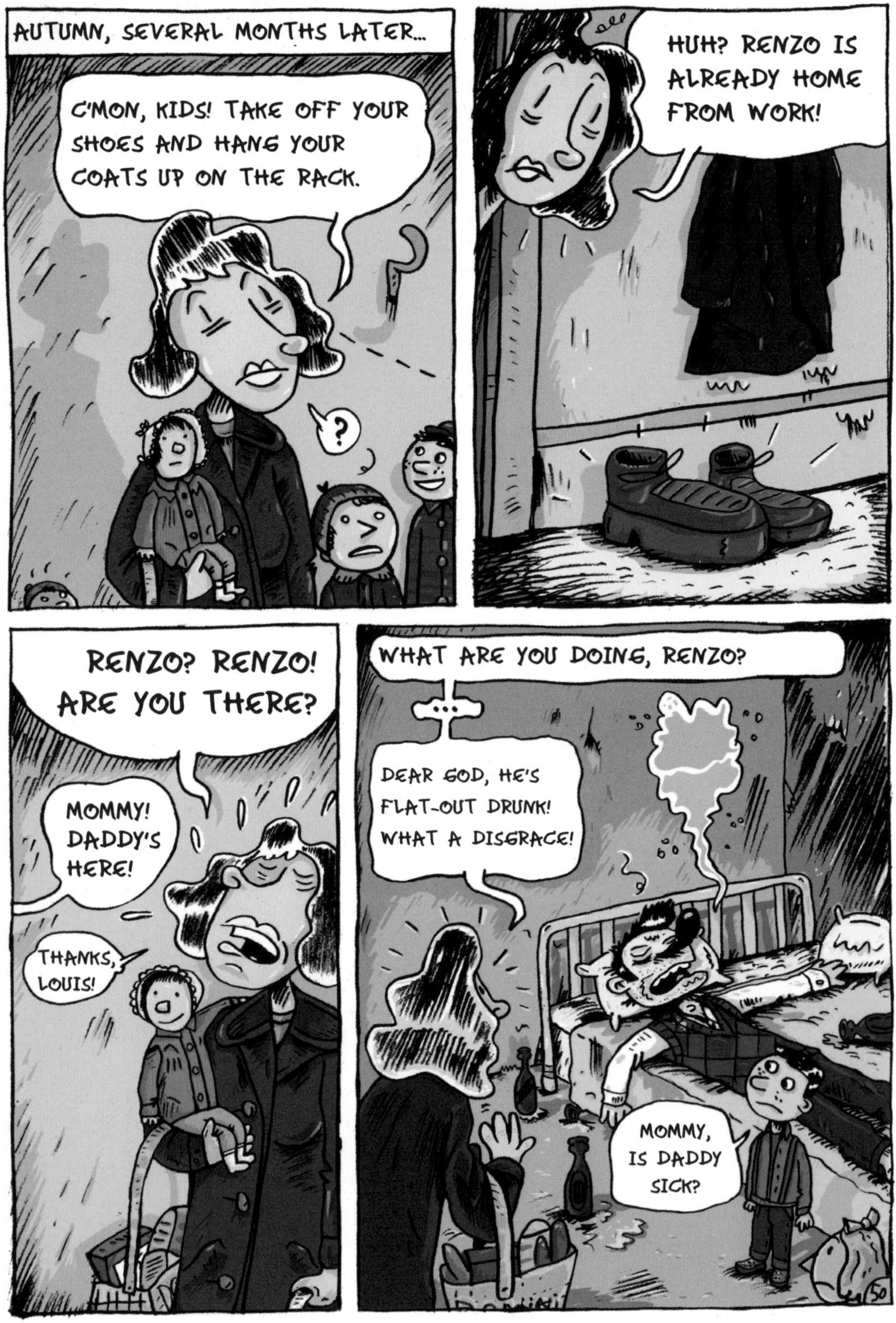
AUTUMN, SEVERAL MONTHS LATER...
C'MON, KIDS! TAKE OFF YOUR SHOES AND HANG YOUR COATS UP ON THE RACK.
?
HUH? RENZO IS ALREADY HOME FROM WORK!
RENZO? RENZO! ARE YOU THERE?
MOMMY! DADDY'S HERE!
THANKS, LOUIS!
WHAT ARE YOU DOING, RENZO?
...
DEAR GOD, HE'S FLAT-OUT DRUNK! WHAT A DISGRACE!
MOMMY, IS DADDY SICK?
50

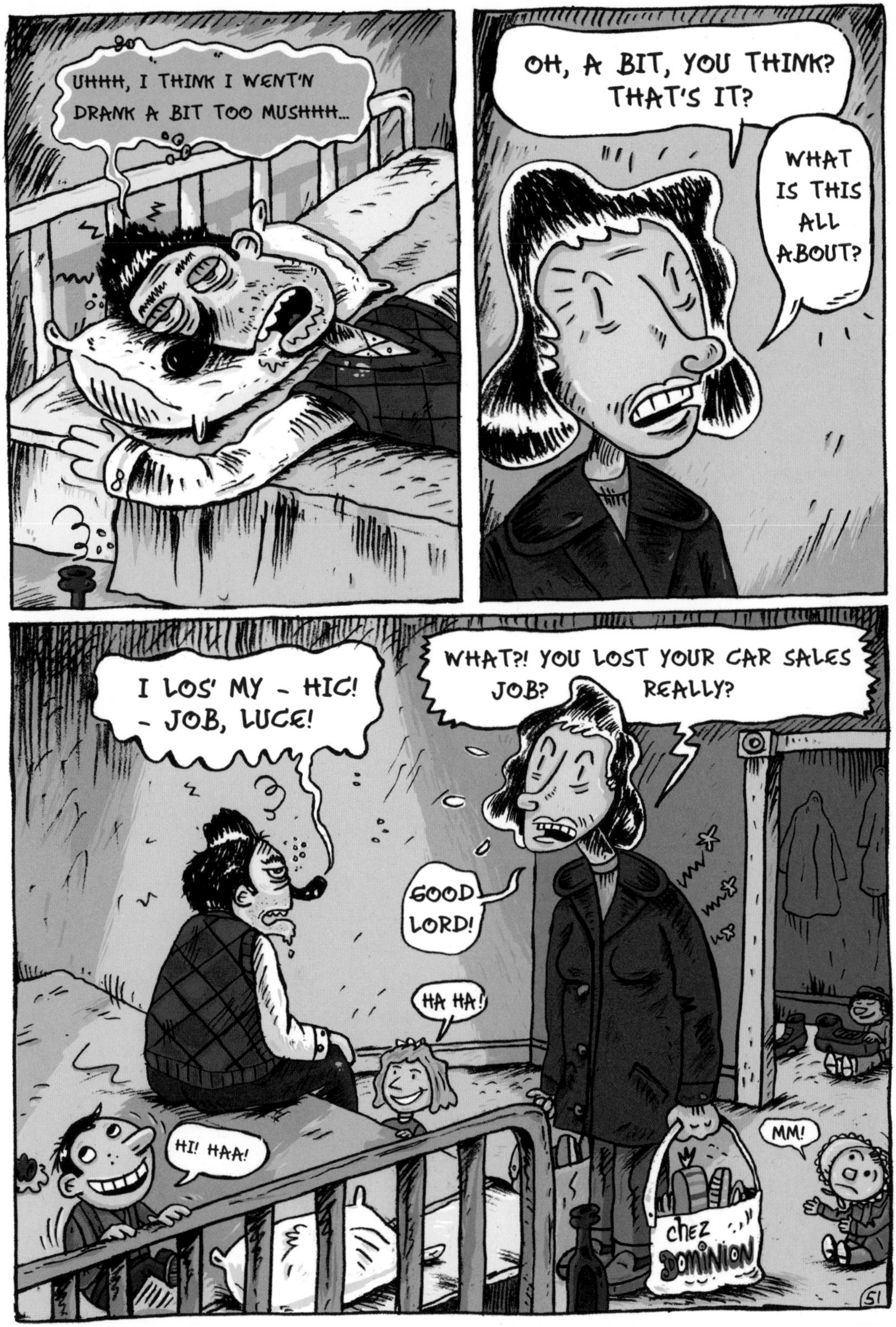
UHHH, I THINK I WENT'N DRANK A BIT TOO MUSHHH...
OH, A BIT, YOU THINK? THAT'S IT?
WHAT IS THIS ALL ABOUT?
I LOS' MY - HIC! - JOB, LUCE!
WHAT?! YOU LOST YOUR CAR SALES JOB? REALLY?
GOOD LORD!
HA HA!
HI! HAA!
MM!
chez DOMINION
51

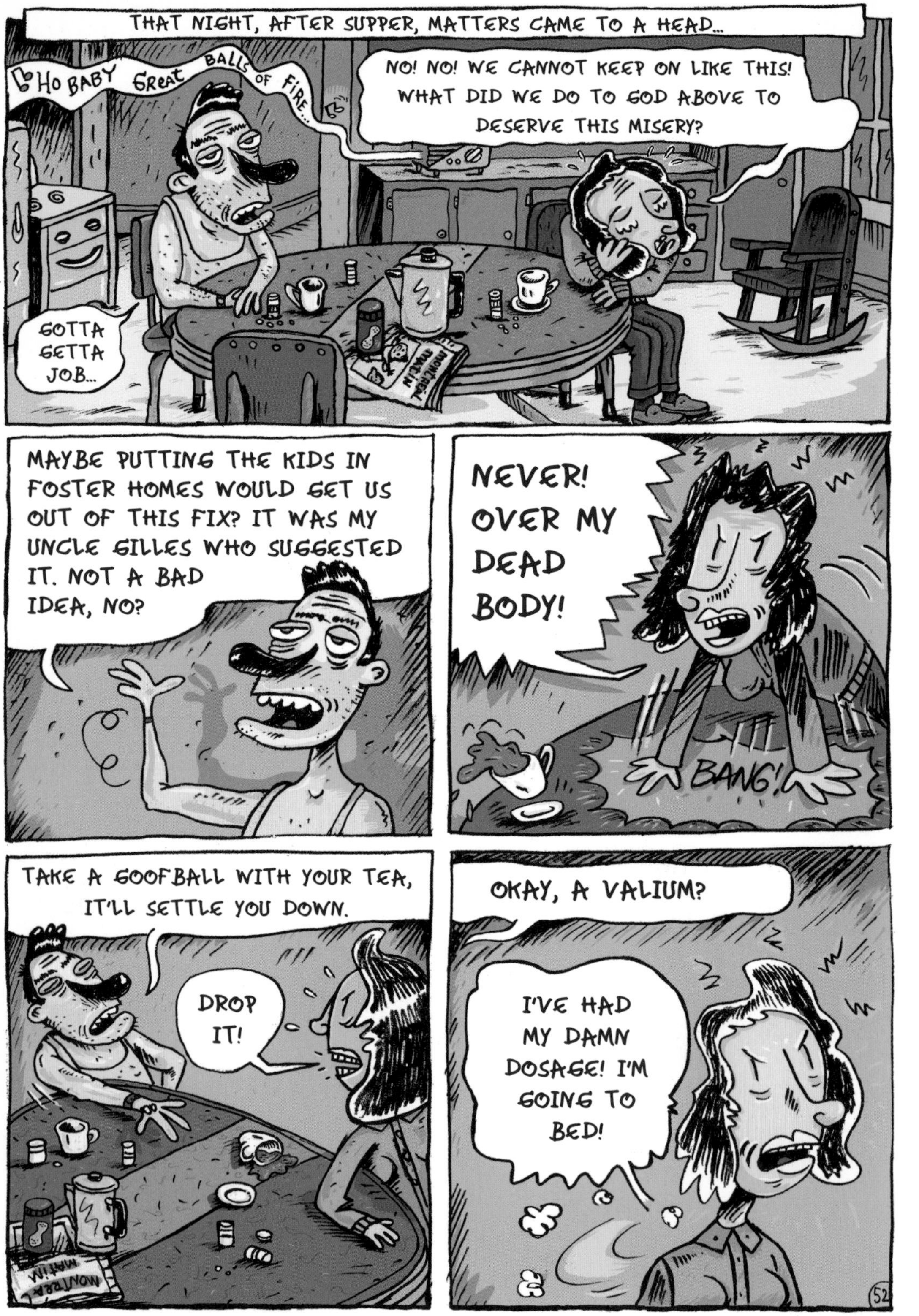
THAT NIGHT, AFTER SUPPER, MATTERS CAME TO A HEAD...
HO BABY GREAT BALLS OF FIRE...
NO! NO! WE CANNOT KEEP ON LIKE THIS! WHAT DID WE DO TO GOD ABOVE TO DESERVE THIS MISERY?
GOTTA GETTA JOB...
MONTREAL MATIN
MAYBE PUTTING THE KIDS IN FOSTER HOMES WOULD GET US OUT OF THIS FIX? IT WAS MY UNCLE GILLES WHO SUGGESTED IT. NOT A BAD IDEA, NO?
NEVER! OVER MY DEAD BODY!
BANG!
TAKE A GOOFBALL WITH YOUR TEA, IT'LL SETTLE YOU DOWN.
DROP IT!
MONTREAL MATIN
OKAY, A VALIUM?
I'VE HAD MY DAMN DOSAGE! I'M GOING TO BED!
52

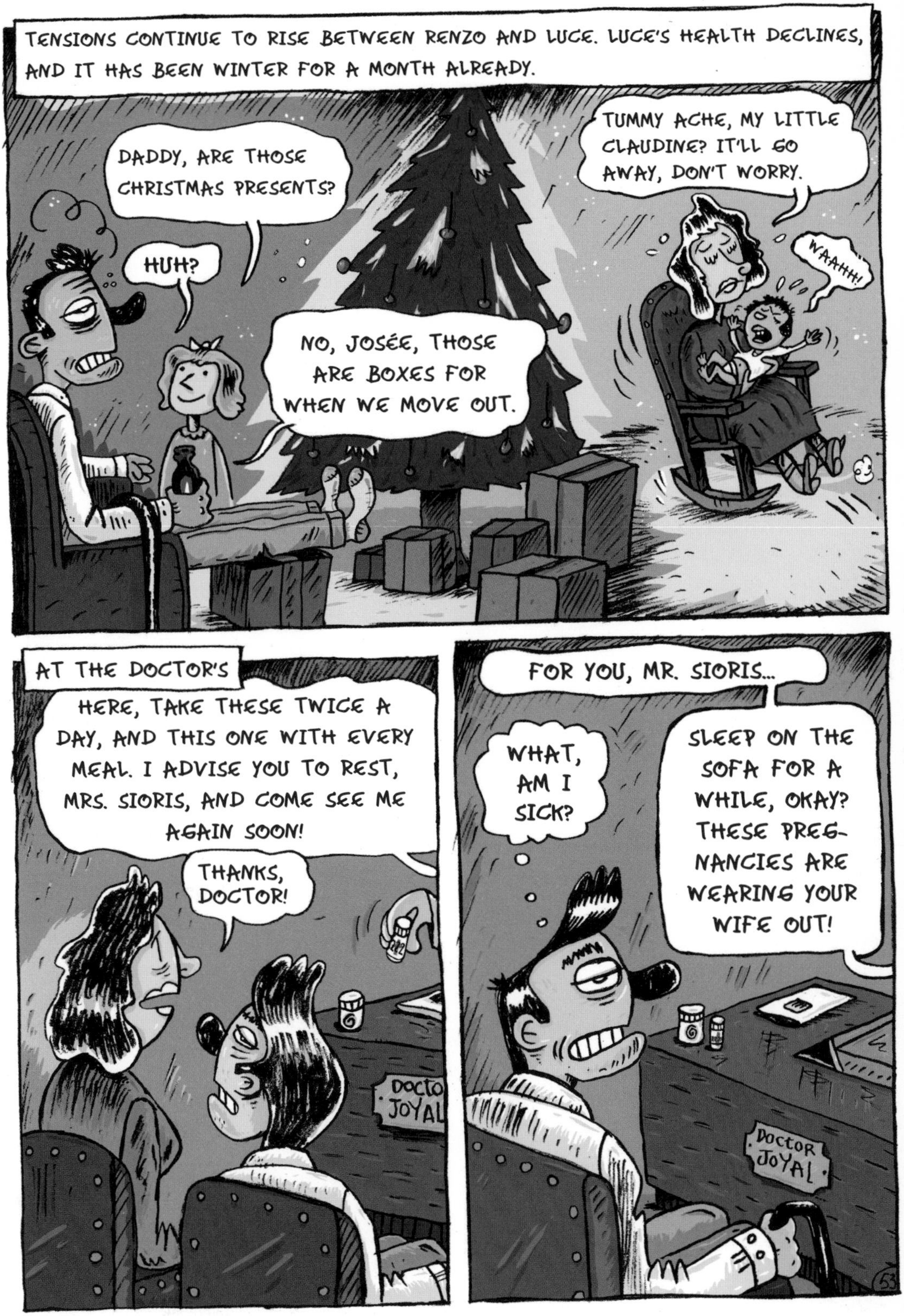
TENSIONS CONTINUE TO RISE BETWEEN RENZO AND LUCE. LUCE'S HEALTH DECLINES, AND IT HAS BEEN WINTER FOR A MONTH ALREADY.
DADDY, ARE THOSE CHRISTMAS PRESENTS?
HUH?
NO, JOSÉE, THOSE ARE BOXES FOR WHEN WE MOVE OUT.
TUMMY ACHE, MY LITTLE CLAUDINE? IT'LL GO AWAY, DON'T WORRY.
WAAHH!
AT THE DOCTOR'S
HERE, TAKE THESE TWICE A DAY, AND THIS ONE WITH EVERY MEAL. I ADVISE YOU TO REST, MRS. SIORIS, AND COME SEE ME AGAIN SOON!
THANKS, DOCTOR!
DOCTOR JOYAL
FOR YOU, MR. SIORIS...
WHAT, AM I SICK?
SLEEP ON THE SOFA FOR A WHILE, OKAY? THESE PREGNANCIES ARE WEARING YOUR WIFE OUT!
DOCTOR JOYAL
53

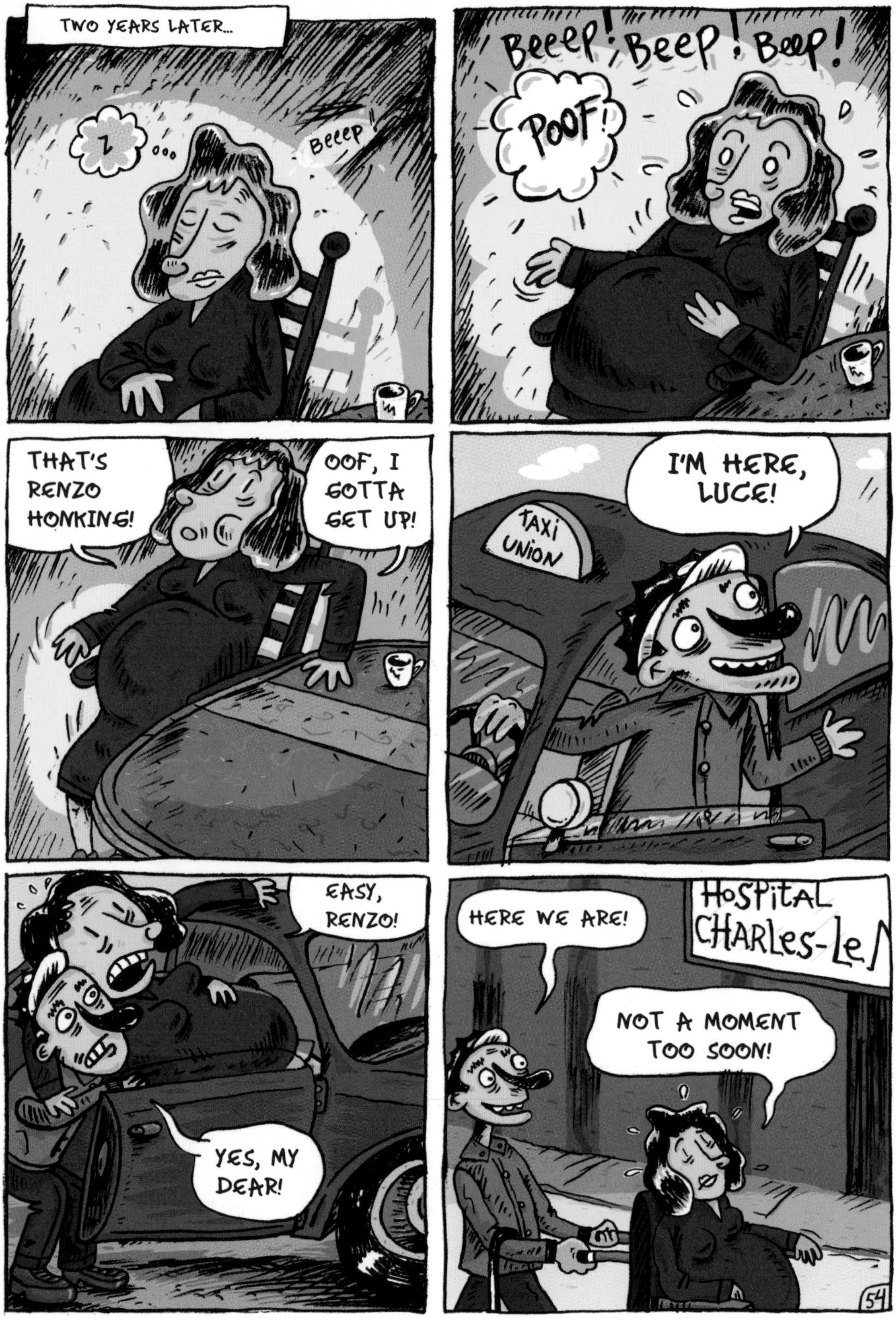
TWO YEARS LATER...
Z
Beeep!
Beeep! Beep! Beep!
POOF!
THAT'S RENZO HONKING!
OOF, I GOTTA GET UP!
TAXI UNION
I'M HERE, LUCE!
EASY, RENZO!
YES, MY DEAR!
HERE WE ARE!
HOSPITAL CHARLES-LE
NOT A MOMENT TOO SOON!
54

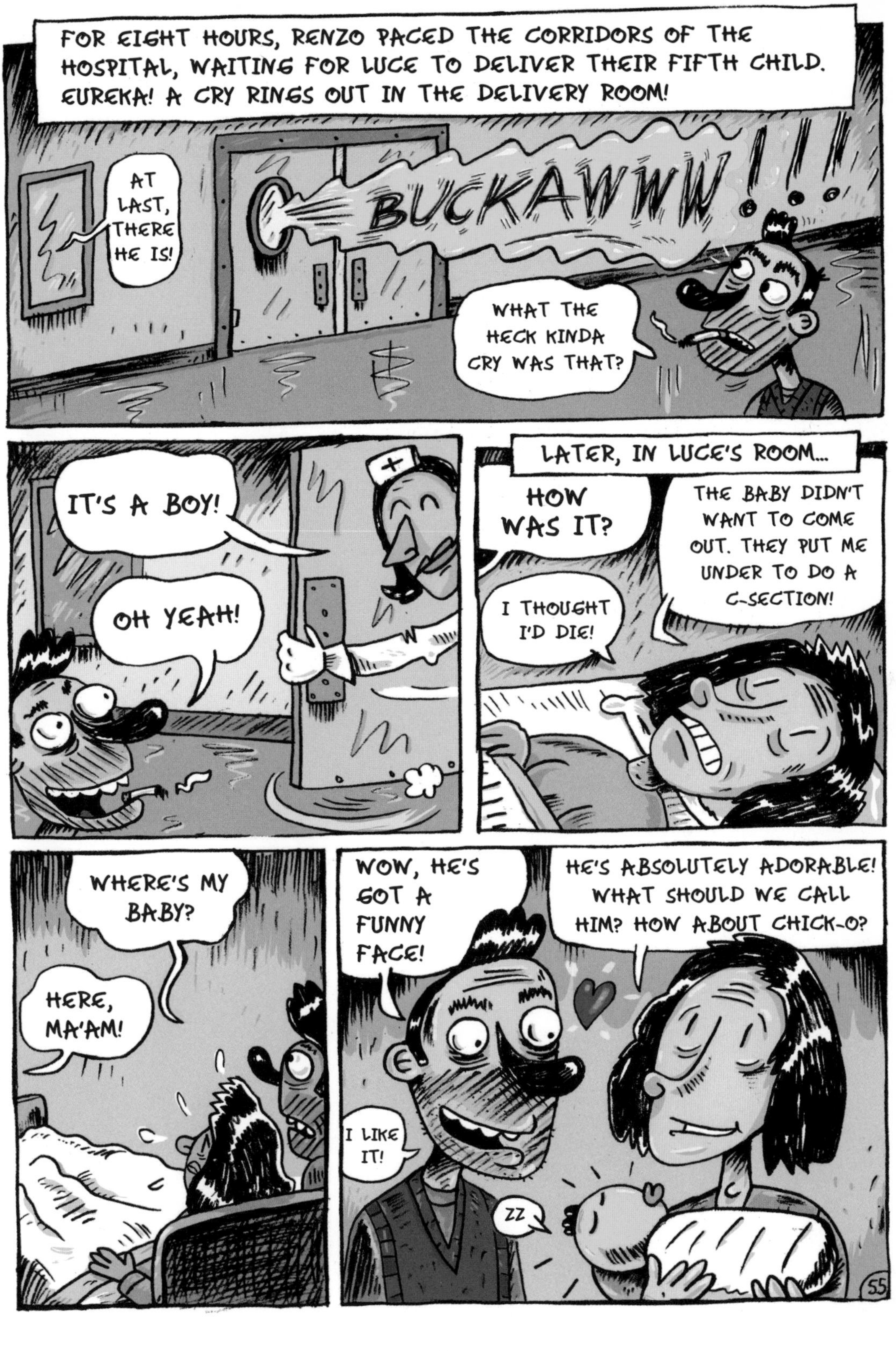
FOR EIGHT HOURS, RENZO PACED THE CORRIDORS OF THE HOSPITAL, WAITING FOR LUCE TO DELIVER THEIR FIFTH CHILD. EUREKA! A CRY RINGS OUT IN THE DELIVERY ROOM!
AT LAST, THERE HE IS!
BUCKAWWW!!!
WHAT THE HECK KINDA CRY WAS THAT?
IT'S A BOY!
OH YEAH!
LATER, IN LUCE'S ROOM...
HOW WAS IT?
THE BABY DIDN'T WANT TO COME OUT. THEY PUT ME UNDER TO DO A C-SECTION!
I THOUGHT I'D DIE!
WHERE'S MY BABY?
HERE, MA'AM!
WOW, HE'S GOT A FUNNY FACE!
HE'S ABSOLUTELY ADORABLE! WHAT SHOULD WE CALL HIM? HOW ABOUT CHICK-O?
I LIKE IT!
ZZ
55

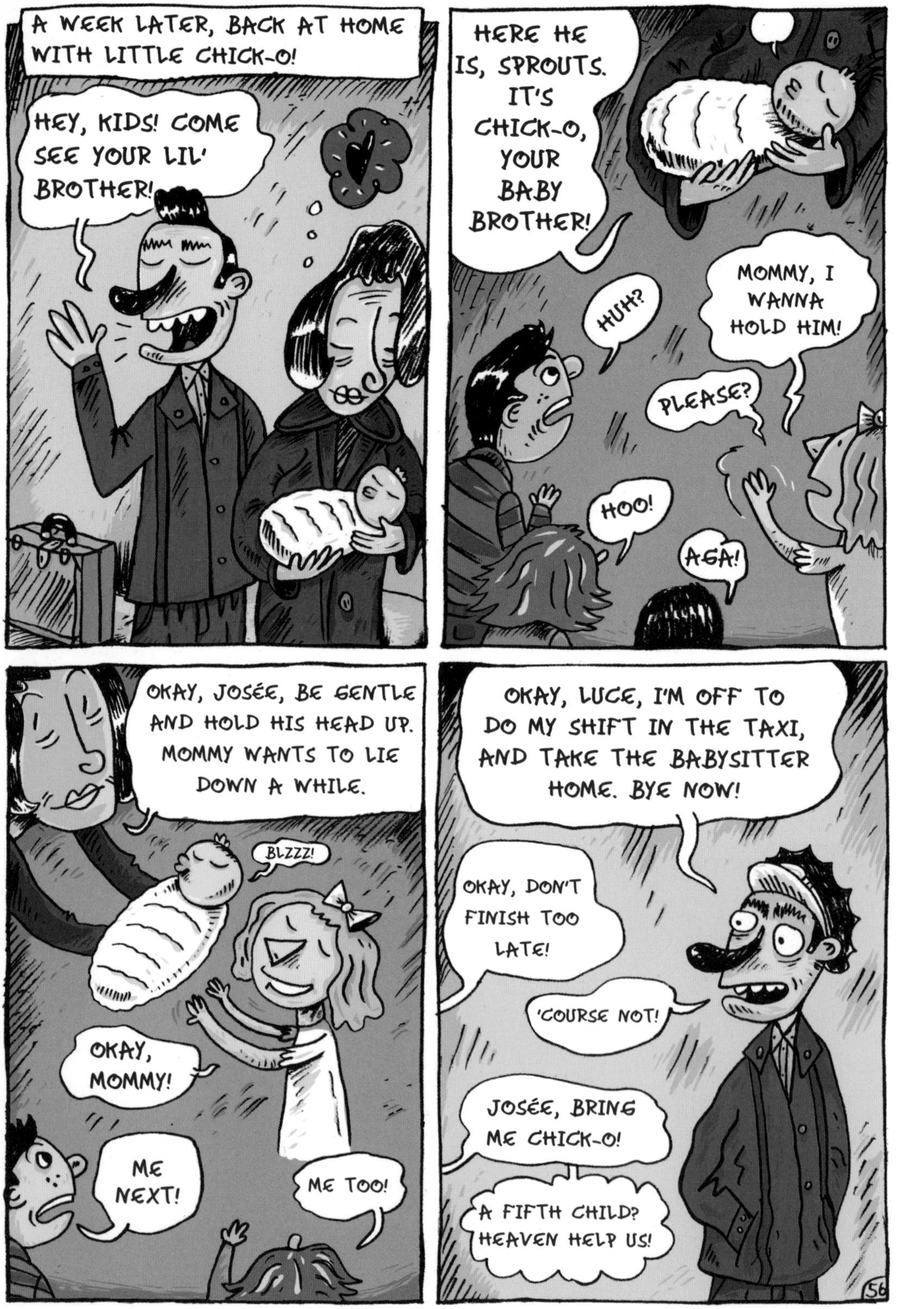
A WEEK LATER, BACK AT HOME WITH LITTLE CHICK-O!
HEY, KIDS! COME SEE YOUR LIL' BROTHER!
HERE HE IS, SPROUTS. IT'S CHICK-O, YOUR BABY BROTHER!
HUH?
MOMMY, I WANNA HOLD HIM!
PLEASE?
HOO!
AGA!
OKAY, JOSÉE, BE GENTLE AND HOLD HIS HEAD UP. MOMMY WANTS TO LIE DOWN A WHILE.
BLZZZ!
OKAY, MOMMY!
ME NEXT!
ME TOO!
OKAY, LUCE, I'M OFF TO DO MY SHIFT IN THE TAXI, AND TAKE THE BABYSITTER HOME. BYE NOW!
OKAY, DON'T FINISH TOO LATE!
'COURSE NOT!
JOSÉE, BRING ME CHICK-O!
A FIFTH CHILD? HEAVEN HELP US!
56

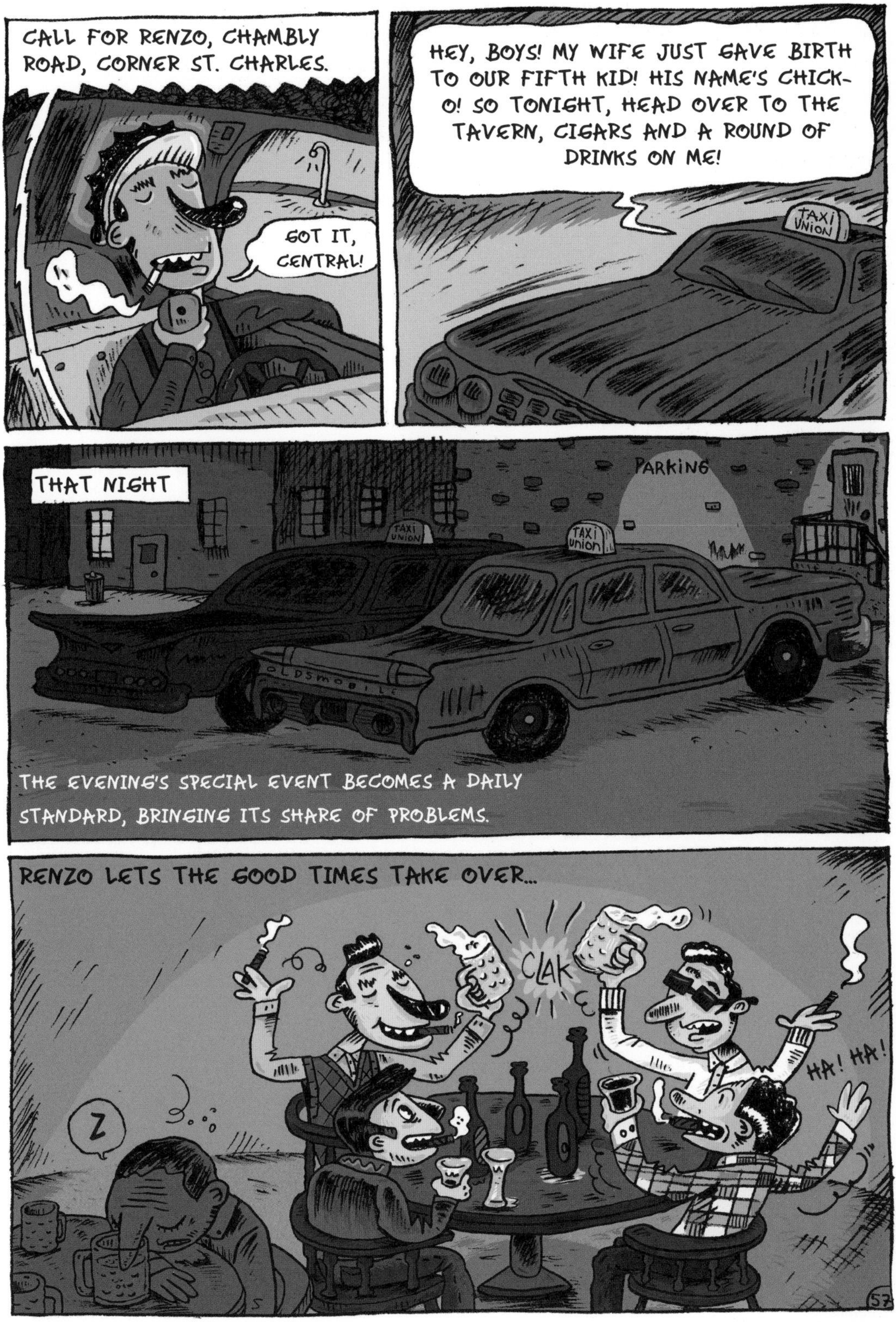
CALL FOR RENZO, CHAMBLY ROAD, CORNER ST. CHARLES.
GOT IT, CENTRAL!
HEY, BOYS! MY WIFE JUST GAVE BIRTH TO OUR FIFTH KID! HIS NAME'S CHICK-O! SO TONIGHT, HEAD OVER TO THE TAVERN, CIGARS AND A ROUND OF DRINKS ON ME!
TAXI UNION
THAT NIGHT
PARKING
TAXI UNION
TAXI UNION
OLDSMOBILE
THE EVENING'S SPECIAL EVENT BECOMES A DAILY STANDARD, BRINGING ITS SHARE OF PROBLEMS.
RENZO LETS THE GOOD TIMES TAKE OVER...
CLAK
HA! HA!
Z

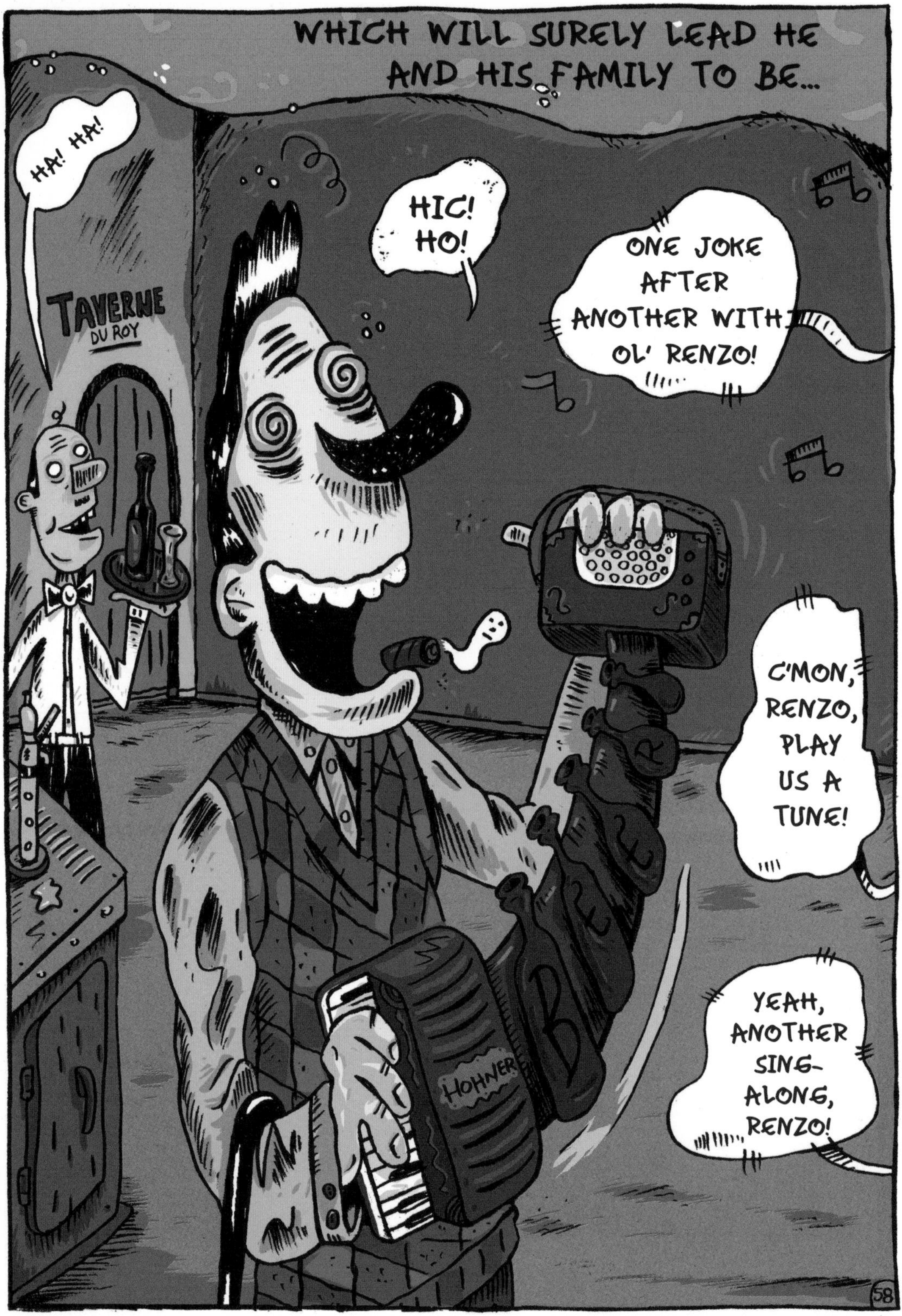
WHICH WILL SURELY LEAD HE AND HIS FAMILY TO BE...
HA! HA!
TAVERNE DU ROY
HIC! HO!
ONE JOKE AFTER ANOTHER WITH OL' RENZO!
C'MON, RENZO, PLAY US A TUNE!
YEAH, ANOTHER SING-ALONG, RENZO!
HOHNER
BEER
58

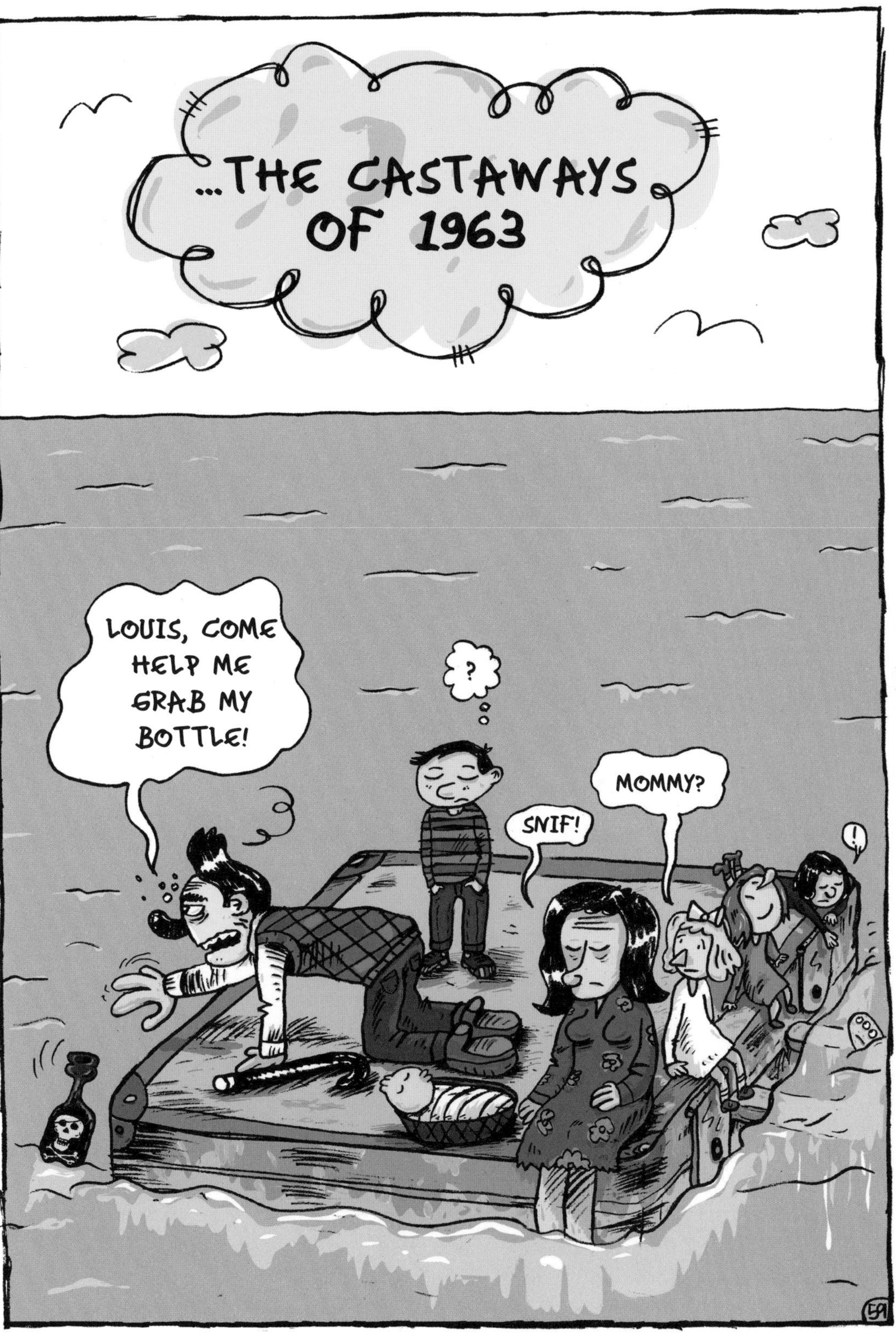
...THE CASTAWAYS OF 1963
LOUIS, COME HELP ME GRAB MY BOTTLE!
?
SNIF!
MOMMY?
!

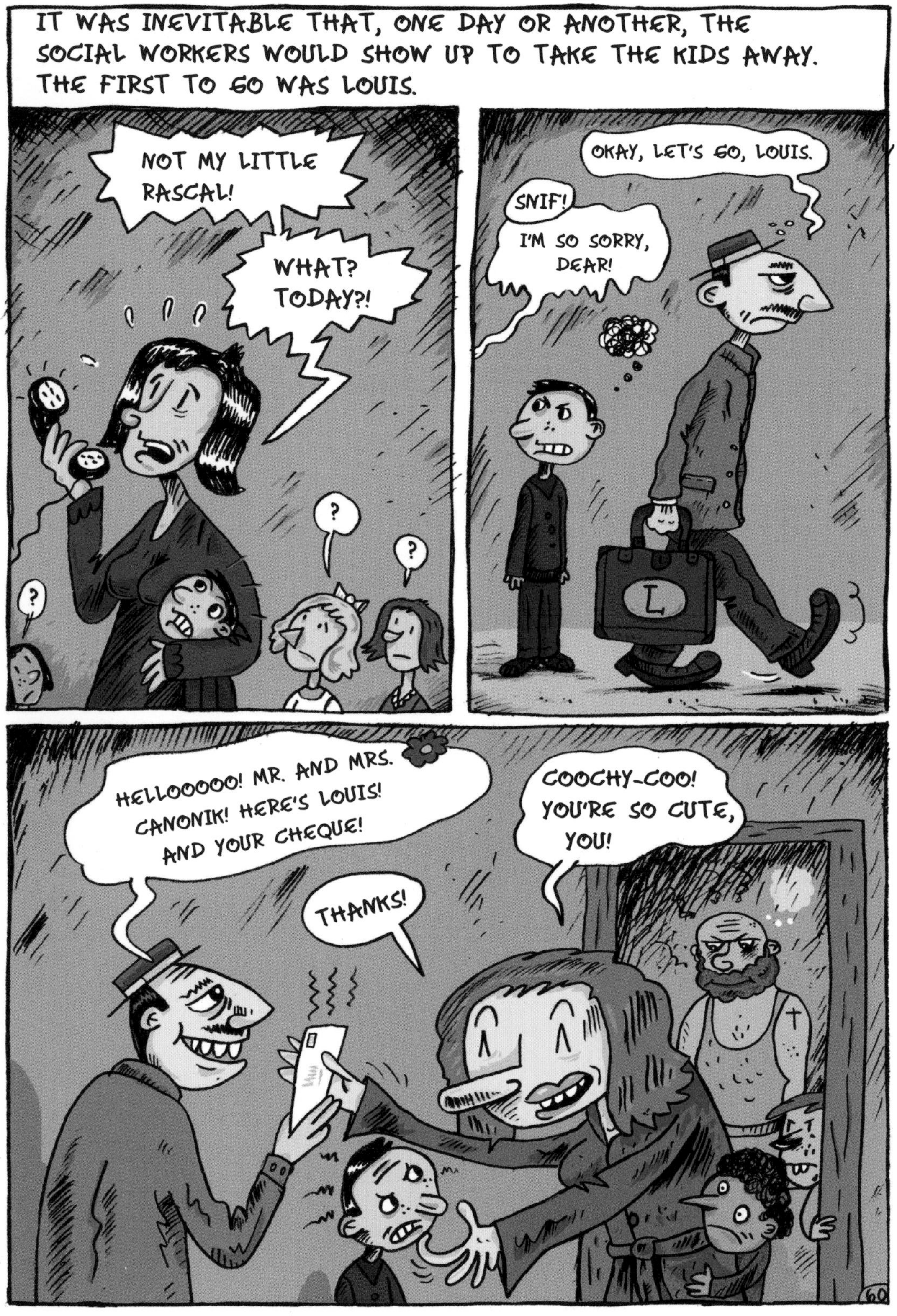
IT WAS INEVITABLE THAT, ONE DAY OR ANOTHER, THE SOCIAL WORKERS WOULD SHOW UP TO TAKE THE KIDS AWAY. THE FIRST TO GO WAS LOUIS.
NOT MY LITTLE RASCAL!
WHAT? TODAY?!
?
?
?
OKAY, LET'S GO, LOUIS.
SNIF!
I'M SO SORRY, DEAR!
L
HELLOOOOO! MR. AND MRS. CANONIK! HERE'S LOUIS! AND YOUR CHEQUE!
COOCHY-COO! YOU'RE SO CUTE, YOU!
THANKS!

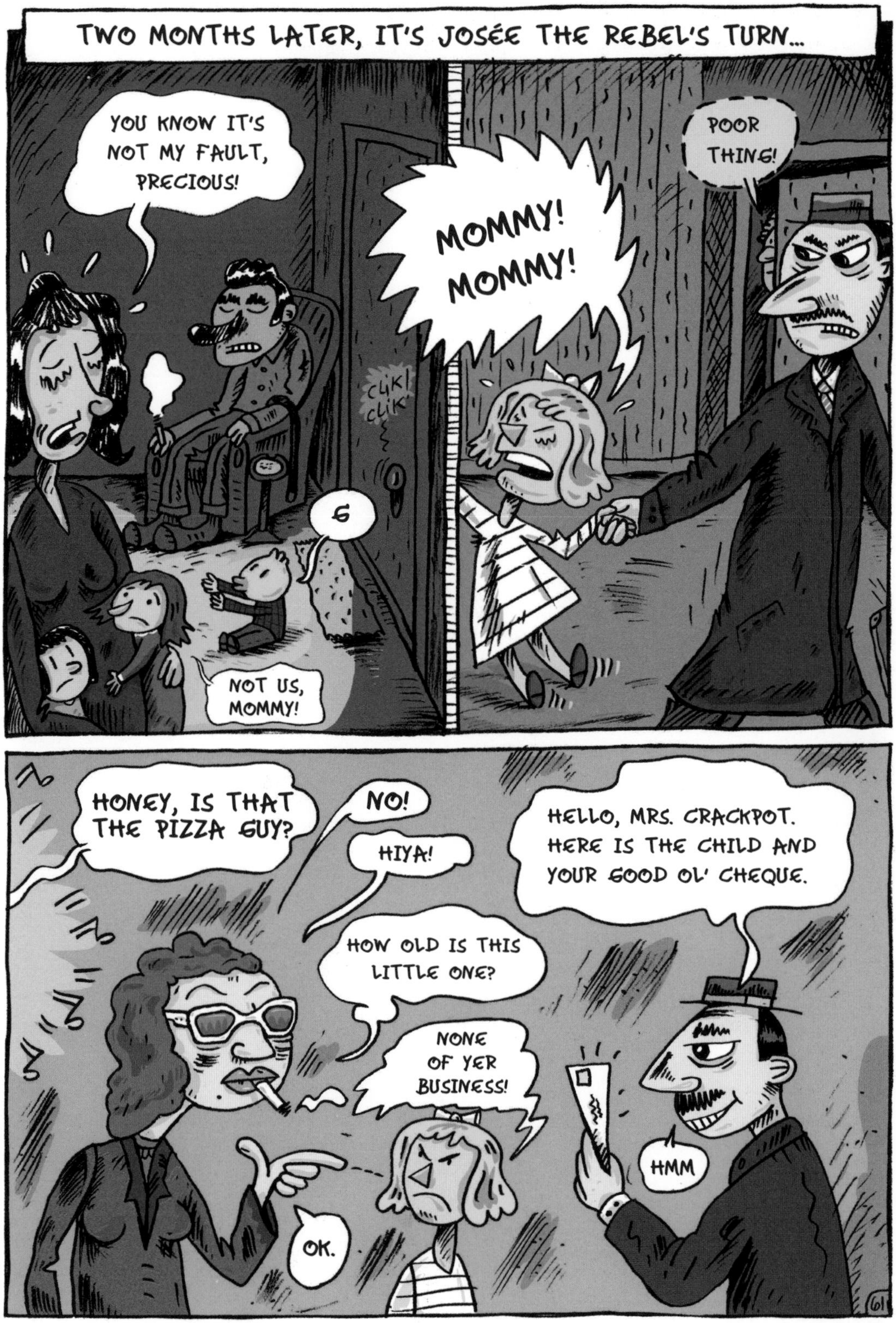
TWO MONTHS LATER, IT'S JOSÉE THE REBEL'S TURN...
YOU KNOW IT'S NOT MY FAULT, PRECIOUS!
G
NOT US, MOMMY!
CLIK! CLIK
MOMMY! MOMMY!
POOR THING!
HONEY, IS THAT THE PIZZA GUY?
NO!
HIYA!
HOW OLD IS THIS LITTLE ONE?
NONE OF YER BUSINESS!
OK.
HELLO, MRS. CRACKPOT. HERE IS THE CHILD AND YOUR GOOD OL' CHEQUE.
HMM
61

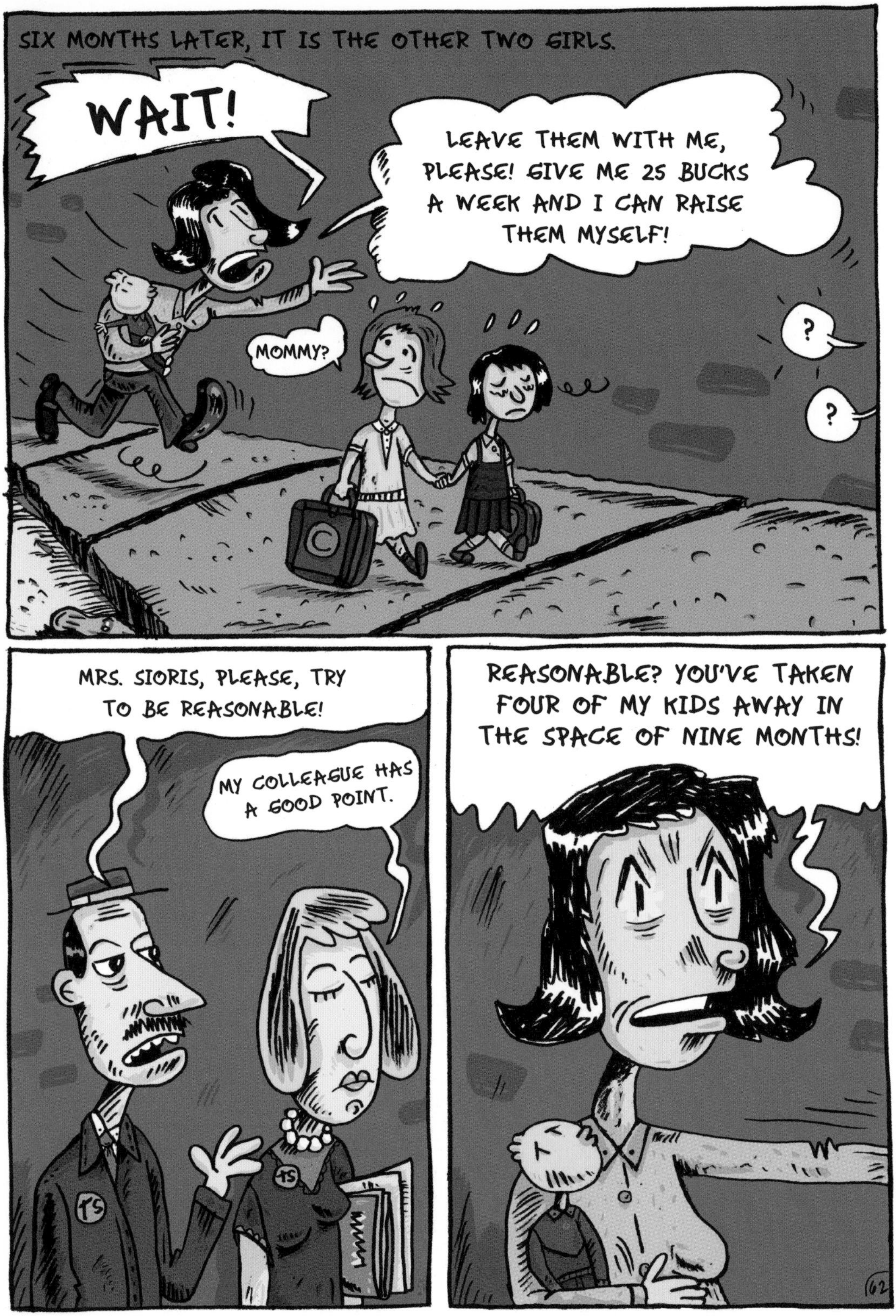
SIX MONTHS LATER, IT IS THE OTHER TWO GIRLS.
WAIT!
LEAVE THEM WITH ME, PLEASE! GIVE ME 25 BUCKS A WEEK AND I CAN RAISE THEM MYSELF!
MOMMY?
?
?
MRS. SIORIS, PLEASE, TRY TO BE REASONABLE!
MY COLLEAGUE HAS A GOOD POINT.
REASONABLE? YOU'VE TAKEN FOUR OF MY KIDS AWAY IN THE SPACE OF NINE MONTHS!

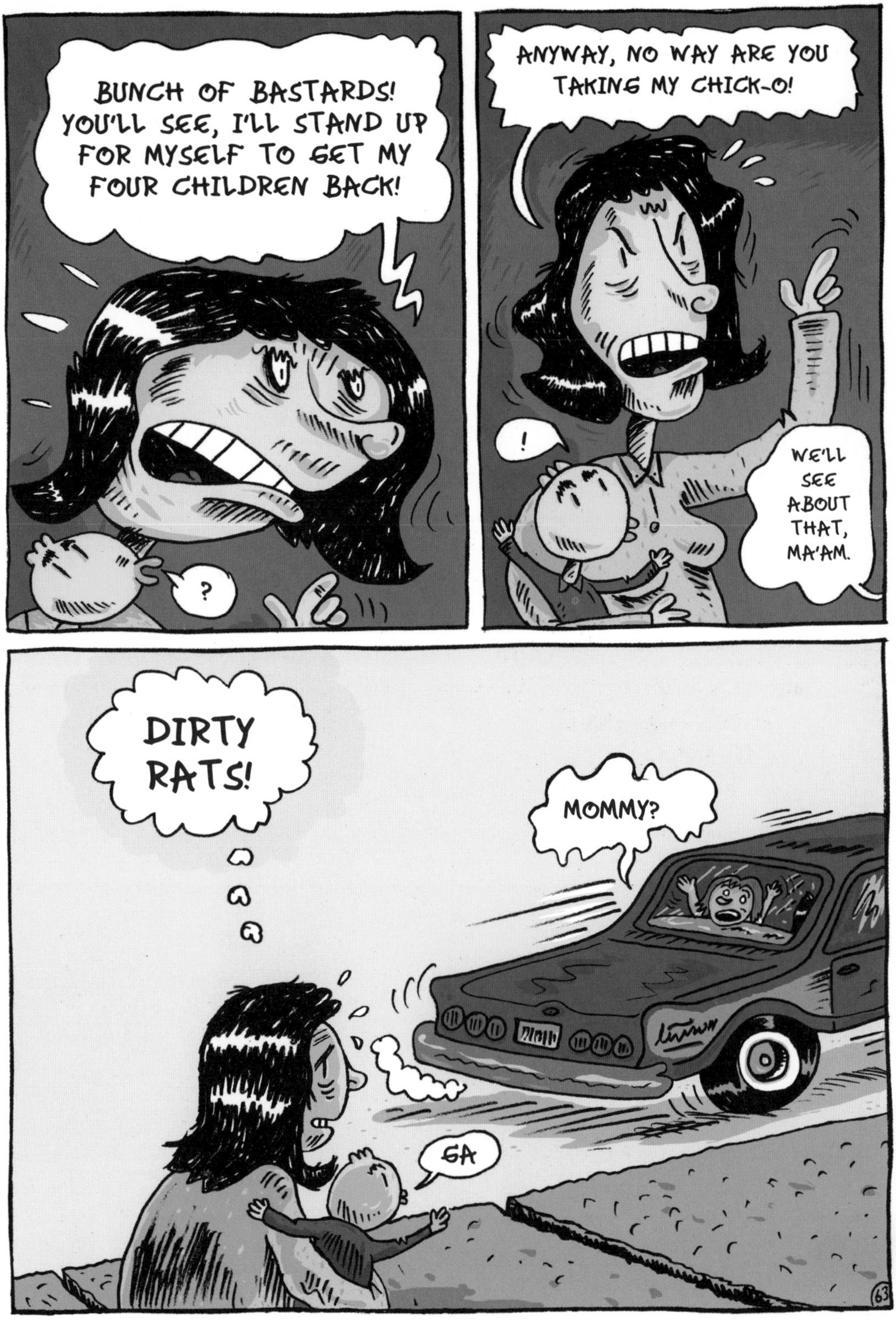
BUNCH OF BASTARDS! YOU'LL SEE, I'LL STAND UP FOR MYSELF TO GET MY FOUR CHILDREN BACK!
?
ANYWAY, NO WAY ARE YOU TAKING MY CHICK-O!
!
WE'LL SEE ABOUT THAT, MA'AM.
DIRTY RATS!
MOMMY?
GA
63

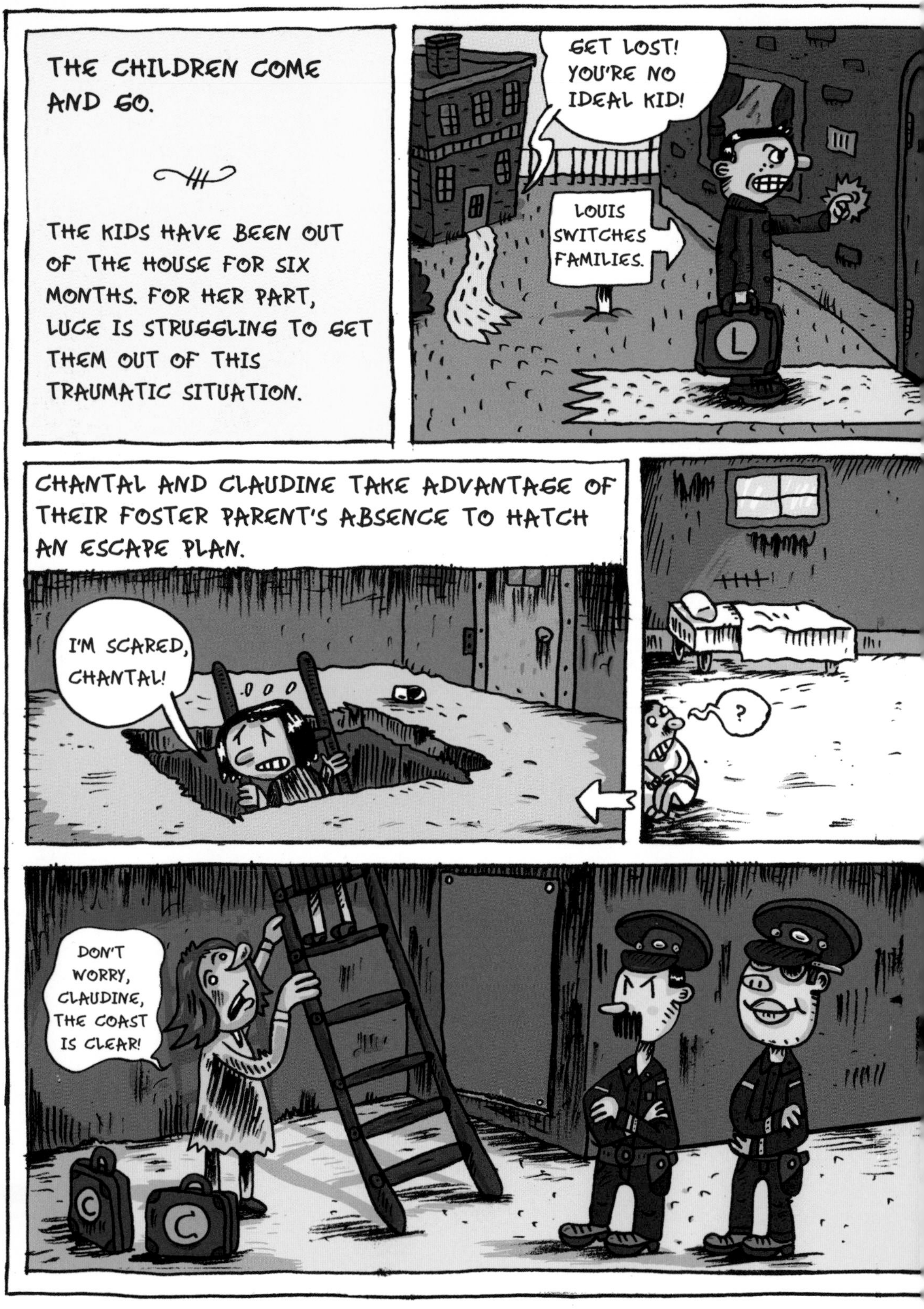
THE CHILDREN COME AND GO.
THE KIDS HAVE BEEN OUT OF THE HOUSE FOR SIX MONTHS. FOR HER PART, LUCE IS STRUGGLING TO GET THEM OUT OF THIS TRAUMATIC SITUATION.
GET LOST! YOU'RE NO IDEAL KID!
LOUIS SWITCHES FAMILIES.
L
CHANTAL AND CLAUDINE TAKE ADVANTAGE OF THEIR FOSTER PARENT'S ABSENCE TO HATCH AN ESCAPE PLAN.
I'M SCARED, CHANTAL!
?
DON'T WORRY, CLAUDINE, THE COAST IS CLEAR!
C
C

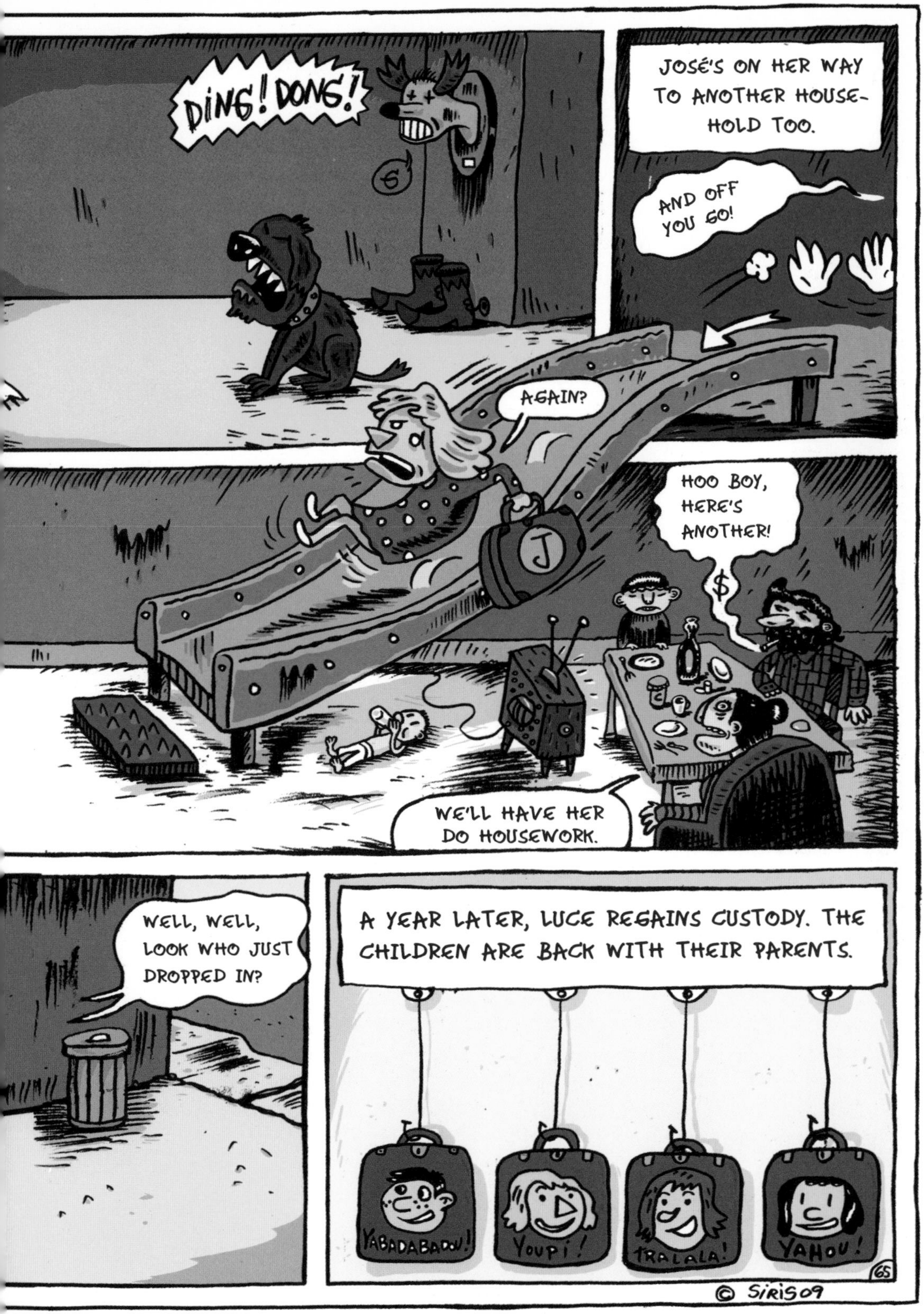
DING! DONG!
JOSÉ'S ON HER WAY TO ANOTHER HOUSE-HOLD TOO.
AND OFF YOU GO!
AGAIN?
HOO BOY, HERE'S ANOTHER!
WE'LL HAVE HER DO HOUSEWORK.
WELL, WELL, LOOK WHO JUST DROPPED IN?
A YEAR LATER, LUCE REGAINS CUSTODY. THE CHILDREN ARE BACK WITH THEIR PARENTS.
YABADABADOU!
YOUPI!
TRALALA!
YAHOU!
65
© SIRIS 09

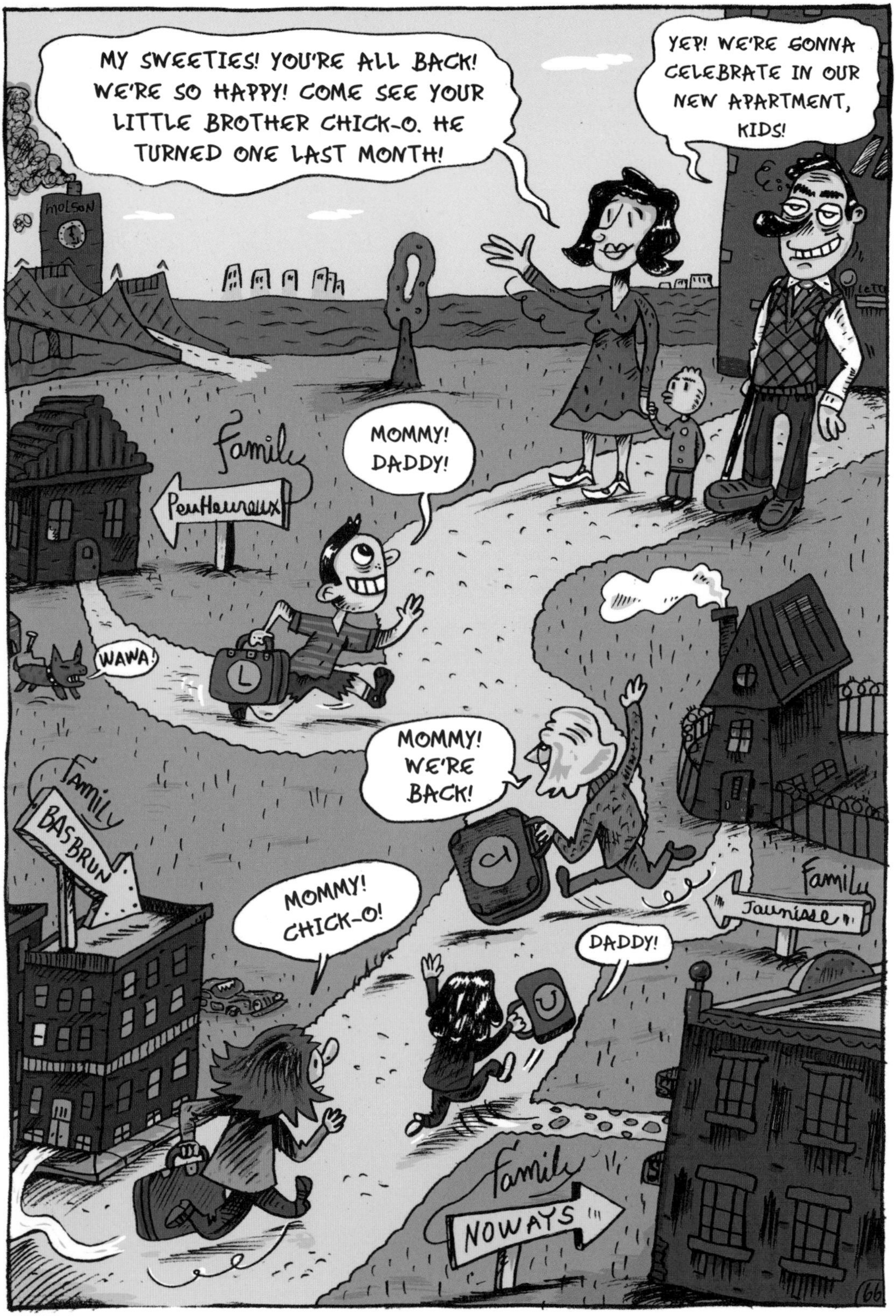

MY SWEETIES! YOU'RE ALL BACK! WE'RE SO HAPPY! COME SEE YOUR LITTLE BROTHER CHICK-O. HE TURNED ONE LAST MONTH!
YEP! WE'RE GONNA CELEBRATE IN OUR NEW APARTMENT, KIDS!
MOLSON
Family
PeuHeureux
MOMMY! DADDY!
WAWA!
MOMMY! WE'RE BACK!
Family
BASBRUN
MOMMY! CHICK-O!
DADDY!
Family
Jaunisse
Family
NOWAYS
66

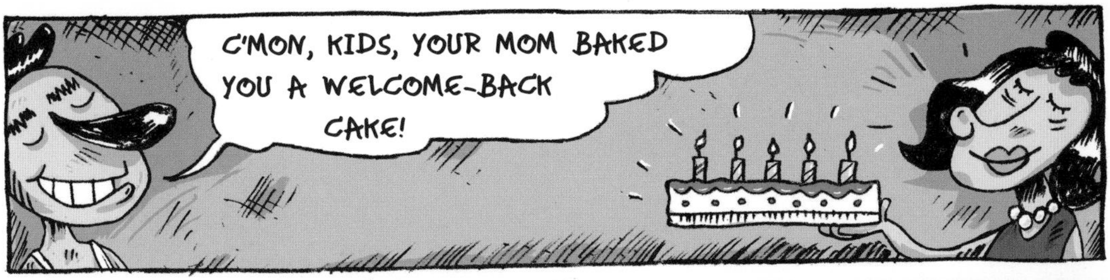
C'MON, KIDS, YOUR MOM BAKED YOU A WELCOME-BACK CAKE!

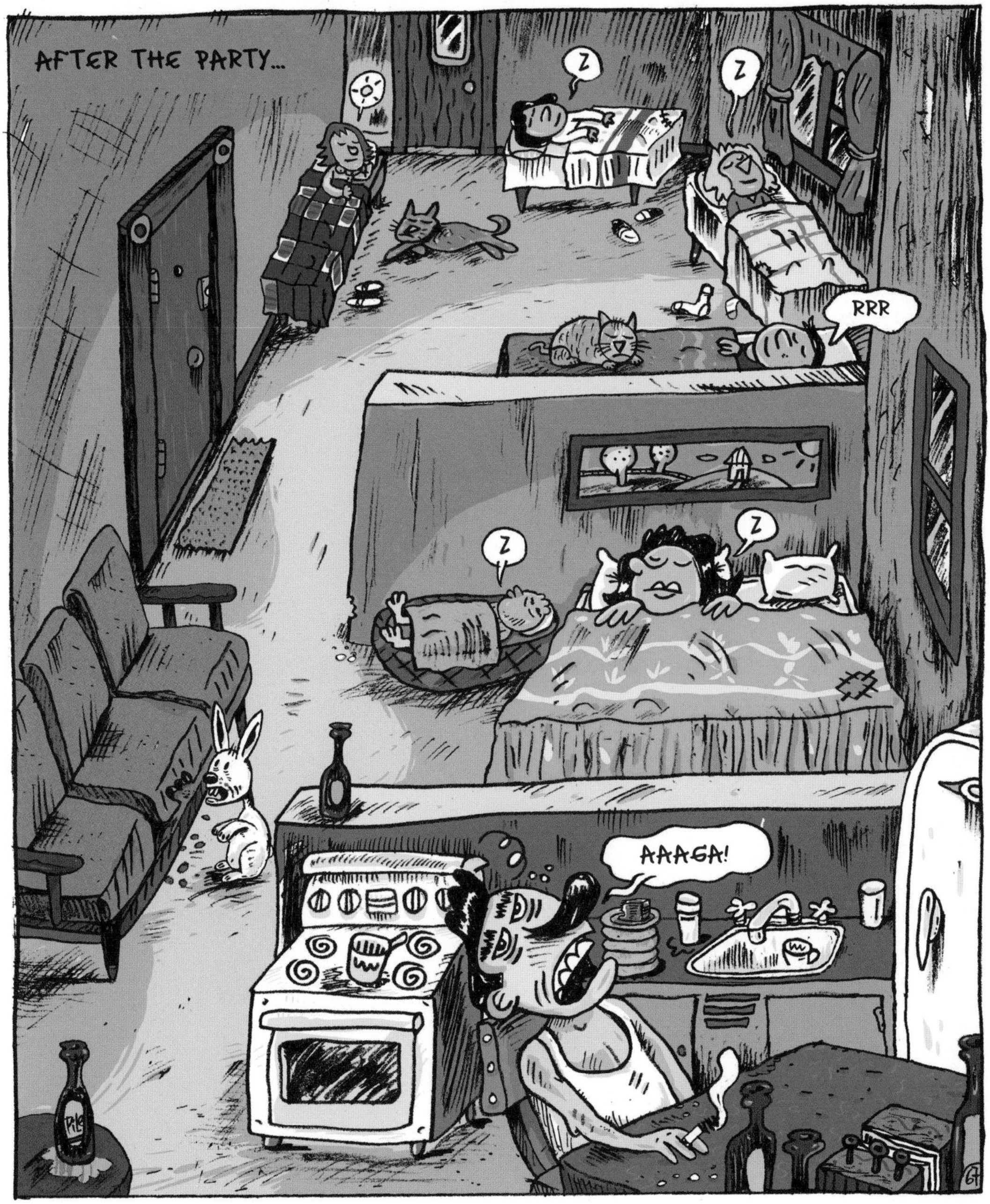
AFTER THE PARTY...
Z
Z
RRR
Z
Z
AAAGA!

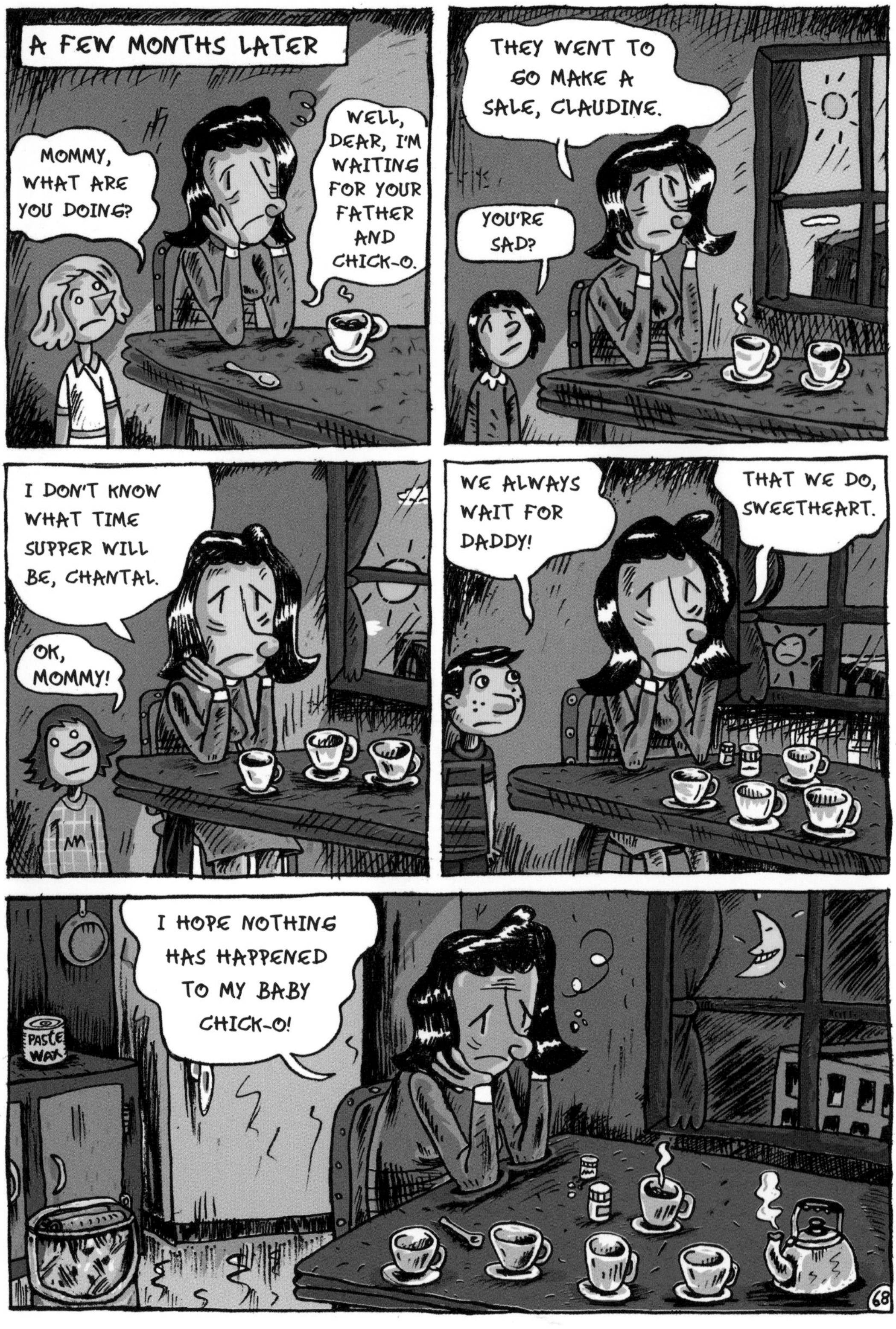
A FEW MONTHS LATER
MOMMY, WHAT ARE YOU DOING?
WELL, DEAR, I'M WAITING FOR YOUR FATHER AND CHICK-O.
THEY WENT TO GO MAKE A SALE, CLAUDINE.
YOU'RE SAD?
I DON'T KNOW WHAT TIME SUPPER WILL BE, CHANTAL.
OK, MOMMY!
WE ALWAYS WAIT FOR DADDY!
THAT WE DO, SWEETHEART.
I HOPE NOTHING HAS HAPPENED TO MY BABY CHICK-O!
PASTE WAX
68

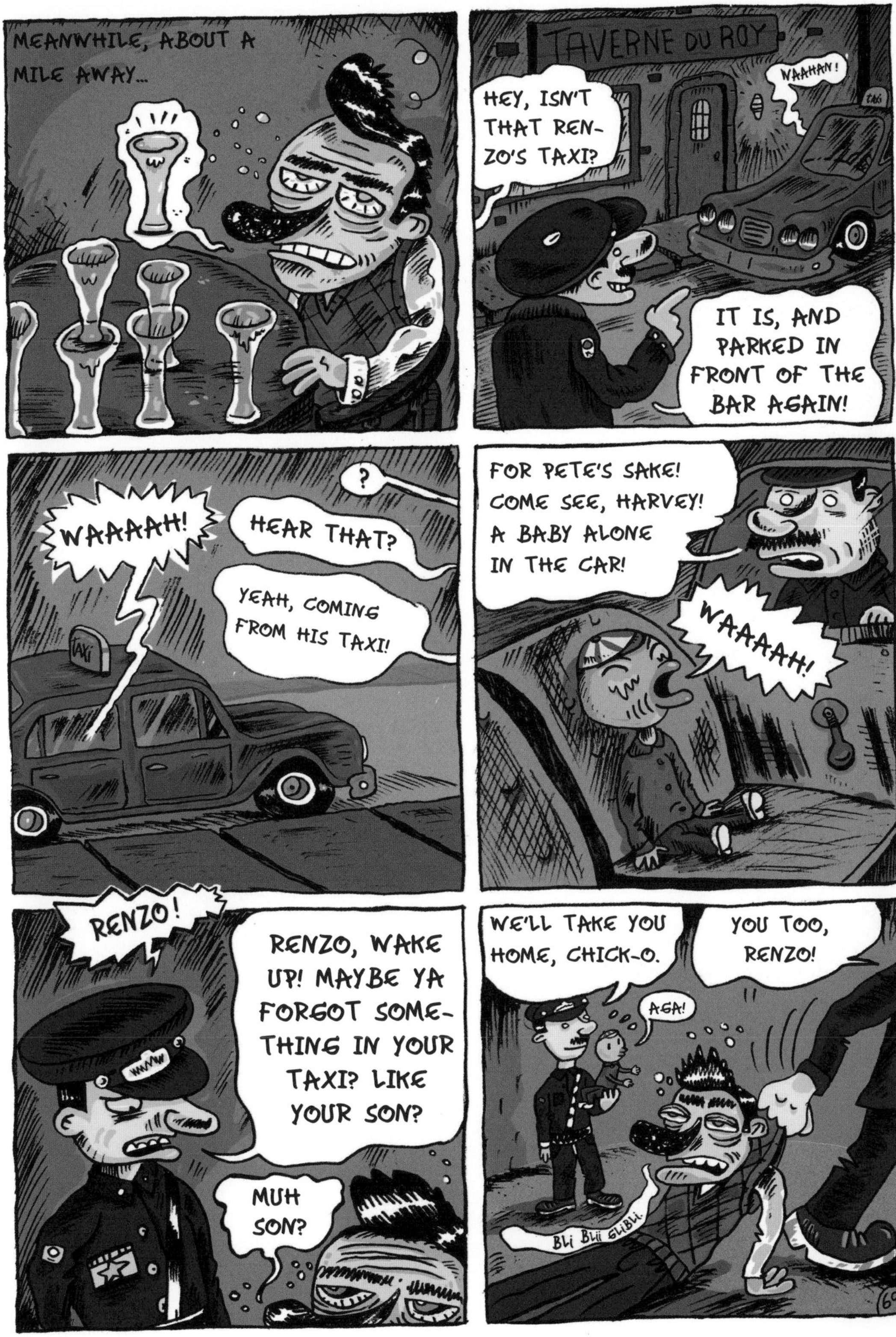
MEANWHILE, ABOUT A MILE AWAY...
TAVERNE DU ROY
HEY, ISN'T THAT REN-ZO'S TAXI?
WAAHAH!
TAXI
IT IS, AND PARKED IN FRONT OF THE BAR AGAIN!
WAAAAH!
?
HEAR THAT?
YEAH, COMING FROM HIS TAXI!
TAXI
FOR PETE'S SAKE! COME SEE, HARVEY! A BABY ALONE IN THE CAR!
WAAAAAH!
RENZO!
RENZO, WAKE UP! MAYBE YA FORGOT SOME-THING IN YOUR TAXI? LIKE YOUR SON?
MUH SON?
WE'LL TAKE YOU HOME, CHICK-O.
YOU TOO, RENZO!
AGA!
BLi BLii GLiBLi.
69

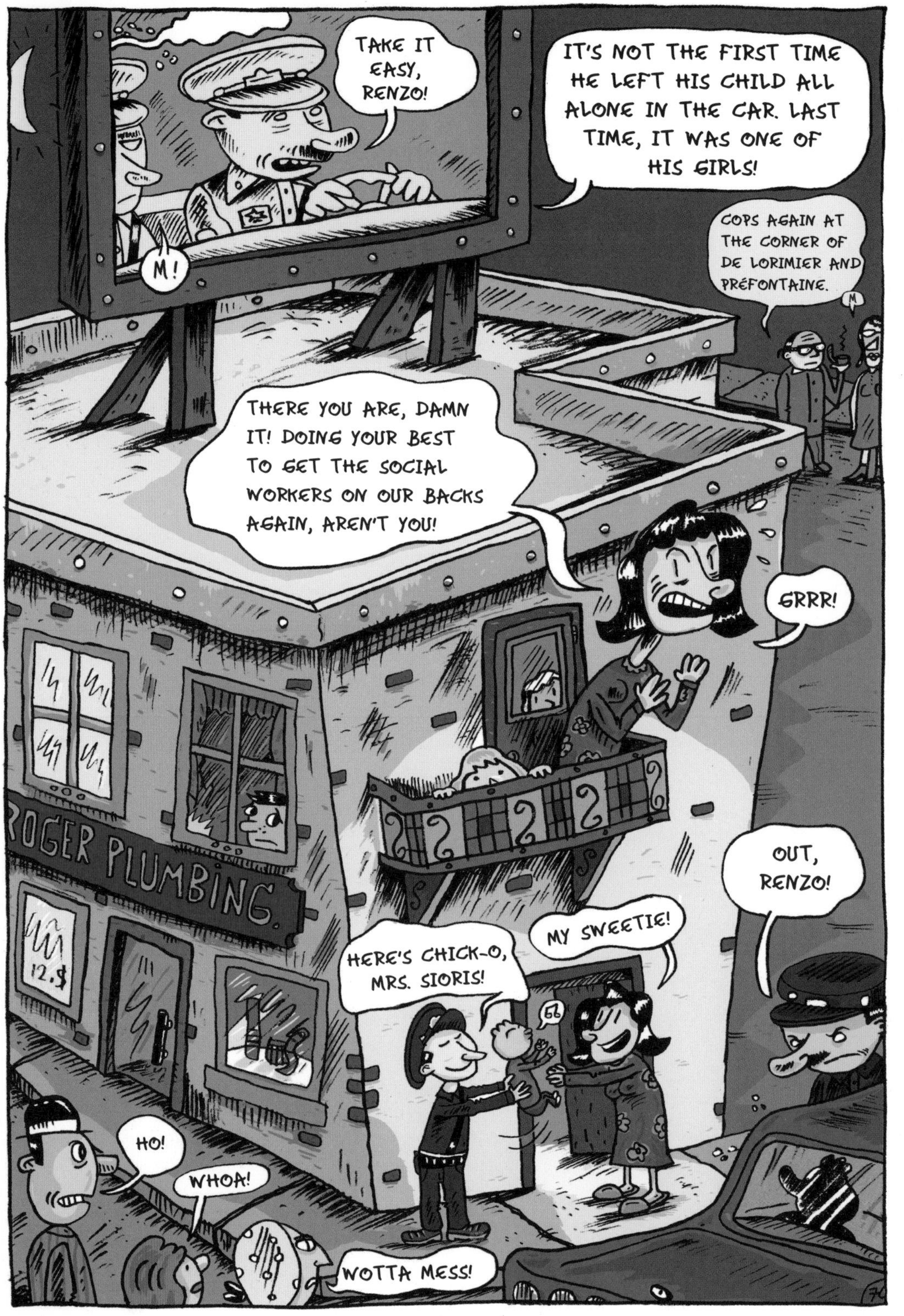
TAKE IT EASY, RENZO!
M!
IT'S NOT THE FIRST TIME HE LEFT HIS CHILD ALL ALONE IN THE CAR. LAST TIME, IT WAS ONE OF HIS GIRLS!
COPS AGAIN AT THE CORNER OF DE LORIMIER AND PRÉFONTAINE.
M
THERE YOU ARE, DAMN IT! DOING YOUR BEST TO GET THE SOCIAL WORKERS ON OUR BACKS AGAIN, AREN'T YOU!
GRRR!
ROGER PLUMBING.
12.$
OUT, RENZO!
MY SWEETIE!
HERE'S CHICK-O, MRS. SIORIS!
GG
HO!
WHOA!
WOTTA MESS!

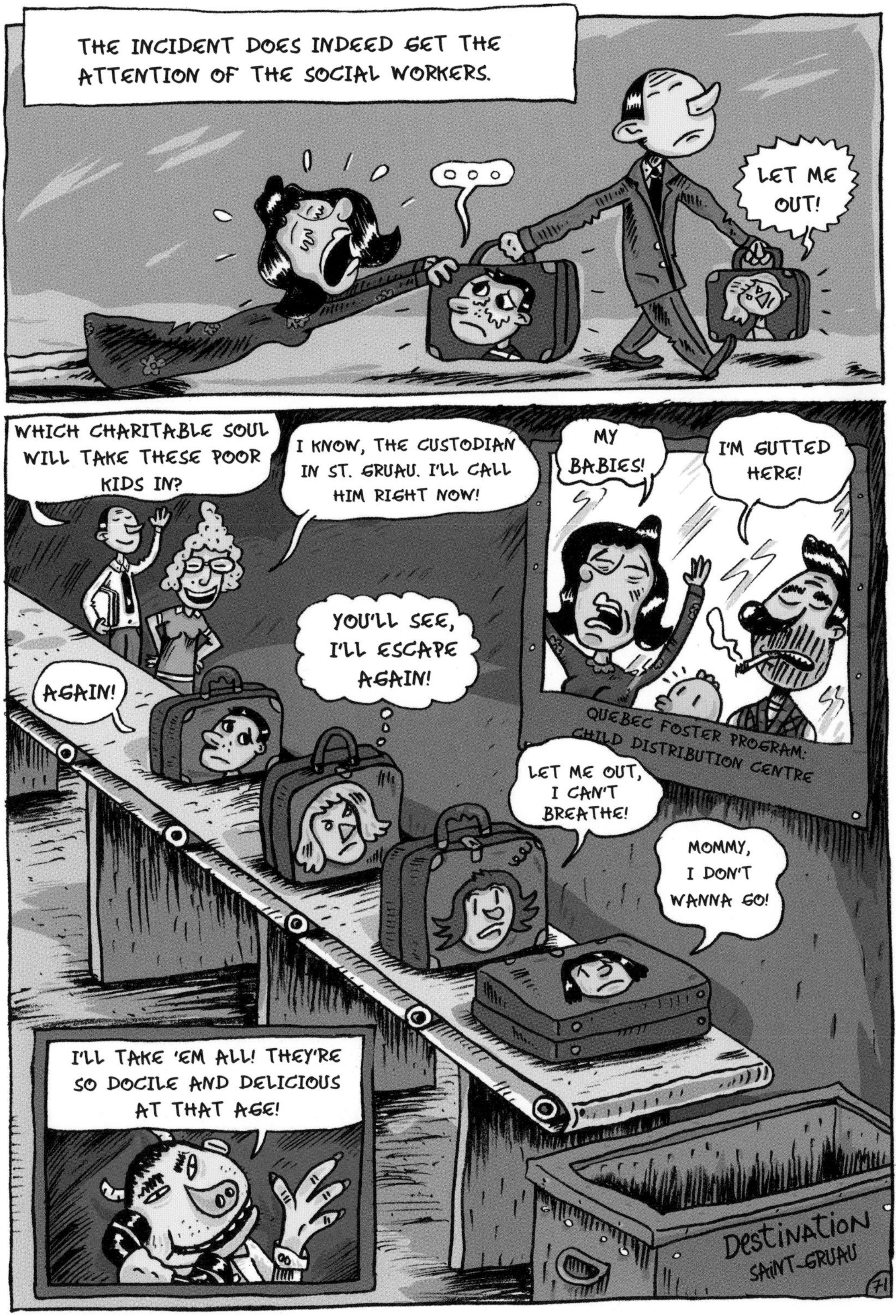
THE INCIDENT DOES INDEED GET THE ATTENTION OF THE SOCIAL WORKERS.
LET ME OUT!
WHICH CHARITABLE SOUL WILL TAKE THESE POOR KIDS IN?
I KNOW, THE CUSTODIAN IN ST. GRUAU. I'LL CALL HIM RIGHT NOW!
MY BABIES!
I'M GUTTED HERE!
QUEBEC FOSTER PROGRAM: CHILD DISTRIBUTION CENTRE
AGAIN!
YOU'LL SEE, I'LL ESCAPE AGAIN!
LET ME OUT, I CAN'T BREATHE!
MOMMY, I DON'T WANNA GO!
I'LL TAKE 'EM ALL! THEY'RE SO DOCILE AND DELICIOUS AT THAT AGE!
Destination SAINT-GRUAU
71

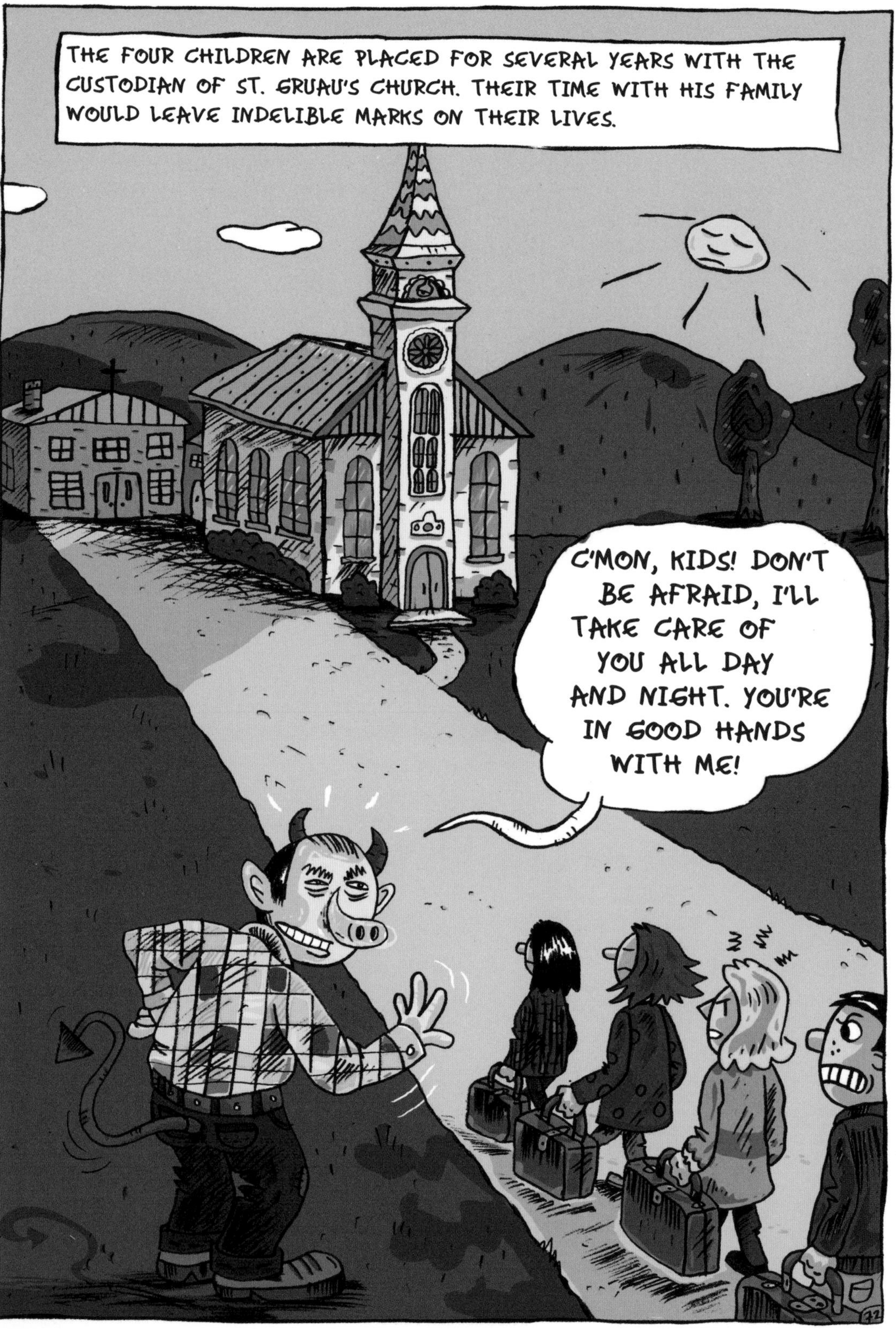
THE FOUR CHILDREN ARE PLACED FOR SEVERAL YEARS WITH THE CUSTODIAN OF ST. GRUAU'S CHURCH. THEIR TIME WITH HIS FAMILY WOULD LEAVE INDELIBLE MARKS ON THEIR LIVES.
C'MON, KIDS! DON'T BE AFRAID, I'LL TAKE CARE OF YOU ALL DAY AND NIGHT. YOU'RE IN GOOD HANDS WITH ME!

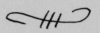

ONE YEAR LATER...

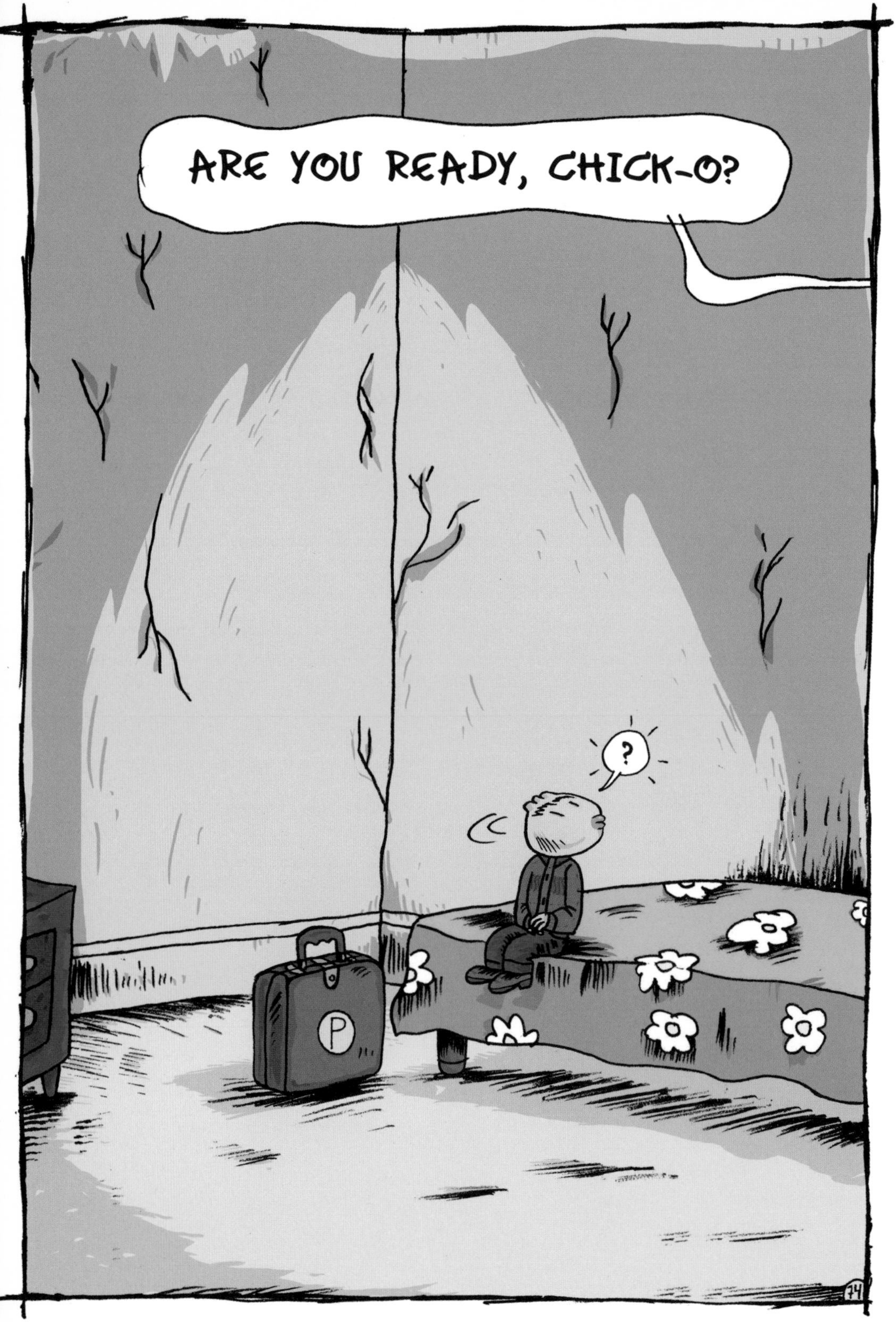
ARE YOU READY, CHICK-O?
?
74

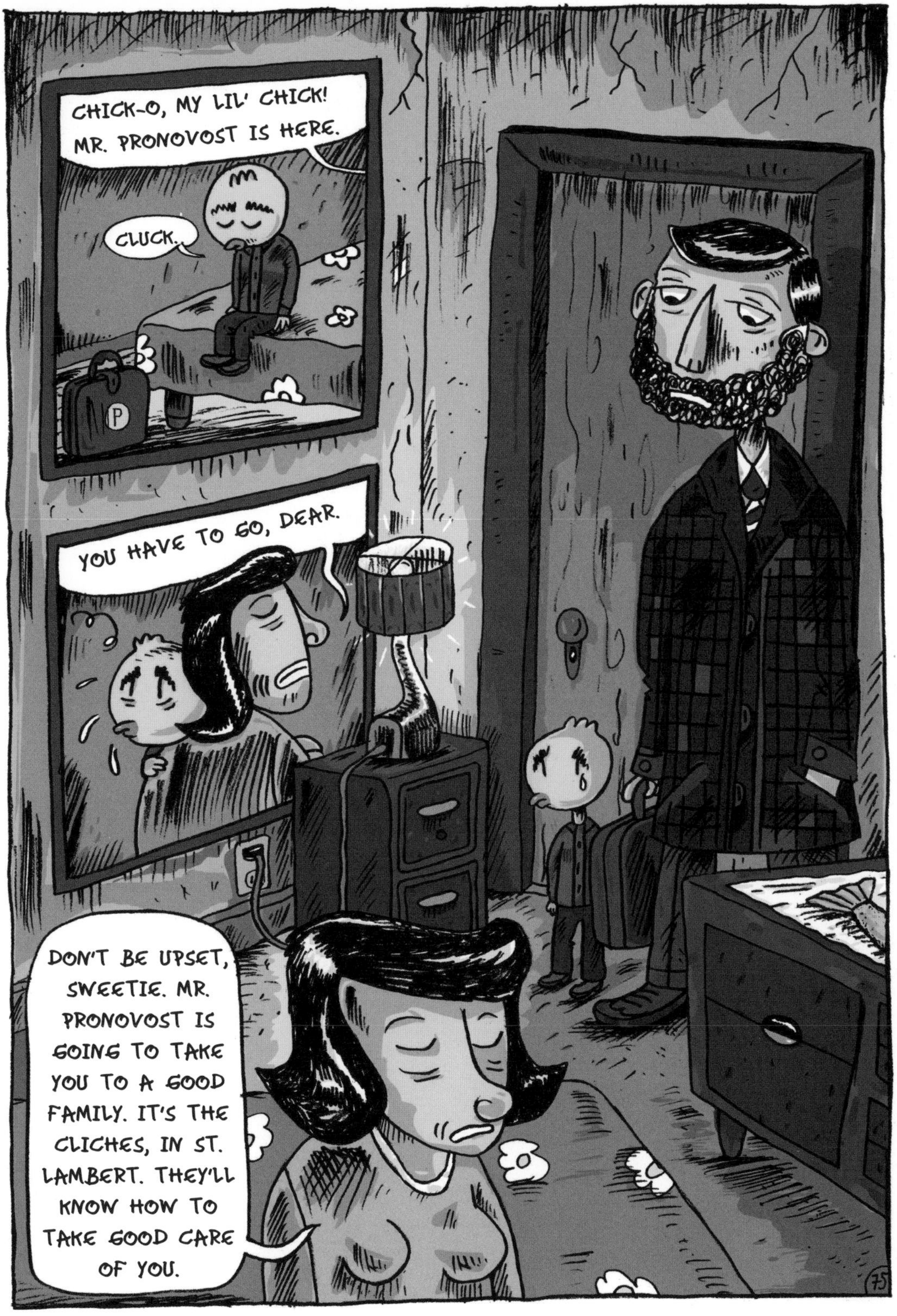
CHICK-O, MY LIL' CHICK! MR. PRONOVOST IS HERE.
CLUCK.
P
YOU HAVE TO GO, DEAR.
DON'T BE UPSET, SWEETIE. MR. PRONOVOST IS GOING TO TAKE YOU TO A GOOD FAMILY. IT'S THE CLICHES, IN ST. LAMBERT. THEY'LL KNOW HOW TO TAKE GOOD CARE OF YOU.
75

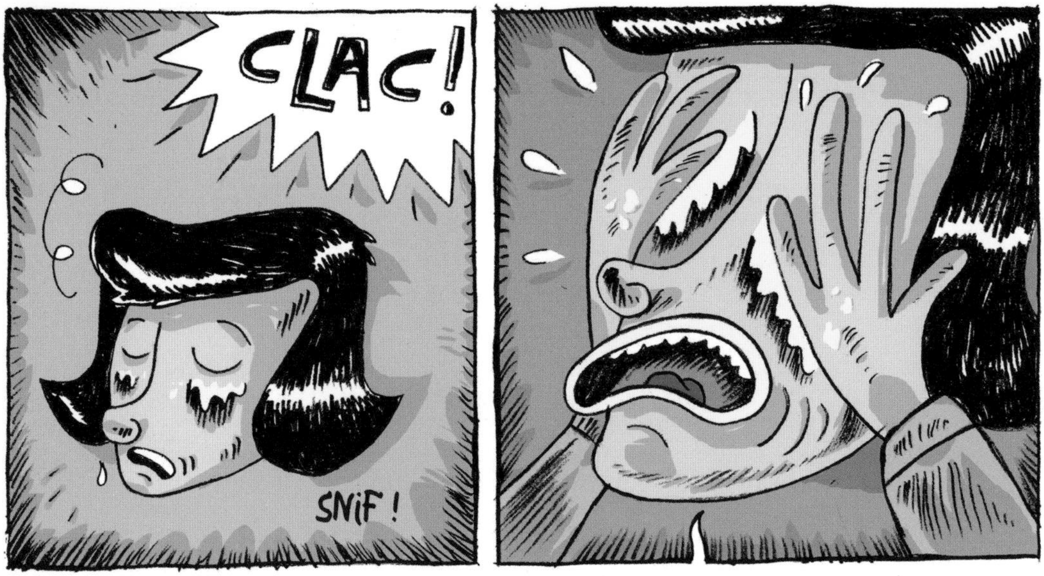
CLAC!
SNIF!

BOO-HOO-HOOO! MY PRECIOUS LITTLE CHICK, THE LAST OF MY FIVE CHILDREN! THEY TOOK HIM AWAY TOO! WHAT AM I GOING TO HAVE TO DEAL WITH NEXT?

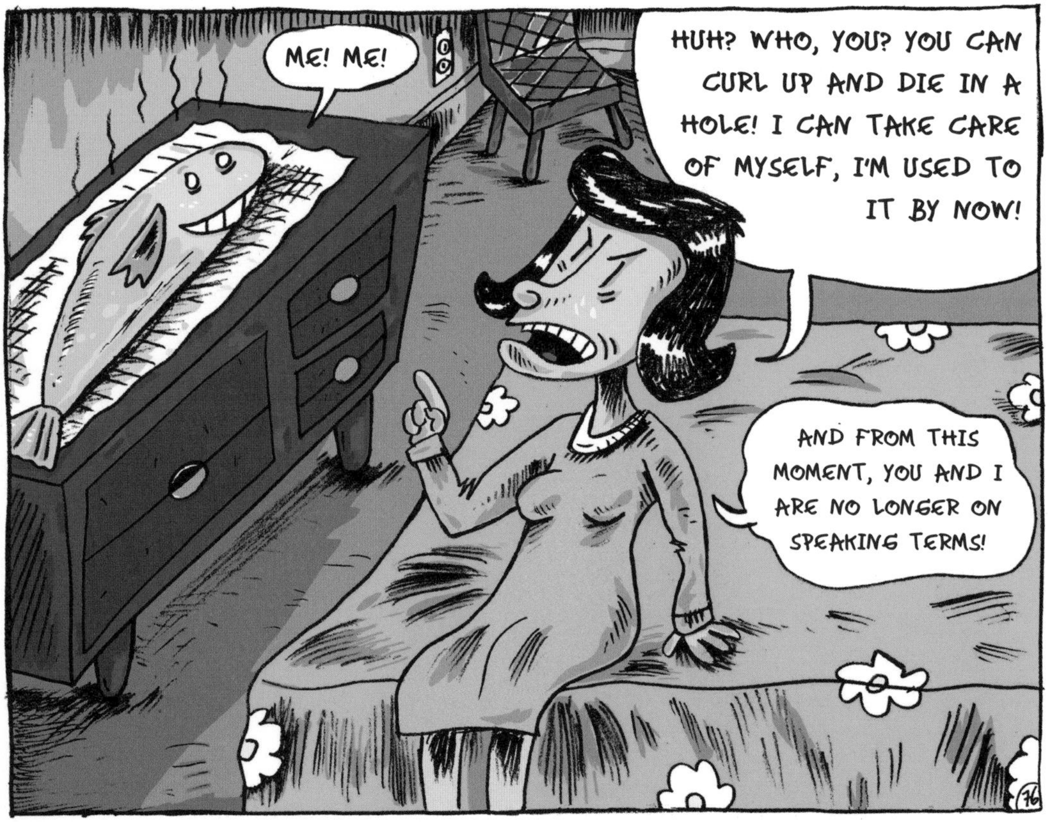
ME! ME!
HUH? WHO, YOU? YOU CAN CURL UP AND DIE IN A HOLE! I CAN TAKE CARE OF MYSELF, I'M USED TO IT BY NOW!
AND FROM THIS MOMENT, YOU AND I ARE NO LONGER ON SPEAKING TERMS!

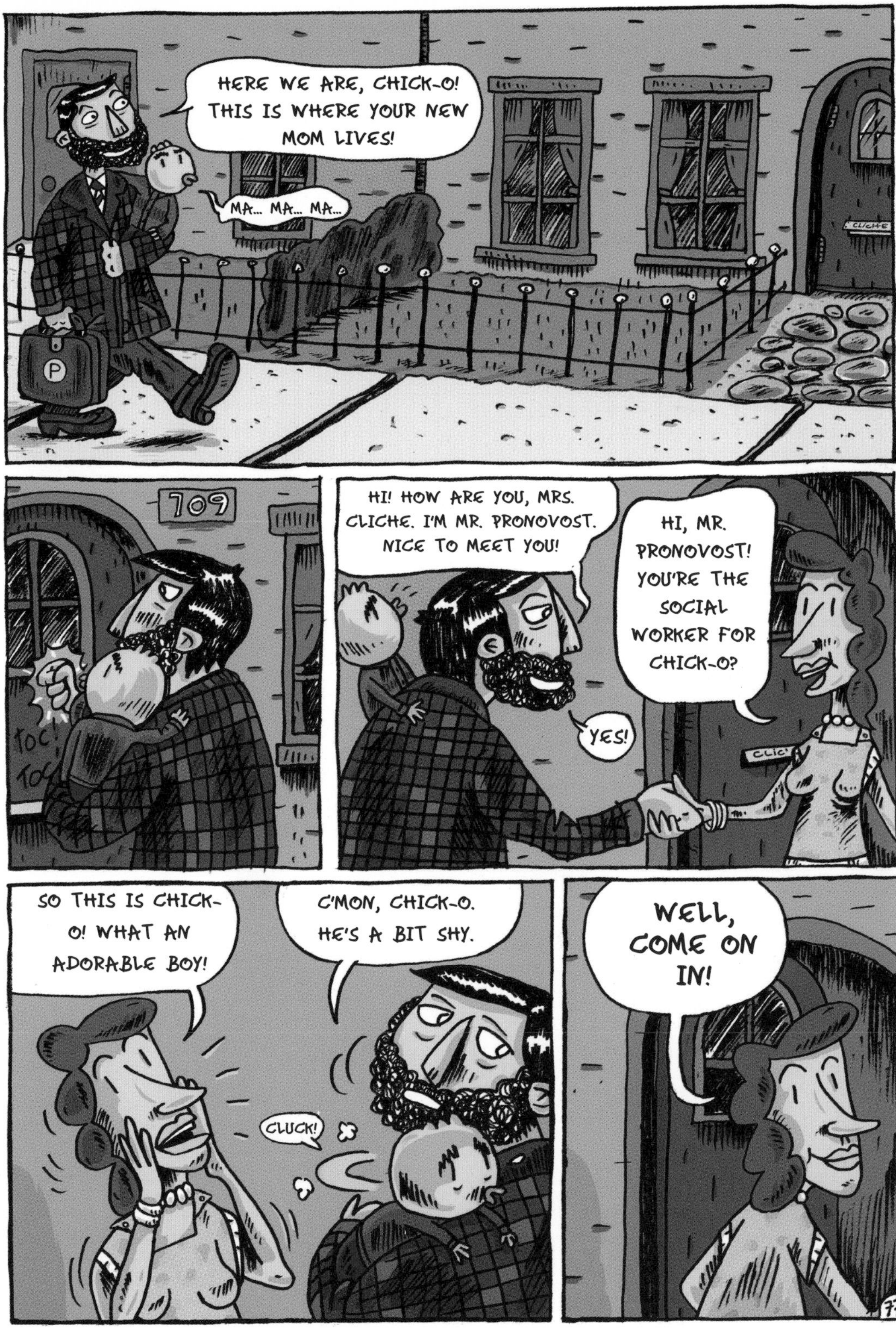
HERE WE ARE, CHICK-O! THIS IS WHERE YOUR NEW MOM LIVES!
MA... MA... MA...
CLICHE
709
TOC! TOC!
HI! HOW ARE YOU, MRS. CLICHE. I'M MR. PRONOVOST. NICE TO MEET YOU!
HI, MR. PRONOVOST! YOU'RE THE SOCIAL WORKER FOR CHICK-O?
YES!
SO THIS IS CHICK-O! WHAT AN ADORABLE BOY!
C'MON, CHICK-O. HE'S A BIT SHY.
CLUCK!
WELL, COME ON IN!
77

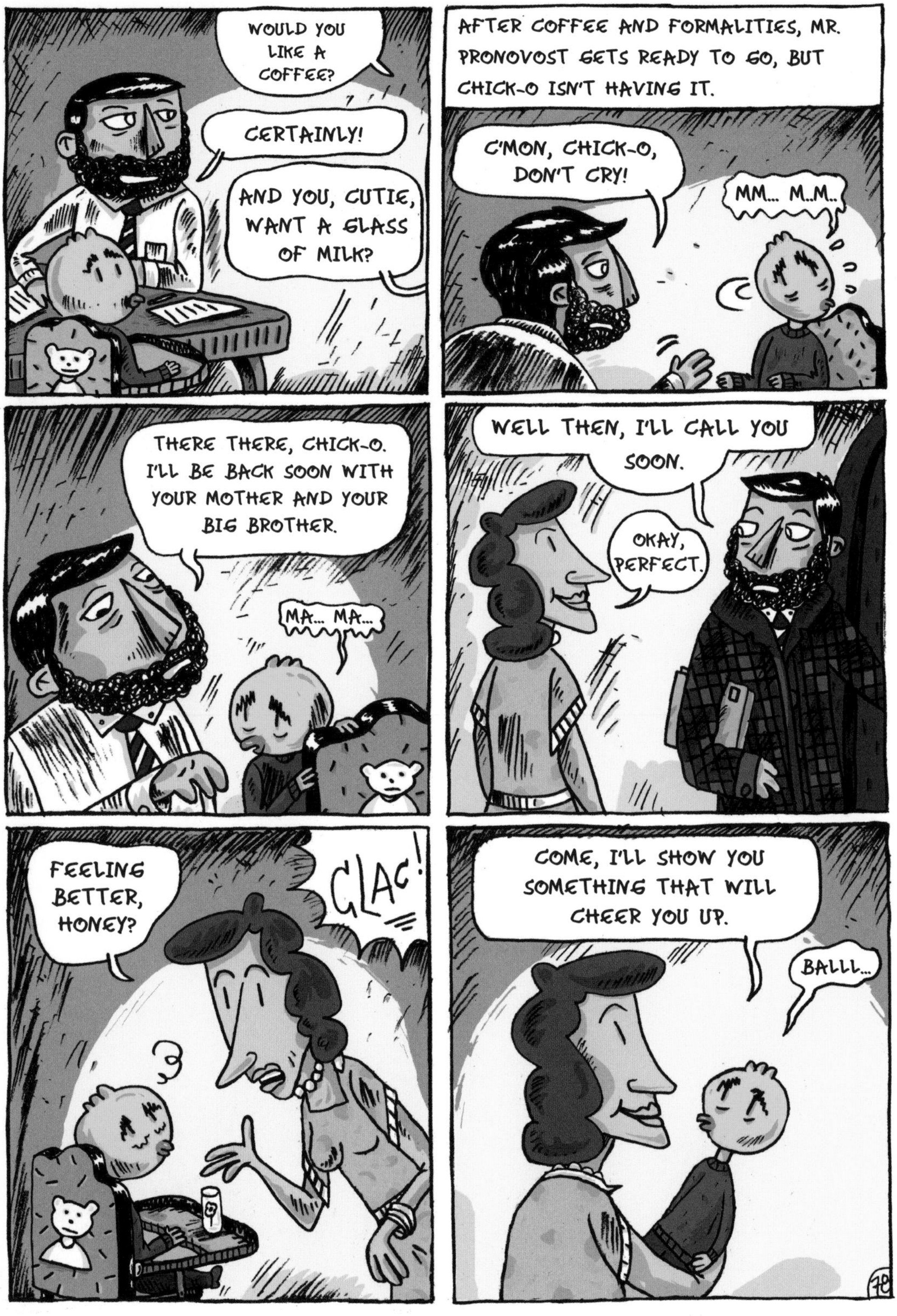
WOULD YOU LIKE A COFFEE?
CERTAINLY!
AND YOU, CUTIE, WANT A GLASS OF MILK?
AFTER COFFEE AND FORMALITIES, MR. PRONOVOST GETS READY TO GO, BUT CHICK-O ISN'T HAVING IT.
C'MON, CHICK-O, DON'T CRY!
MM... M..M..
THERE THERE, CHICK-O. I'LL BE BACK SOON WITH YOUR MOTHER AND YOUR BIG BROTHER.
MA... MA...
WELL THEN, I'LL CALL YOU SOON.
OKAY, PERFECT.
FEELING BETTER, HONEY?
GLAC!
COME, I'LL SHOW YOU SOMETHING THAT WILL CHEER YOU UP.
BALLL...

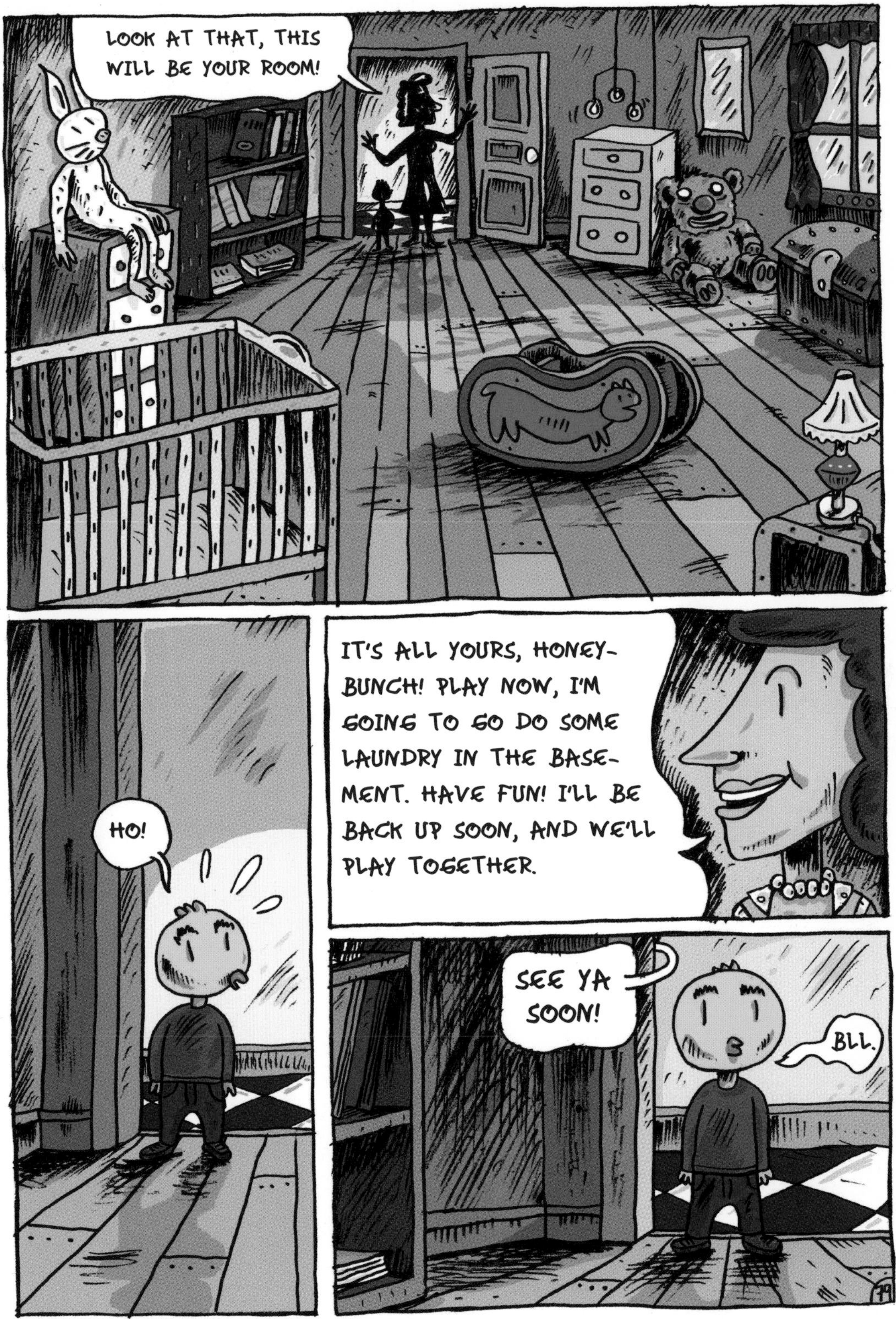
LOOK AT THAT, THIS WILL BE YOUR ROOM!
IT'S ALL YOURS, HONEY-BUNCH! PLAY NOW, I'M GOING TO GO DO SOME LAUNDRY IN THE BASE-MENT. HAVE FUN! I'LL BE BACK UP SOON, AND WE'LL PLAY TOGETHER.
HO!
SEE YA SOON!
BLL.

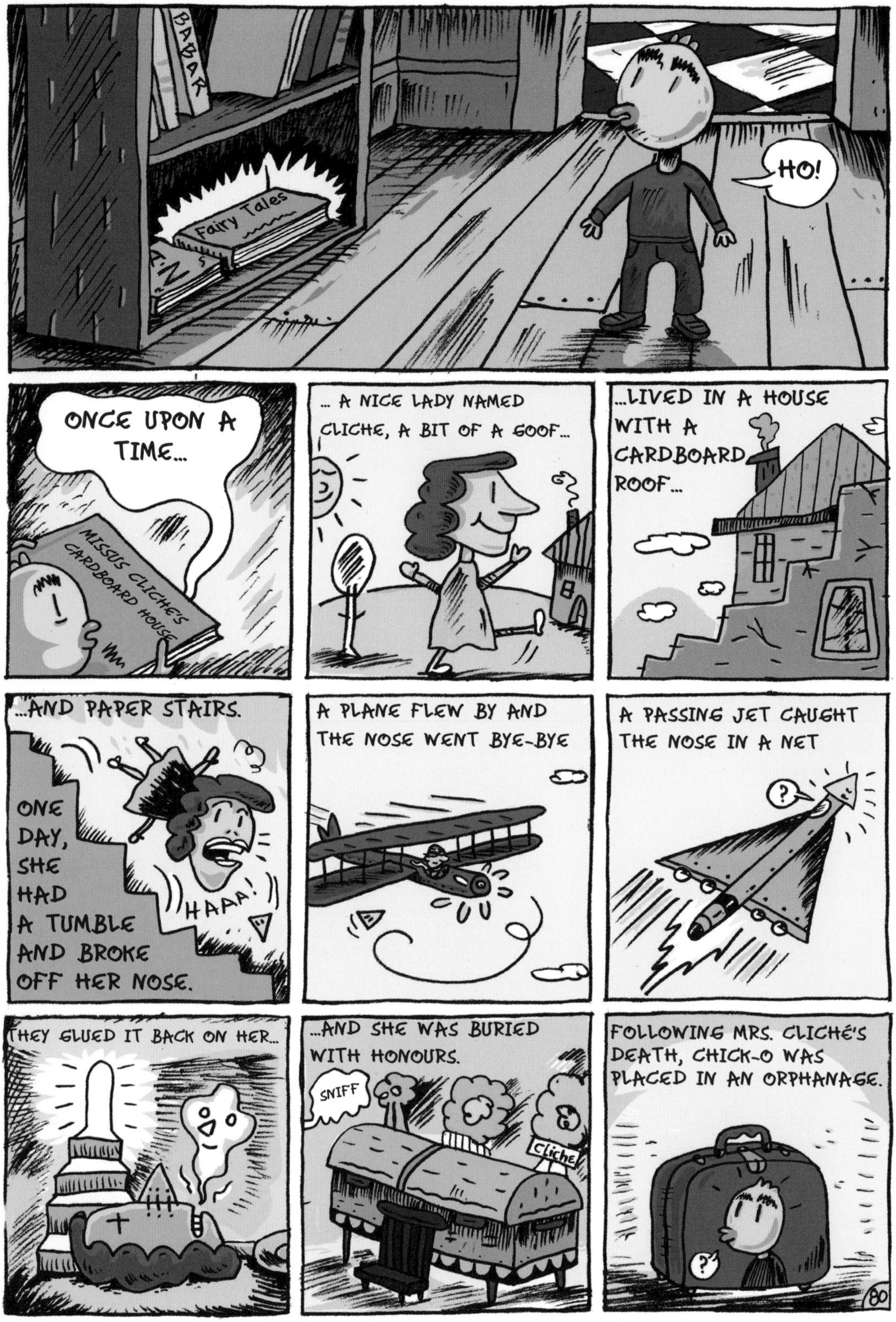
BABAR
Fairy Tales
HO!
ONCE UPON A TIME...
MISSUS CLICHE'S CARDBOARD HOUSE
... A NICE LADY NAMED CLICHE, A BIT OF A GOOF...
...LIVED IN A HOUSE WITH A CARDBOARD ROOF...
...AND PAPER STAIRS.
ONE DAY, SHE HAD A TUMBLE AND BROKE OFF HER NOSE.
HAAA!
A PLANE FLEW BY AND THE NOSE WENT BYE-BYE
A PASSING JET CAUGHT THE NOSE IN A NET
?
THEY GLUED IT BACK ON HER...
...AND SHE WAS BURIED WITH HONOURS.
SNIFF
Cliche
FOLLOWING MRS. CLICHÉ'S DEATH, CHICK-O WAS PLACED IN AN ORPHANAGE.
?
80

CHICK-O AT THE ITALIAN SISTERS' ORPHANAGE

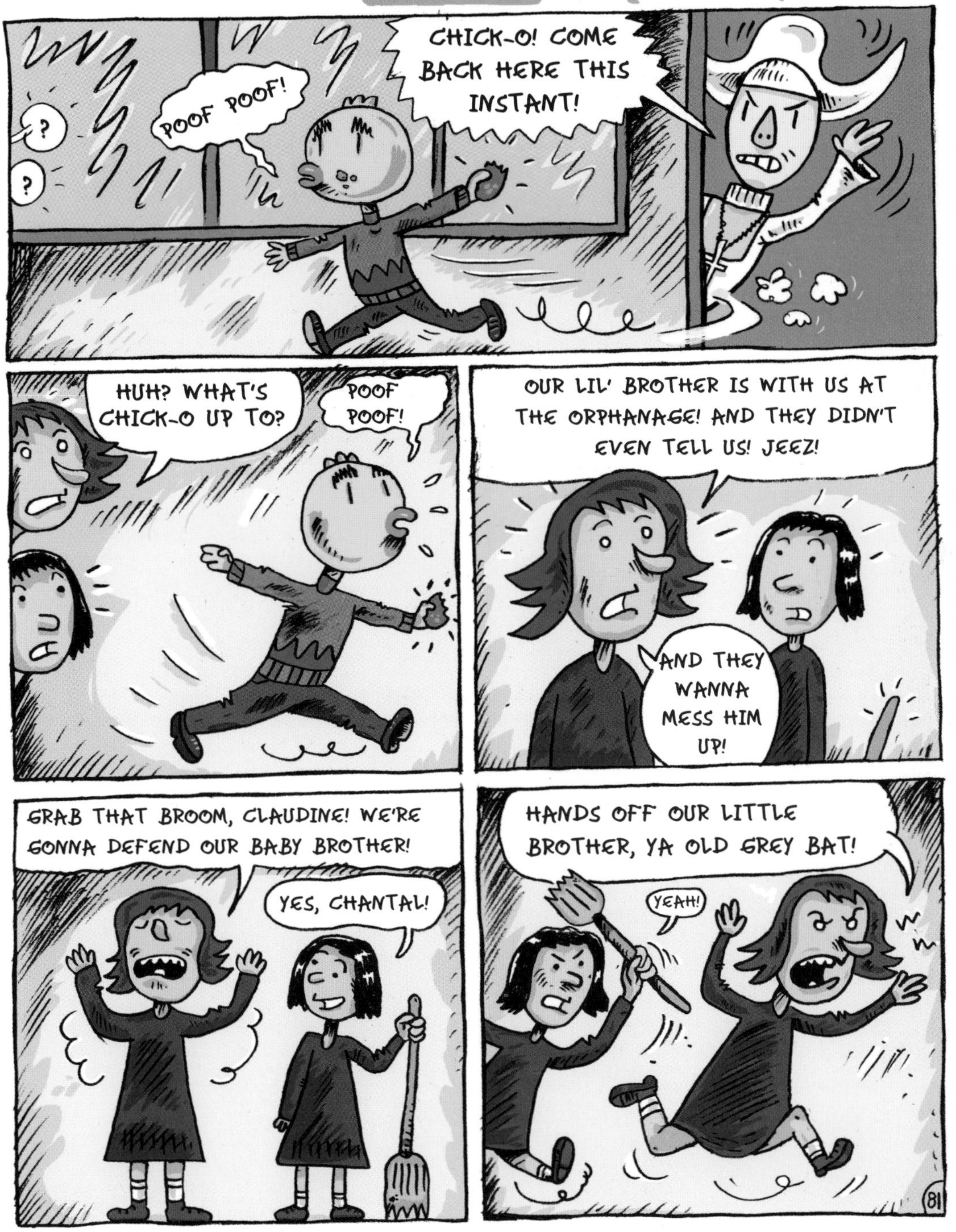
?
?
POOF POOF!
CHICK-O! COME BACK HERE THIS INSTANT!
HUH? WHAT'S CHICK-O UP TO?
POOF POOF!
OUR LIL' BROTHER IS WITH US AT THE ORPHANAGE! AND THEY DIDN'T EVEN TELL US! JEEZ!
AND THEY WANNA MESS HIM UP!
GRAB THAT BROOM, CLAUDINE! WE'RE GONNA DEFEND OUR BABY BROTHER!
YES, CHANTAL!
HANDS OFF OUR LITTLE BROTHER, YA OLD GREY BAT!
YEAH!

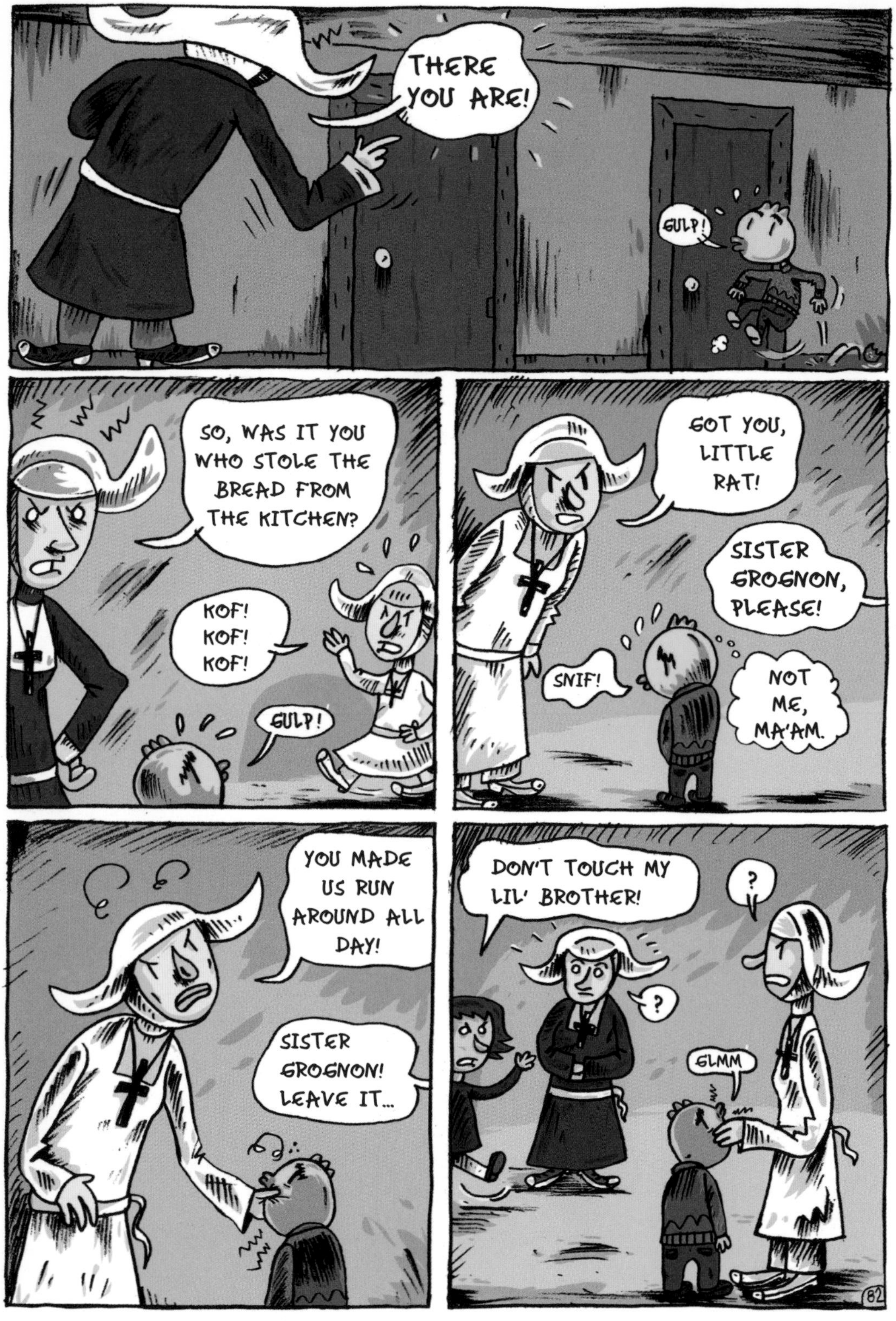
THERE YOU ARE!
GULP!
SO, WAS IT YOU WHO STOLE THE BREAD FROM THE KITCHEN?
KOF! KOF! KOF!
GULP!
GOT YOU, LITTLE RAT!
SISTER GROGNON, PLEASE!
SNIF!
NOT ME, MA'AM.
YOU MADE US RUN AROUND ALL DAY!
SISTER GROGNON! LEAVE IT...
DON'T TOUCH MY LIL' BROTHER!
?
?
GLMM
82

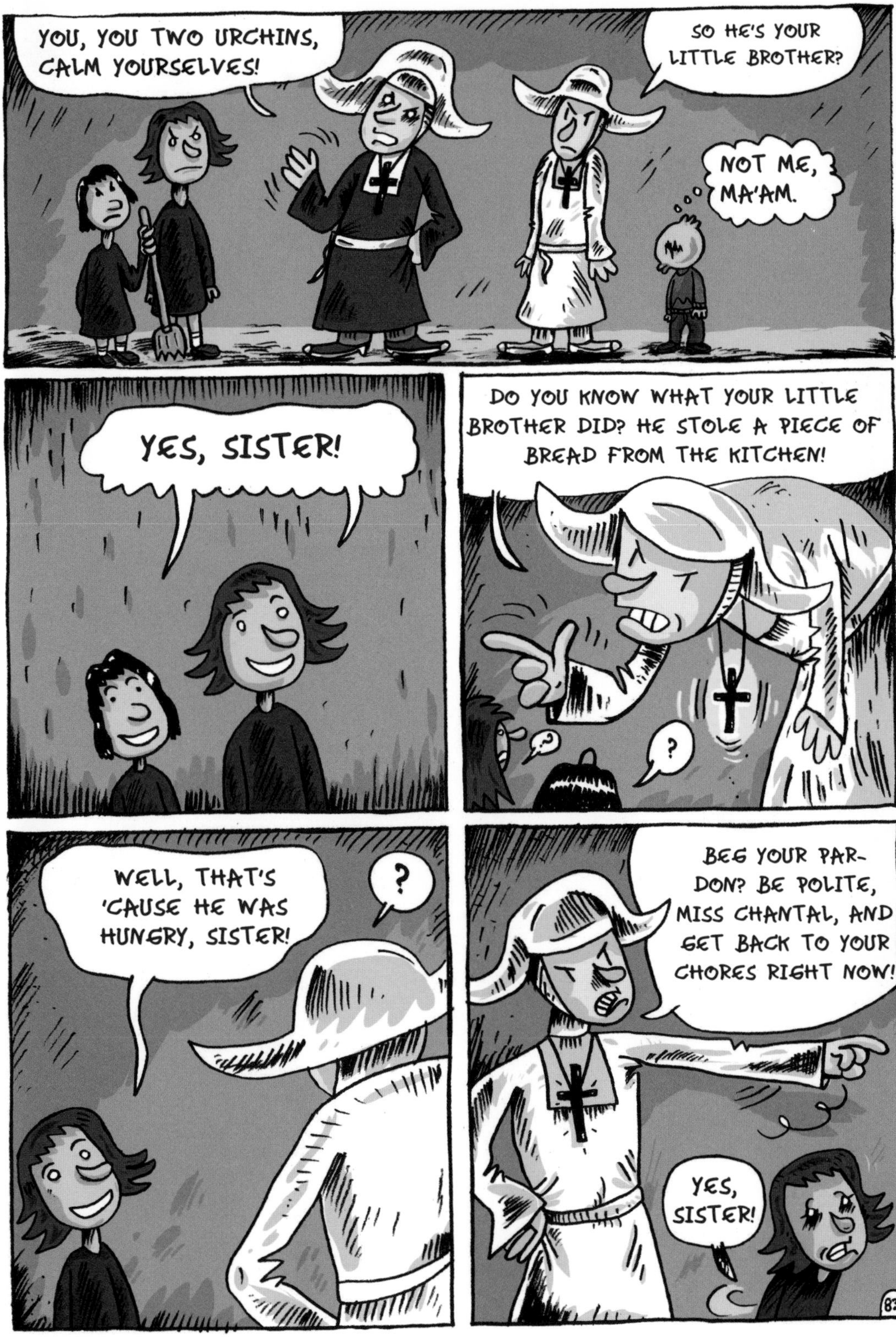
YOU, YOU TWO URCHINS, CALM YOURSELVES!
SO HE'S YOUR LITTLE BROTHER?
NOT ME, MA'AM.
YES, SISTER!
DO YOU KNOW WHAT YOUR LITTLE BROTHER DID? HE STOLE A PIECE OF BREAD FROM THE KITCHEN!
?
?
WELL, THAT'S 'CAUSE HE WAS HUNGRY, SISTER!
?
BEG YOUR PARDON? BE POLITE, MISS CHANTAL, AND GET BACK TO YOUR CHORES RIGHT NOW!
YES, SISTER!
83

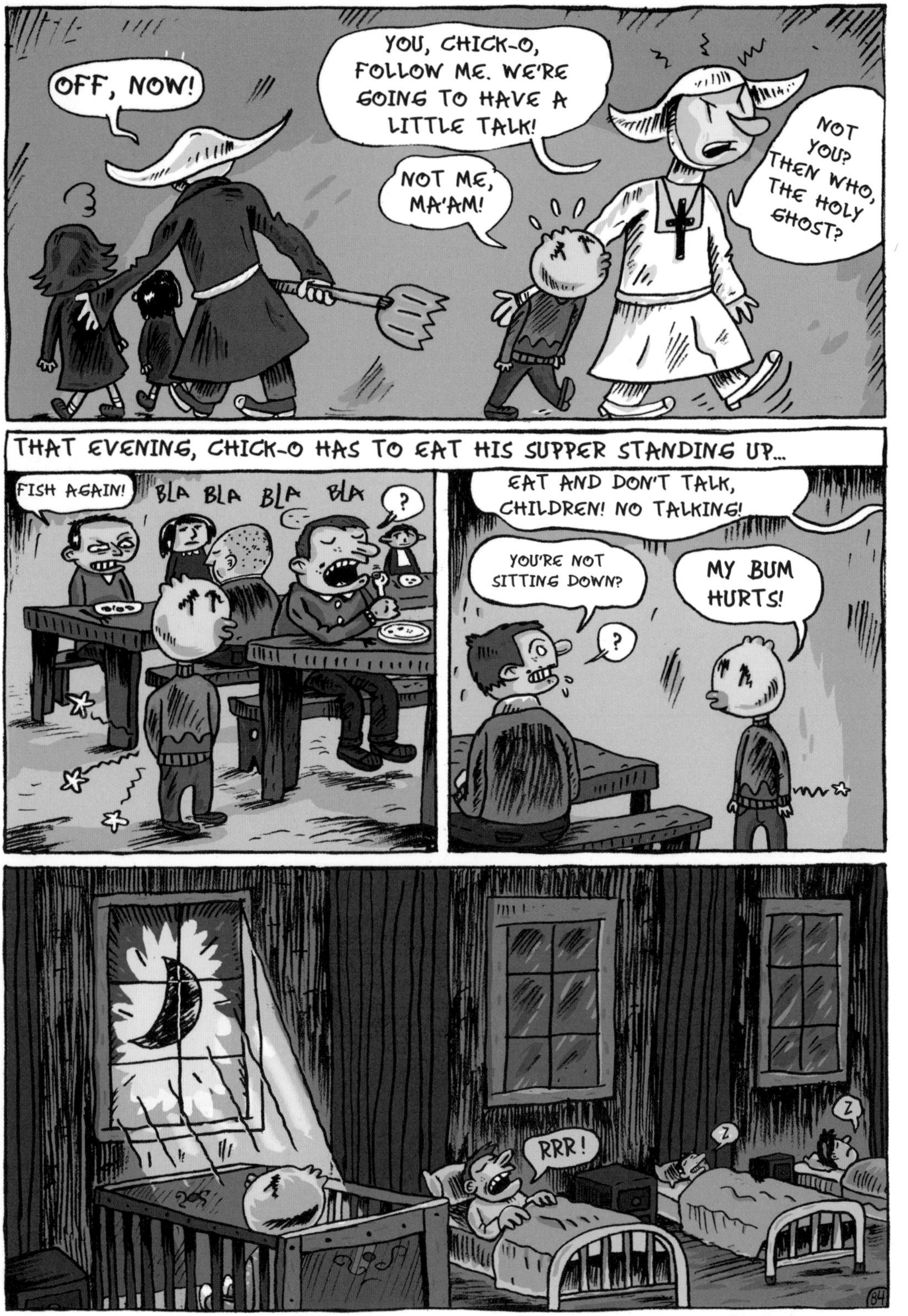

OFF, NOW!
YOU, CHICK-O, FOLLOW ME. WE'RE GOING TO HAVE A LITTLE TALK!
NOT ME, MA'AM!
NOT YOU? THEN WHO, THE HOLY GHOST?
THAT EVENING, CHICK-O HAS TO EAT HIS SUPPER STANDING UP...
FISH AGAIN!
BLA BLA BLA BLA
?
EAT AND DON'T TALK, CHILDREN! NO TALKING!
YOU'RE NOT SITTING DOWN?
?
MY BUM HURTS!
RRR!
Z
Z
84

A YEAR TRICKLES BY AT THE ORPHANAGE. CHICK-O GETS USED TO THE DAILY LITANY OF ORDERS.

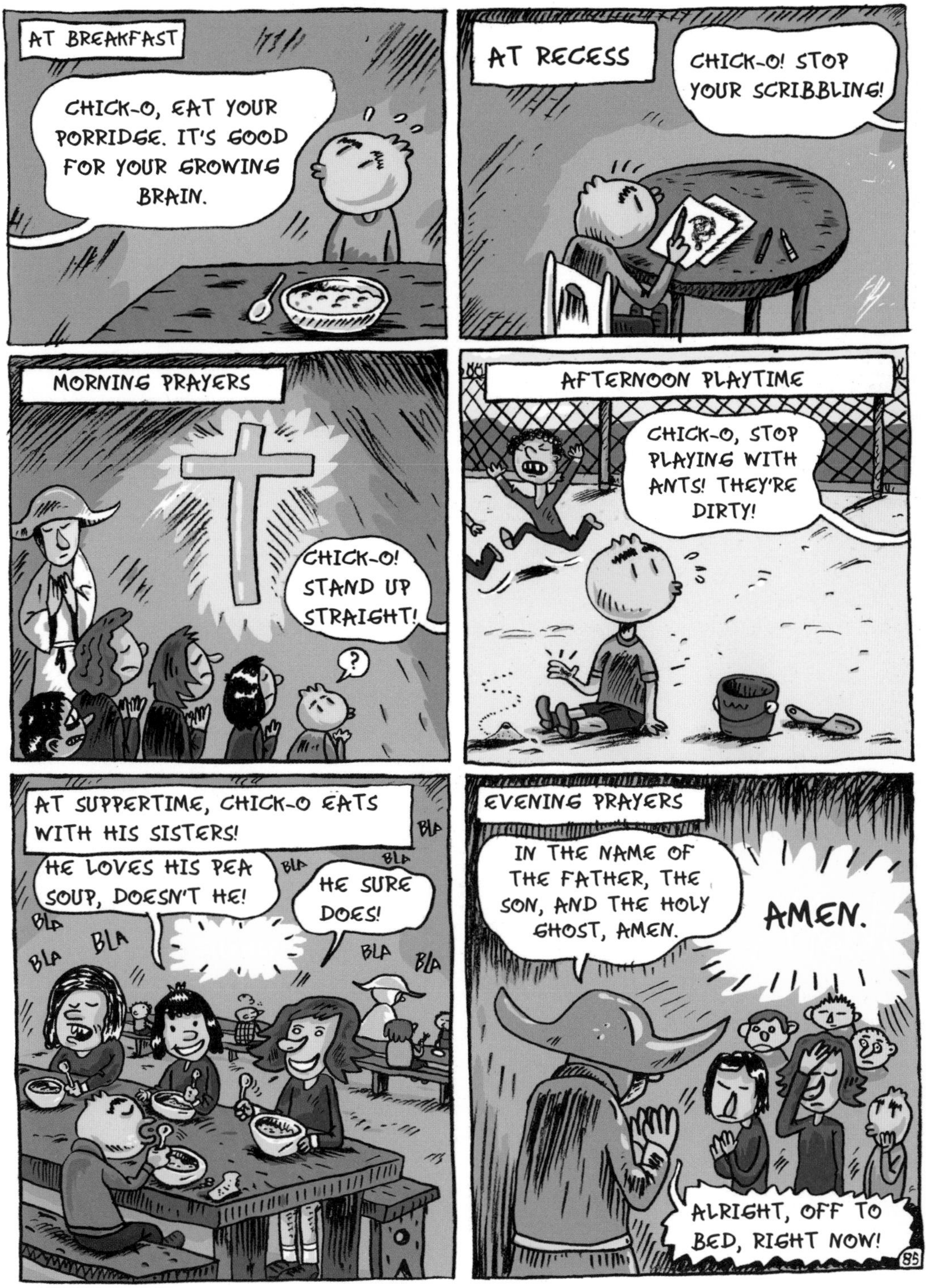
AT BREAKFAST
CHICK-O, EAT YOUR PORRIDGE. IT'S GOOD FOR YOUR GROWING BRAIN.
AT RECESS
CHICK-O! STOP YOUR SCRIBBLING!
MORNING PRAYERS
CHICK-O! STAND UP STRAIGHT!
?
AFTERNOON PLAYTIME
CHICK-O, STOP PLAYING WITH ANTS! THEY'RE DIRTY!
AT SUPPERTIME, CHICK-O EATS WITH HIS SISTERS!
HE LOVES HIS PEA SOUP, DOESN'T HE!
HE SURE DOES!
BLA BLA BLA BLA BLA BLA BLA BLA
EVENING PRAYERS
IN THE NAME OF THE FATHER, THE SON, AND THE HOLY GHOST, AMEN.
AMEN.
ALRIGHT, OFF TO BED, RIGHT NOW!

CHICK-O'S SISTERS HAVE SOME BAD NEWS FOR THEIR LITTLE BROTHER.

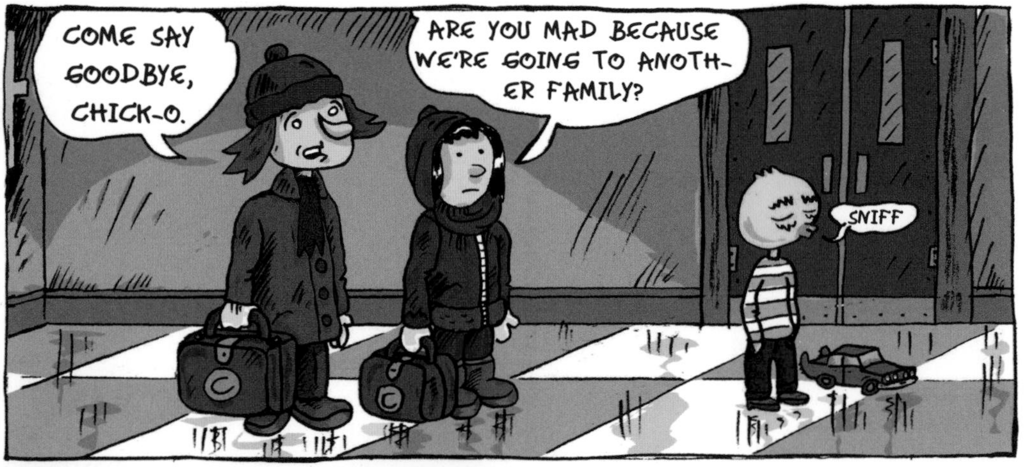
COME SAY GOODBYE, CHICK-O.
ARE YOU MAD BECAUSE WE'RE GOING TO ANOTH-ER FAMILY?
SNIFF

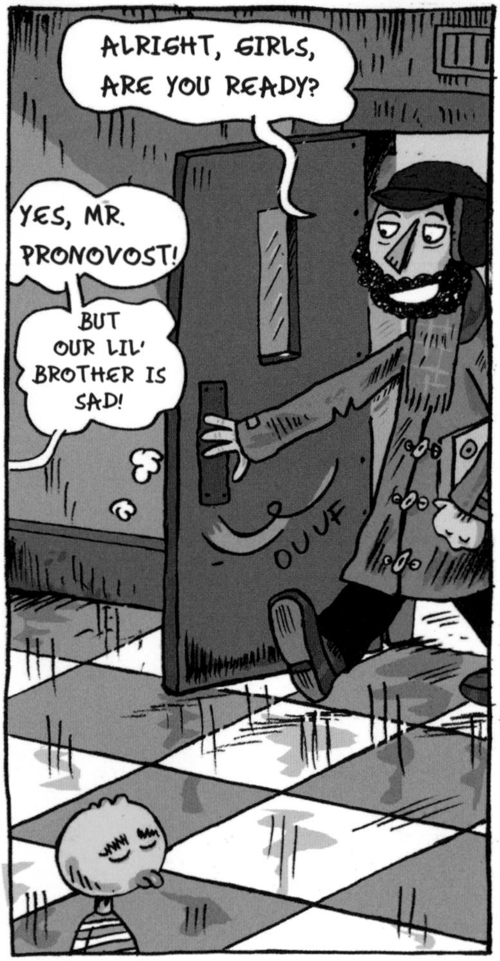
ALRIGHT, GIRLS, ARE YOU READY?
YES, MR. PRONOVOST!
BUT OUR LIL' BROTHER IS SAD!
OUUF

MR. PRONOVOST HANDLES THE CASES OF ALL THE SIORIS CHIL-DREN. THE PARENTS TRUSTED MR. PRONOVOST TO PLACE THEIR KIDS IN HOMES WHERE THEY WOULDN'T BE ABUSED PHYSICALLY OR PSYCHOLOGICALLY.

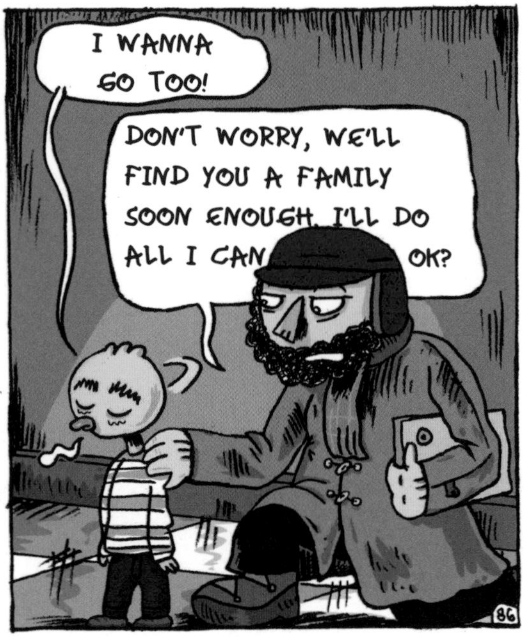
I WANNA GO TOO!
DON'T WORRY, WE'LL FIND YOU A FAMILY SOON ENOUGH. I'LL DO ALL I CAN OK?
86

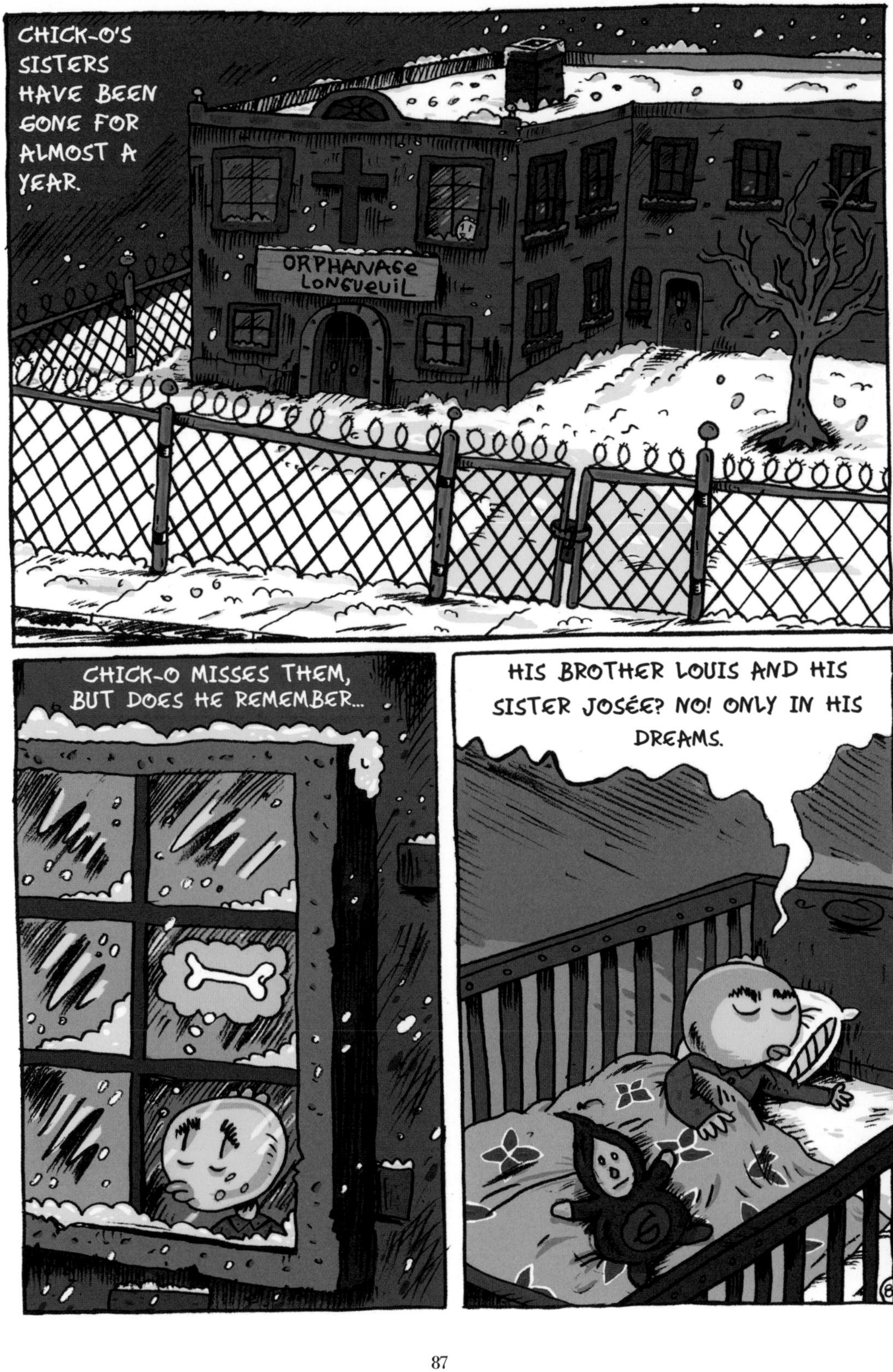
CHICK-O'S SISTERS HAVE BEEN GONE FOR ALMOST A YEAR.
ORPHANAGE LONGUEUIL
CHICK-O MISSES THEM, BUT DOES HE REMEMBER...
HIS BROTHER LOUIS AND HIS SISTER JOSÉE? NO! ONLY IN HIS DREAMS.

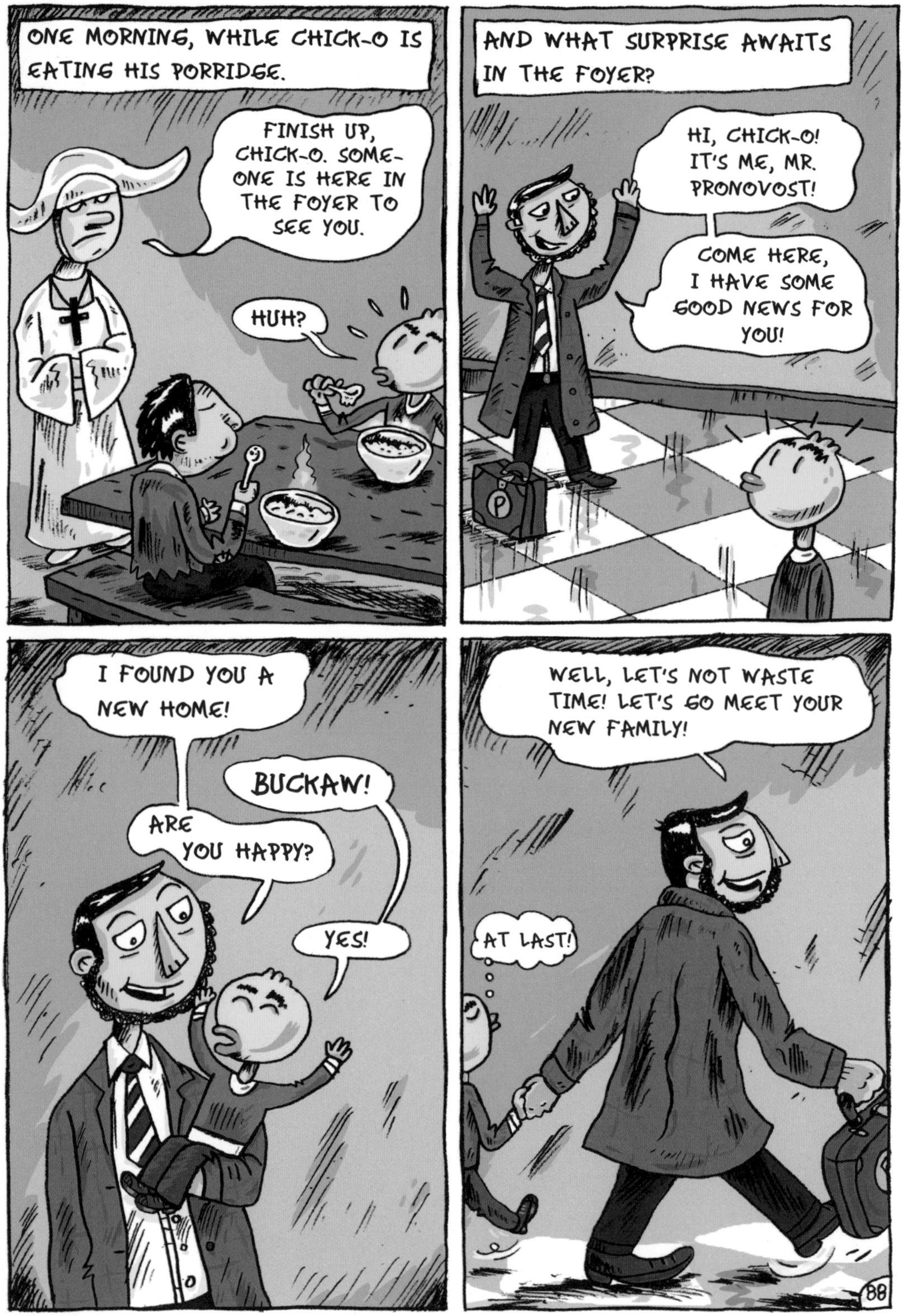
ONE MORNING, WHILE CHICK-O IS EATING HIS PORRIDGE.
FINISH UP, CHICK-O. SOME-ONE IS HERE IN THE FOYER TO SEE YOU.
HUH?
AND WHAT SURPRISE AWAITS IN THE FOYER?
HI, CHICK-O! IT'S ME, MR. PRONOVOST!
COME HERE, I HAVE SOME GOOD NEWS FOR YOU!
I FOUND YOU A NEW HOME!
ARE YOU HAPPY?
BUCKAW!
YES!
WELL, LET'S NOT WASTE TIME! LET'S GO MEET YOUR NEW FAMILY!
AT LAST!
88

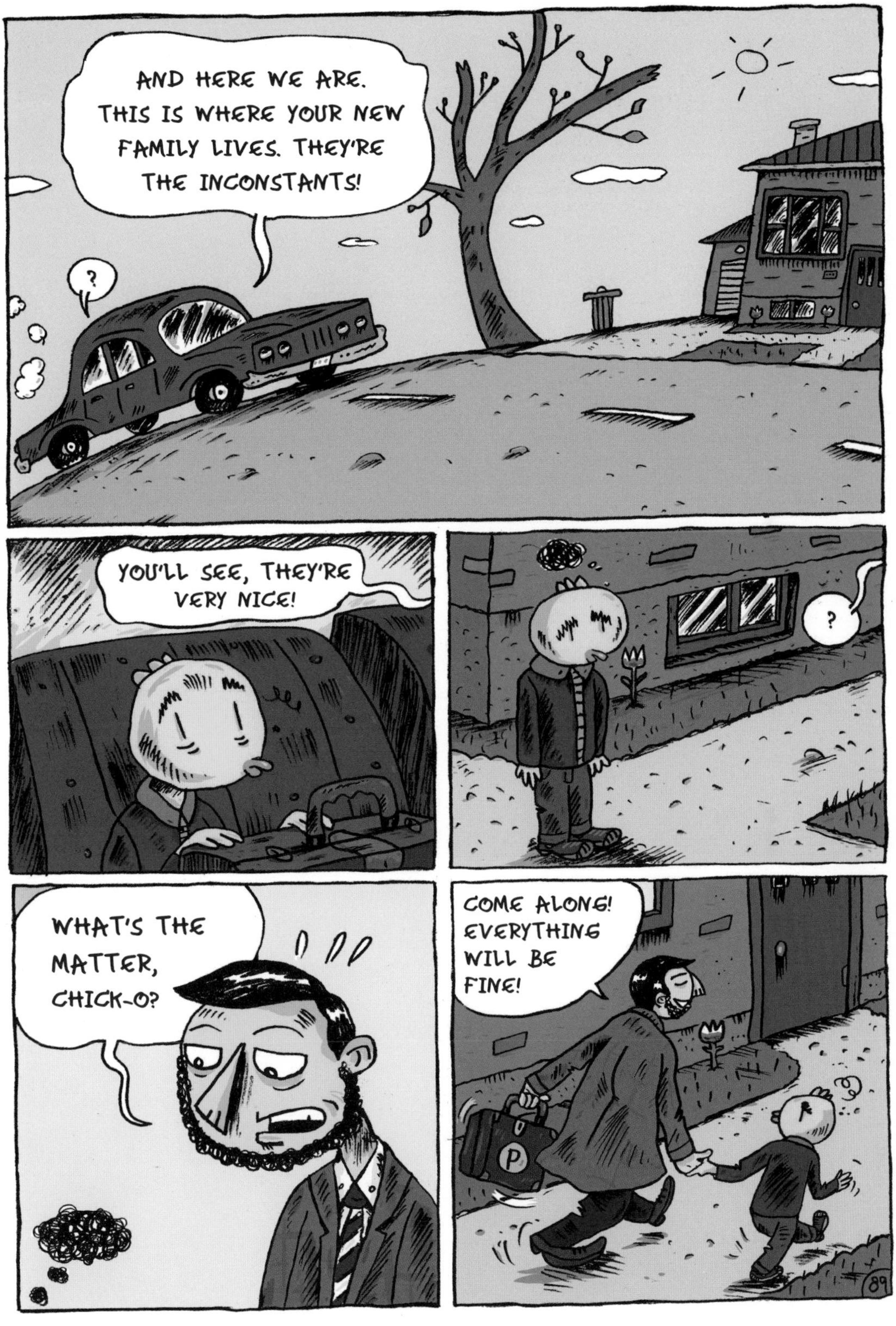
AND HERE WE ARE. THIS IS WHERE YOUR NEW FAMILY LIVES. THEY'RE THE INCONSTANTS!
?
YOU'LL SEE, THEY'RE VERY NICE!
?
WHAT'S THE MATTER, CHICK-O?
COME ALONG! EVERYTHING WILL BE FINE!
P
89

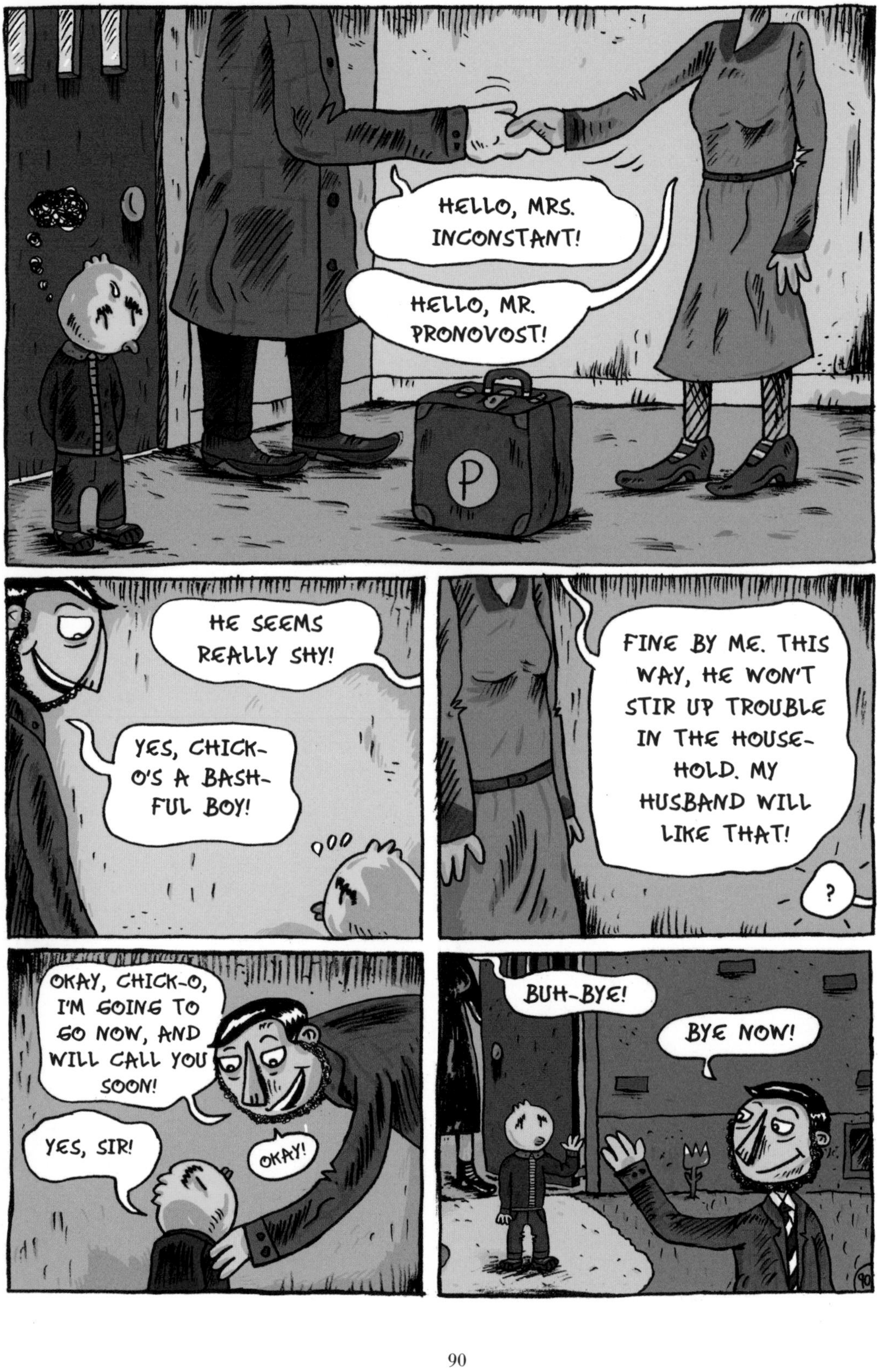
HELLO, MRS. INCONSTANT!
HELLO, MR. PRONOVOST!
P
HE SEEMS REALLY SHY!
YES, CHICK-O'S A BASHFUL BOY!
FINE BY ME. THIS WAY, HE WON'T STIR UP TROUBLE IN THE HOUSEHOLD. MY HUSBAND WILL LIKE THAT!
?
OKAY, CHICK-O, I'M GOING TO GO NOW, AND WILL CALL YOU SOON!
YES, SIR!
OKAY!
BUH-BYE!
BYE NOW!

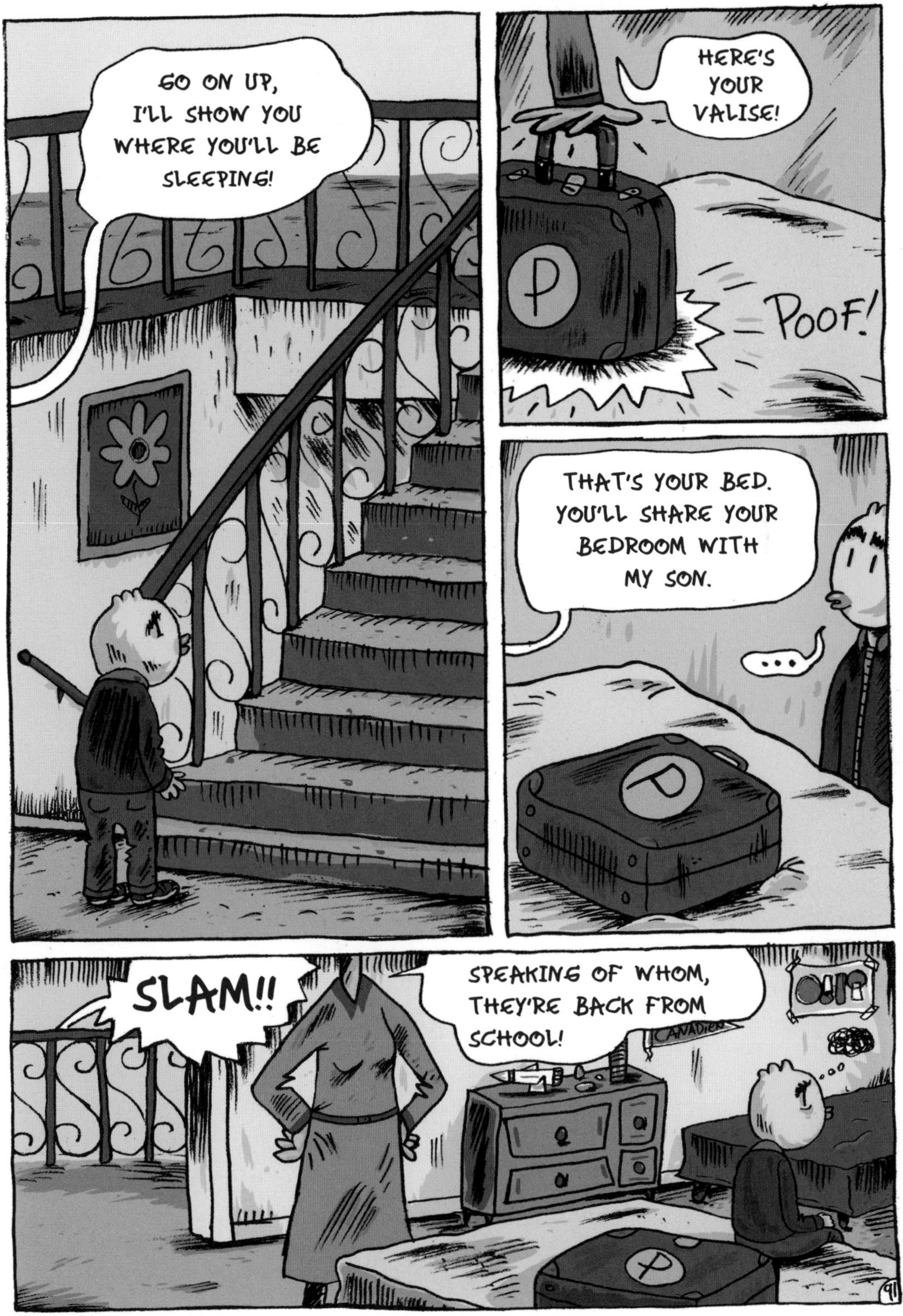
GO ON UP, I'LL SHOW YOU WHERE YOU'LL BE SLEEPING!
HERE'S YOUR VALISE!
POOF!
THAT'S YOUR BED. YOU'LL SHARE YOUR BEDROOM WITH MY SON.
...
SLAM!!
SPEAKING OF WHOM, THEY'RE BACK FROM SCHOOL!
CANADIEN
91

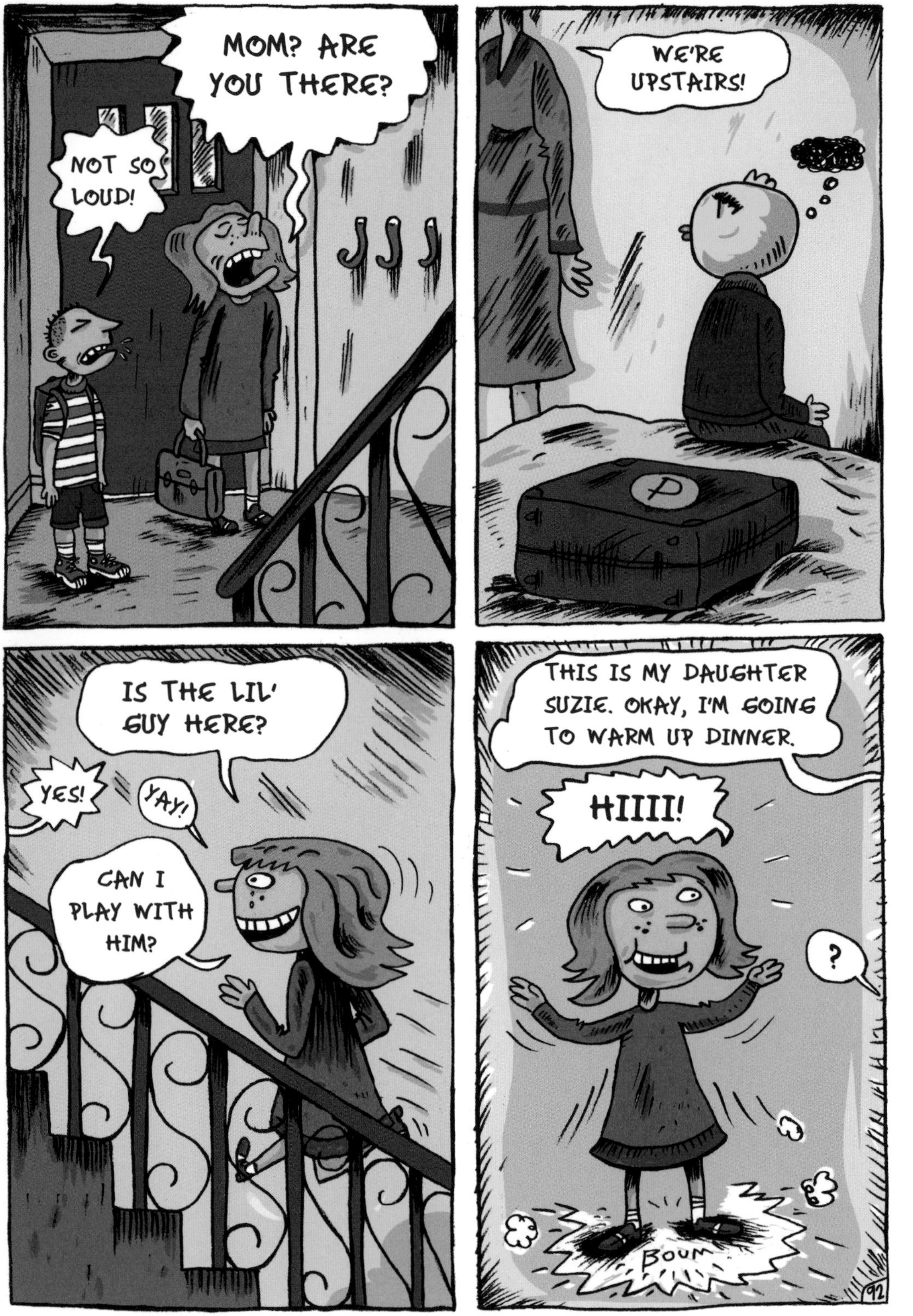
MOM? ARE YOU THERE?
NOT SO LOUD!
WE'RE UPSTAIRS!
IS THE LIL' GUY HERE?
YES!
YAY!
CAN I PLAY WITH HIM?
THIS IS MY DAUGHTER SUZIE. OKAY, I'M GOING TO WARM UP DINNER.
HIIII!
?
BOUM
92

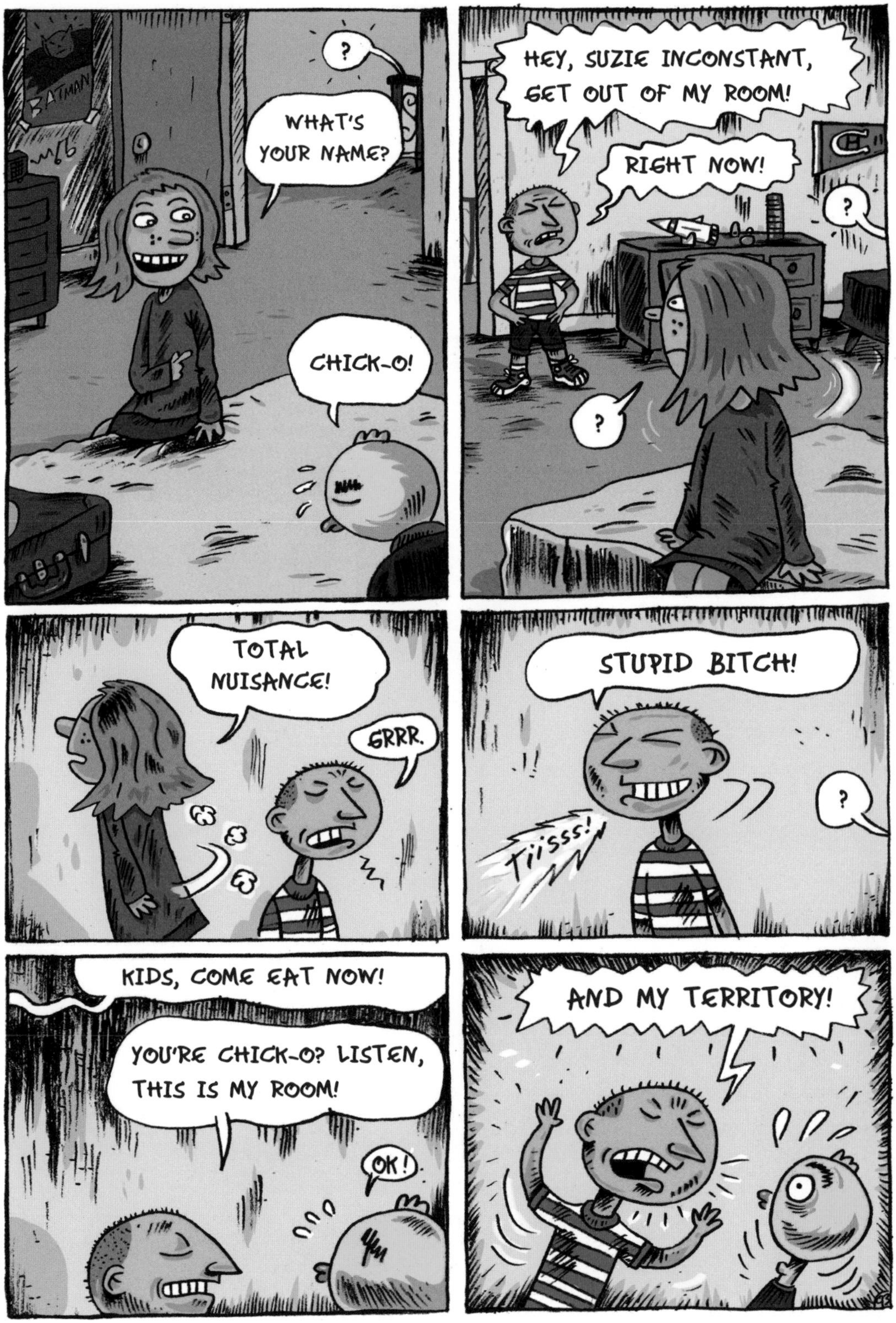
?
WHAT'S YOUR NAME?
CHICK-O!
HEY, SUZIE INCONSTANT, GET OUT OF MY ROOM!
RIGHT NOW!
?
?
TOTAL NUISANCE!
GRRR.
STUPID BITCH!
Tiisss!
?
KIDS, COME EAT NOW!
YOU'RE CHICK-O? LISTEN, THIS IS MY ROOM!
OK!
AND MY TERRITORY!

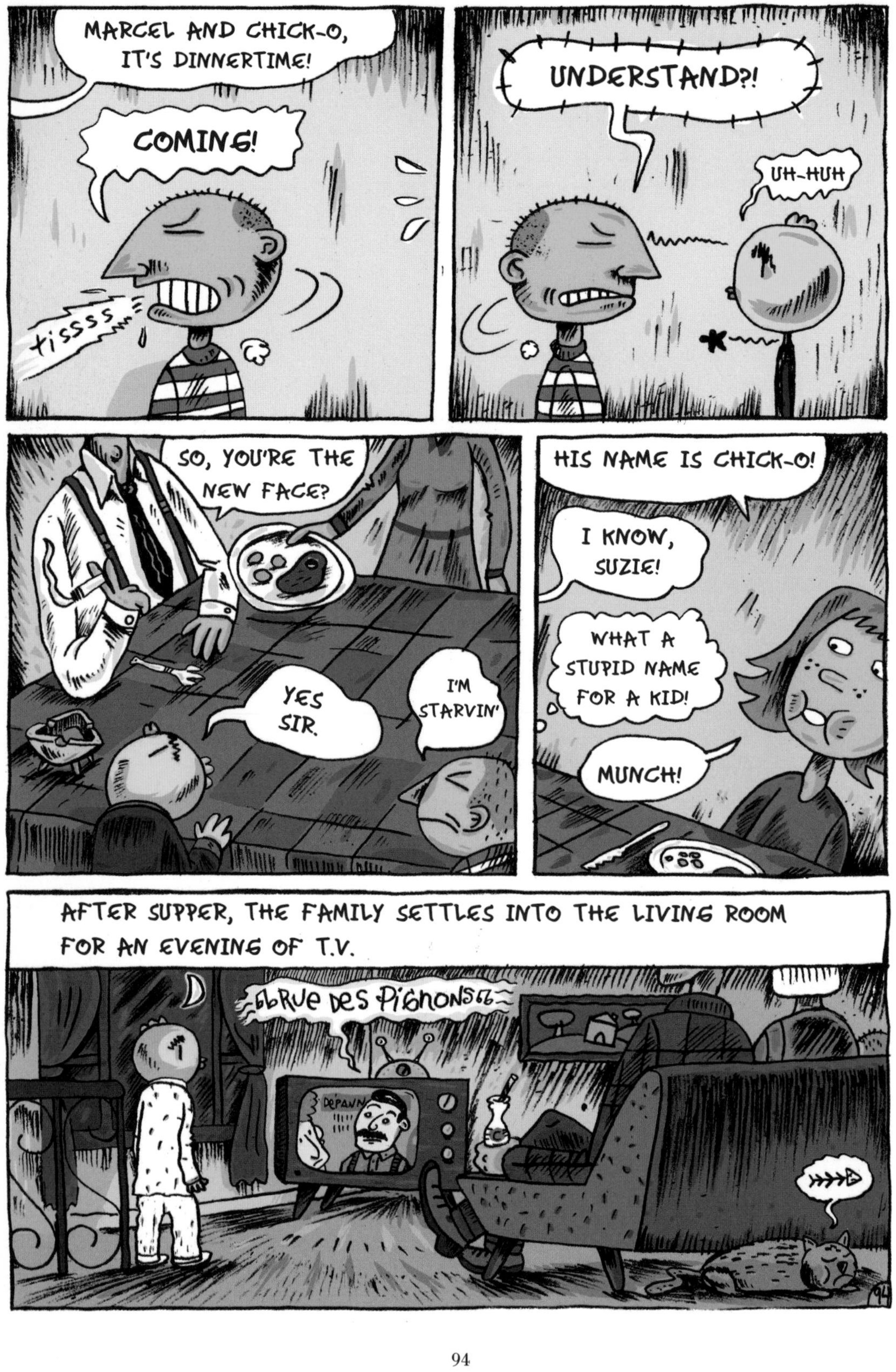
MARCEL AND CHICK-O, IT'S DINNERTIME!
COMING!
tissss
UNDERSTAND?!
UH-HUH
SO, YOU'RE THE NEW FACE?
YES SIR.
I'M STARVIN'
HIS NAME IS CHICK-O!
I KNOW, SUZIE!
WHAT A STUPID NAME FOR A KID!
MUNCH!
AFTER SUPPER, THE FAMILY SETTLES INTO THE LIVING ROOM FOR AN EVENING OF T.V.
rue des Pignons

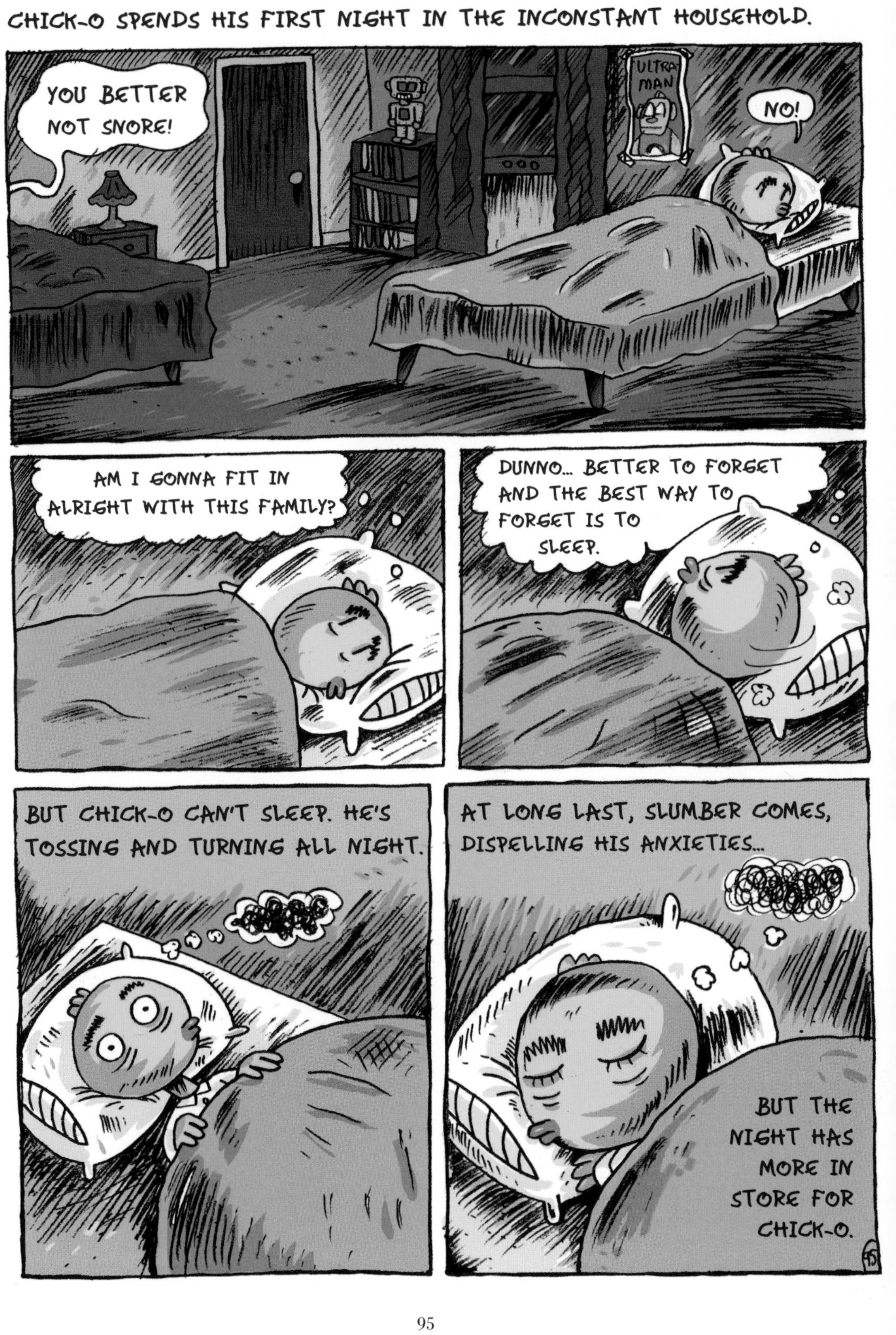
CHICK-O SPENDS HIS FIRST NIGHT IN THE INCONSTANT HOUSEHOLD.
YOU BETTER NOT SNORE!
ULTRA MAN
NO!
AM I GONNA FIT IN ALRIGHT WITH THIS FAMILY?
DUNNO... BETTER TO FORGET AND THE BEST WAY TO FORGET IS TO SLEEP.
BUT CHICK-O CAN'T SLEEP. HE'S TOSSING AND TURNING ALL NIGHT.
AT LONG LAST, SLUMBER COMES, DISPELLING HIS ANXIETIES...
BUT THE NIGHT HAS MORE IN STORE FOR CHICK-O.
95

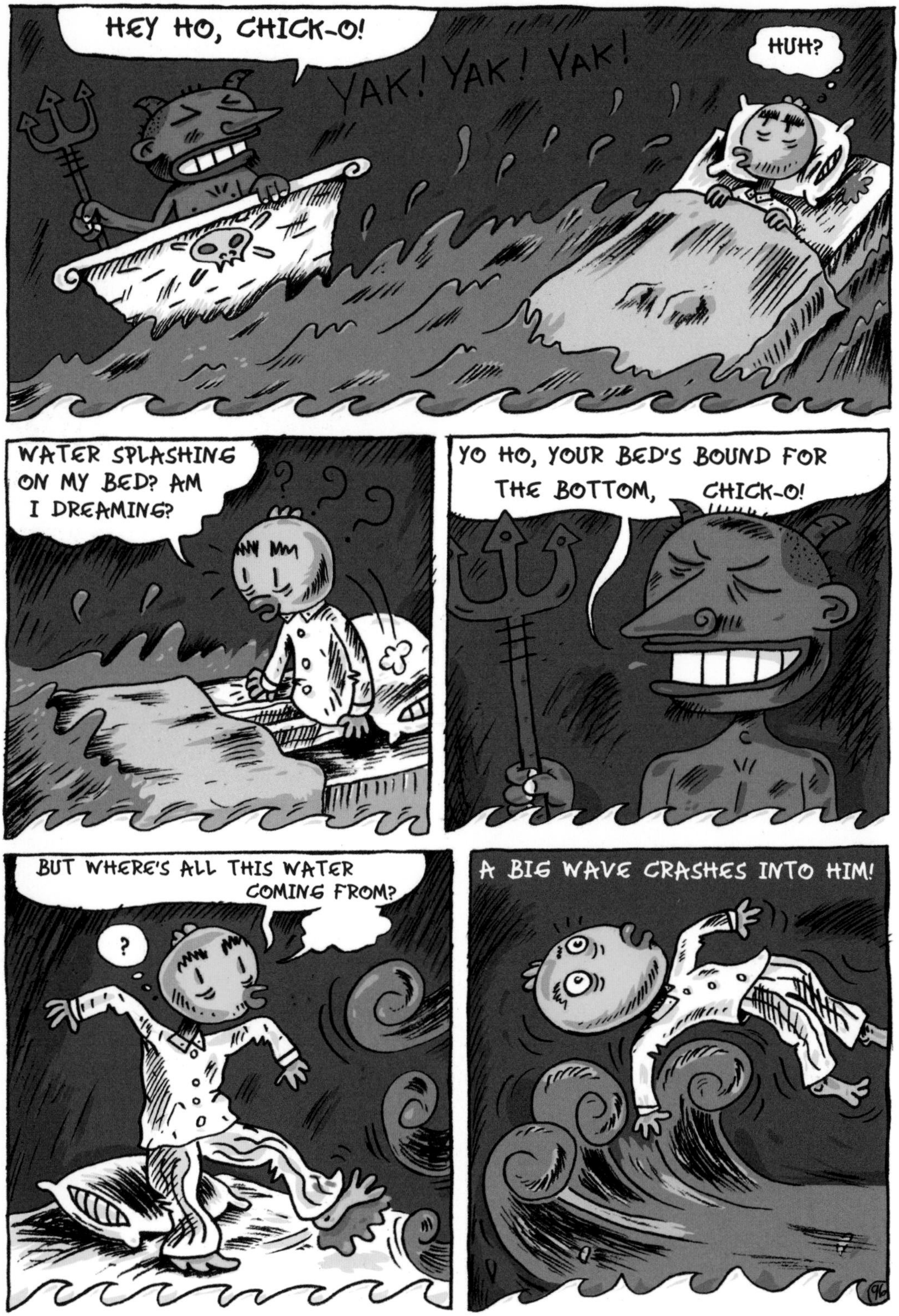
HEY HO, CHICK-O!
YAK! YAK! YAK!
HUH?
WATER SPLASHING ON MY BED? AM I DREAMING?
YO HO, YOUR BED'S BOUND FOR THE BOTTOM, CHICK-O!
BUT WHERE'S ALL THIS WATER COMING FROM?
?
A BIG WAVE CRASHES INTO HIM!
96

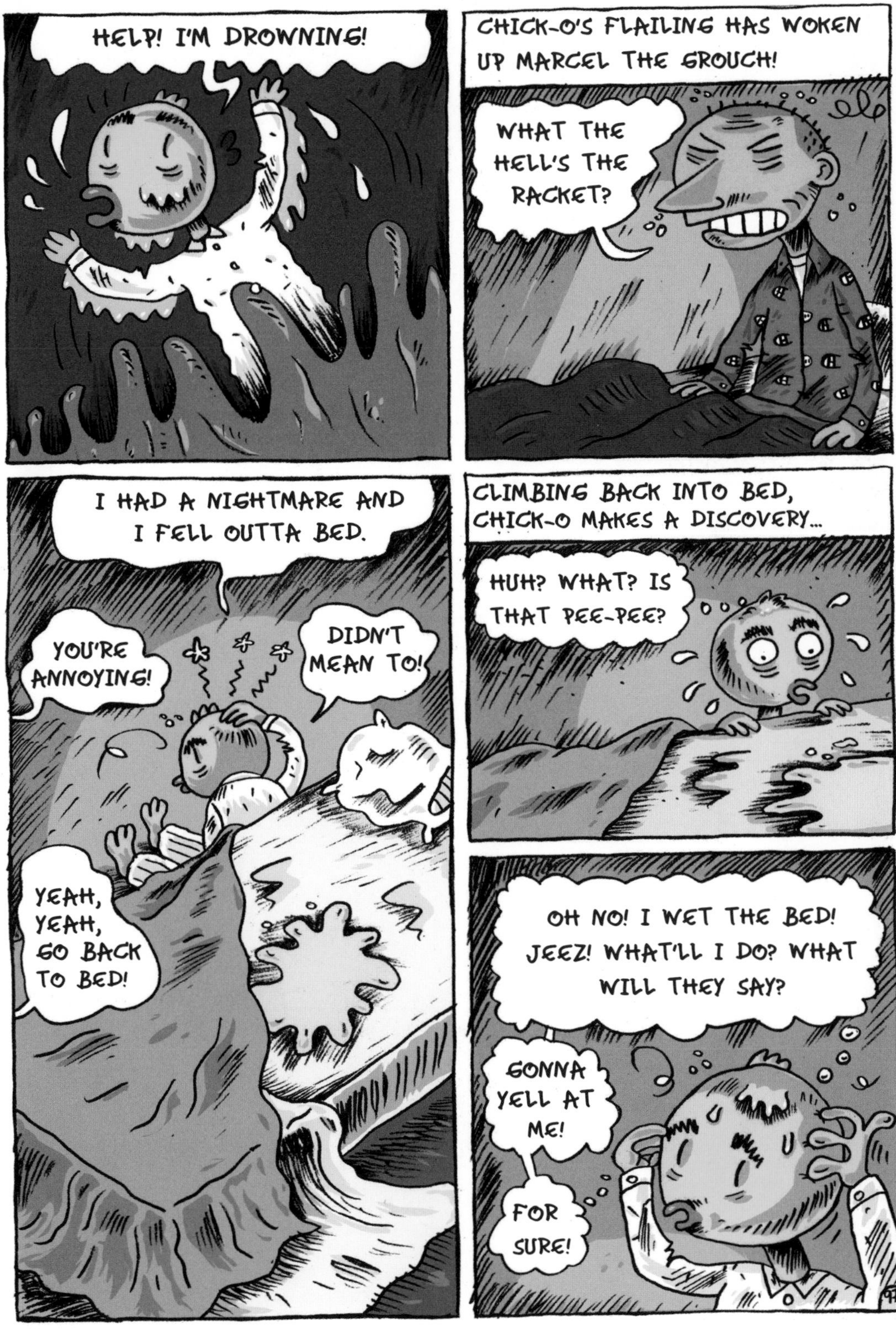
HELP! I'M DROWNING!
CHICK-O'S FLAILING HAS WOKEN UP MARCEL THE GROUCH!
WHAT THE HELL'S THE RACKET?
I HAD A NIGHTMARE AND I FELL OUTTA BED.
YOU'RE ANNOYING!
DIDN'T MEAN TO!
YEAH, YEAH, GO BACK TO BED!
CLIMBING BACK INTO BED, CHICK-O MAKES A DISCOVERY...
HUH? WHAT? IS THAT PEE-PEE?
OH NO! I WET THE BED! JEEZ! WHAT'LL I DO? WHAT WILL THEY SAY?
GONNA YELL AT ME!
FOR SURE!

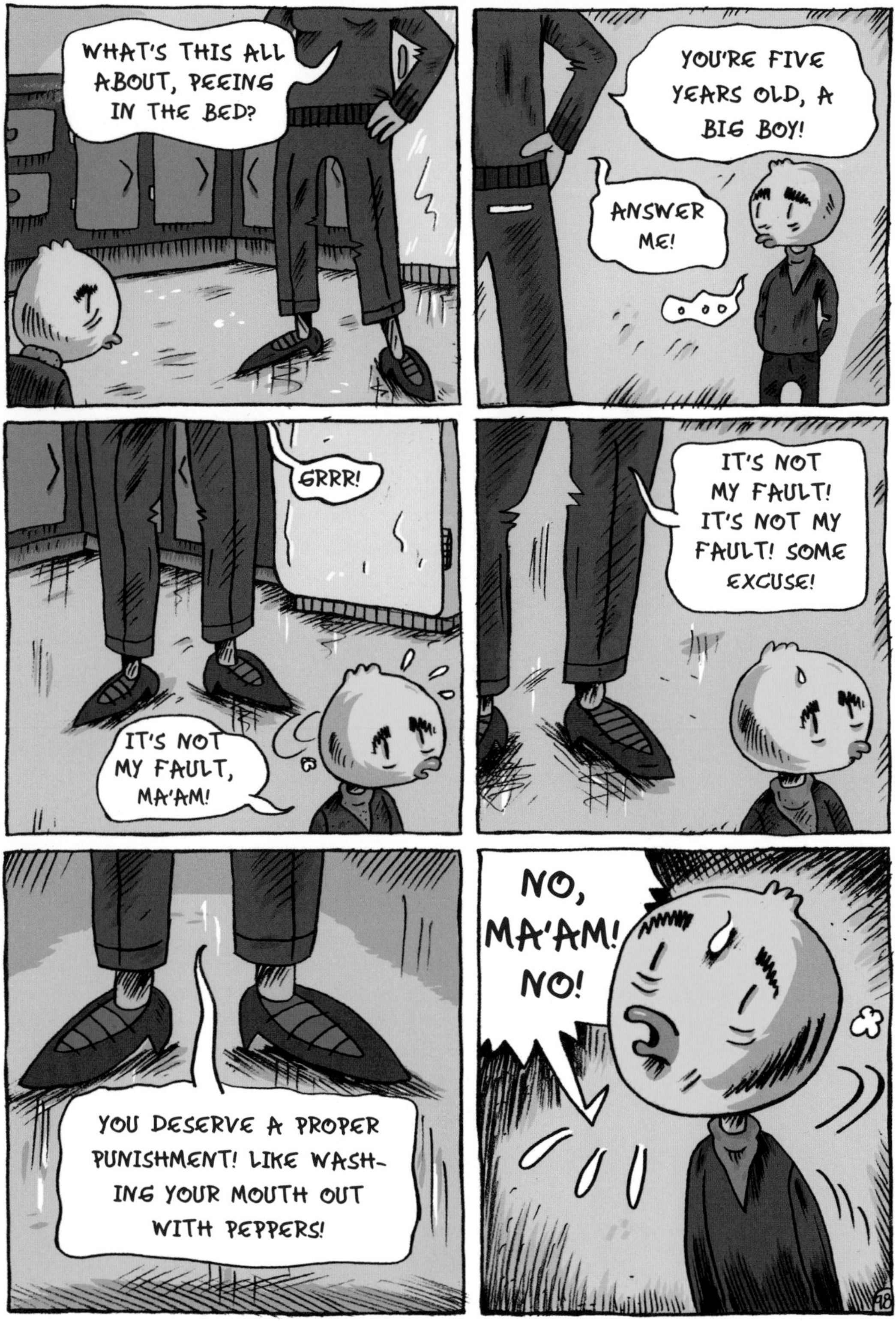
WHAT'S THIS ALL ABOUT, PEEING IN THE BED?
YOU'RE FIVE YEARS OLD, A BIG BOY!
ANSWER ME!
...
GRRR!
IT'S NOT MY FAULT, MA'AM!
IT'S NOT MY FAULT! IT'S NOT MY FAULT! SOME EXCUSE!
YOU DESERVE A PROPER PUNISHMENT! LIKE WASH-ING YOUR MOUTH OUT WITH PEPPERS!
NO, MA'AM! NO!
98

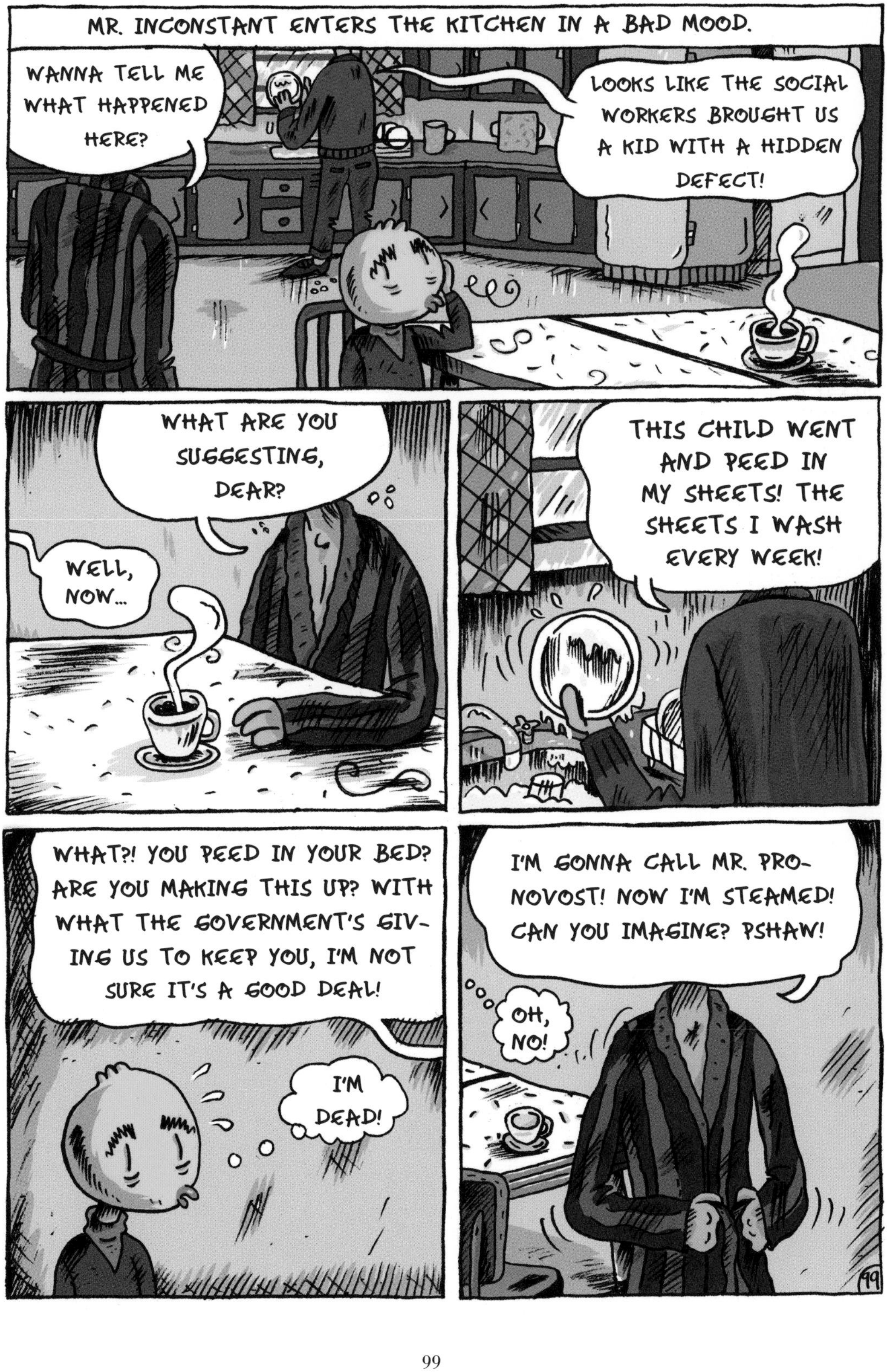
MR. INCONSTANT ENTERS THE KITCHEN IN A BAD MOOD.
WANNA TELL ME WHAT HAPPENED HERE?
LOOKS LIKE THE SOCIAL WORKERS BROUGHT US A KID WITH A HIDDEN DEFECT!
WHAT ARE YOU SUGGESTING, DEAR?
WELL, NOW...
THIS CHILD WENT AND PEED IN MY SHEETS! THE SHEETS I WASH EVERY WEEK!
WHAT?! YOU PEED IN YOUR BED? ARE YOU MAKING THIS UP? WITH WHAT THE GOVERNMENT'S GIV-ING US TO KEEP YOU, I'M NOT SURE IT'S A GOOD DEAL!
I'M DEAD!
I'M GONNA CALL MR. PRO-NOVOST! NOW I'M STEAMED! CAN YOU IMAGINE? PSHAW!
OH, NO!
99

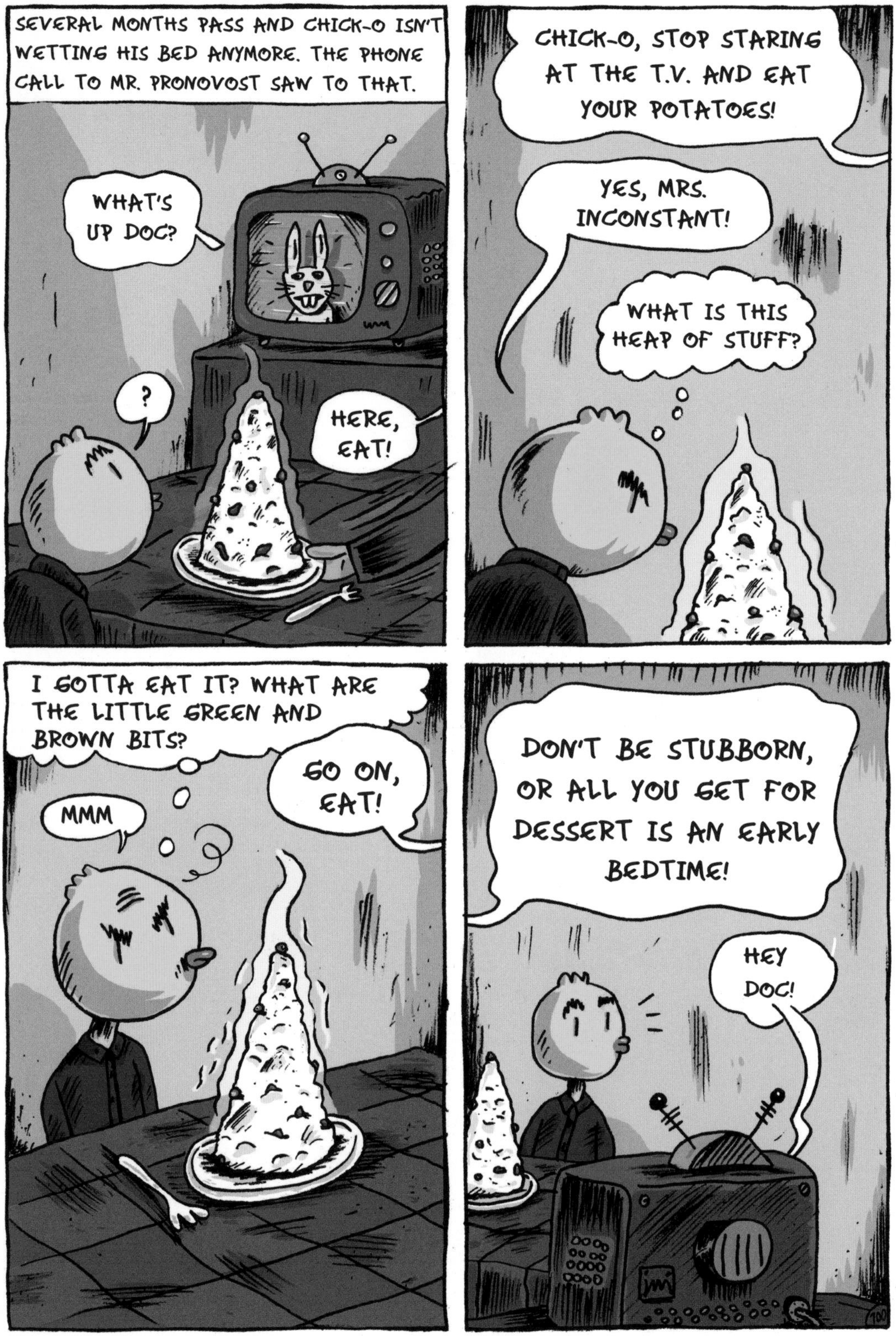
SEVERAL MONTHS PASS AND CHICK-O ISN'T WETTING HIS BED ANYMORE. THE PHONE CALL TO MR. PRONOVOST SAW TO THAT.
WHAT'S UP DOC?
?
HERE, EAT!
CHICK-O, STOP STARING AT THE T.V. AND EAT YOUR POTATOES!
YES, MRS. INCONSTANT!
WHAT IS THIS HEAP OF STUFF?
I GOTTA EAT IT? WHAT ARE THE LITTLE GREEN AND BROWN BITS?
GO ON, EAT!
MMM
DON'T BE STUBBORN, OR ALL YOU GET FOR DESSERT IS AN EARLY BEDTIME!
HEY DOC!

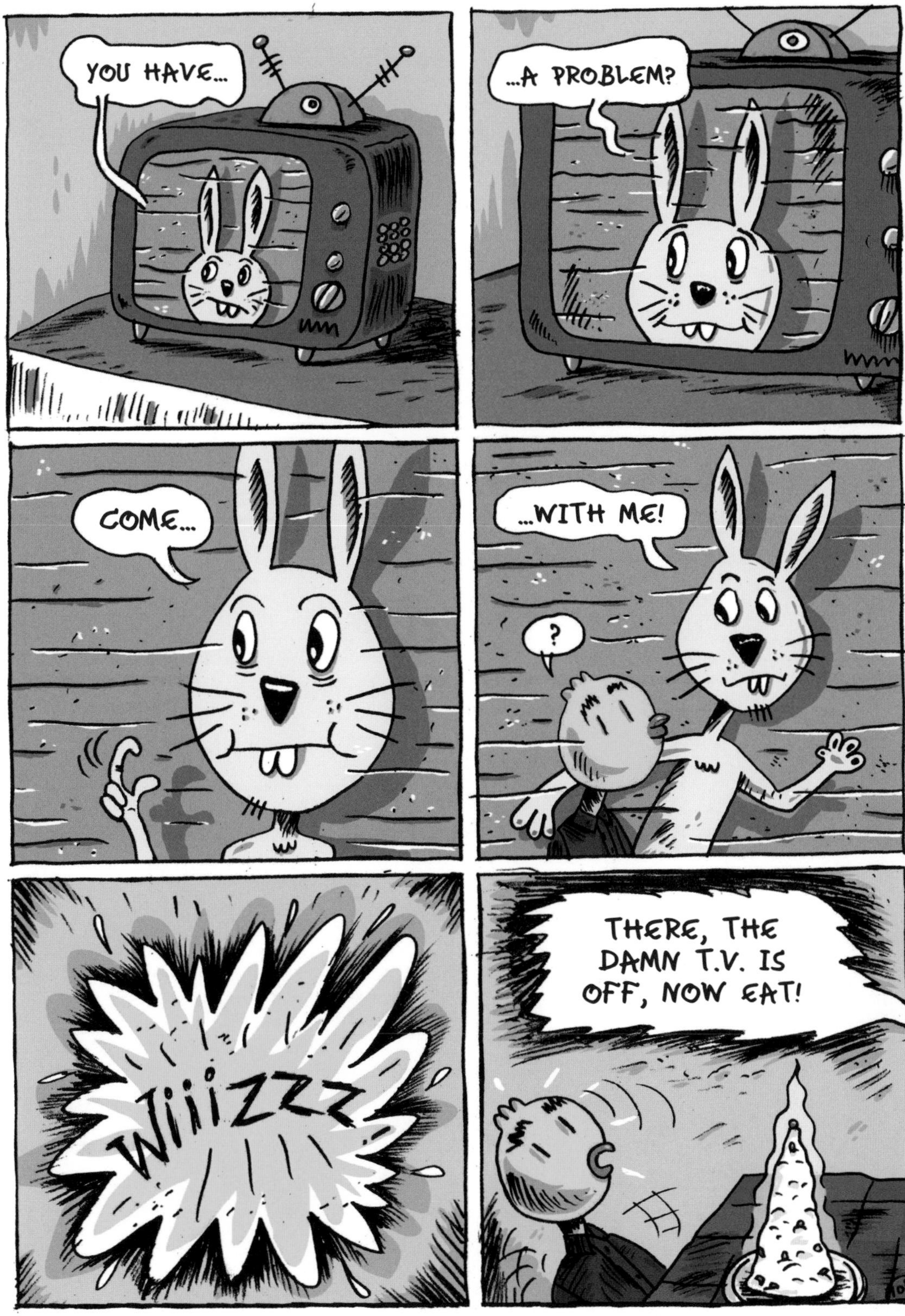
YOU HAVE...
...A PROBLEM?
COME...
...WITH ME!
?
WIIIZZZZ
THERE, THE DAMN T.V. IS OFF, NOW EAT!

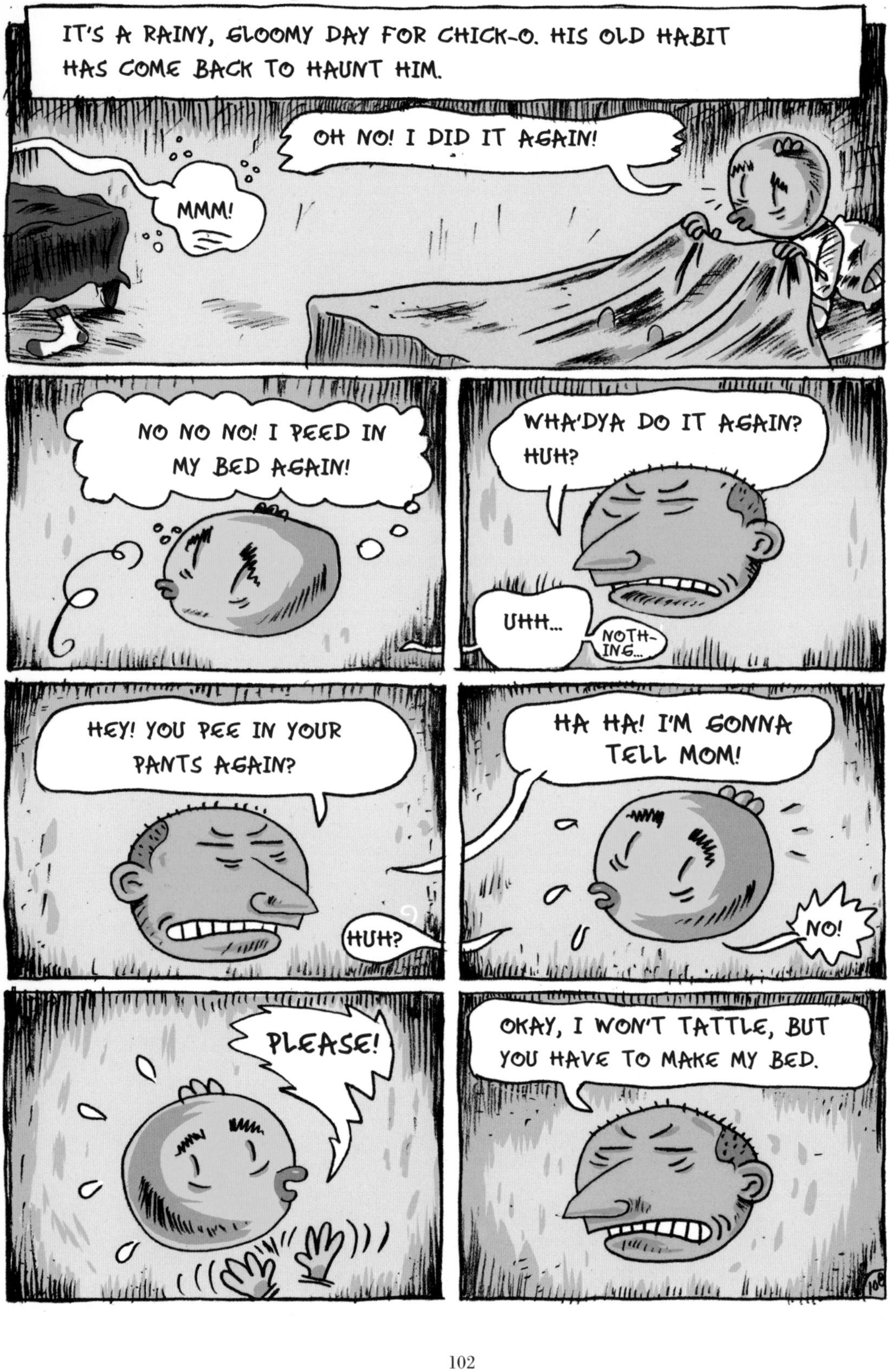
IT'S A RAINY, GLOOMY DAY FOR CHICK-O. HIS OLD HABIT HAS COME BACK TO HAUNT HIM.
OH NO! I DID IT AGAIN!
MMM!
NO NO NO! I PEED IN MY BED AGAIN!
WHA'DYA DO IT AGAIN? HUH?
UHH...
NOTH-ING...
HEY! YOU PEE IN YOUR PANTS AGAIN?
HUH?
HA HA! I'M GONNA TELL MOM!
NO!
PLEASE!
OKAY, I WON'T TATTLE, BUT YOU HAVE TO MAKE MY BED.

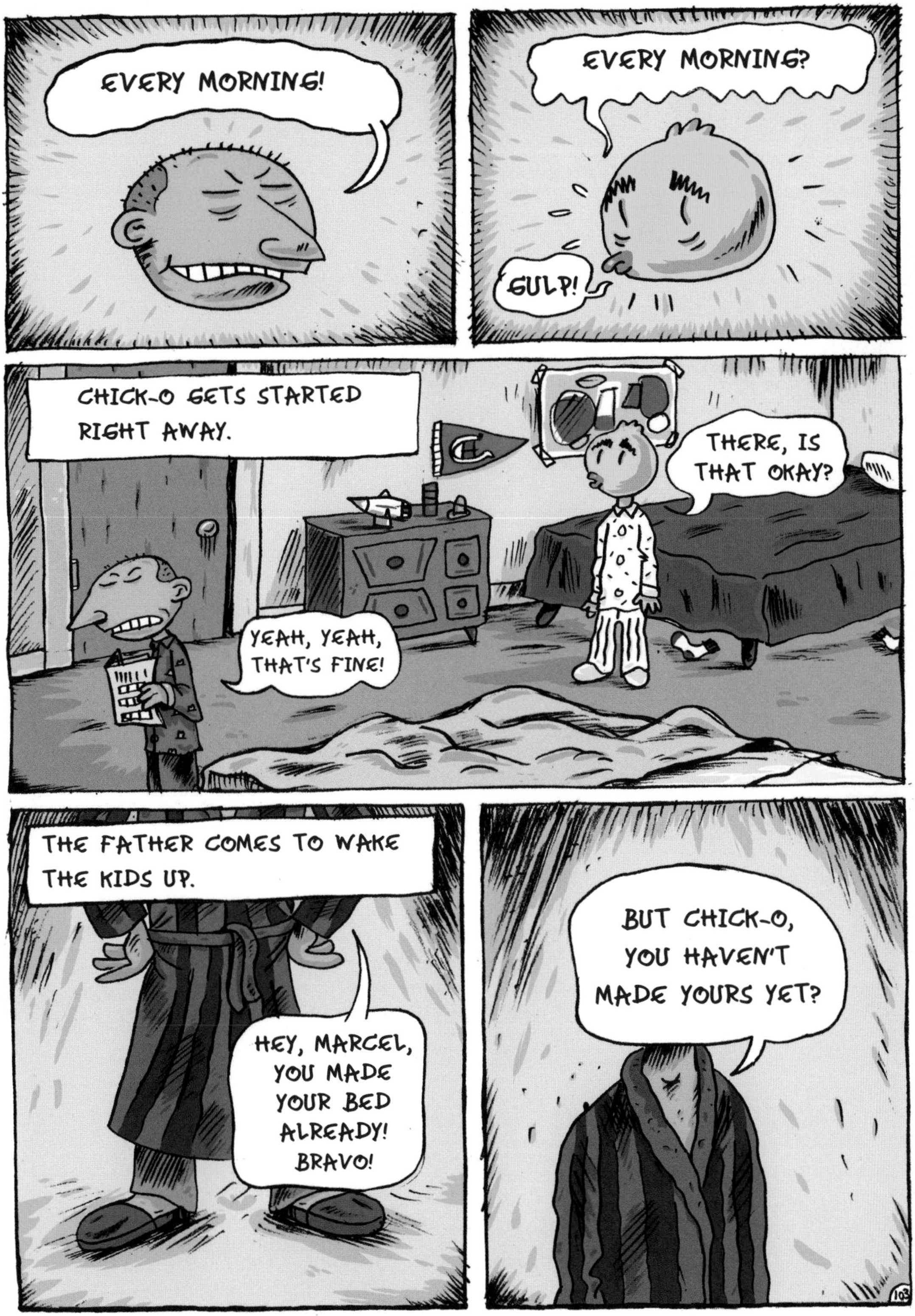
EVERY MORNING!
EVERY MORNING?
GULP!
CHICK-O GETS STARTED RIGHT AWAY.
THERE, IS THAT OKAY?
YEAH, YEAH, THAT'S FINE!
THE FATHER COMES TO WAKE THE KIDS UP.
HEY, MARCEL, YOU MADE YOUR BED ALREADY! BRAVO!
BUT CHICK-O, YOU HAVEN'T MADE YOURS YET?
103

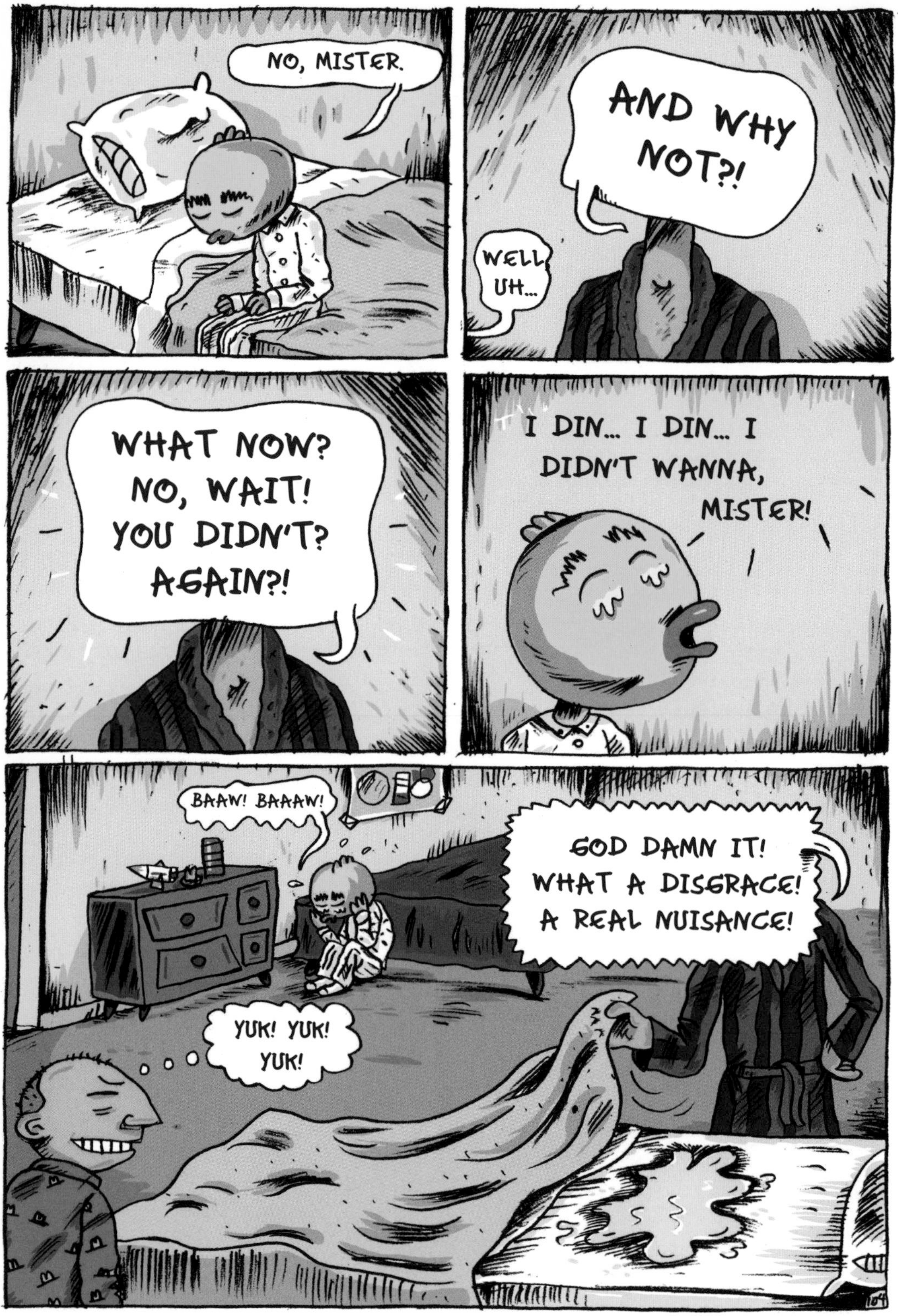
NO, MISTER.
AND WHY NOT?!
WELL UH...
WHAT NOW? NO, WAIT! YOU DIDN'T? AGAIN?!
I DIN... I DIN... I DIDN'T WANNA, MISTER!
BAAW! BAAAW!
GOD DAMN IT! WHAT A DISGRACE! A REAL NUISANCE!
YUK! YUK! YUK!

CHICK-O HAS BEEN WETTING THE BED MORE AND MORE FREQUENTLY OVER THE PAST YEAR. THE TENSION BETWEEN HE AND HIS FOSTER PARENTS HAS BECOME WORSE THAT EVER. THE INCONSTANTS HOLD A SECRET MEETING TO DISCUSS THE SITUATION.

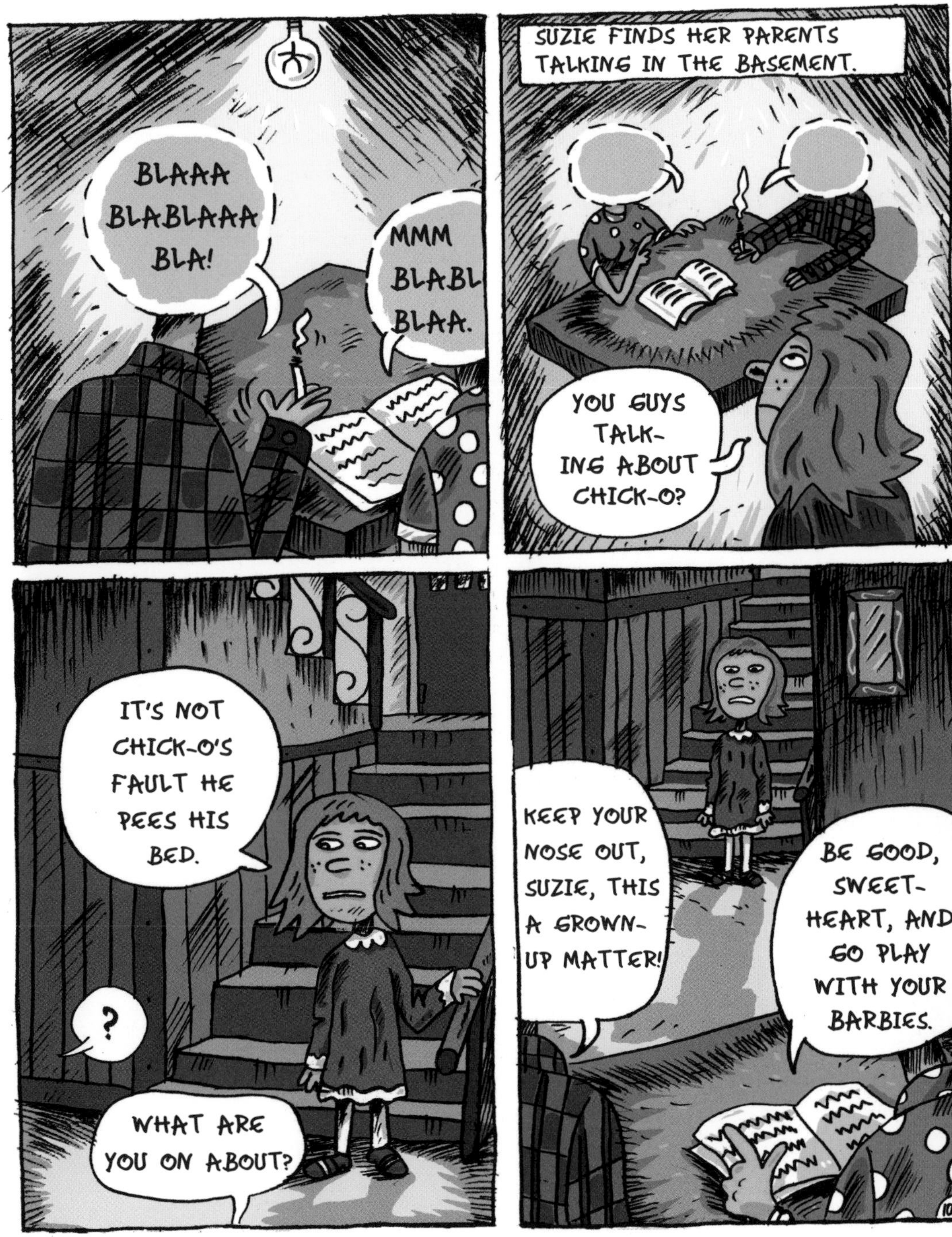
BLAAA BLABLAAA BLA!
MMM BLABL BLAA.
SUZIE FINDS HER PARENTS TALKING IN THE BASEMENT.
YOU GUYS TALK-ING ABOUT CHICK-O?
IT'S NOT CHICK-O'S FAULT HE PEES HIS BED.
?
WHAT ARE YOU ON ABOUT?
KEEP YOUR NOSE OUT, SUZIE, THIS A GROWN-UP MATTER!
BE GOOD, SWEET-HEART, AND GO PLAY WITH YOUR BARBIES.
105

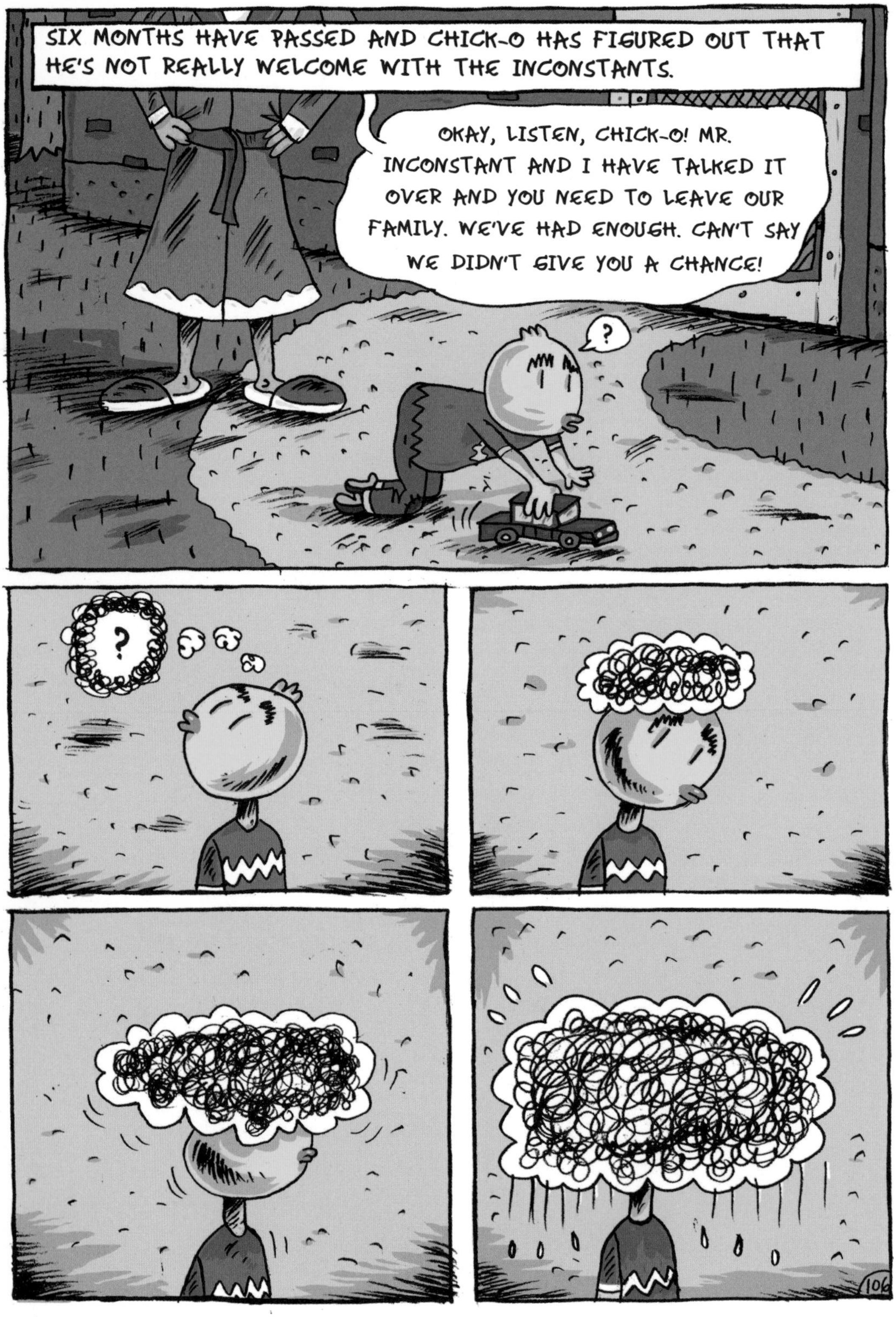
SIX MONTHS HAVE PASSED AND CHICK-O HAS FIGURED OUT THAT HE'S NOT REALLY WELCOME WITH THE INCONSTANTS.
OKAY, LISTEN, CHICK-O! MR. INCONSTANT AND I HAVE TALKED IT OVER AND YOU NEED TO LEAVE OUR FAMILY. WE'VE HAD ENOUGH. CAN'T SAY WE DIDN'T GIVE YOU A CHANCE!
?
?
106

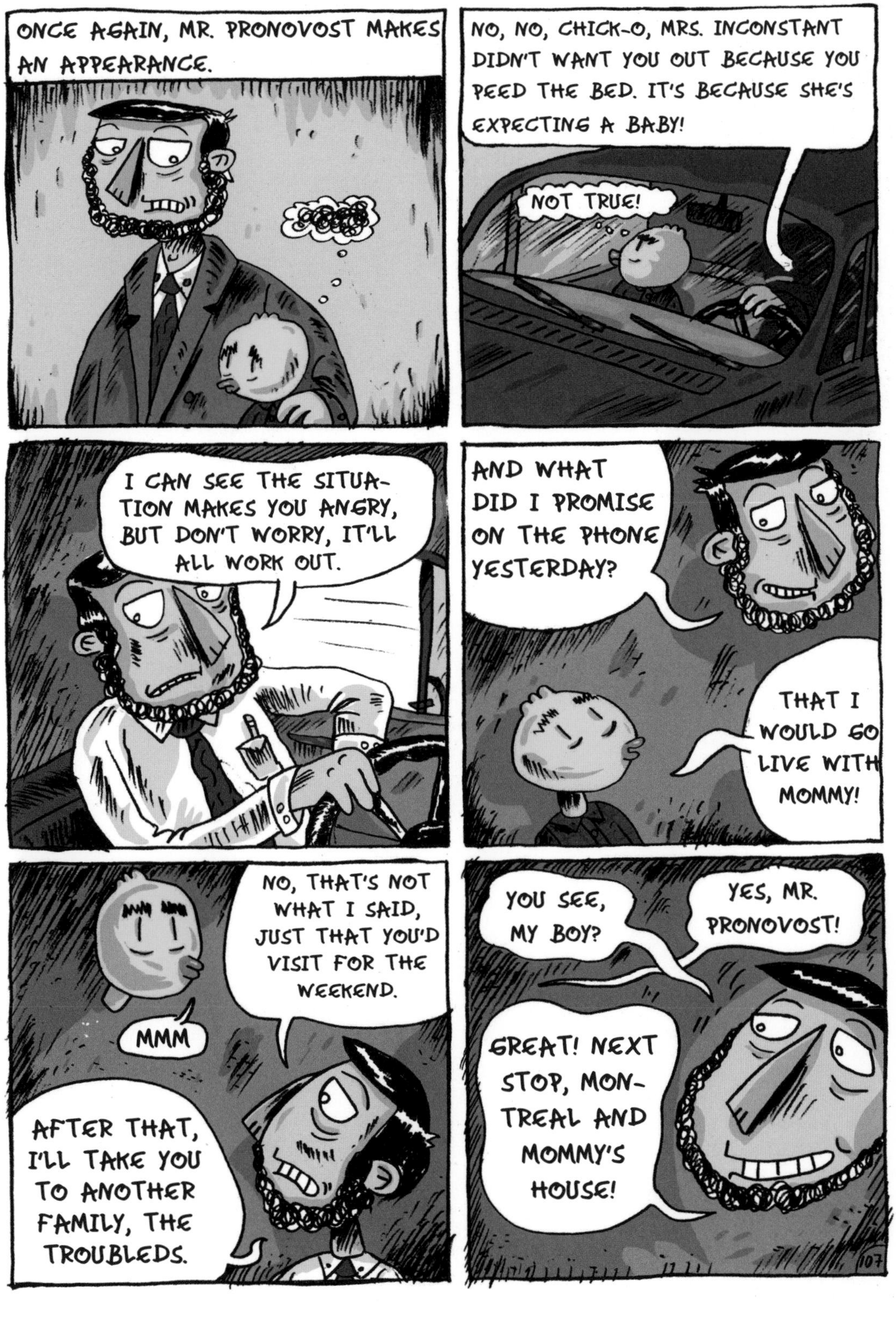
ONCE AGAIN, MR. PRONOVOST MAKES AN APPEARANCE.
NO, NO, CHICK-O, MRS. INCONSTANT DIDN'T WANT YOU OUT BECAUSE YOU PEED THE BED. IT'S BECAUSE SHE'S EXPECTING A BABY!
NOT TRUE!
I CAN SEE THE SITUATION MAKES YOU ANGRY, BUT DON'T WORRY, IT'LL ALL WORK OUT.
AND WHAT DID I PROMISE ON THE PHONE YESTERDAY?
THAT I WOULD GO LIVE WITH MOMMY!
NO, THAT'S NOT WHAT I SAID, JUST THAT YOU'D VISIT FOR THE WEEKEND.
MMM
AFTER THAT, I'LL TAKE YOU TO ANOTHER FAMILY, THE TROUBLEDS.
YOU SEE, MY BOY?
YES, MR. PRONOVOST!
GREAT! NEXT STOP, MONTREAL AND MOMMY'S HOUSE!
107

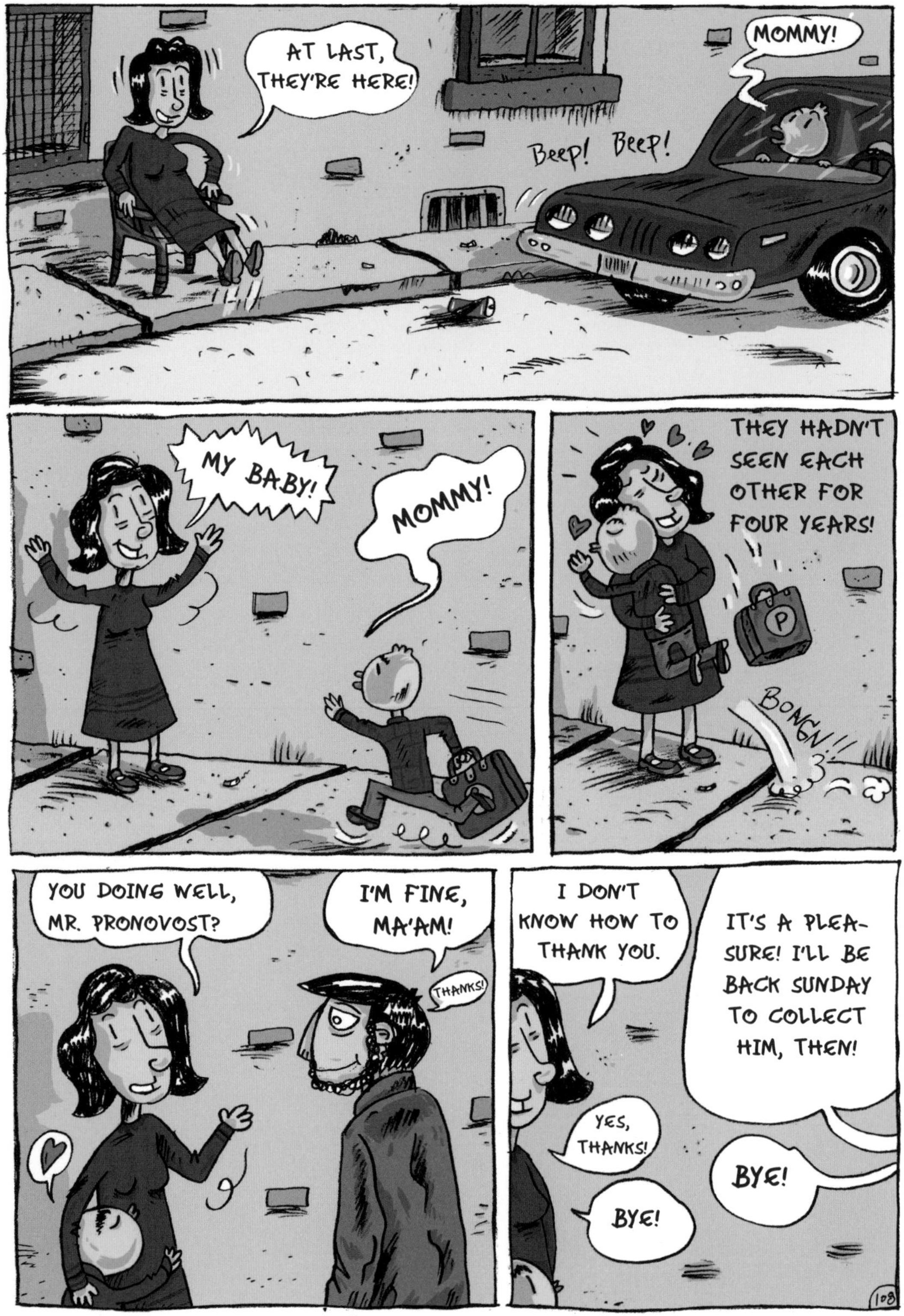
AT LAST, THEY'RE HERE!
MOMMY!
Beep! Beep!
MY BABY!
MOMMY!
THEY HADN'T SEEN EACH OTHER FOR FOUR YEARS!
BONGN!
YOU DOING WELL, MR. PRONOVOST?
I'M FINE, MA'AM!
THANKS!
I DON'T KNOW HOW TO THANK YOU.
IT'S A PLEA-SURE! I'LL BE BACK SUNDAY TO COLLECT HIM, THEN!
YES, THANKS!
BYE!
BYE!
108

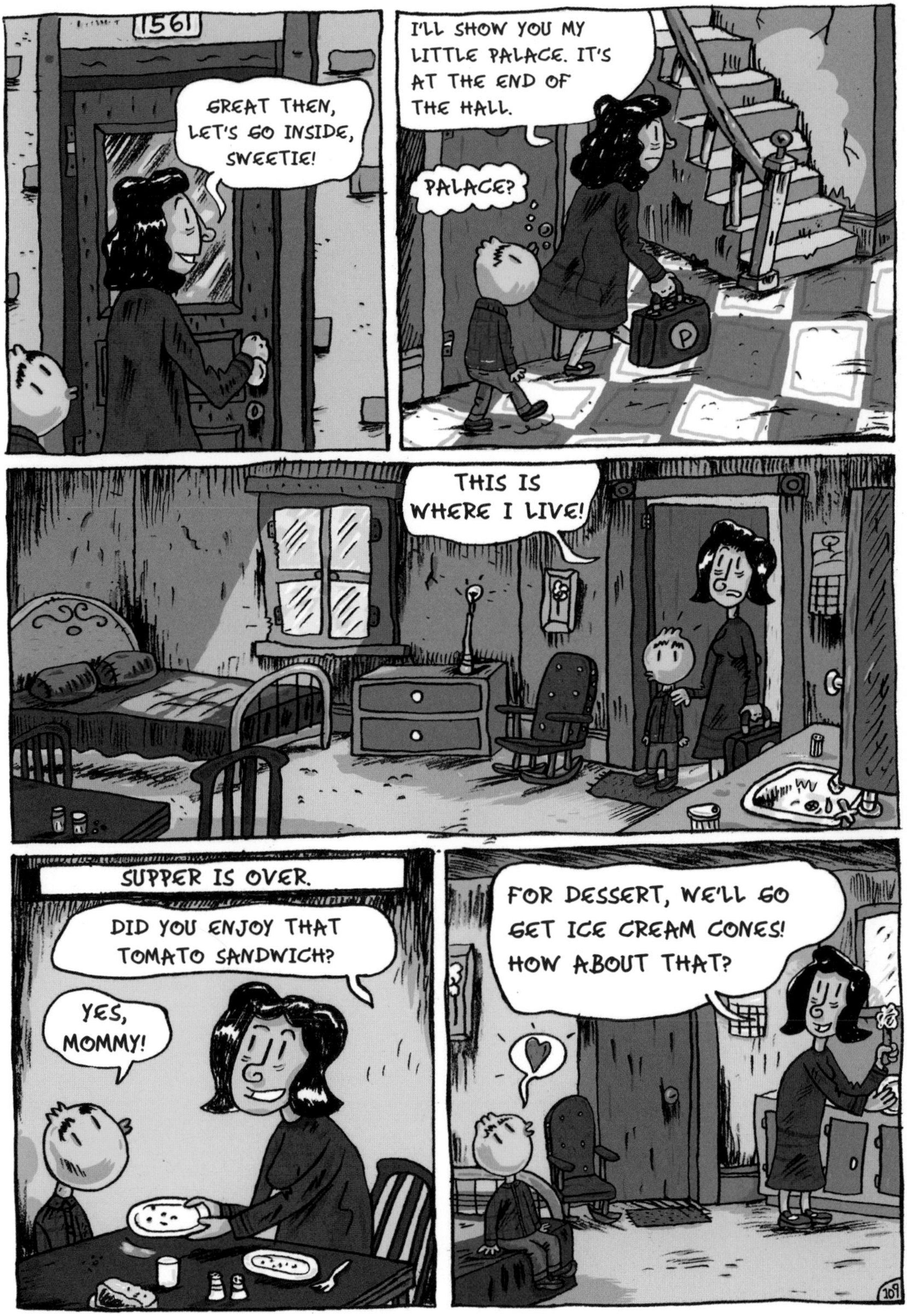
1561
GREAT THEN, LET'S GO INSIDE, SWEETIE!
I'LL SHOW YOU MY LITTLE PALACE. IT'S AT THE END OF THE HALL.
PALACE?
THIS IS WHERE I LIVE!
SUPPER IS OVER.
DID YOU ENJOY THAT TOMATO SANDWICH?
YES, MOMMY!
FOR DESSERT, WE'LL GO GET ICE CREAM CONES! HOW ABOUT THAT?
109

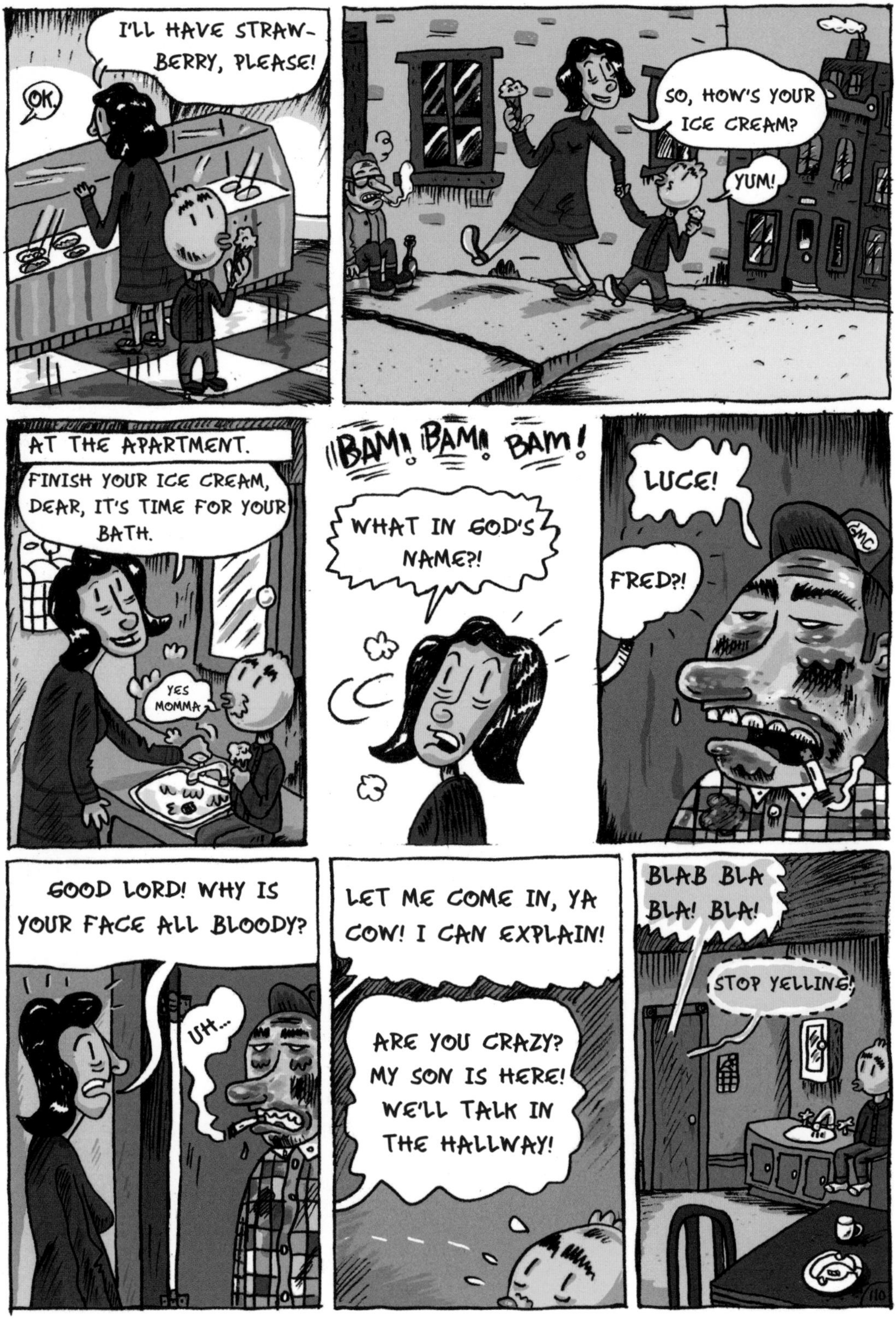
I'LL HAVE STRAW-BERRY, PLEASE!
OK.
SO, HOW'S YOUR ICE CREAM?
YUM!
AT THE APARTMENT.
FINISH YOUR ICE CREAM, DEAR, IT'S TIME FOR YOUR BATH.
YES MOMMA
BAM! BAM! BAM!
WHAT IN GOD'S NAME?!
LUCE!
FRED?!
GMC
GOOD LORD! WHY IS YOUR FACE ALL BLOODY?
UH...
LET ME COME IN, YA COW! I CAN EXPLAIN!
ARE YOU CRAZY? MY SON IS HERE! WE'LL TALK IN THE HALLWAY!
BLAB BLA BLA! BLA!
STOP YELLING!

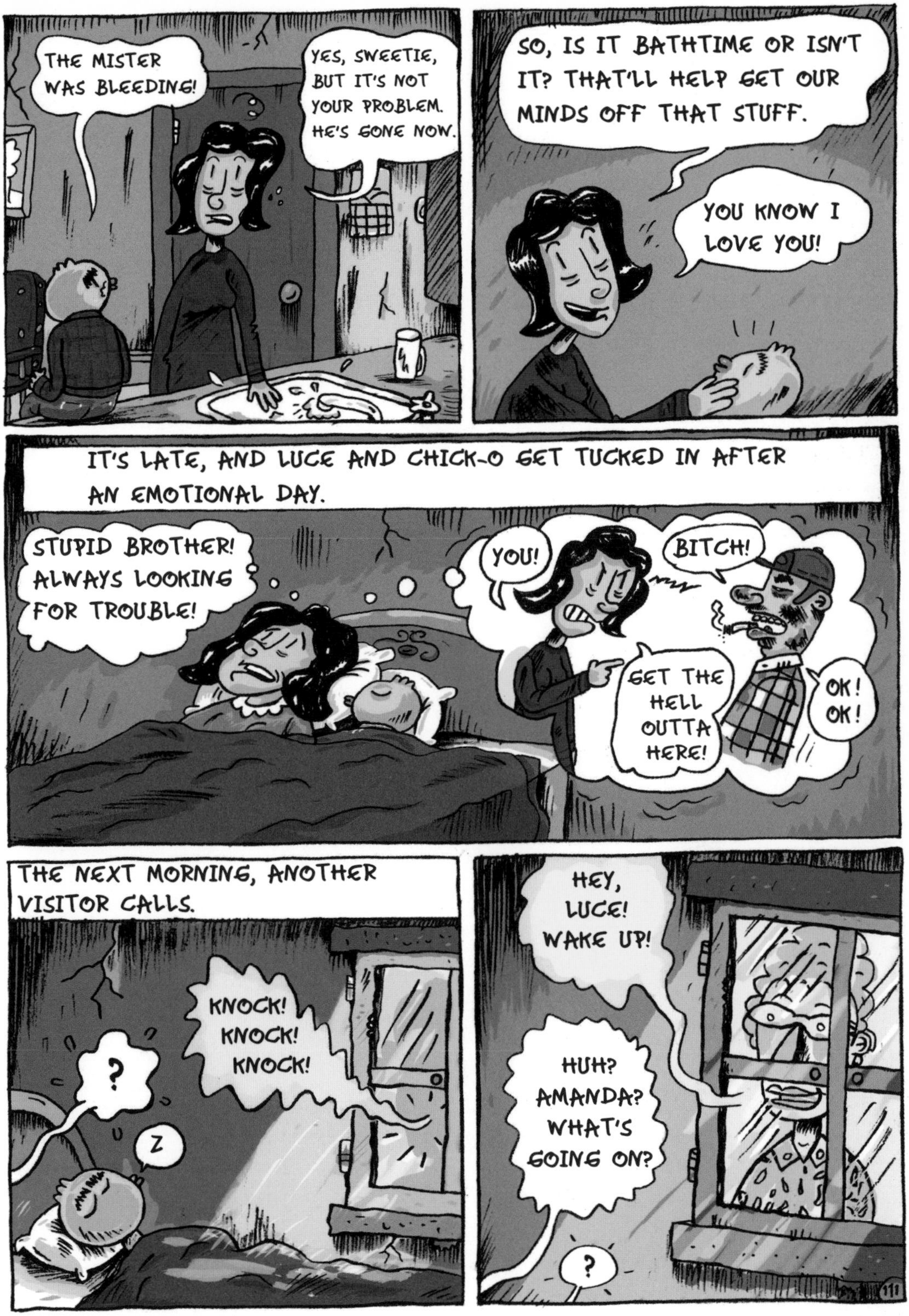

THE MISTER WAS BLEEDING!
YES, SWEETIE, BUT IT'S NOT YOUR PROBLEM. HE'S GONE NOW.
SO, IS IT BATHTIME OR ISN'T IT? THAT'LL HELP GET OUR MINDS OFF THAT STUFF.
YOU KNOW I LOVE YOU!
IT'S LATE, AND LUCE AND CHICK-O GET TUCKED IN AFTER AN EMOTIONAL DAY.
STUPID BROTHER! ALWAYS LOOKING FOR TROUBLE!
YOU!
BITCH!
GET THE HELL OUTTA HERE!
OK! OK!
THE NEXT MORNING, ANOTHER VISITOR CALLS.
?
Z
KNOCK! KNOCK! KNOCK!
HEY, LUCE! WAKE UP!
HUH? AMANDA? WHAT'S GOING ON?
?

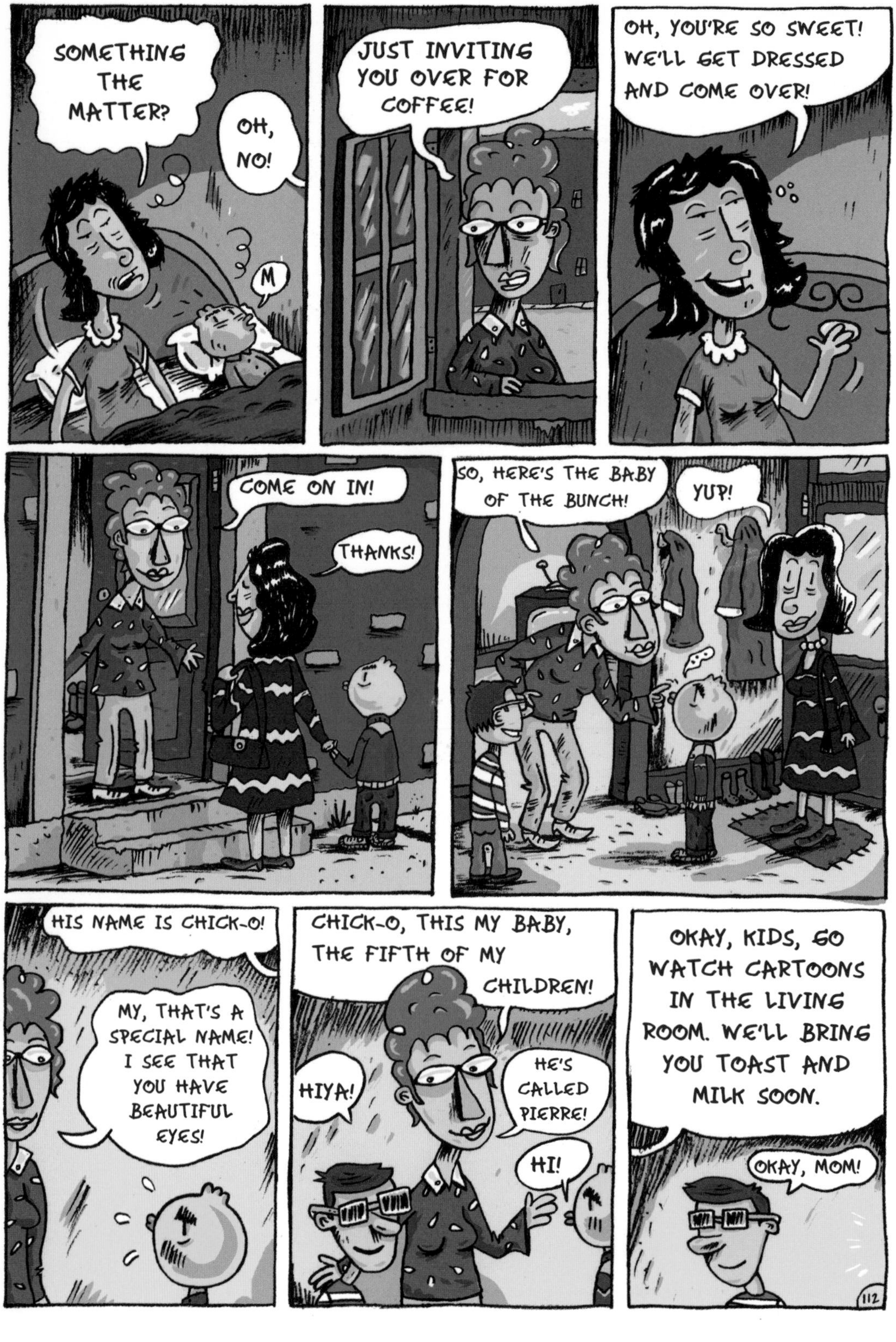
SOMETHING THE MATTER?
OH, NO!
M
JUST INVITING YOU OVER FOR COFFEE!
OH, YOU'RE SO SWEET! WE'LL GET DRESSED AND COME OVER!
COME ON IN!
THANKS!
SO, HERE'S THE BABY OF THE BUNCH!
YUP!
HIS NAME IS CHICK-O!
MY, THAT'S A SPECIAL NAME! I SEE THAT YOU HAVE BEAUTIFUL EYES!
CHICK-O, THIS MY BABY, THE FIFTH OF MY CHILDREN!
HIYA!
HE'S CALLED PIERRE!
HI!
OKAY, KIDS, GO WATCH CARTOONS IN THE LIVING ROOM. WE'LL BRING YOU TOAST AND MILK SOON.
OKAY, MOM!
112

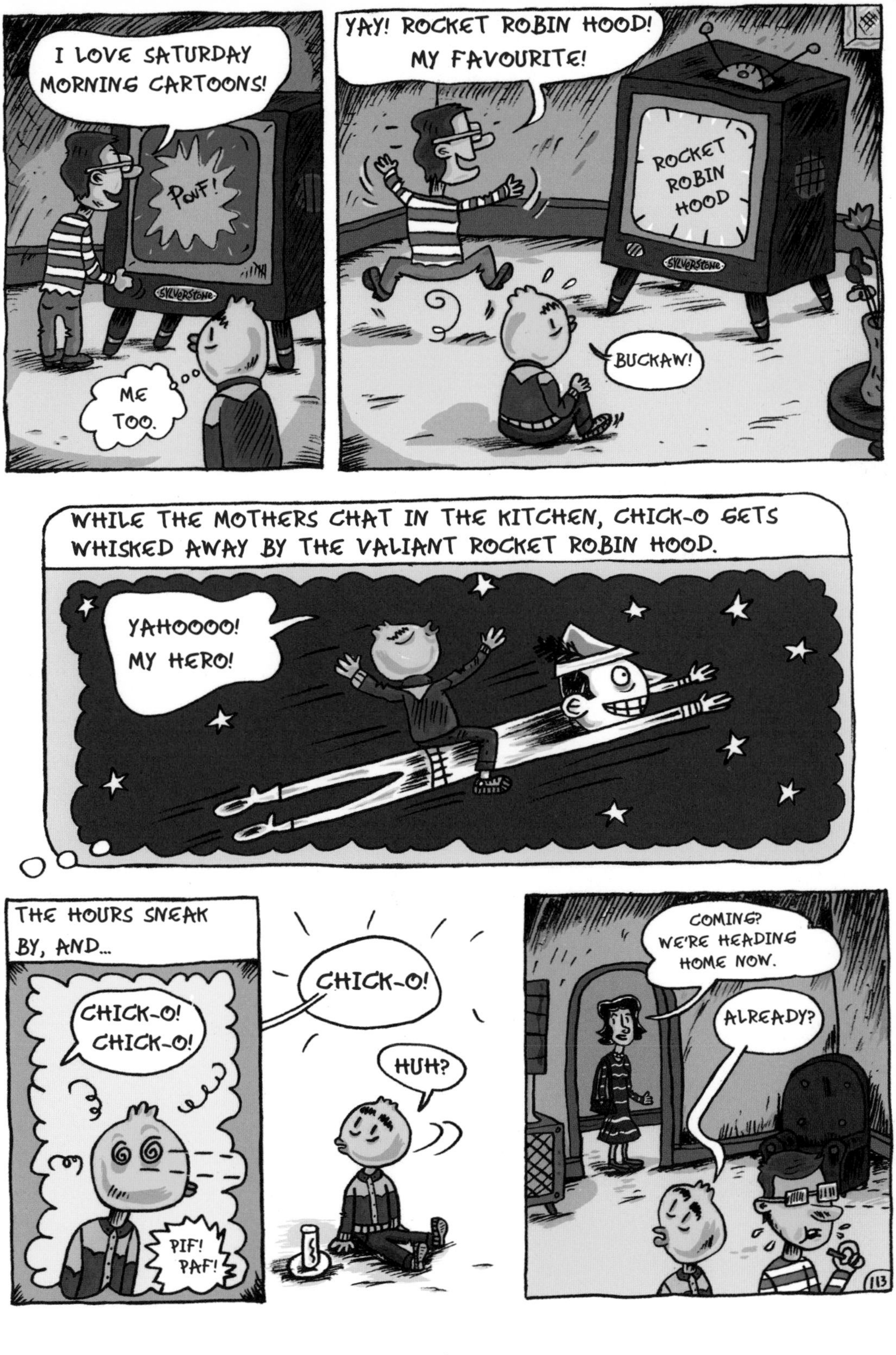
I LOVE SATURDAY MORNING CARTOONS!
POUF!
SYLVERSTONE
ME TOO.
YAY! ROCKET ROBIN HOOD! MY FAVOURITE!
ROCKET ROBIN HOOD
SYLVERSTONE
BUCKAW!
WHILE THE MOTHERS CHAT IN THE KITCHEN, CHICK-O GETS WHISKED AWAY BY THE VALIANT ROCKET ROBIN HOOD.
YAHOOOO! MY HERO!
THE HOURS SNEAK BY, AND...
CHICK-O! CHICK-O!
PIF! PAF!
CHICK-O!
HUH?
COMING? WE'RE HEADING HOME NOW.
ALREADY?
113

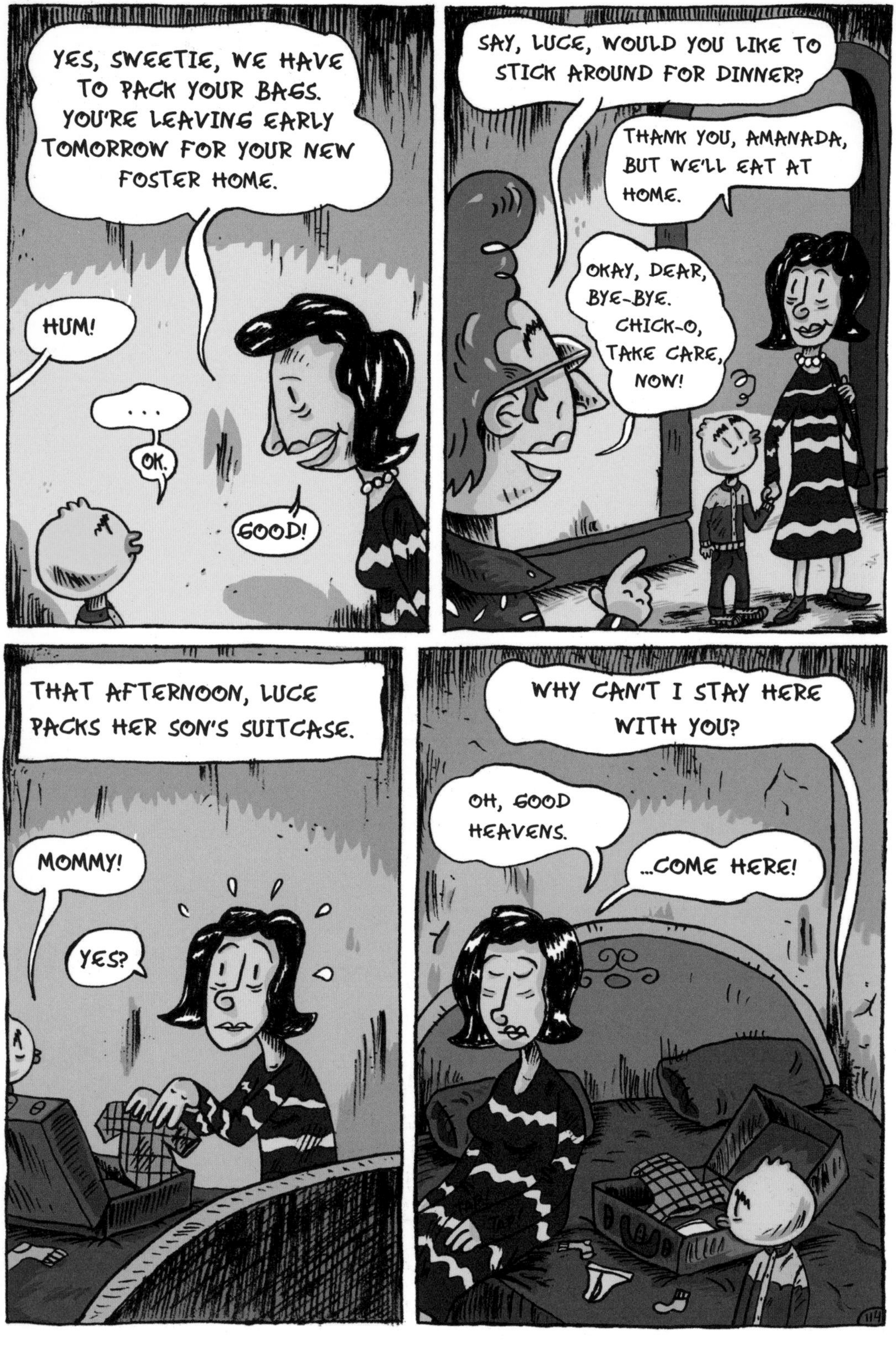
YES, SWEETIE, WE HAVE TO PACK YOUR BAGS. YOU'RE LEAVING EARLY TOMORROW FOR YOUR NEW FOSTER HOME.
HUM!
...
OK.
GOOD!
SAY, LUCE, WOULD YOU LIKE TO STICK AROUND FOR DINNER?
THANK YOU, AMANADA, BUT WE'LL EAT AT HOME.
OKAY, DEAR, BYE-BYE. CHICK-O, TAKE CARE, NOW!
THAT AFTERNOON, LUCE PACKS HER SON'S SUITCASE.
MOMMY!
YES?
WHY CAN'T I STAY HERE WITH YOU?
OH, GOOD HEAVENS.
...COME HERE!

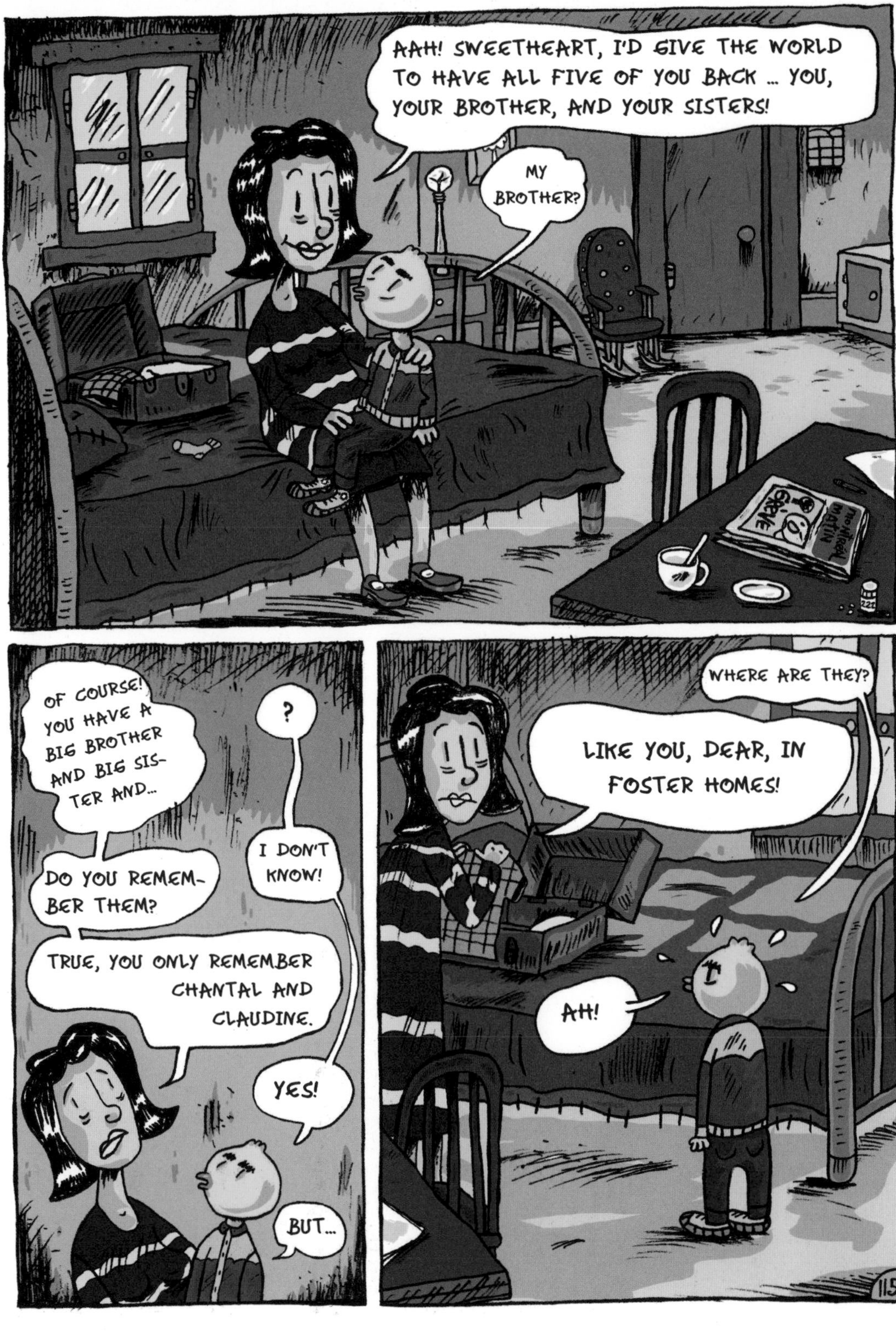
AAH! SWEETHEART, I'D GIVE THE WORLD TO HAVE ALL FIVE OF YOU BACK ... YOU, YOUR BROTHER, AND YOUR SISTERS!
MY BROTHER?
OF COURSE! YOU HAVE A BIG BROTHER AND BIG SIS- TER AND...
?
DO YOU REMEM- BER THEM?
I DON'T KNOW!
TRUE, YOU ONLY REMEMBER CHANTAL AND CLAUDINE.
YES!
BUT...
WHERE ARE THEY?
LIKE YOU, DEAR, IN FOSTER HOMES!
AH!

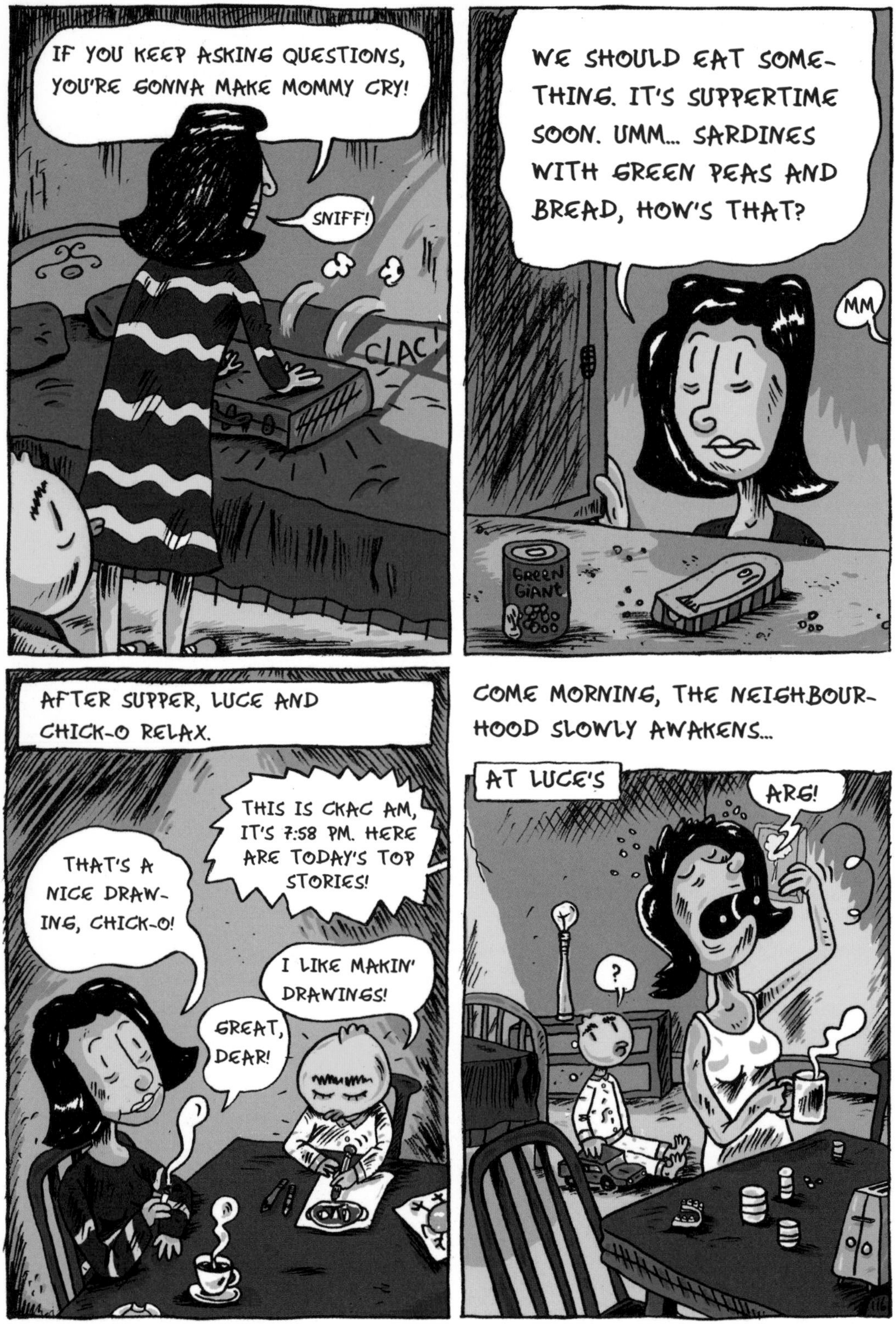
IF YOU KEEP ASKING QUESTIONS, YOU'RE GONNA MAKE MOMMY CRY!
SNIFF!
CLAC!
WE SHOULD EAT SOMETHING. IT'S SUPPERTIME SOON. UMM... SARDINES WITH GREEN PEAS AND BREAD, HOW'S THAT?
MM
GREEN GIANT
AFTER SUPPER, LUCE AND CHICK-O RELAX.
THAT'S A NICE DRAWING, CHICK-O!
THIS IS CKAC AM, IT'S 7:58 PM. HERE ARE TODAY'S TOP STORIES!
I LIKE MAKIN' DRAWINGS!
GREAT, DEAR!
COME MORNING, THE NEIGHBOURHOOD SLOWLY AWAKENS...
AT LUCE'S
ARG!
?

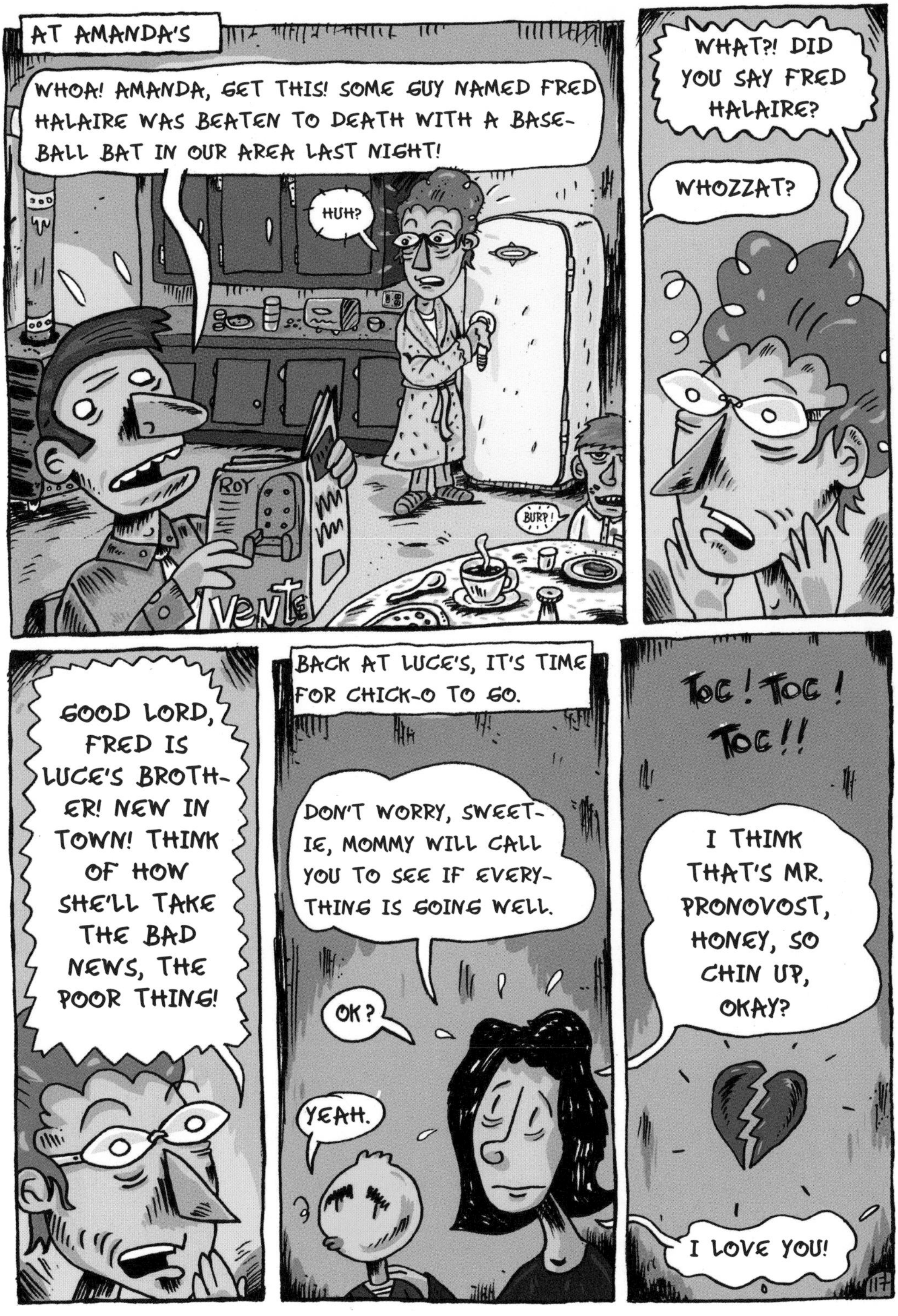
AT AMANDA'S
WHOA! AMANDA, GET THIS! SOME GUY NAMED FRED HALAIRE WAS BEATEN TO DEATH WITH A BASE-BALL BAT IN OUR AREA LAST NIGHT!
HUH?
ROY
VENTE
BURP!
WHAT?! DID YOU SAY FRED HALAIRE?
WHOZZAT?
GOOD LORD, FRED IS LUCE'S BROTH-ER! NEW IN TOWN! THINK OF HOW SHE'LL TAKE THE BAD NEWS, THE POOR THING!
BACK AT LUCE'S, IT'S TIME FOR CHICK-O TO GO.
DON'T WORRY, SWEET-IE, MOMMY WILL CALL YOU TO SEE IF EVERY-THING IS GOING WELL.
OK?
YEAH.
TOC! TOC! TOC!!
I THINK THAT'S MR. PRONOVOST, HONEY, SO CHIN UP, OKAY?
I LOVE YOU!
117

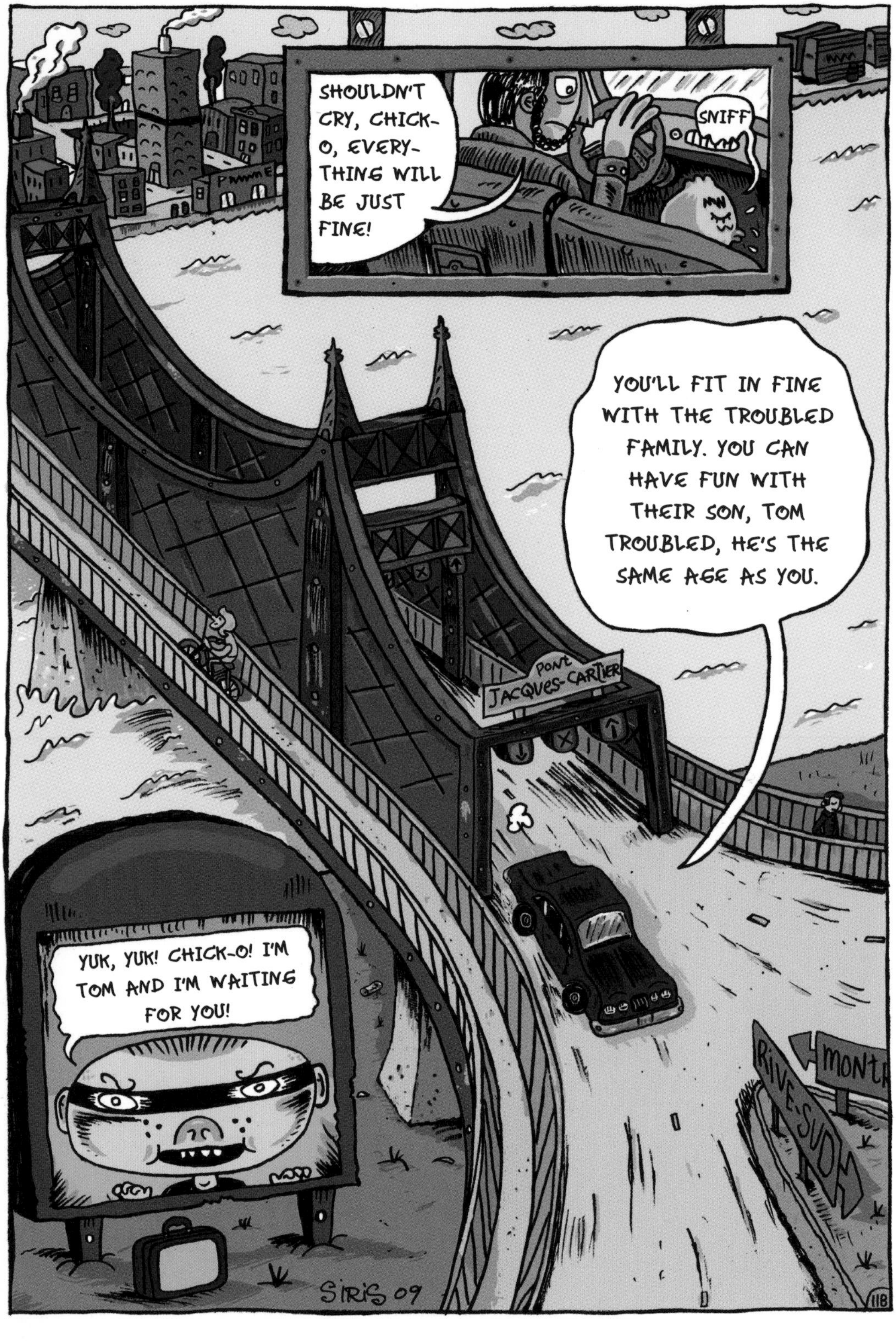
SHOULDN'T CRY, CHICK-O, EVERY-THING WILL BE JUST FINE!
SNIFF
YOU'LL FIT IN FINE WITH THE TROUBLED FAMILY. YOU CAN HAVE FUN WITH THEIR SON, TOM TROUBLED, HE'S THE SAME AGE AS YOU.
Pont JACQUES-CARTIER
YUK, YUK! CHICK-O! I'M TOM AND I'M WAITING FOR YOU!
RIVE-SUD
montr
SIRIS 09
118

CHAPTER 2

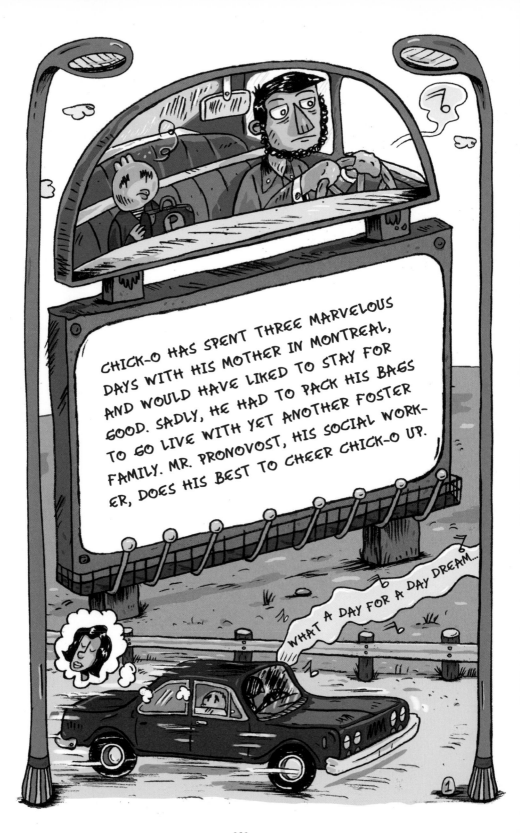

CHICK-O HAS SPENT THREE MARVELOUS DAYS WITH HIS MOTHER IN MONTREAL, AND WOULD HAVE LIKED TO STAY FOR GOOD. SADLY, HE HAD TO PACK HIS BAGS TO GO LIVE WITH YET ANOTHER FOSTER FAMILY. MR. PRONOVOST, HIS SOCIAL WORKER, DOES HIS BEST TO CHEER CHICK-O UP.

WHAT A DAY FOR A DAY DREAM...

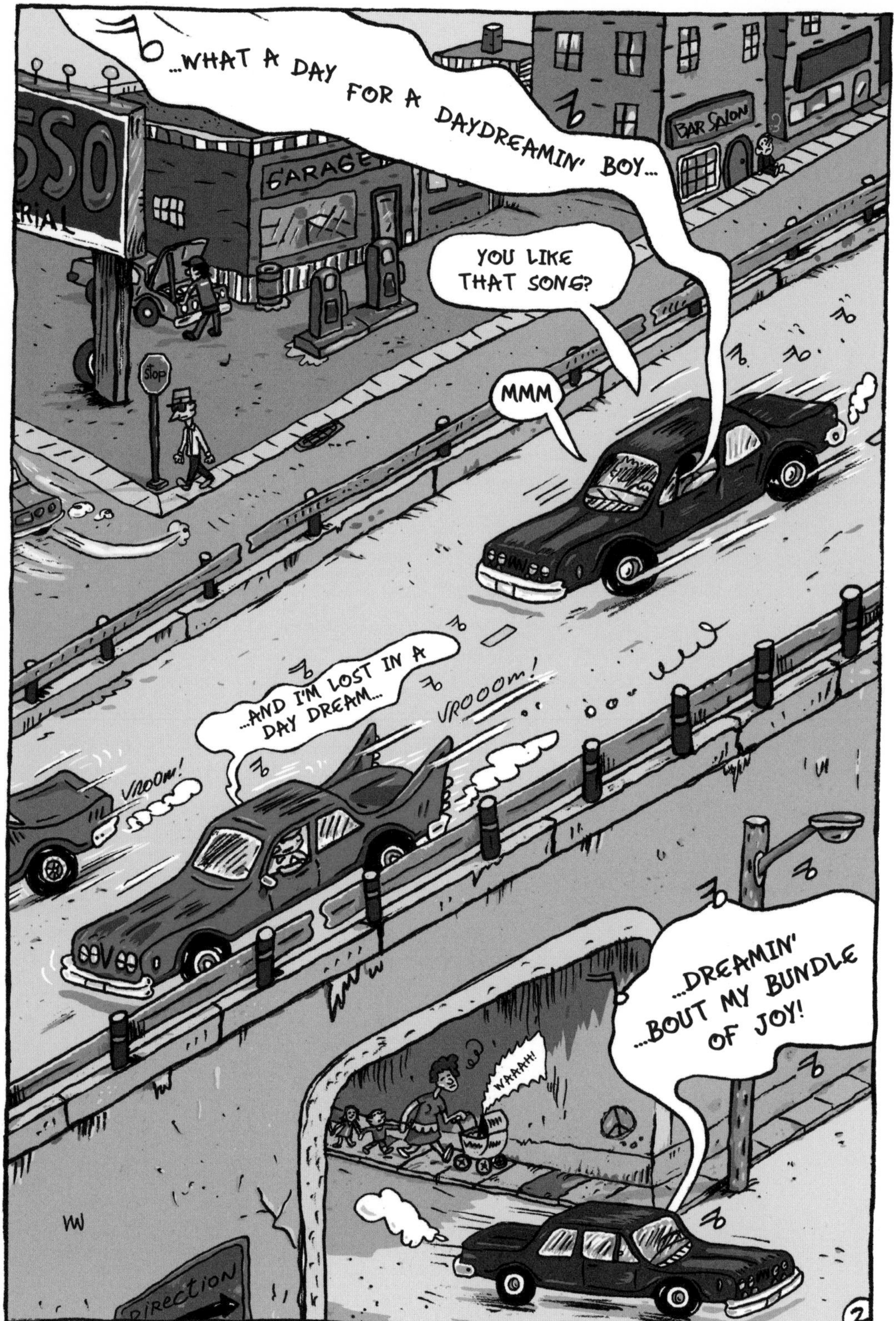
...WHAT A DAY FOR A DAYDREAMIN' BOY...
GARAGE
BAR SALON
STOP
YOU LIKE THAT SONG?
MMM
...AND I'M LOST IN A DAY DREAM...
VROOOM!
VROOM!
...DREAMIN' ...BOUT MY BUNDLE OF JOY!
WAAAH!
Direction
2

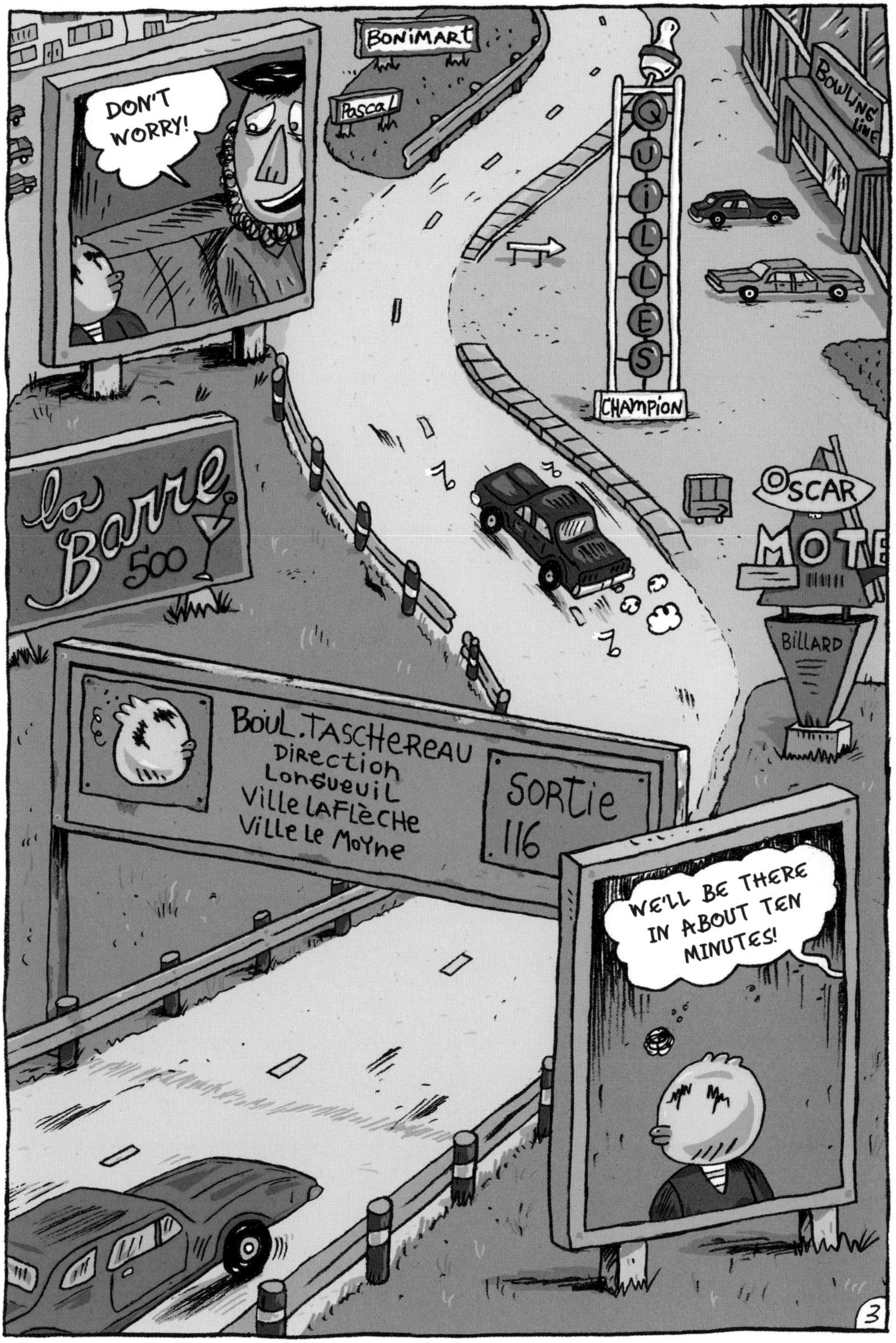
DON'T WORRY!
BONIMART
Pascal
QUILLES
CHAMPION
BOWLING LINE
la Barre 500
OSCAR
MOTE
BILLARD
BOUL. TASCHEREAU
Direction
Longueuil
Ville LaFlèche
Ville Le Moyne
SORTIE 116
WE'LL BE THERE IN ABOUT TEN MINUTES!
3

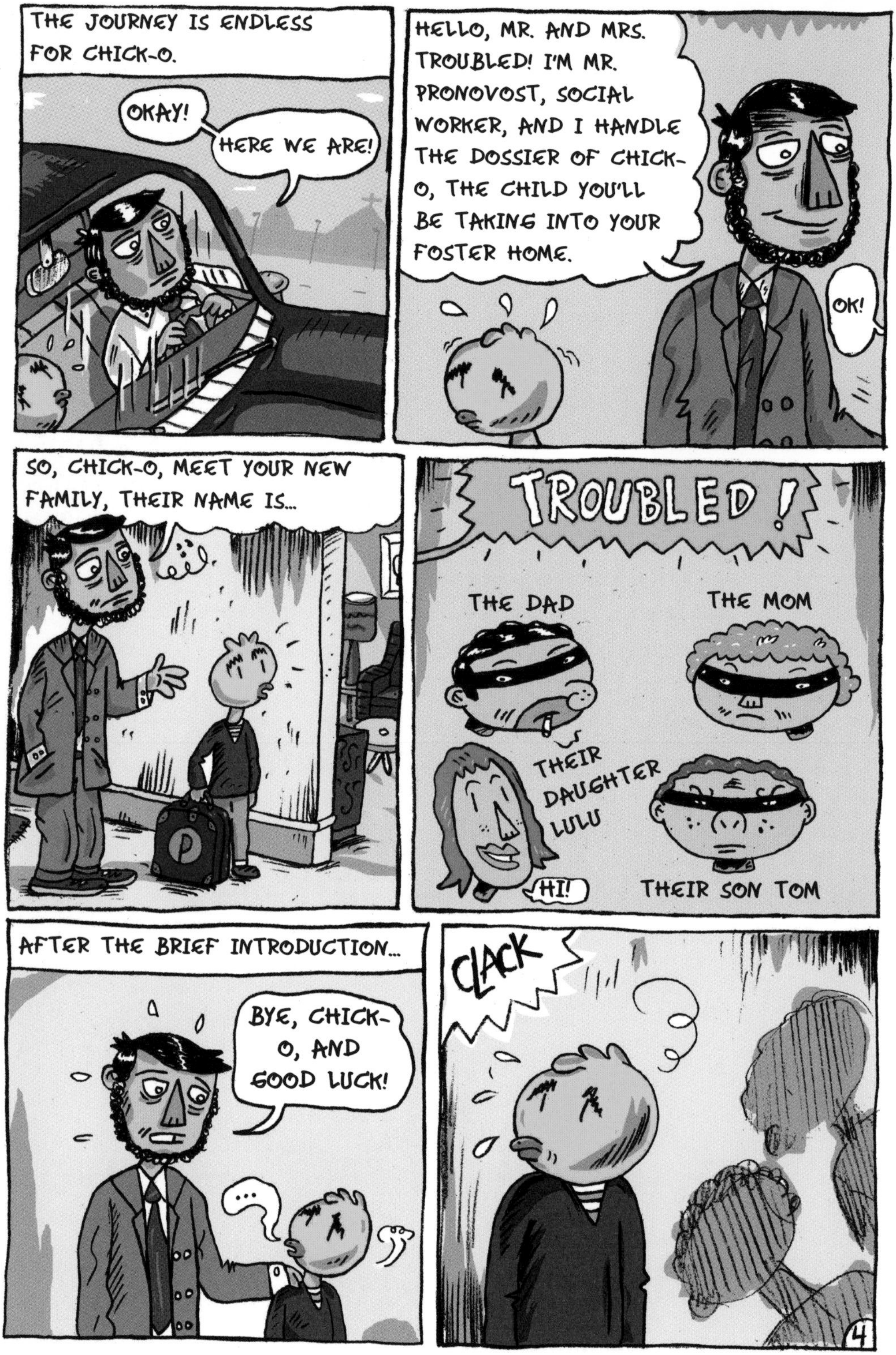
THE JOURNEY IS ENDLESS FOR CHICK-O.
OKAY!
HERE WE ARE!
HELLO, MR. AND MRS. TROUBLED! I'M MR. PRONOVOST, SOCIAL WORKER, AND I HANDLE THE DOSSIER OF CHICK-O, THE CHILD YOU'LL BE TAKING INTO YOUR FOSTER HOME.
OK!
SO, CHICK-O, MEET YOUR NEW FAMILY, THEIR NAME IS...
TROUBLED!
THE DAD
THE MOM
THEIR DAUGHTER LULU
HI!
THEIR SON TOM
AFTER THE BRIEF INTRODUCTION...
BYE, CHICK-O, AND GOOD LUCK!
...
CLACK
4

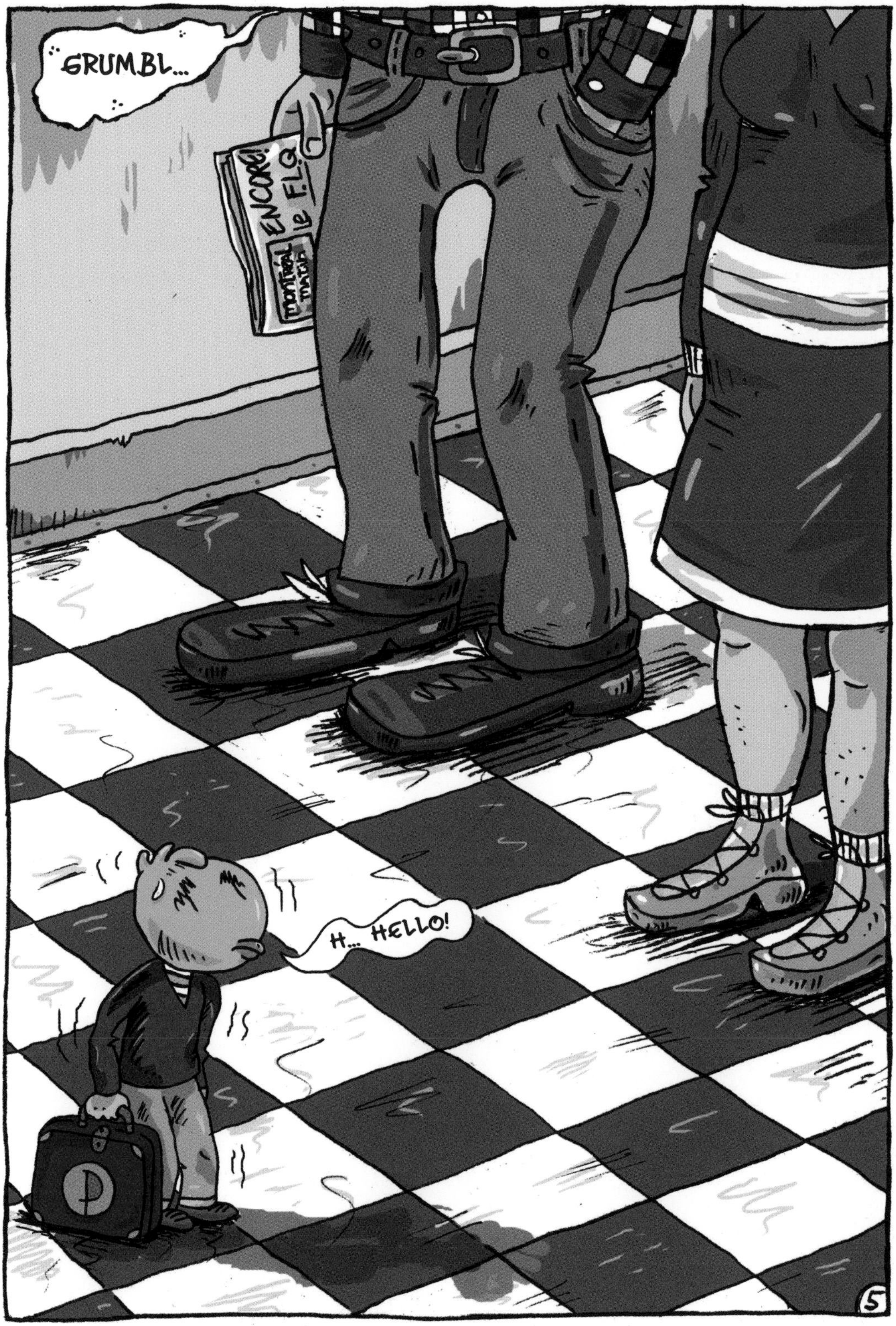
GRUMBL...
ENCORE! le F.L.Q.
Montréal Matin
H... HELLO!
5

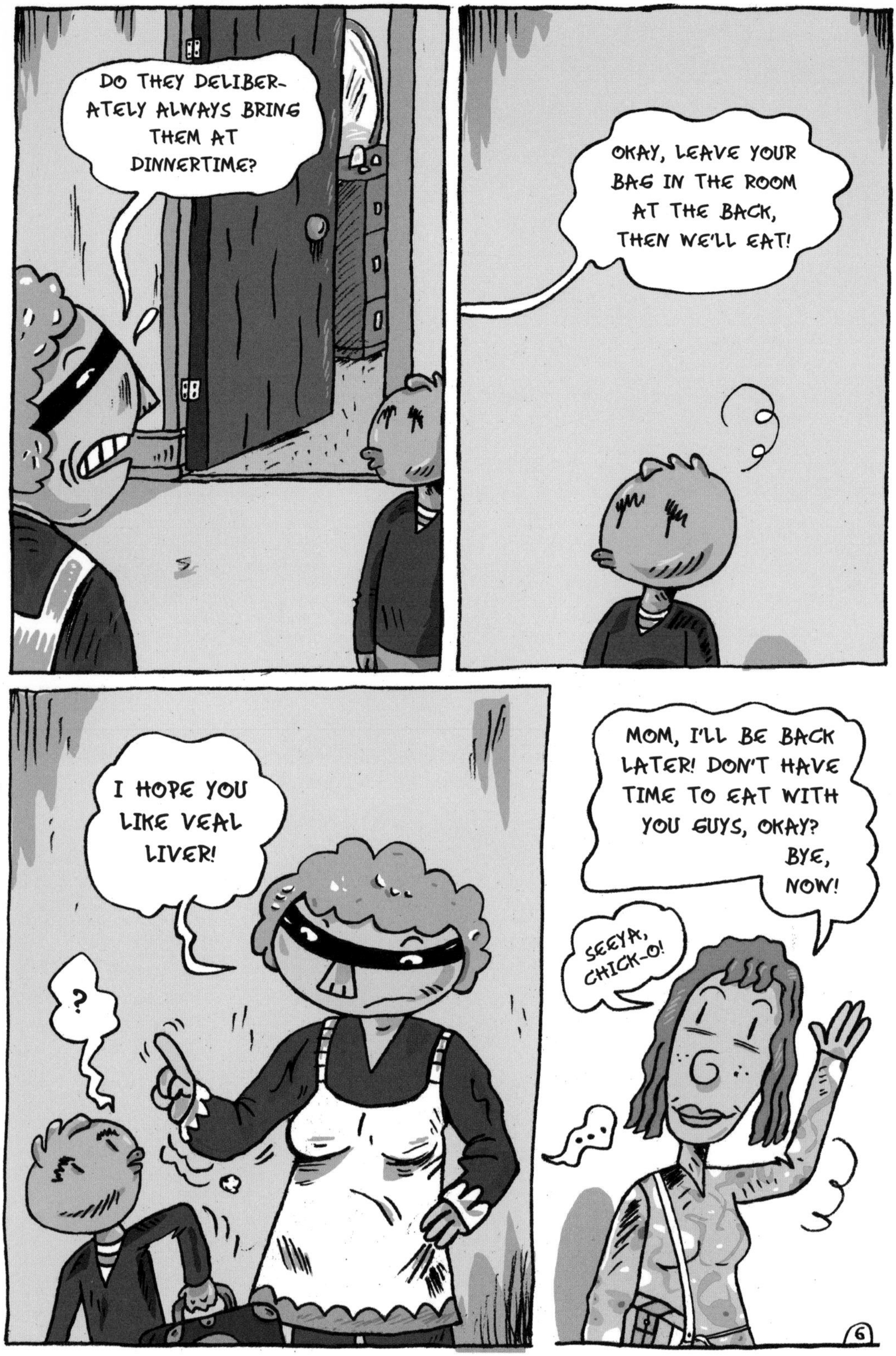
DO THEY DELIBER-ATELY ALWAYS BRING THEM AT DINNERTIME?
OKAY, LEAVE YOUR BAG IN THE ROOM AT THE BACK, THEN WE'LL EAT!
I HOPE YOU LIKE VEAL LIVER!
?
MOM, I'LL BE BACK LATER! DON'T HAVE TIME TO EAT WITH YOU GUYS, OKAY? BYE, NOW!
SEEYA, CHICK-O!
6

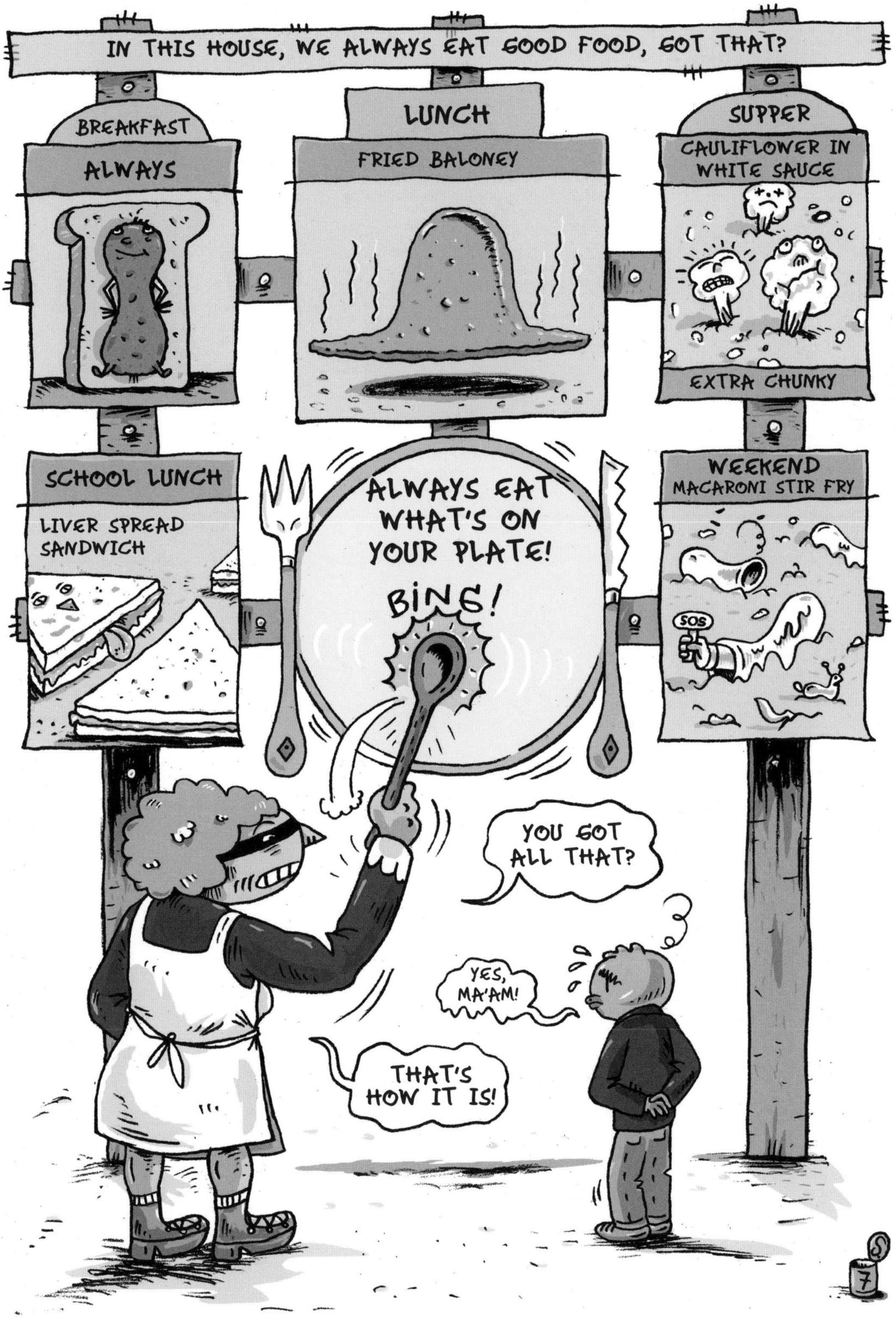

IN THIS HOUSE, WE ALWAYS EAT GOOD FOOD, GOT THAT?
BREAKFAST
ALWAYS
LUNCH
FRIED BALONEY
SUPPER
CAULIFLOWER IN WHITE SAUCE
EXTRA CHUNKY
SCHOOL LUNCH
LIVER SPREAD SANDWICH
ALWAYS EAT WHAT'S ON YOUR PLATE!
BING!
WEEKEND
MACARONI STIR FRY
SOS
YOU GOT ALL THAT?
YES, MA'AM!
THAT'S HOW IT IS!

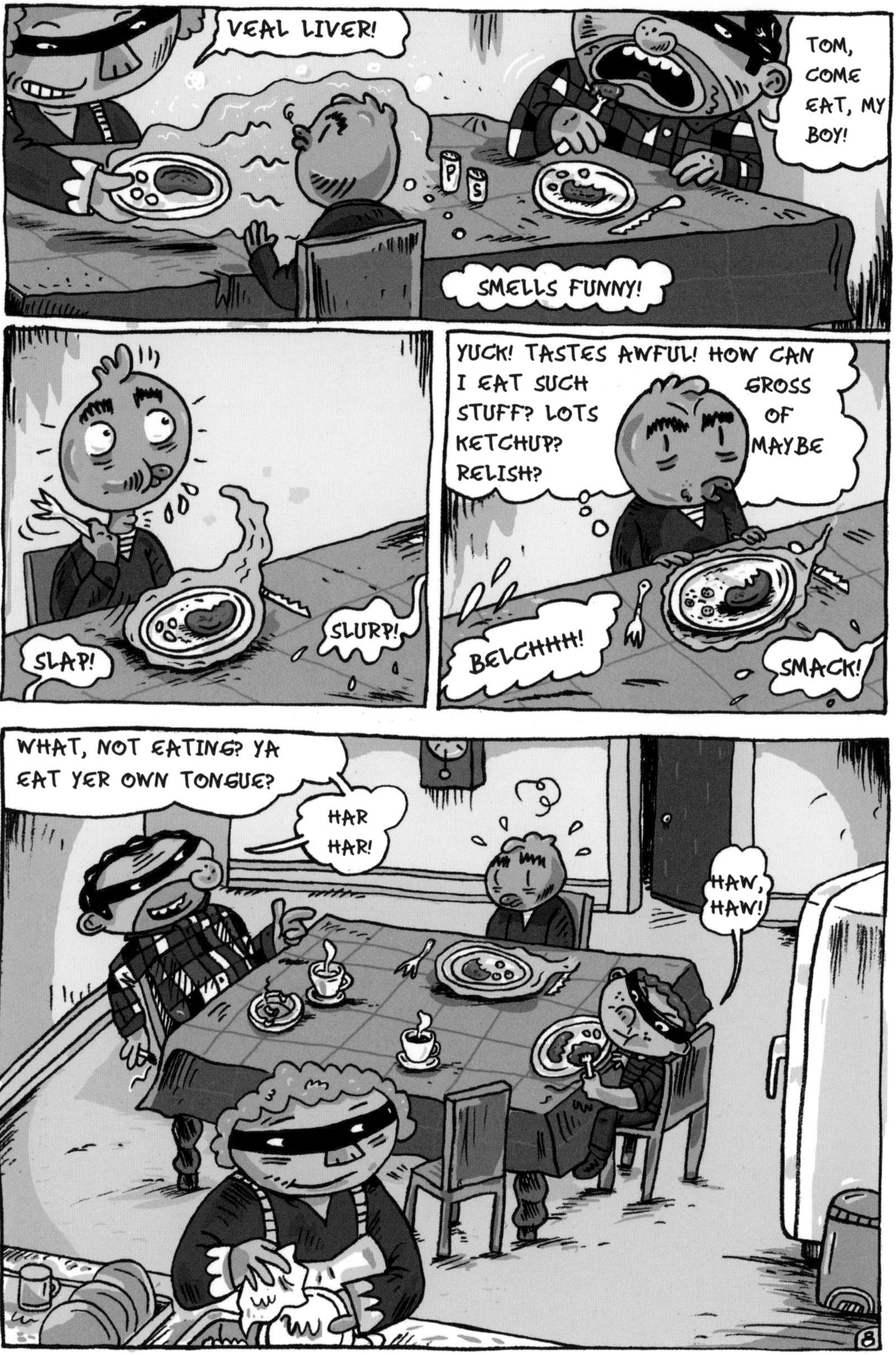
VEAL LIVER!
TOM, COME EAT, MY BOY!
SMELLS FUNNY!
SLAP!
SLURP!
YUCK! TASTES AWFUL! HOW CAN I EAT SUCH GROSS STUFF? LOTS OF KETCHUP? MAYBE RELISH?
BELCHHH!
SMACK!
WHAT, NOT EATING? YA EAT YER OWN TONGUE?
HAR HAR!
HAW, HAW!
8

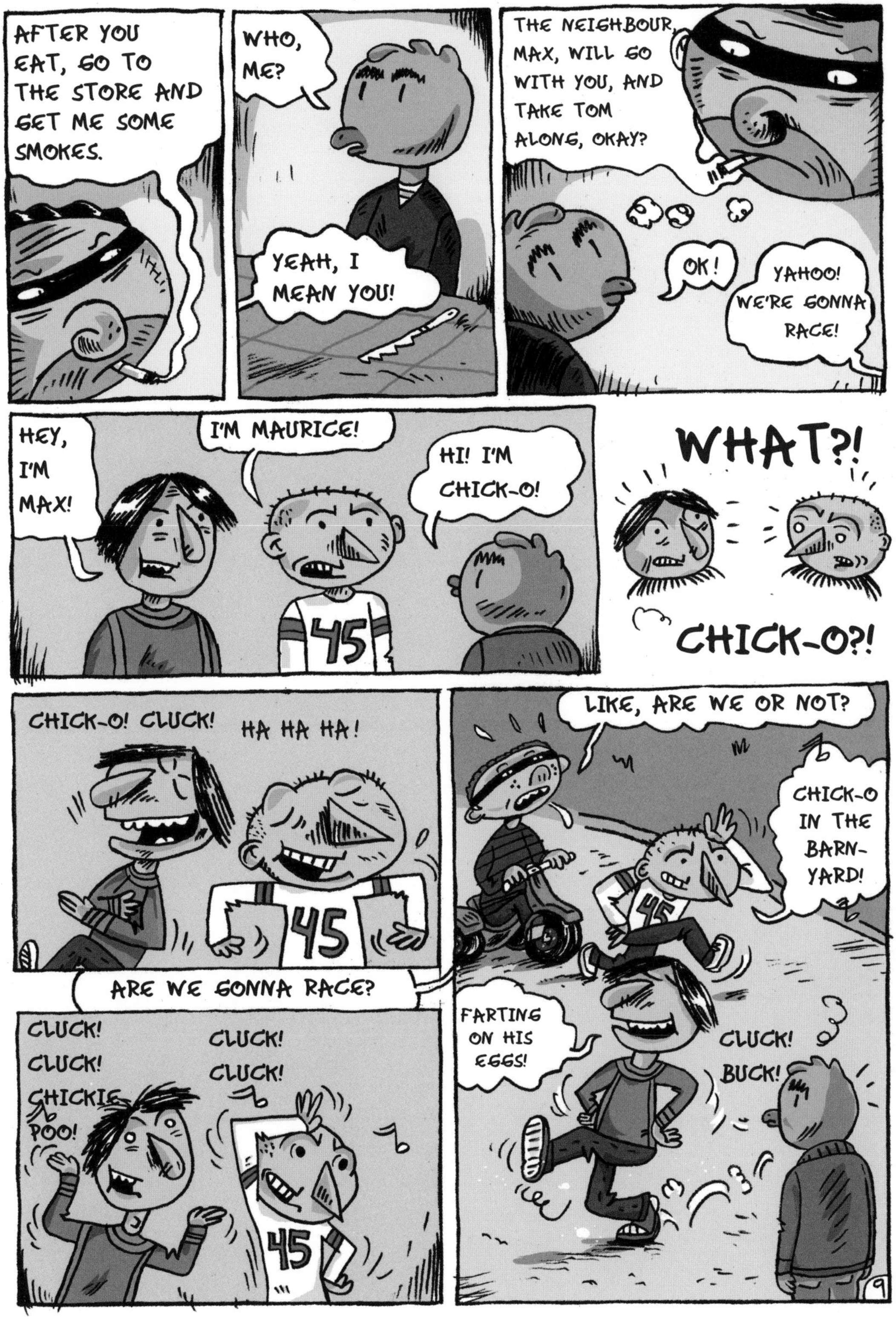
AFTER YOU EAT, GO TO THE STORE AND GET ME SOME SMOKES.
WHO, ME?
YEAH, I MEAN YOU!
THE NEIGHBOUR, MAX, WILL GO WITH YOU, AND TAKE TOM ALONG, OKAY?
OK!
YAHOO! WE'RE GONNA RACE!
HEY, I'M MAX!
I'M MAURICE!
HI! I'M CHICK-O!
WHAT?!
CHICK-O?!
CHICK-O! CLUCK!
HA HA HA!
ARE WE GONNA RACE?
LIKE, ARE WE OR NOT?
CHICK-O IN THE BARN-YARD!
CLUCK! CLUCK! CHICKIE-POO!
CLUCK! CLUCK!
FARTING ON HIS EGGS!
CLUCK! BUCK!
9

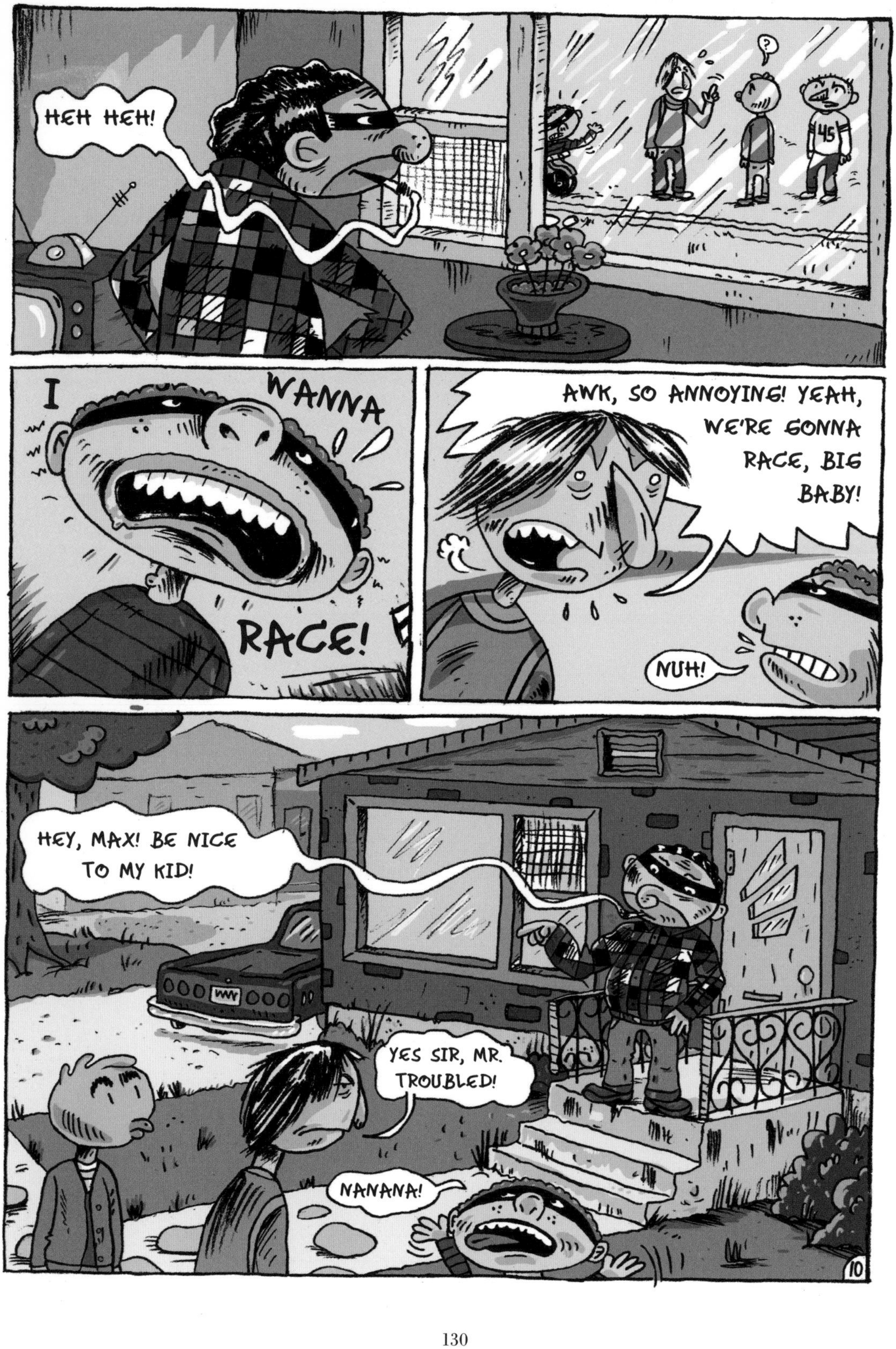
HEH HEH!
?
45
I WANNA RACE!
AWK, SO ANNOYING! YEAH, WE'RE GONNA RACE, BIG BABY!
NUH!
HEY, MAX! BE NICE TO MY KID!
YES SIR, MR. TROUBLED!
NANANA!
10

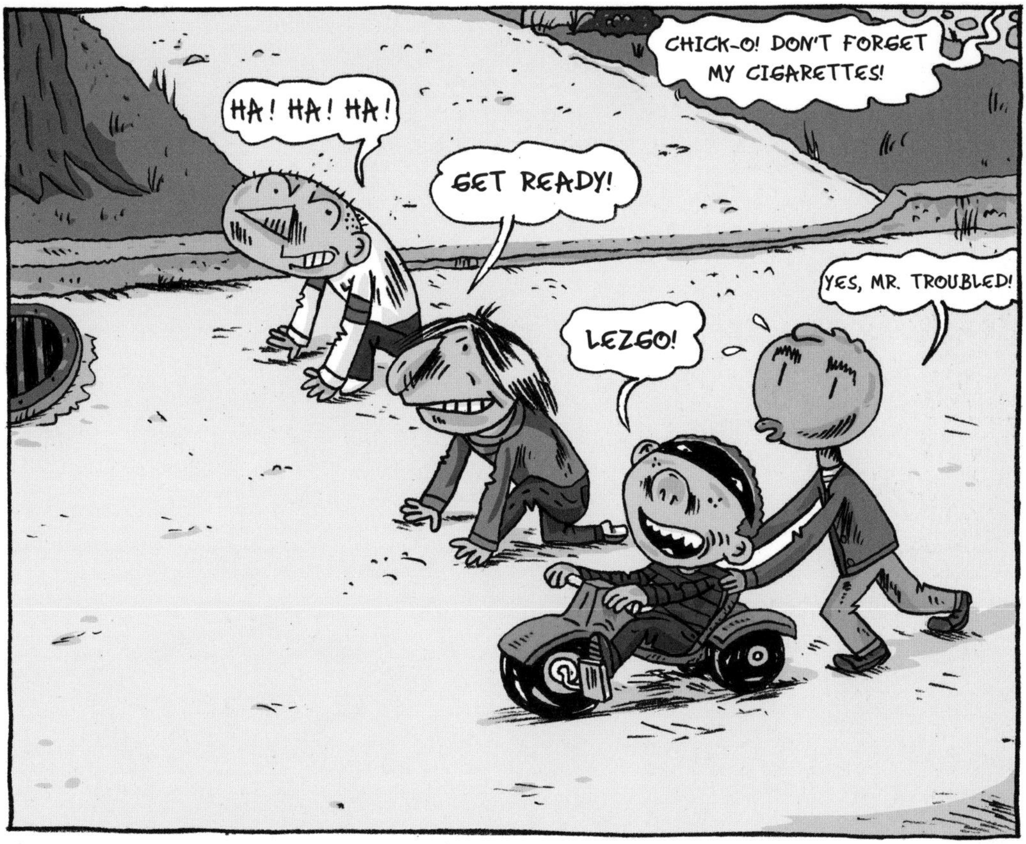
HA! HA! HA!
GET READY!
CHICK-O! DON'T FORGET MY CIGARETTES!
LEZGO!
YES, MR. TROUBLED!

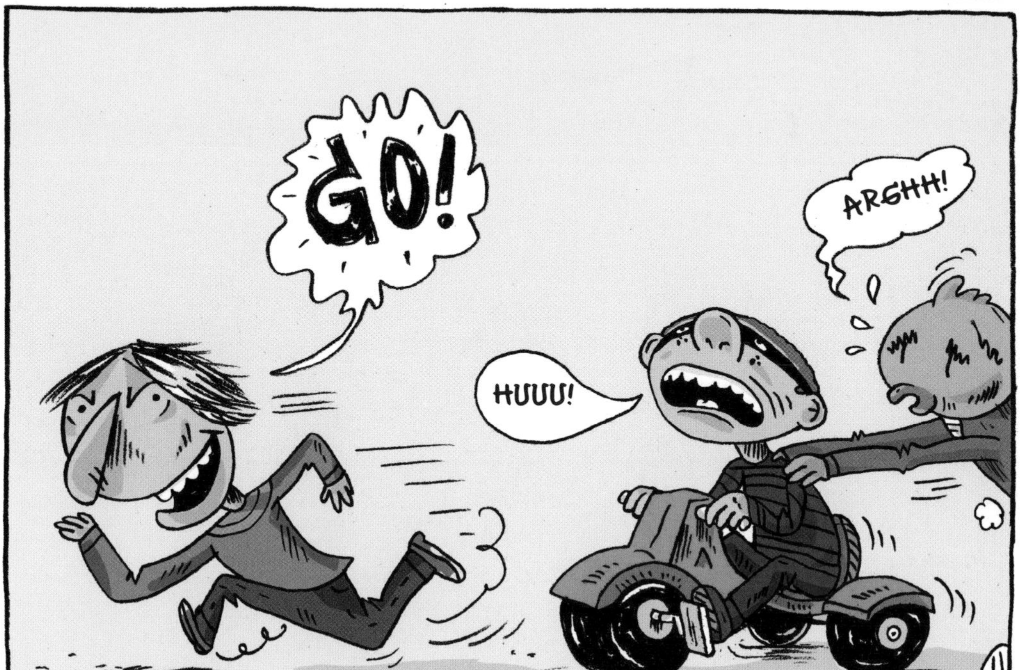
GO!
HUUU!
ARGHH!

PUSH! PUSH IT FASTER, DUMMY!
POOF! POOF!!!
I'M GONNA WIN!
WHAAAAA?!
...
?
BANG!!
12

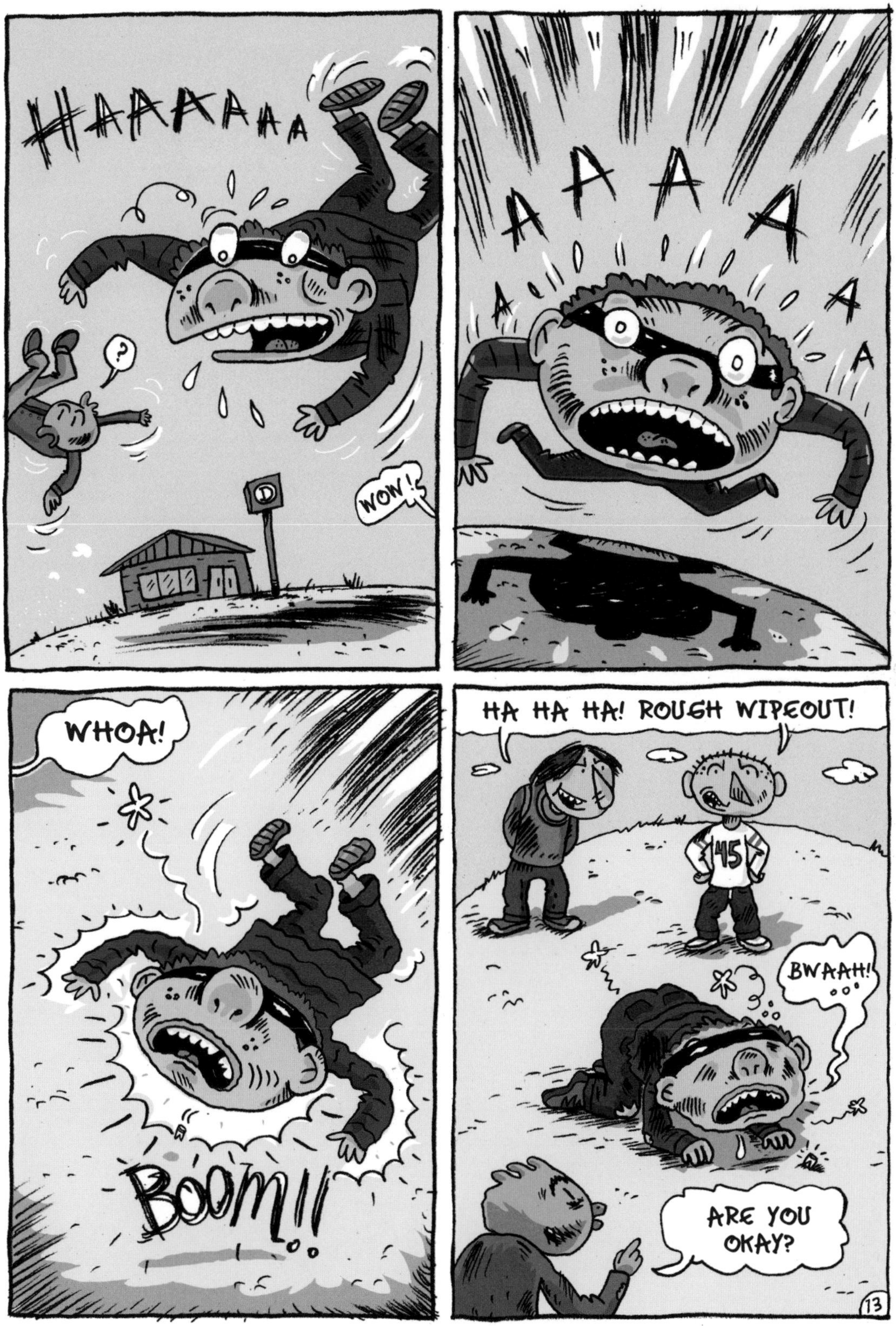
HAAAAAA
?
WOW!
AAAAAAAA
WHOA!
BOOM!!
HA HA HA! ROUGH WIPEOUT!
BWAAH!
ARE YOU OKAY?
13

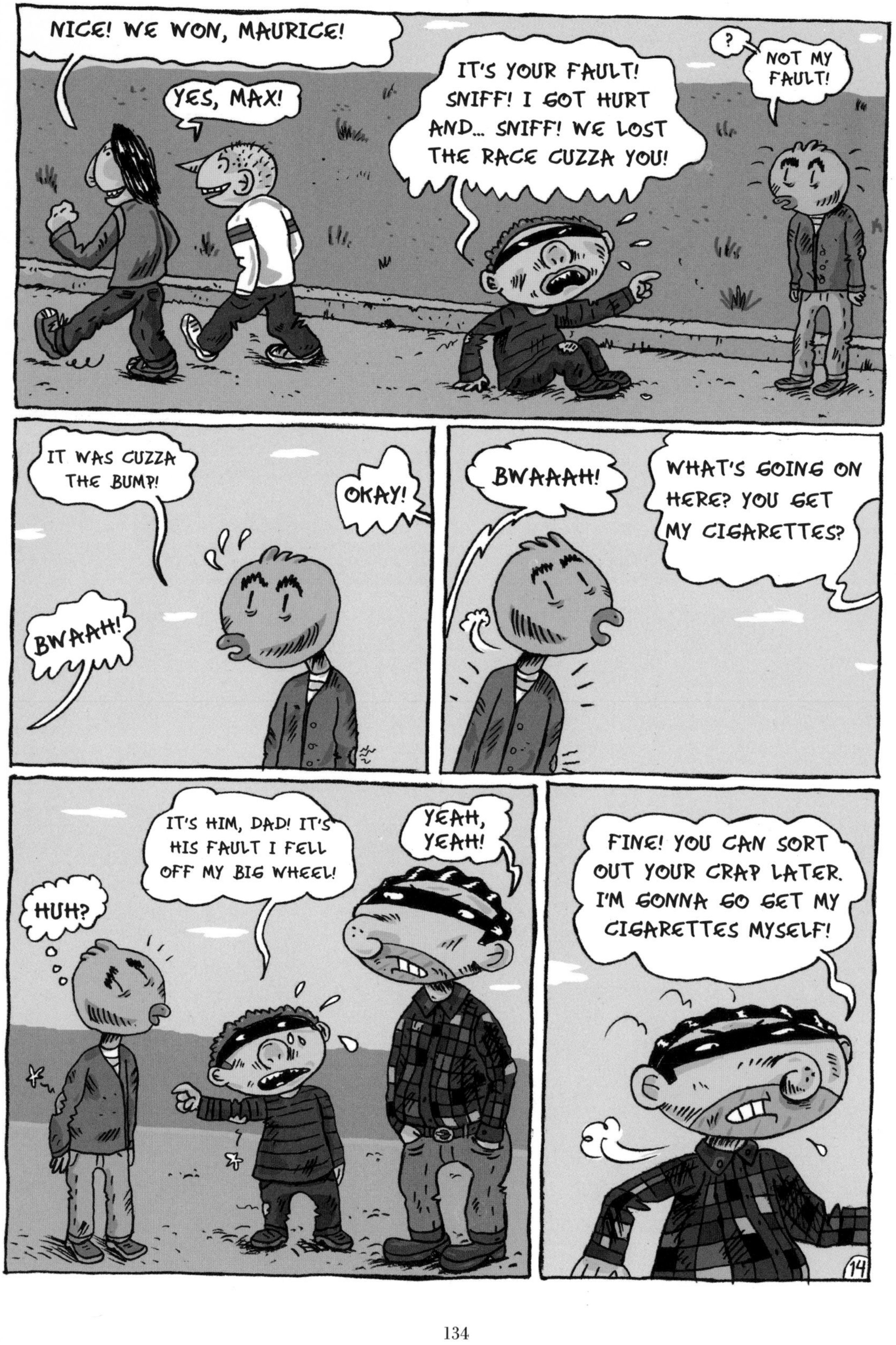
NICE! WE WON, MAURICE!
YES, MAX!
IT'S YOUR FAULT! SNIFF! I GOT HURT AND... SNIFF! WE LOST THE RACE CUZZA YOU!
?
NOT MY FAULT!
IT WAS CUZZA THE BUMP!
OKAY!
BWAAH!
BWAAAH!
WHAT'S GOING ON HERE? YOU GET MY CIGARETTES?
HUH?
IT'S HIM, DAD! IT'S HIS FAULT I FELL OFF MY BIG WHEEL!
YEAH, YEAH!
FINE! YOU CAN SORT OUT YOUR CRAP LATER. I'M GONNA GO GET MY CIGARETTES MYSELF!
14

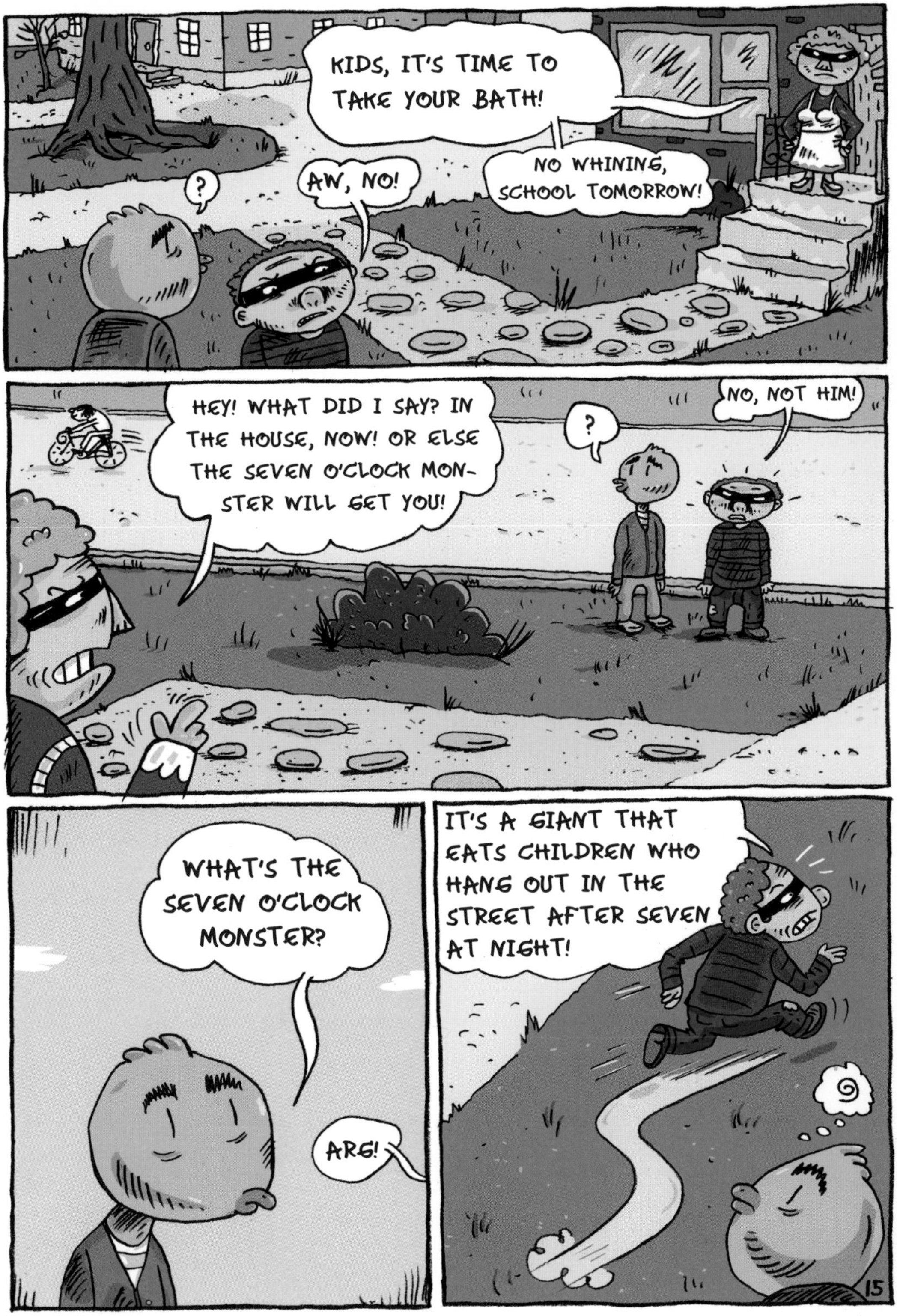
KIDS, IT'S TIME TO TAKE YOUR BATH!
?
AW, NO!
NO WHINING, SCHOOL TOMORROW!
HEY! WHAT DID I SAY? IN THE HOUSE, NOW! OR ELSE THE SEVEN O'CLOCK MON-STER WILL GET YOU!
?
NO, NOT HIM!
WHAT'S THE SEVEN O'CLOCK MONSTER?
ARG!
IT'S A GIANT THAT EATS CHILDREN WHO HANG OUT IN THE STREET AFTER SEVEN AT NIGHT!
15

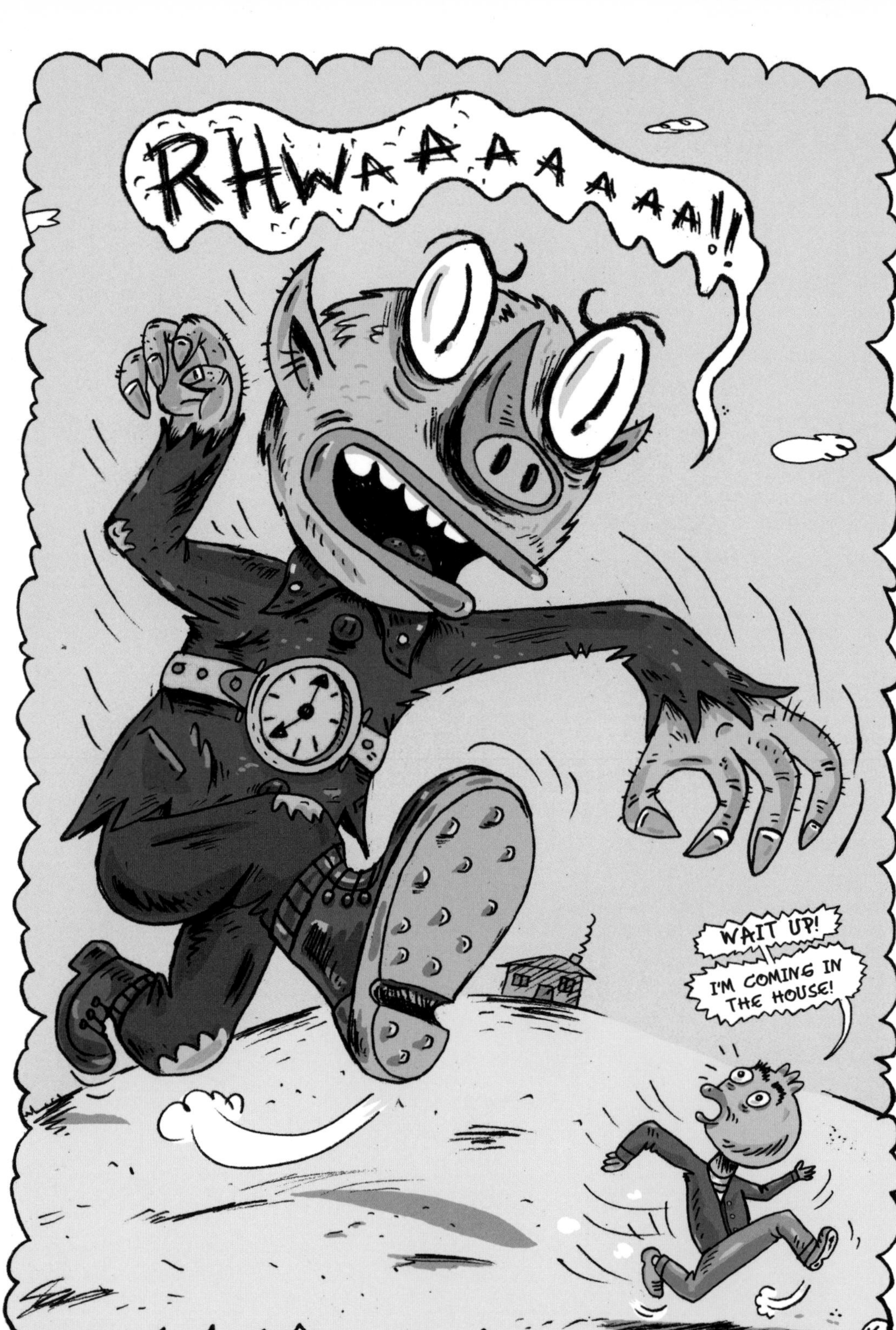
RHWAAAAAAAA!!
WAIT UP!
I'M COMING IN THE HOUSE!
16

THE NEXT DAY, CHICK-O ARRIVES AT HIS NEW SCHOOL.

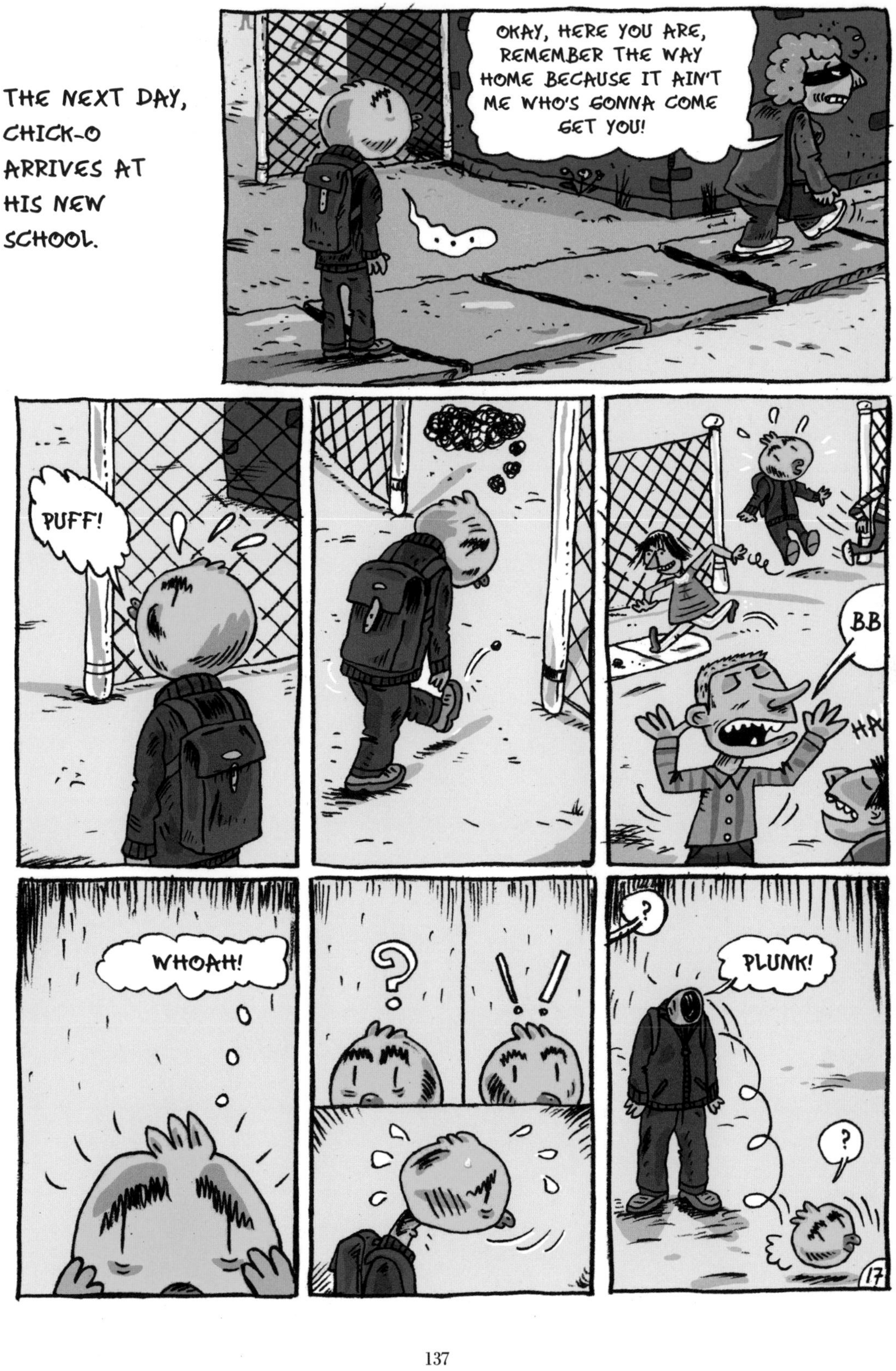
OKAY, HERE YOU ARE, REMEMBER THE WAY HOME BECAUSE IT AIN'T ME WHO'S GONNA COME GET YOU!
PUFF!
BB
HA
WHOAH!
?
PLUNK!
?
17

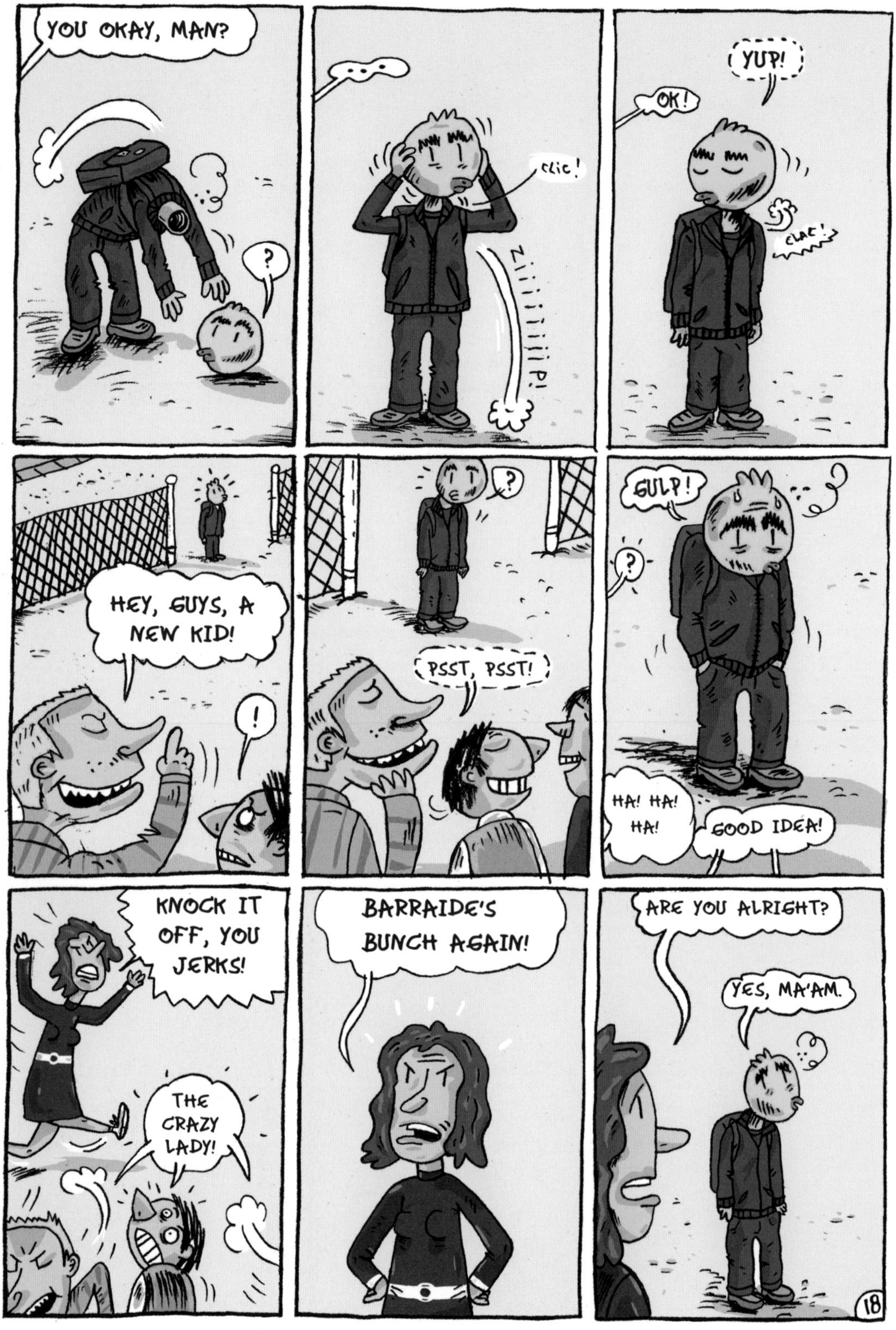
YOU OKAY, MAN?
?
clic!
ZIIIIIIIIIIP!
OK!
YUP!
CLAC!
HEY, GUYS, A NEW KID!
!
?
PSST, PSST!
GULP!
?
HA! HA! HA!
GOOD IDEA!
KNOCK IT OFF, YOU JERKS!
THE CRAZY LADY!
BARRAIDE'S BUNCH AGAIN!
ARE YOU ALRIGHT?
YES, MA'AM.
18

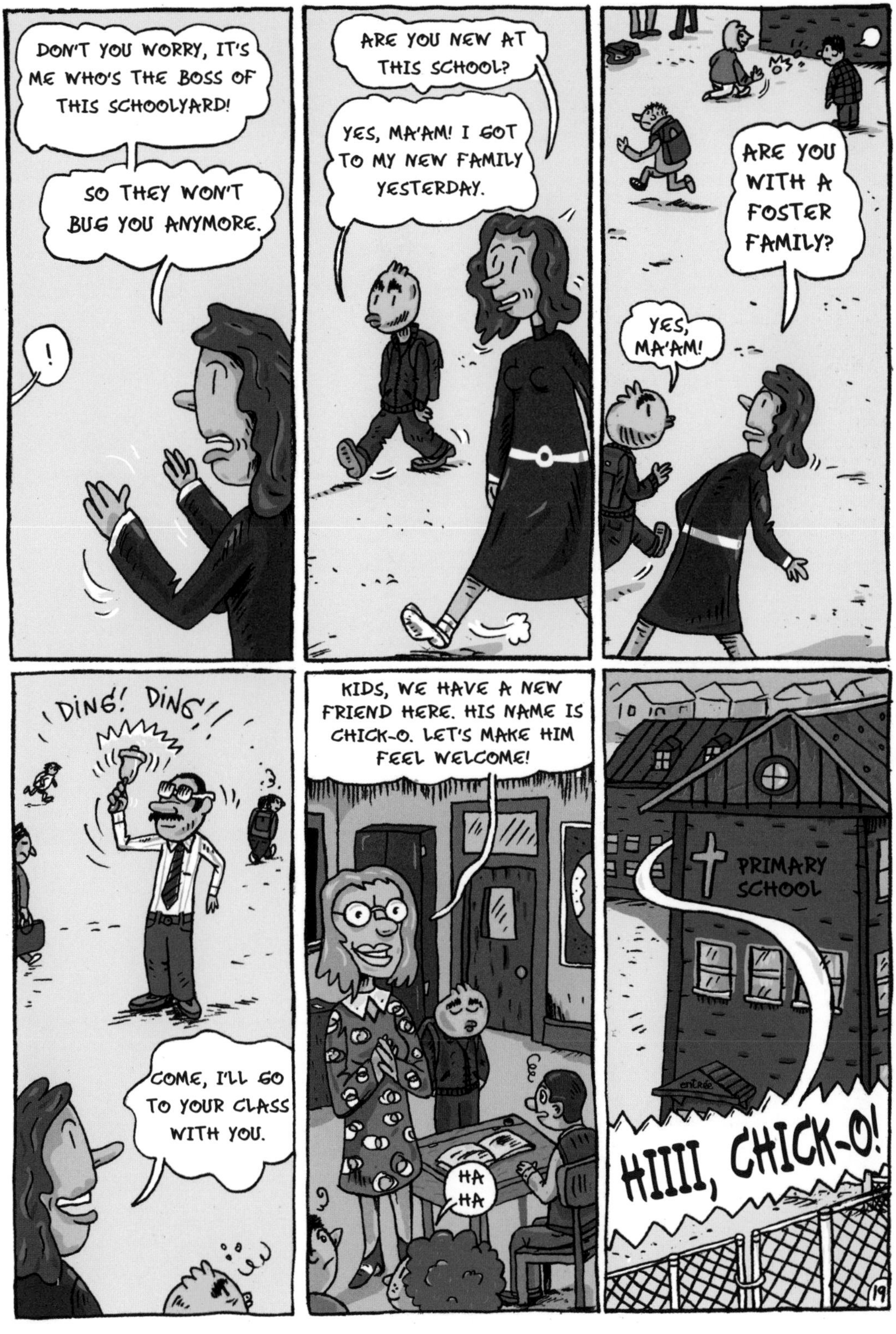
DON'T YOU WORRY, IT'S ME WHO'S THE BOSS OF THIS SCHOOLYARD!
SO THEY WON'T BUG YOU ANYMORE.
!
ARE YOU NEW AT THIS SCHOOL?
YES, MA'AM! I GOT TO MY NEW FAMILY YESTERDAY.
ARE YOU WITH A FOSTER FAMILY?
YES, MA'AM!
DING! DING!
COME, I'LL GO TO YOUR CLASS WITH YOU.
KIDS, WE HAVE A NEW FRIEND HERE. HIS NAME IS CHICK-O. LET'S MAKE HIM FEEL WELCOME!
HA HA
PRIMARY SCHOOL
entrée
HIIII, CHICK-O!
19

ON HIS WAY HOME, CHICK-O IS JOINED BY MARY, ANOTHER STUDENT IN HIS CLASS.

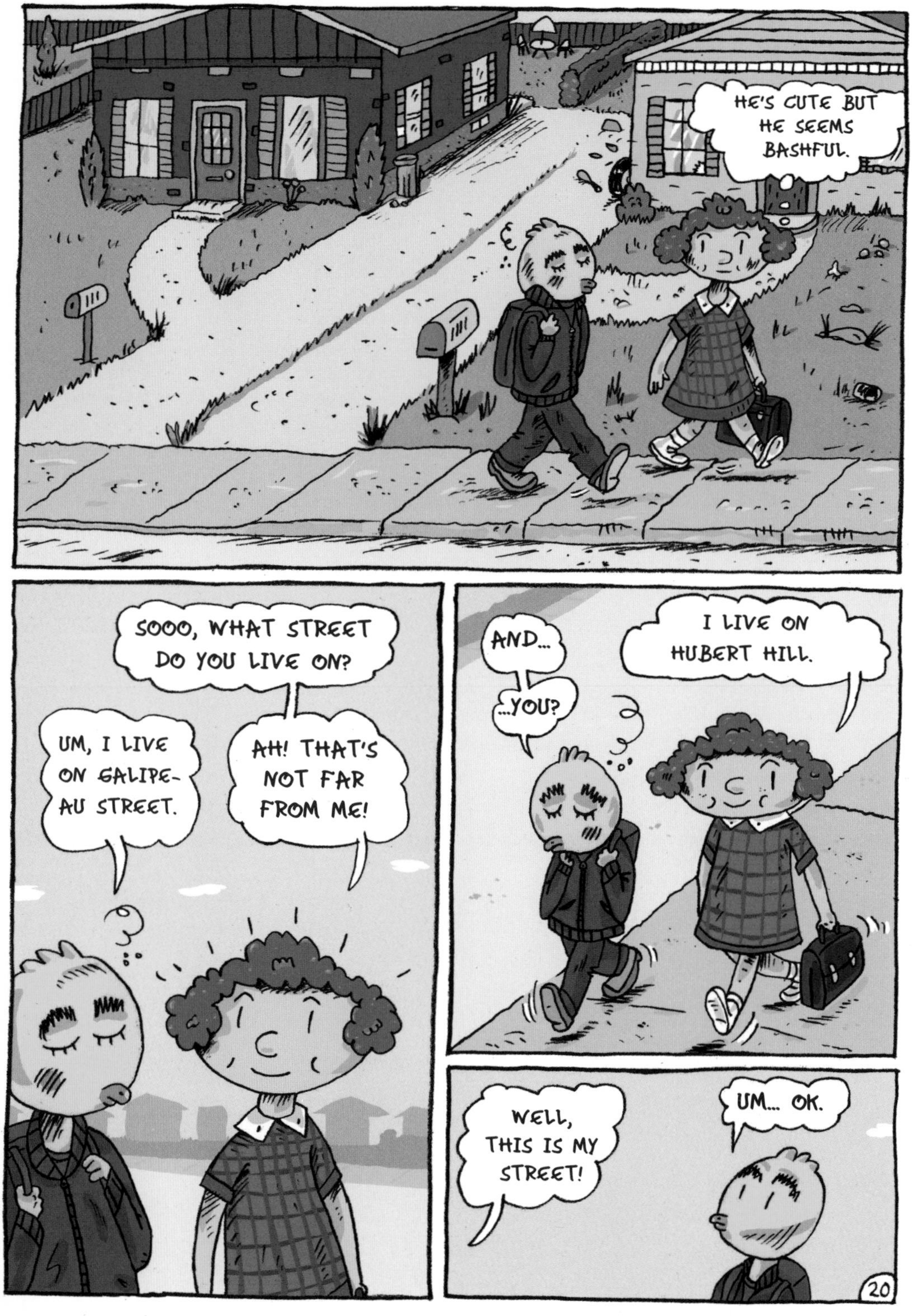
HE'S CUTE BUT HE SEEMS BASHFUL.
SOOO, WHAT STREET DO YOU LIVE ON?
UM, I LIVE ON GALIPE-AU STREET.
AH! THAT'S NOT FAR FROM ME!
I LIVE ON HUBERT HILL.
AND...
...YOU?
WELL, THIS IS MY STREET!
UM... OK.
20

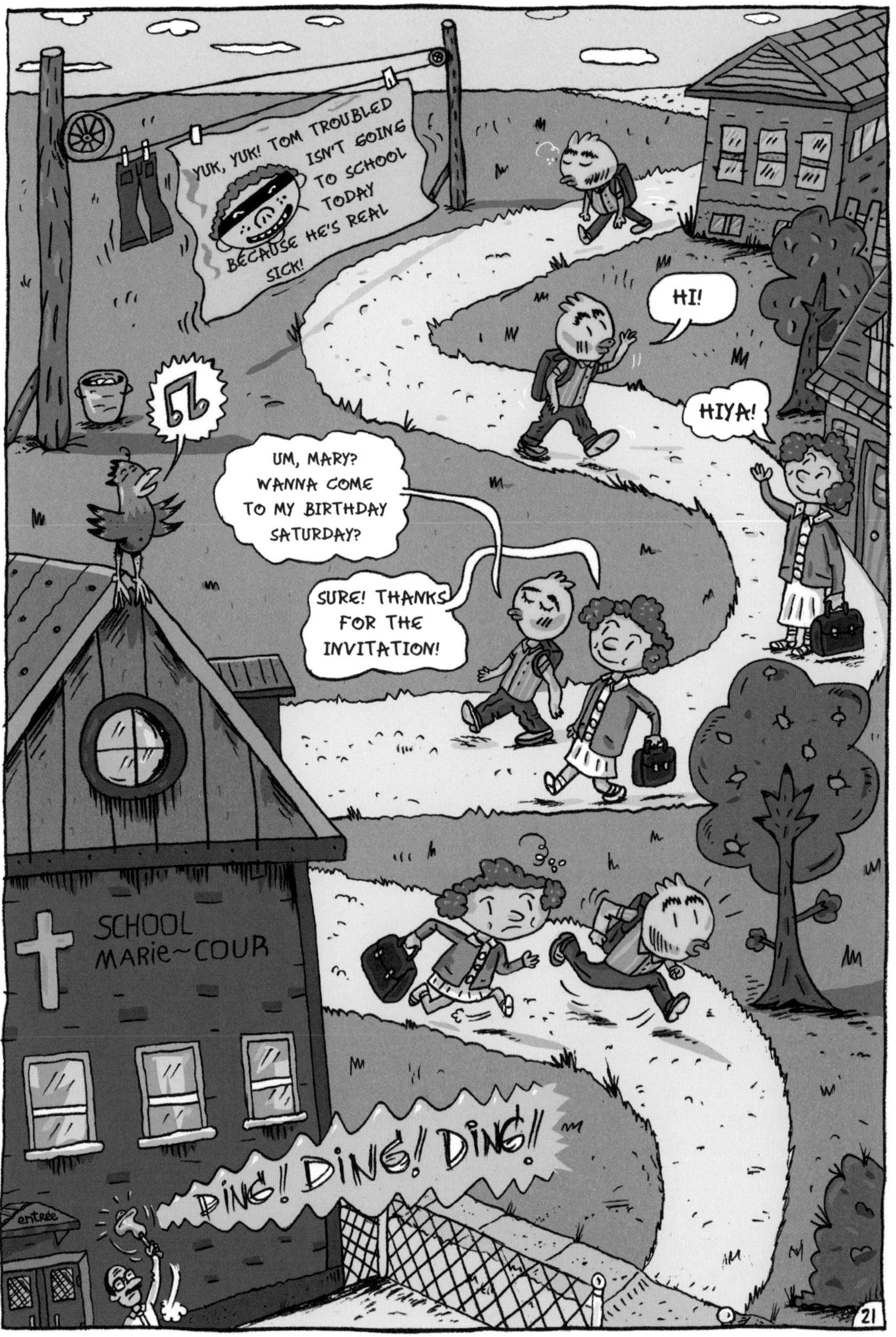
YUK, YUK! TOM TROUBLED ISN'T GOING TO SCHOOL TODAY BECAUSE HE'S REAL SICK!
HI!
HIYA!
UM, MARY? WANNA COME TO MY BIRTHDAY SATURDAY?
SURE! THANKS FOR THE INVITATION!
SCHOOL MARIE~COUR
entrée
DING! DING! DING!
21

22

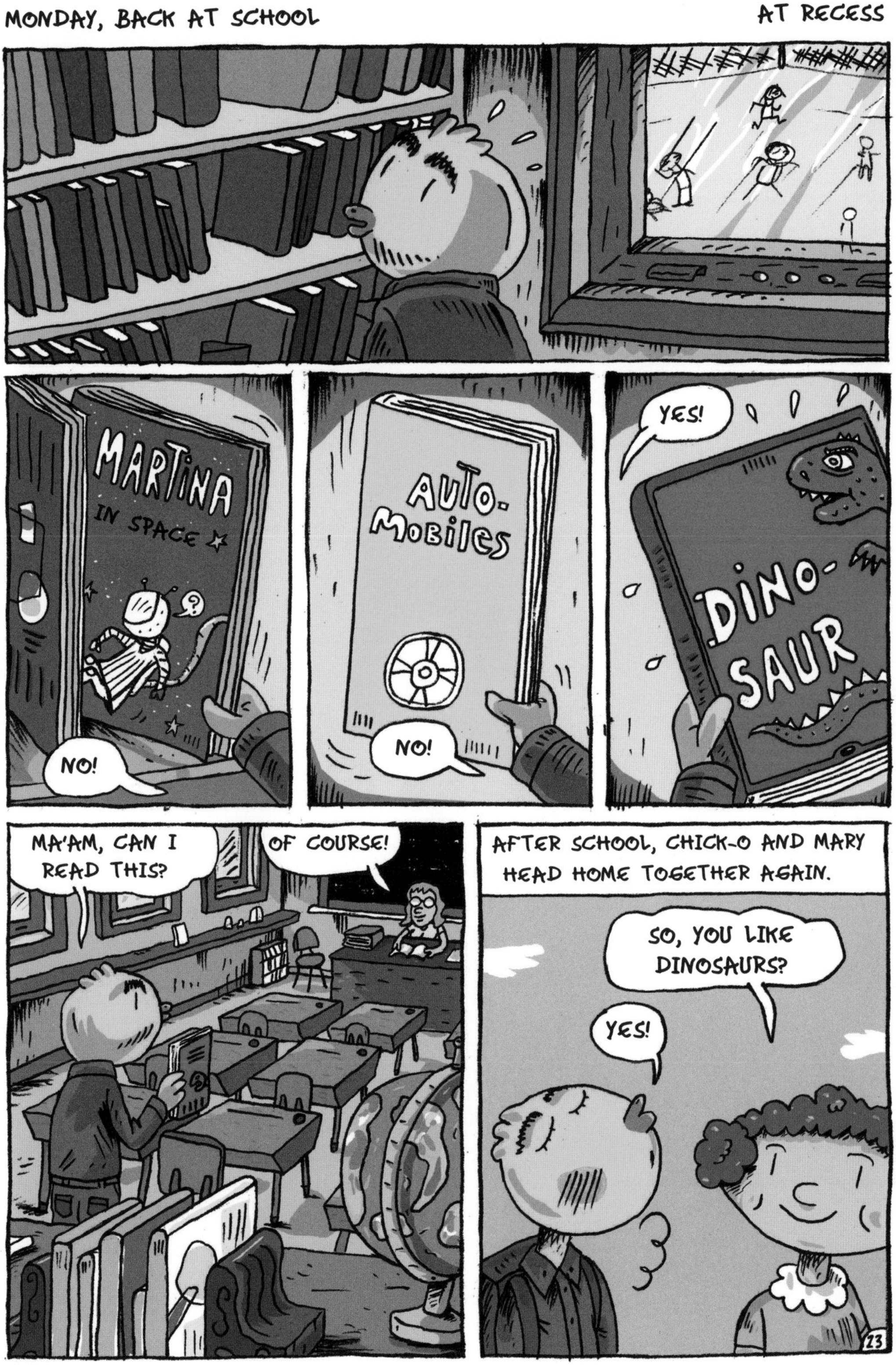
MONDAY, BACK AT SCHOOL
AT RECESS
MARTINA IN SPACE
NO!
AUTO-MOBILES
NO!
YES!
DINO-SAUR
MA'AM, CAN I READ THIS?
OF COURSE!
AFTER SCHOOL, CHICK-O AND MARY HEAD HOME TOGETHER AGAIN.
SO, YOU LIKE DINOSAURS?
YES!
23

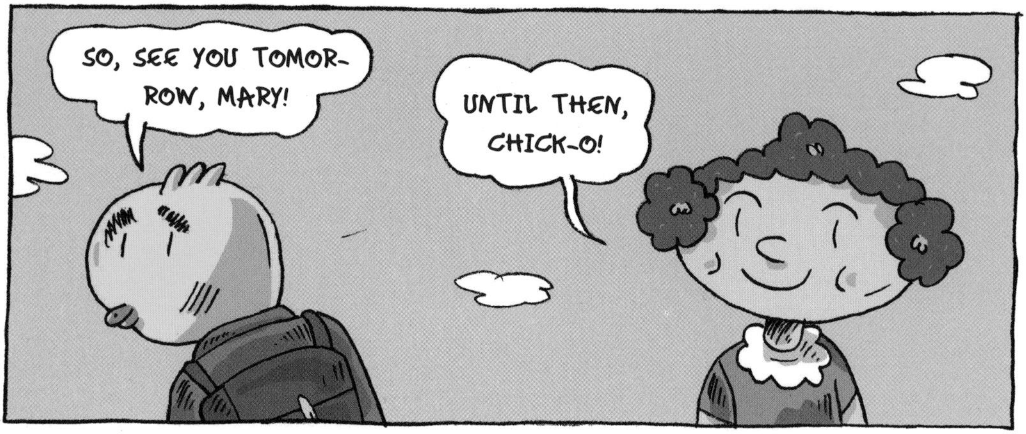
SO, SEE YOU TOMOR-
ROW, MARY!
UNTIL THEN,
CHICK-O!

BACK AT HOME, CHICK-O SLOGS THROUGH HIS HOMEWORK UNDER MRS. TROUBLED'S STERN EYE. AFTER SUPPER, HE DRIES THE DISHES AND SWEEPS AND THEN FINDS SOME TIME TO DRAW BEFORE BED.

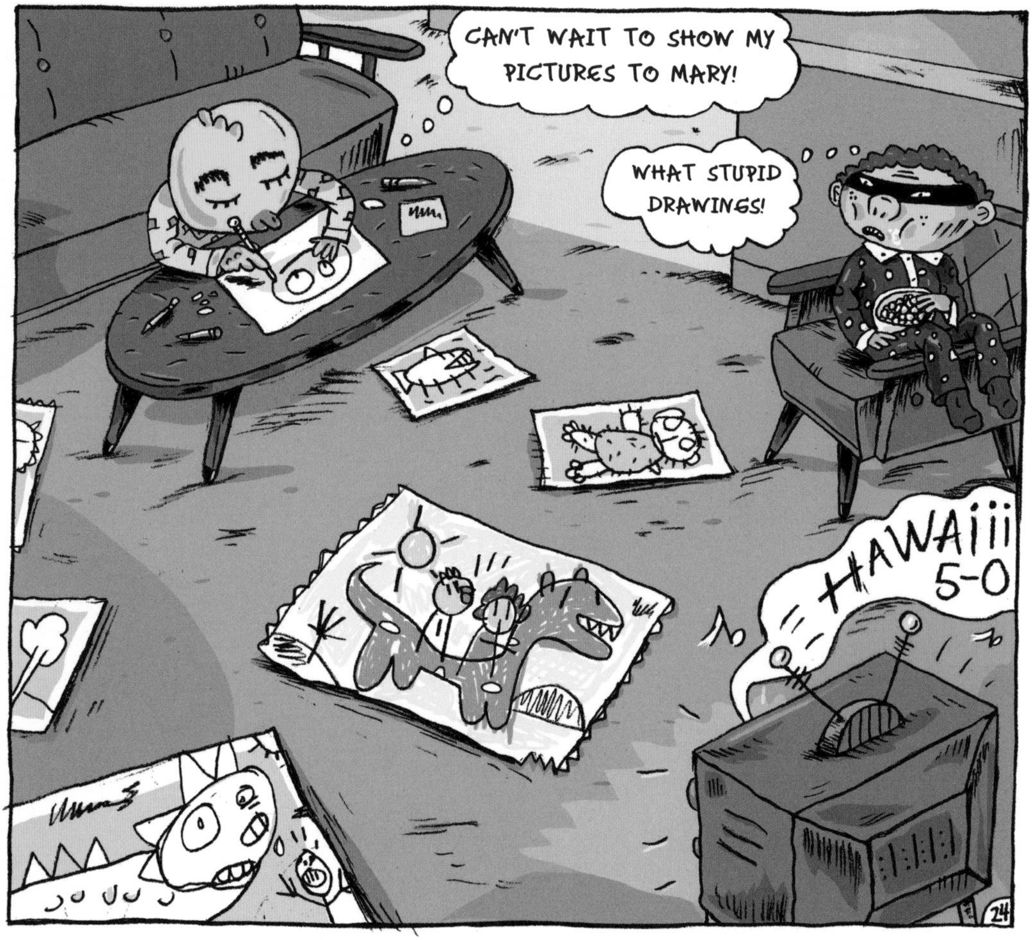
CAN'T WAIT TO SHOW MY
PICTURES TO MARY!
WHAT STUPID
DRAWINGS!
HAWAiii
5-0

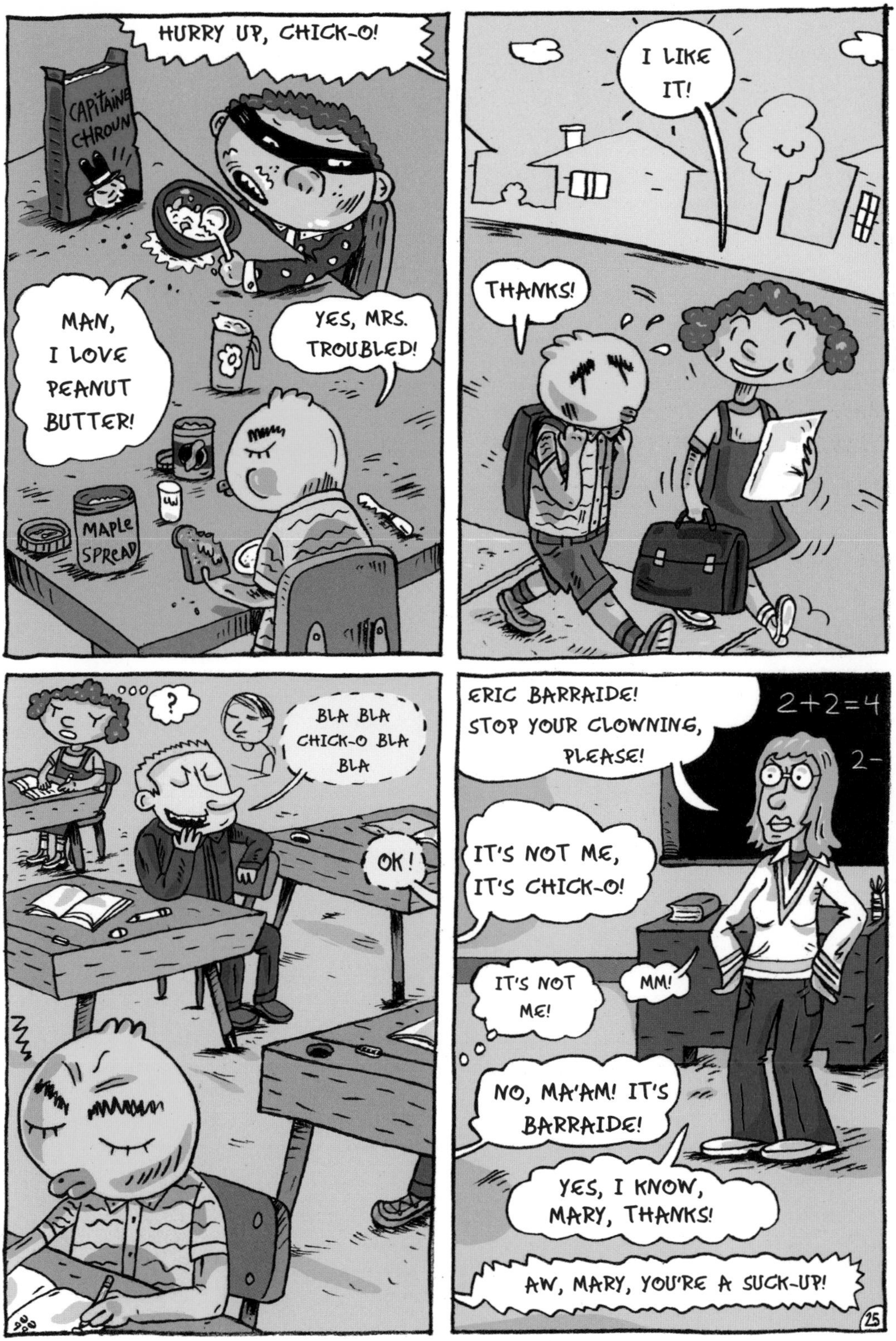
HURRY UP, CHICK-O!
CAPITAINE CHROUN
MAN, I LOVE PEANUT BUTTER!
YES, MRS. TROUBLED!
MAPLE SPREAD
I LIKE IT!
THANKS!
BLA BLA CHICK-O BLA BLA
OK!
ERIC BARRAIDE! STOP YOUR CLOWNING, PLEASE!
2+2=4
IT'S NOT ME, IT'S CHICK-O!
IT'S NOT ME!
MM!
NO, MA'AM! IT'S BARRAIDE!
YES, I KNOW, MARY, THANKS!
AW, MARY, YOU'RE A SUCK-UP!
25

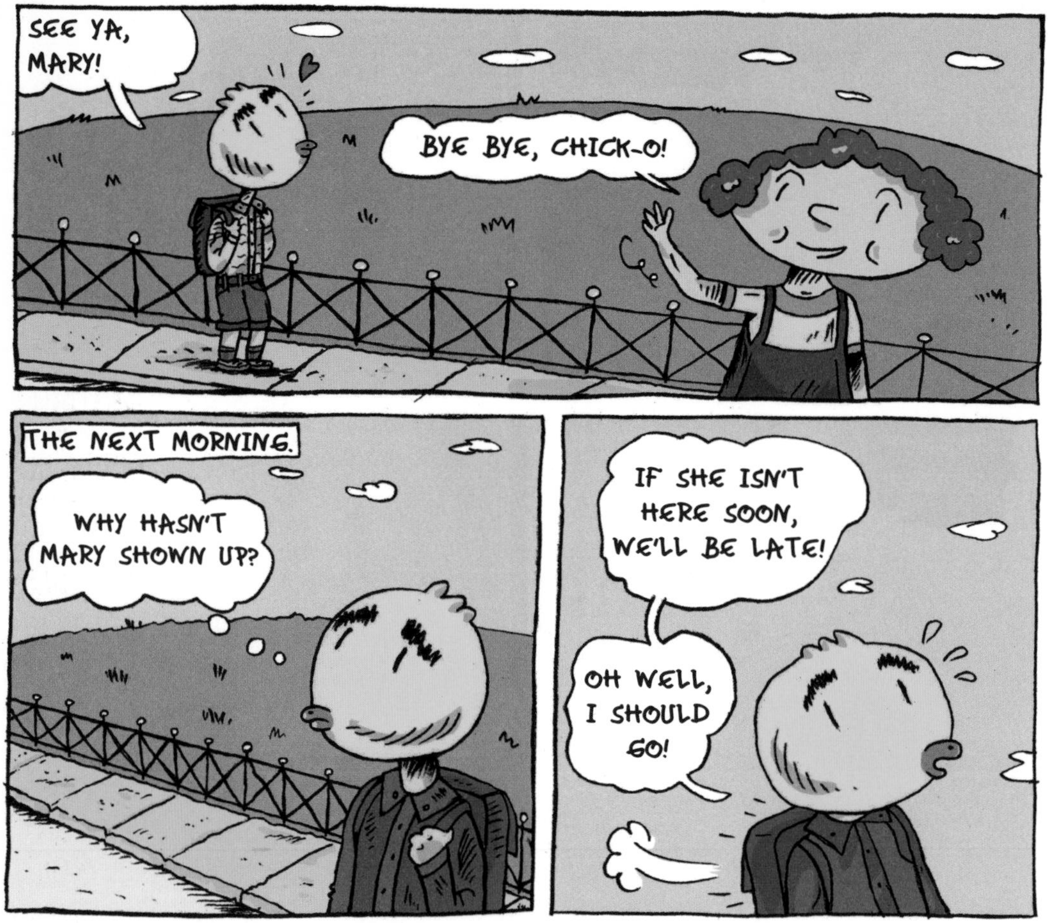
SEE YA, MARY!
BYE BYE, CHICK-O!
THE NEXT MORNING.
WHY HASN'T MARY SHOWN UP?
IF SHE ISN'T HERE SOON, WE'LL BE LATE!
OH WELL, I SHOULD GO!

IN THE SCHOOLYARD, THE KIDS ARE ALL ON EDGE.

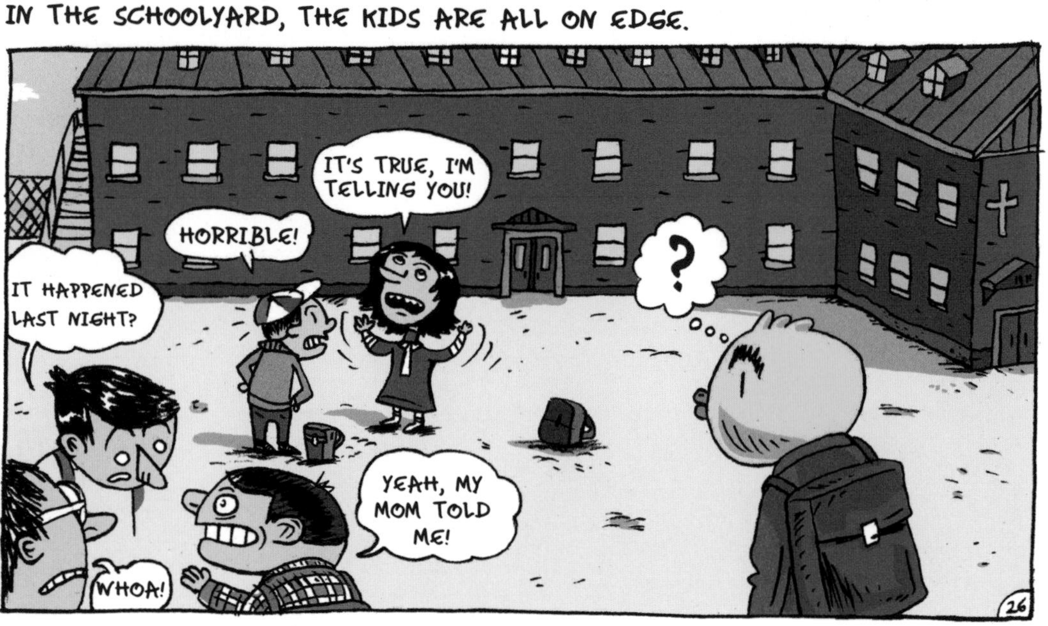
IT'S TRUE, I'M TELLING YOU!
HORRIBLE!
IT HAPPENED LAST NIGHT?
?
YEAH, MY MOM TOLD ME!
WHOA!
26

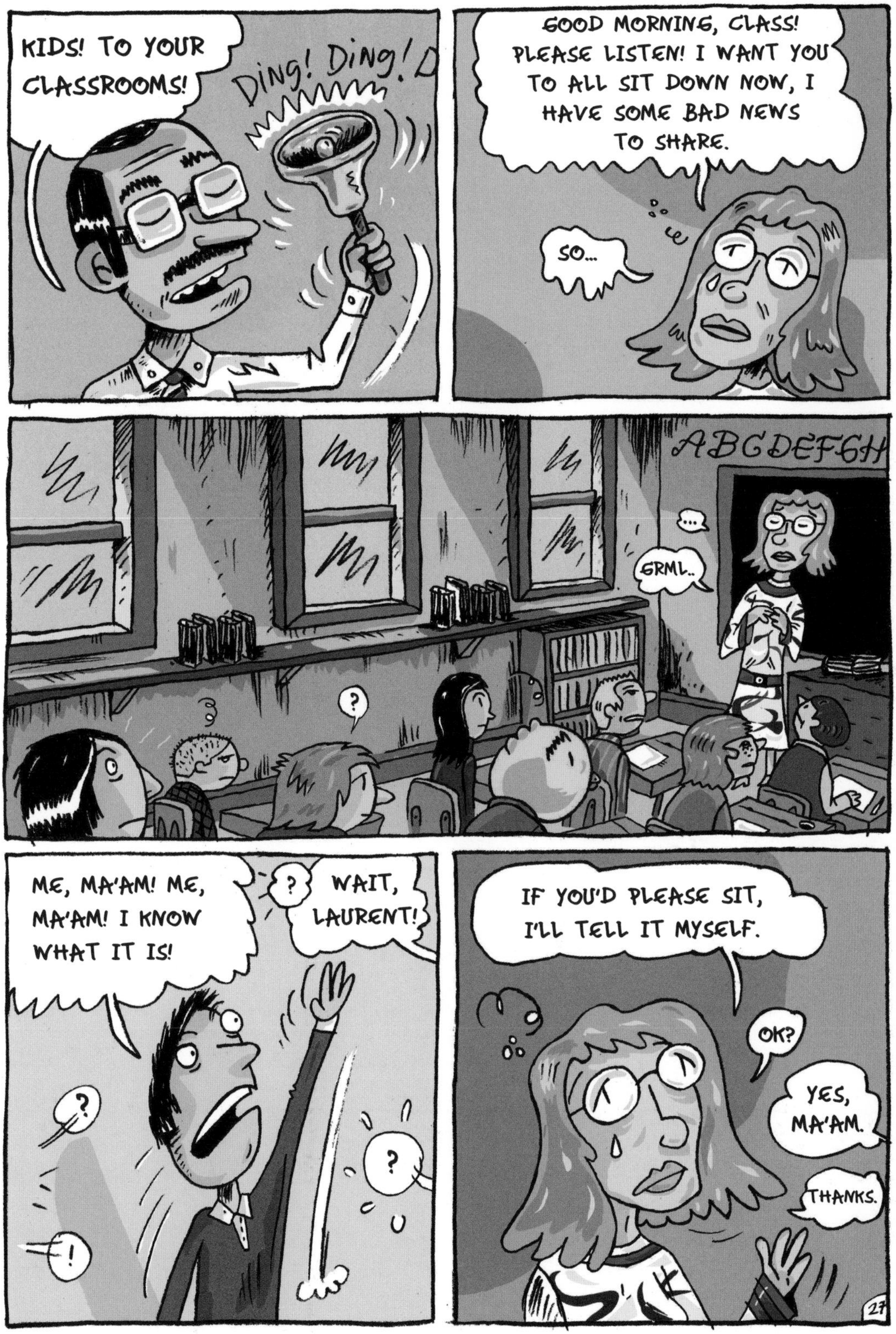
KIDS! TO YOUR CLASSROOMS!
DING! DING! D
GOOD MORNING, CLASS! PLEASE LISTEN! I WANT YOU TO ALL SIT DOWN NOW, I HAVE SOME BAD NEWS TO SHARE.
SO...
ABCDEFGH
...
GRML..
?
ME, MA'AM! ME, MA'AM! I KNOW WHAT IT IS!
?
WAIT, LAURENT!
?
?
!
IF YOU'D PLEASE SIT, I'LL TELL IT MYSELF.
OK?
YES, MA'AM.
THANKS.
27

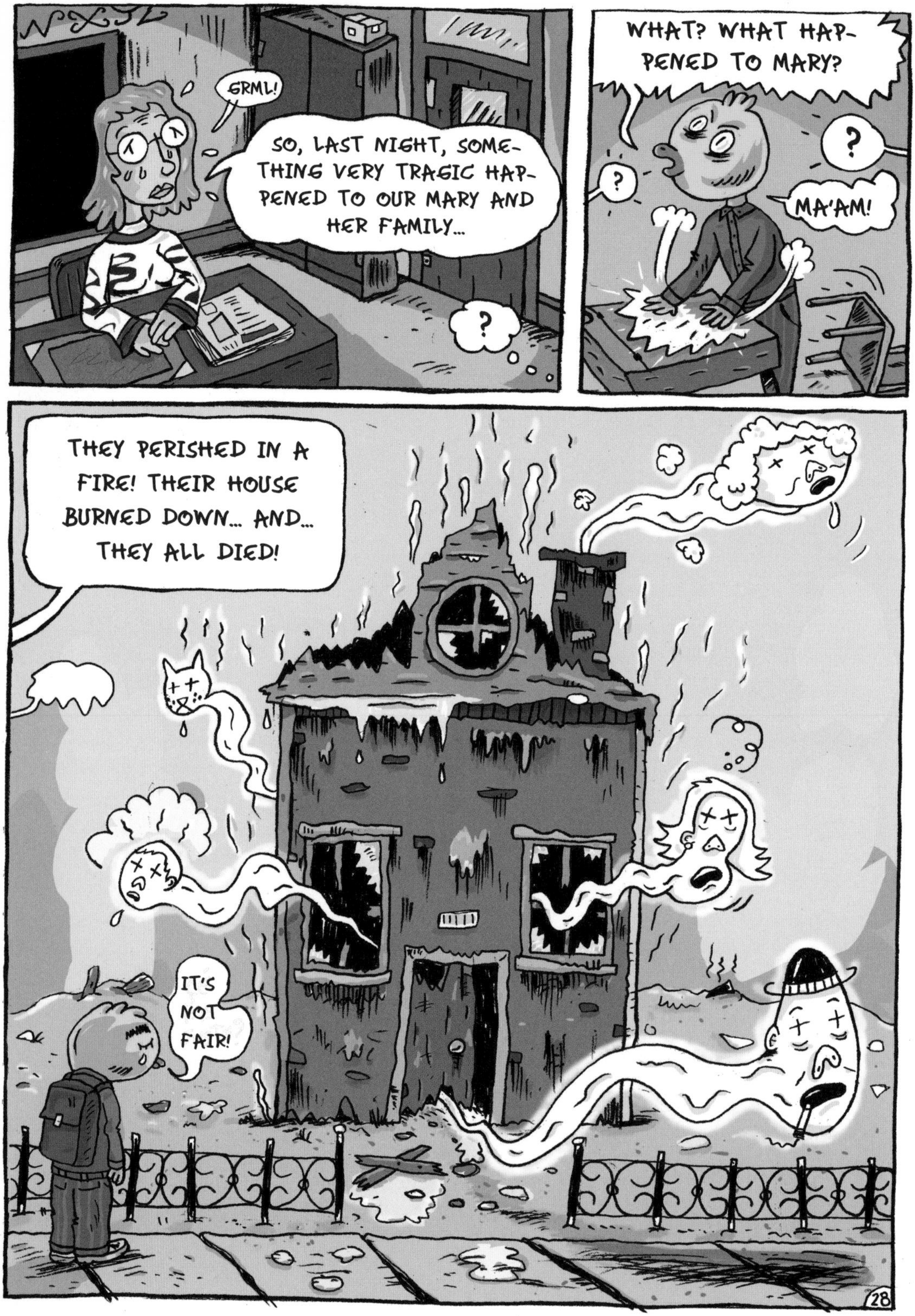
GRML!
SO, LAST NIGHT, SOMETHING VERY TRAGIC HAPPENED TO OUR MARY AND HER FAMILY...
?
WHAT? WHAT HAPPENED TO MARY?
?
?
MA'AM!
THEY PERISHED IN A FIRE! THEIR HOUSE BURNED DOWN... AND... THEY ALL DIED!
IT'S NOT FAIR!
28

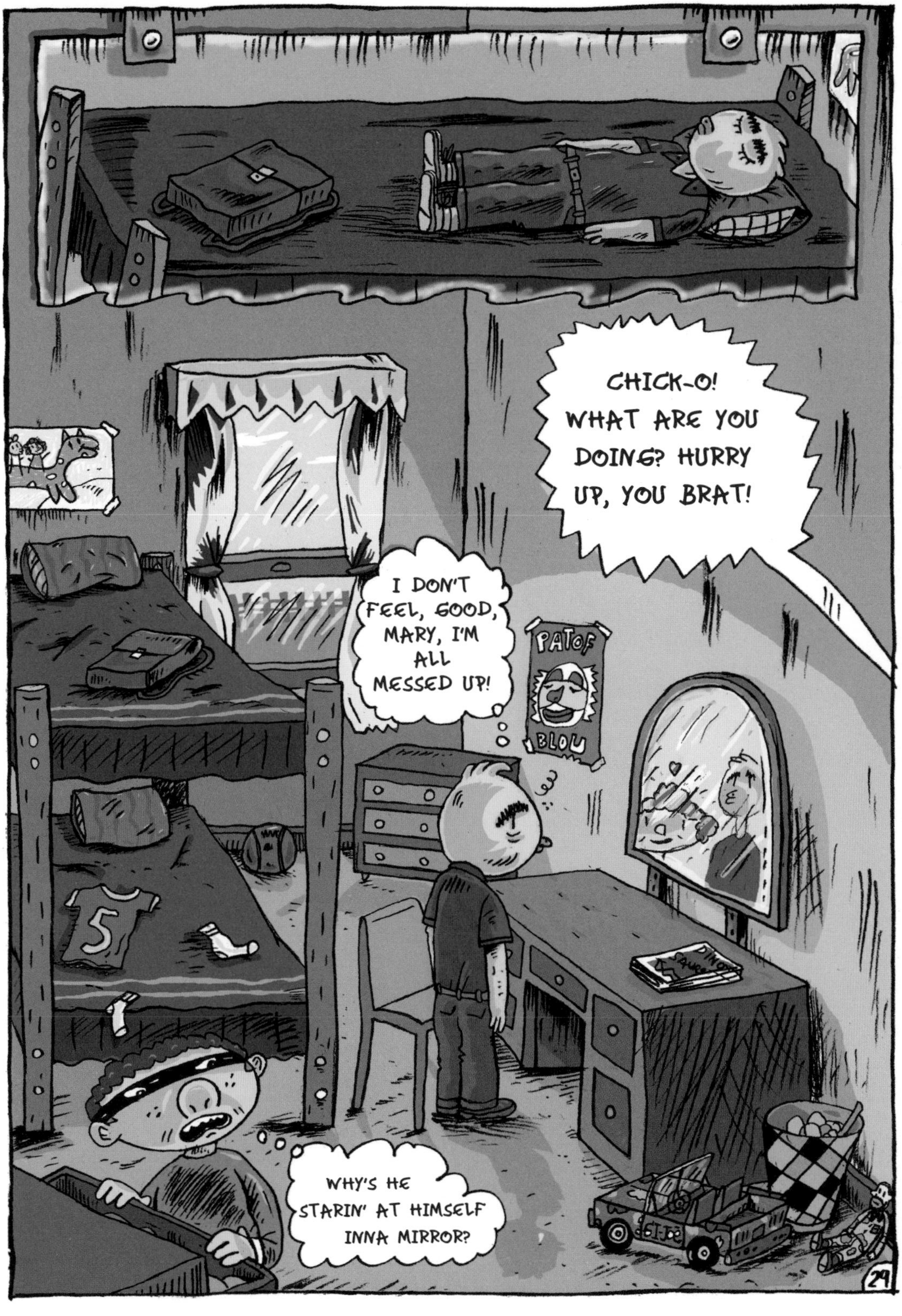
CHICK-O! WHAT ARE YOU DOING? HURRY UP, YOU BRAT!
I DON'T FEEL, GOOD, MARY, I'M ALL MESSED UP!
PATOF
BLOU
WHY'S HE STARIN' AT HIMSELF INNA MIRROR?
29

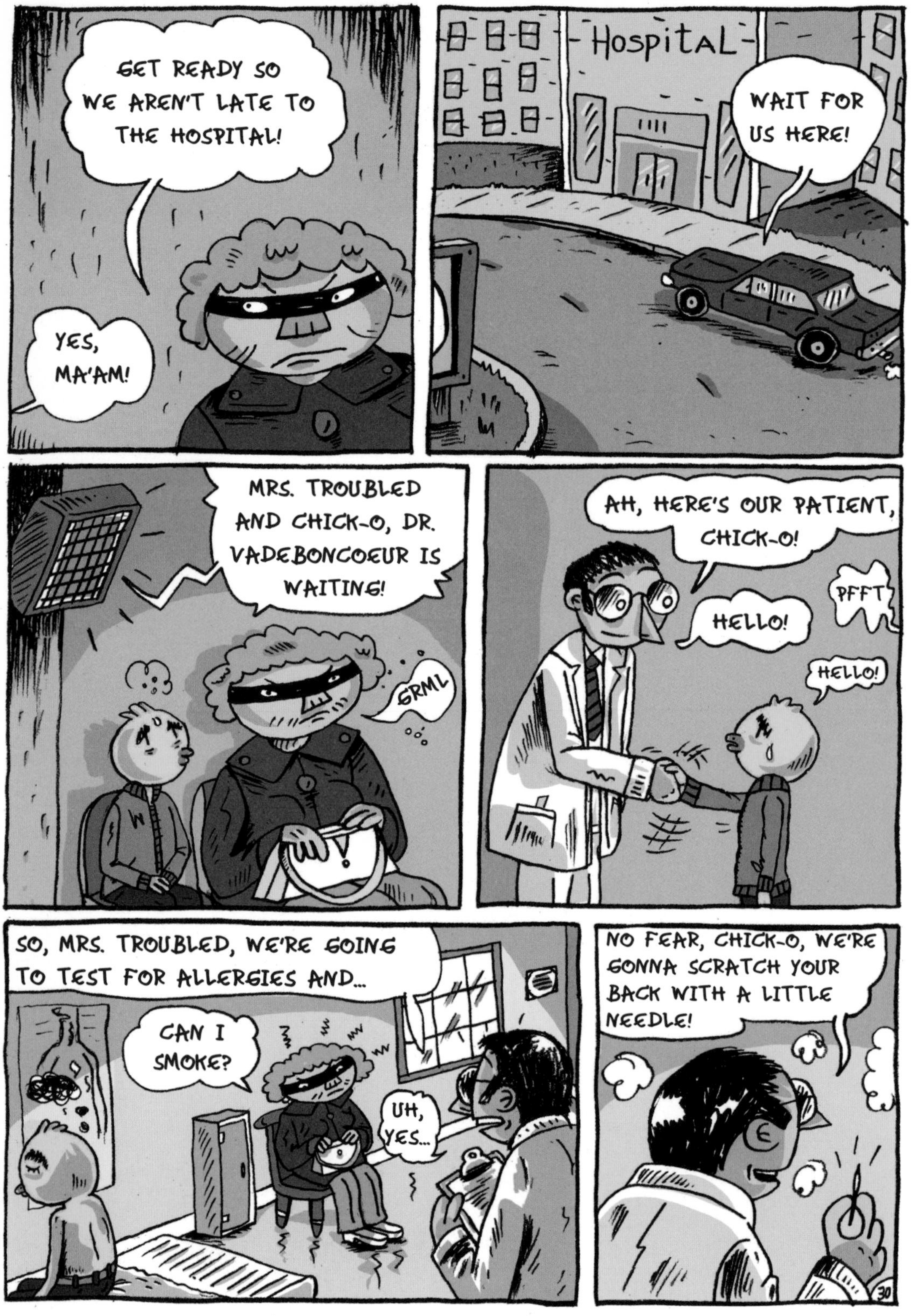
GET READY SO WE AREN'T LATE TO THE HOSPITAL!
YES, MA'AM!
Hospital
WAIT FOR US HERE!
MRS. TROUBLED AND CHICK-O, DR. VADEBONCOEUR IS WAITING!
GRML
AH, HERE'S OUR PATIENT, CHICK-O!
PFFT
HELLO!
HELLO!
SO, MRS. TROUBLED, WE'RE GOING TO TEST FOR ALLERGIES AND...
CAN I SMOKE?
UH, YES...
NO FEAR, CHICK-O, WE'RE GONNA SCRATCH YOUR BACK WITH A LITTLE NEEDLE!
30

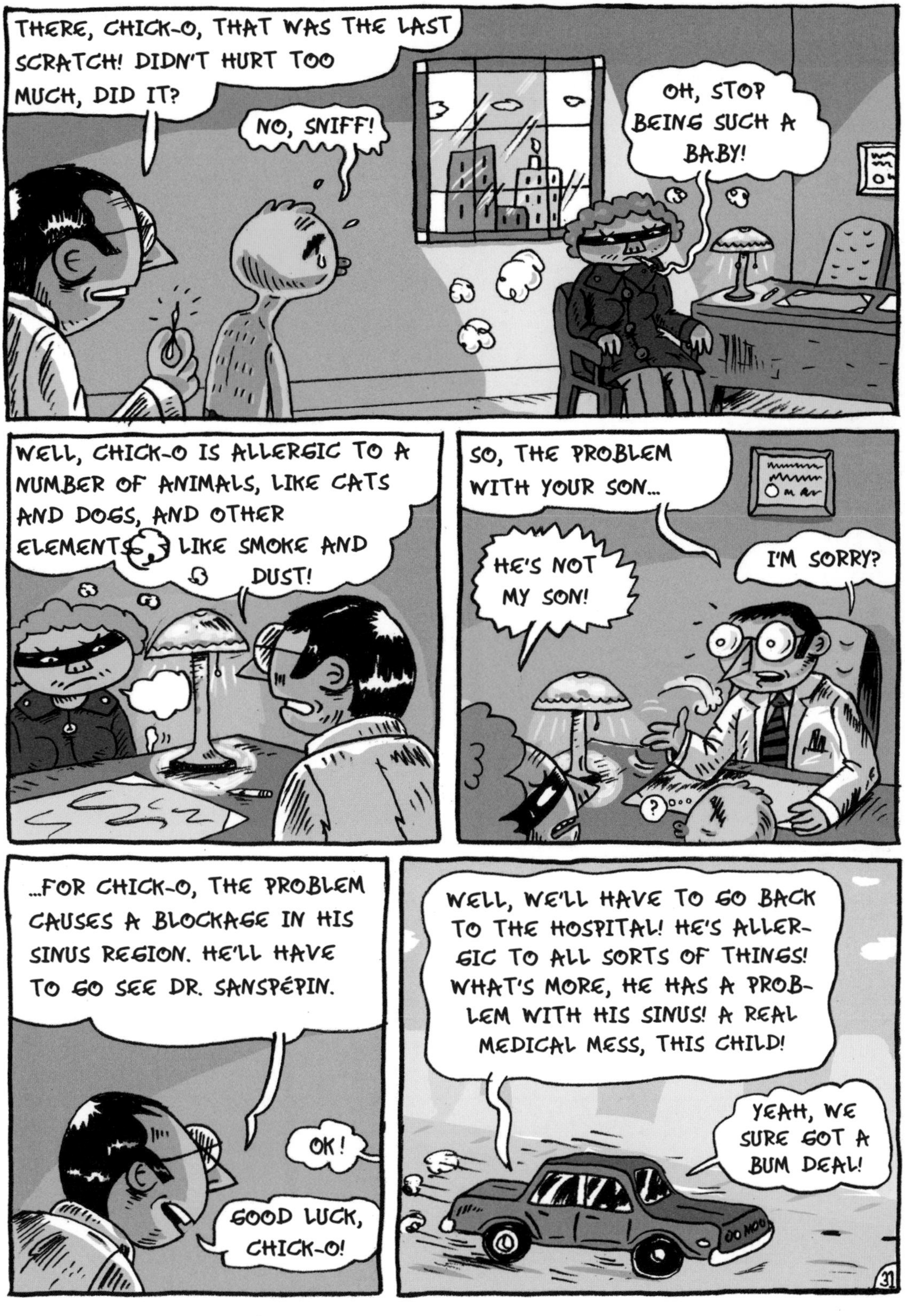
THERE, CHICK-O, THAT WAS THE LAST SCRATCH! DIDN'T HURT TOO MUCH, DID IT?
NO, SNIFF!
OH, STOP BEING SUCH A BABY!
WELL, CHICK-O IS ALLERGIC TO A NUMBER OF ANIMALS, LIKE CATS AND DOGS, AND OTHER ELEMENTS, LIKE SMOKE AND DUST!
SO, THE PROBLEM WITH YOUR SON...
HE'S NOT MY SON!
I'M SORRY?
...FOR CHICK-O, THE PROBLEM CAUSES A BLOCKAGE IN HIS SINUS REGION. HE'LL HAVE TO GO SEE DR. SANSPÉPIN.
OK!
GOOD LUCK, CHICK-O!
WELL, WE'LL HAVE TO GO BACK TO THE HOSPITAL! HE'S ALLER-GIC TO ALL SORTS OF THINGS! WHAT'S MORE, HE HAS A PROB-LEM WITH HIS SINUS! A REAL MEDICAL MESS, THIS CHILD!
YEAH, WE SURE GOT A BUM DEAL!
31

A FEW MONTHS LATER, CHICK-O GOES IN FOR HIS OPERATION.

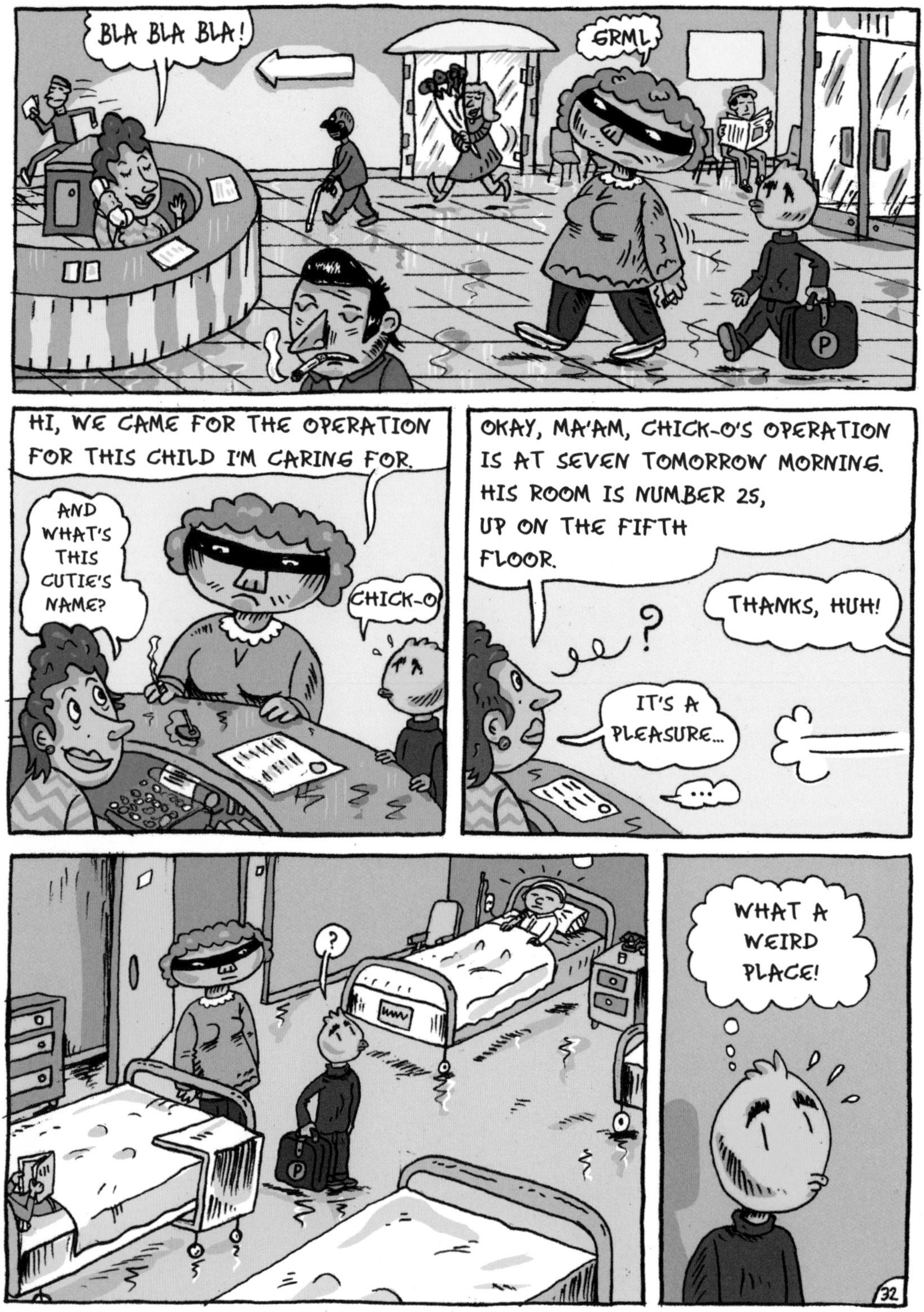
BLA BLA BLA!
GRML
HI, WE CAME FOR THE OPERATION FOR THIS CHILD I'M CARING FOR.
AND WHAT'S THIS CUTIE'S NAME?
CHICK-O
OKAY, MA'AM, CHICK-O'S OPERATION IS AT SEVEN TOMORROW MORNING. HIS ROOM IS NUMBER 25, UP ON THE FIFTH FLOOR.
THANKS, HUH!
?
IT'S A PLEASURE...
...
?
WHAT A WEIRD PLACE!
32

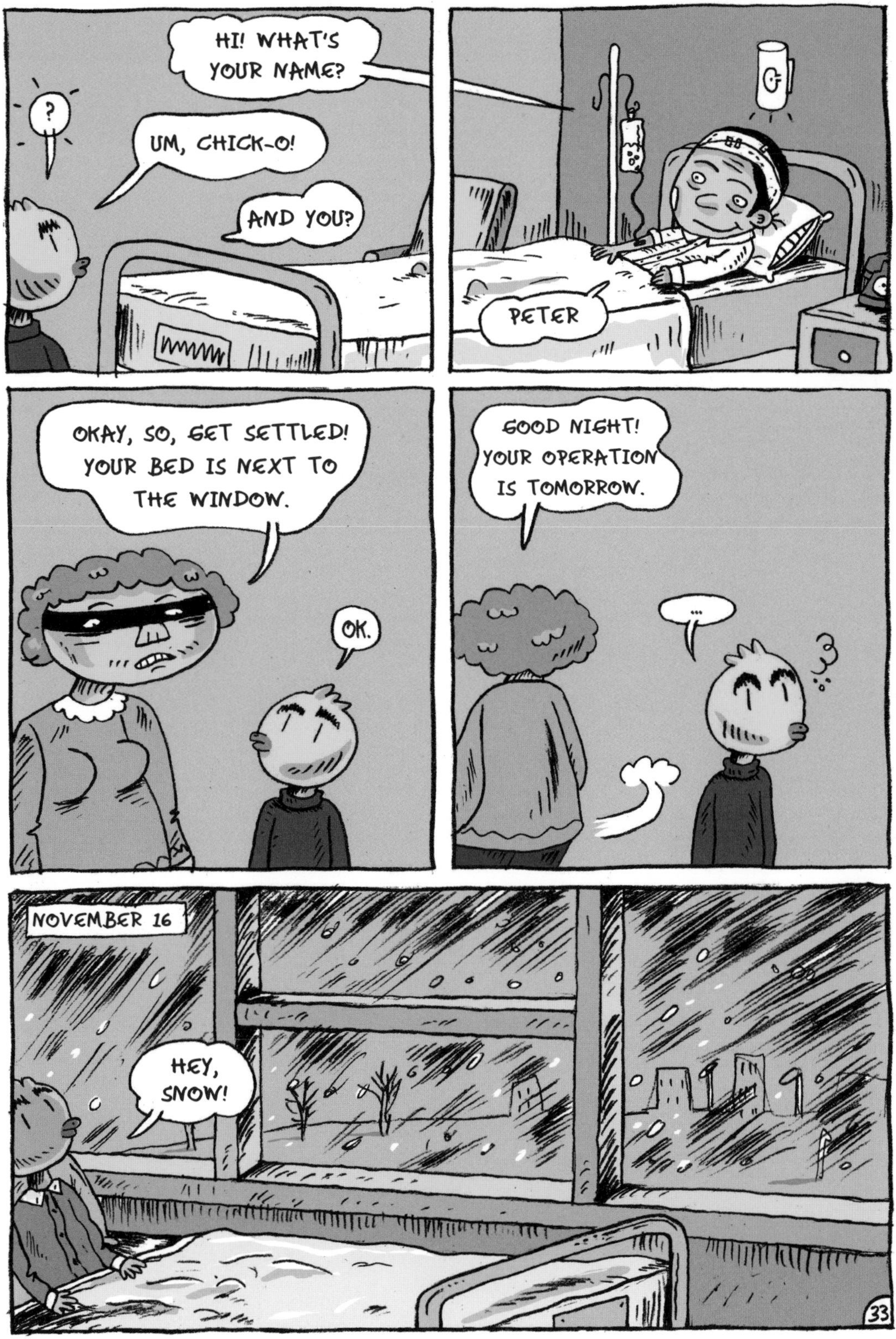

?
HI! WHAT'S YOUR NAME?
UM, CHICK-O!
AND YOU?
PETER
OKAY, SO, GET SETTLED! YOUR BED IS NEXT TO THE WINDOW.
OK.
GOOD NIGHT! YOUR OPERATION IS TOMORROW.
...
NOVEMBER 16
HEY, SNOW!
33

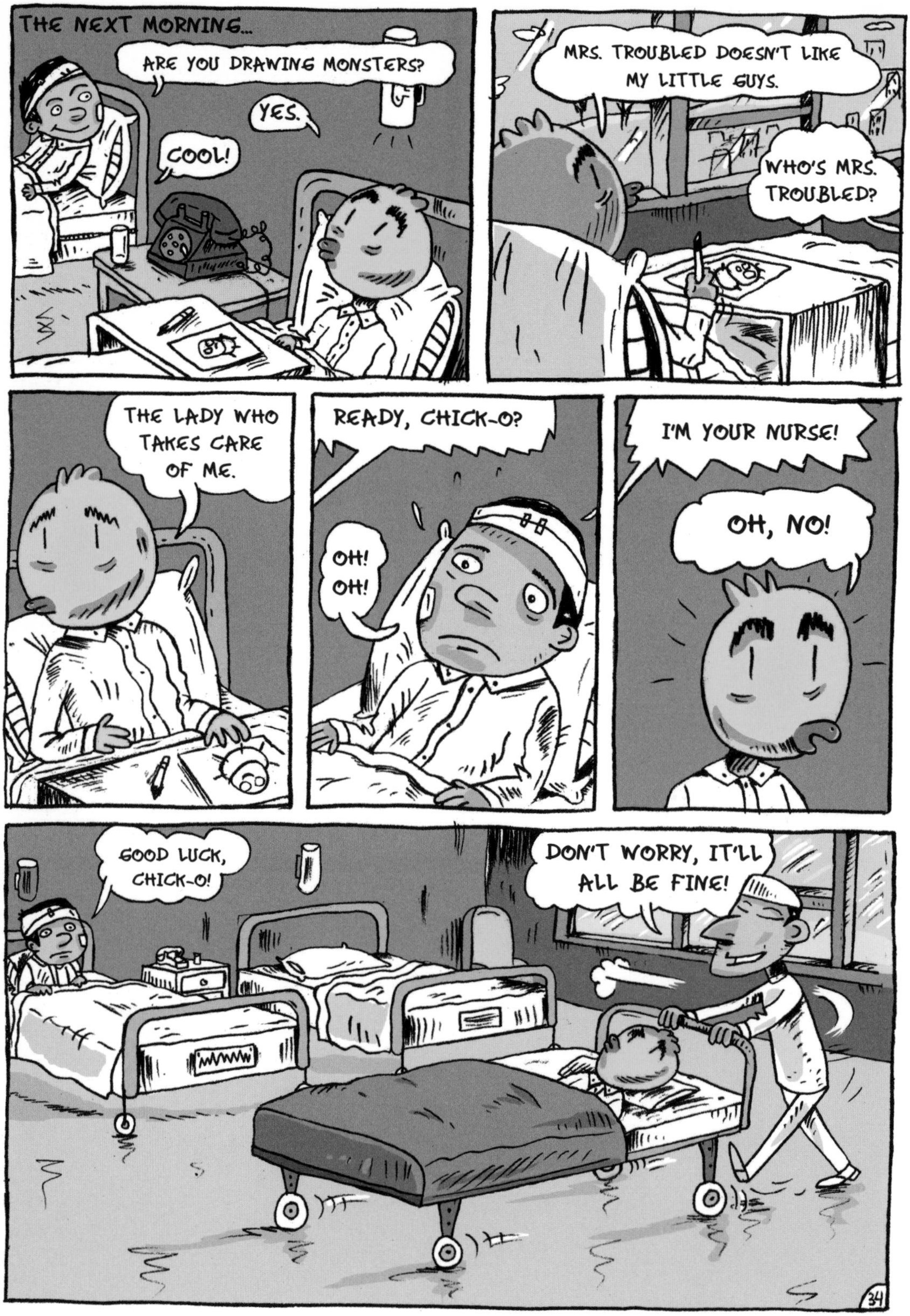
THE NEXT MORNING...
ARE YOU DRAWING MONSTERS?
YES.
COOL!
MRS. TROUBLED DOESN'T LIKE MY LITTLE GUYS.
WHO'S MRS. TROUBLED?
THE LADY WHO TAKES CARE OF ME.
READY, CHICK-O?
OH! OH!
I'M YOUR NURSE!
OH, NO!
GOOD LUCK, CHICK-O!
DON'T WORRY, IT'LL ALL BE FINE!
34

WHAT'S THIS WEIRD TUBE?
SO, IS OUR LITTLE PATIENT AWAKE?
UH, WHERE... AM I... MA'AM?
YOU'RE IN THE RECOVERY ROOM!
WHAT'D THEY DO TO ME?
35

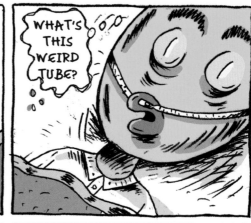

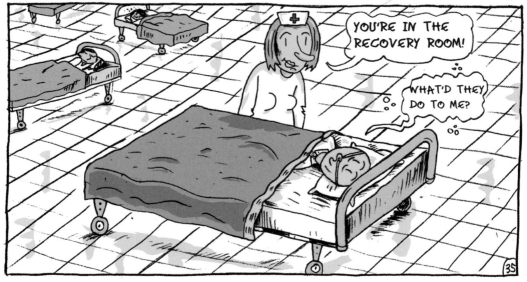

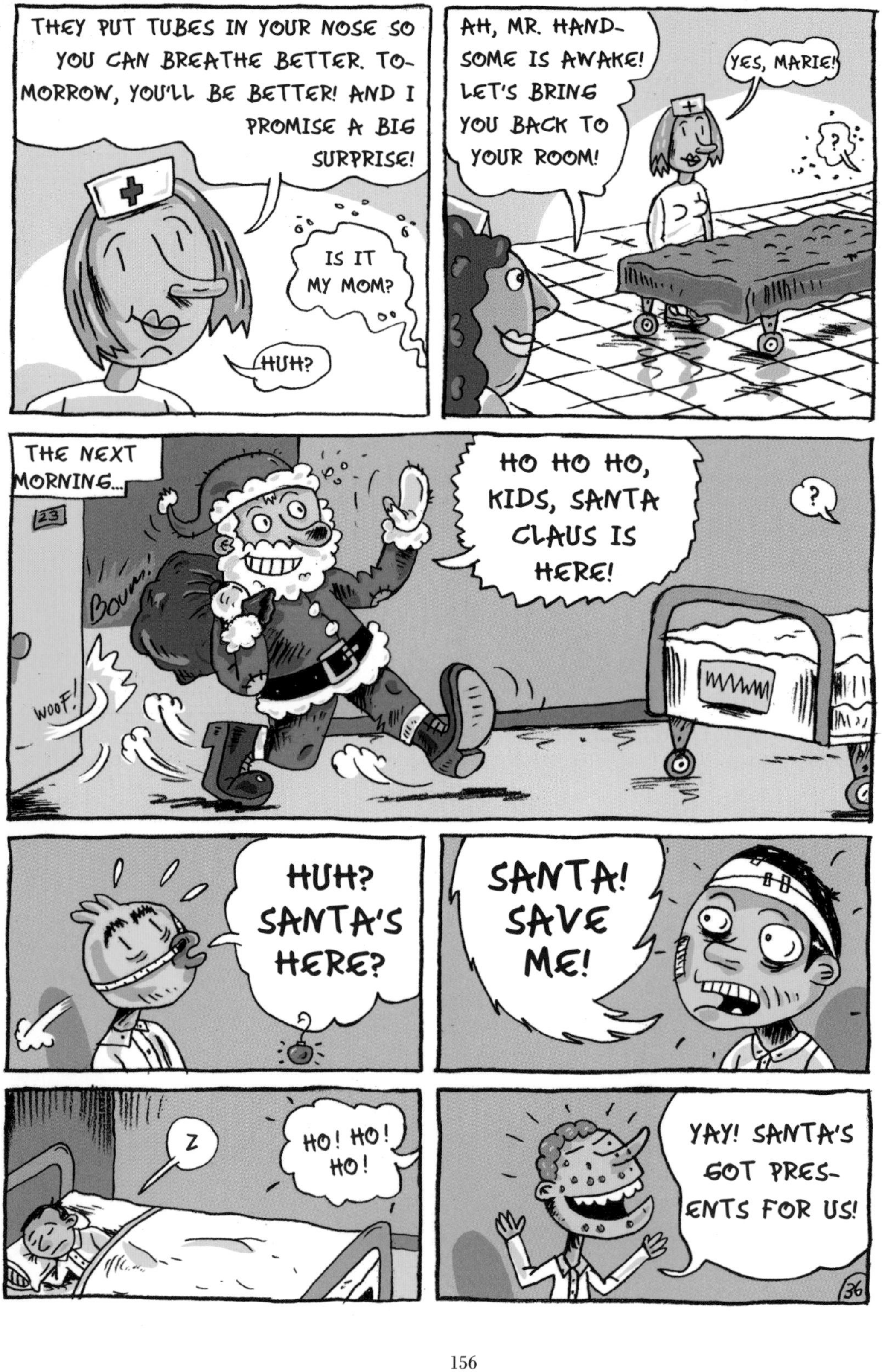
THEY PUT TUBES IN YOUR NOSE SO YOU CAN BREATHE BETTER. TO-MORROW, YOU'LL BE BETTER! AND I PROMISE A BIG SURPRISE!
IS IT MY MOM?
HUH?
AH, MR. HAND-SOME IS AWAKE! LET'S BRING YOU BACK TO YOUR ROOM!
YES, MARIE!
?
THE NEXT MORNING...
23
BOUM!
WOOF!
HO HO HO, KIDS, SANTA CLAUS IS HERE!
?
HUH? SANTA'S HERE?
SANTA! SAVE ME!
Z
HO! HO! HO!
YAY! SANTA'S GOT PRES-ENTS FOR US!
36

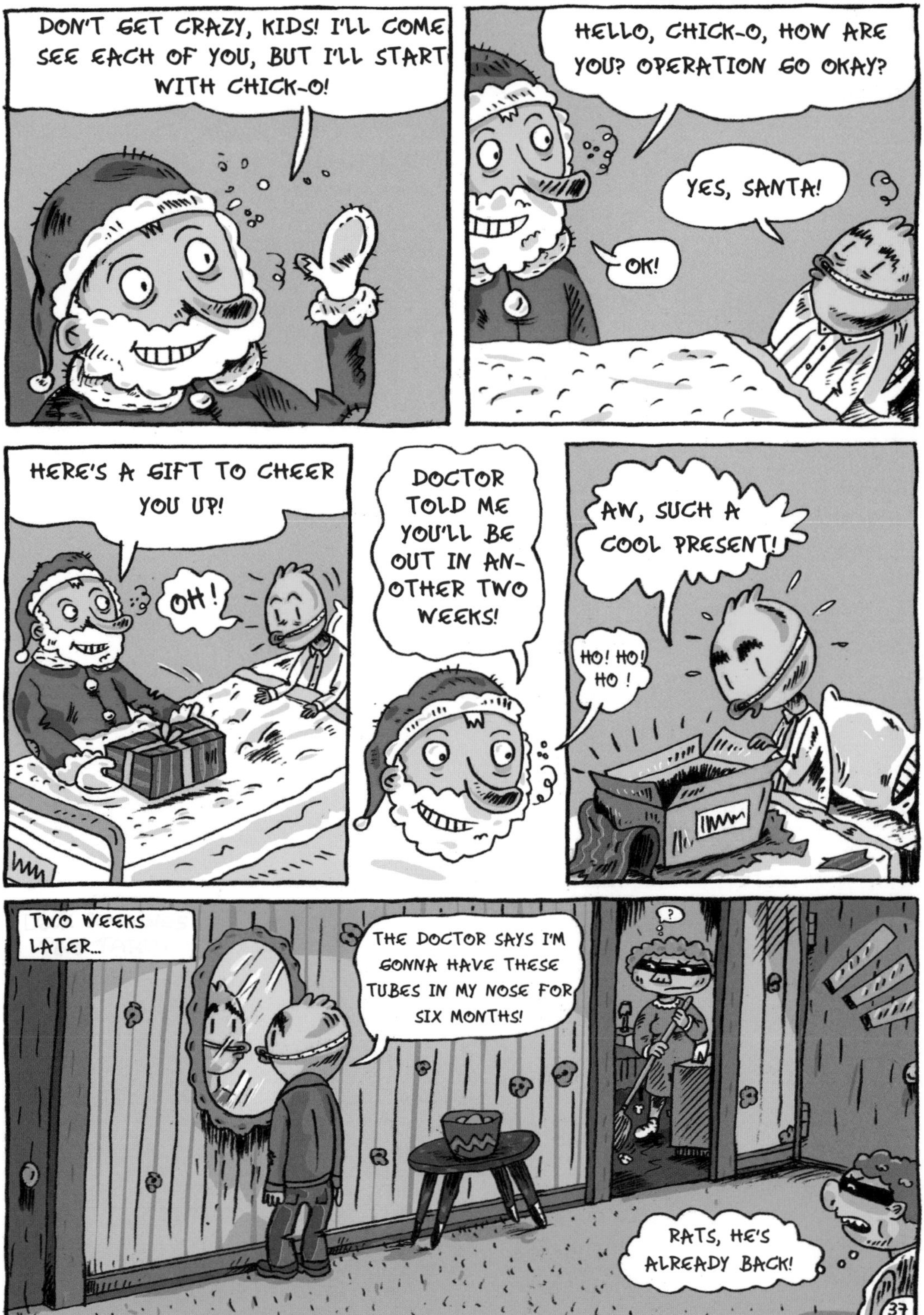
DON'T GET CRAZY, KIDS! I'LL COME SEE EACH OF YOU, BUT I'LL START WITH CHICK-O!
HELLO, CHICK-O, HOW ARE YOU? OPERATION GO OKAY?
YES, SANTA!
OK!
HERE'S A GIFT TO CHEER YOU UP!
OH!
DOCTOR TOLD ME YOU'LL BE OUT IN ANOTHER TWO WEEKS!
AW, SUCH A COOL PRESENT!
HO! HO! HO!
TWO WEEKS LATER...
THE DOCTOR SAYS I'M GONNA HAVE THESE TUBES IN MY NOSE FOR SIX MONTHS!
?
RATS, HE'S ALREADY BACK!
37

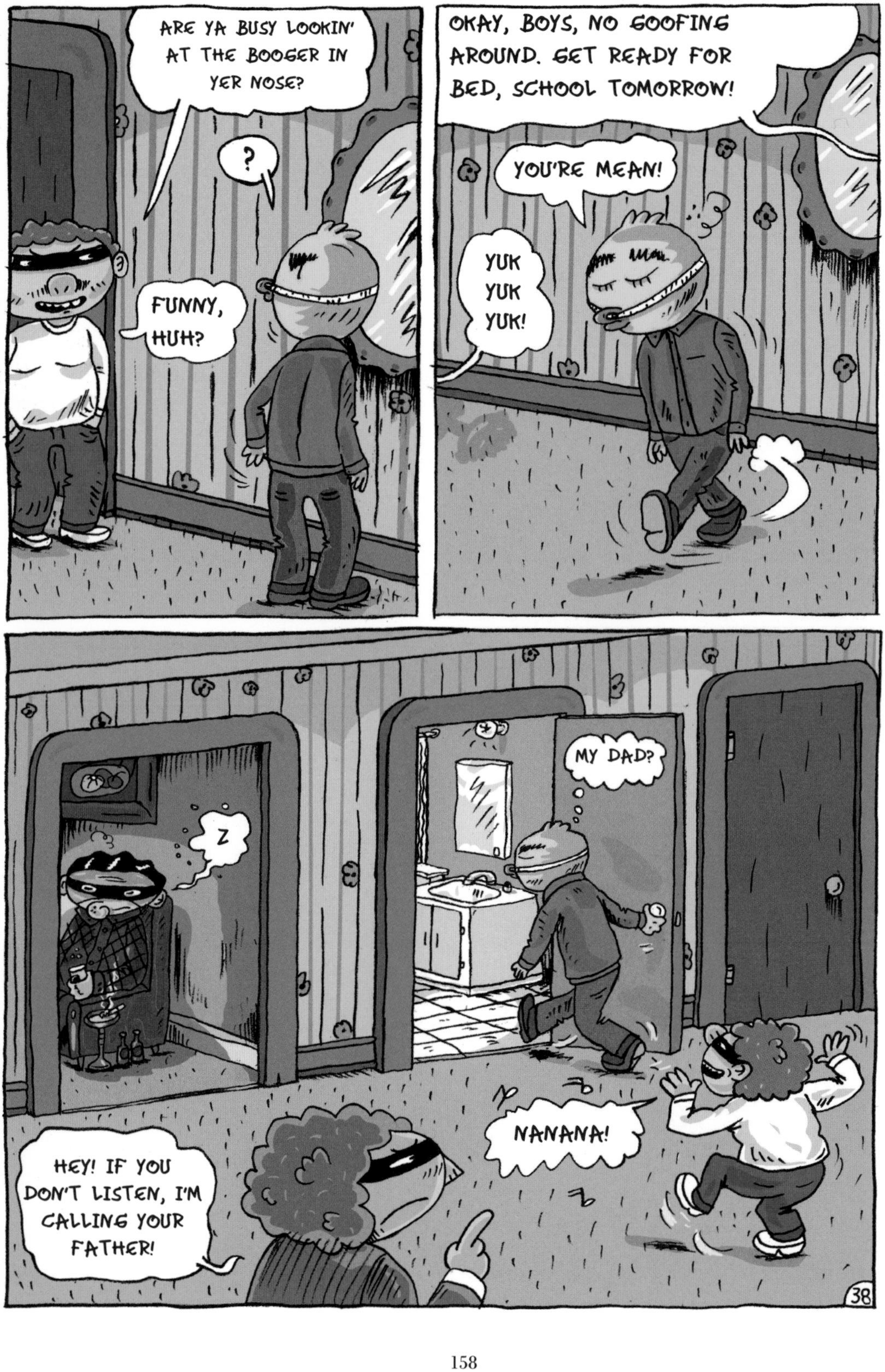
ARE YA BUSY LOOKIN' AT THE BOOGER IN YER NOSE?
?
FUNNY, HUH?
OKAY, BOYS, NO GOOFING AROUND. GET READY FOR BED, SCHOOL TOMORROW!
YOU'RE MEAN!
YUK YUK YUK!
Z
MY DAD?
HEY! IF YOU DON'T LISTEN, I'M CALLING YOUR FATHER!
NANANA!
38

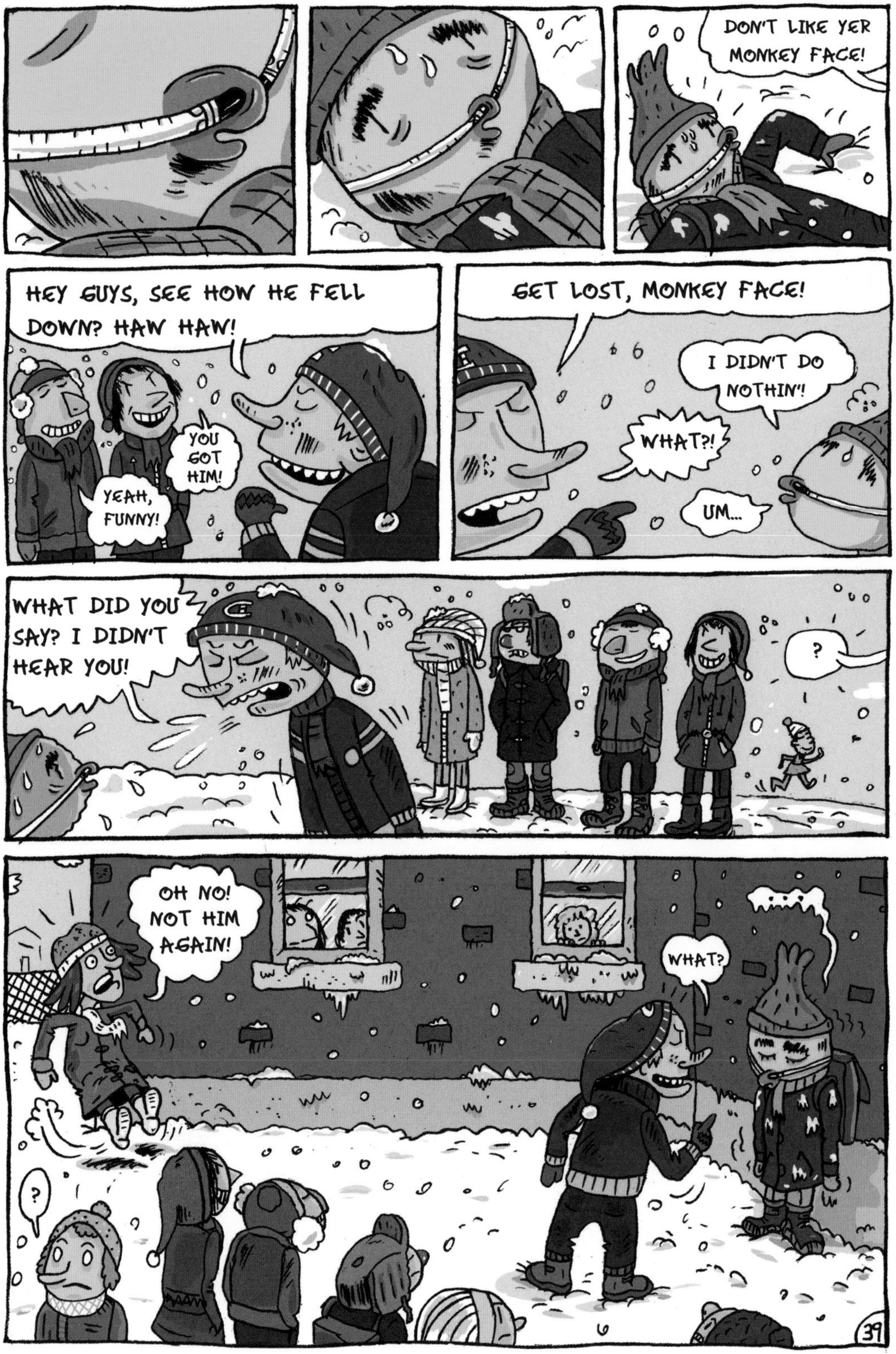
DON'T LIKE YER MONKEY FACE!
HEY GUYS, SEE HOW HE FELL DOWN? HAW HAW!
YOU GOT HIM!
YEAH, FUNNY!
GET LOST, MONKEY FACE!
I DIDN'T DO NOTHIN'!
WHAT?!
UM...
WHAT DID YOU SAY? I DIDN'T HEAR YOU!
?
OH NO! NOT HIM AGAIN!
WHAT?
?
39

OUCH!

GOD, YOU'RE SUCH A JERK, BARRAIDE! YOU ALWAYS PICK ON THE LITTLE GUYS!

OW, YOU'RE HURTING ME!

AND WHAT, YOU'RE NOT HURTING OTHERS, YOUNG MAN?

IT AIN'T ME WHO STARTED IT, MA'AM!

TELL IT TO THE PRINCIPAL, BUSTER!

CHICK-O, YOU CAN GO TO CLASS, RECESS IS OVER!

PHEW!

MAN, THAT SUCKS! BARRAIDE IS GONNA GET DETENTION!

YA, THAT SUCKS!

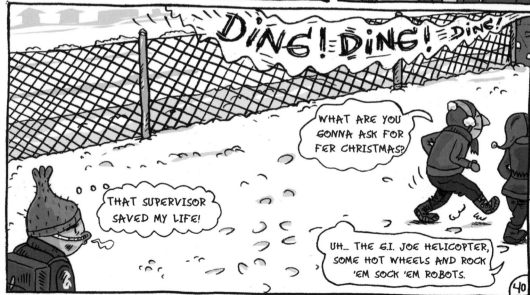

DING! DING! DING!

WHAT ARE YOU GONNA ASK FOR FER CHRISTMAS?

THAT SUPERVISOR SAVED MY LIFE!

UH... THE G.I. JOE HELICOPTER, SOME HOT WHEELS AND ROCK 'EM SOCK 'EM ROBOTS.

40

41

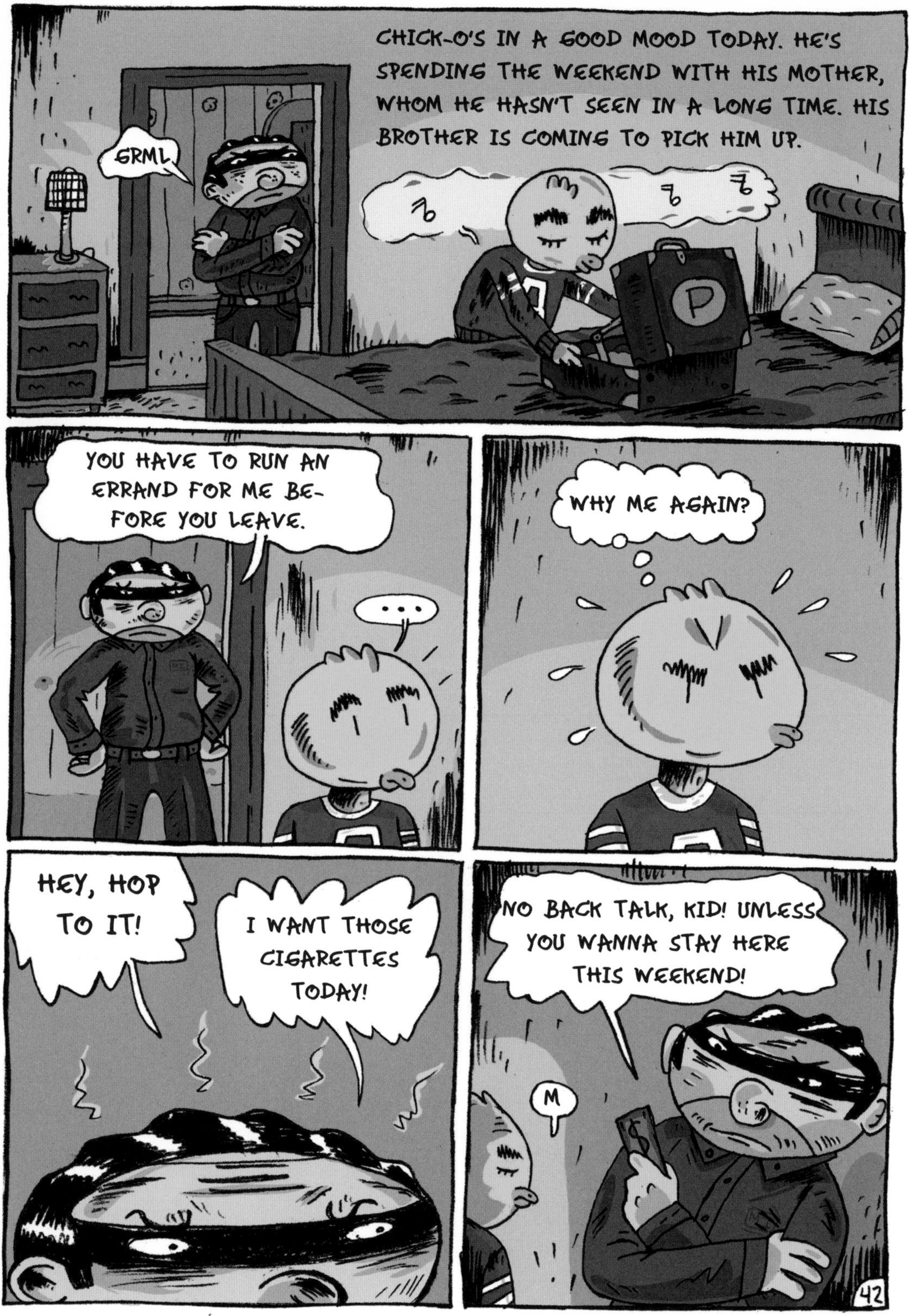
CHICK-O'S IN A GOOD MOOD TODAY. HE'S SPENDING THE WEEKEND WITH HIS MOTHER, WHOM HE HASN'T SEEN IN A LONG TIME. HIS BROTHER IS COMING TO PICK HIM UP.
GRML
Z
Z
Z
YOU HAVE TO RUN AN ERRAND FOR ME BE-FORE YOU LEAVE.
...
WHY ME AGAIN?
HEY, HOP TO IT!
I WANT THOSE CIGARETTES TODAY!
NO BACK TALK, KID! UNLESS YOU WANNA STAY HERE THIS WEEKEND!
M
42

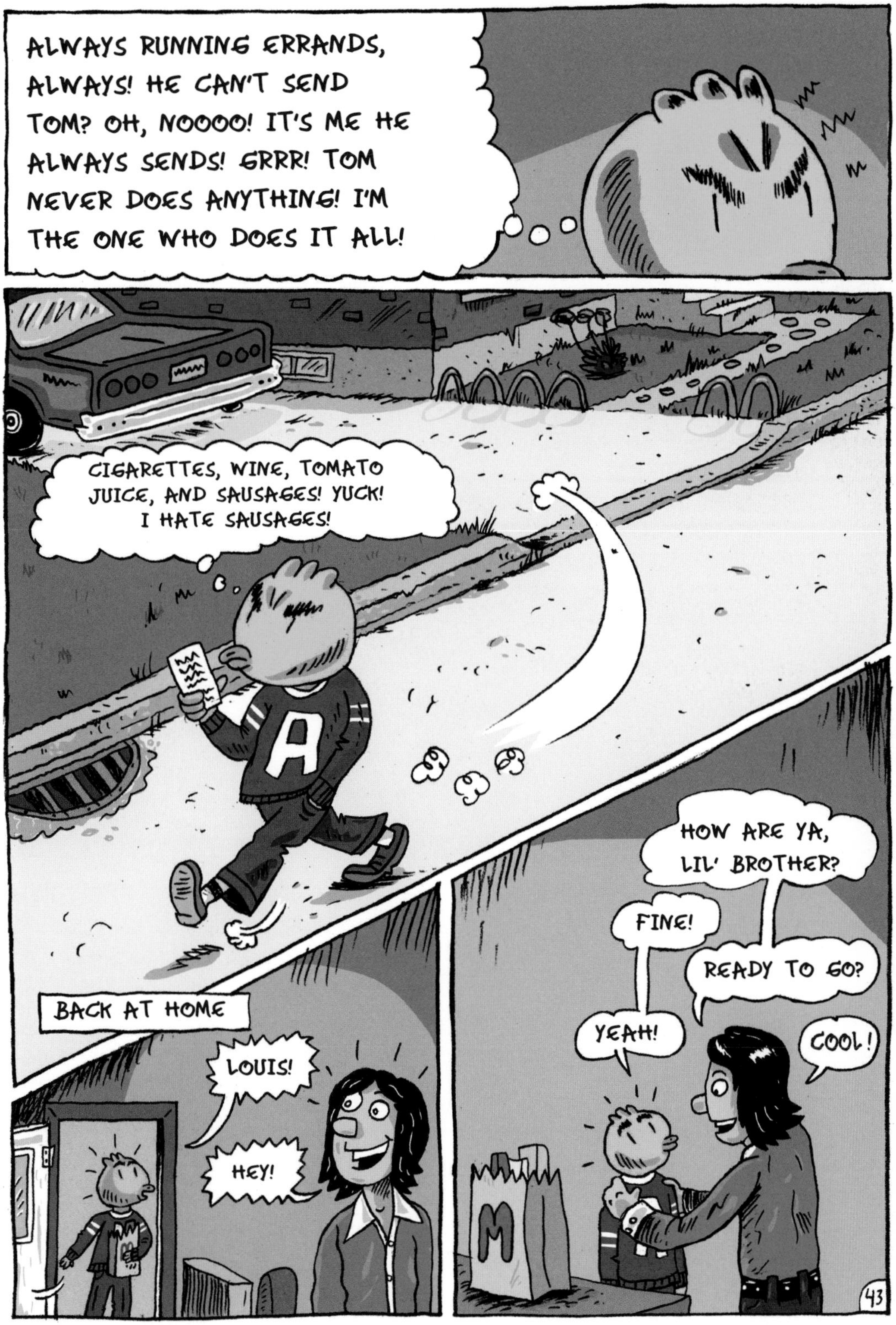
ALWAYS RUNNING ERRANDS, ALWAYS! HE CAN'T SEND TOM? OH, NOOOO! IT'S ME HE ALWAYS SENDS! GRRR! TOM NEVER DOES ANYTHING! I'M THE ONE WHO DOES IT ALL!
CIGARETTES, WINE, TOMATO JUICE, AND SAUSAGES! YUCK! I HATE SAUSAGES!
BACK AT HOME
LOUIS!
HEY!
HOW ARE YA, LIL' BROTHER?
FINE!
READY TO GO?
YEAH!
COOL!
43

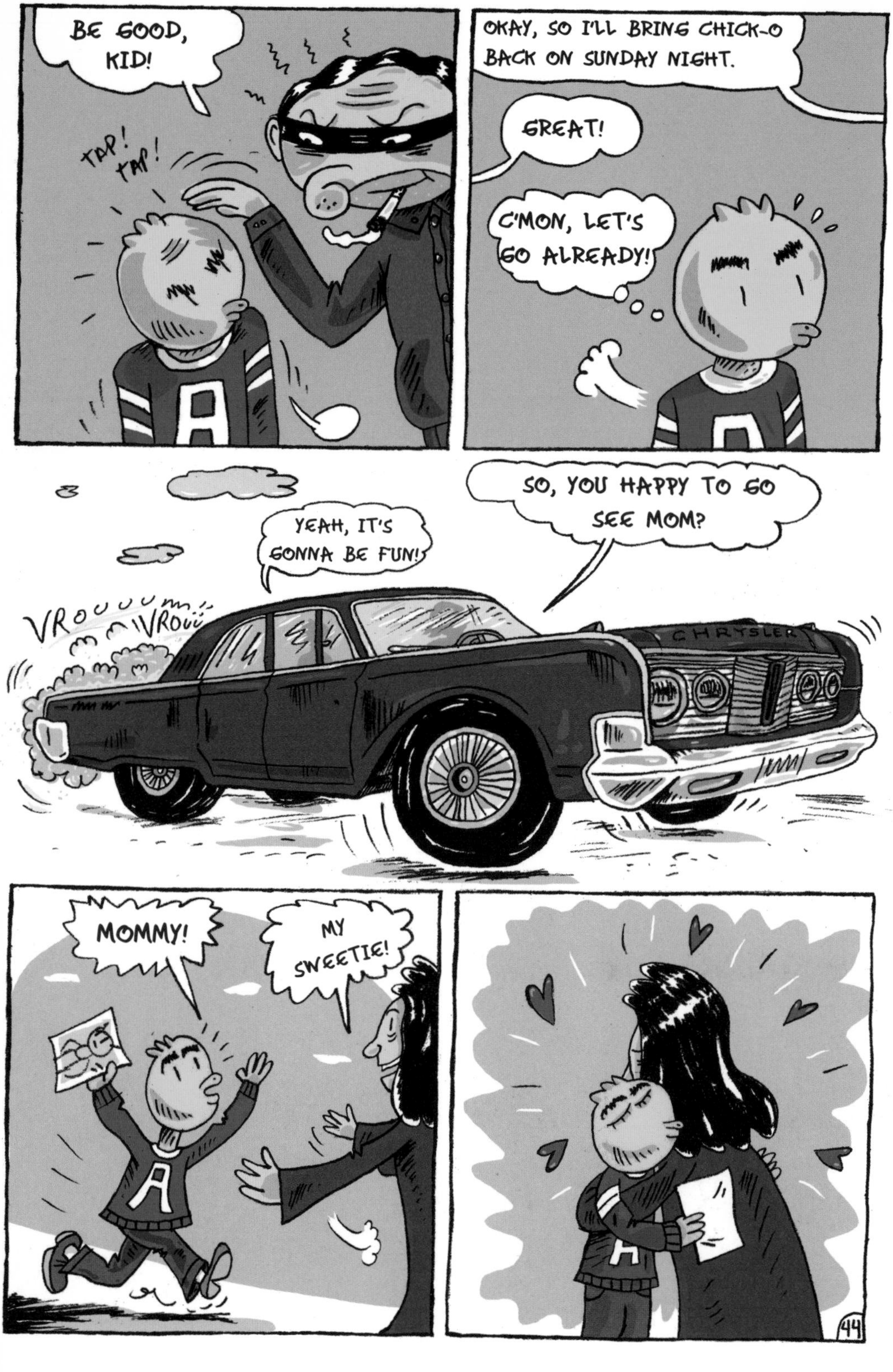
BE GOOD, KID!
TAP! TAP!
OKAY, SO I'LL BRING CHICK-O BACK ON SUNDAY NIGHT.
GREAT!
C'MON, LET'S GO ALREADY!
SO, YOU HAPPY TO GO SEE MOM?
YEAH, IT'S GONNA BE FUN!
VROOOOOM... VROUU
CHRYSLER
MOMMY!
MY SWEETIE!
44

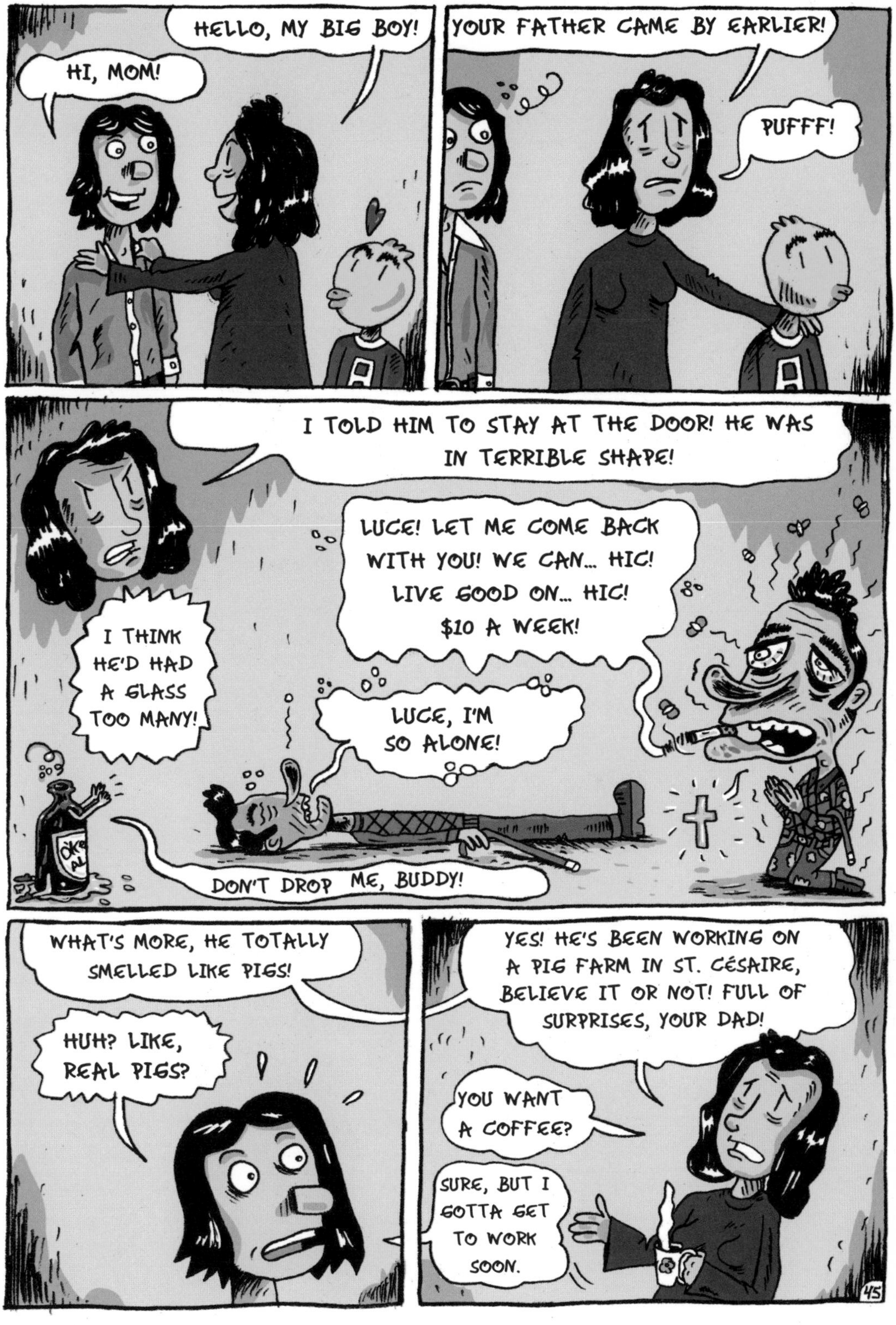
HI, MOM!
HELLO, MY BIG BOY!
YOUR FATHER CAME BY EARLIER!
PUFFF!
I TOLD HIM TO STAY AT THE DOOR! HE WAS IN TERRIBLE SHAPE!
I THINK HE'D HAD A GLASS TOO MANY!
LUCE! LET ME COME BACK WITH YOU! WE CAN... HIC! LIVE GOOD ON... HIC! $10 A WEEK!
LUCE, I'M SO ALONE!
DON'T DROP ME, BUDDY!
WHAT'S MORE, HE TOTALLY SMELLED LIKE PIGS!
HUH? LIKE, REAL PIGS?
YES! HE'S BEEN WORKING ON A PIG FARM IN ST. CÉSAIRE, BELIEVE IT OR NOT! FULL OF SURPRISES, YOUR DAD!
YOU WANT A COFFEE?
SURE, BUT I GOTTA GET TO WORK SOON.
45

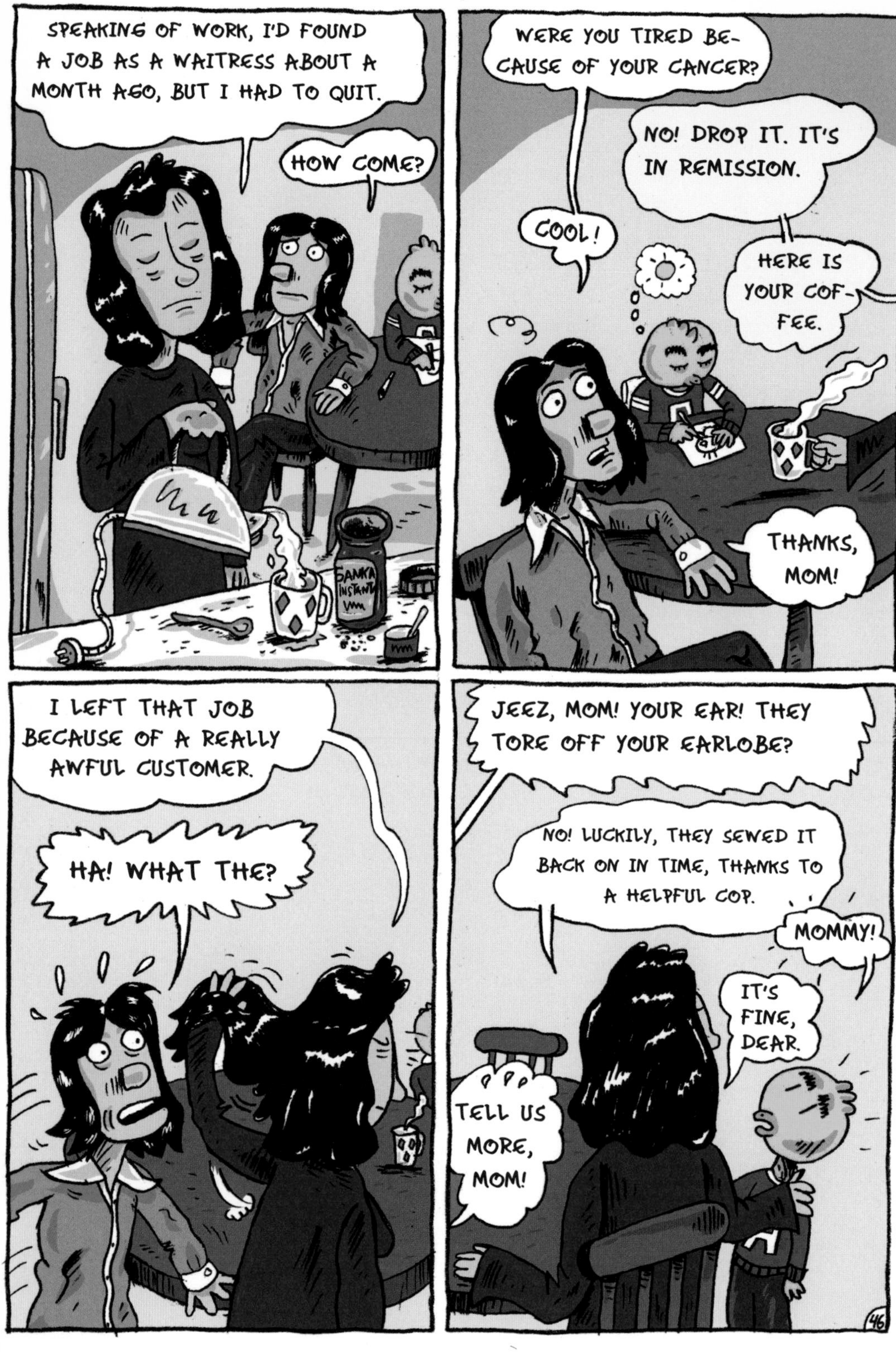

SPEAKING OF WORK, I'D FOUND A JOB AS A WAITRESS ABOUT A MONTH AGO, BUT I HAD TO QUIT.
HOW COME?
SANKA INSTANT
WERE YOU TIRED BE-CAUSE OF YOUR CANCER?
NO! DROP IT. IT'S IN REMISSION.
COOL!
HERE IS YOUR COF-FEE.
THANKS, MOM!
I LEFT THAT JOB BECAUSE OF A REALLY AWFUL CUSTOMER.
HA! WHAT THE?
JEEZ, MOM! YOUR EAR! THEY TORE OFF YOUR EARLOBE?
NO! LUCKILY, THEY SEWED IT BACK ON IN TIME, THANKS TO A HELPFUL COP.
MOMMY!
IT'S FINE, DEAR.
TELL US MORE, MOM!
46

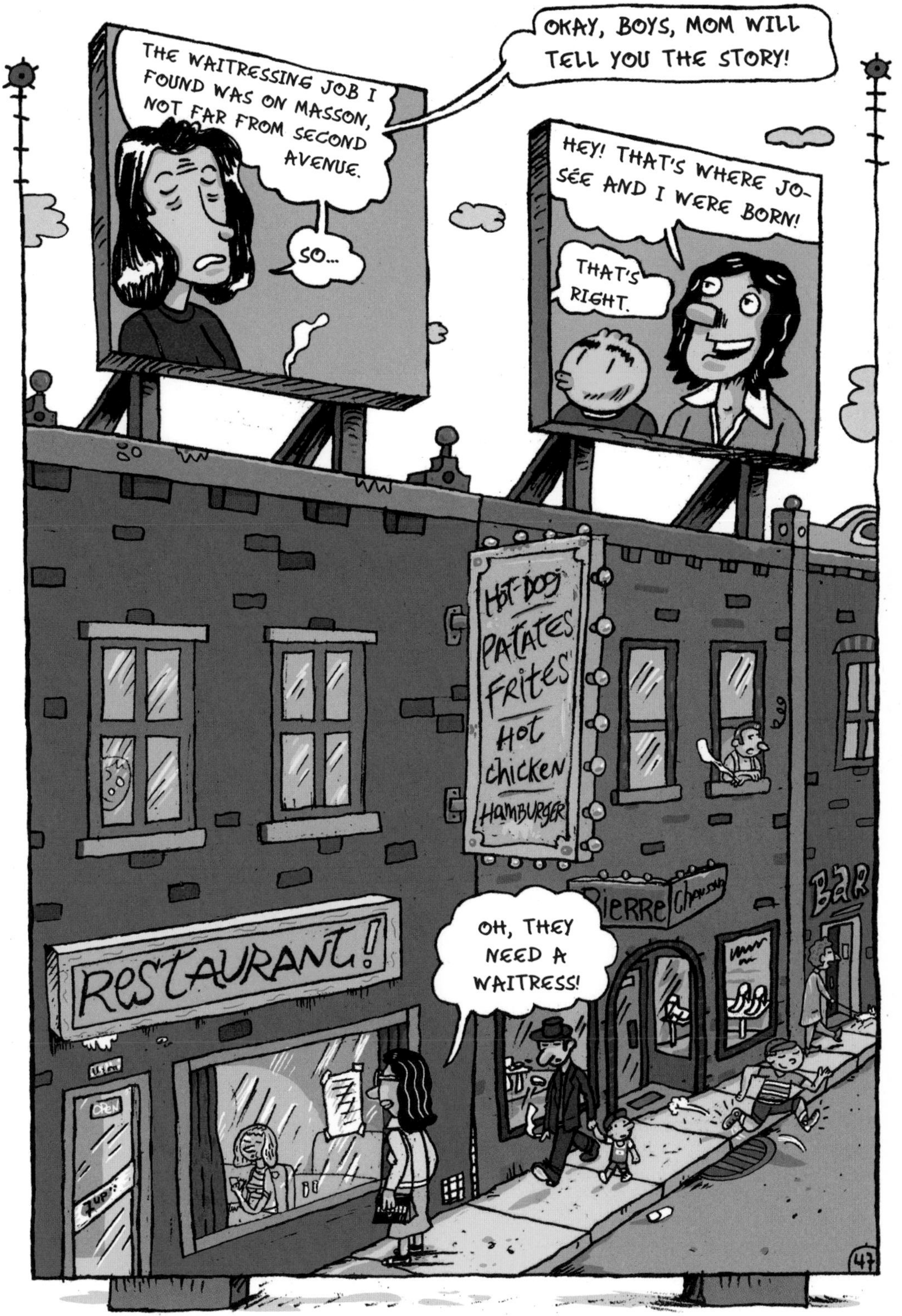
THE WAITRESSING JOB I FOUND WAS ON MASSON, NOT FAR FROM SECOND AVENUE.
OKAY, BOYS, MOM WILL TELL YOU THE STORY!
SO...
HEY! THAT'S WHERE JO-SÉE AND I WERE BORN!
THAT'S RIGHT.
HOT-DOG
PATATES FRITES
HOT CHICKEN
HAMBURGER
RESTAURANT!
Pierre
BAR
OH, THEY NEED A WAITRESS!
47

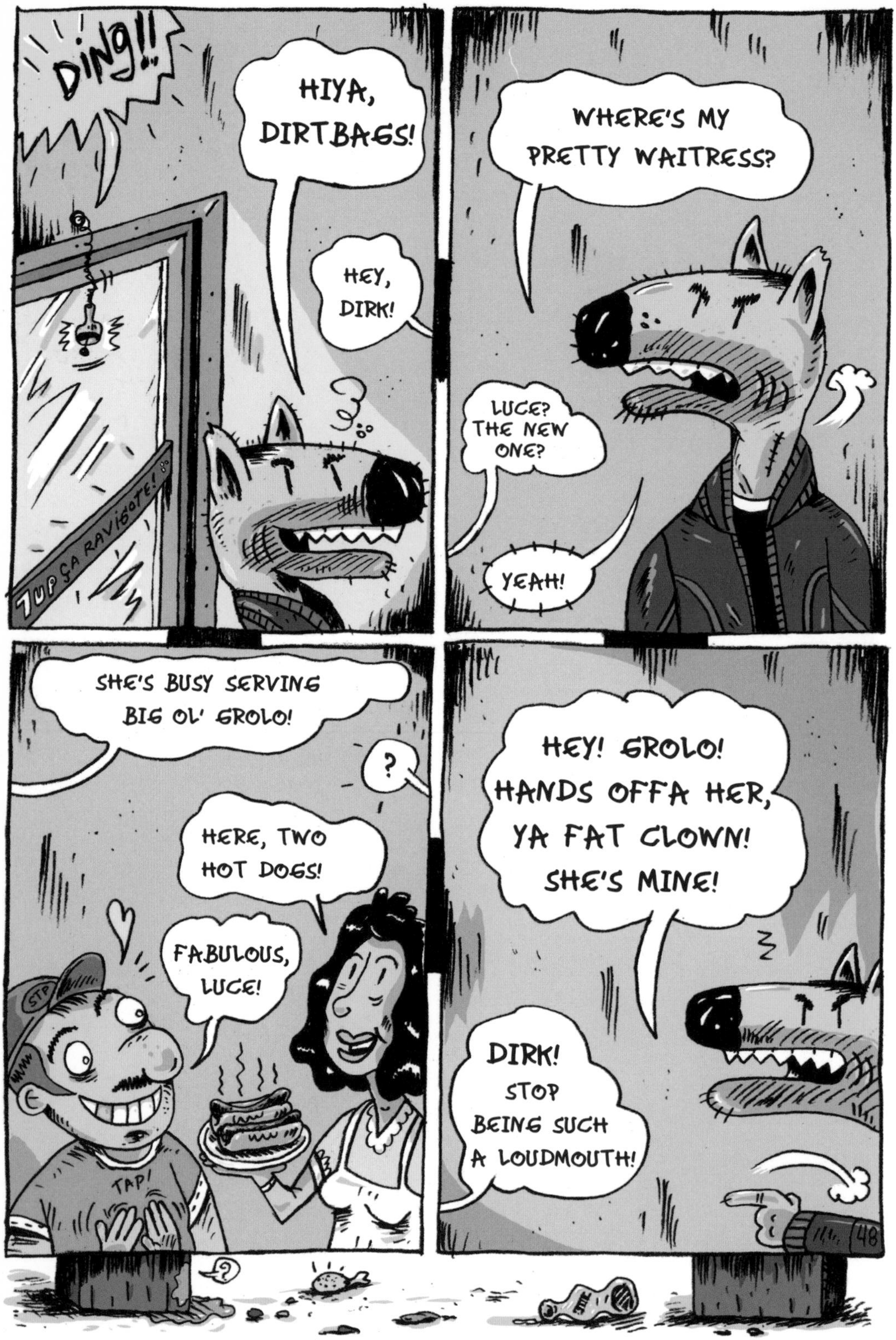
DING!!
HIYA, DIRTBAGS!
HEY, DIRK!
JUP ÇA RAVIGOTE!
WHERE'S MY PRETTY WAITRESS?
LUCE? THE NEW ONE?
YEAH!
SHE'S BUSY SERVING BIG OL' GROLO!
?
HERE, TWO HOT DOGS!
FABULOUS, LUCE!
STP
TAP!
HEY! GROLO! HANDS OFFA HER, YA FAT CLOWN! SHE'S MINE!
DIRK! STOP BEING SUCH A LOUDMOUTH!
48

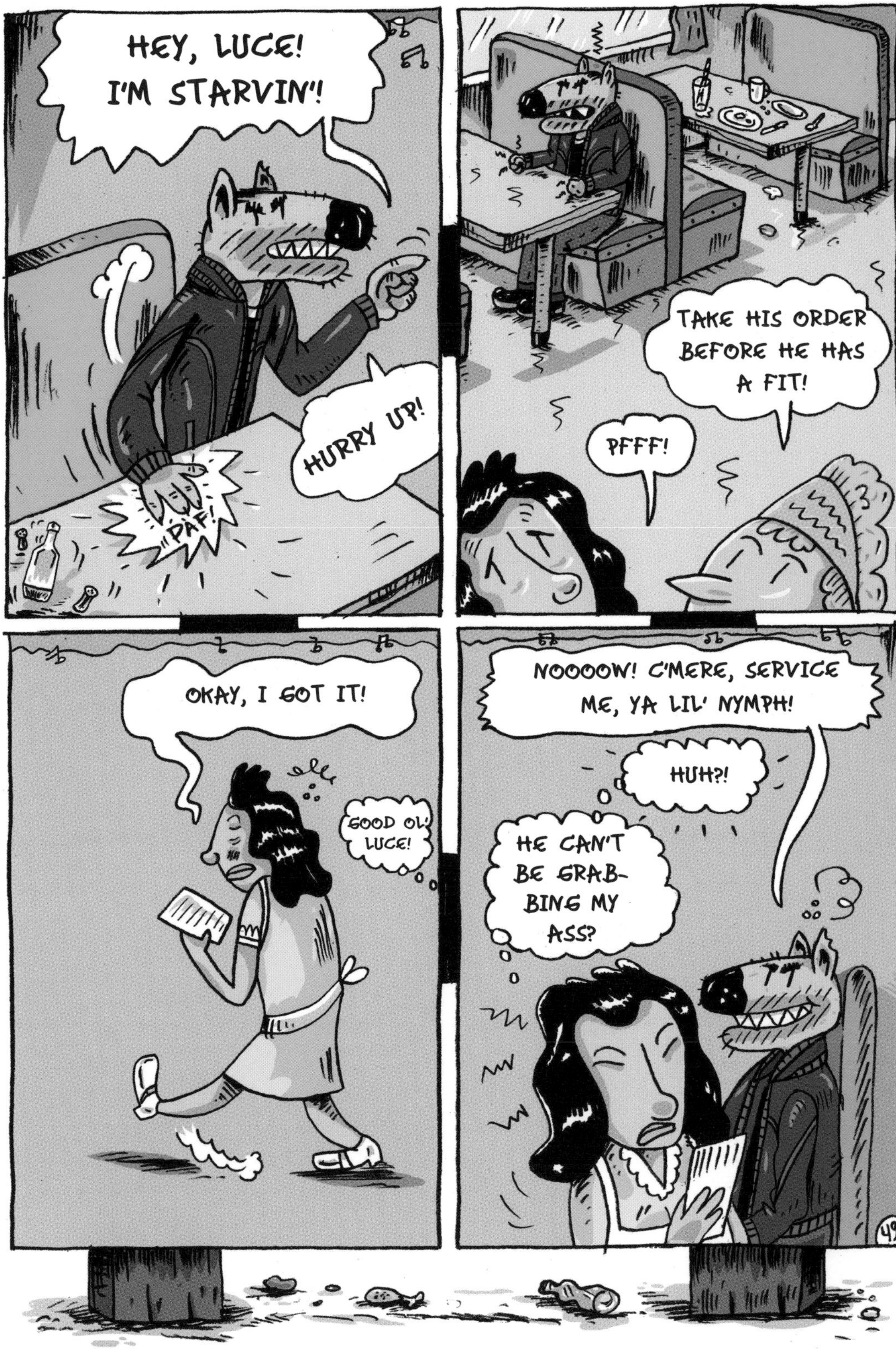
HEY, LUCE! I'M STARVIN'!
PAF!
HURRY UP!
TAKE HIS ORDER BEFORE HE HAS A FIT!
PFFF!
OKAY, I GOT IT!
GOOD OL' LUCE!
NOOOOW! C'MERE, SERVICE ME, YA LIL' NYMPH!
HUH?!
HE CAN'T BE GRAB-BING MY ASS?
49

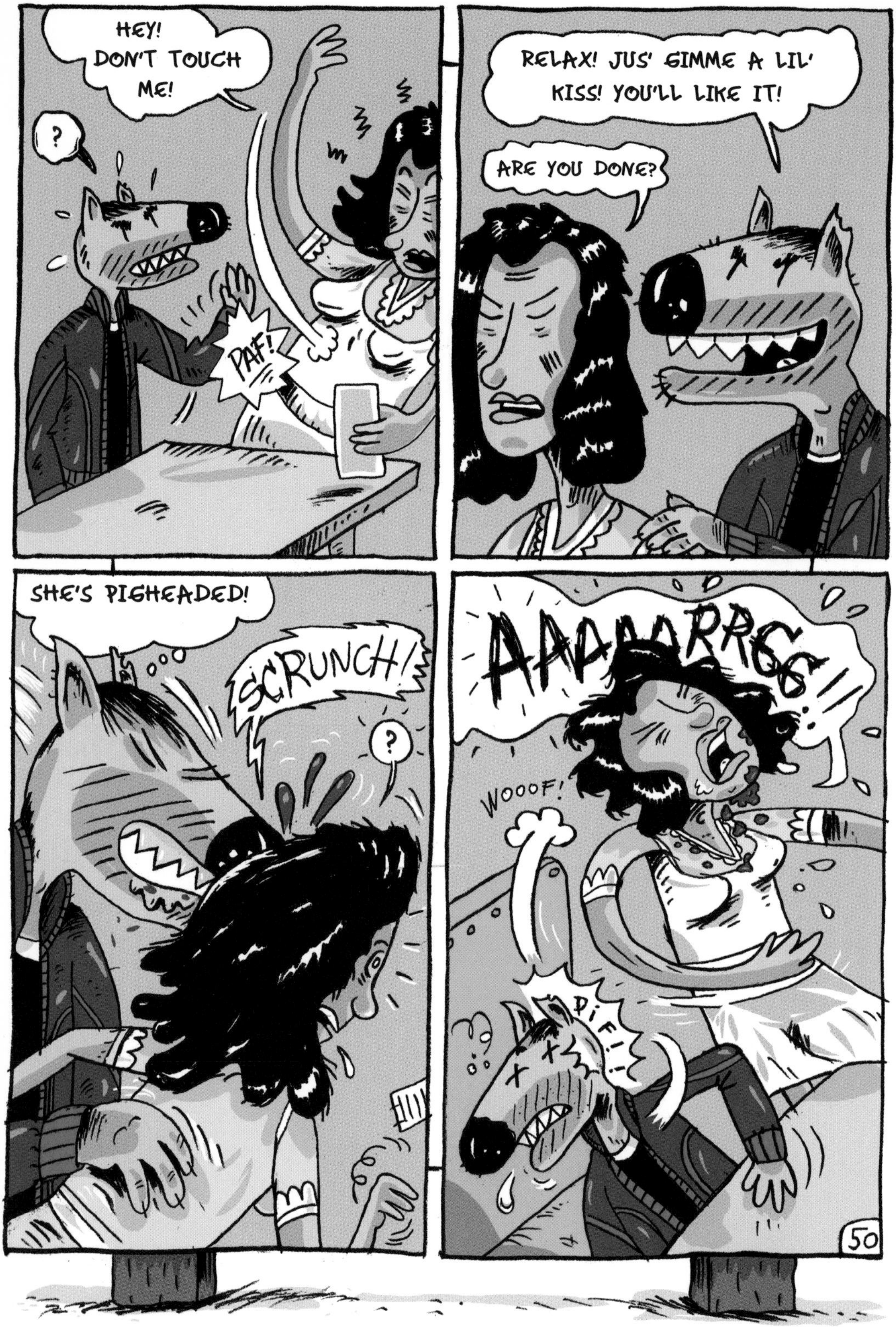
HEY! DON'T TOUCH ME!
?
PAF!
RELAX! JUS' GIMME A LIL' KISS! YOU'LL LIKE IT!
ARE YOU DONE?
SHE'S PIGHEADED!
SCRUNCH!
?
AAAAARRGG
WOOOF!
PIF!
50

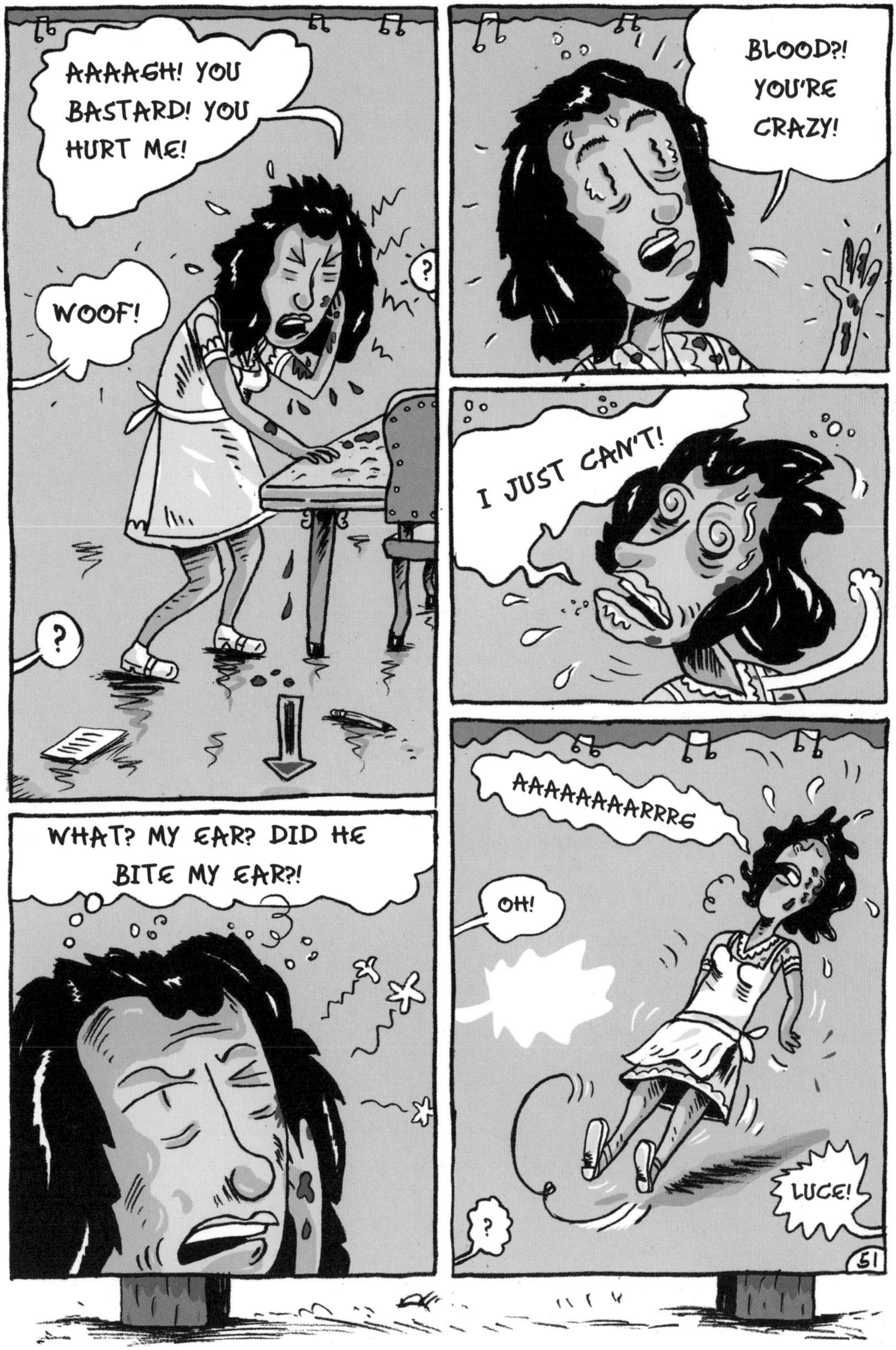
AAAAGH! YOU BASTARD! YOU HURT ME!
WOOF!
?
?
BLOOD?! YOU'RE CRAZY!
I JUST CAN'T!
WHAT? MY EAR? DID HE BITE MY EAR?!
AAAAAAAAARRRG
OH!
LUCE!
?
51

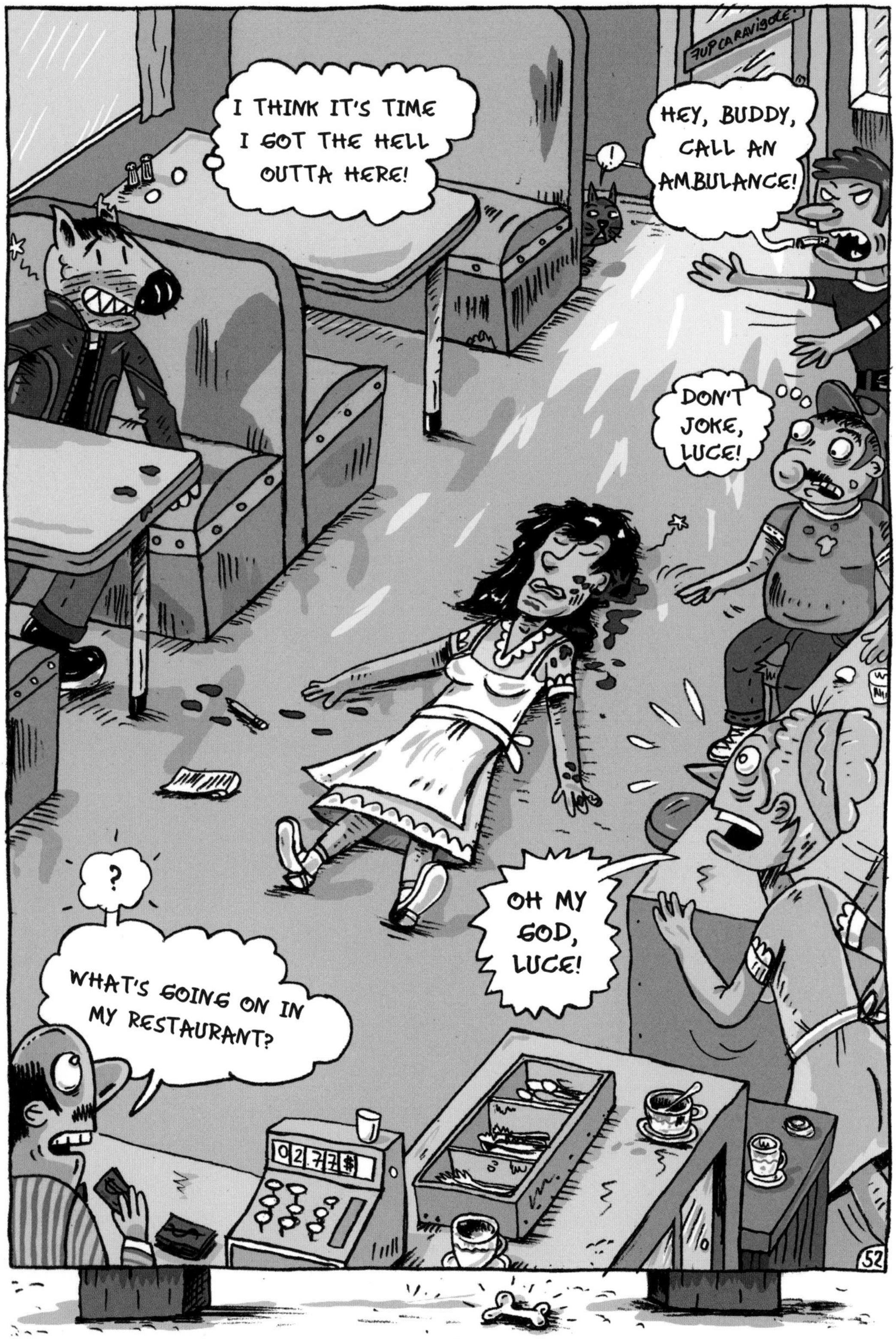
I THINK IT'S TIME I GOT THE HELL OUTTA HERE!
!
HEY, BUDDY, CALL AN AMBULANCE!
DON'T JOKE, LUCE!
OH MY GOD, LUCE!
?
WHAT'S GOING ON IN MY RESTAURANT?
52

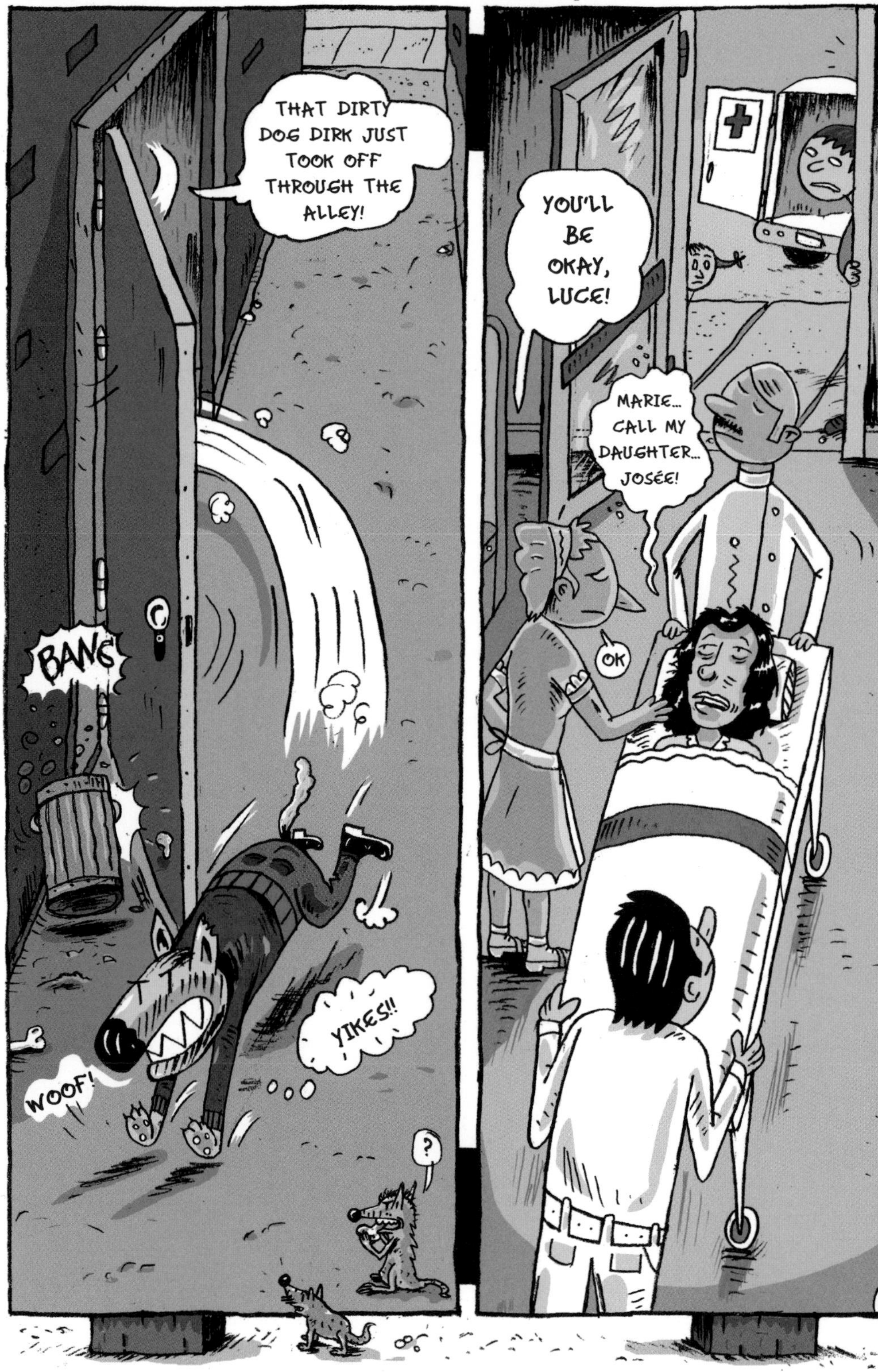
THAT DIRTY DOG DIRK JUST TOOK OFF THROUGH THE ALLEY!
BANG
YIKES!!
WOOF!
?
YOU'LL BE OKAY, LUCE!
MARIE... CALL MY DAUGHTER... JOSÉE!
OK
53

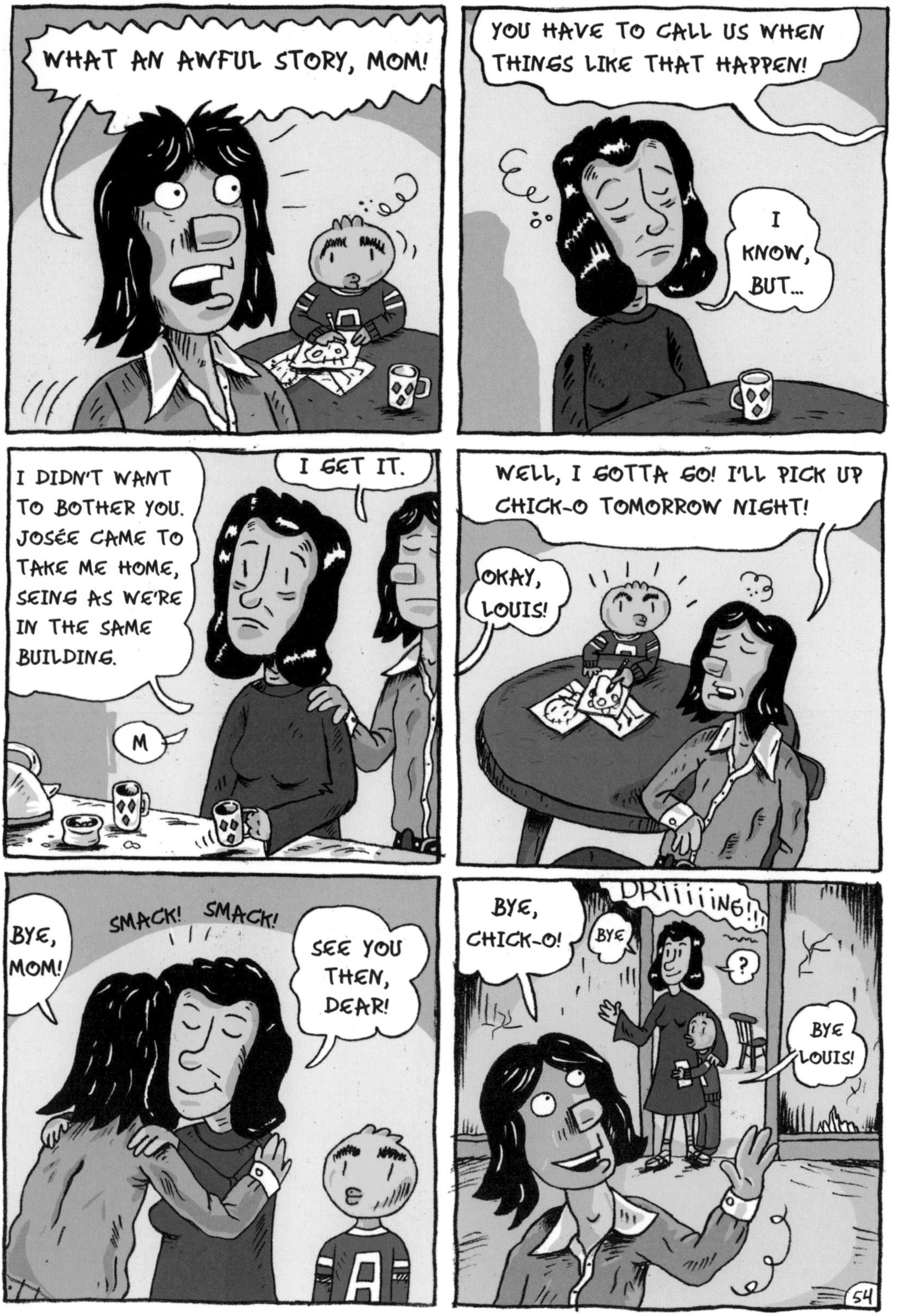
WHAT AN AWFUL STORY, MOM!
YOU HAVE TO CALL US WHEN THINGS LIKE THAT HAPPEN!
I KNOW, BUT...
I DIDN'T WANT TO BOTHER YOU. JOSÉE CAME TO TAKE ME HOME, SEING AS WE'RE IN THE SAME BUILDING.
I GET IT.
M
WELL, I GOTTA GO! I'LL PICK UP CHICK-O TOMORROW NIGHT!
OKAY, LOUIS!
BYE, MOM!
SMACK! SMACK!
SEE YOU THEN, DEAR!
BYE, CHICK-O!
DRIIIIING!!!
BYE
?
BYE LOUIS!
54

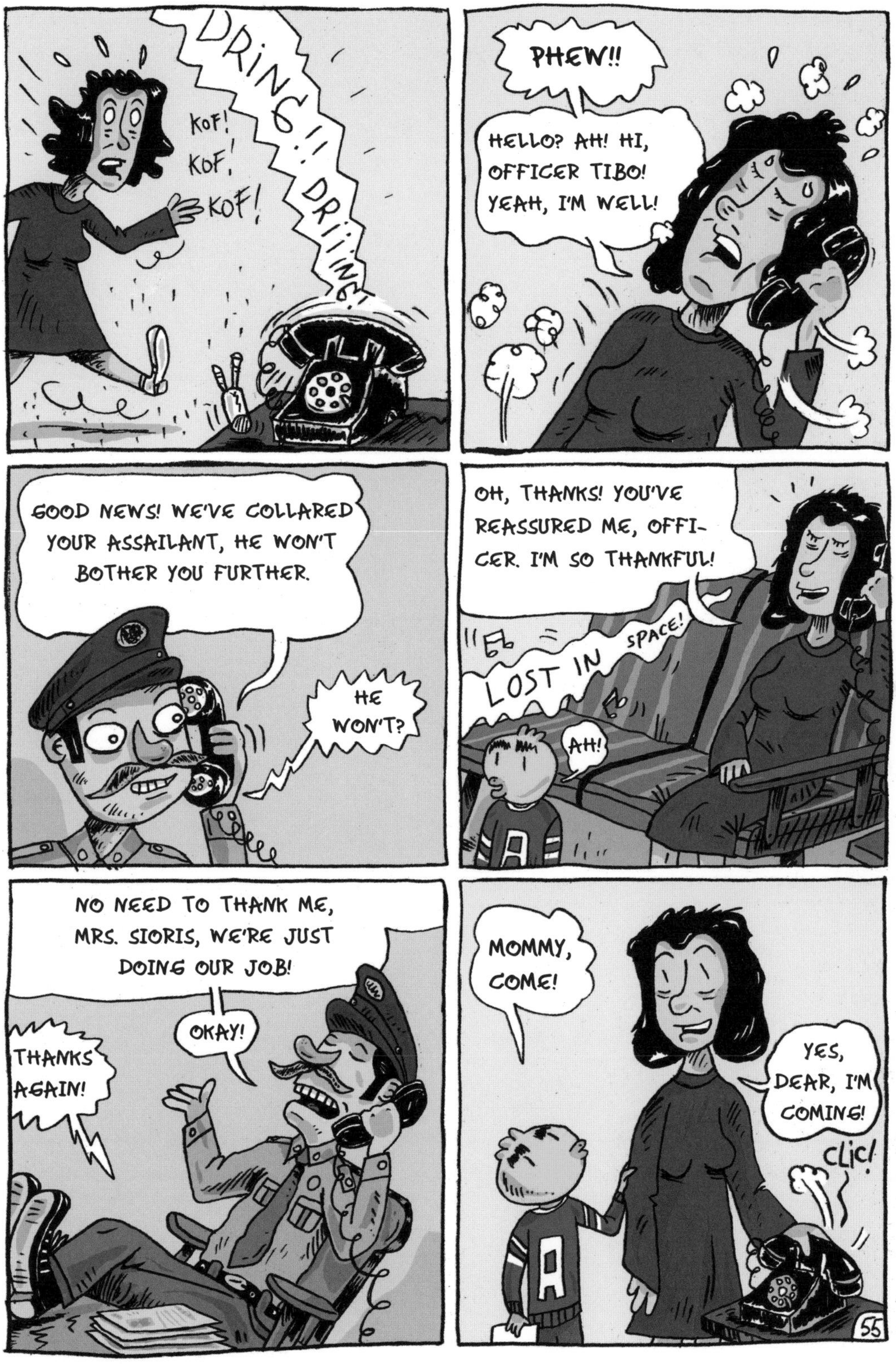
DRING!!! DRIIING!
KOF! KOF! KOF!
PHEW!!
HELLO? AH! HI, OFFICER TIBO! YEAH, I'M WELL!
GOOD NEWS! WE'VE COLLARED YOUR ASSAILANT, HE WON'T BOTHER YOU FURTHER.
HE WON'T?
OH, THANKS! YOU'VE REASSURED ME, OFFI-CER. I'M SO THANKFUL!
LOST IN SPACE!
AH!
NO NEED TO THANK ME, MRS. SIORIS, WE'RE JUST DOING OUR JOB!
THANKS AGAIN!
OKAY!
MOMMY, COME!
YES, DEAR, I'M COMING!
CLIC!
55

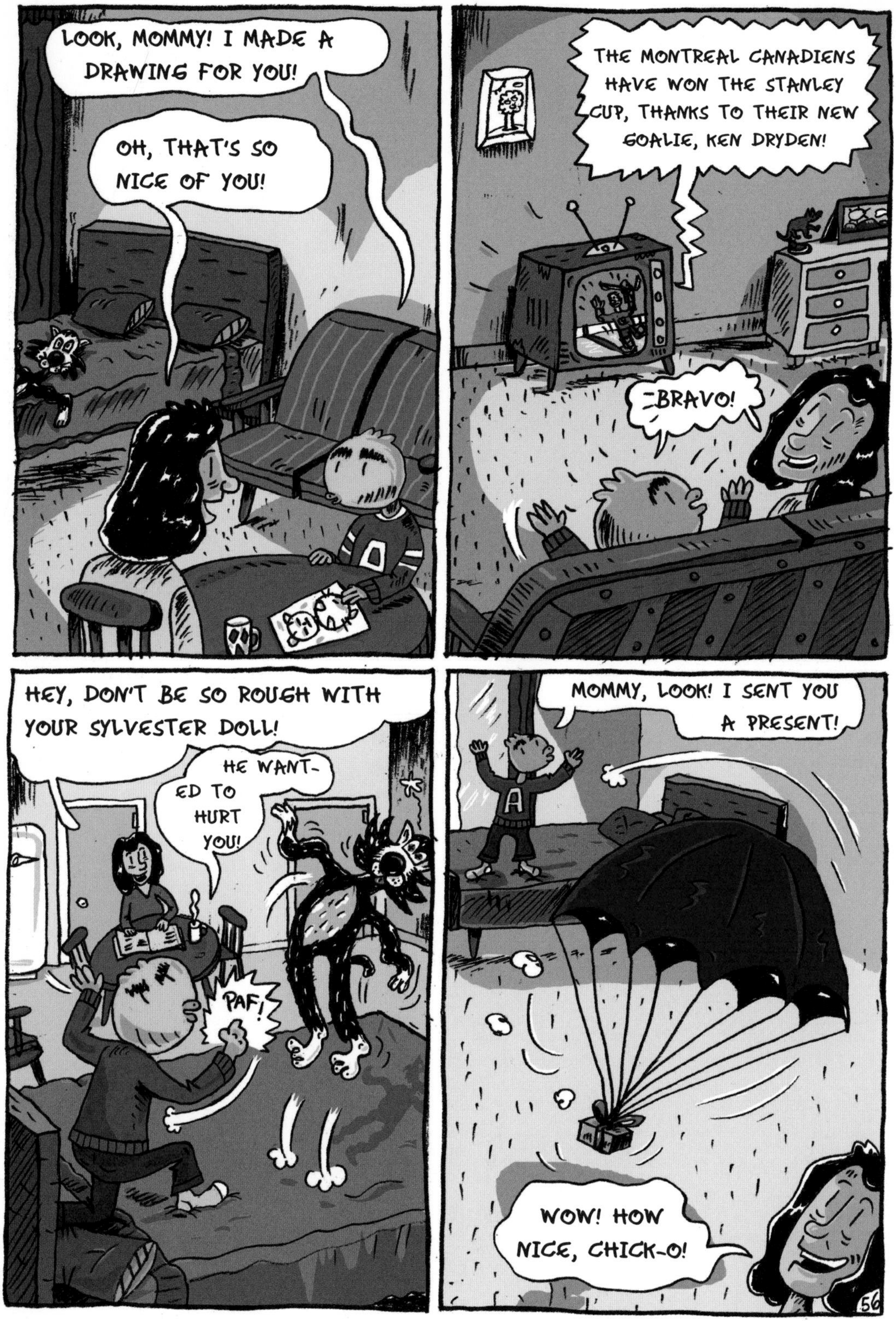
LOOK, MOMMY! I MADE A DRAWING FOR YOU!
OH, THAT'S SO NICE OF YOU!
THE MONTREAL CANADIENS HAVE WON THE STANLEY CUP, THANKS TO THEIR NEW GOALIE, KEN DRYDEN!
BRAVO!
HEY, DON'T BE SO ROUGH WITH YOUR SYLVESTER DOLL!
HE WANTED TO HURT YOU!
PAF!
MOMMY, LOOK! I SENT YOU A PRESENT!
WOW! HOW NICE, CHICK-O!
56

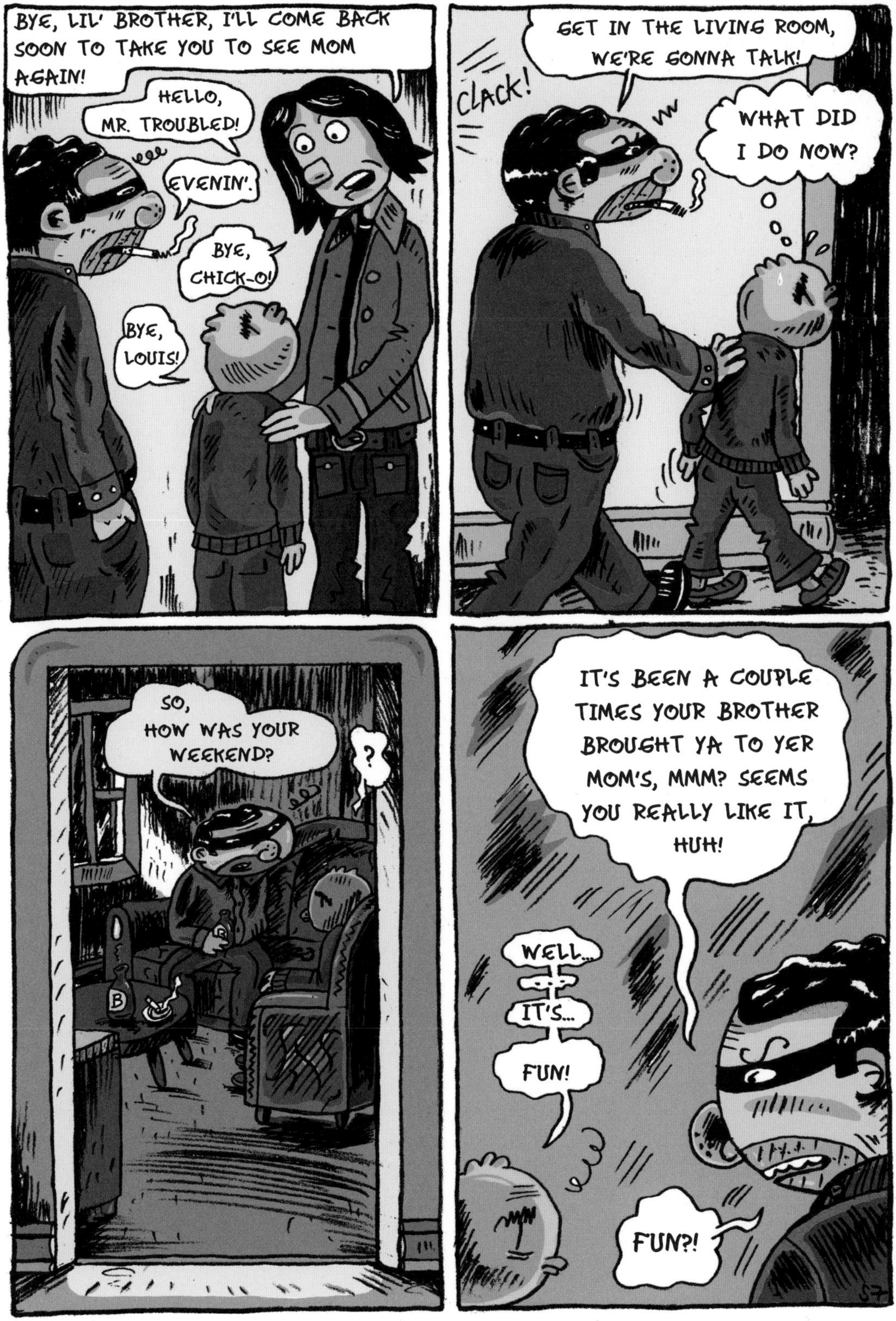
BYE, LIL' BROTHER, I'LL COME BACK SOON TO TAKE YOU TO SEE MOM AGAIN!
HELLO, MR. TROUBLED!
EVENIN'.
BYE, CHICK-O!
BYE, LOUIS!
CLACK!
GET IN THE LIVING ROOM, WE'RE GONNA TALK!
WHAT DID I DO NOW?
SO, HOW WAS YOUR WEEKEND?
?
IT'S BEEN A COUPLE TIMES YOUR BROTHER BROUGHT YA TO YER MOM'S, MMM? SEEMS YOU REALLY LIKE IT, HUH!
WELL...
IT'S...
FUN!
FUN?!

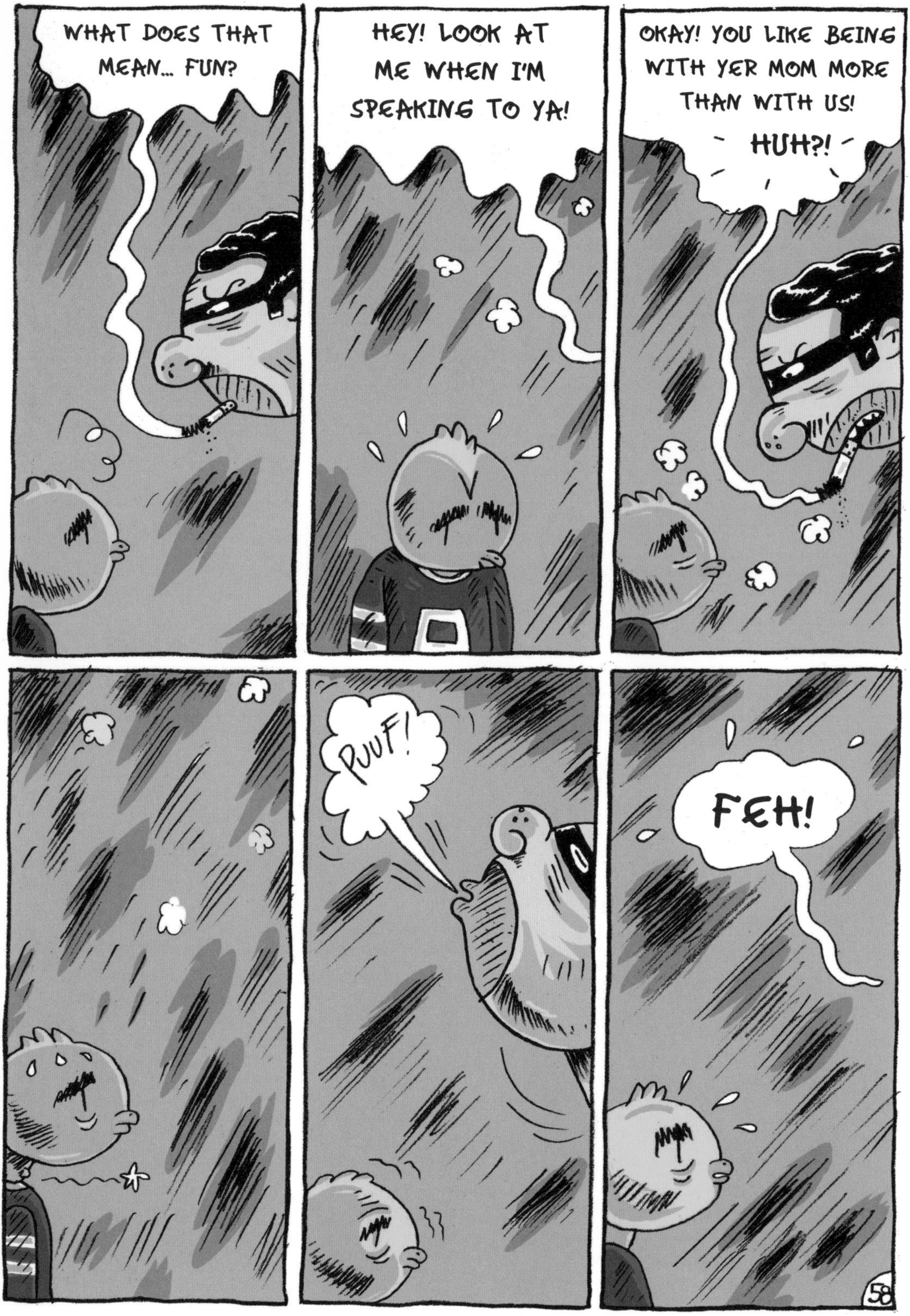
WHAT DOES THAT MEAN... FUN?
HEY! LOOK AT ME WHEN I'M SPEAKING TO YA!
OKAY! YOU LIKE BEING WITH YER MOM MORE THAN WITH US!
HUH?!
PUUF!
FEH!
58

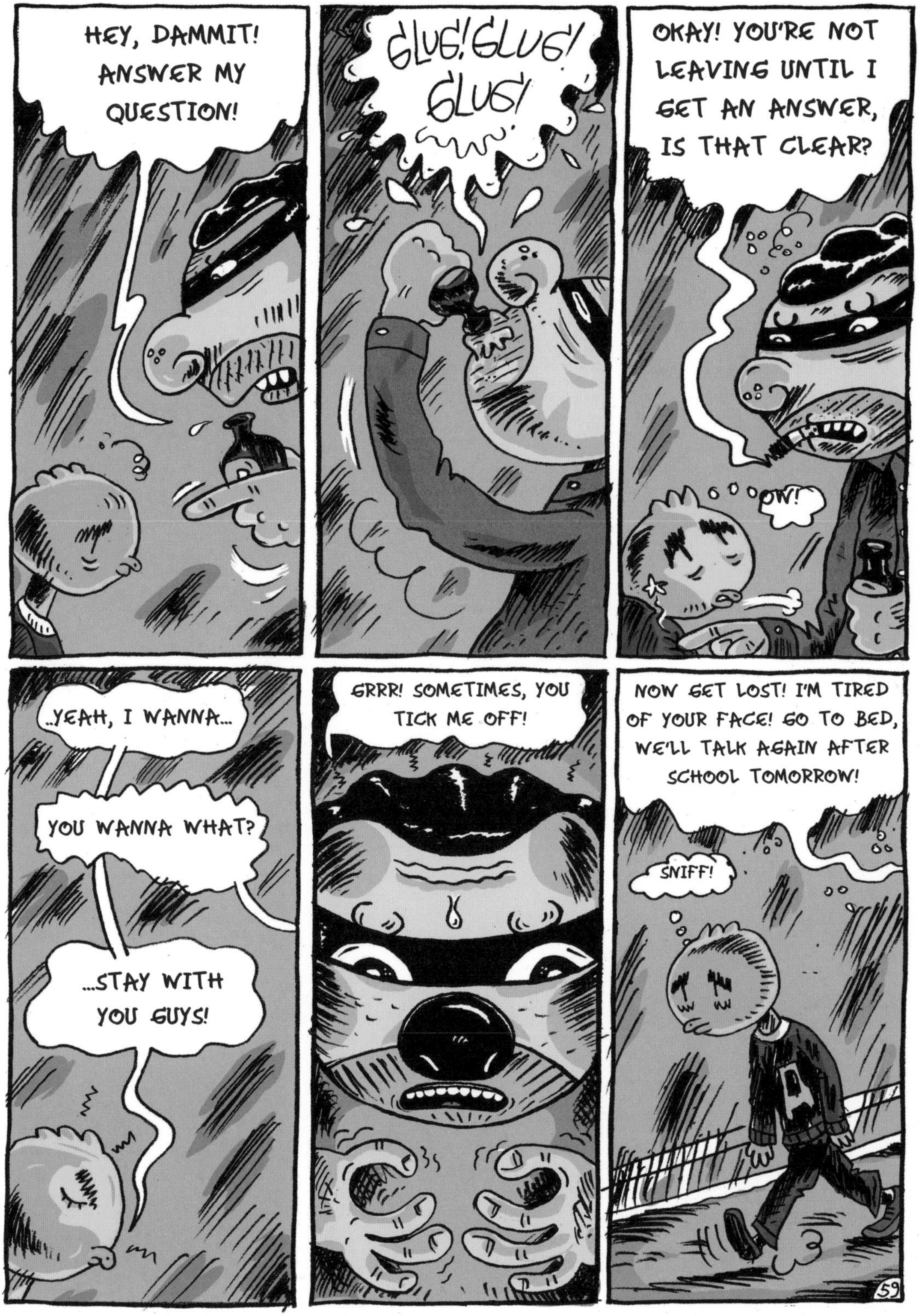
HEY, DAMMIT! ANSWER MY QUESTION!
GLUG! GLUG! GLUG!
OKAY! YOU'RE NOT LEAVING UNTIL I GET AN ANSWER, IS THAT CLEAR?
OOOW!
...YEAH, I WANNA...
YOU WANNA WHAT?
...STAY WITH YOU GUYS!
GRRR! SOMETIMES, YOU TICK ME OFF!
NOW GET LOST! I'M TIRED OF YOUR FACE! GO TO BED, WE'LL TALK AGAIN AFTER SCHOOL TOMORROW!
SNIFF!
59

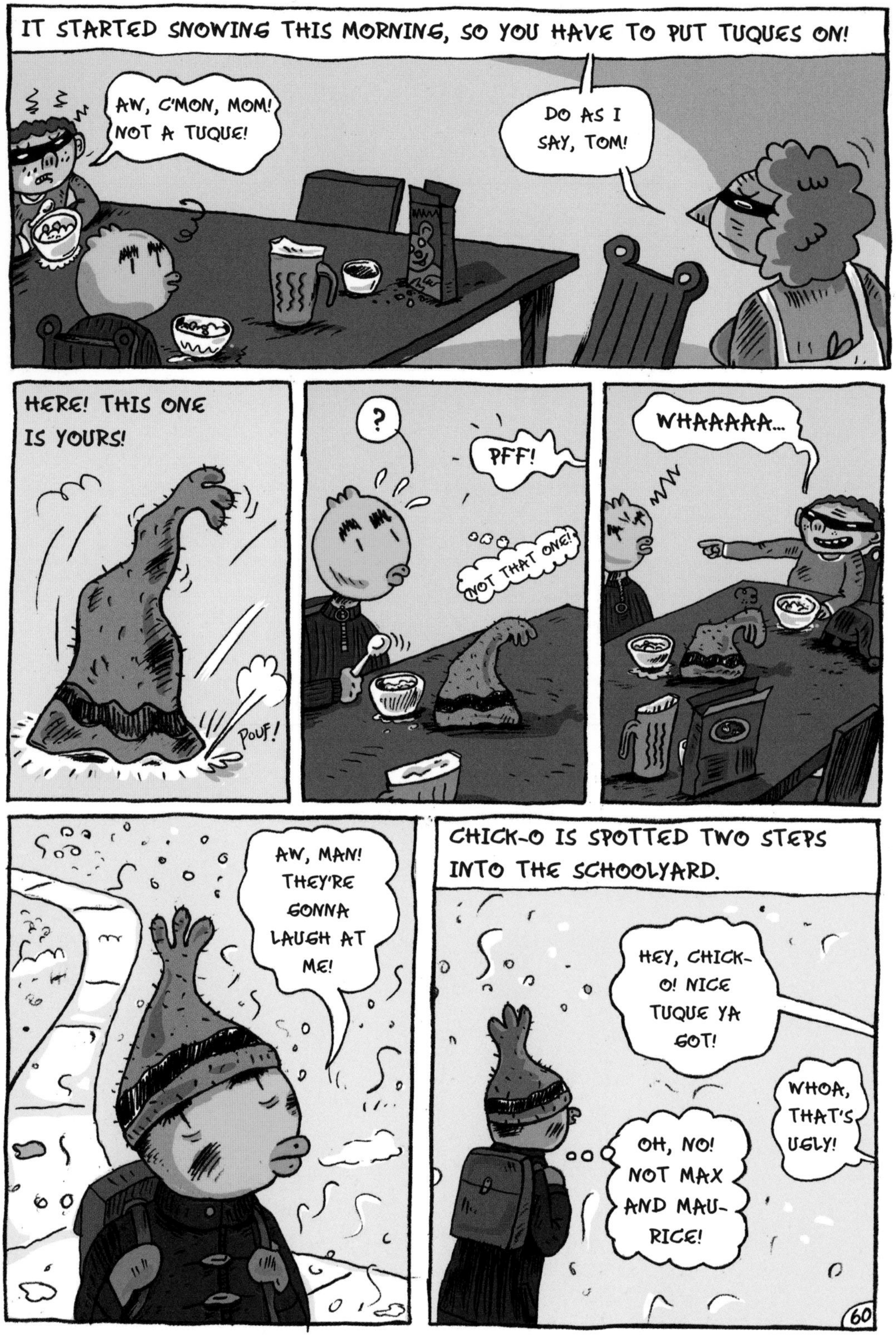

IT STARTED SNOWING THIS MORNING, SO YOU HAVE TO PUT TUQUES ON!
AW, C'MON, MOM! NOT A TUQUE!
DO AS I SAY, TOM!
HERE! THIS ONE IS YOURS!
POUF!
?
PFF!
NOT THAT ONE!
WHAAAAA...
AW, MAN! THEY'RE GONNA LAUGH AT ME!
CHICK-O IS SPOTTED TWO STEPS INTO THE SCHOOLYARD.
HEY, CHICK-O! NICE TUQUE YA GOT!
WHOA, THAT'S UGLY!
OH, NO! NOT MAX AND MAU-RICE!
60

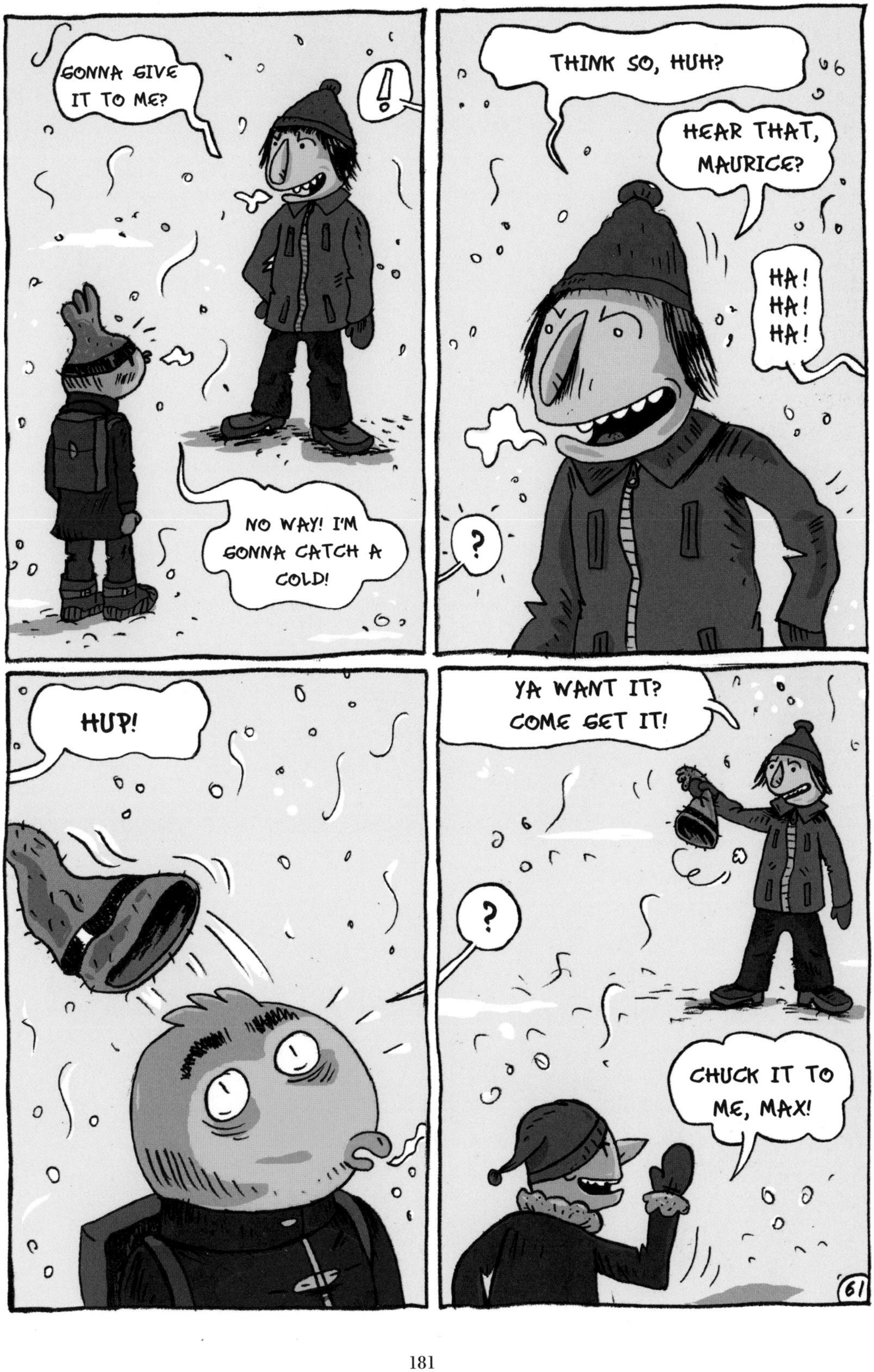
GONNA GIVE IT TO ME?
!
NO WAY! I'M GONNA CATCH A COLD!
THINK SO, HUH?
HEAR THAT, MAURICE?
HA! HA! HA!
?
HUP!
YA WANT IT? COME GET IT!
?
CHUCK IT TO ME, MAX!
61

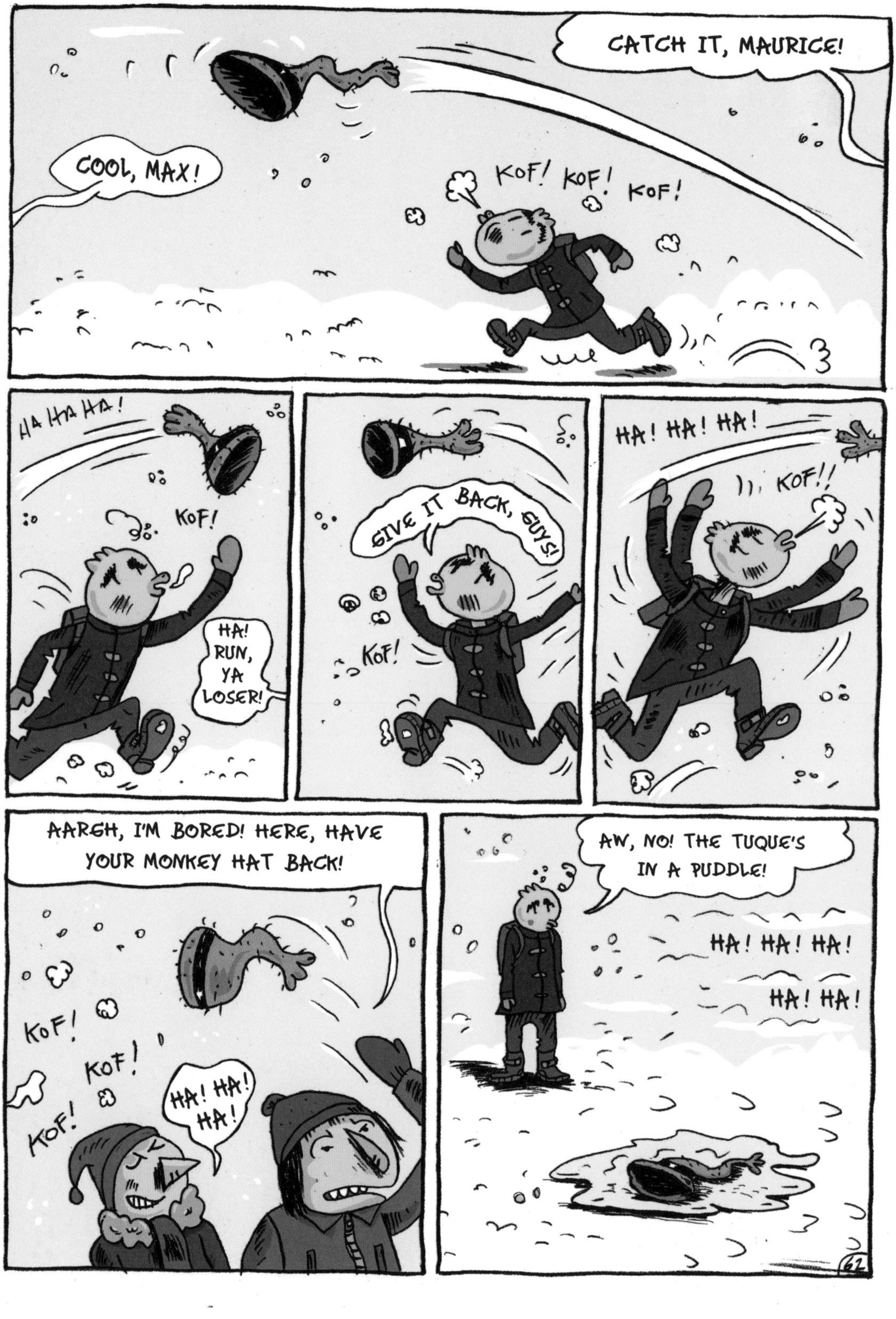
CATCH IT, MAURICE!
COOL, MAX!
KOF! KOF! KOF!
HA HA HA HA!
KOF!
HA! RUN, YA LOSER!
GIVE IT BACK, GUYS!
KOF!
HA! HA! HA!
KOF!!
AARGH, I'M BORED! HERE, HAVE YOUR MONKEY HAT BACK!
KOF!
KOF!
KOF!
HA! HA! HA!
AW, NO! THE TUQUE'S IN A PUDDLE!
HA! HA! HA!
HA! HA!
62

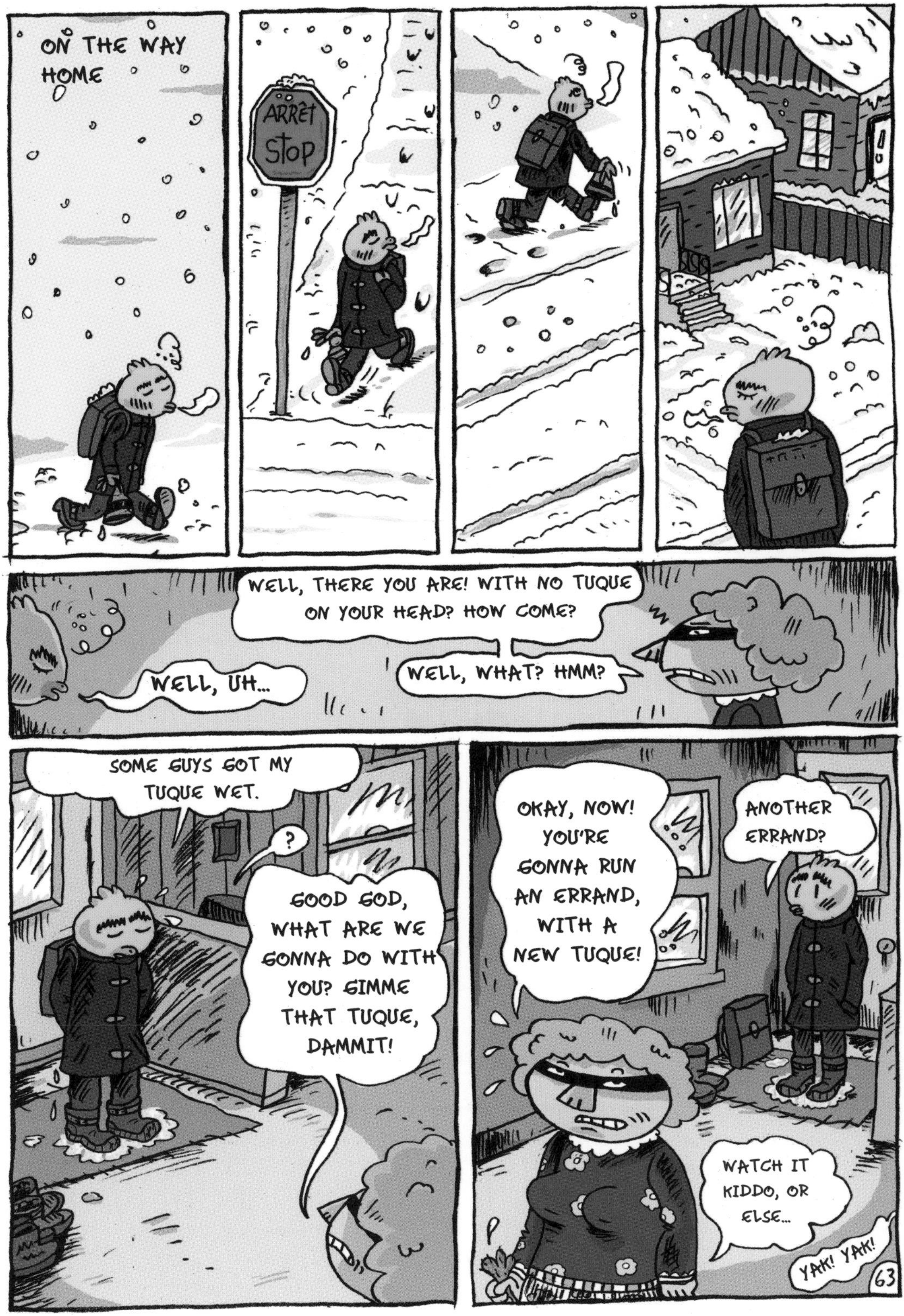
ON THE WAY HOME
ARRÊT STOP
WELL, THERE YOU ARE! WITH NO TUQUE ON YOUR HEAD? HOW COME?
WELL, UH...
WELL, WHAT? HMM?
SOME GUYS GOT MY TUQUE WET.
?
GOOD GOD, WHAT ARE WE GONNA DO WITH YOU? GIMME THAT TUQUE, DAMMIT!
OKAY, NOW! YOU'RE GONNA RUN AN ERRAND, WITH A NEW TUQUE!
ANOTHER ERRAND?
WATCH IT KIDDO, OR ELSE...
YAK! YAK!
63

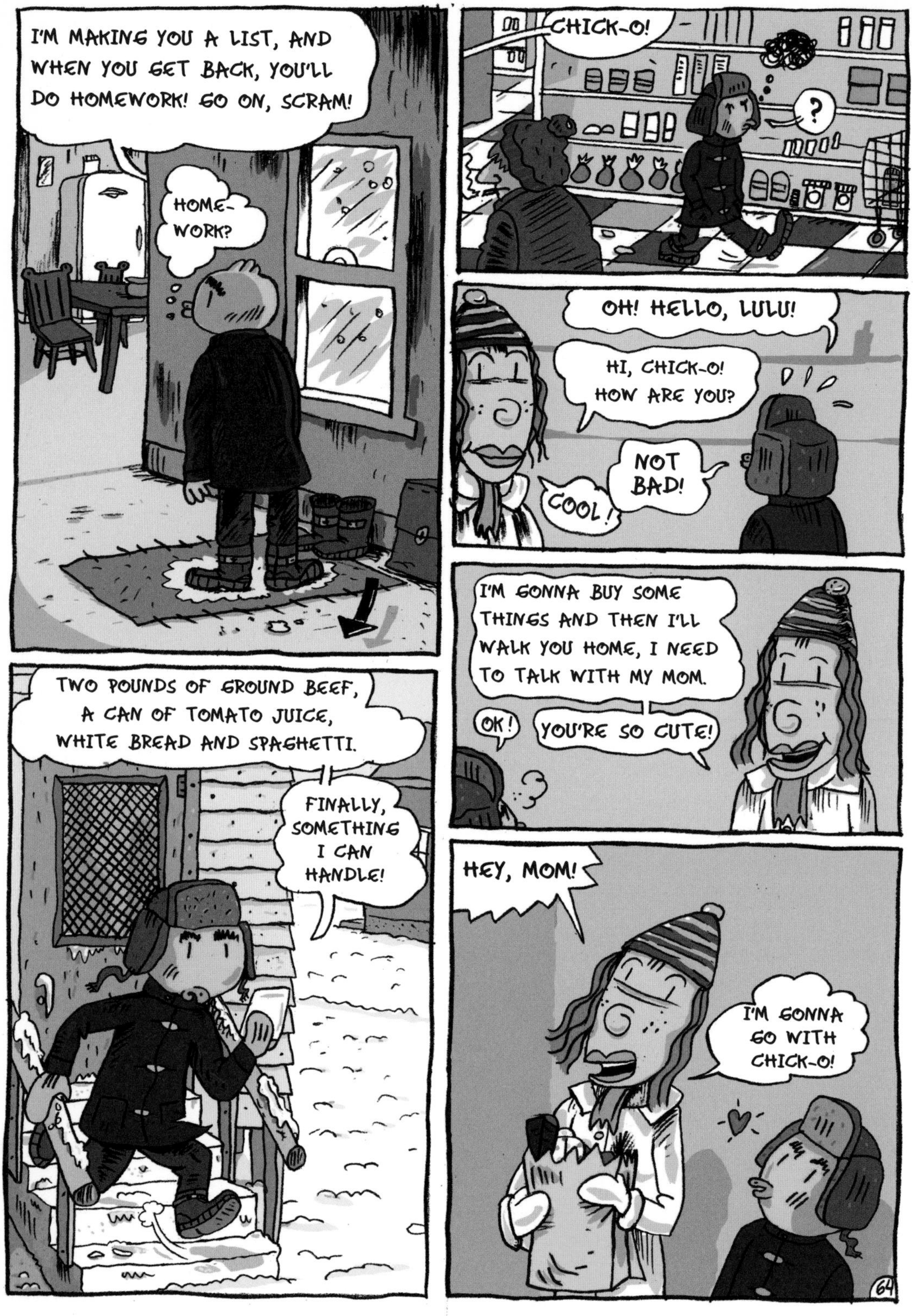
I'M MAKING YOU A LIST, AND WHEN YOU GET BACK, YOU'LL DO HOMEWORK! GO ON, SCRAM!
HOME-WORK?
CHICK-O!
?
OH! HELLO, LULU!
HI, CHICK-O! HOW ARE YOU?
NOT BAD!
COOL!
TWO POUNDS OF GROUND BEEF, A CAN OF TOMATO JUICE, WHITE BREAD AND SPAGHETTI.
FINALLY, SOMETHING I CAN HANDLE!
I'M GONNA BUY SOME THINGS AND THEN I'LL WALK YOU HOME, I NEED TO TALK WITH MY MOM.
OK!
YOU'RE SO CUTE!
HEY, MOM!
I'M GONNA GO WITH CHICK-O!
64

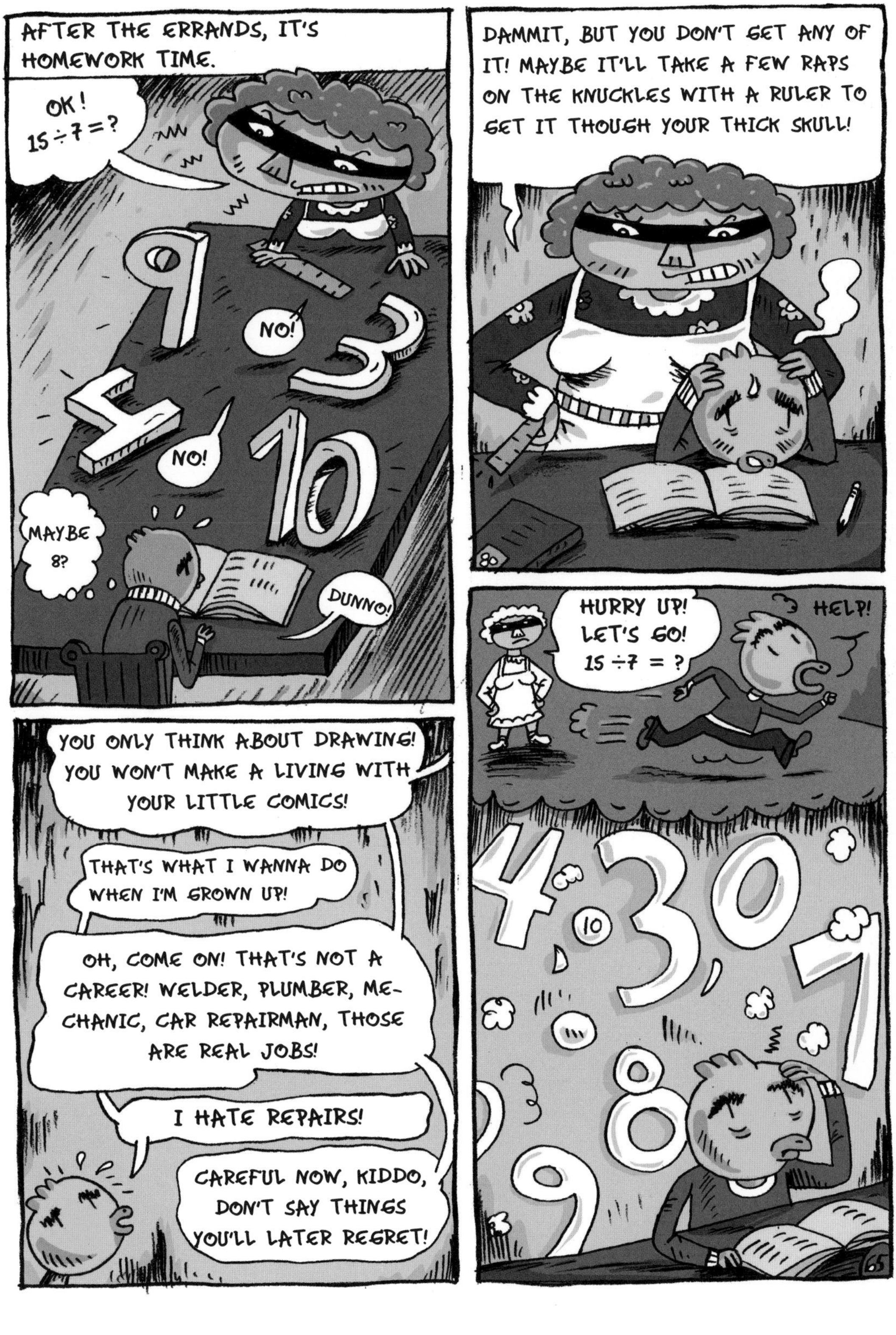
AFTER THE ERRANDS, IT'S HOMEWORK TIME.
OK! 15 ÷ 7 = ?
NO!
NO!
MAYBE 8?
DUNNO!
DAMMIT, BUT YOU DON'T GET ANY OF IT! MAYBE IT'LL TAKE A FEW RAPS ON THE KNUCKLES WITH A RULER TO GET IT THOUGH YOUR THICK SKULL!
YOU ONLY THINK ABOUT DRAWING! YOU WON'T MAKE A LIVING WITH YOUR LITTLE COMICS!
THAT'S WHAT I WANNA DO WHEN I'M GROWN UP!
OH, COME ON! THAT'S NOT A CAREER! WELDER, PLUMBER, MECHANIC, CAR REPAIRMAN, THOSE ARE REAL JOBS!
I HATE REPAIRS!
CAREFUL NOW, KIDDO, DON'T SAY THINGS YOU'LL LATER REGRET!
HURRY UP! LET'S GO! 15 ÷ 7 = ?
HELP!

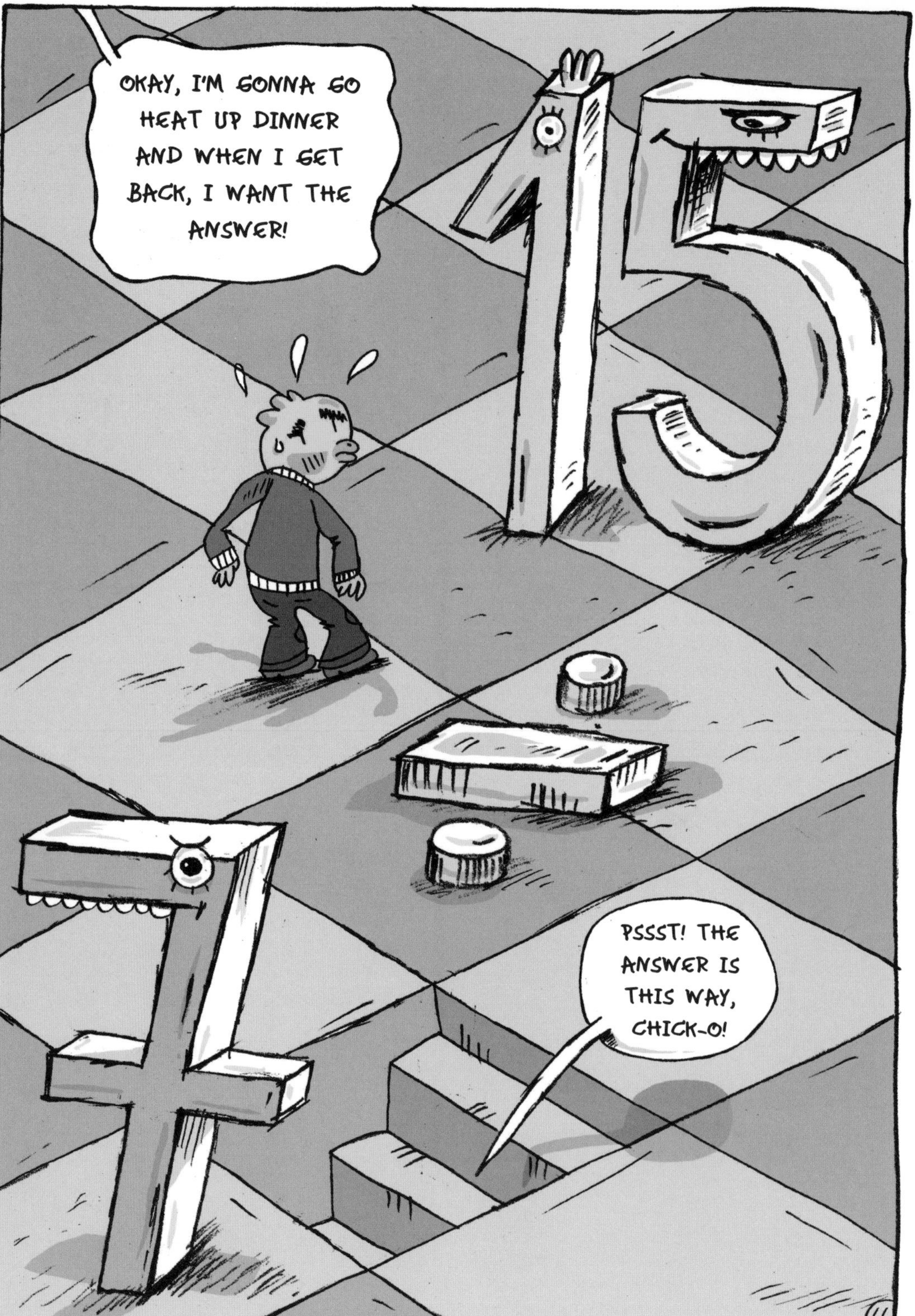
OKAY, I'M GONNA GO HEAT UP DINNER AND WHEN I GET BACK, I WANT THE ANSWER!
PSSST! THE ANSWER IS THIS WAY, CHICK-O!
66

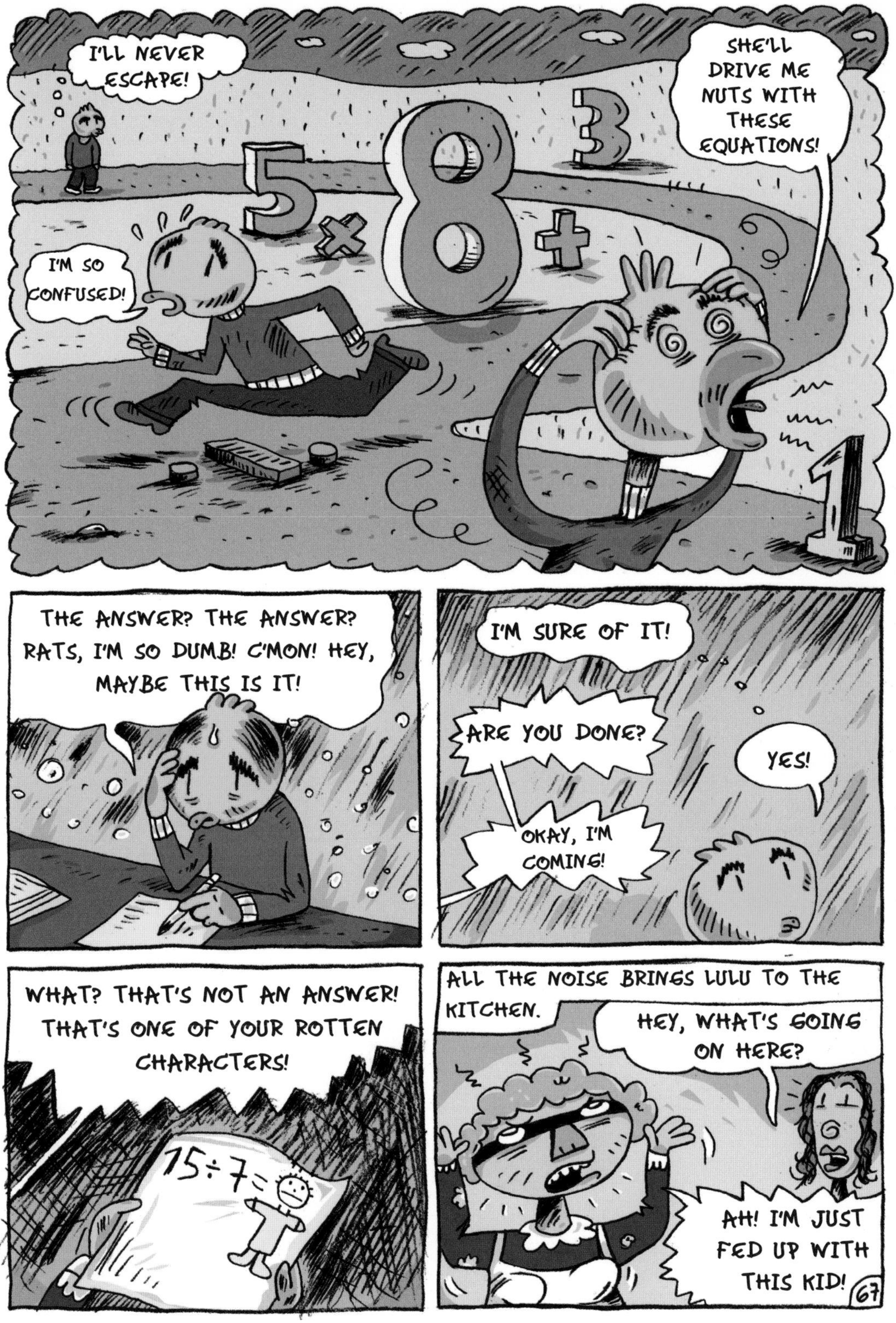
I'LL NEVER ESCAPE!
SHE'LL DRIVE ME NUTS WITH THESE EQUATIONS!
I'M SO CONFUSED!
THE ANSWER? THE ANSWER? RATS, I'M SO DUMB! C'MON! HEY, MAYBE THIS IS IT!
I'M SURE OF IT!
ARE YOU DONE?
YES!
OKAY, I'M COMING!
WHAT? THAT'S NOT AN ANSWER! THAT'S ONE OF YOUR ROTTEN CHARACTERS!
75÷7=
ALL THE NOISE BRINGS LULU TO THE KITCHEN.
HEY, WHAT'S GOING ON HERE?
AH! I'M JUST FED UP WITH THIS KID!
67

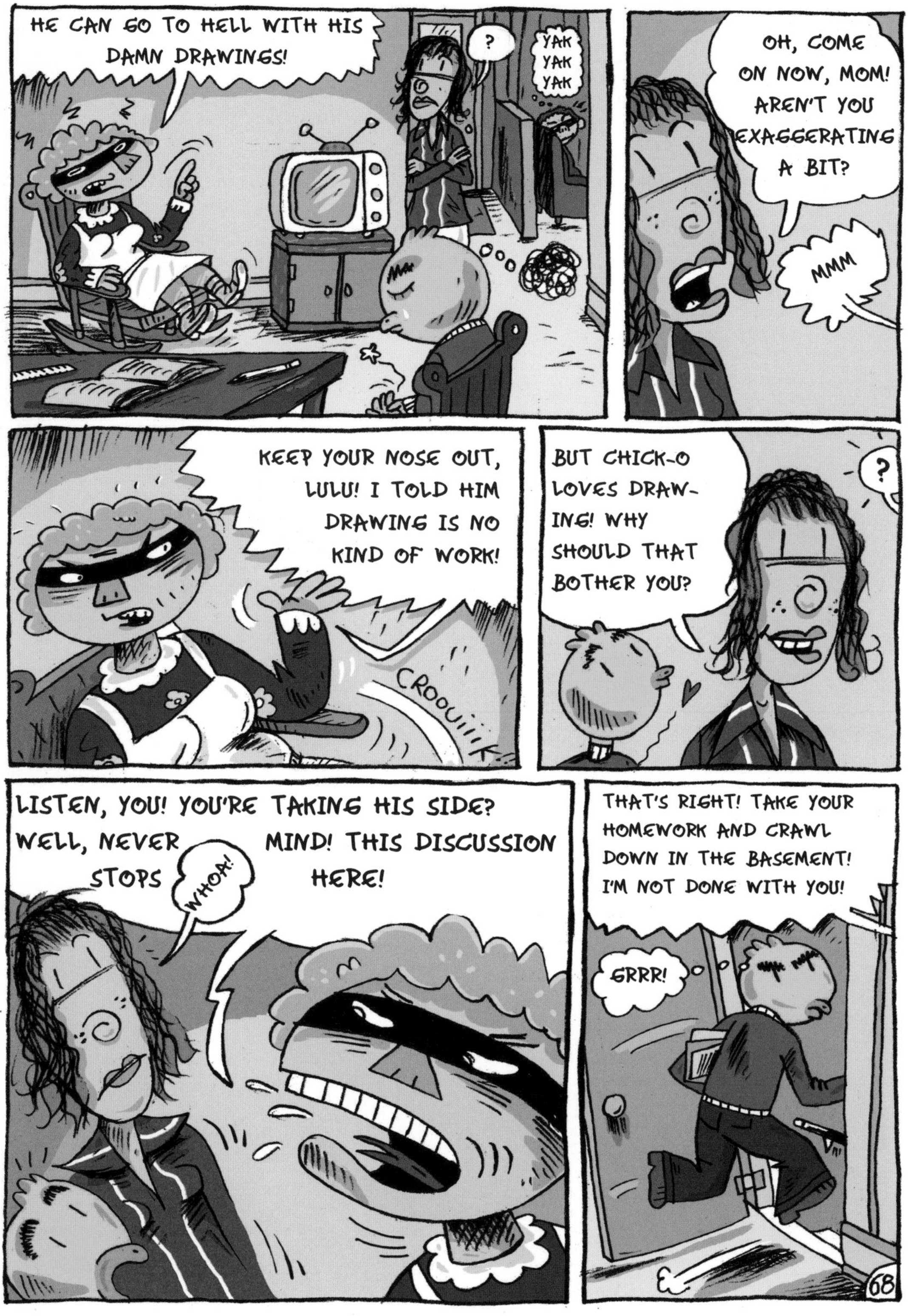
HE CAN GO TO HELL WITH HIS DAMN DRAWINGS!
?
YAK YAK YAK
OH, COME ON NOW, MOM! AREN'T YOU EXAGGERATING A BIT?
MMM
KEEP YOUR NOSE OUT, LULU! I TOLD HIM DRAWING IS NO KIND OF WORK!
CROOUIK
BUT CHICK-O LOVES DRAWING! WHY SHOULD THAT BOTHER YOU?
?
LISTEN, YOU! YOU'RE TAKING HIS SIDE? WELL, NEVER MIND! THIS DISCUSSION STOPS HERE!
WHOA!
THAT'S RIGHT! TAKE YOUR HOMEWORK AND CRAWL DOWN IN THE BASEMENT! I'M NOT DONE WITH YOU!
GRRR!
68

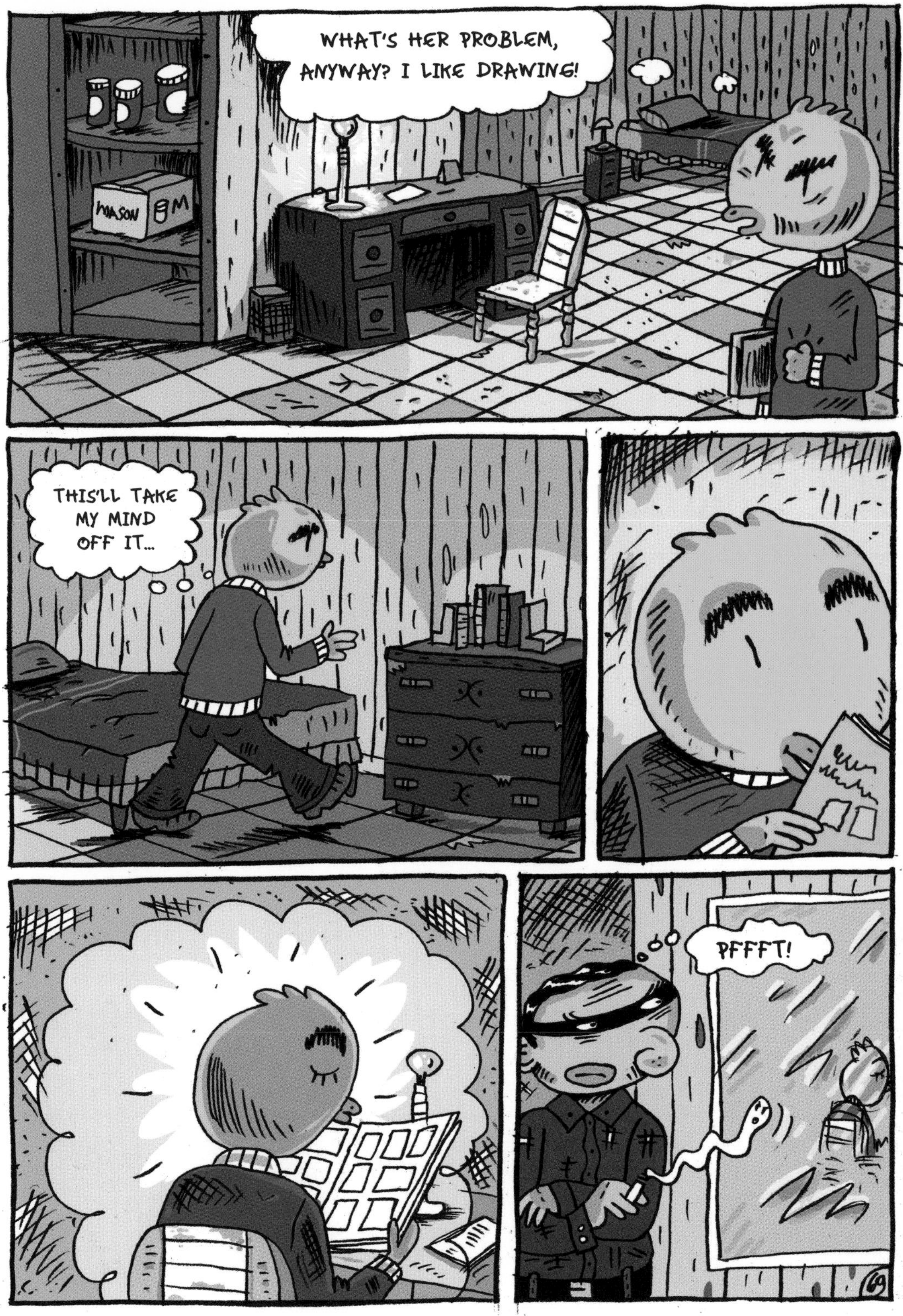
WHAT'S HER PROBLEM, ANYWAY? I LIKE DRAWING!
MASON
THIS'LL TAKE MY MIND OFF IT...
PFFFT!
69

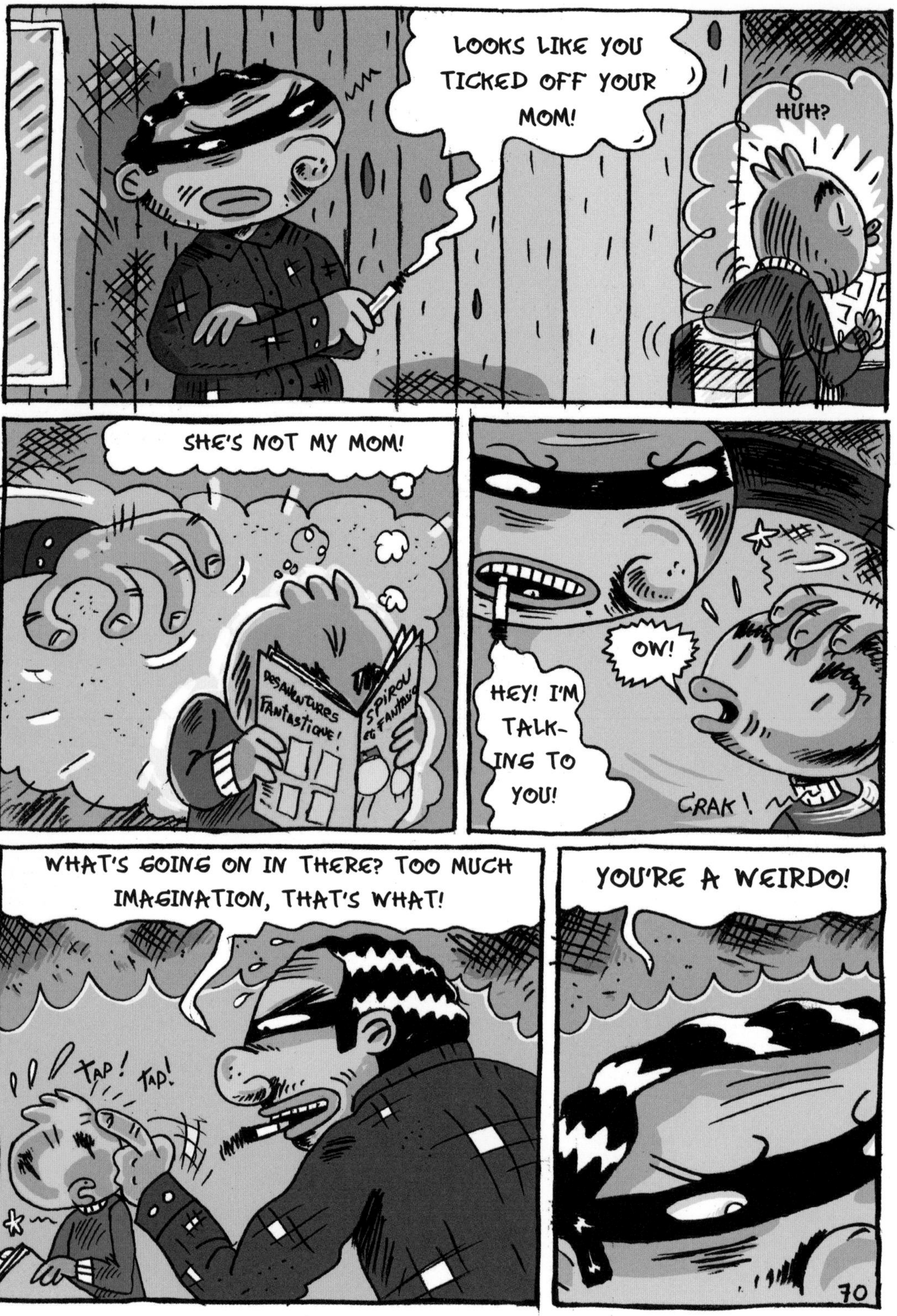
LOOKS LIKE YOU TICKED OFF YOUR MOM!
HUH?
SHE'S NOT MY MOM!
DES AVENTURES FANTASTIQUE!
SPIROU ET FANTASIO
OW!
HEY! I'M TALK-ING TO YOU!
CRAK!
WHAT'S GOING ON IN THERE? TOO MUCH IMAGINATION, THAT'S WHAT!
TAP! TAP!
YOU'RE A WEIRDO!
70

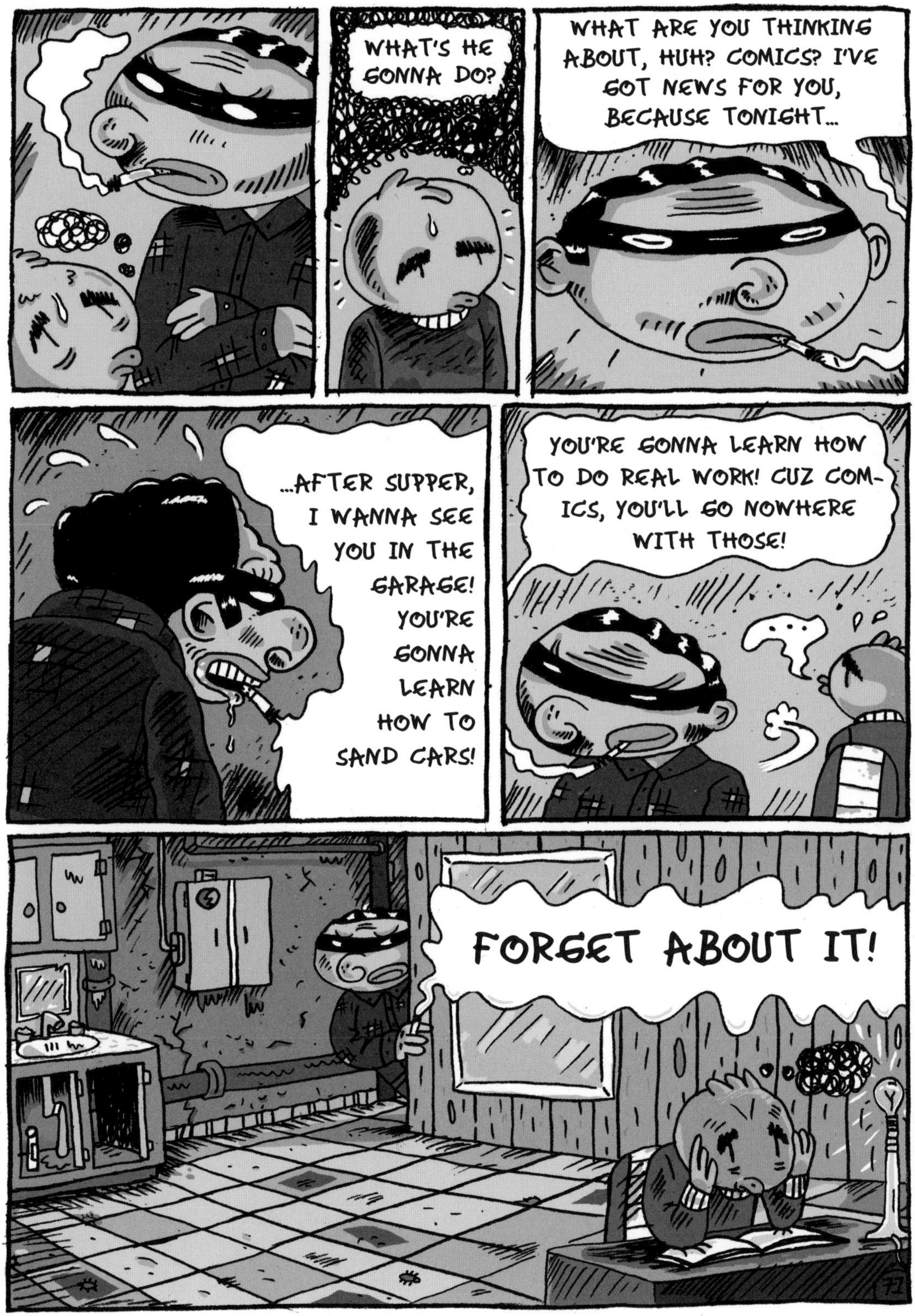
WHAT'S HE GONNA DO?
WHAT ARE YOU THINKING ABOUT, HUH? COMICS? I'VE GOT NEWS FOR YOU, BECAUSE TONIGHT...
...AFTER SUPPER, I WANNA SEE YOU IN THE GARAGE! YOU'RE GONNA LEARN HOW TO SAND CARS!
YOU'RE GONNA LEARN HOW TO DO REAL WORK! CUZ COM-ICS, YOU'LL GO NOWHERE WITH THOSE!
FORGET ABOUT IT!

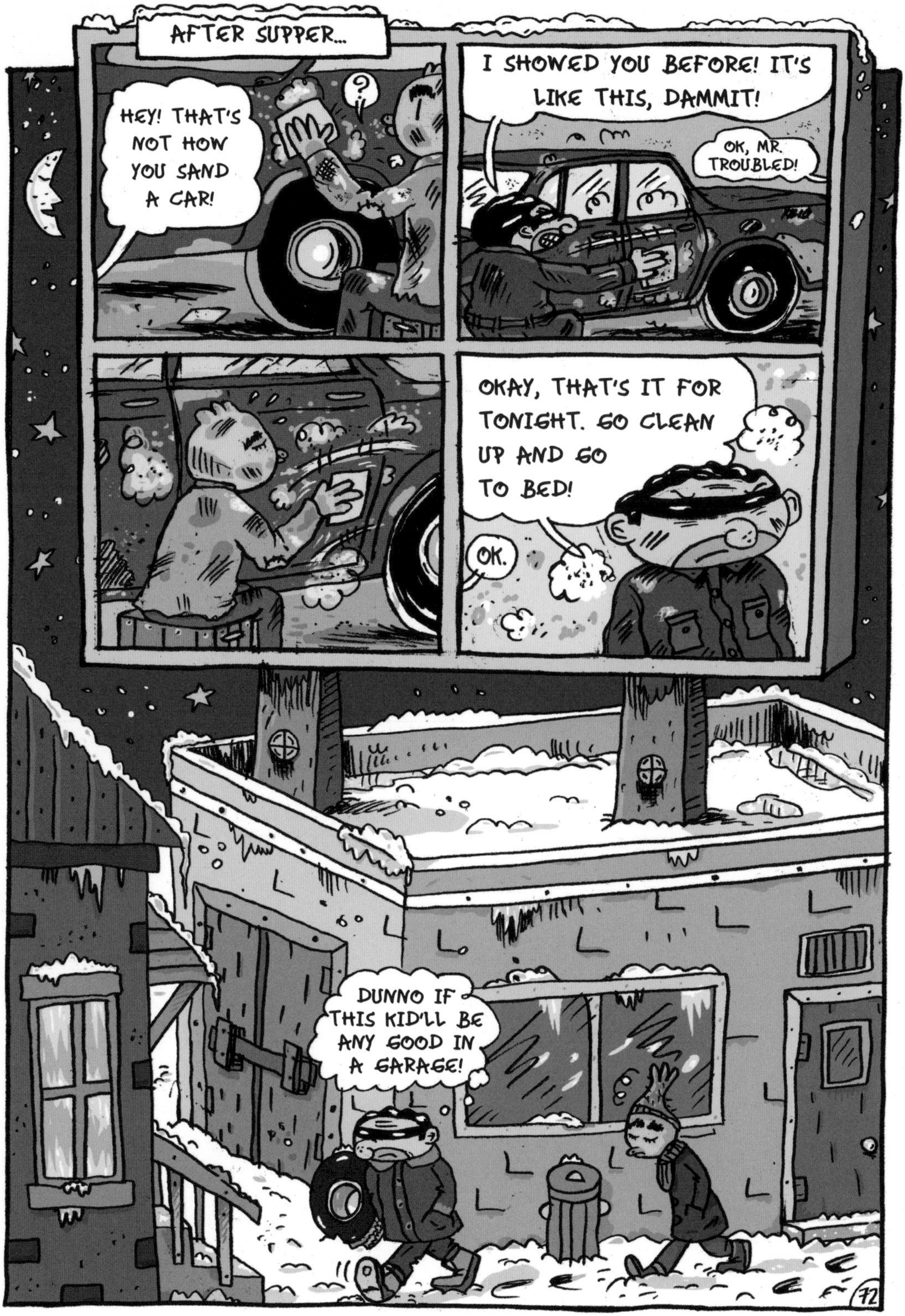
AFTER SUPPER...
HEY! THAT'S NOT HOW YOU SAND A CAR!
?
I SHOWED YOU BEFORE! IT'S LIKE THIS, DAMMIT!
OK, MR. TROUBLED!
OKAY, THAT'S IT FOR TONIGHT. GO CLEAN UP AND GO TO BED!
OK.
DUNNO IF THIS KID'LL BE ANY GOOD IN A GARAGE!
72

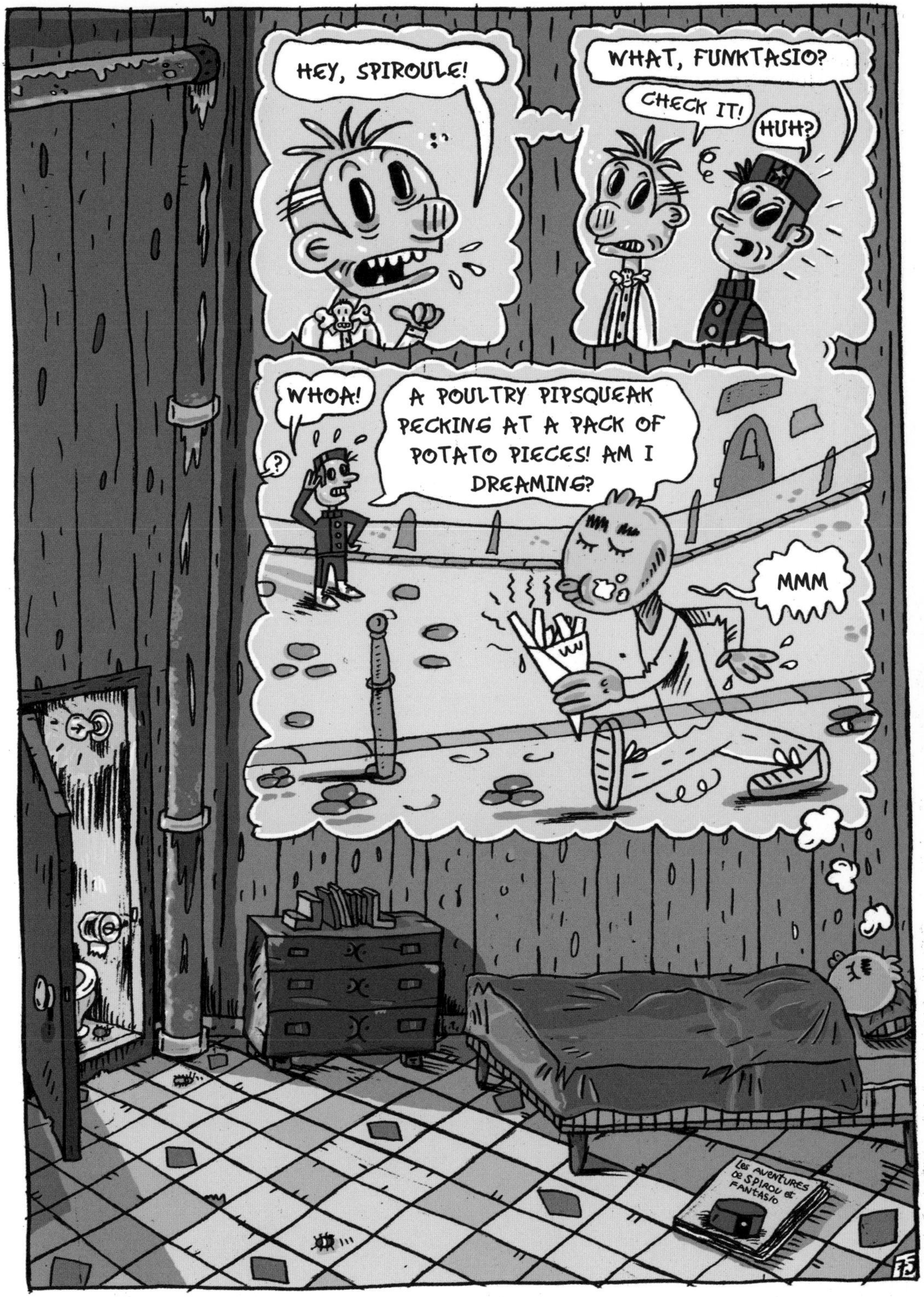
HEY, SPIROULE!
WHAT, FUNKTASIO?
CHECK IT!
HUH?
WHOA!
A POULTRY PIPSQUEAK PECKING AT A PACK OF POTATO PIECES! AM I DREAMING?
MMM
LES AVENTURES DE SPIROU ET FANTASIO

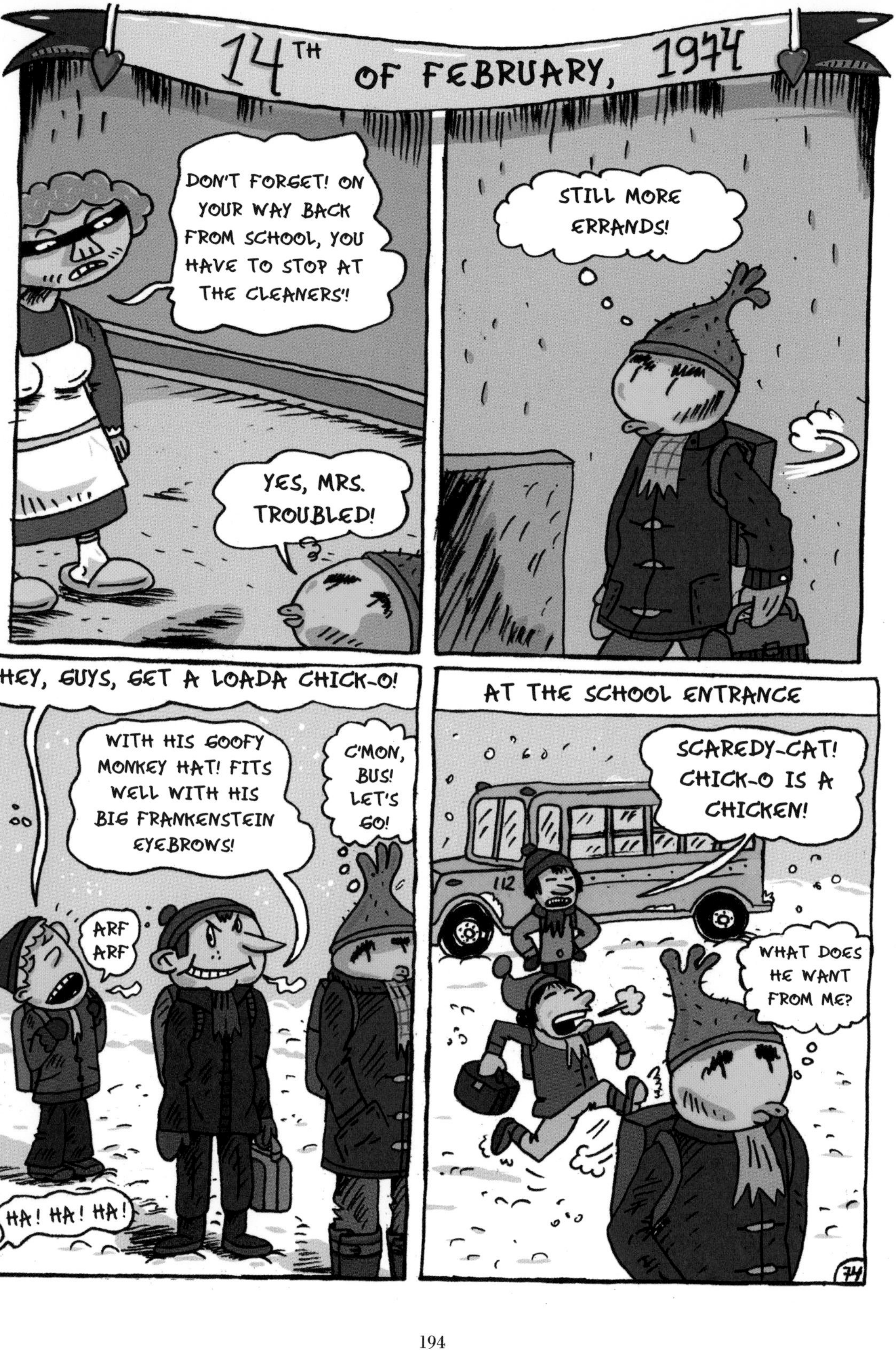
14TH OF FEBRUARY, 1974
DON'T FORGET! ON YOUR WAY BACK FROM SCHOOL, YOU HAVE TO STOP AT THE CLEANERS'!
YES, MRS. TROUBLED!
STILL MORE ERRANDS!
HEY, GUYS, GET A LOADA CHICK-O!
WITH HIS GOOFY MONKEY HAT! FITS WELL WITH HIS BIG FRANKENSTEIN EYEBROWS!
C'MON, BUS! LET'S GO!
ARF ARF
HA! HA! HA!
AT THE SCHOOL ENTRANCE
SCAREDY-CAT! CHICK-O IS A CHICKEN!
112
WHAT DOES HE WANT FROM ME?
74

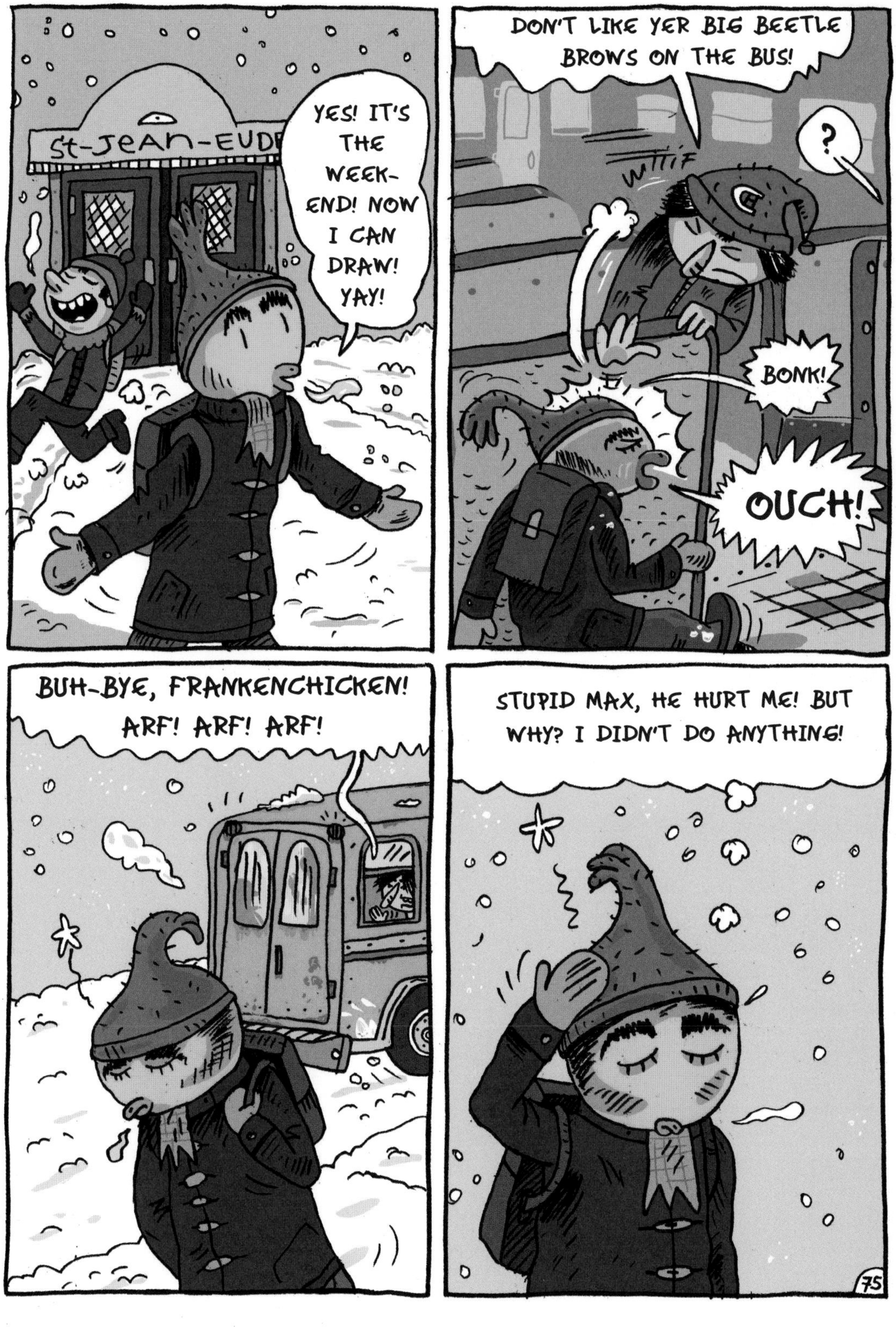
St-Jean-Eude
YES! IT'S THE WEEK-END! NOW I CAN DRAW! YAY!
DON'T LIKE YER BIG BEETLE BROWS ON THE BUS!
WHIIF
?
BONK!
OUCH!
BUH-BYE, FRANKENCHICKEN! ARF! ARF! ARF!
STUPID MAX, HE HURT ME! BUT WHY? I DIDN'T DO ANYTHING!
75

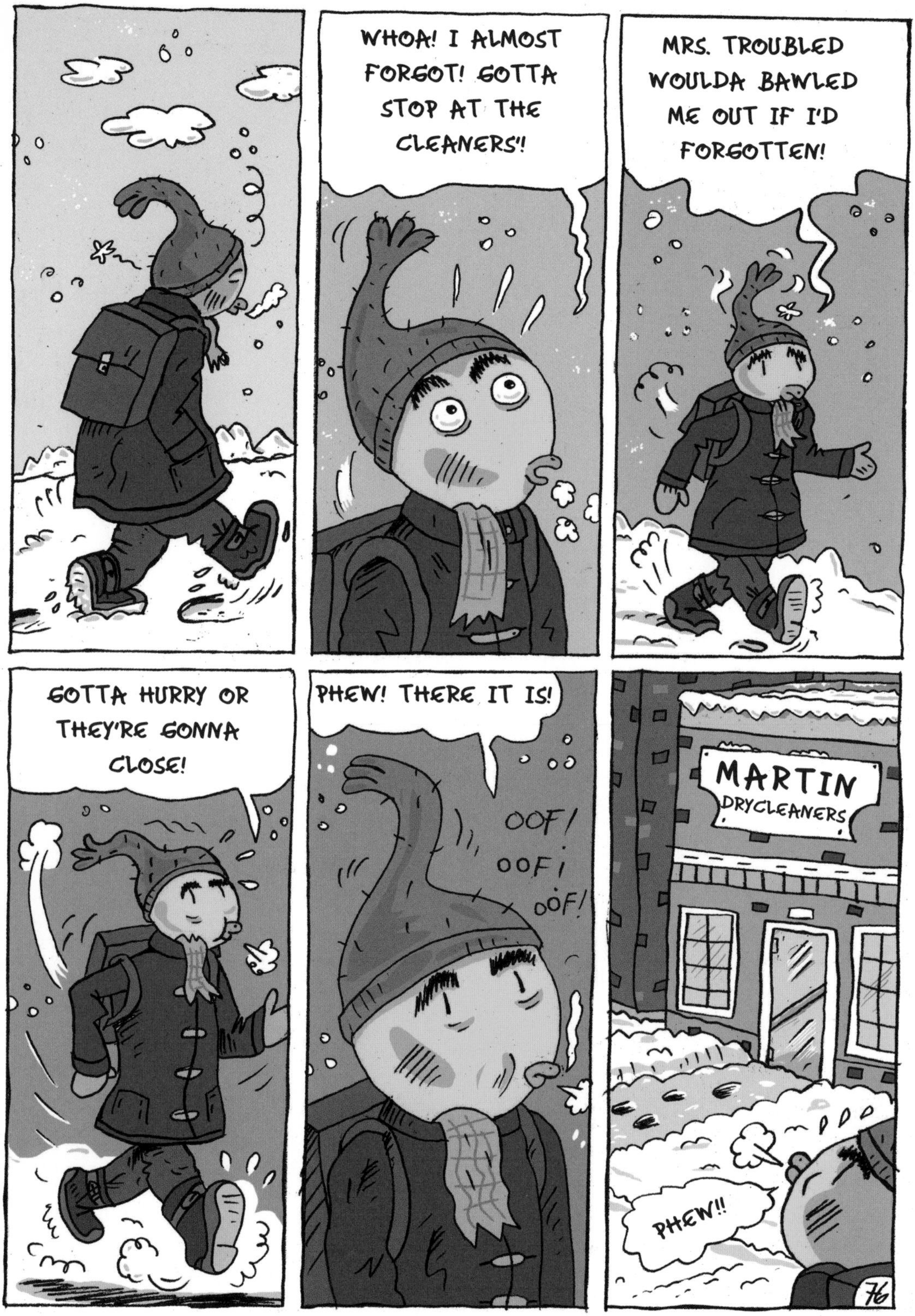
WHOA! I ALMOST FORGOT! GOTTA STOP AT THE CLEANERS'!
MRS. TROUBLED WOULDA BAWLED ME OUT IF I'D FORGOTTEN!
GOTTA HURRY OR THEY'RE GONNA CLOSE!
PHEW! THERE IT IS!
OOF!
OOF!
OOF!
MARTIN DRYCLEANERS
PHEW!!

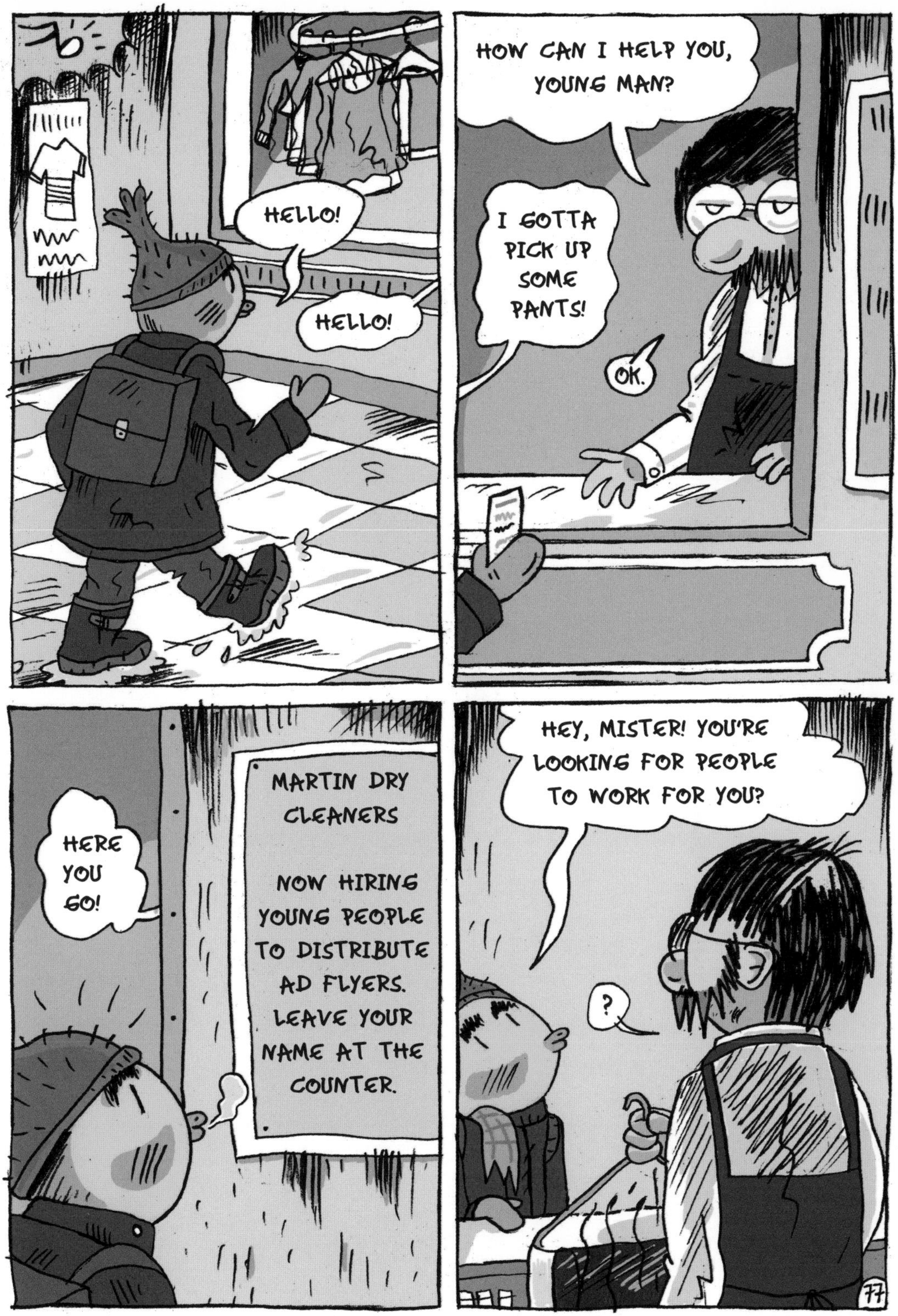
HELLO!
HELLO!
HOW CAN I HELP YOU, YOUNG MAN?
I GOTTA PICK UP SOME PANTS!
OK.
HERE YOU GO!
MARTIN DRY CLEANERS
NOW HIRING YOUNG PEOPLE TO DISTRIBUTE AD FLYERS. LEAVE YOUR NAME AT THE COUNTER.
HEY, MISTER! YOU'RE LOOKING FOR PEOPLE TO WORK FOR YOU?
?

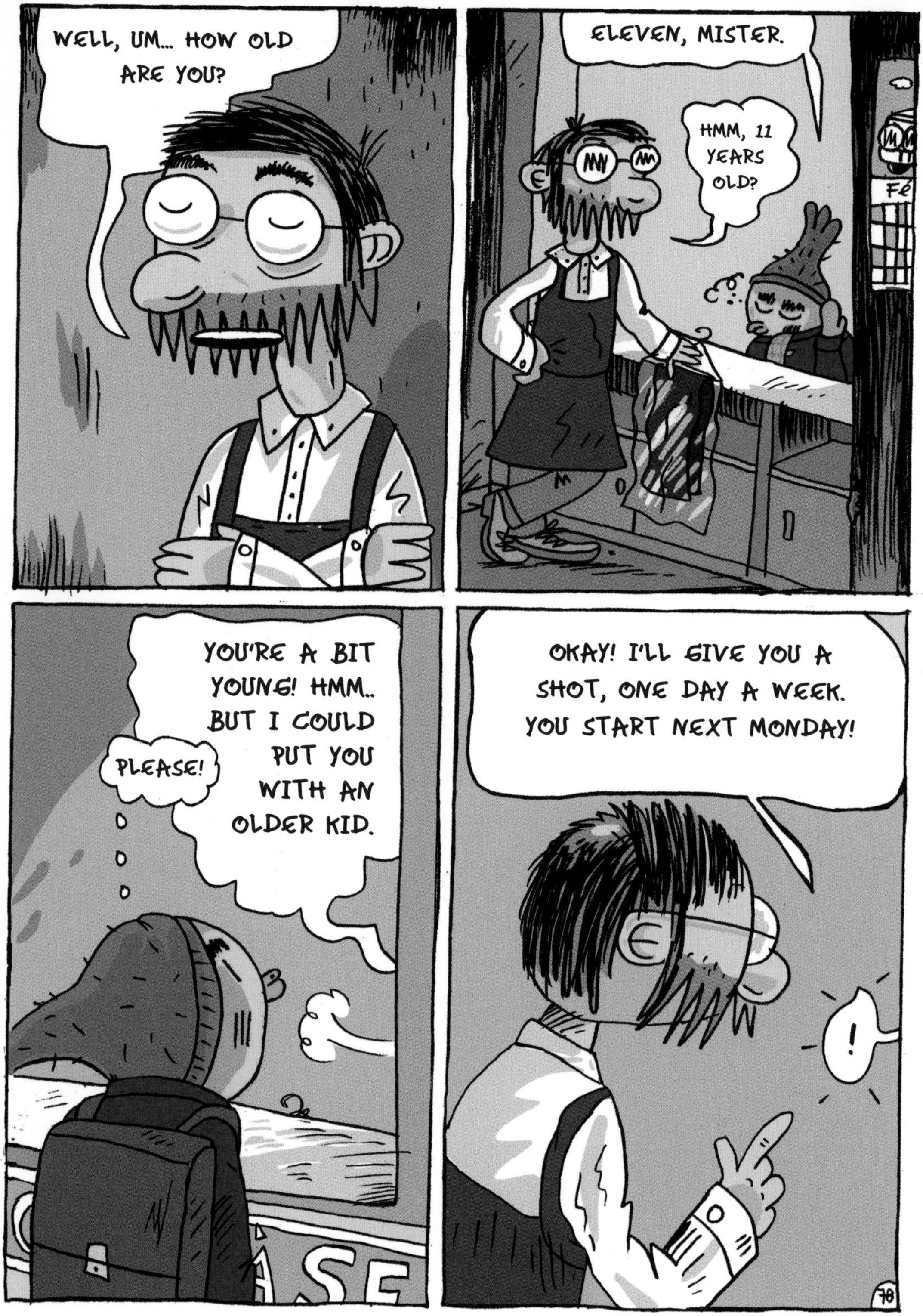
WELL, UM... HOW OLD ARE YOU?
ELEVEN, MISTER.
HMM, 11 YEARS OLD?
YOU'RE A BIT YOUNG! HMM.. BUT I COULD PUT YOU WITH AN OLDER KID.
PLEASE!
OKAY! I'LL GIVE YOU A SHOT, ONE DAY A WEEK. YOU START NEXT MONDAY!
!

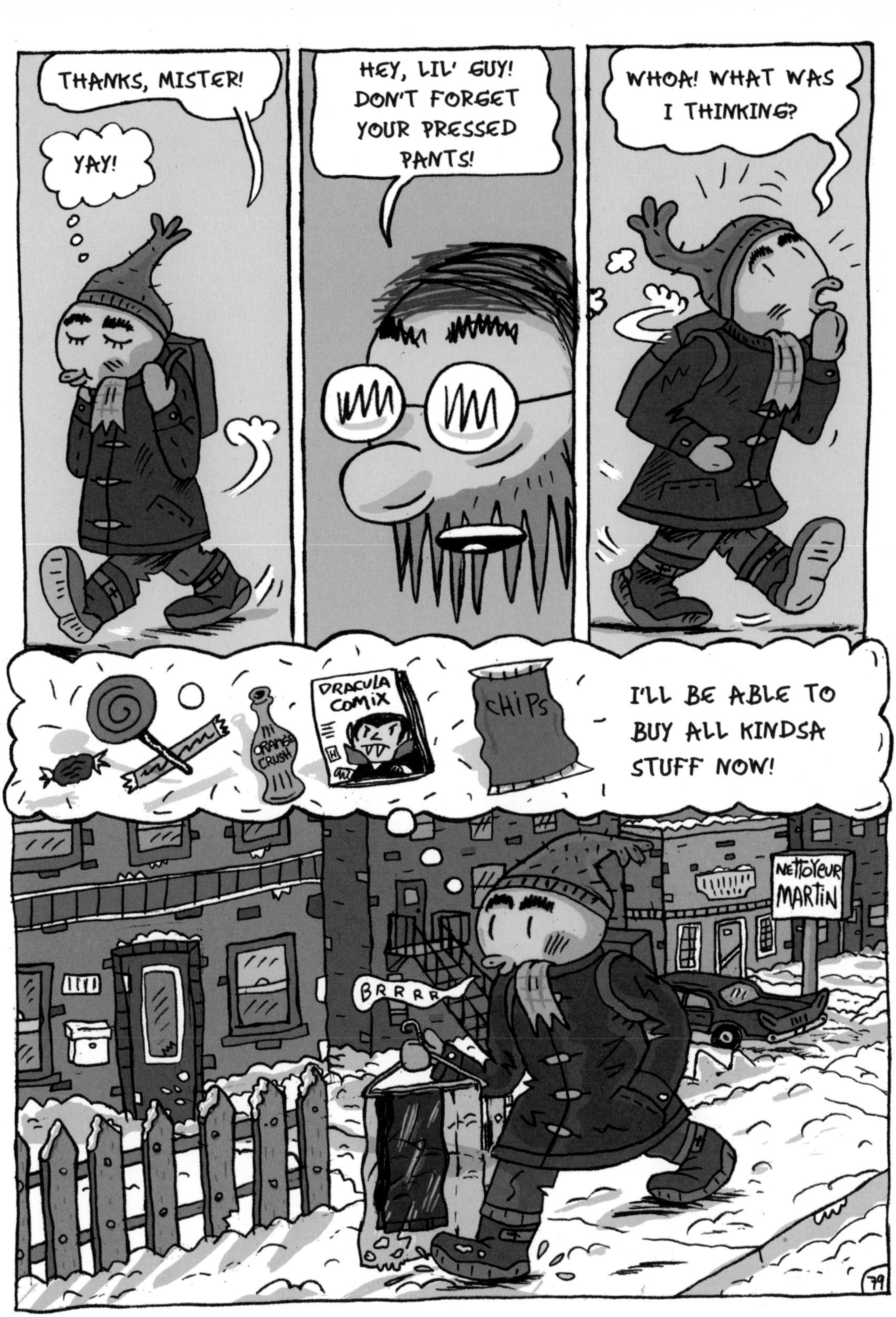
THANKS, MISTER!
YAY!
HEY, LIL' GUY! DON'T FORGET YOUR PRESSED PANTS!
WHOA! WHAT WAS I THINKING?
DRACULA COMIX
ORANGE CRUSH
CHIPS
I'LL BE ABLE TO BUY ALL KINDSA STUFF NOW!
NETTOYEUR MARTIN
BRRRRR
79

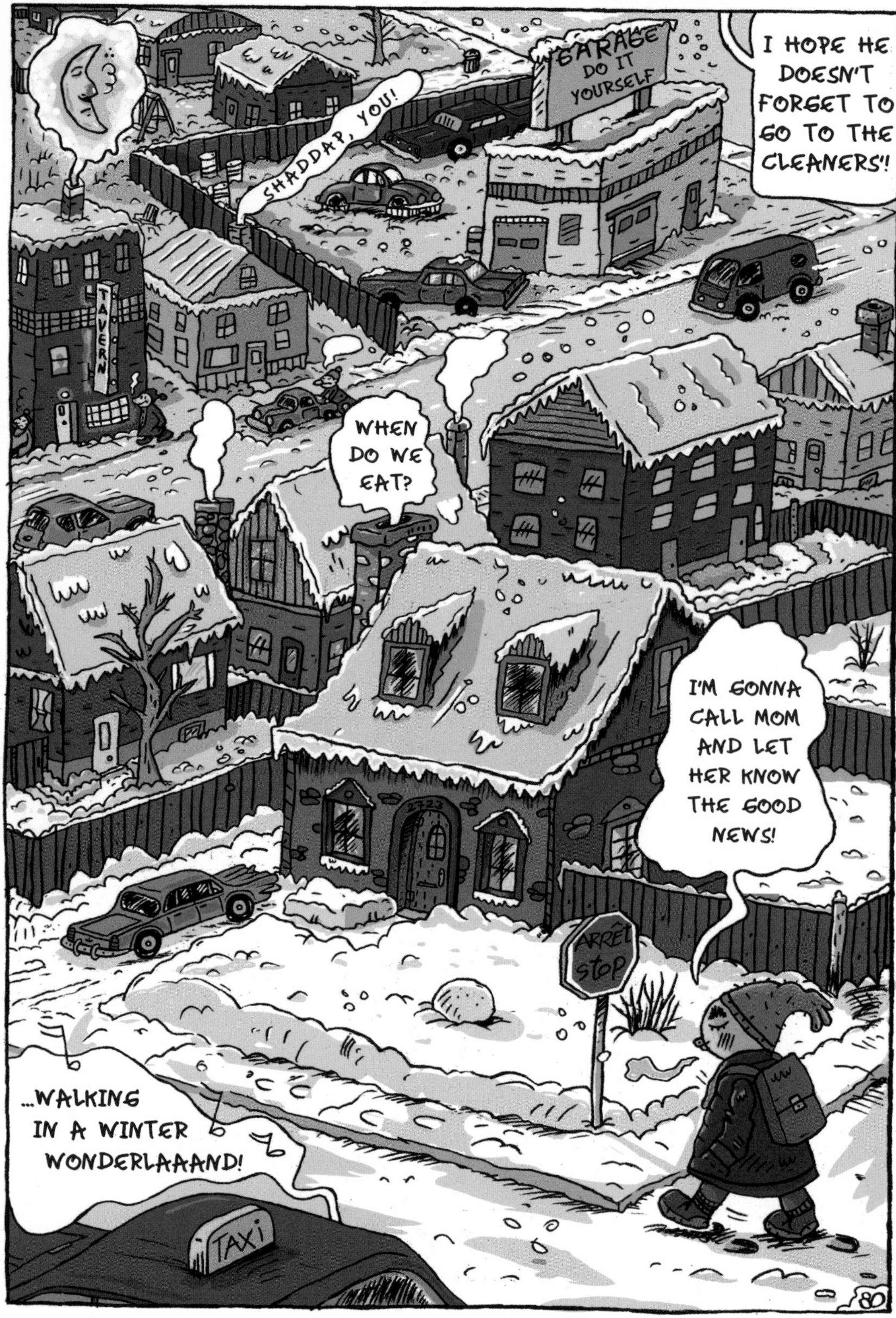
SHADDAP, YOU!
GARAGE
DO IT YOURSELF
I HOPE HE DOESN'T FORGET TO GO TO THE CLEANERS'!
TAVERN
WHEN DO WE EAT?
I'M GONNA CALL MOM AND LET HER KNOW THE GOOD NEWS!
2723
ARRÊT
stop
...WALKING IN A WINTER WONDERLAAAND!
TAXI

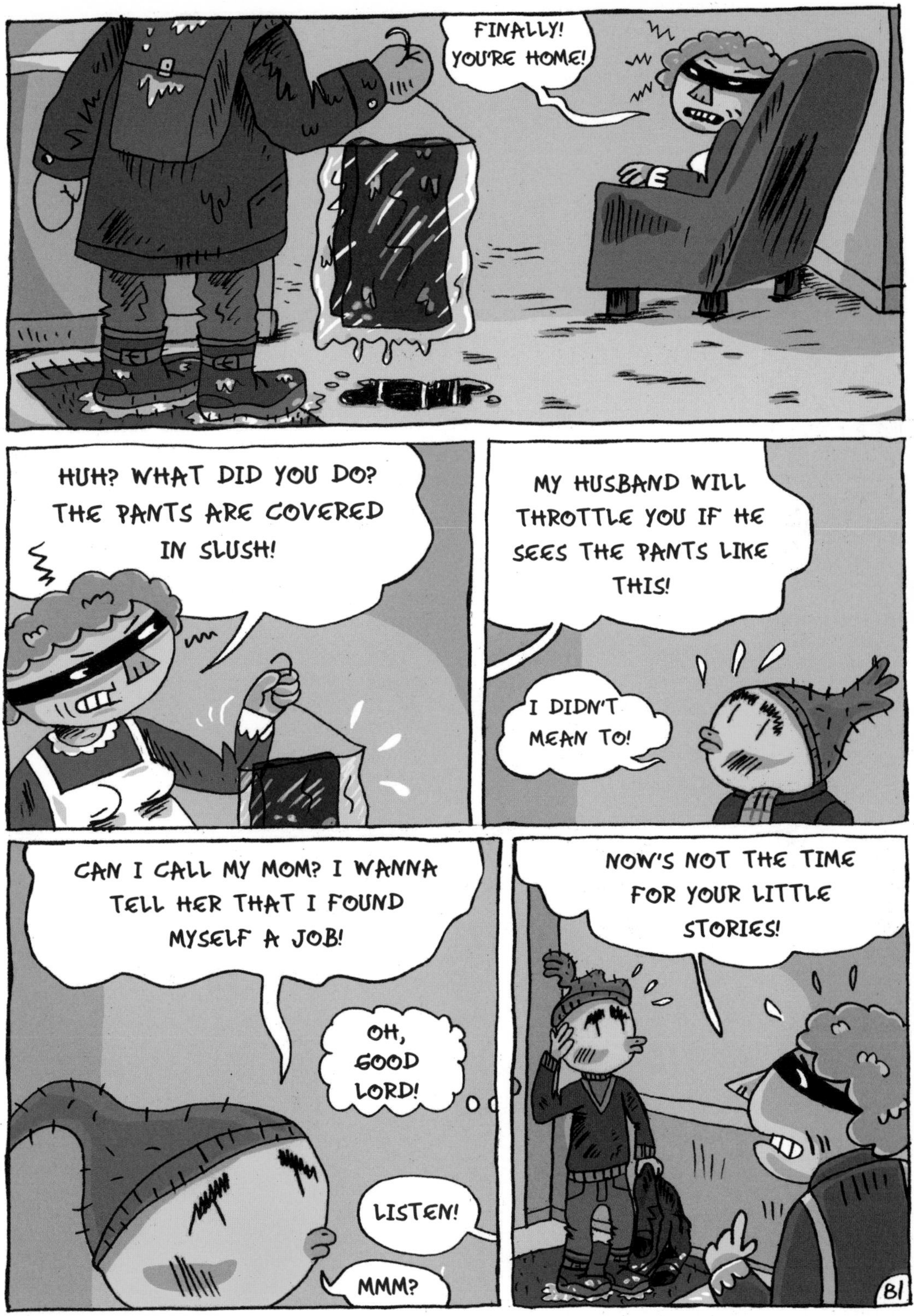
FINALLY! YOU'RE HOME!
HUH? WHAT DID YOU DO? THE PANTS ARE COVERED IN SLUSH!
MY HUSBAND WILL THROTTLE YOU IF HE SEES THE PANTS LIKE THIS!
I DIDN'T MEAN TO!
CAN I CALL MY MOM? I WANNA TELL HER THAT I FOUND MYSELF A JOB!
OH, GOOD LORD!
LISTEN!
MMM?
NOW'S NOT THE TIME FOR YOUR LITTLE STORIES!
81

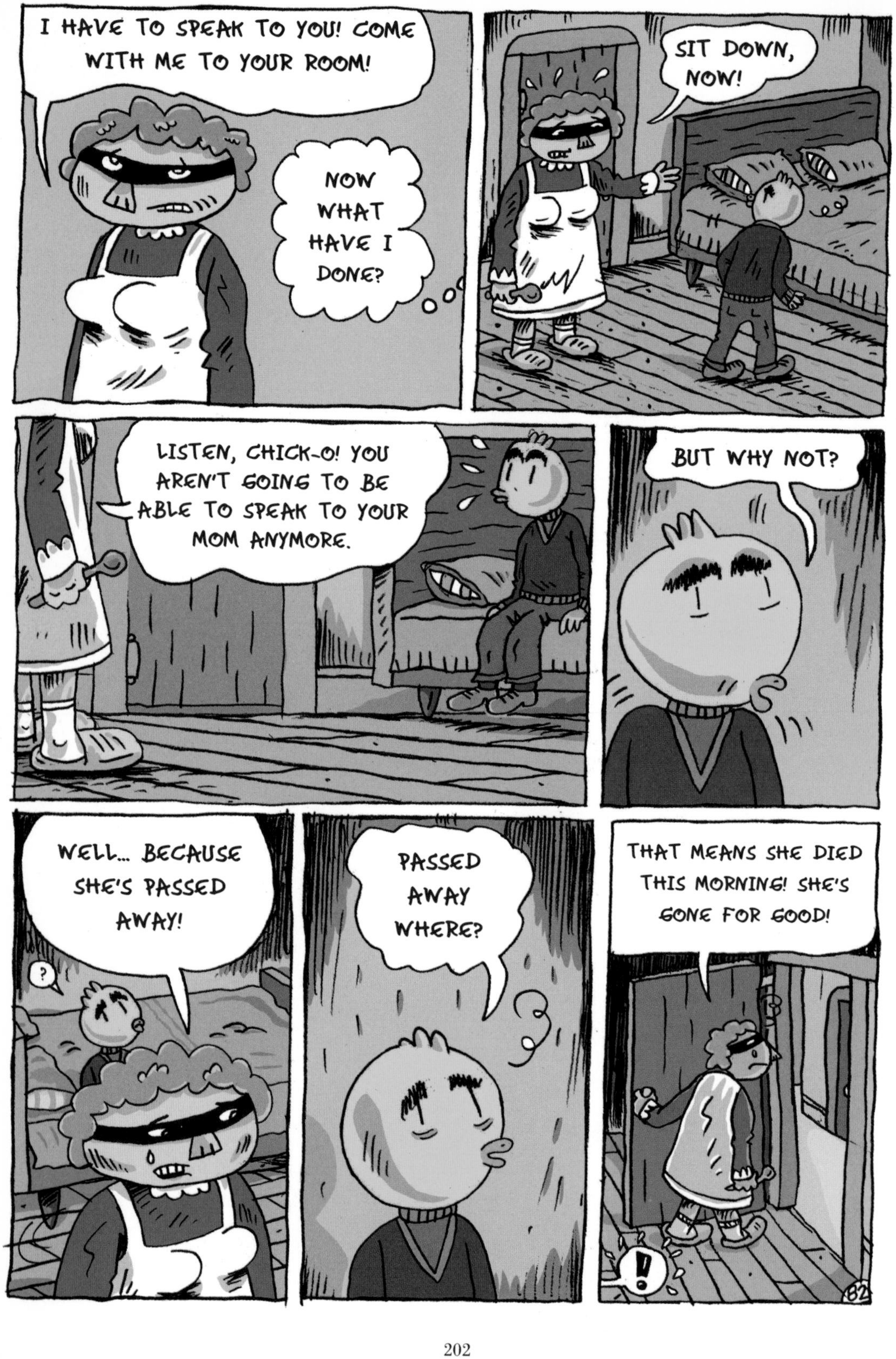
I HAVE TO SPEAK TO YOU! COME WITH ME TO YOUR ROOM!
NOW WHAT HAVE I DONE?
SIT DOWN, NOW!
LISTEN, CHICK-O! YOU AREN'T GOING TO BE ABLE TO SPEAK TO YOUR MOM ANYMORE.
BUT WHY NOT?
WELL... BECAUSE SHE'S PASSED AWAY!
?
PASSED AWAY WHERE?
THAT MEANS SHE DIED THIS MORNING! SHE'S GONE FOR GOOD!
!

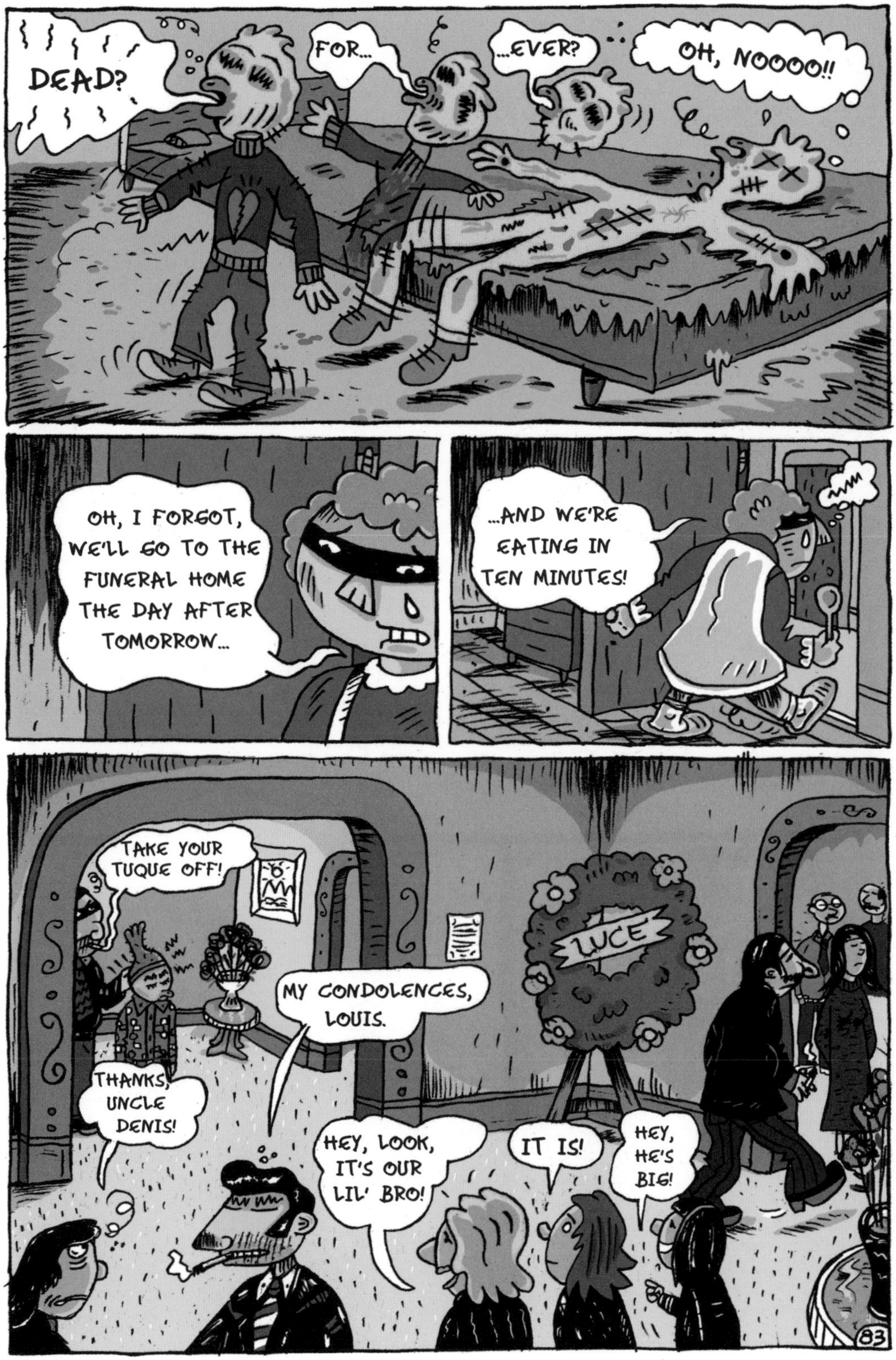
DEAD?
FOR...
...EVER?
OH, NOOOO!!
OH, I FORGOT, WE'LL GO TO THE FUNERAL HOME THE DAY AFTER TOMORROW...
...AND WE'RE EATING IN TEN MINUTES!
TAKE YOUR TUQUE OFF!
LUCE
MY CONDOLENCES, LOUIS.
THANKS, UNCLE DENIS!
HEY, LOOK, IT'S OUR LIL' BRO!
IT IS!
HEY, HE'S BIG!
83

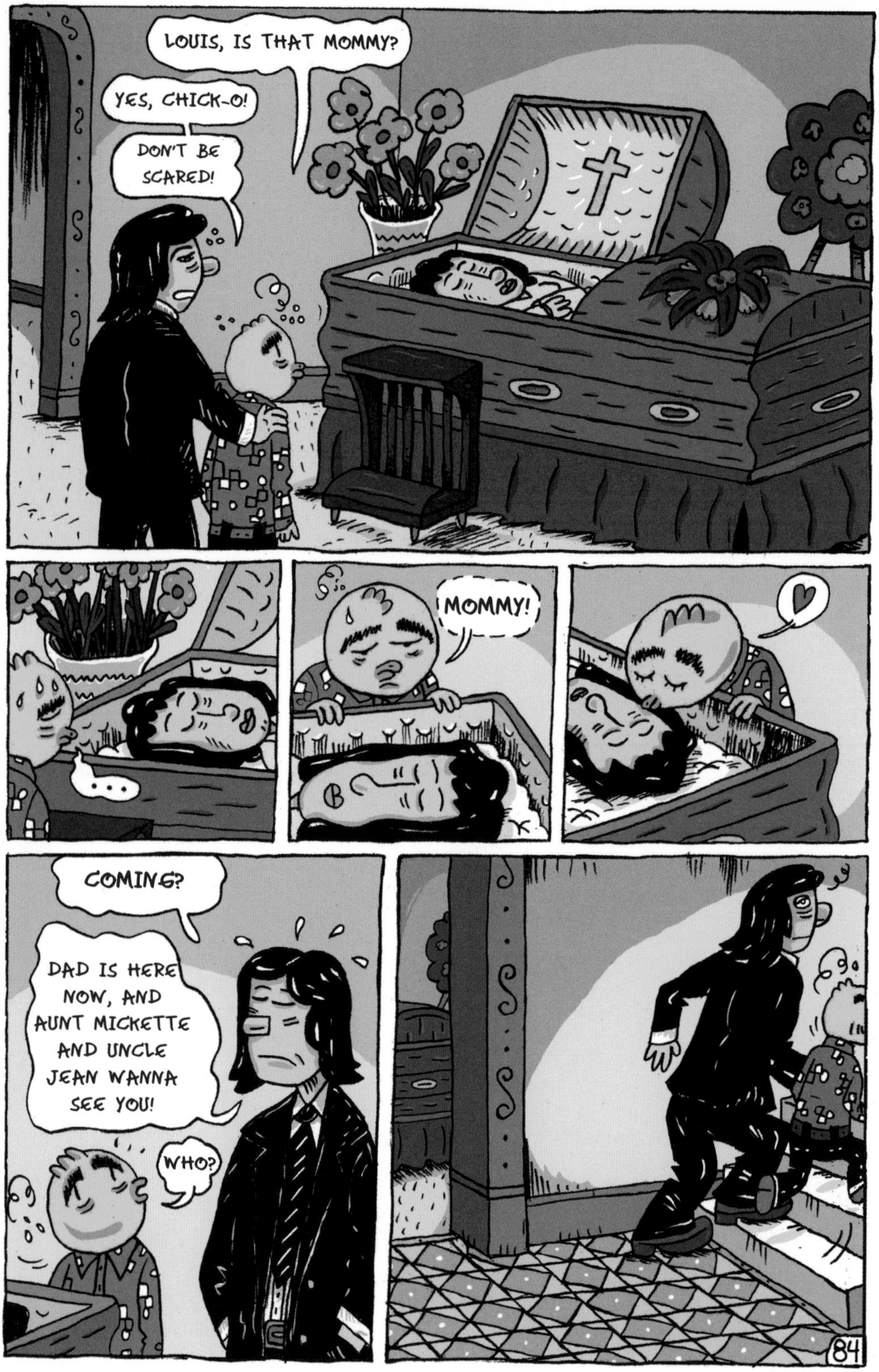
LOUIS, IS THAT MOMMY?
YES, CHICK-O!
DON'T BE SCARED!
...
MOMMY!
COMING?
DAD IS HERE NOW, AND AUNT MICKETTE AND UNCLE JEAN WANNA SEE YOU!
WHO?
84

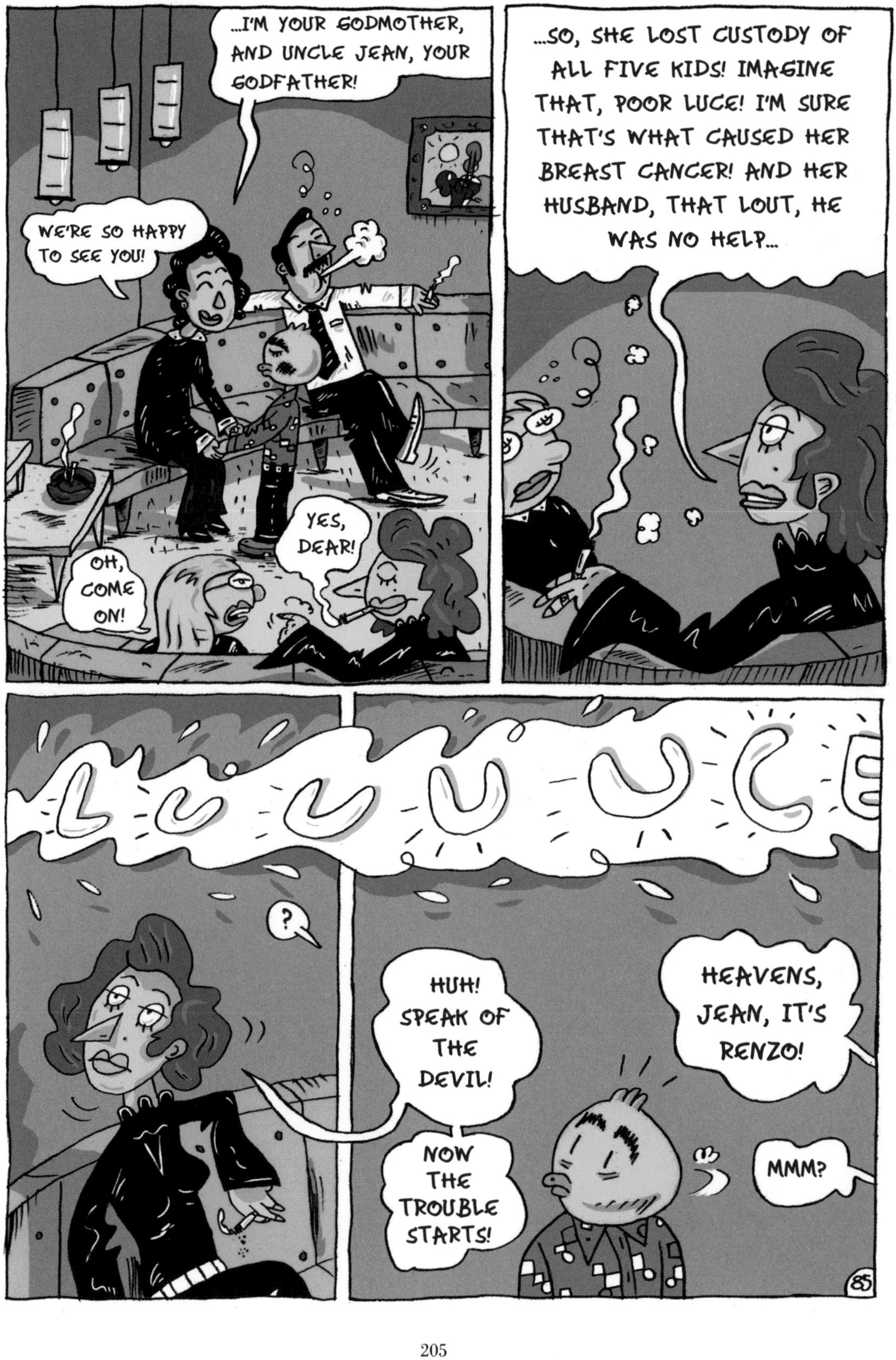

...I'M YOUR GODMOTHER, AND UNCLE JEAN, YOUR GODFATHER!
WE'RE SO HAPPY TO SEE YOU!
YES, DEAR!
OH, COME ON!
...SO, SHE LOST CUSTODY OF ALL FIVE KIDS! IMAGINE THAT, POOR LUCE! I'M SURE THAT'S WHAT CAUSED HER BREAST CANCER! AND HER HUSBAND, THAT LOUT, HE WAS NO HELP...
LUUUUCE
?
HUH! SPEAK OF THE DEVIL!
NOW THE TROUBLE STARTS!
HEAVENS, JEAN, IT'S RENZO!
MMM?
85

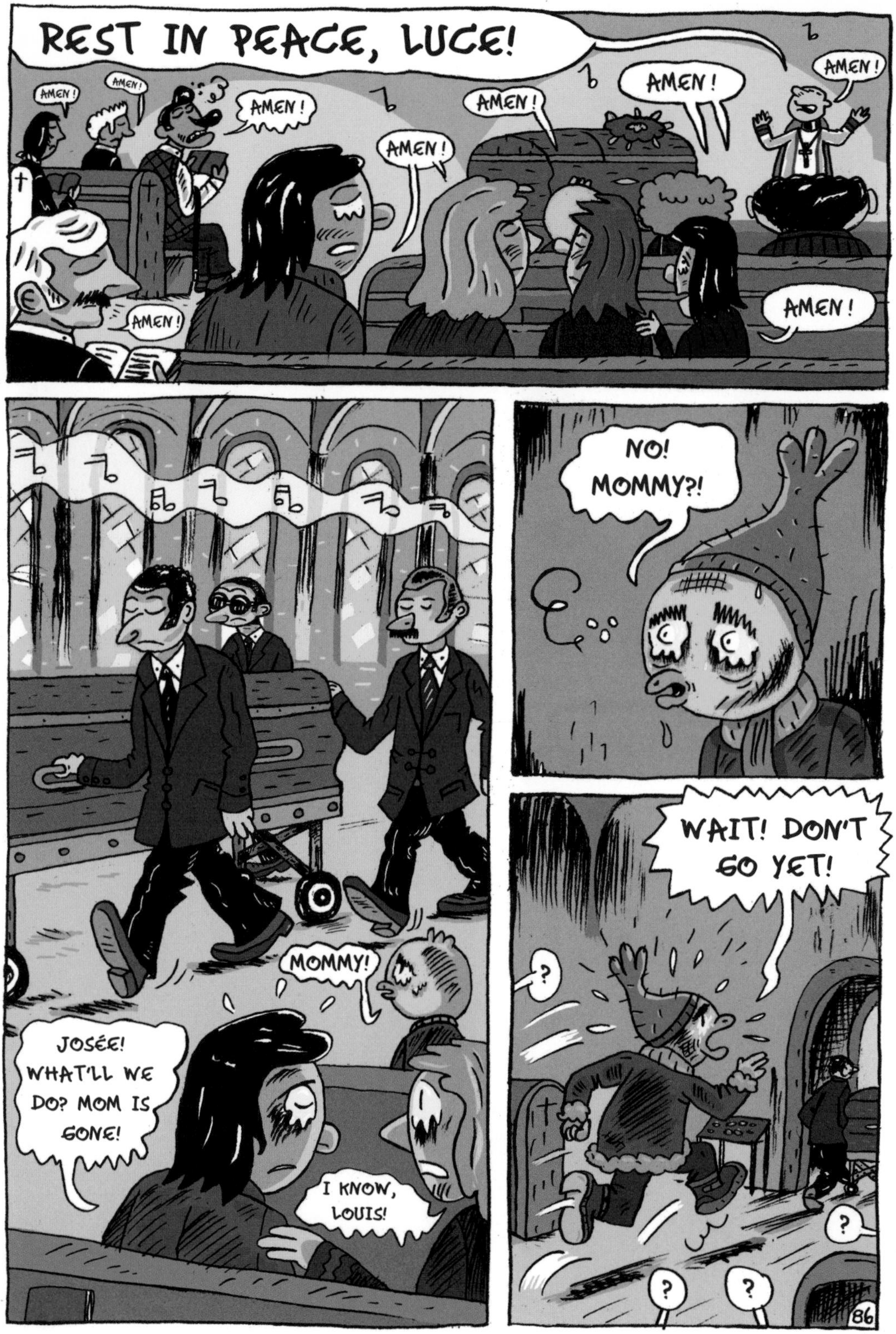
REST IN PEACE, LUCE!
AMEN!
AMEN!
AMEN!
AMEN!
AMEN!
AMEN!
AMEN!
AMEN!
AMEN!
AMEN!
NO! MOMMY?!
MOMMY!
JOSÉE! WHAT'LL WE DO? MOM IS GONE!
I KNOW, LOUIS!
WAIT! DON'T GO YET!
?
?
?
?
86

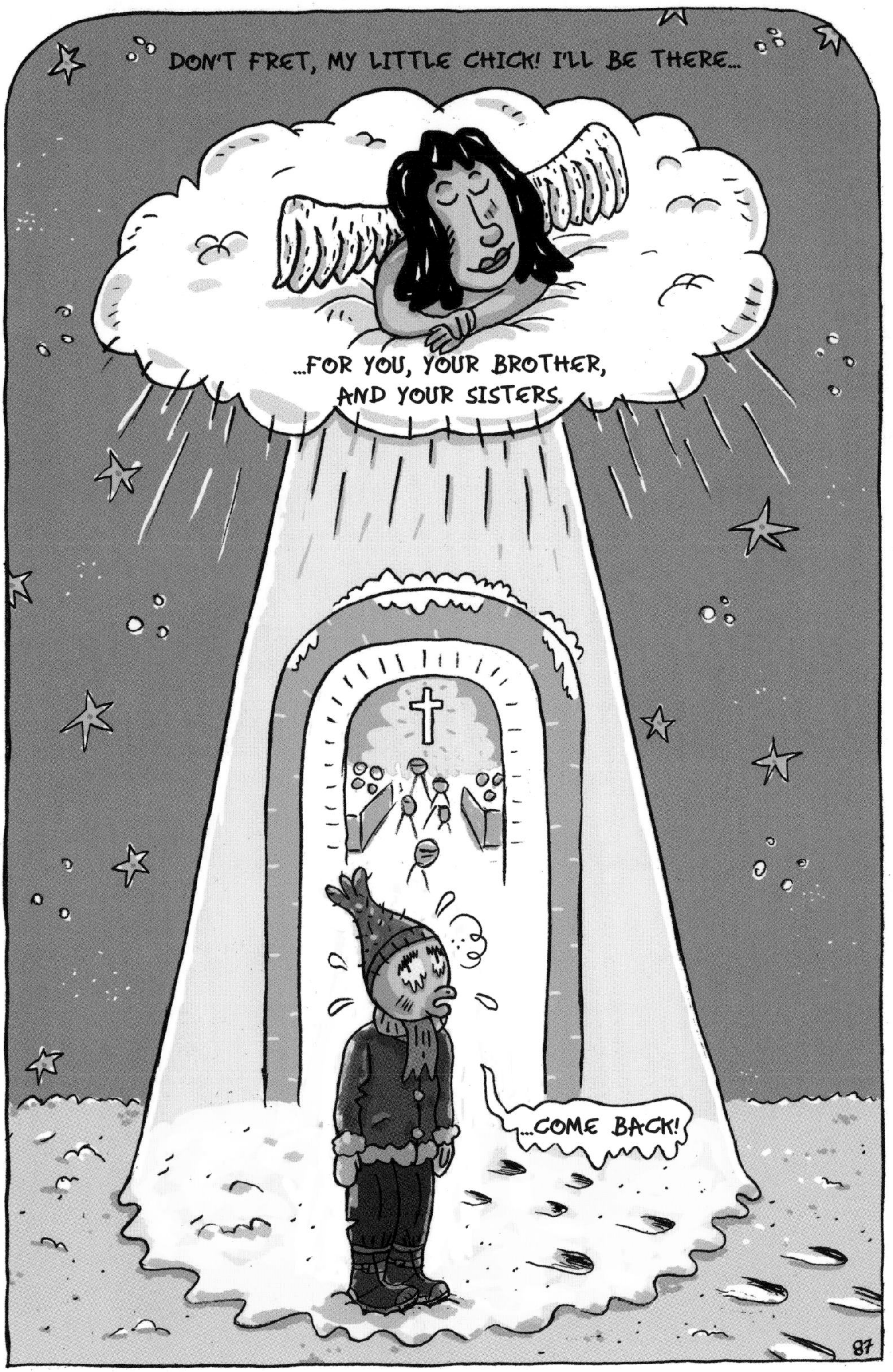
DON'T FRET, MY LITTLE CHICK! I'LL BE THERE...
...FOR YOU, YOUR BROTHER, AND YOUR SISTERS.
...COME BACK!
87

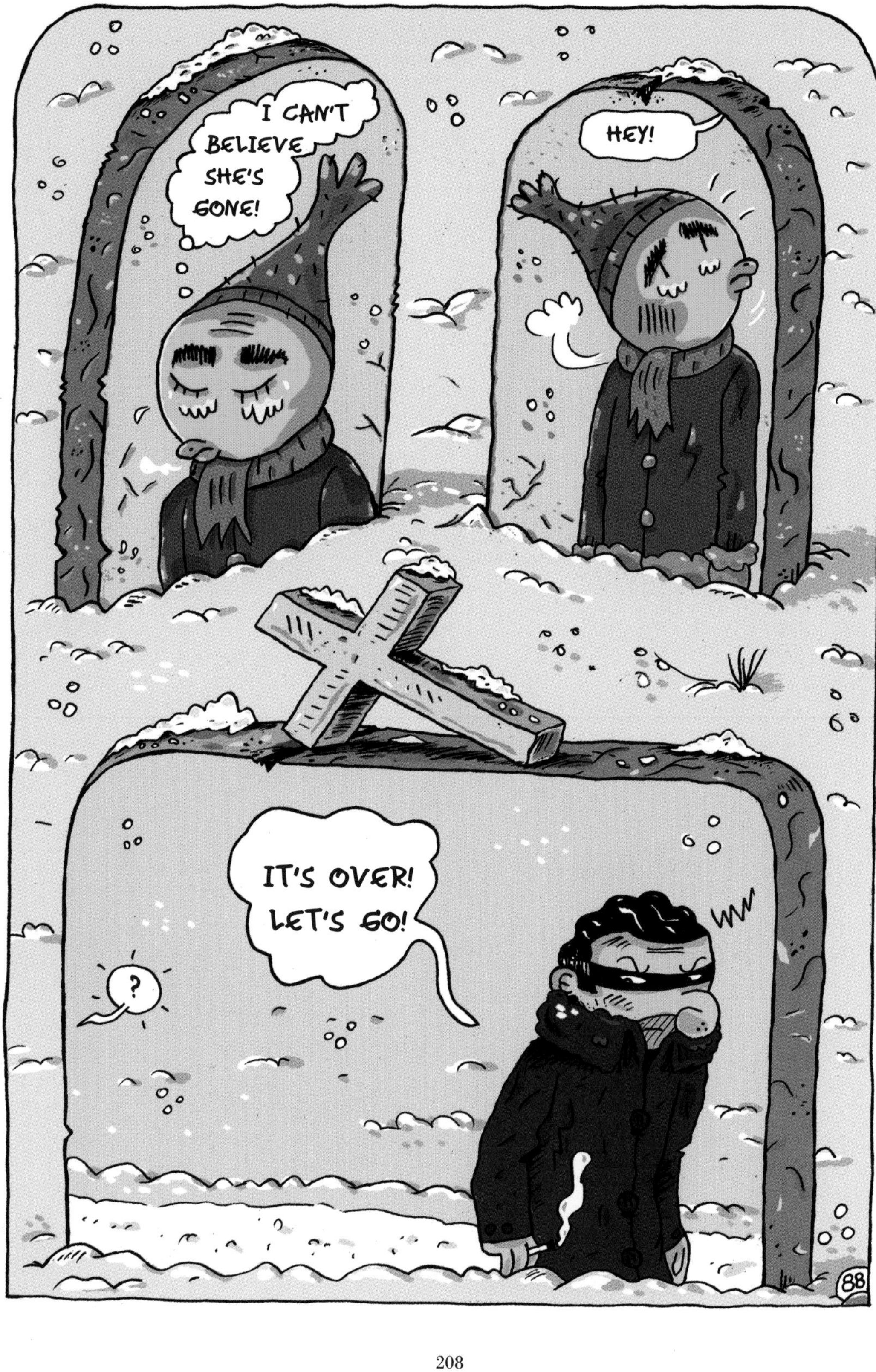
I CAN'T BELIEVE SHE'S GONE!
HEY!
IT'S OVER! LET'S GO!
?
88

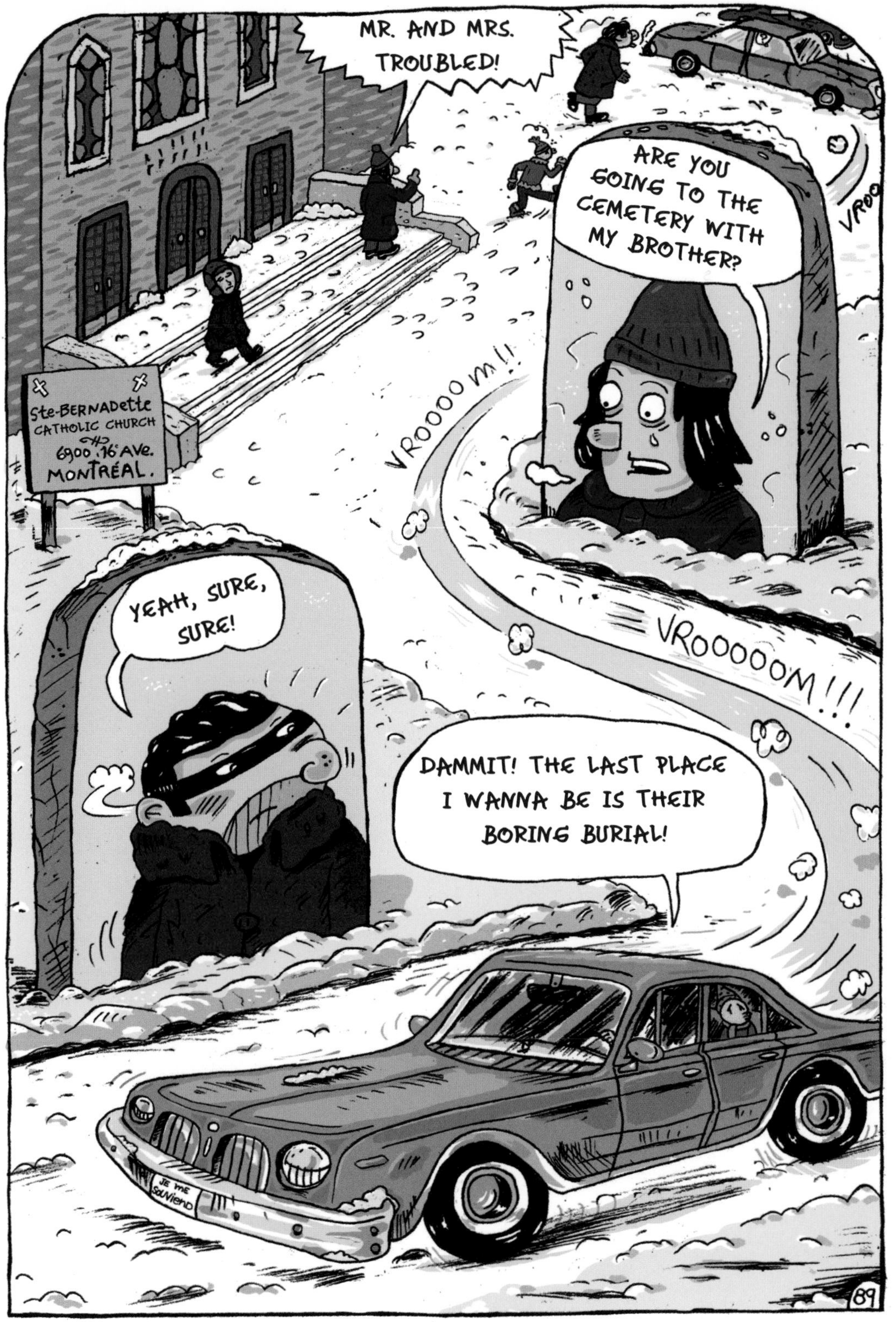
MR. AND MRS. TROUBLED!
Ste-BERNADETTE CATHOLIC CHURCH 6900 16e AVE. MONTRÉAL.
ARE YOU GOING TO THE CEMETERY WITH MY BROTHER?
VROOOOM!!
YEAH, SURE, SURE!
VROOOOOM!!!
DAMMIT! THE LAST PLACE I WANNA BE IS THEIR BORING BURIAL!
JE ME SOUVIENS
89

90

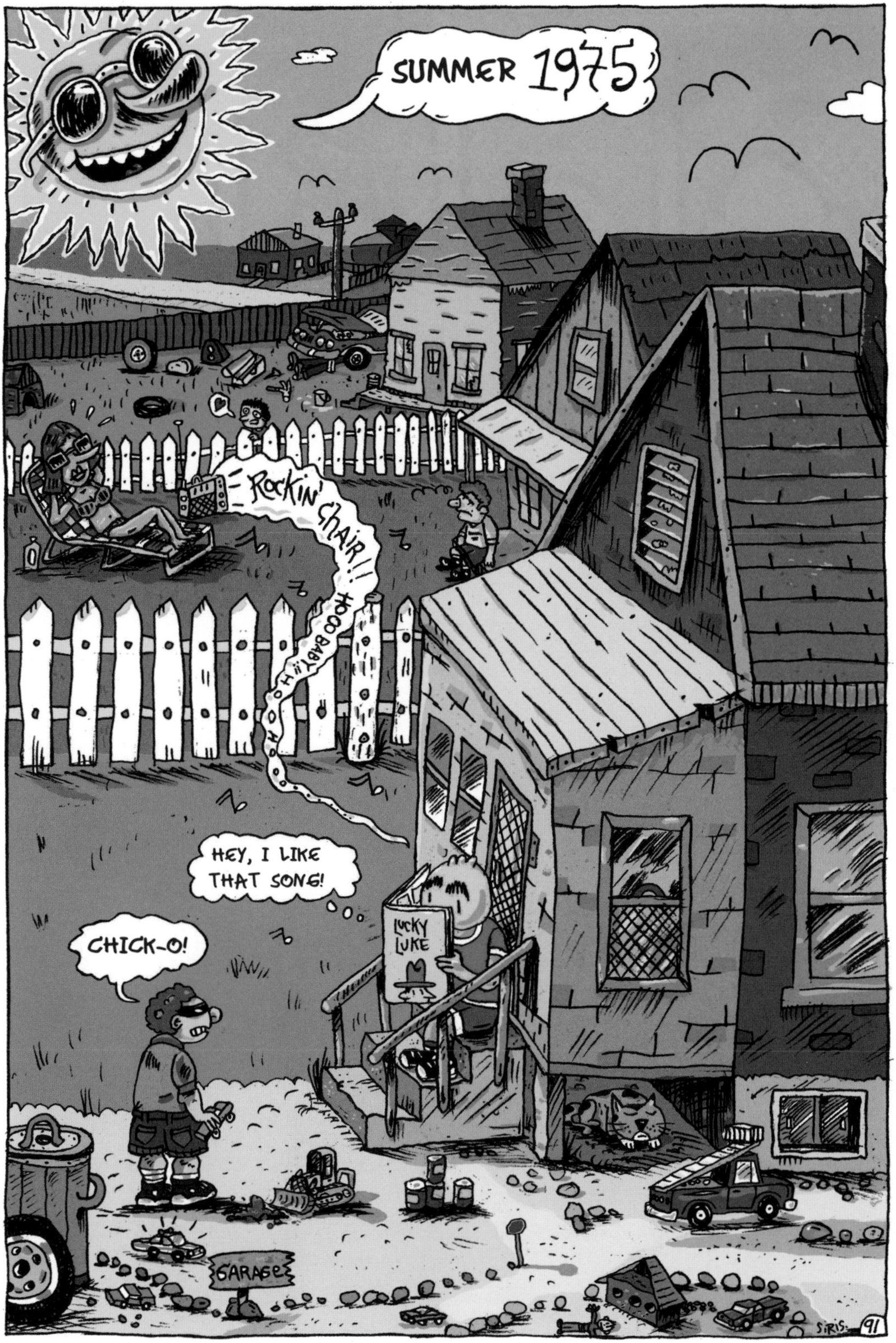
SUMMER 1975
ROCKIN' CHAIR!!
HOO BABY!! HOOOOO
HEY, I LIKE THAT SONG!
CHICK-O!
LUCKY LUKE
GARAGE
SIRIS. 91

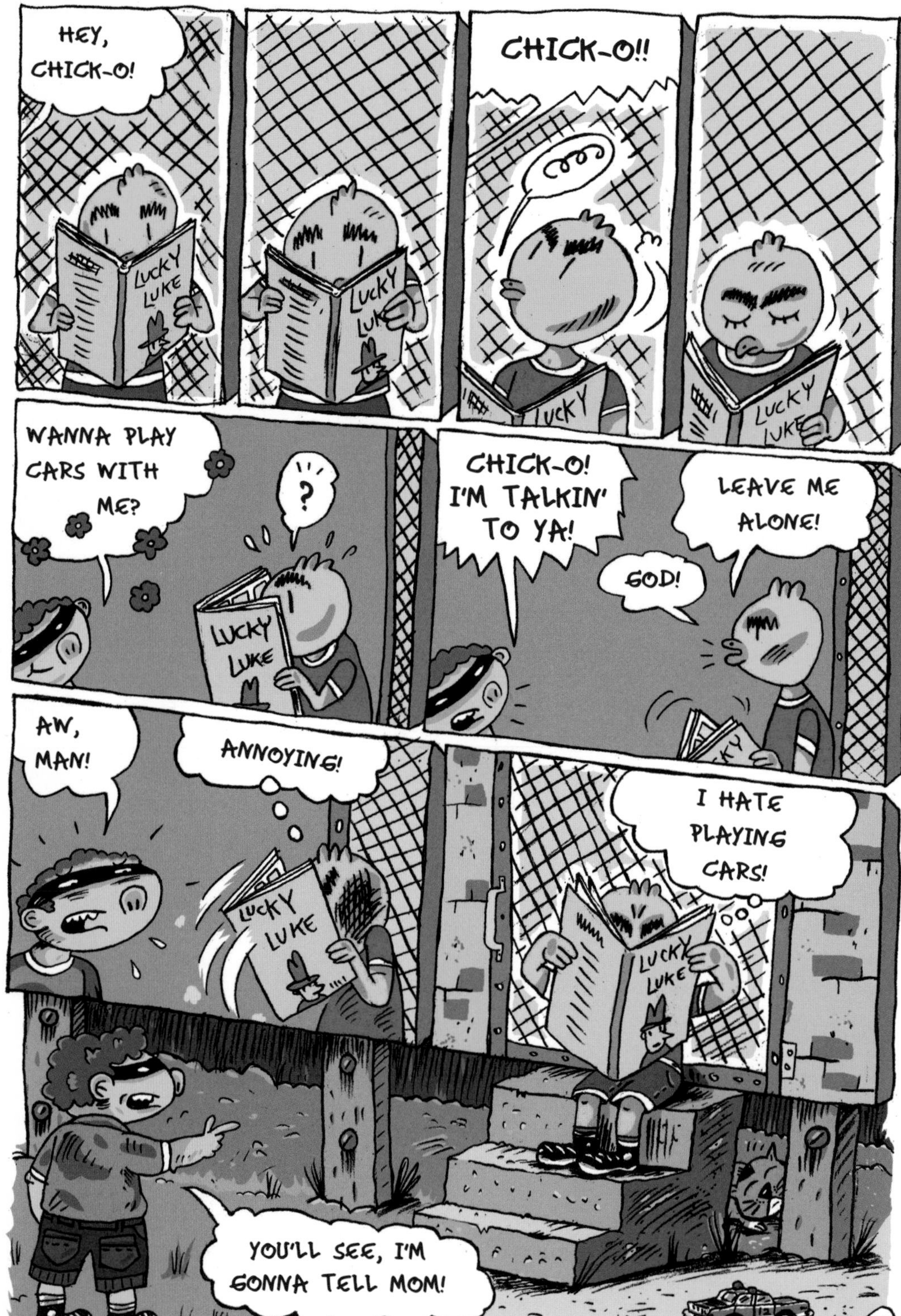
HEY, CHICK-O!
CHICK-O!!
WANNA PLAY CARS WITH ME?
?
CHICK-O! I'M TALKIN' TO YA!
LEAVE ME ALONE!
GOD!
AW, MAN!
ANNOYING!
I HATE PLAYING CARS!
YOU'LL SEE, I'M GONNA TELL MOM!
92

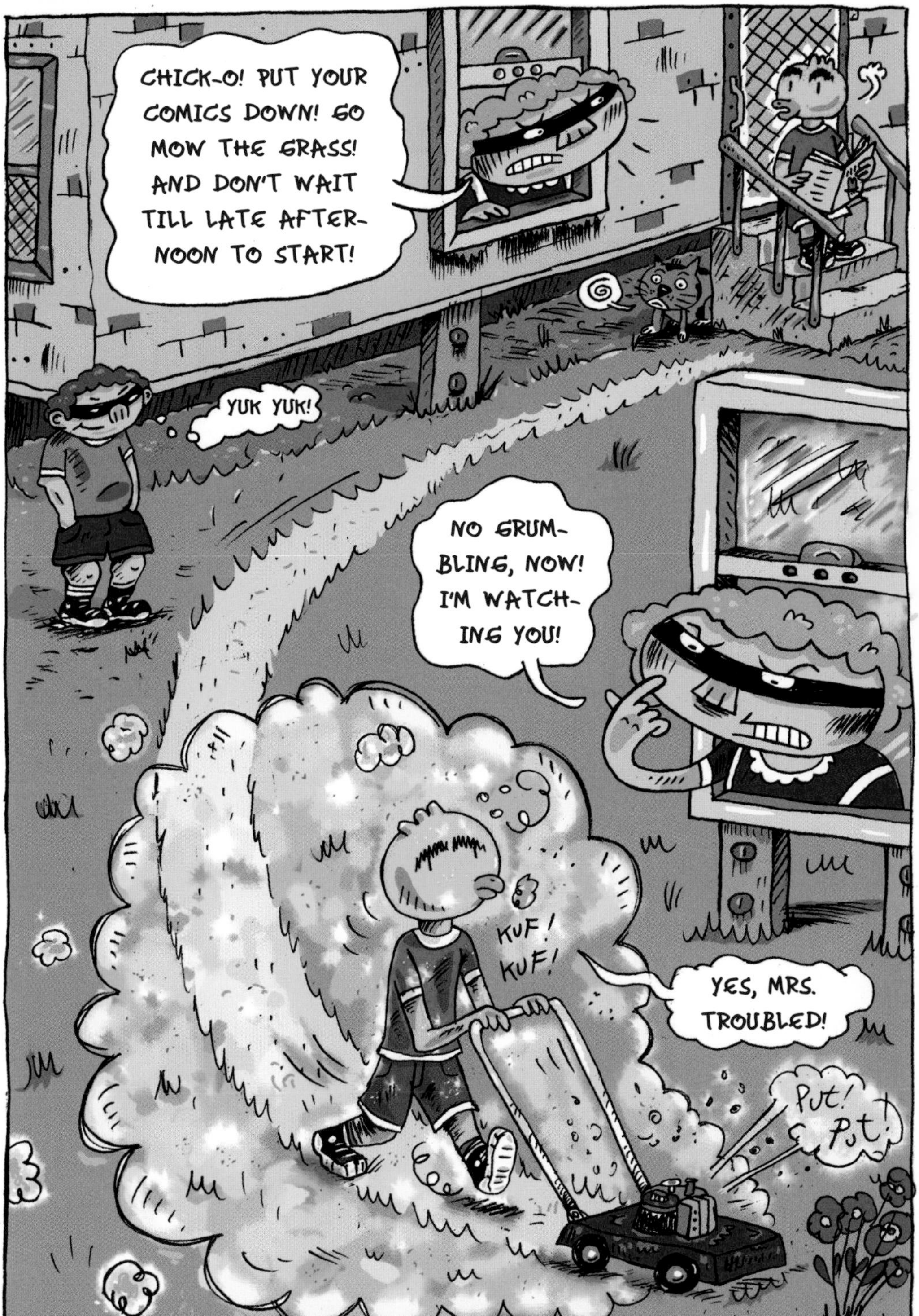
CHICK-O! PUT YOUR COMICS DOWN! GO MOW THE GRASS! AND DON'T WAIT TILL LATE AFTER-NOON TO START!
YUK YUK!
NO GRUM-BLING, NOW! I'M WATCH-ING YOU!
KUF! KUF!
YES, MRS. TROUBLED!
Put! Put!
93

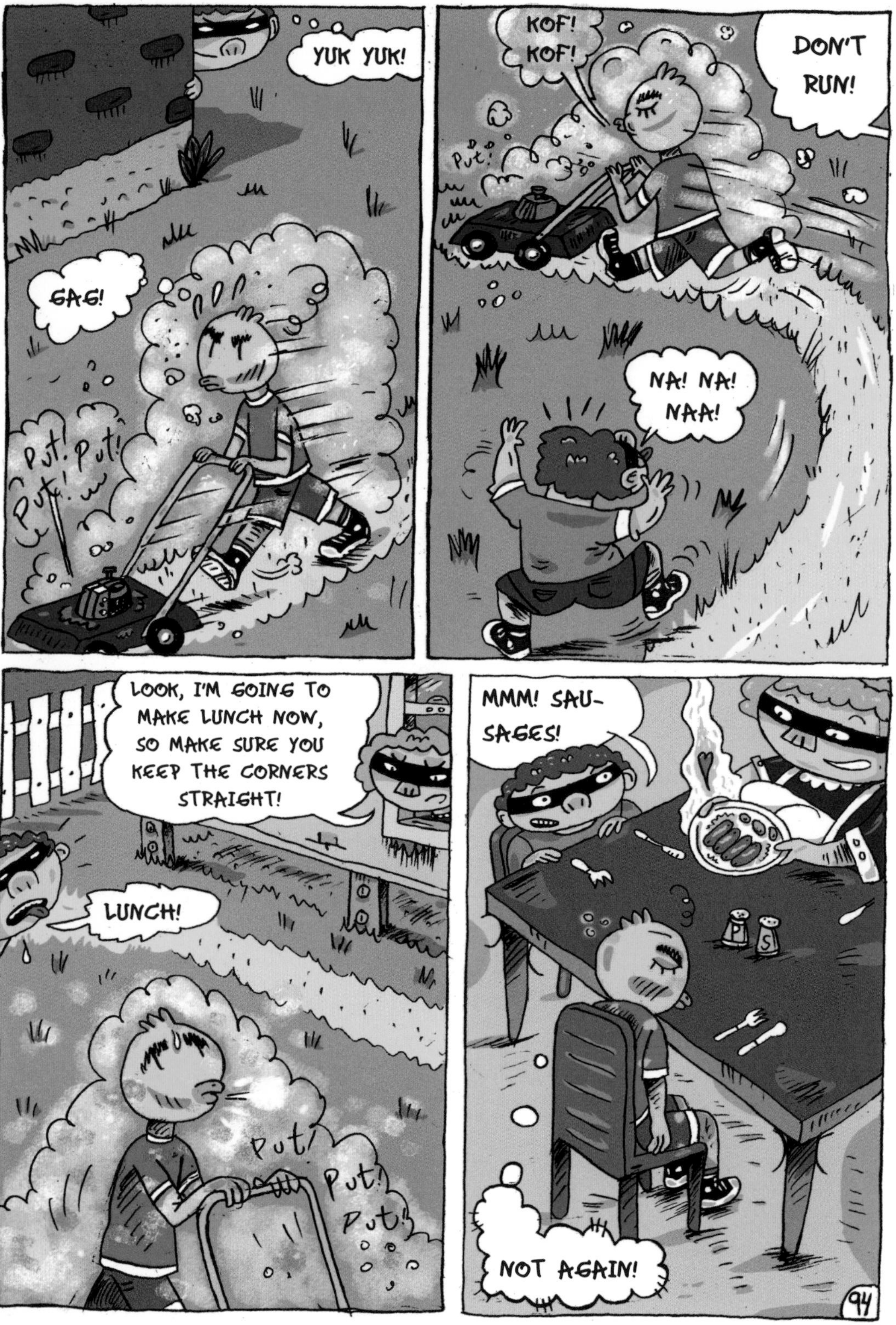
YUK YUK!
GAG!
Put! Put! Put!
KOF! KOF!
Put!
DON'T RUN!
NA! NA! NAA!
LOOK, I'M GOING TO MAKE LUNCH NOW, SO MAKE SURE YOU KEEP THE CORNERS STRAIGHT!
LUNCH!
Put! Put! Put!
MMM! SAU-SAGES!
P
S
NOT AGAIN!
94

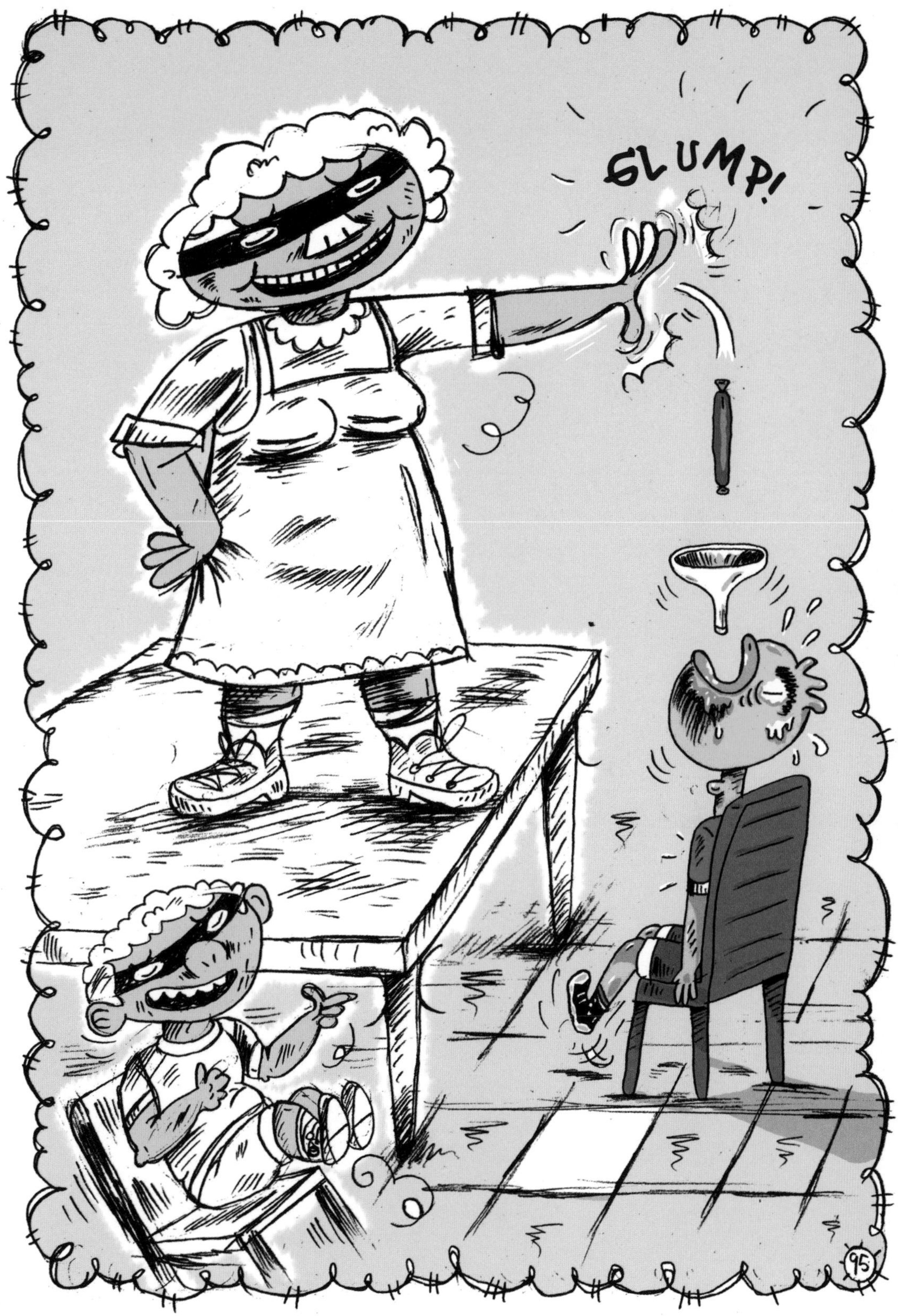
GLUMP!
95

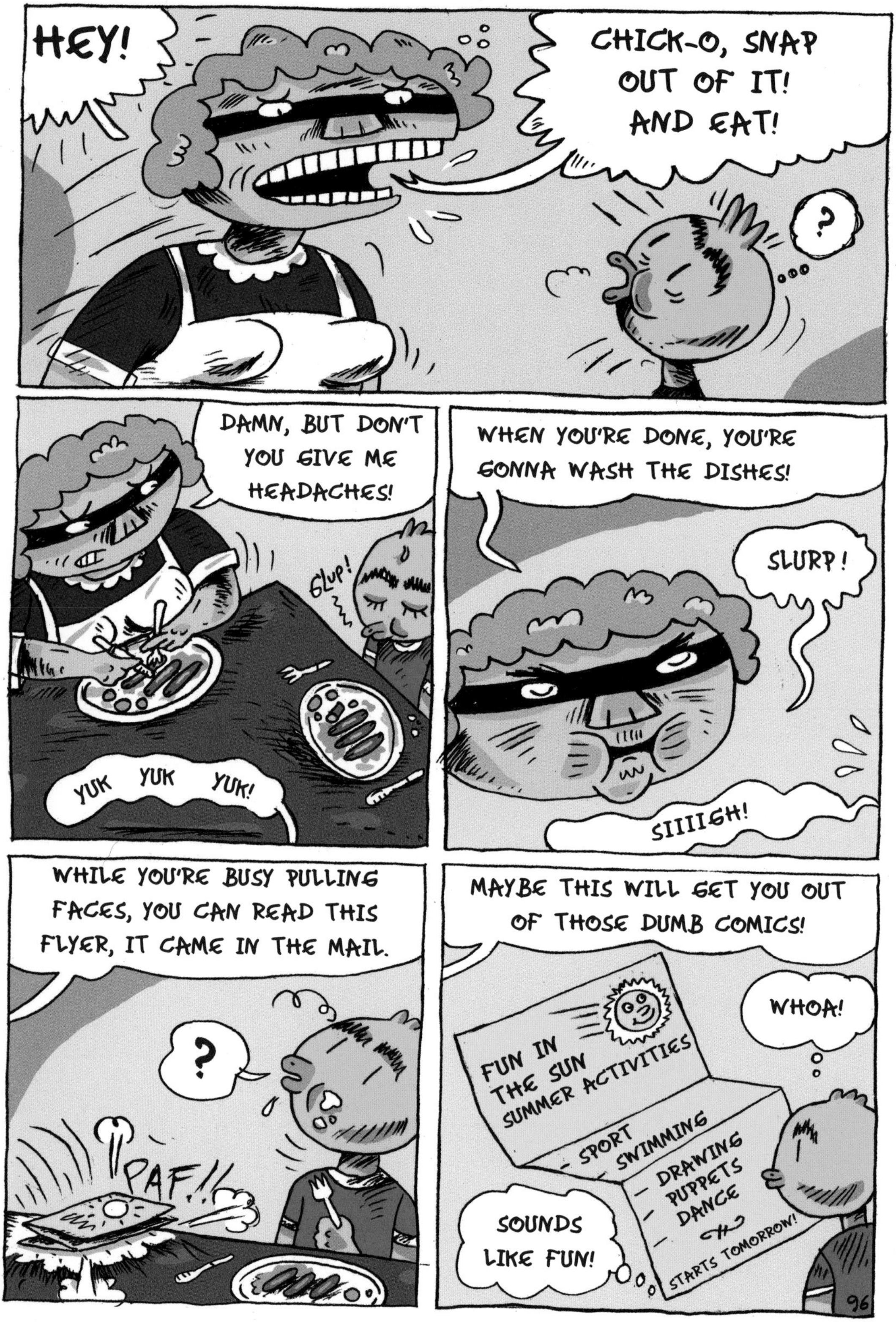
HEY!
CHICK-O, SNAP OUT OF IT! AND EAT!
?
DAMN, BUT DON'T YOU GIVE ME HEADACHES!
SLUP!
YUK YUK YUK!
WHEN YOU'RE DONE, YOU'RE GONNA WASH THE DISHES!
SLURP!
SIIIIGH!
WHILE YOU'RE BUSY PULLING FACES, YOU CAN READ THIS FLYER, IT CAME IN THE MAIL.
?
PAF!
MAYBE THIS WILL GET YOU OUT OF THOSE DUMB COMICS!
FUN IN THE SUN SUMMER ACTIVITIES
SPORT
SWIMMING
DRAWING
PUPPETS
DANCE
STARTS TOMORROW!
WHOA!
SOUNDS LIKE FUN!
96

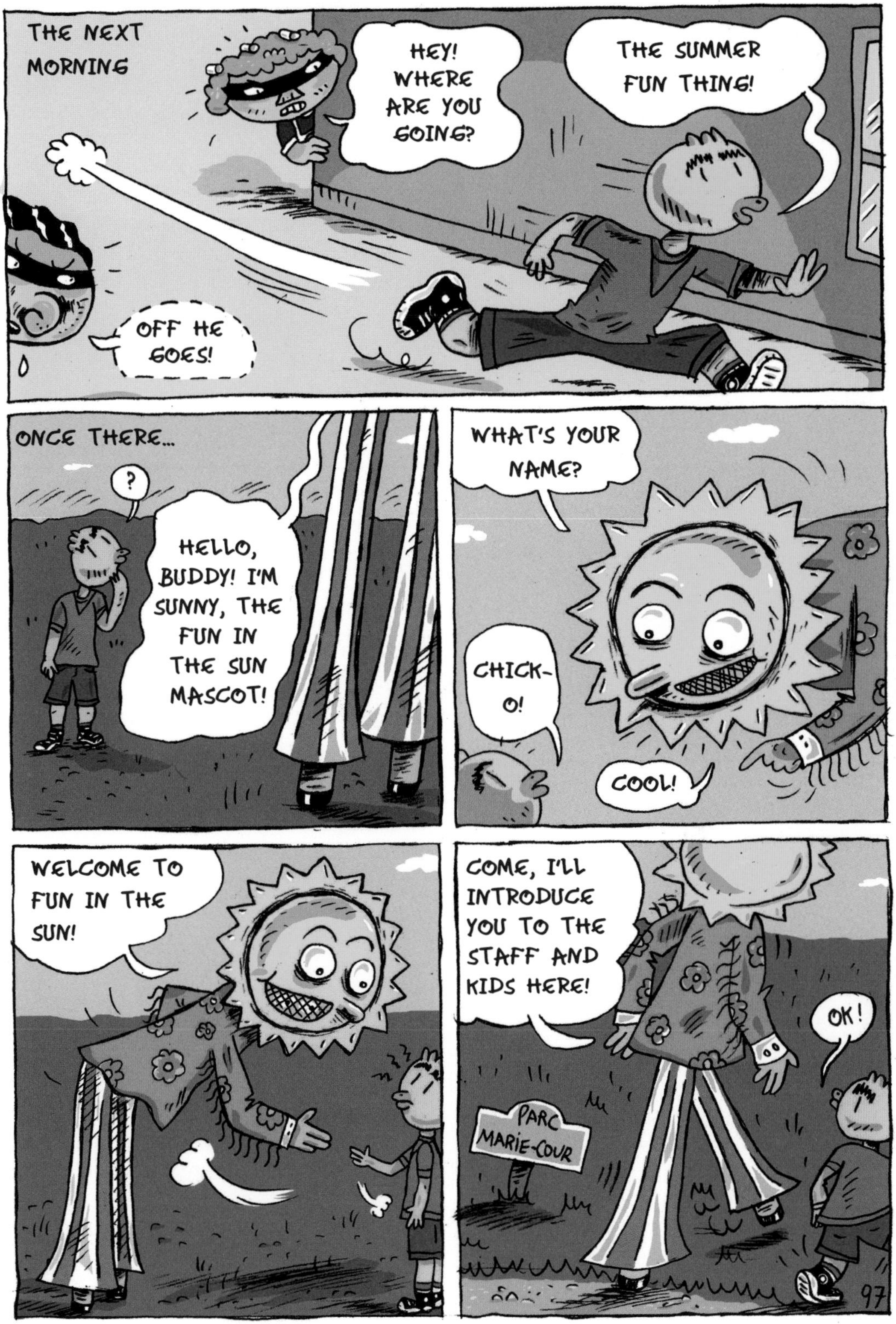
THE NEXT MORNING
HEY! WHERE ARE YOU GOING?
THE SUMMER FUN THING!
OFF HE GOES!
ONCE THERE...
?
HELLO, BUDDY! I'M SUNNY, THE FUN IN THE SUN MASCOT!
WHAT'S YOUR NAME?
CHICK-O!
COOL!
WELCOME TO FUN IN THE SUN!
COME, I'LL INTRODUCE YOU TO THE STAFF AND KIDS HERE!
OK!
PARC MARIE-COUR
97

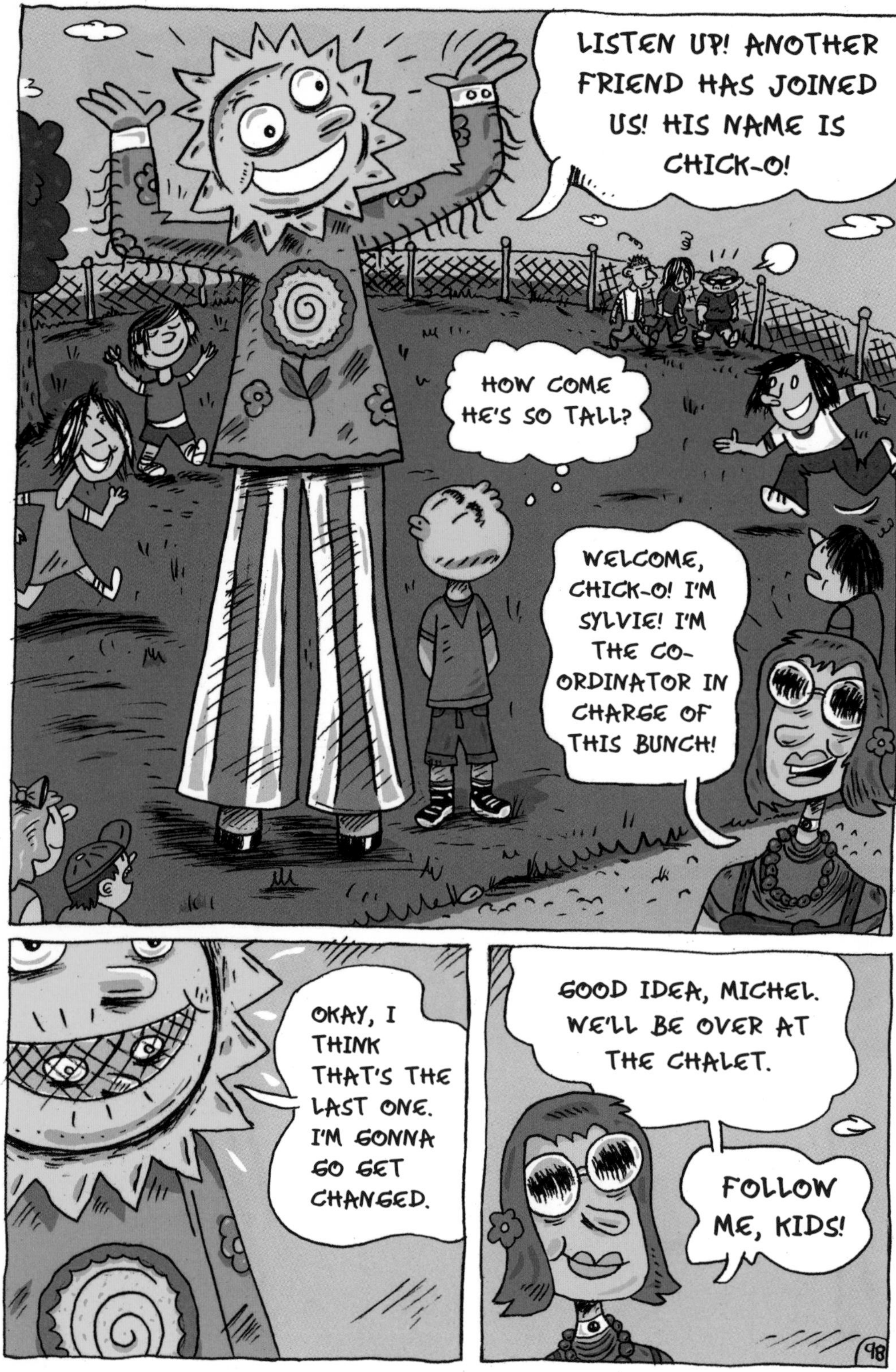
LISTEN UP! ANOTHER FRIEND HAS JOINED US! HIS NAME IS CHICK-O!
HOW COME HE'S SO TALL?
WELCOME, CHICK-O! I'M SYLVIE! I'M THE CO-ORDINATOR IN CHARGE OF THIS BUNCH!
OKAY, I THINK THAT'S THE LAST ONE. I'M GONNA GO GET CHANGED.
GOOD IDEA, MICHEL. WE'LL BE OVER AT THE CHALET.
FOLLOW ME, KIDS!
98

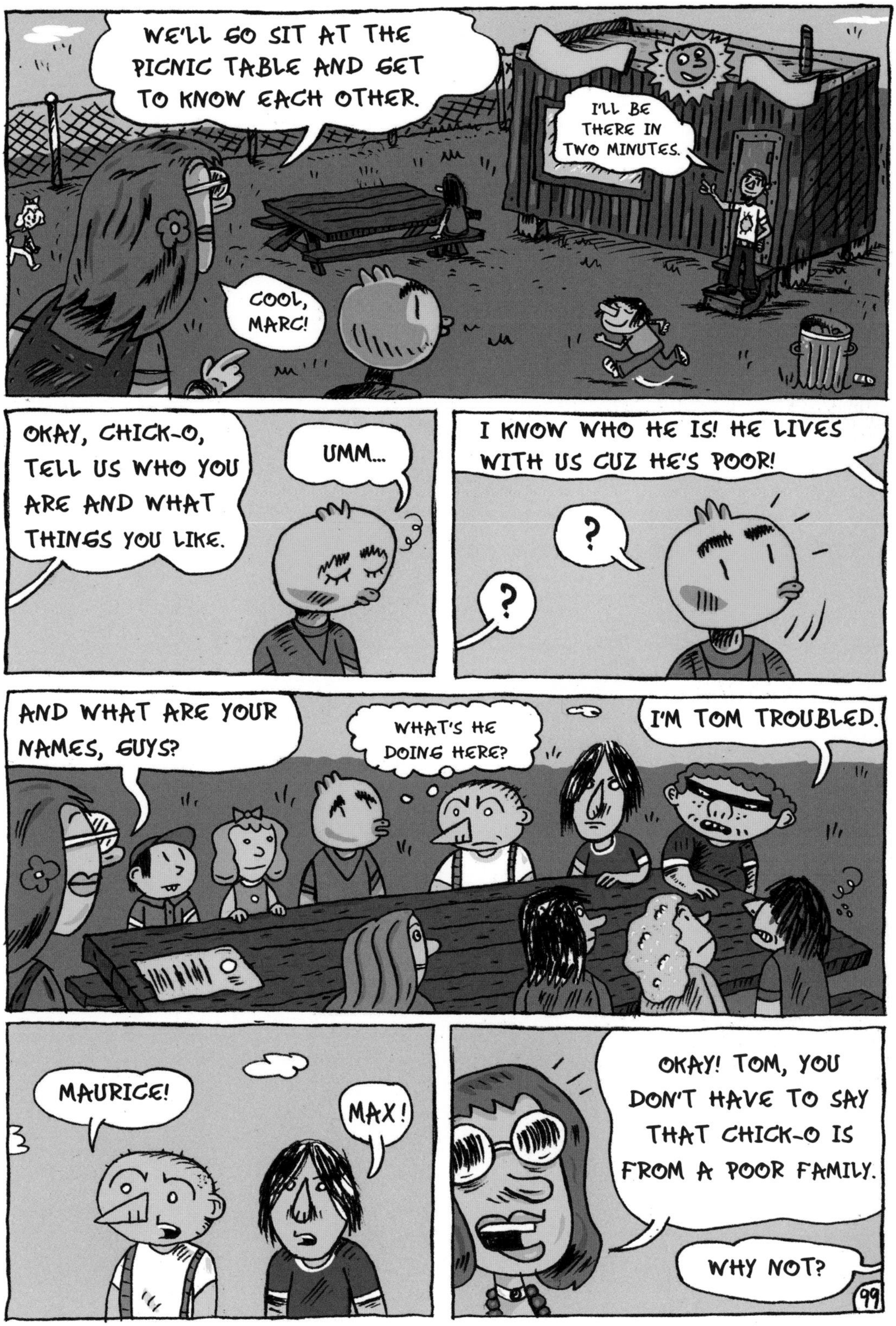
WE'LL GO SIT AT THE PICNIC TABLE AND GET TO KNOW EACH OTHER.
I'LL BE THERE IN TWO MINUTES.
COOL, MARC!
OKAY, CHICK-O, TELL US WHO YOU ARE AND WHAT THINGS YOU LIKE.
UMM...
I KNOW WHO HE IS! HE LIVES WITH US CUZ HE'S POOR!
?
?
AND WHAT ARE YOUR NAMES, GUYS?
WHAT'S HE DOING HERE?
I'M TOM TROUBLED.
MAURICE!
MAX!
OKAY! TOM, YOU DON'T HAVE TO SAY THAT CHICK-O IS FROM A POOR FAMILY.
WHY NOT?
99

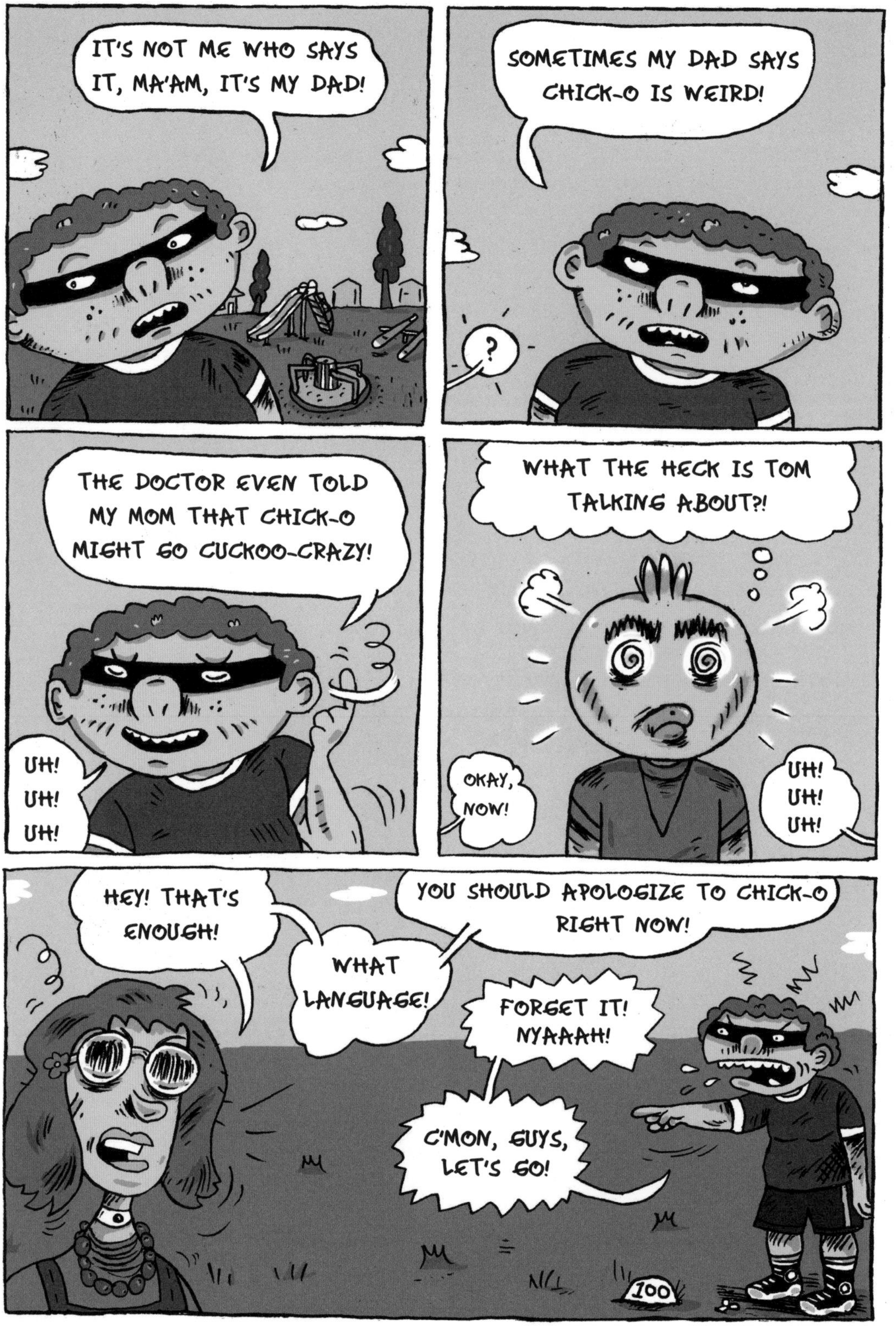

IT'S NOT ME WHO SAYS IT, MA'AM, IT'S MY DAD!
SOMETIMES MY DAD SAYS CHICK-O IS WEIRD!
?
THE DOCTOR EVEN TOLD MY MOM THAT CHICK-O MIGHT GO CUCKOO-CRAZY!
UH! UH! UH!
WHAT THE HECK IS TOM TALKING ABOUT?!
OKAY, NOW!
UH! UH! UH!
HEY! THAT'S ENOUGH!
WHAT LANGUAGE!
YOU SHOULD APOLOGIZE TO CHICK-O RIGHT NOW!
FORGET IT! NYAAAH!
C'MON, GUYS, LET'S GO!
100

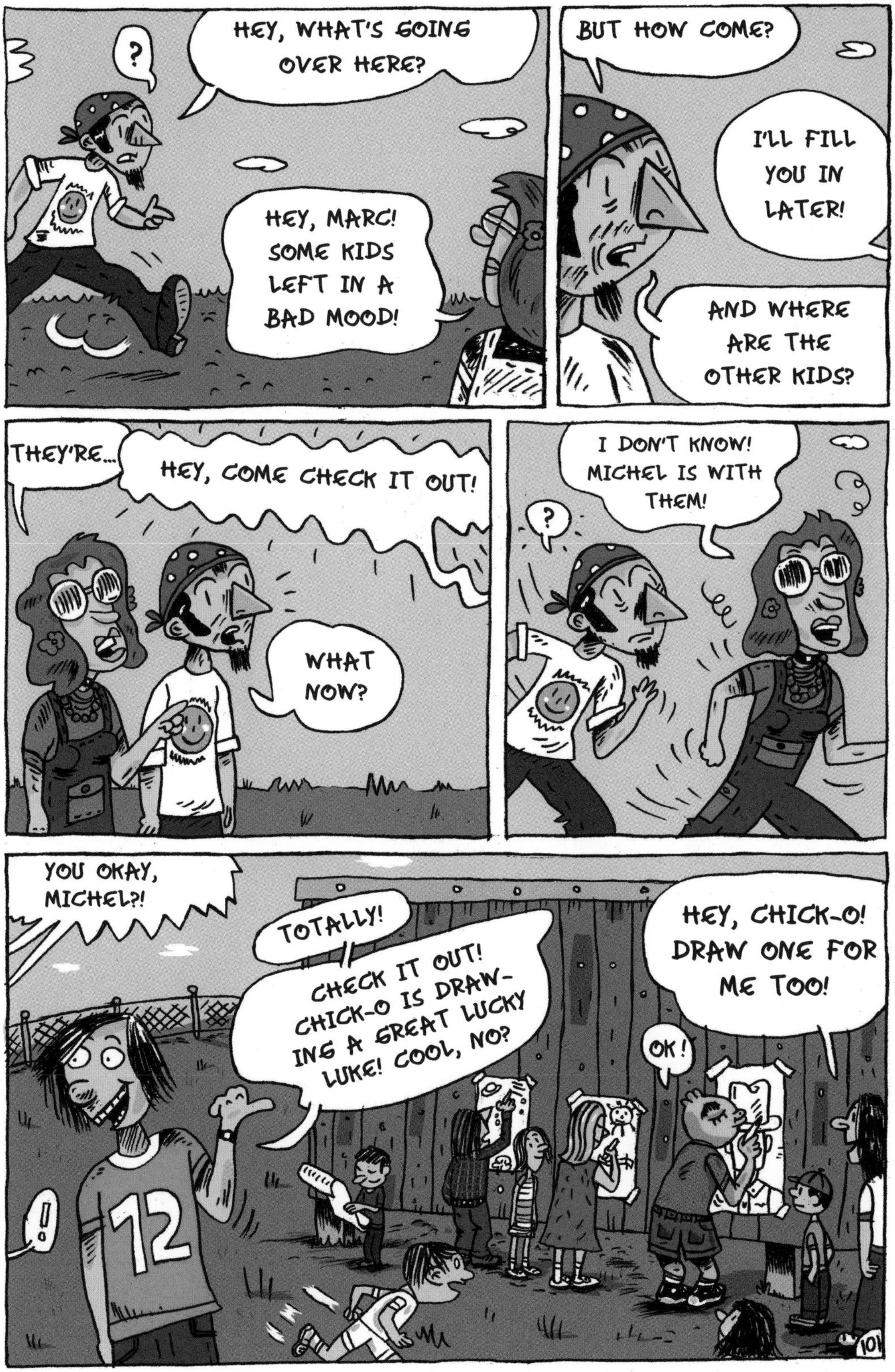
?
HEY, WHAT'S GOING OVER HERE?
HEY, MARC! SOME KIDS LEFT IN A BAD MOOD!
BUT HOW COME?
I'LL FILL YOU IN LATER!
AND WHERE ARE THE OTHER KIDS?
THEY'RE...
HEY, COME CHECK IT OUT!
WHAT NOW?
?
I DON'T KNOW! MICHEL IS WITH THEM!
YOU OKAY, MICHEL?!
TOTALLY!
CHECK IT OUT! CHICK-O IS DRAW-ING A GREAT LUCKY LUKE! COOL, NO?
HEY, CHICK-O! DRAW ONE FOR ME TOO!
OK!
!
12

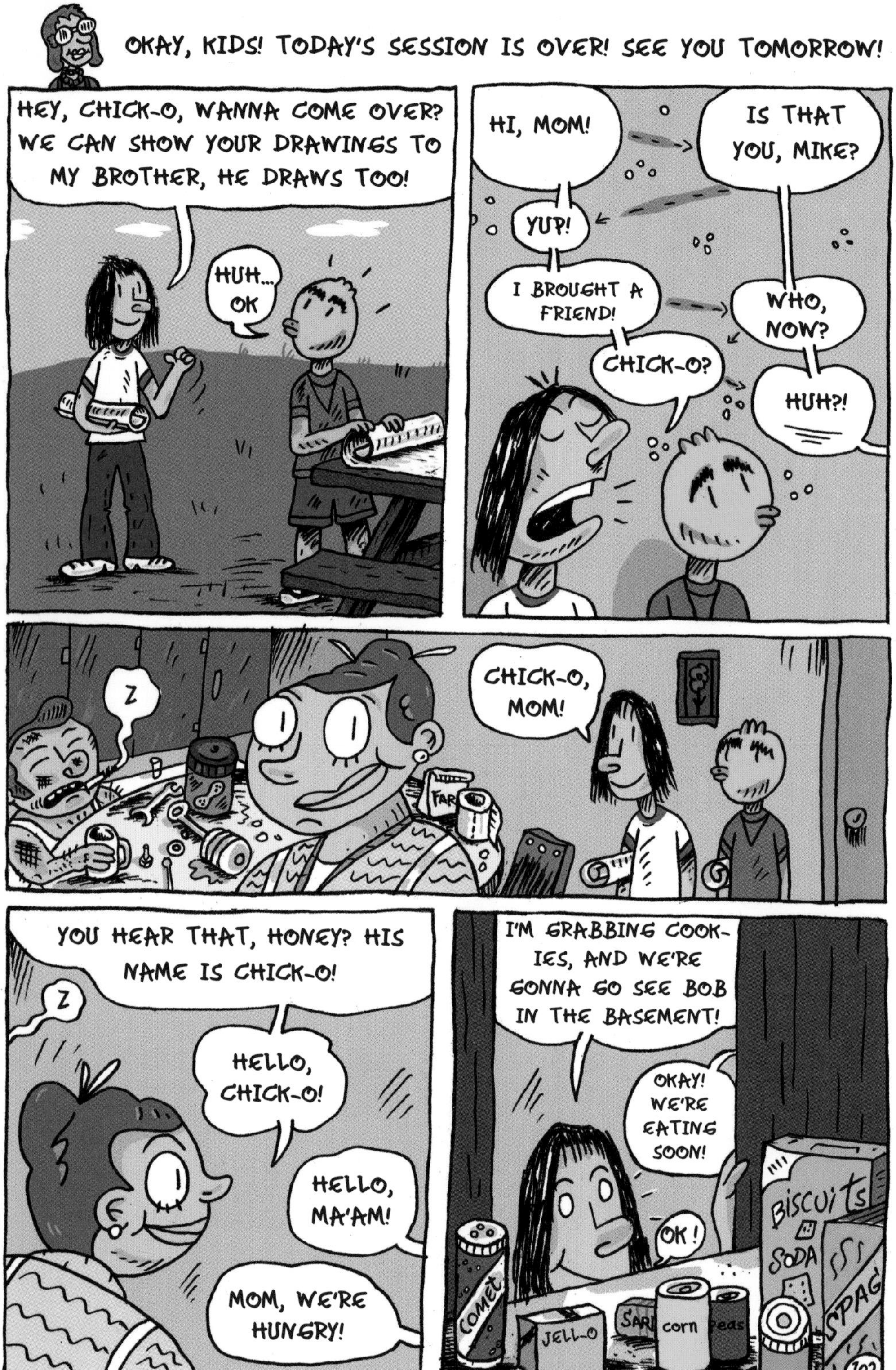
OKAY, KIDS! TODAY'S SESSION IS OVER! SEE YOU TOMORROW!
HEY, CHICK-O, WANNA COME OVER? WE CAN SHOW YOUR DRAWINGS TO MY BROTHER, HE DRAWS TOO!
HUH... OK
HI, MOM!
IS THAT YOU, MIKE?
YUP!
I BROUGHT A FRIEND!
WHO, NOW?
CHICK-O?
HUH?!
Z
CHICK-O, MOM!
FAR
YOU HEAR THAT, HONEY? HIS NAME IS CHICK-O!
Z
HELLO, CHICK-O!
HELLO, MA'AM!
MOM, WE'RE HUNGRY!
I'M GRABBING COOKIES, AND WE'RE GONNA GO SEE BOB IN THE BASEMENT!
OKAY! WE'RE EATING SOON!
OK!
BISCUITS
SODA
SPAG
comet
JELL-O
SAR
corn
peas
102

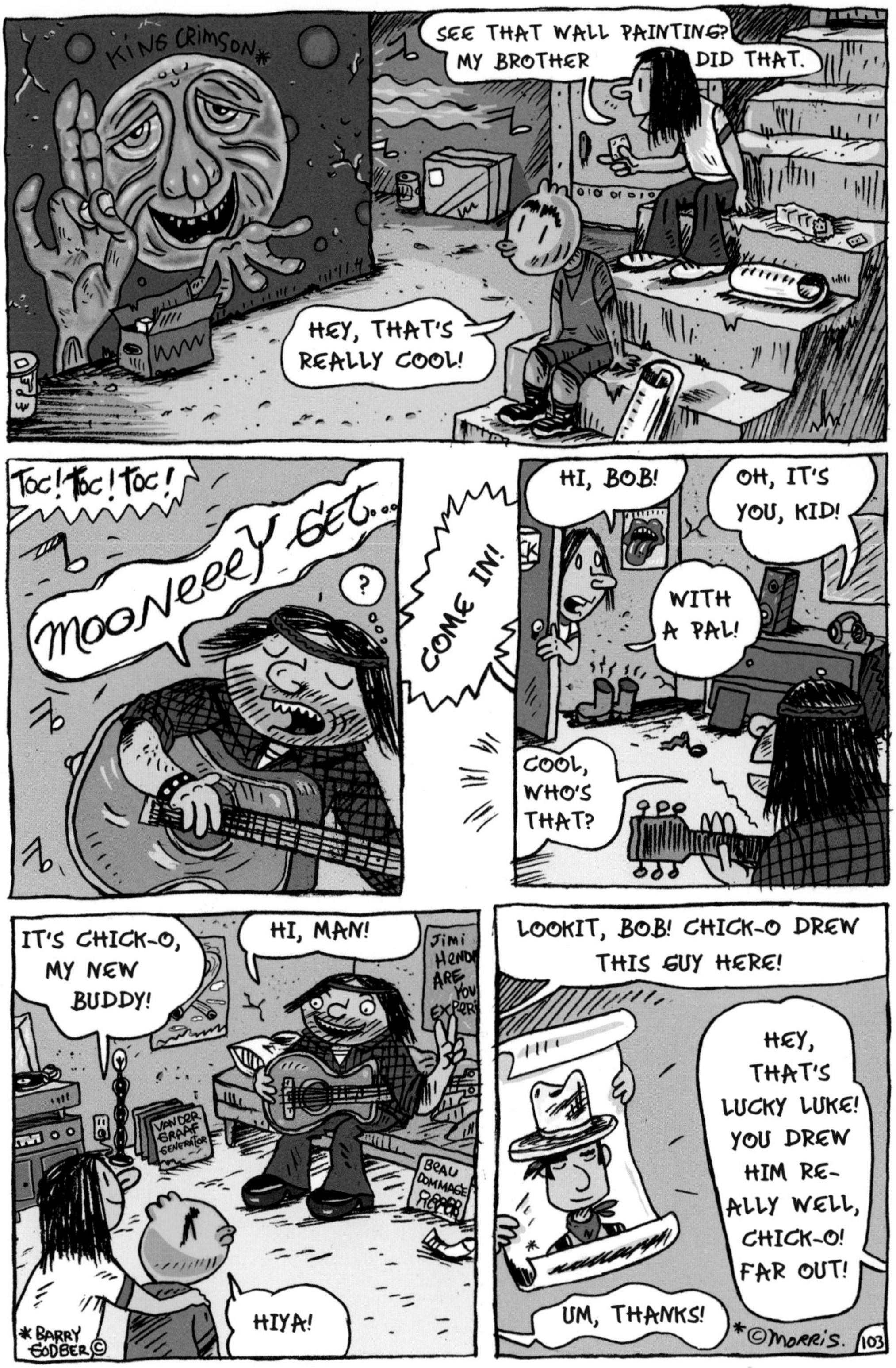
KING CRIMSON
SEE THAT WALL PAINTING? MY BROTHER* DID THAT.
HEY, THAT'S REALLY COOL!
TOC! TOC! TOC!
MOONEEEY GET...
?
COME IN!
HI, BOB!
OH, IT'S YOU, KID!
WITH A PAL!
COOL, WHO'S THAT?
IT'S CHICK-O, MY NEW BUDDY!
HI, MAN!
HIYA!
VAN DER GRAAF GENERATOR
BEAU DOMMAGE
*BARRY GODBER©
LOOKIT, BOB! CHICK-O DREW THIS GUY HERE!
HEY, THAT'S LUCKY LUKE! YOU DREW HIM RE-ALLY WELL, CHICK-O! FAR OUT!
UM, THANKS!
*©MORRIS.
103

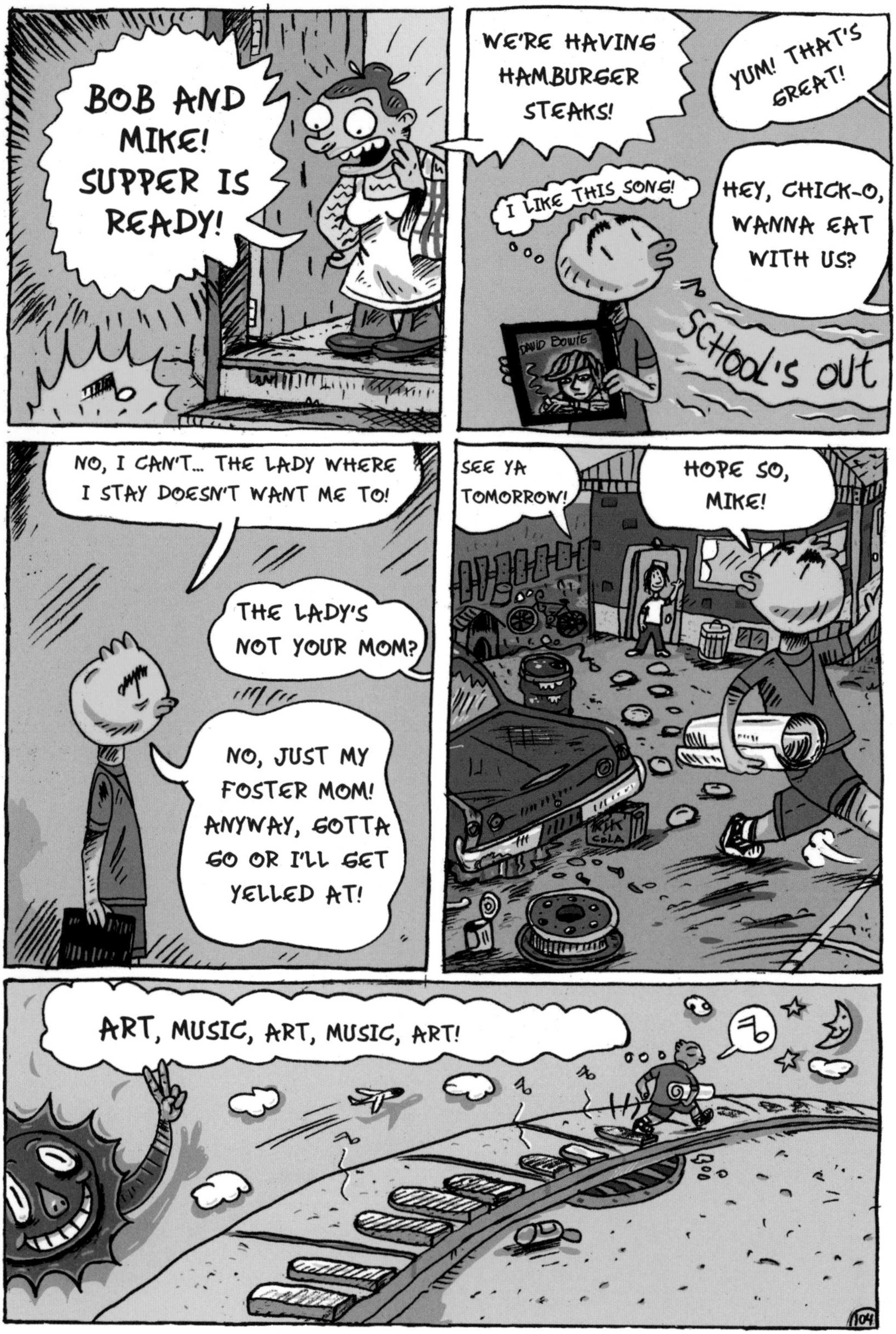
BOB AND MIKE! SUPPER IS READY!
WE'RE HAVING HAMBURGER STEAKS!
YUM! THAT'S GREAT!
I LIKE THIS SONG!
HEY, CHICK-O, WANNA EAT WITH US?
DAVID BOWIE
SCHOOL'S OUT
NO, I CAN'T... THE LADY WHERE I STAY DOESN'T WANT ME TO!
THE LADY'S NOT YOUR MOM?
NO, JUST MY FOSTER MOM! ANYWAY, GOTTA GO OR I'LL GET YELLED AT!
SEE YA TOMORROW!
HOPE SO, MIKE!
KIK COLA
ART, MUSIC, ART, MUSIC, ART!
104

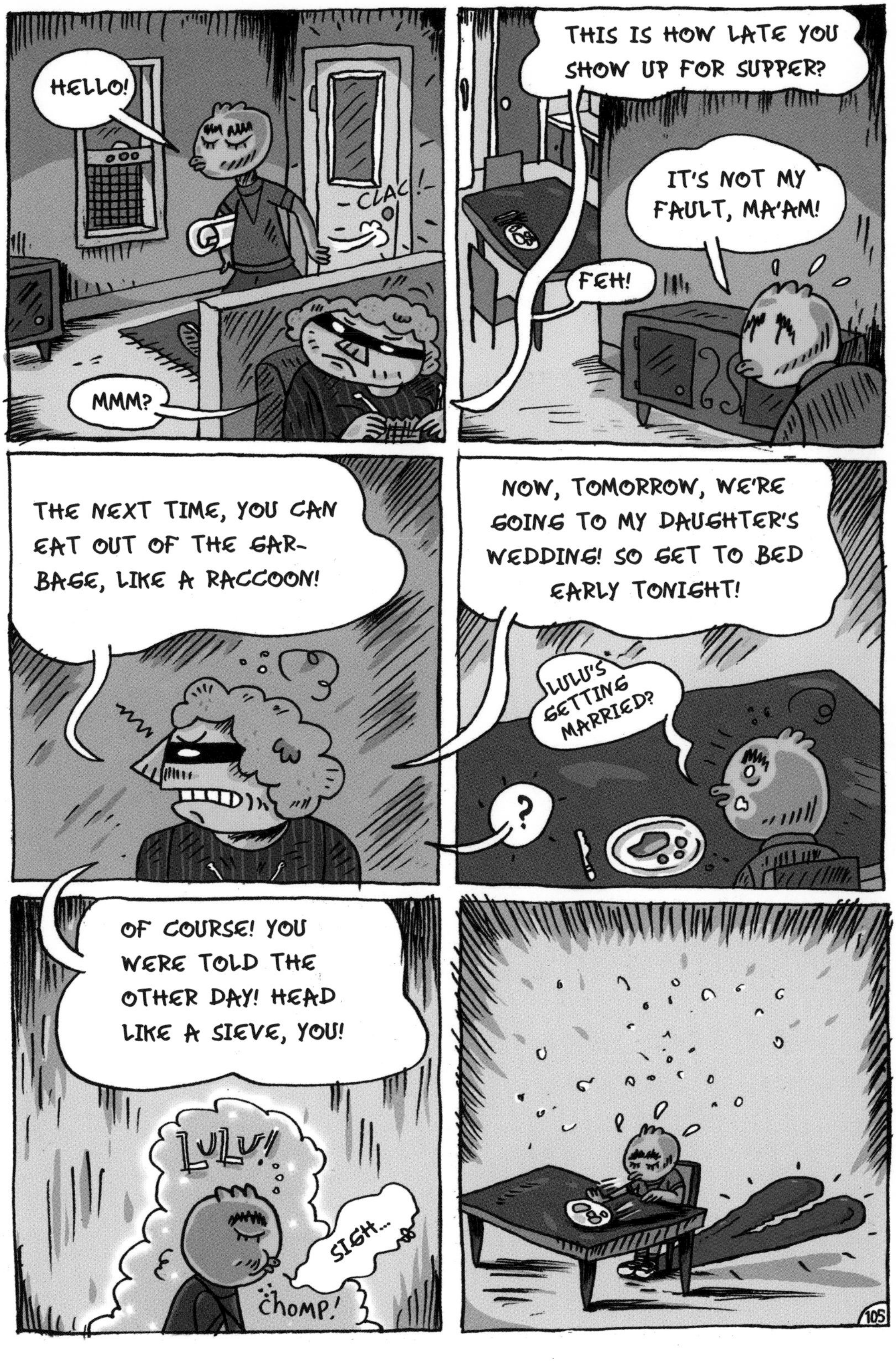
HELLO!
CLAC!
MMM?
THIS IS HOW LATE YOU SHOW UP FOR SUPPER?
IT'S NOT MY FAULT, MA'AM!
FEH!
THE NEXT TIME, YOU CAN EAT OUT OF THE GAR-BAGE, LIKE A RACCOON!
NOW, TOMORROW, WE'RE GOING TO MY DAUGHTER'S WEDDING! SO GET TO BED EARLY TONIGHT!
LULU'S GETTING MARRIED?
?
OF COURSE! YOU WERE TOLD THE OTHER DAY! HEAD LIKE A SIEVE, YOU!
LULU!
SIGH...
CHOMP!
105

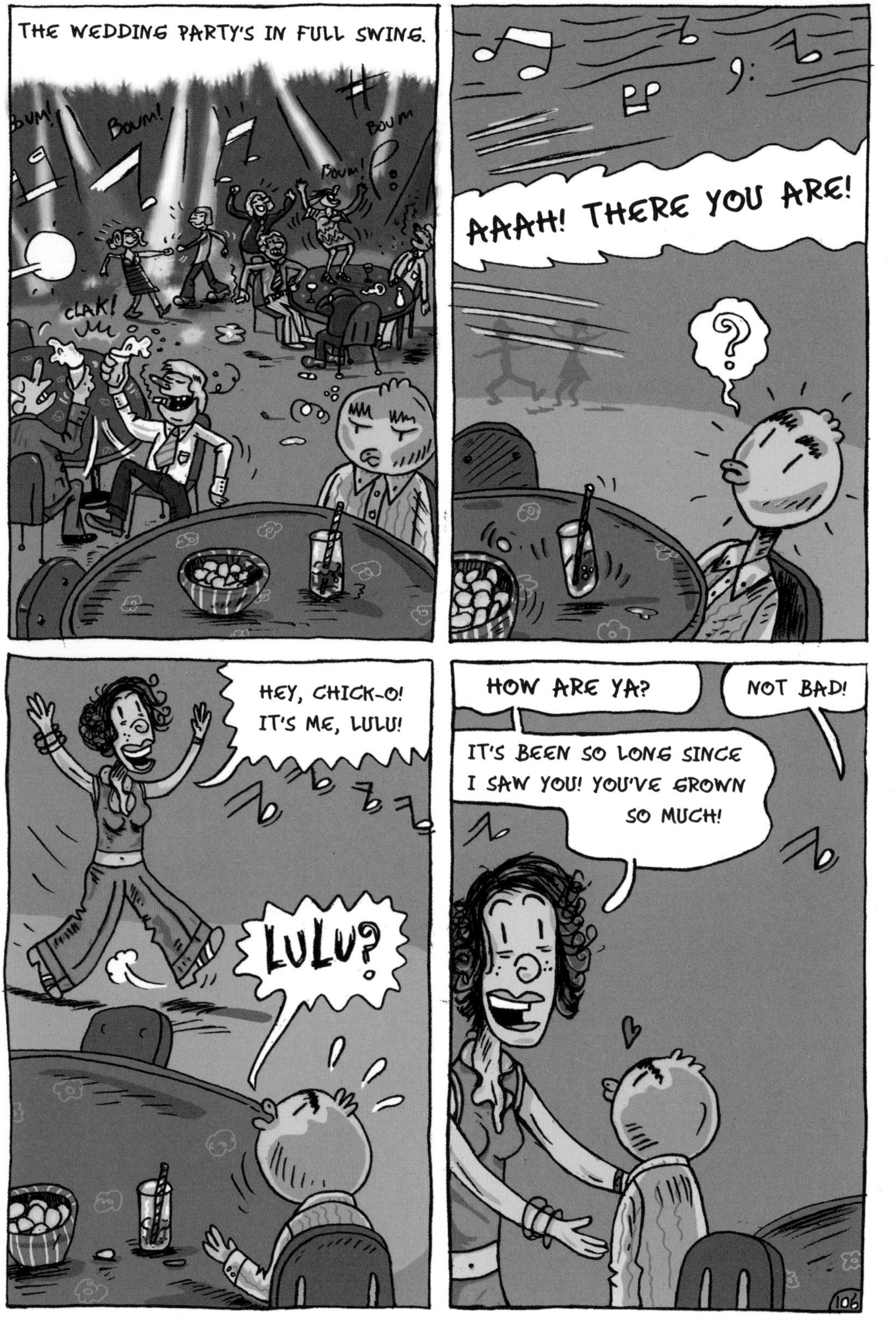
THE WEDDING PARTY'S IN FULL SWING.
BOUM!
BOUM!
BOUM
BOUM!
CLAK!
AAAH! THERE YOU ARE!
?
HEY, CHICK-O! IT'S ME, LULU!
LULU?
HOW ARE YA?
NOT BAD!
IT'S BEEN SO LONG SINCE I SAW YOU! YOU'VE GROWN SO MUCH!
106

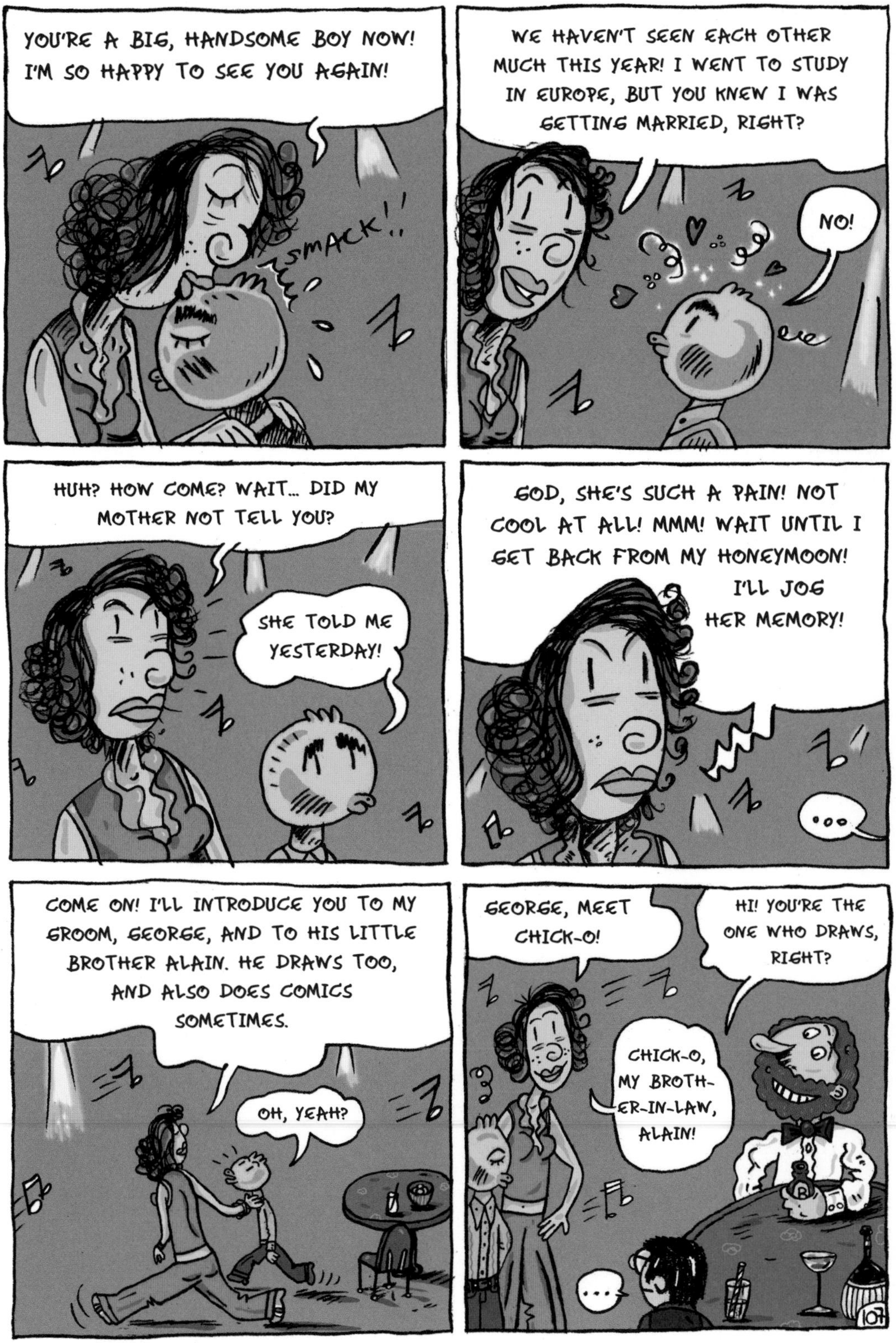
YOU'RE A BIG, HANDSOME BOY NOW! I'M SO HAPPY TO SEE YOU AGAIN!
SMACK!!!
WE HAVEN'T SEEN EACH OTHER MUCH THIS YEAR! I WENT TO STUDY IN EUROPE, BUT YOU KNEW I WAS GETTING MARRIED, RIGHT?
NO!
HUH? HOW COME? WAIT... DID MY MOTHER NOT TELL YOU?
SHE TOLD ME YESTERDAY!
GOD, SHE'S SUCH A PAIN! NOT COOL AT ALL! MMM! WAIT UNTIL I GET BACK FROM MY HONEYMOON!
I'LL JOG HER MEMORY!
...
COME ON! I'LL INTRODUCE YOU TO MY GROOM, GEORGE, AND TO HIS LITTLE BROTHER ALAIN. HE DRAWS TOO, AND ALSO DOES COMICS SOMETIMES.
OH, YEAH?
GEORGE, MEET CHICK-O!
HI! YOU'RE THE ONE WHO DRAWS, RIGHT?
CHICK-O, MY BROTH-ER-IN-LAW, ALAIN!
...
107

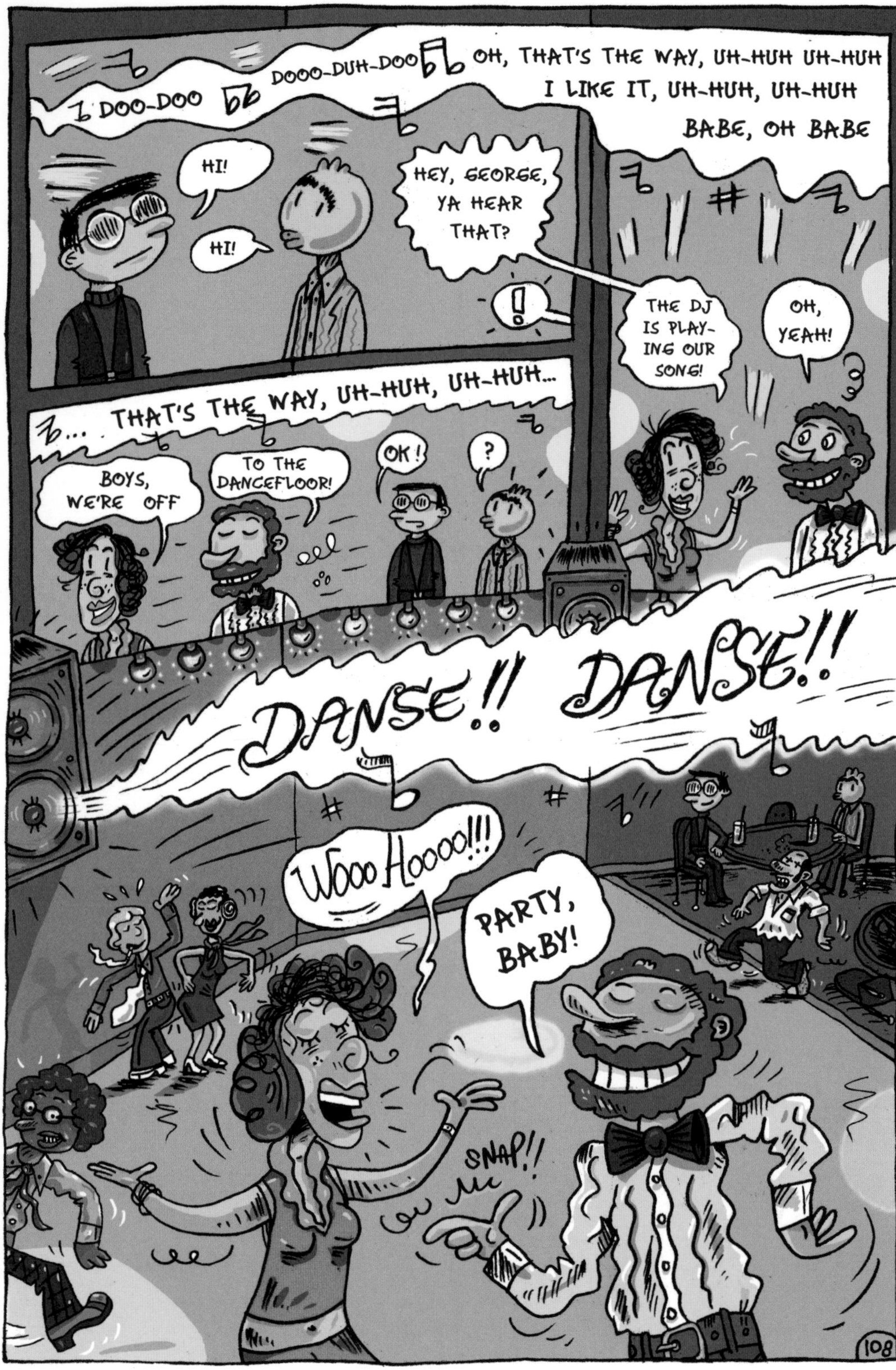
DOO-DOO DOOO-DUH-DOO OH, THAT'S THE WAY, UH-HUH UH-HUH
I LIKE IT, UH-HUH, UH-HUH
BABE, OH BABE
HI!
HI!
HEY, GEORGE, YA HEAR THAT?
!
THE DJ IS PLAY-ING OUR SONG!
OH, YEAH!
... THAT'S THE WAY, UH-HUH, UH-HUH...
BOYS, WE'RE OFF
TO THE DANCEFLOOR!
OK!
?
DANSE!! DANSE!!
WOOO HOOOO!!!
PARTY, BABY!
SNAP!!
108

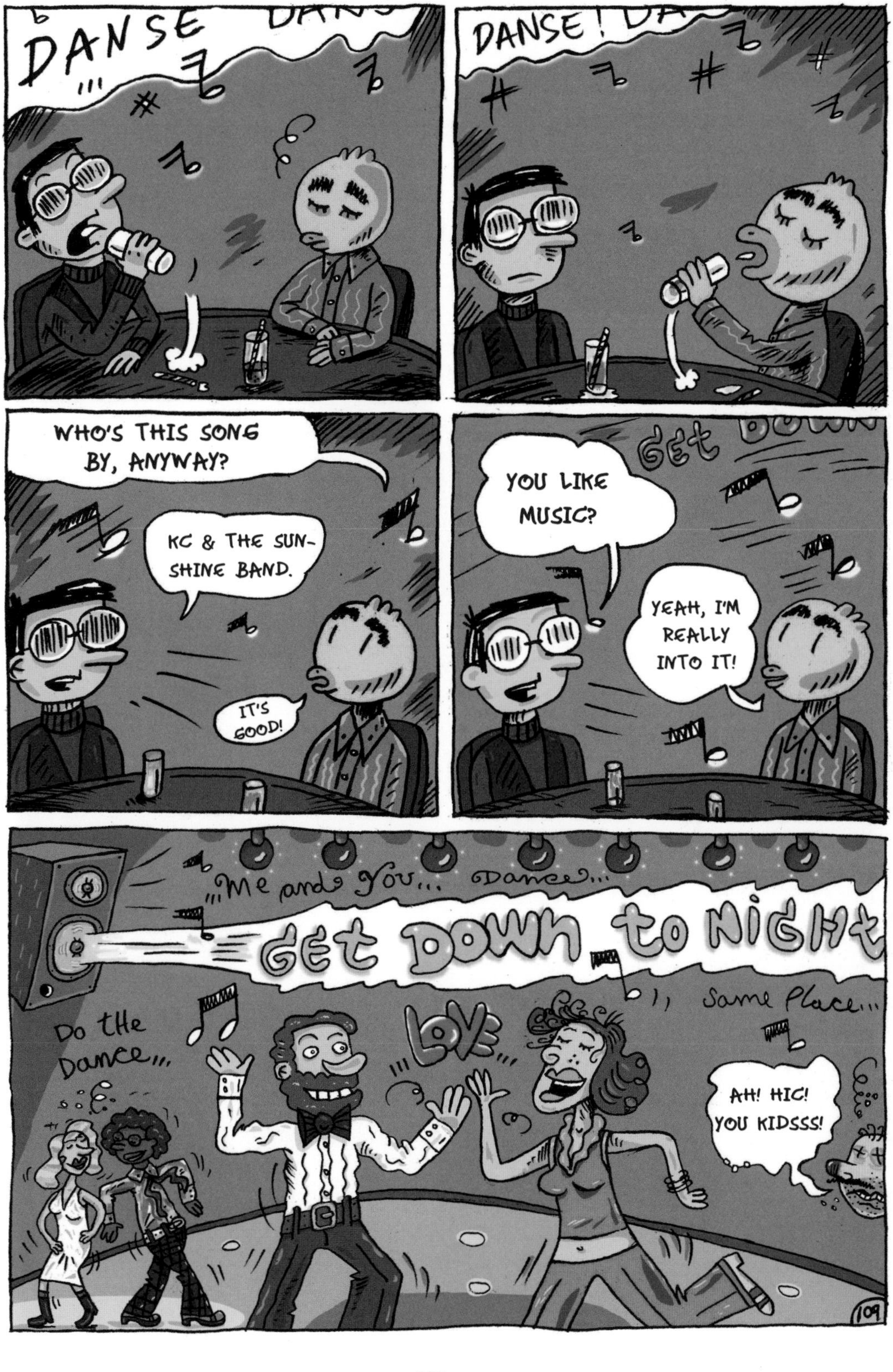
DANSE
DANSE!
WHO'S THIS SONG BY, ANYWAY?
KC & THE SUN-SHINE BAND.
IT'S GOOD!
YOU LIKE MUSIC?
YEAH, I'M REALLY INTO IT!
Me and You... Dance...
GET DOWN TO NIGHT
Same Place...
Do tHe Dance...
LOVE
AH! HIC! YOU KIDSSS!
109

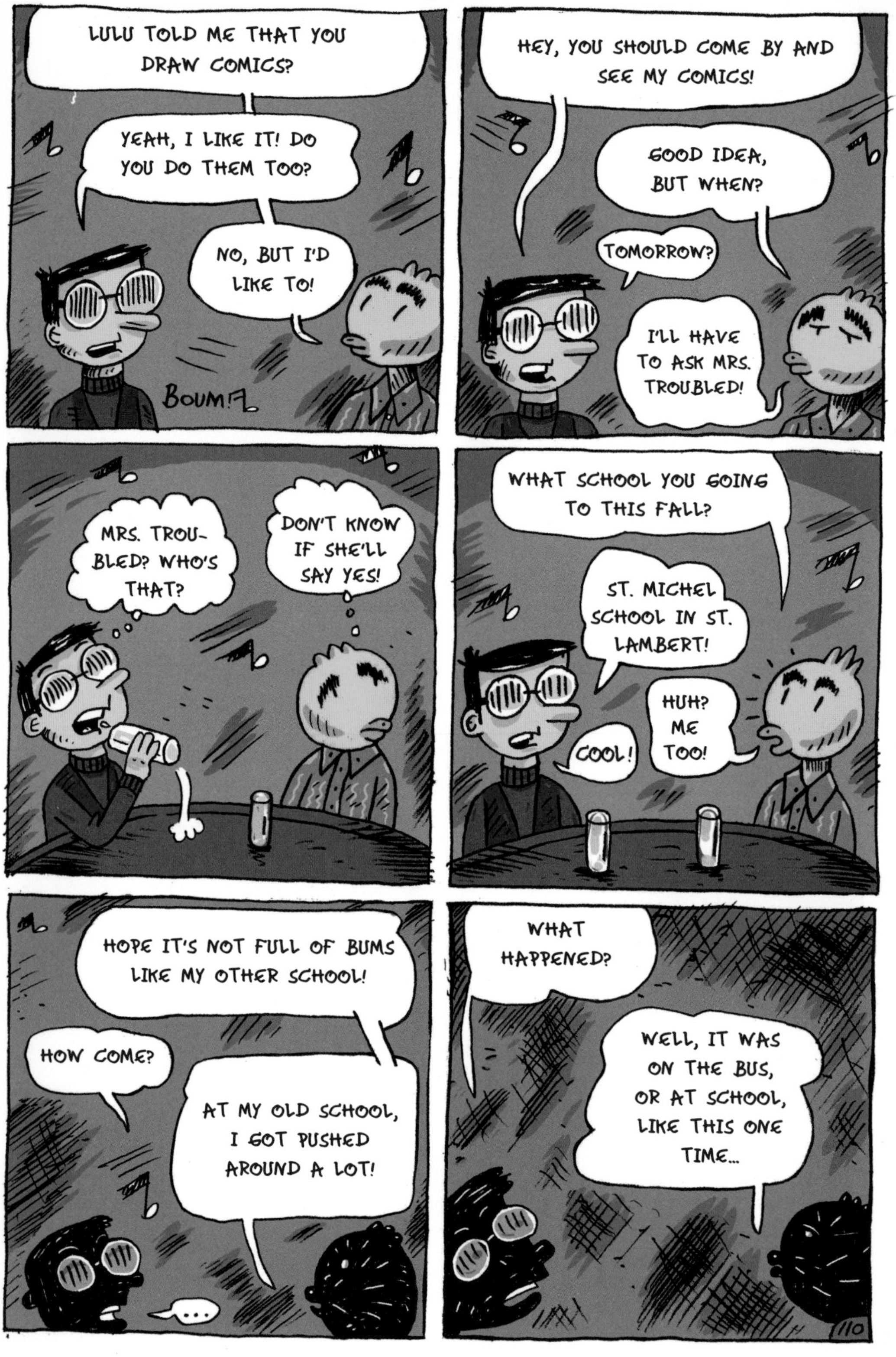
LULU TOLD ME THAT YOU DRAW COMICS?
YEAH, I LIKE IT! DO YOU DO THEM TOO?
NO, BUT I'D LIKE TO!
BOUM!
HEY, YOU SHOULD COME BY AND SEE MY COMICS!
GOOD IDEA, BUT WHEN?
TOMORROW?
I'LL HAVE TO ASK MRS. TROUBLED!
MRS. TROU-BLED? WHO'S THAT?
DON'T KNOW IF SHE'LL SAY YES!
WHAT SCHOOL YOU GOING TO THIS FALL?
ST. MICHEL SCHOOL IN ST. LAMBERT!
COOL!
HUH? ME TOO!
HOPE IT'S NOT FULL OF BUMS LIKE MY OTHER SCHOOL!
HOW COME?
AT MY OLD SCHOOL, I GOT PUSHED AROUND A LOT!
...
WHAT HAPPENED?
WELL, IT WAS ON THE BUS, OR AT SCHOOL, LIKE THIS ONE TIME...
110

ONE DAY, ON MY WAY TO MY LOCKER, THREE OF THE SCHOOL'S THUGS HASSLED ME.

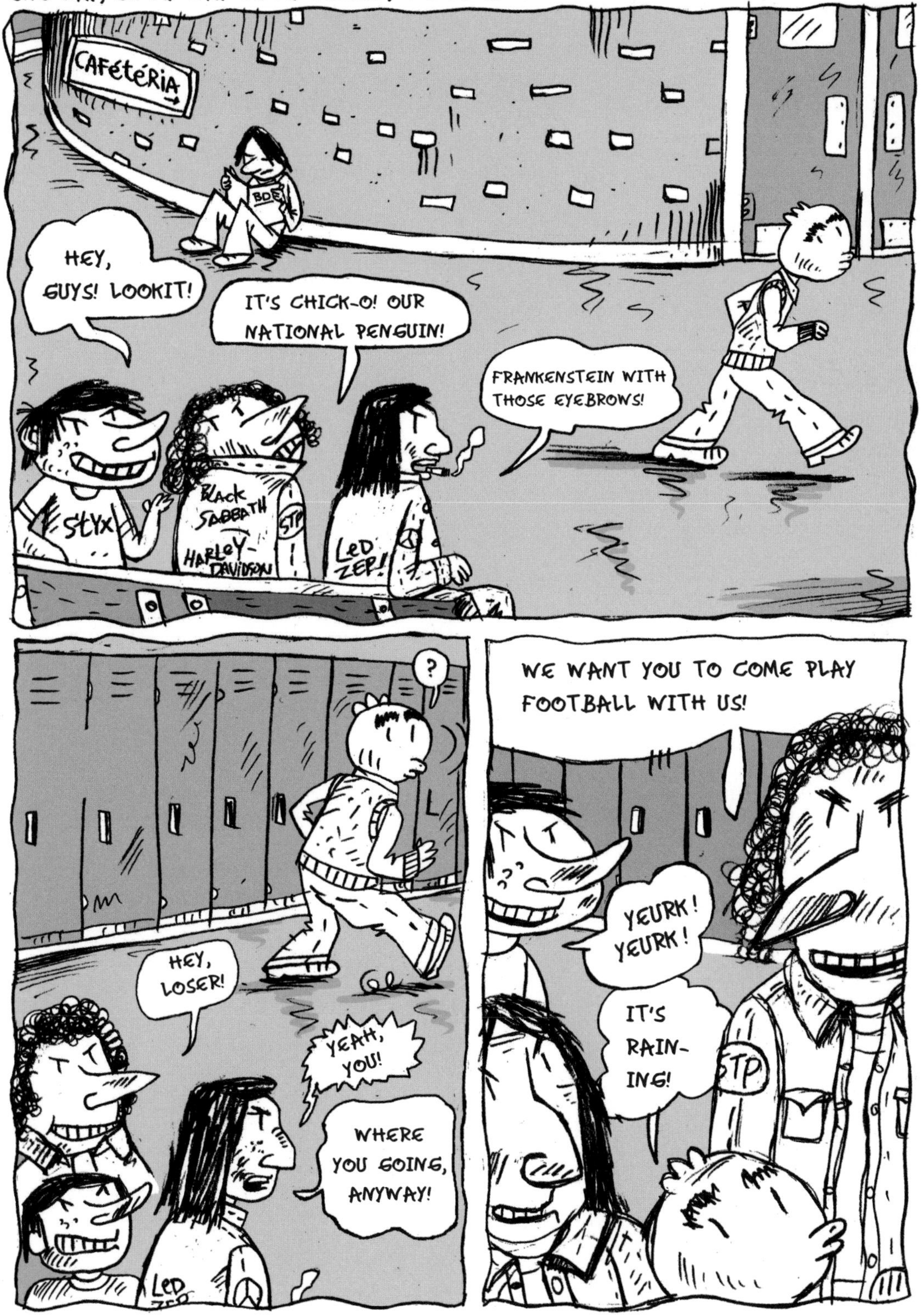
CAFÉTÉRIA
HEY, GUYS! LOOKIT!
IT'S CHICK-O! OUR NATIONAL PENGUIN!
FRANKENSTEIN WITH THOSE EYEBROWS!
STYX
BLACK SABBATH
HARLEY-DAVIDSON
STP
LED ZEP!
?
HEY, LOSER!
YEAH, YOU!
WHERE YOU GOING, ANYWAY!
WE WANT YOU TO COME PLAY FOOTBALL WITH US!
YEURK! YEURK!
IT'S RAIN-ING!
STP

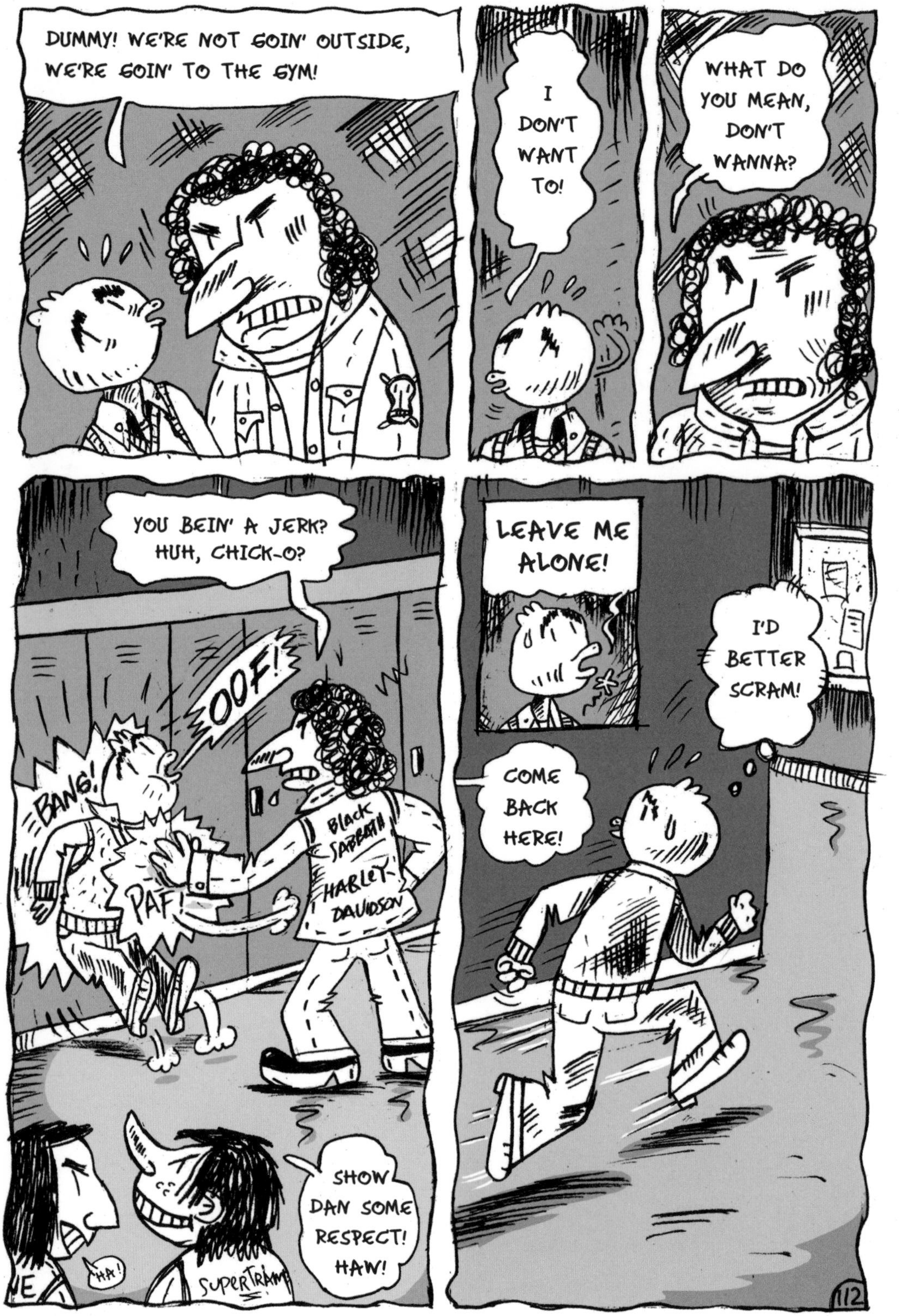
DUMMY! WE'RE NOT GOIN' OUTSIDE, WE'RE GOIN' TO THE GYM!
I DON'T WANT TO!
WHAT DO YOU MEAN, DON'T WANNA?
YOU BEIN' A JERK? HUH, CHICK-O?
OOF!
BANG!
PAF!
BLACK SABBATH
HARLEY-DAVIDSON
HA!
SUPERTRAMP
SHOW DAN SOME RESPECT! HAW!
LEAVE ME ALONE!
I'D BETTER SCRAM!
COME BACK HERE!
112

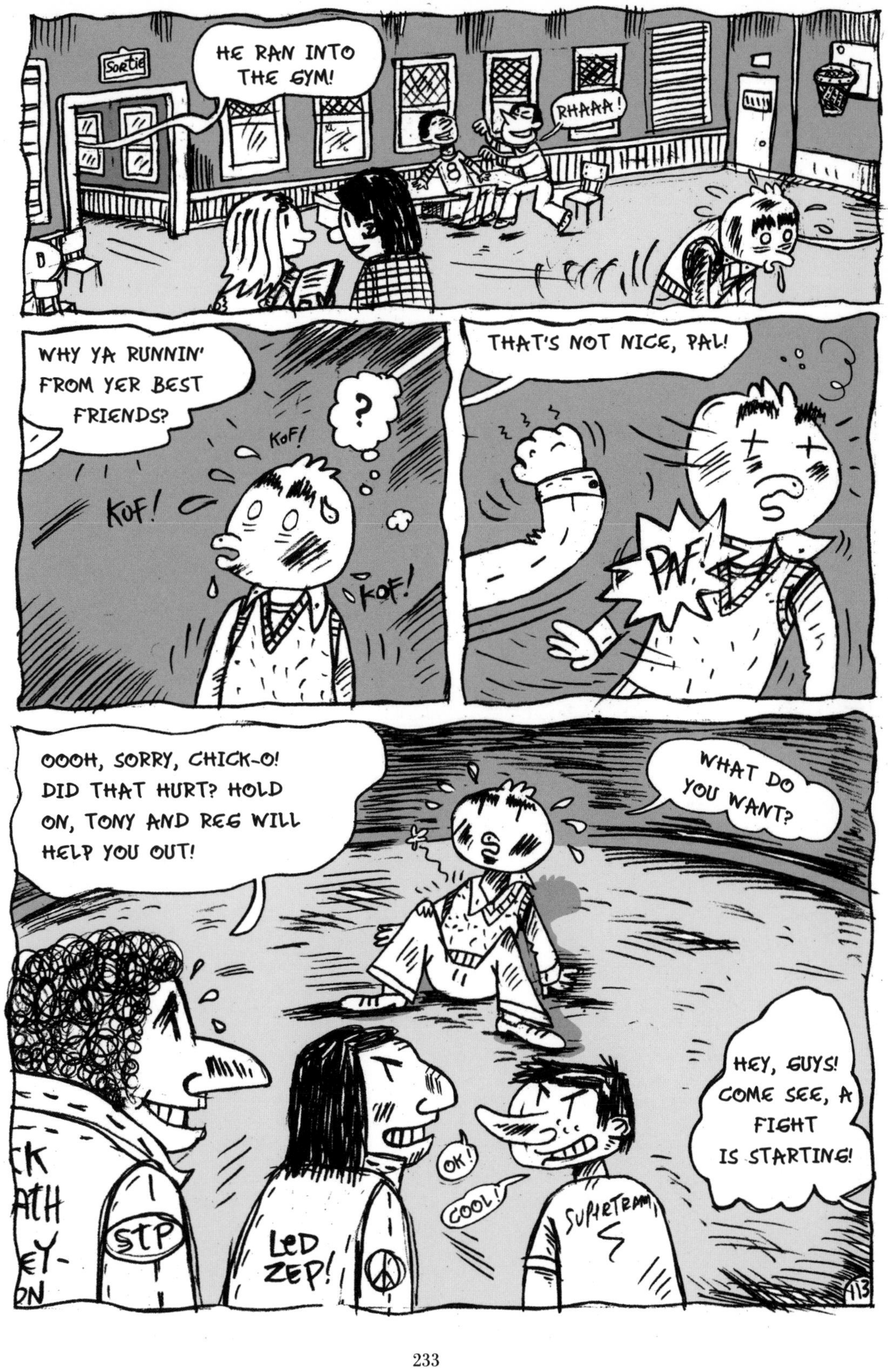
SORTIE
HE RAN INTO THE GYM!
RHAAA!
WHY YA RUNNIN' FROM YER BEST FRIENDS?
KOF!
KOF!
KOF!
?
THAT'S NOT NICE, PAL!
PAF!
OOOH, SORRY, CHICK-O! DID THAT HURT? HOLD ON, TONY AND REG WILL HELP YOU OUT!
WHAT DO YOU WANT?
STP
LED ZEP!
OK!
COOL!
HEY, GUYS! COME SEE, A FIGHT IS STARTING!
113

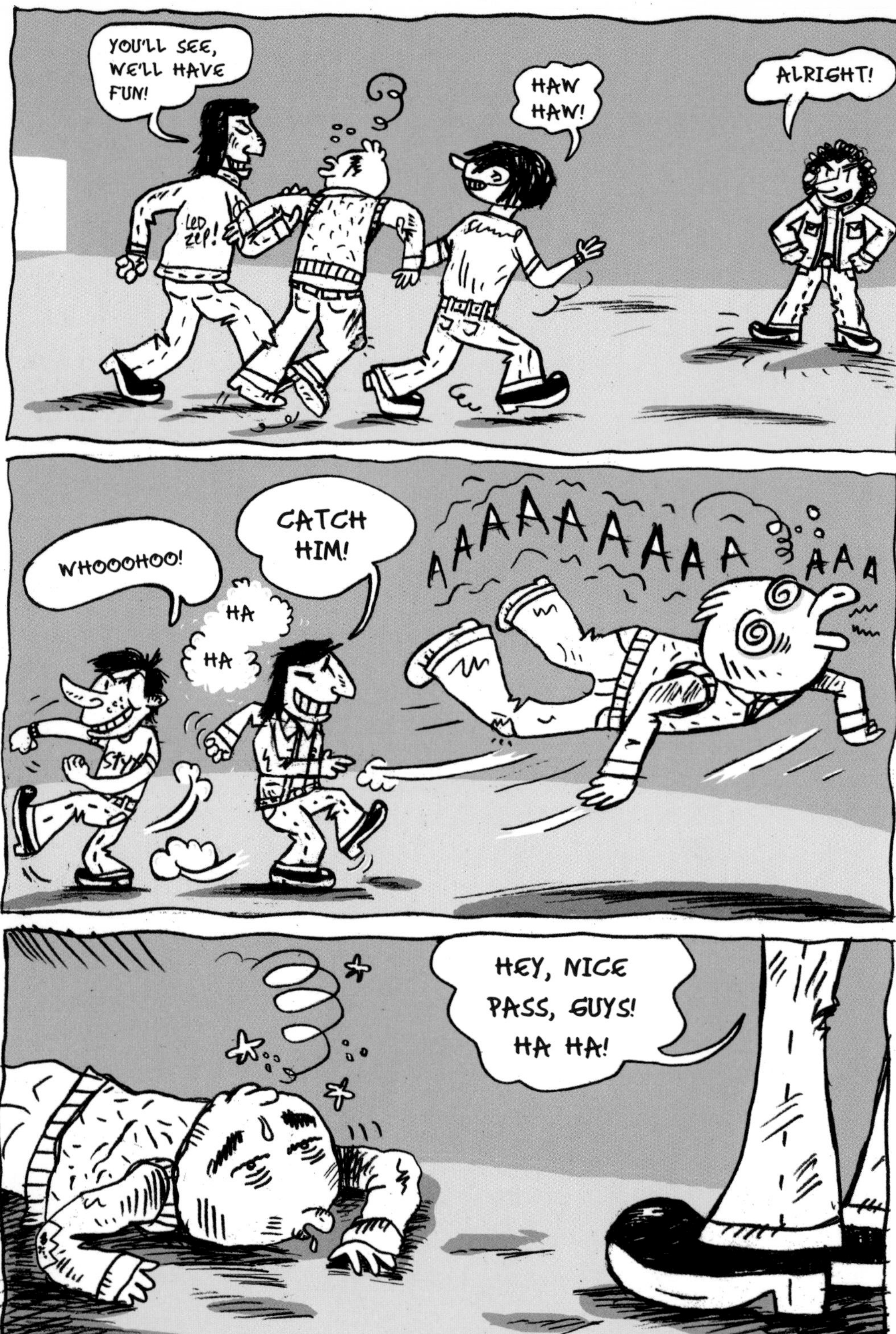
YOU'LL SEE, WE'LL HAVE FUN!
HAW HAW!
ALRIGHT!
LED ZEP!
WHOOOHOO!
HA HA
CATCH HIM!
AAAAAAAAAA AAA
STYX
HEY, NICE PASS, GUYS! HA HA!
114

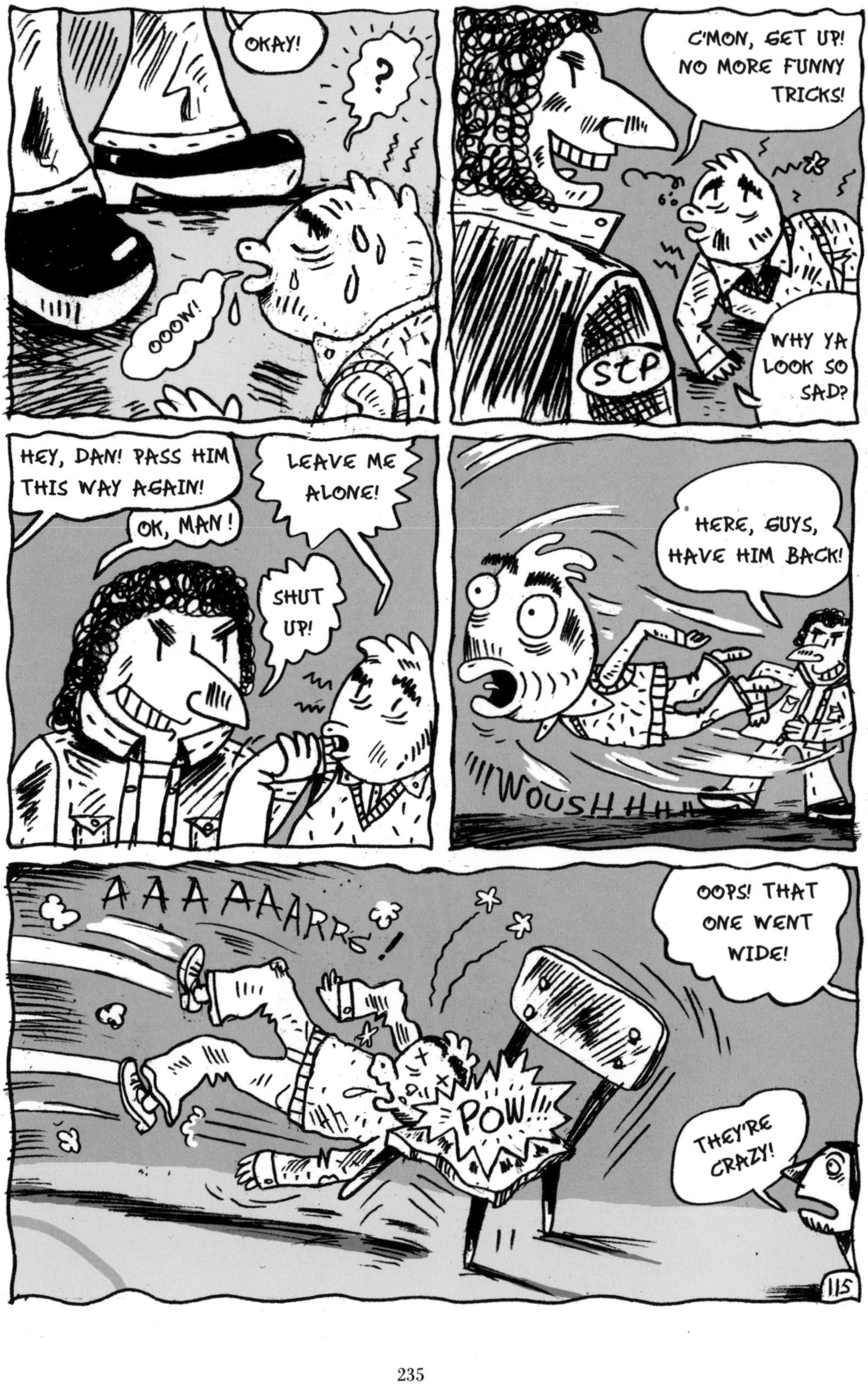
OKAY!
?
OOOW!
C'MON, GET UP! NO MORE FUNNY TRICKS!
STP
WHY YA LOOK SO SAD?
HEY, DAN! PASS HIM THIS WAY AGAIN!
OK, MAN!
LEAVE ME ALONE!
SHUT UP!
HERE, GUYS, HAVE HIM BACK!
WOUSHHHH
AAAAAARRG!
POW!
OOPS! THAT ONE WENT WIDE!
THEY'RE CRAZY!
115

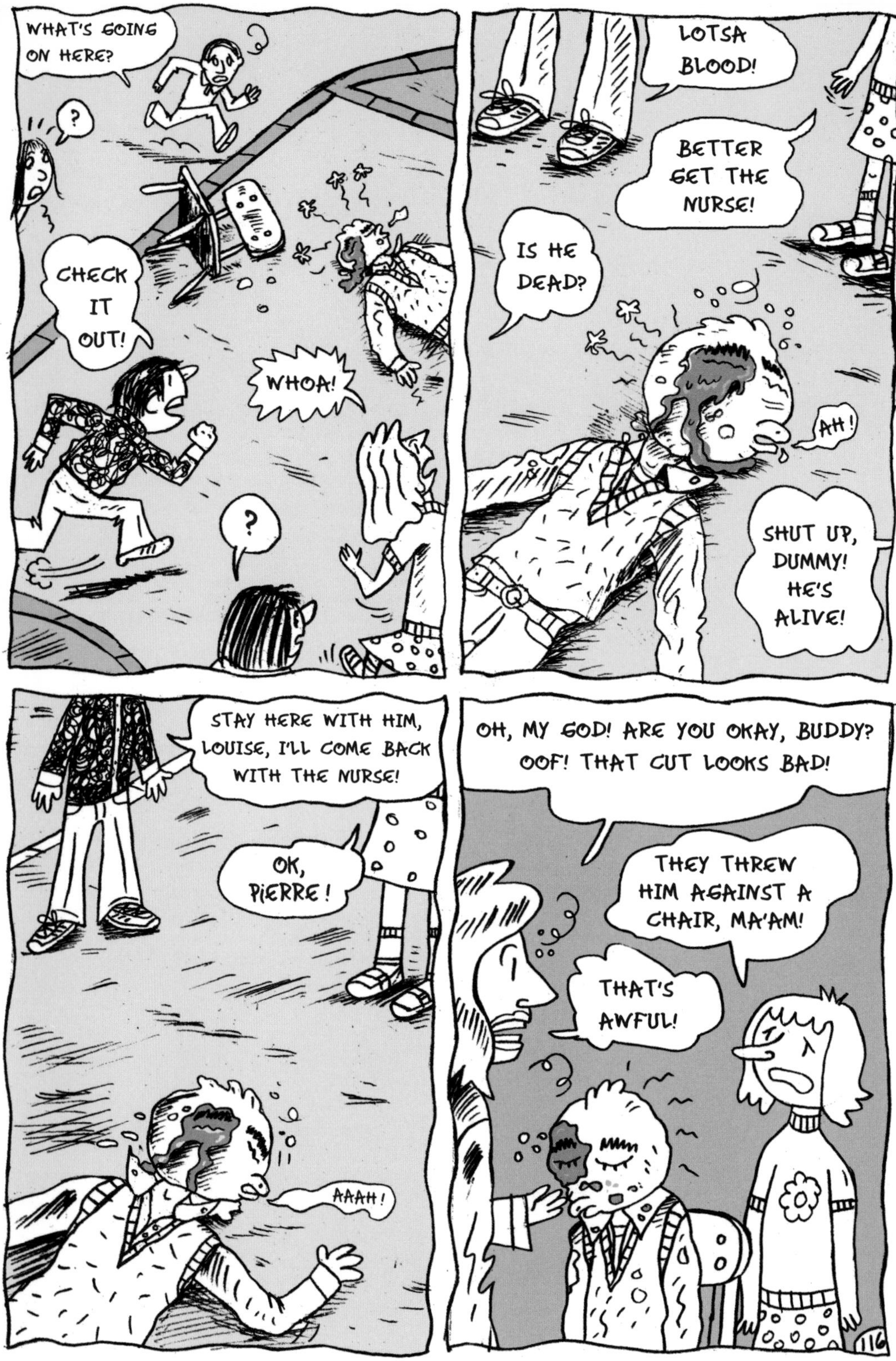
WHAT'S GOING ON HERE?
?
CHECK IT OUT!
WHOA!
?
LOTSA BLOOD!
BETTER GET THE NURSE!
IS HE DEAD?
AH!
SHUT UP, DUMMY! HE'S ALIVE!
STAY HERE WITH HIM, LOUISE, I'LL COME BACK WITH THE NURSE!
OK, PIERRE!
AAAH!
OH, MY GOD! ARE YOU OKAY, BUDDY? OOF! THAT CUT LOOKS BAD!
THEY THREW HIM AGAINST A CHAIR, MA'AM!
THAT'S AWFUL!
116

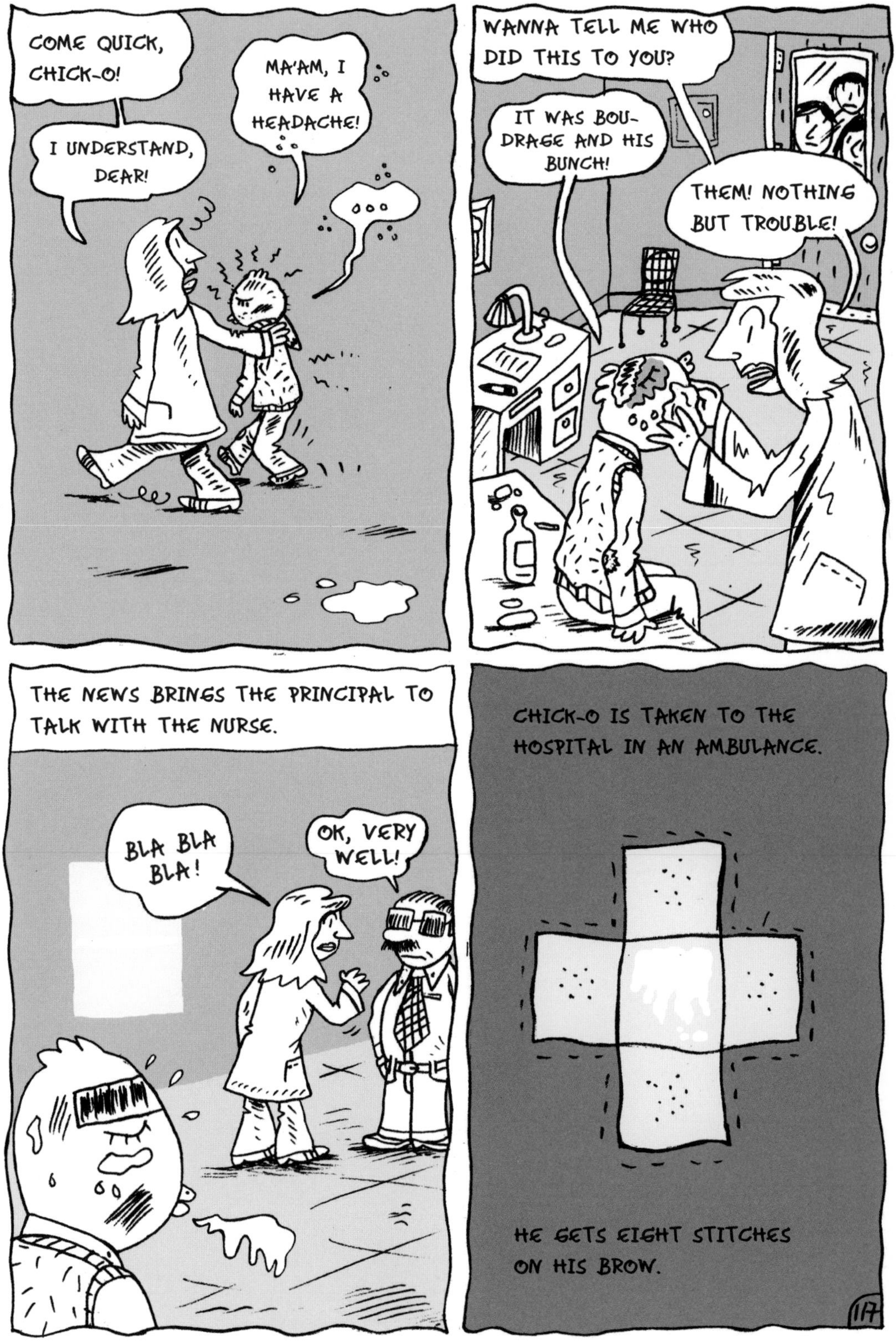
COME QUICK, CHICK-O!
I UNDERSTAND, DEAR!
MA'AM, I HAVE A HEADACHE!
WANNA TELL ME WHO DID THIS TO YOU?
IT WAS BOUDRAGE AND HIS BUNCH!
THEM! NOTHING BUT TROUBLE!
THE NEWS BRINGS THE PRINCIPAL TO TALK WITH THE NURSE.
BLA BLA BLA!
OK, VERY WELL!
CHICK-O IS TAKEN TO THE HOSPITAL IN AN AMBULANCE.
HE GETS EIGHT STITCHES ON HIS BROW.
117

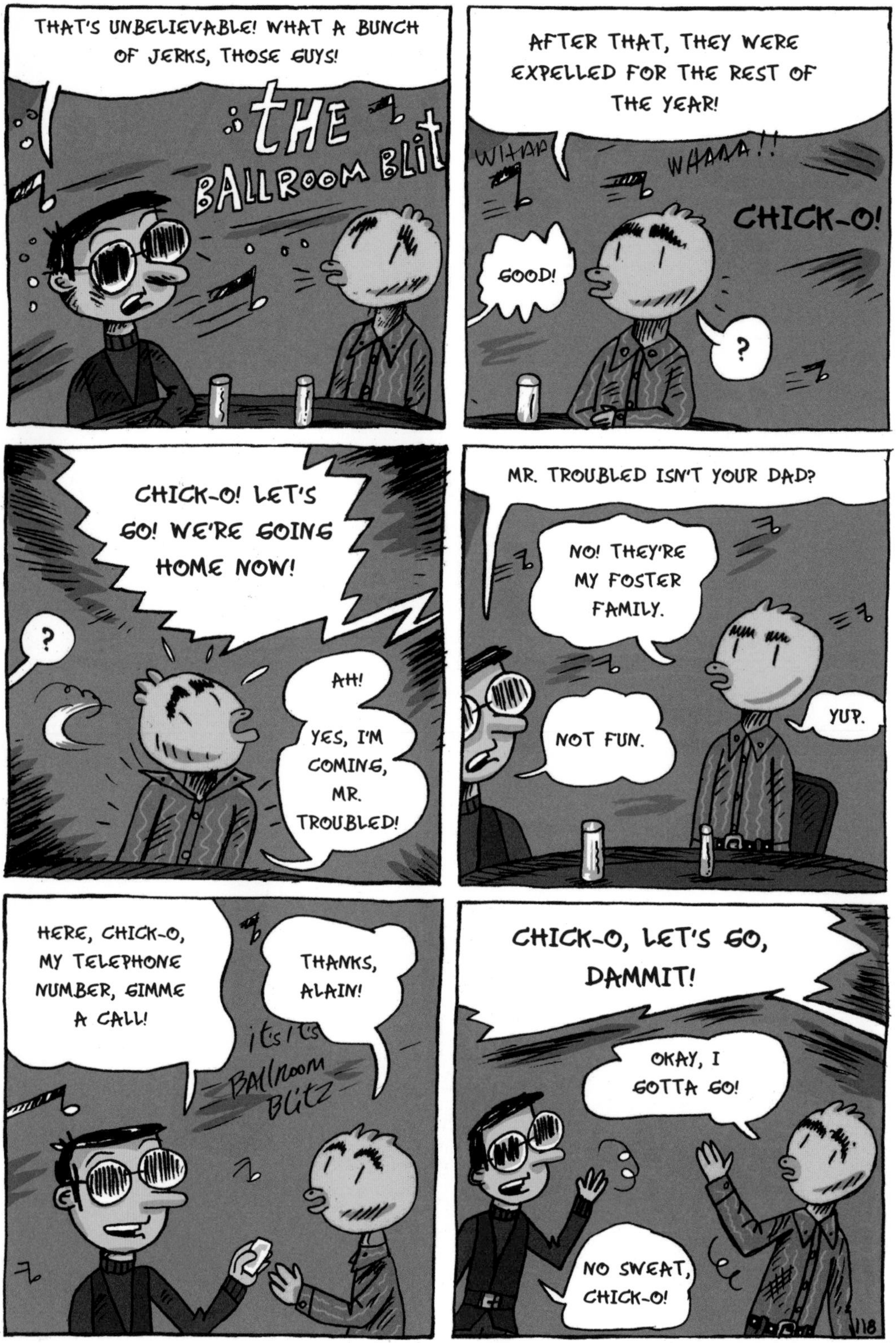
THAT'S UNBELIEVABLE! WHAT A BUNCH OF JERKS, THOSE GUYS!
THE BALLROOM BLIT
AFTER THAT, THEY WERE EXPELLED FOR THE REST OF THE YEAR!
WHAAA!!
CHICK-O!
GOOD!
?
CHICK-O! LET'S GO! WE'RE GOING HOME NOW!
?
AH!
YES, I'M COMING, MR. TROUBLED!
MR. TROUBLED ISN'T YOUR DAD?
NO! THEY'RE MY FOSTER FAMILY.
NOT FUN.
YUP.
HERE, CHICK-O, MY TELEPHONE NUMBER, GIMME A CALL!
THANKS, ALAIN!
it's / it's BALLROOM BLITZ
CHICK-O, LET'S GO, DAMMIT!
OKAY, I GOTTA GO!
NO SWEAT, CHICK-O!
118

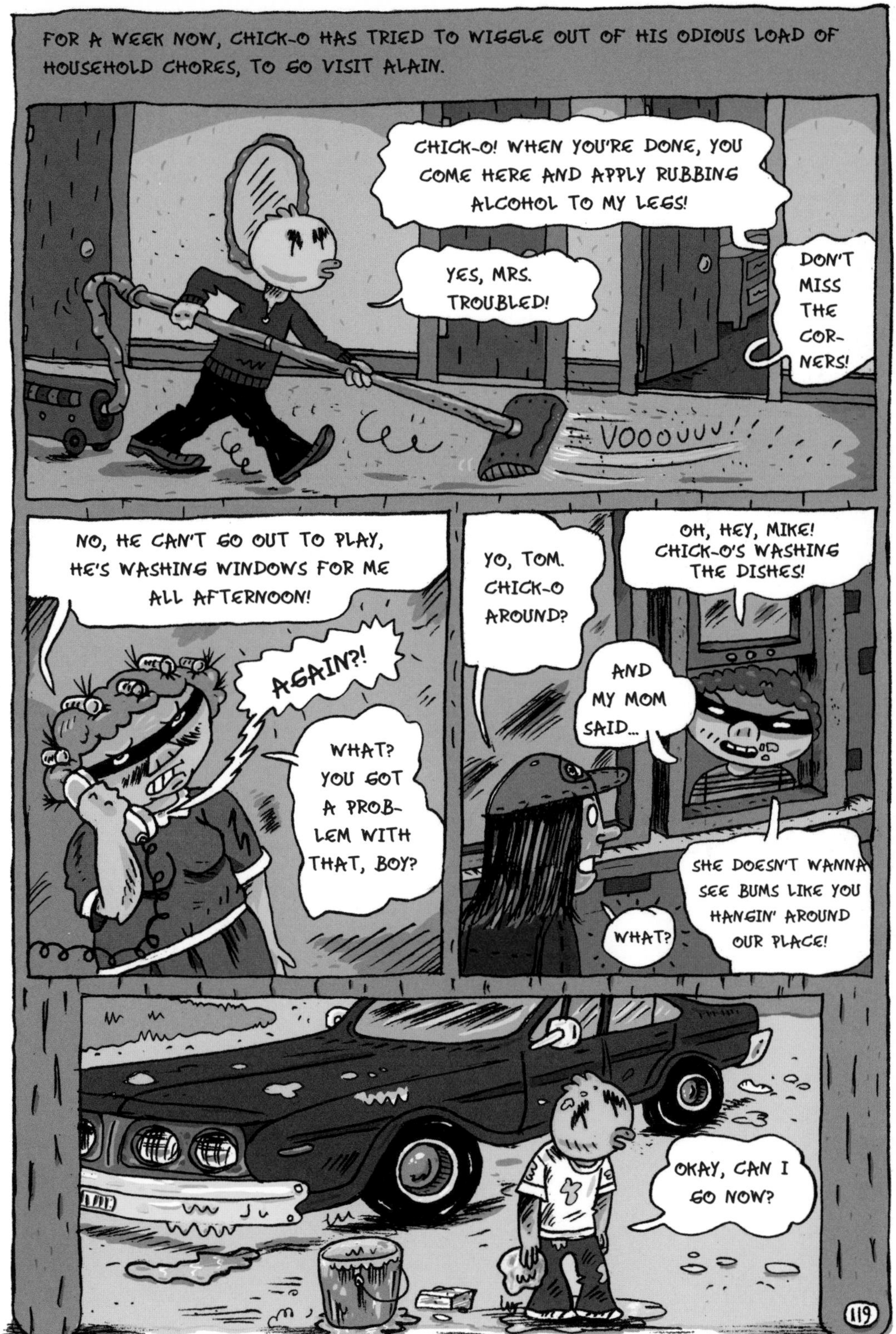
FOR A WEEK NOW, CHICK-O HAS TRIED TO WIGGLE OUT OF HIS ODIOUS LOAD OF HOUSEHOLD CHORES, TO GO VISIT ALAIN.
CHICK-O! WHEN YOU'RE DONE, YOU COME HERE AND APPLY RUBBING ALCOHOL TO MY LEGS!
YES, MRS. TROUBLED!
DON'T MISS THE COR-NERS!
VOOOUUV!
NO, HE CAN'T GO OUT TO PLAY, HE'S WASHING WINDOWS FOR ME ALL AFTERNOON!
AGAIN?!
WHAT? YOU GOT A PROB-LEM WITH THAT, BOY?
YO, TOM. CHICK-O AROUND?
OH, HEY, MIKE! CHICK-O'S WASHING THE DISHES!
AND MY MOM SAID...
SHE DOESN'T WANNA SEE BUMS LIKE YOU HANGIN' AROUND OUR PLACE!
WHAT?
OKAY, CAN I GO NOW?
119

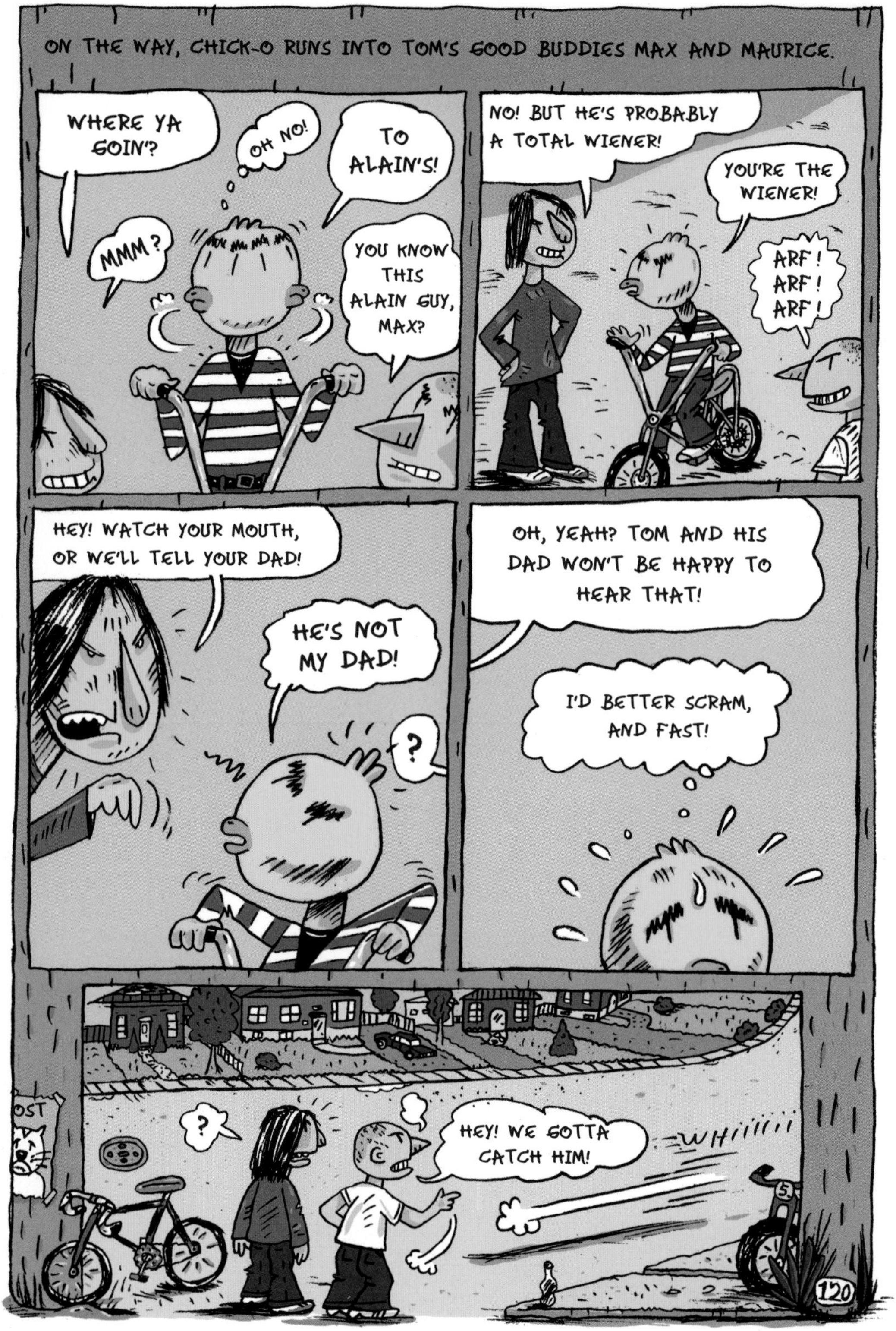
ON THE WAY, CHICK-O RUNS INTO TOM'S GOOD BUDDIES MAX AND MAURICE.
WHERE YA GOIN'?
MMM?
OH NO!
TO ALAIN'S!
YOU KNOW THIS ALAIN GUY, MAX?
NO! BUT HE'S PROBABLY A TOTAL WIENER!
YOU'RE THE WIENER!
ARF! ARF! ARF!
HEY! WATCH YOUR MOUTH, OR WE'LL TELL YOUR DAD!
HE'S NOT MY DAD!
?
OH, YEAH? TOM AND HIS DAD WON'T BE HAPPY TO HEAR THAT!
I'D BETTER SCRAM, AND FAST!
?
HEY! WE GOTTA CATCH HIM!
WHIIII
120

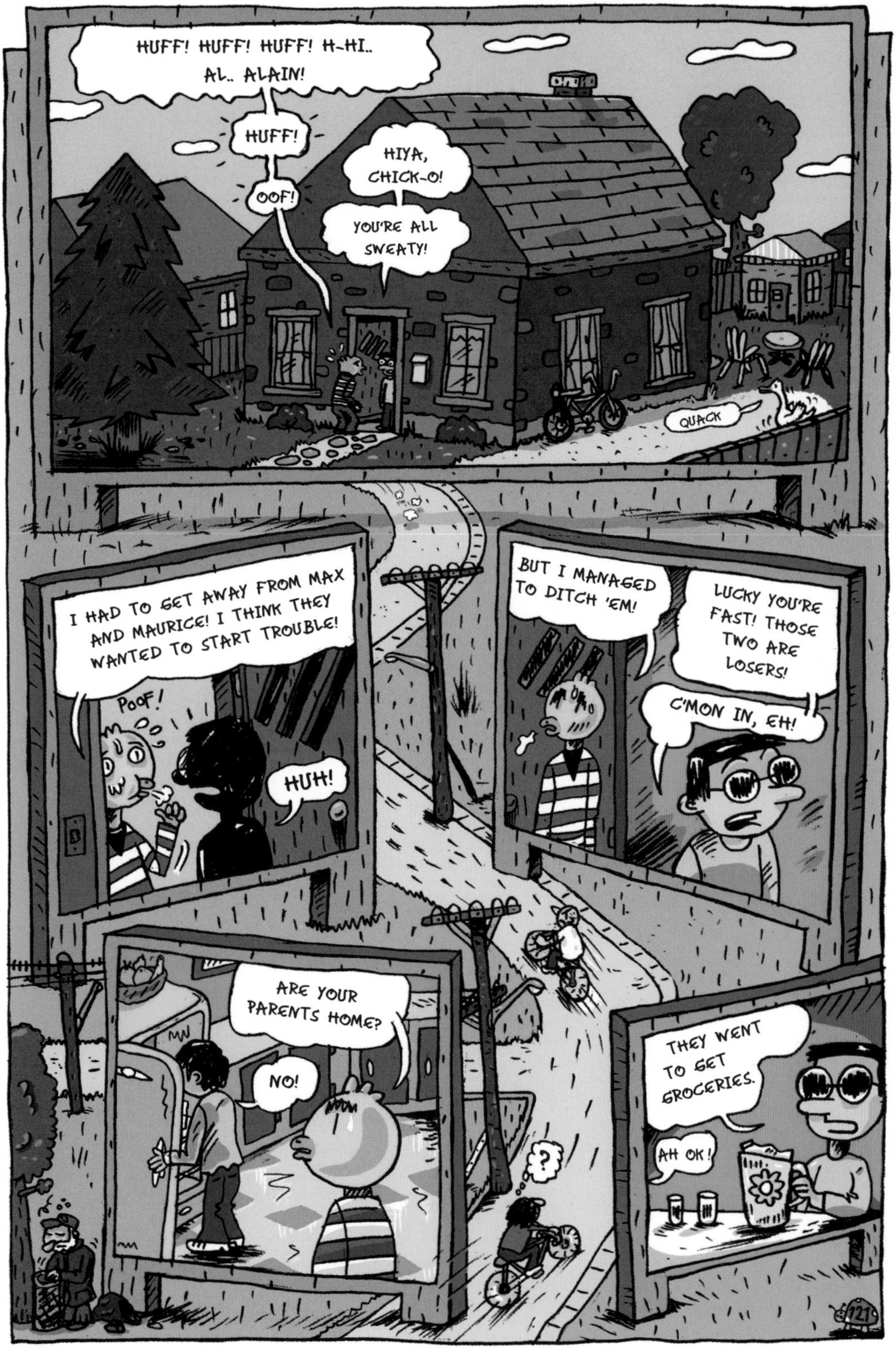
HUFF! HUFF! HUFF! H-HI.. AL.. ALAIN!
HUFF!
OOF!
HIYA, CHICK-O!
YOU'RE ALL SWEATY!
QUACK
I HAD TO GET AWAY FROM MAX AND MAURICE! I THINK THEY WANTED TO START TROUBLE!
POOF!
HUH!
BUT I MANAGED TO DITCH 'EM!
LUCKY YOU'RE FAST! THOSE TWO ARE LOSERS!
C'MON IN, EH!
ARE YOUR PARENTS HOME?
NO!
?
THEY WENT TO GET GROCERIES.
AH OK!
121

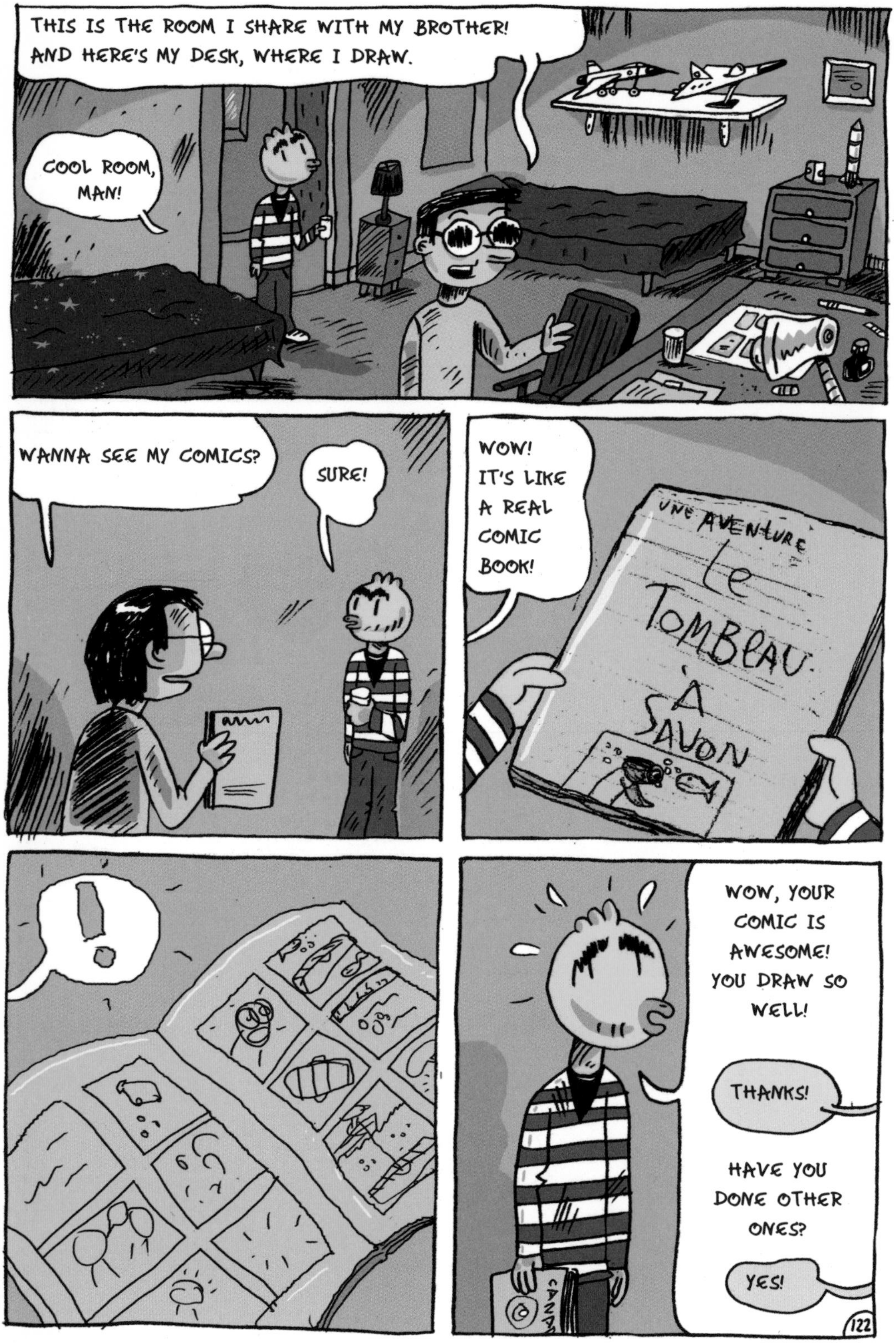
THIS IS THE ROOM I SHARE WITH MY BROTHER! AND HERE'S MY DESK, WHERE I DRAW.
COOL ROOM, MAN!
WANNA SEE MY COMICS?
SURE!
WOW! IT'S LIKE A REAL COMIC BOOK!
UNE AVENTURE
LE TOMBEAU À SAVON
!
WOW, YOUR COMIC IS AWESOME! YOU DRAW SO WELL!
THANKS!
HAVE YOU DONE OTHER ONES?
YES!
122

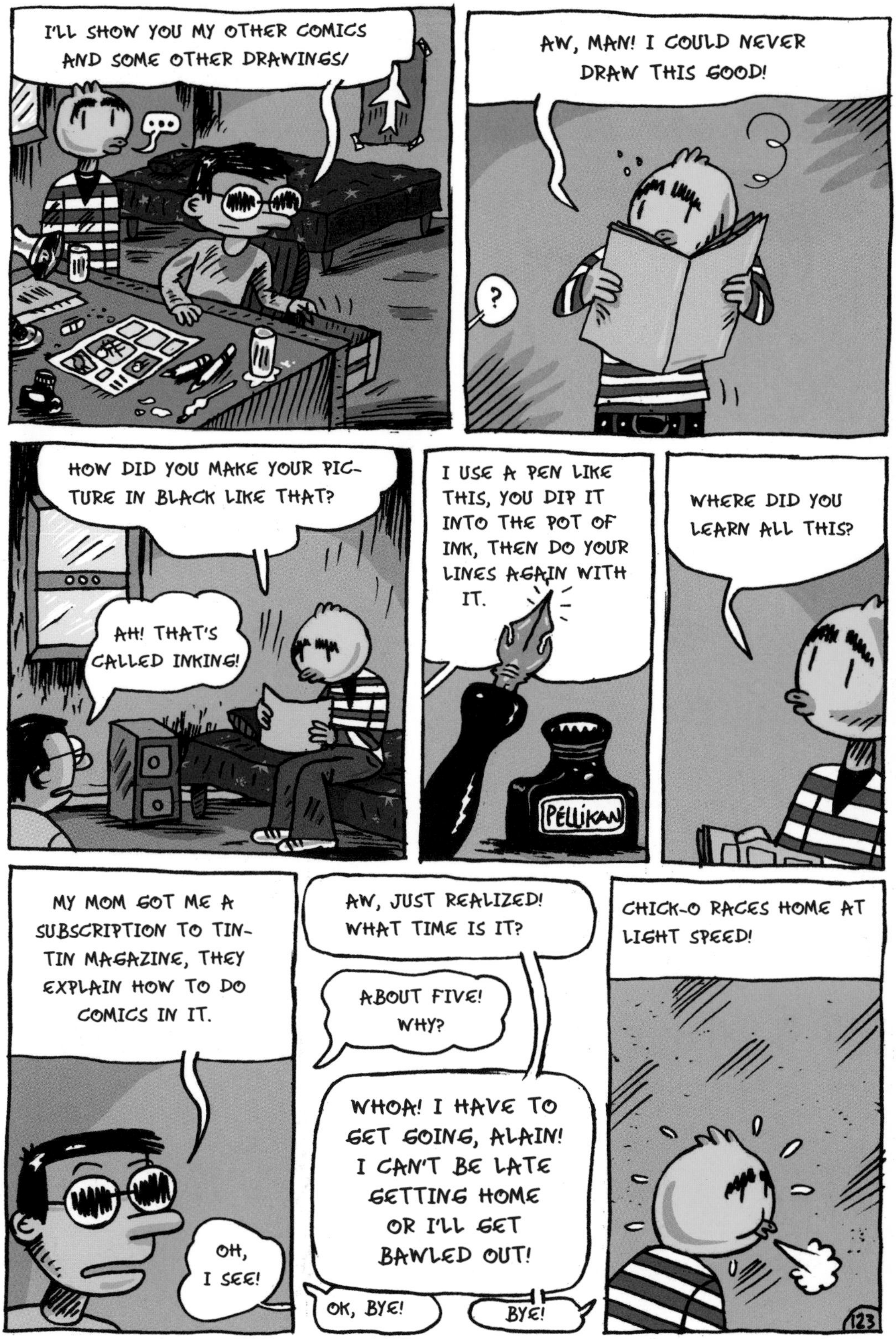
I'LL SHOW YOU MY OTHER COMICS AND SOME OTHER DRAWINGS!
AW, MAN! I COULD NEVER DRAW THIS GOOD!
?
HOW DID YOU MAKE YOUR PICTURE IN BLACK LIKE THAT?
AH! THAT'S CALLED INKING!
I USE A PEN LIKE THIS, YOU DIP IT INTO THE POT OF INK, THEN DO YOUR LINES AGAIN WITH IT.
PELLIKAN
WHERE DID YOU LEARN ALL THIS?
MY MOM GOT ME A SUBSCRIPTION TO TINTIN MAGAZINE, THEY EXPLAIN HOW TO DO COMICS IN IT.
OH, I SEE!
AW, JUST REALIZED! WHAT TIME IS IT?
ABOUT FIVE! WHY?
WHOA! I HAVE TO GET GOING, ALAIN! I CAN'T BE LATE GETTING HOME OR I'LL GET BAWLED OUT!
OK, BYE!
BYE!
CHICK-O RACES HOME AT LIGHT SPEED!
123

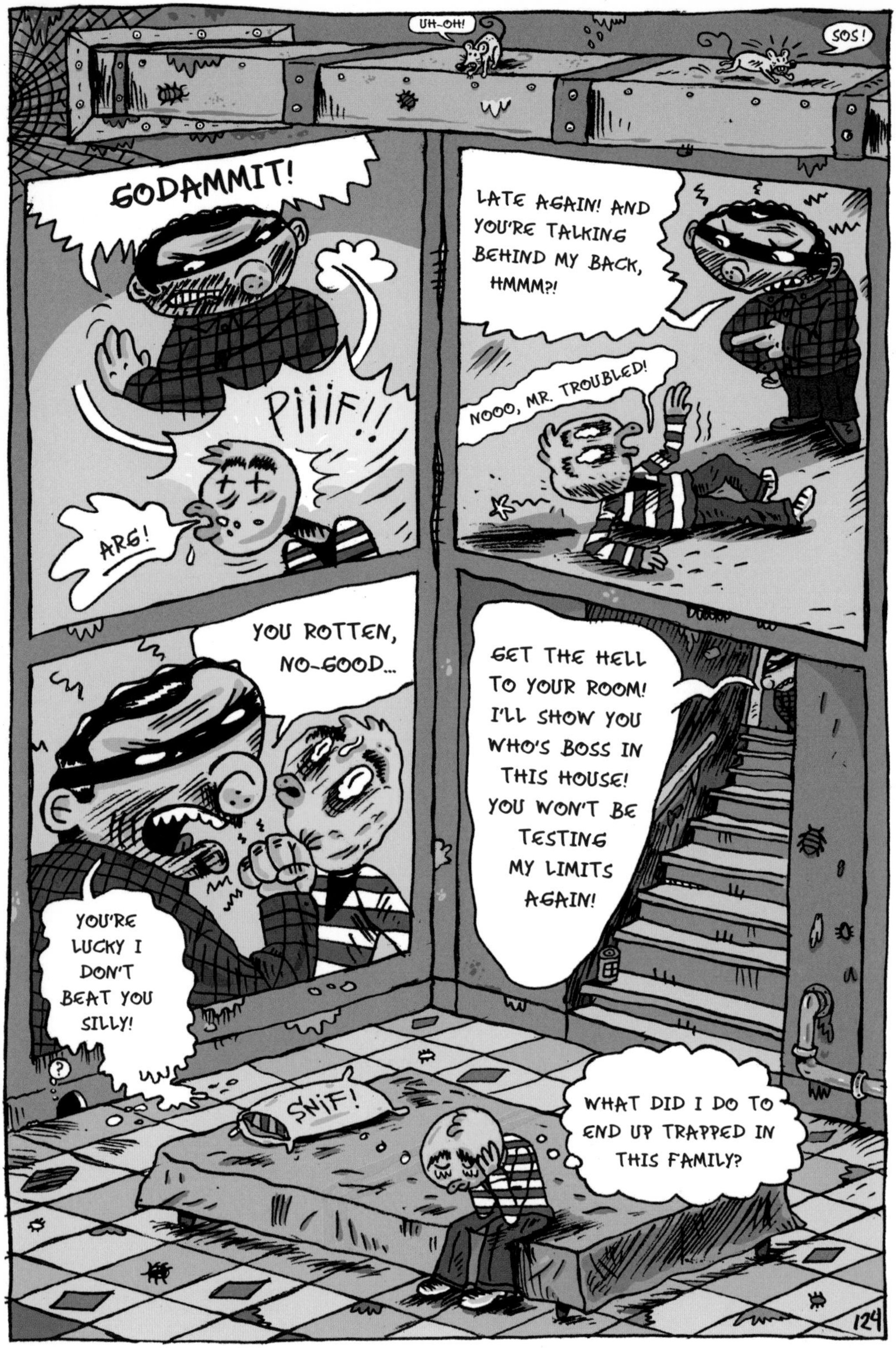
UH-OH!
SOS!
GODAMMIT!
PIIIF!!
ARG!
LATE AGAIN! AND YOU'RE TALKING BEHIND MY BACK, HMMM?!
NOOO, MR. TROUBLED!
YOU ROTTEN, NO-GOOD...
YOU'RE LUCKY I DON'T BEAT YOU SILLY!
GET THE HELL TO YOUR ROOM! I'LL SHOW YOU WHO'S BOSS IN THIS HOUSE! YOU WON'T BE TESTING MY LIMITS AGAIN!
?
SNIF!
WHAT DID I DO TO END UP TRAPPED IN THIS FAMILY?
124

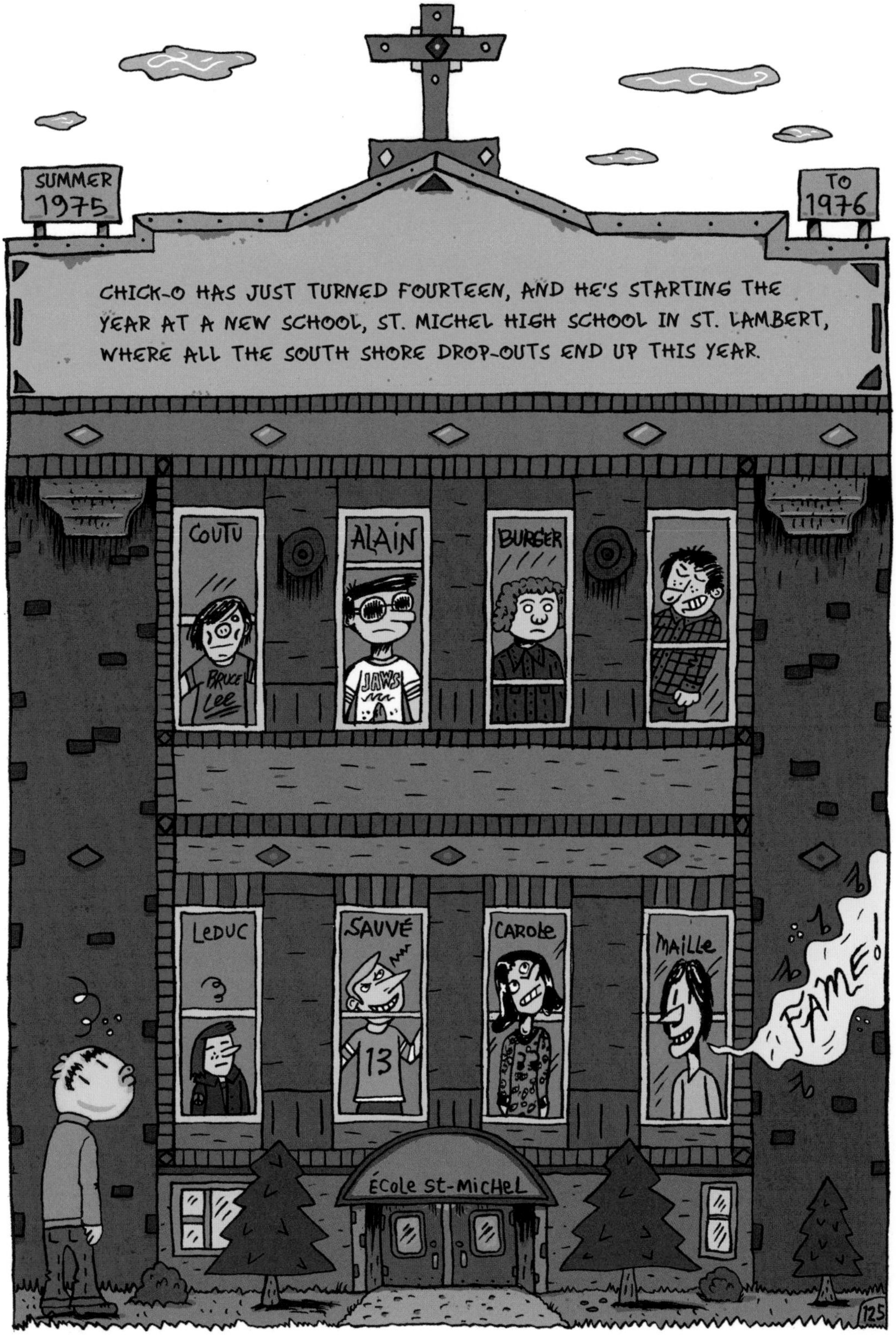
SUMMER 1975
TO 1976
CHICK-O HAS JUST TURNED FOURTEEN, AND HE'S STARTING THE YEAR AT A NEW SCHOOL, ST. MICHEL HIGH SCHOOL IN ST. LAMBERT, WHERE ALL THE SOUTH SHORE DROP-OUTS END UP THIS YEAR.
COUTU
BRUCE LEE
ALAIN
JAWS
BURGER
LEDUC
SAUVÉ
13
CAROLE
MAILLE
FAME!
ÉCOLE ST-MICHEL
125

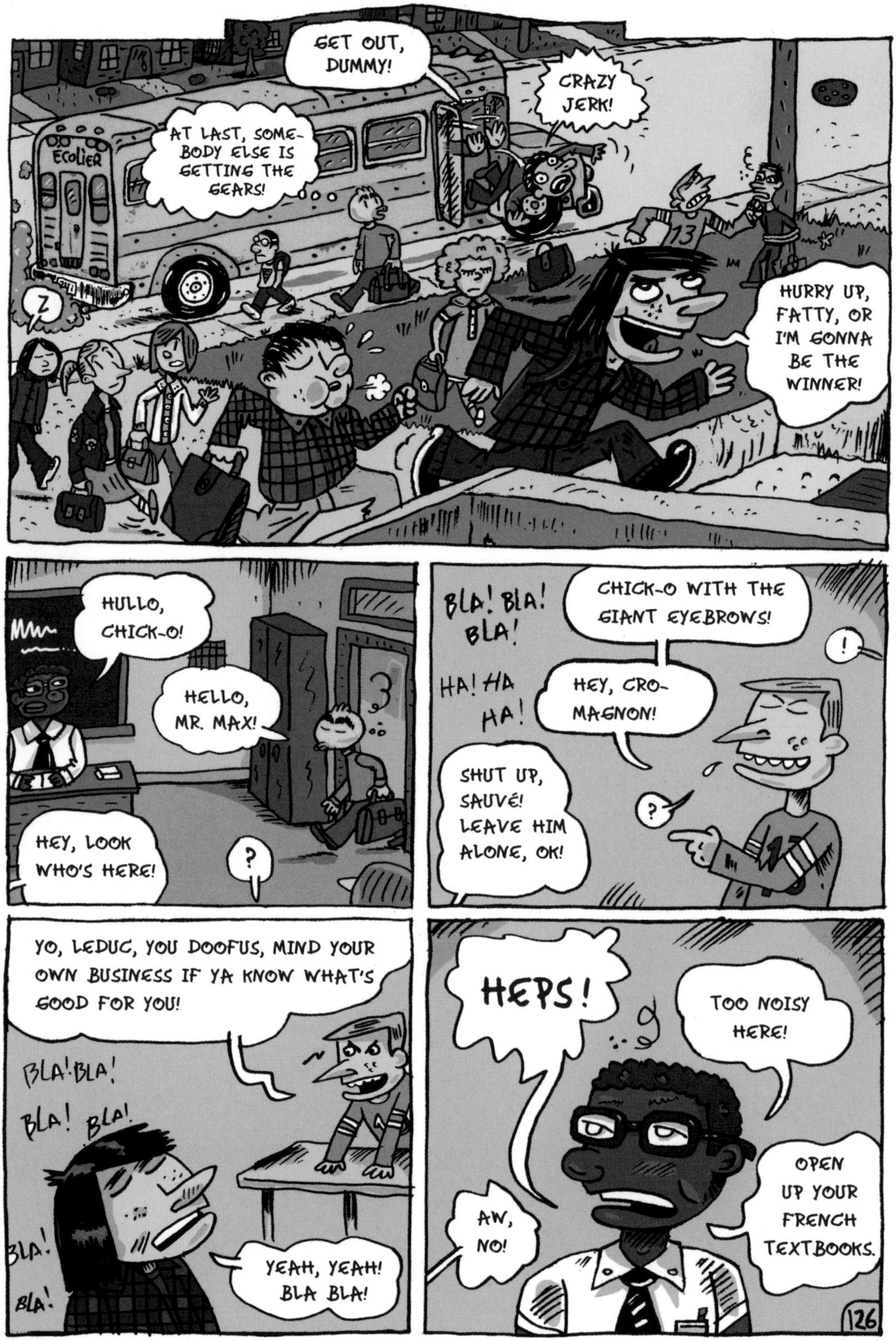
GET OUT, DUMMY!
AT LAST, SOMEBODY ELSE IS GETTING THE GEARS!
CRAZY JERK!
ECOLIER
HURRY UP, FATTY, OR I'M GONNA BE THE WINNER!
HULLO, CHICK-O!
HELLO, MR. MAX!
HEY, LOOK WHO'S HERE!
?
BLA! BLA! BLA!
CHICK-O WITH THE GIANT EYEBROWS!
!
HA! HA HA!
HEY, CRO-MAGNON!
SHUT UP, SAUVÉ! LEAVE HIM ALONE, OK!
?
YO, LEDUC, YOU DOOFUS, MIND YOUR OWN BUSINESS IF YA KNOW WHAT'S GOOD FOR YOU!
BLA! BLA! BLA! BLA!
BLA! BLA!
YEAH, YEAH! BLA BLA!
HEPS!
TOO NOISY HERE!
AW, NO!
OPEN UP YOUR FRENCH TEXTBOOKS.
126

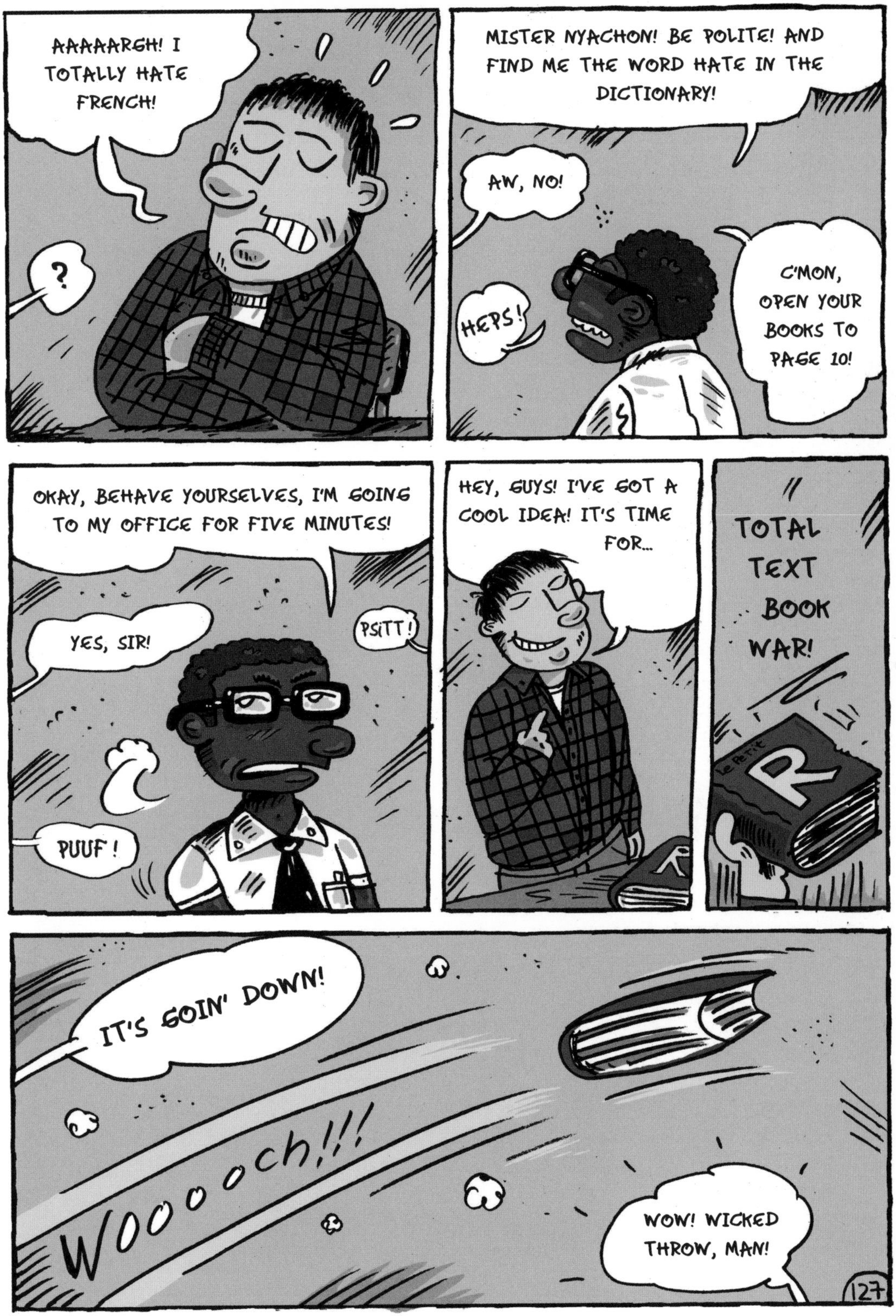
AAAAARGH! I TOTALLY HATE FRENCH!
?
MISTER NYACHON! BE POLITE! AND FIND ME THE WORD HATE IN THE DICTIONARY!
AW, NO!
HEPS!
C'MON, OPEN YOUR BOOKS TO PAGE 10!
OKAY, BEHAVE YOURSELVES, I'M GOING TO MY OFFICE FOR FIVE MINUTES!
YES, SIR!
PSITT!
PUUF!
HEY, GUYS! I'VE GOT A COOL IDEA! IT'S TIME FOR...
TOTAL TEXT BOOK WAR!
le Petit R
IT'S GOIN' DOWN!
Woooooch!!!
WOW! WICKED THROW, MAN!
127

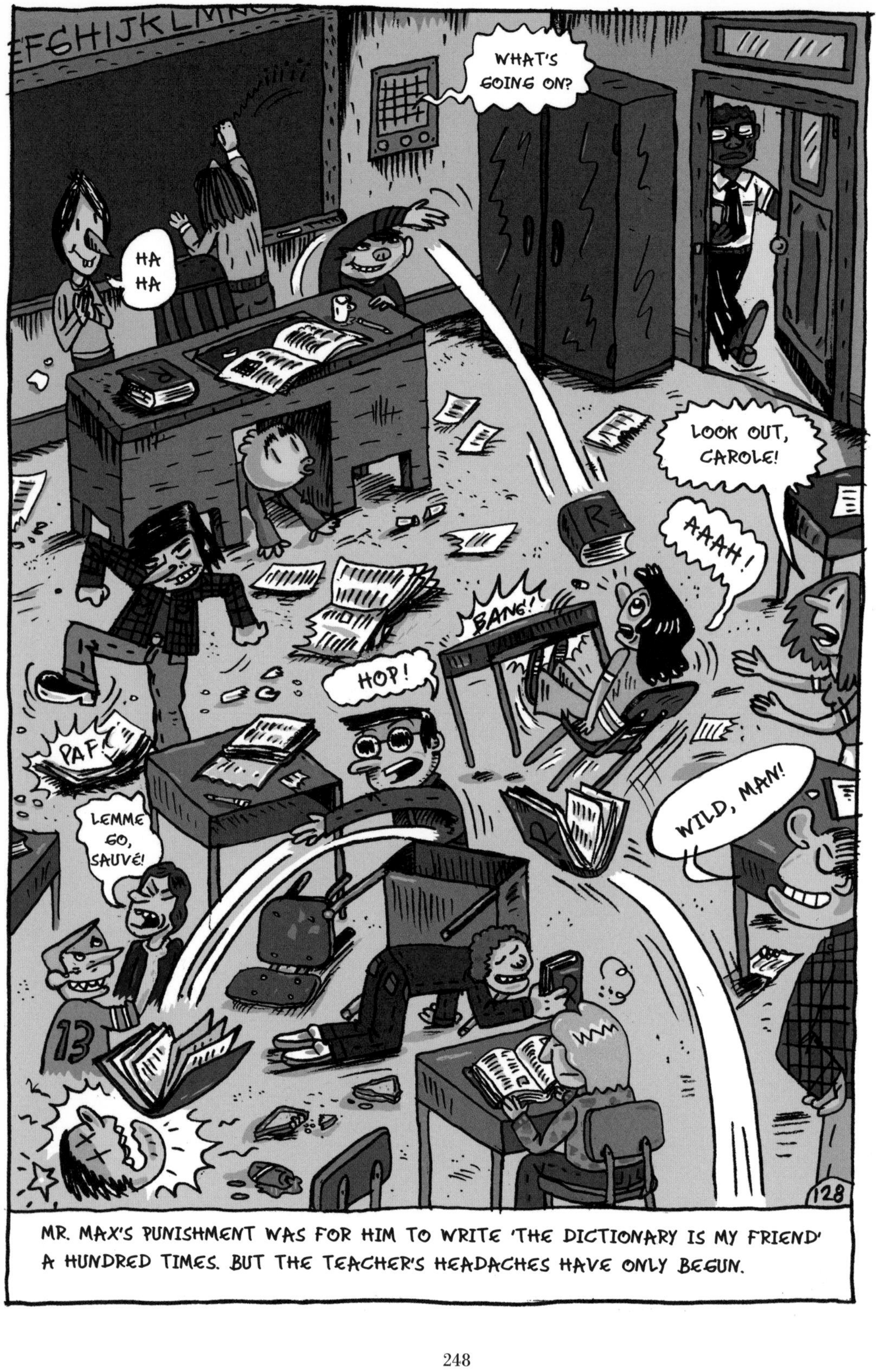
WHAT'S GOING ON?
HA HA
LOOK OUT, CAROLE!
AAAH!
BANG!
HOP!
PAF!
LEMME GO, SAUVÉ!
WILD, MAN!
MR. MAX'S PUNISHMENT WAS FOR HIM TO WRITE 'THE DICTIONARY IS MY FRIEND' A HUNDRED TIMES. BUT THE TEACHER'S HEADACHES HAVE ONLY BEGUN.

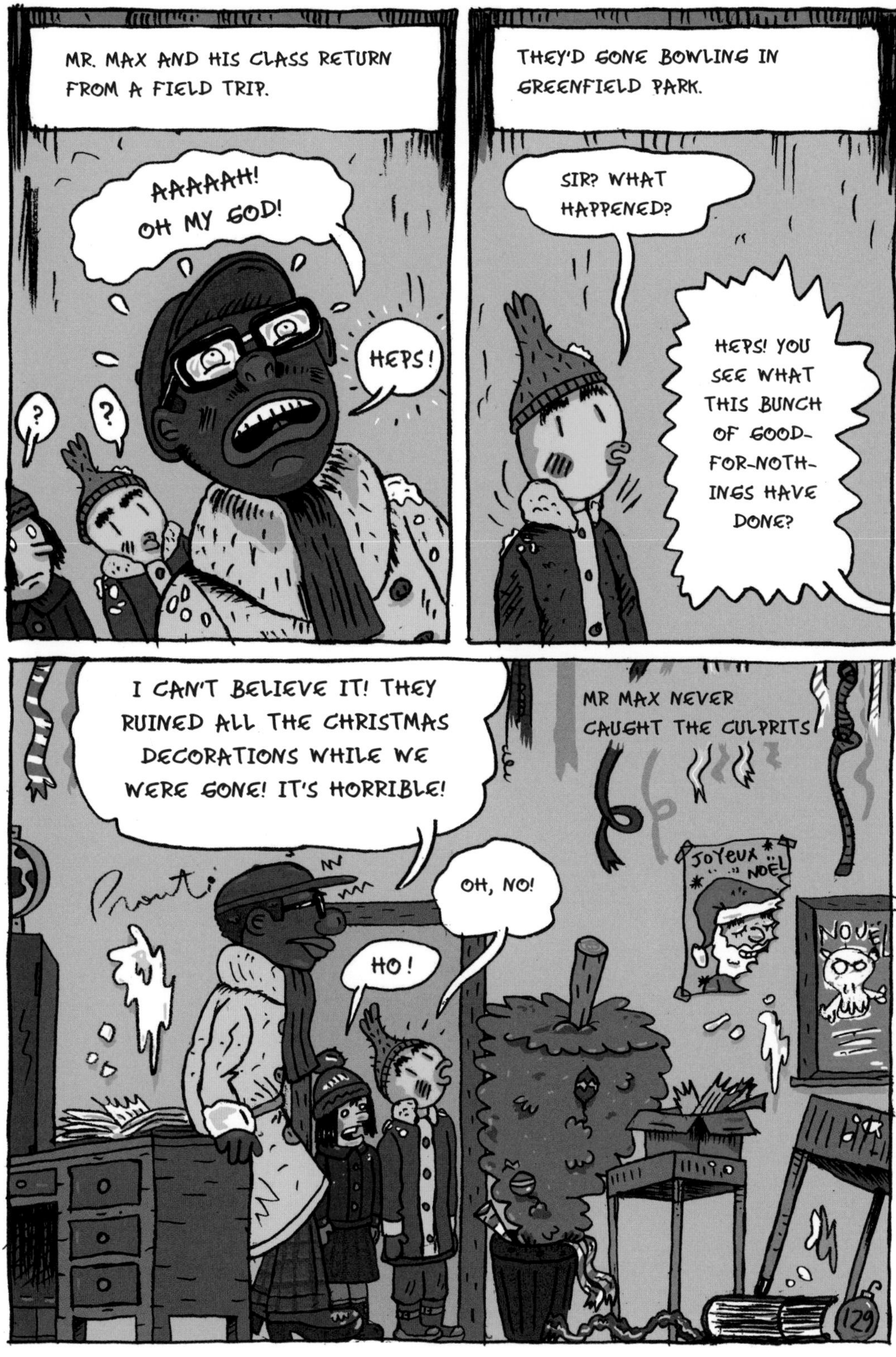
MR. MAX AND HIS CLASS RETURN FROM A FIELD TRIP.
AAAAAH! OH MY GOD!
HEPS!
?
?
THEY'D GONE BOWLING IN GREENFIELD PARK.
SIR? WHAT HAPPENED?
HEPS! YOU SEE WHAT THIS BUNCH OF GOOD-FOR-NOTHINGS HAVE DONE?
I CAN'T BELIEVE IT! THEY RUINED ALL THE CHRISTMAS DECORATIONS WHILE WE WERE GONE! IT'S HORRIBLE!
MR MAX NEVER CAUGHT THE CULPRITS
OH, NO!
HO!
JOYEUX NOEL
NOEL
129

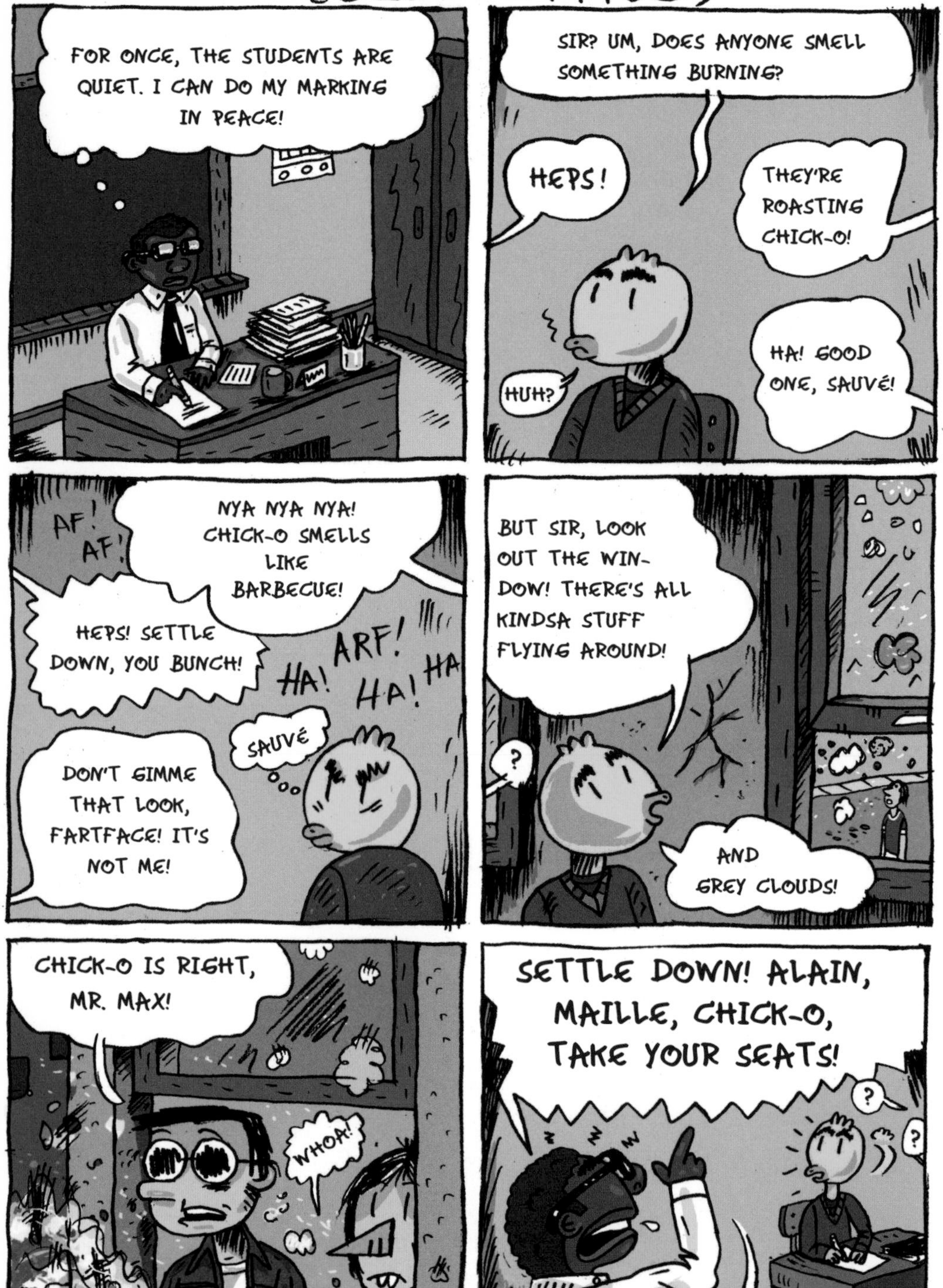
FOR ONCE, THE STUDENTS ARE QUIET. I CAN DO MY MARKING IN PEACE!
SIR? UM, DOES ANYONE SMELL SOMETHING BURNING?
HEPS!
THEY'RE ROASTING CHICK-O!
HUH?
HA! GOOD ONE, SAUVÉ!
AF! AF!
NYA NYA NYA! CHICK-O SMELLS LIKE BARBECUE!
HEPS! SETTLE DOWN, YOU BUNCH!
HA! ARF! HA! HA
SAUVÉ
DON'T GIMME THAT LOOK, FARTFACE! IT'S NOT ME!
BUT SIR, LOOK OUT THE WIN-DOW! THERE'S ALL KINDSA STUFF FLYING AROUND!
?
AND GREY CLOUDS!
CHICK-O IS RIGHT, MR. MAX!
WHOA!
SETTLE DOWN! ALAIN, MAILLE, CHICK-O, TAKE YOUR SEATS!
?
?
130

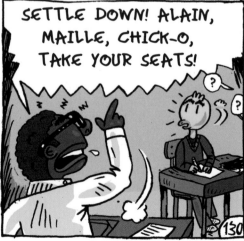

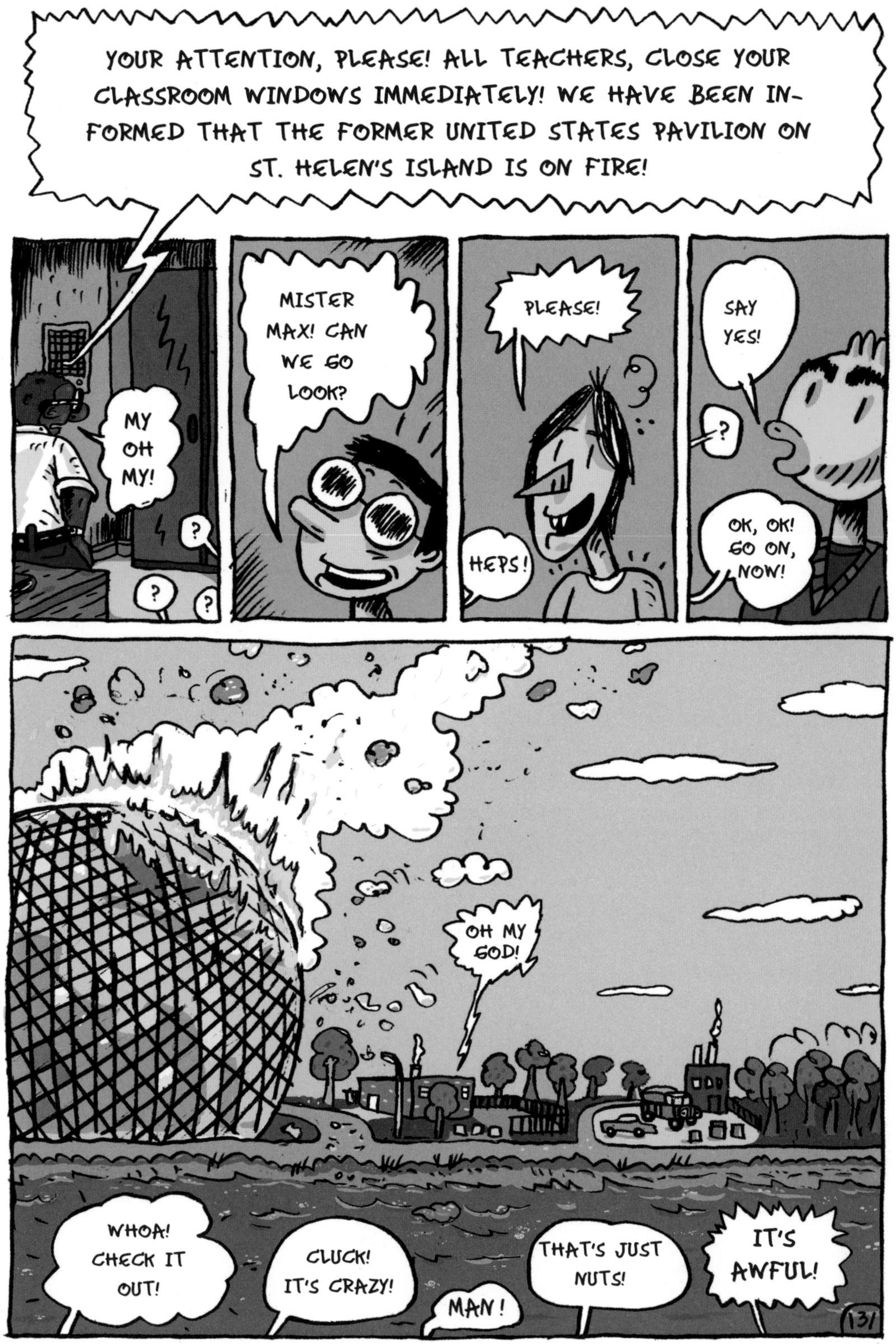
YOUR ATTENTION, PLEASE! ALL TEACHERS, CLOSE YOUR CLASSROOM WINDOWS IMMEDIATELY! WE HAVE BEEN IN-FORMED THAT THE FORMER UNITED STATES PAVILION ON ST. HELEN'S ISLAND IS ON FIRE!
MY OH MY!
?
?
?
MISTER MAX! CAN WE GO LOOK?
PLEASE!
HEPS!
SAY YES!
?
OK, OK! GO ON, NOW!
OH MY GOD!
WHOA! CHECK IT OUT!
CLUCK! IT'S CRAZY!
MAN!
THAT'S JUST NUTS!
IT'S AWFUL!
131

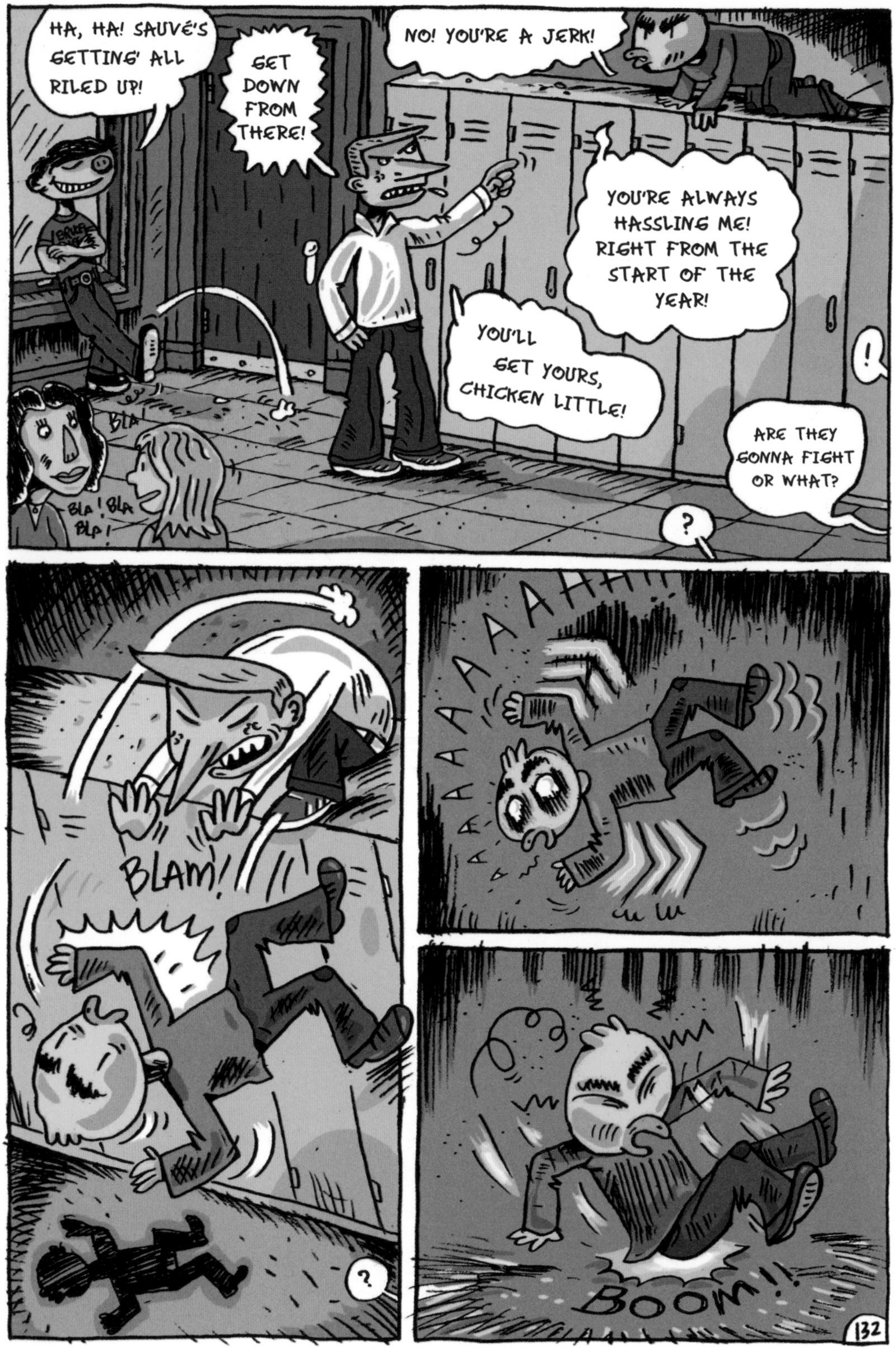
HA, HA! SAUVÉ'S GETTING ALL RILED UP!
GET DOWN FROM THERE!
NO! YOU'RE A JERK!
YOU'RE ALWAYS HASSLING ME! RIGHT FROM THE START OF THE YEAR!
YOU'LL GET YOURS, CHICKEN LITTLE!
!
BLA! BLA! BLA! BLA!
ARE THEY GONNA FIGHT OR WHAT?
?
BLAM!
?
AAAAAAAAAAAAHH!!!
BOOM!!
132

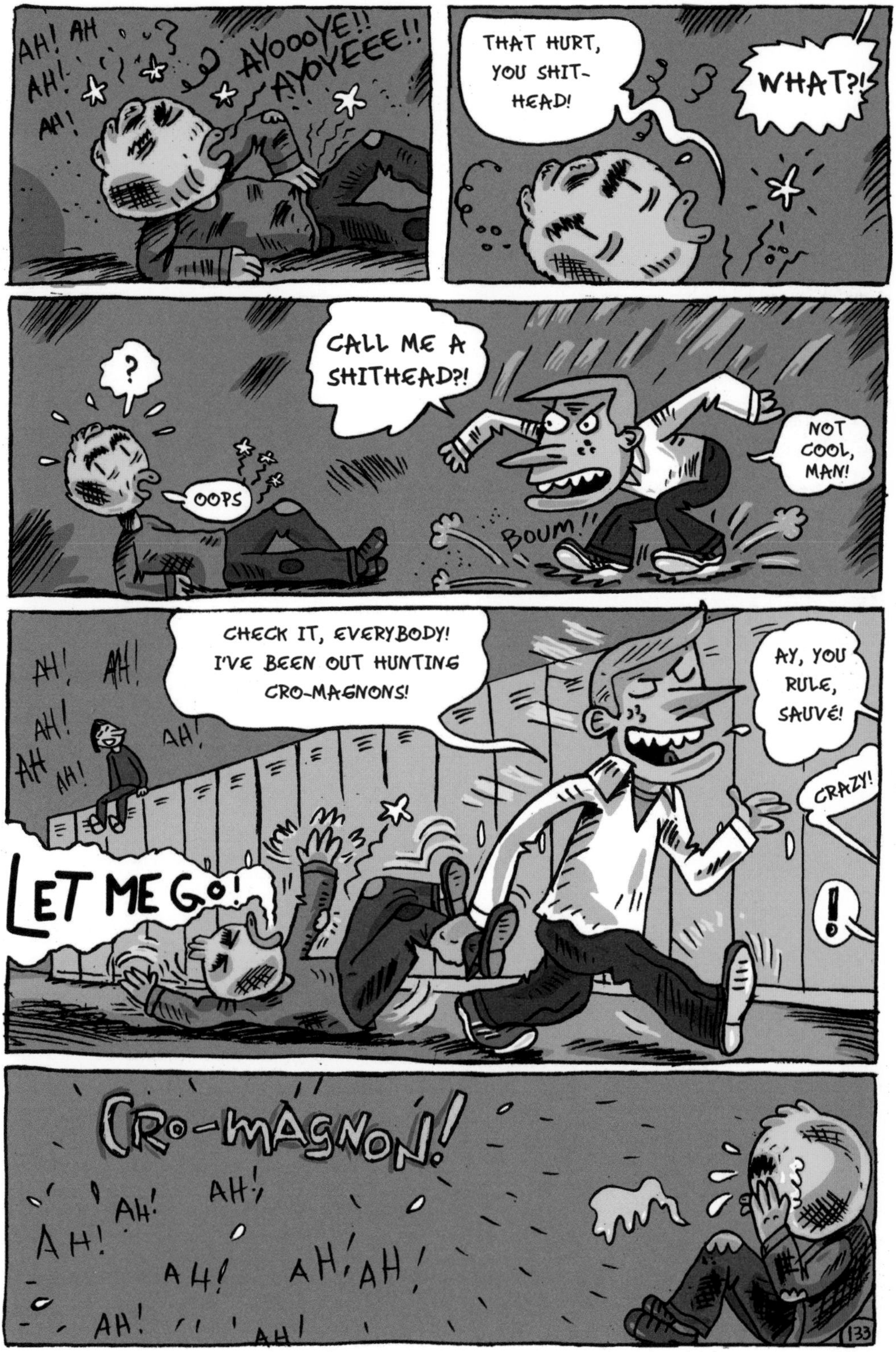
AH! AH
AH!
AH!
AYOOOYE!!
AYOYEEE!!
THAT HURT, YOU SHIT-HEAD!
WHAT?!
?
CALL ME A SHITHEAD?!
OOPS
NOT COOL, MAN!
BOUM!
CHECK IT, EVERYBODY! I'VE BEEN OUT HUNTING CRO-MAGNONS!
AY, YOU RULE, SAUVÉ!
AH! AH!
AH!
AH!
AH
AH!
CRAZY!
LET ME GO!
!
CRO-MAGNON!
AH!
AH!
AH!
AH!
AH! AH!
AH!
AH!
133

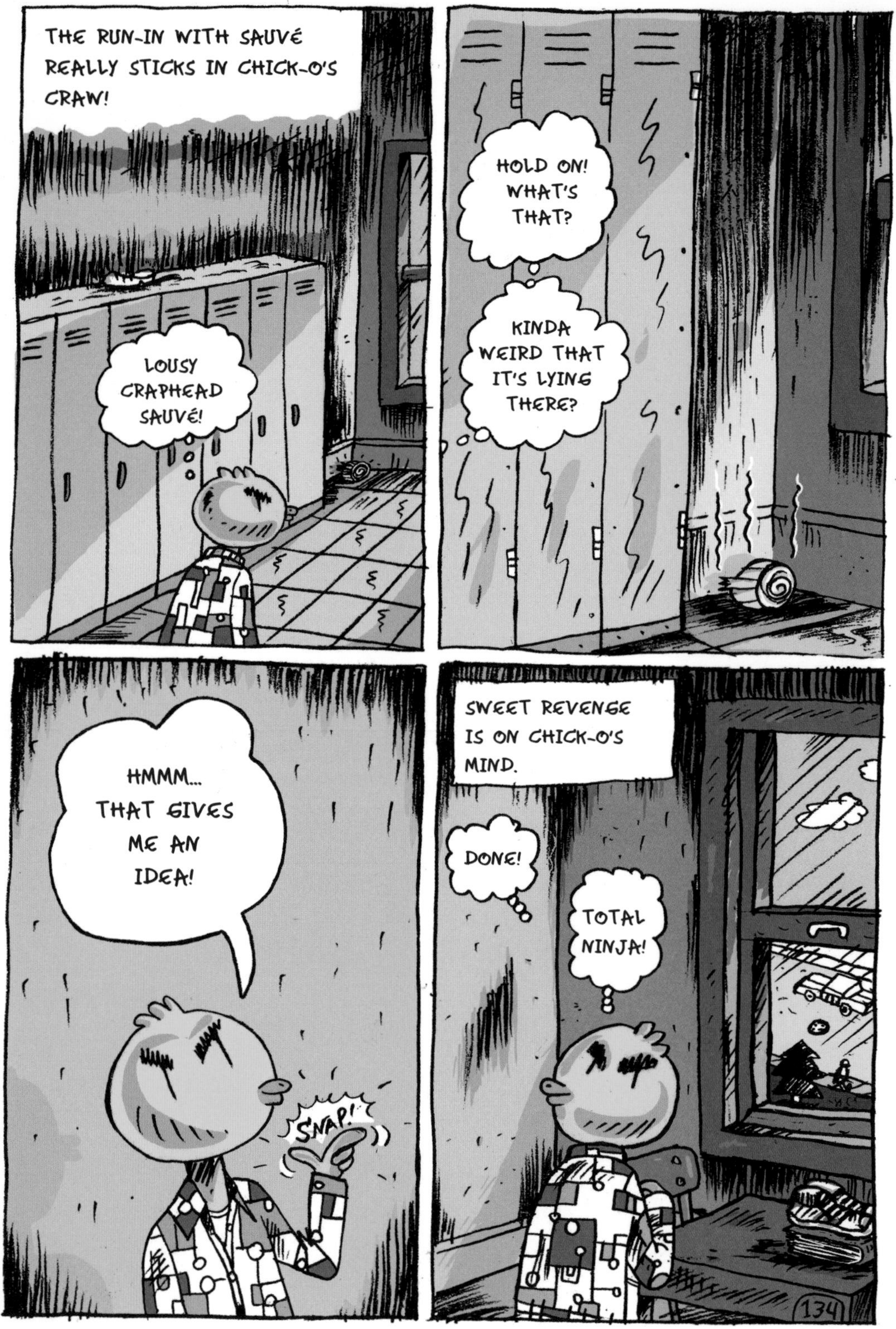
THE RUN-IN WITH SAUVÉ REALLY STICKS IN CHICK-O'S CRAW!
LOUSY CRAPHEAD SAUVÉ!
HOLD ON! WHAT'S THAT?
KINDA WEIRD THAT IT'S LYING THERE?
HMMM... THAT GIVES ME AN IDEA!
SNAP!
SWEET REVENGE IS ON CHICK-O'S MIND.
DONE!
TOTAL NINJA!
134

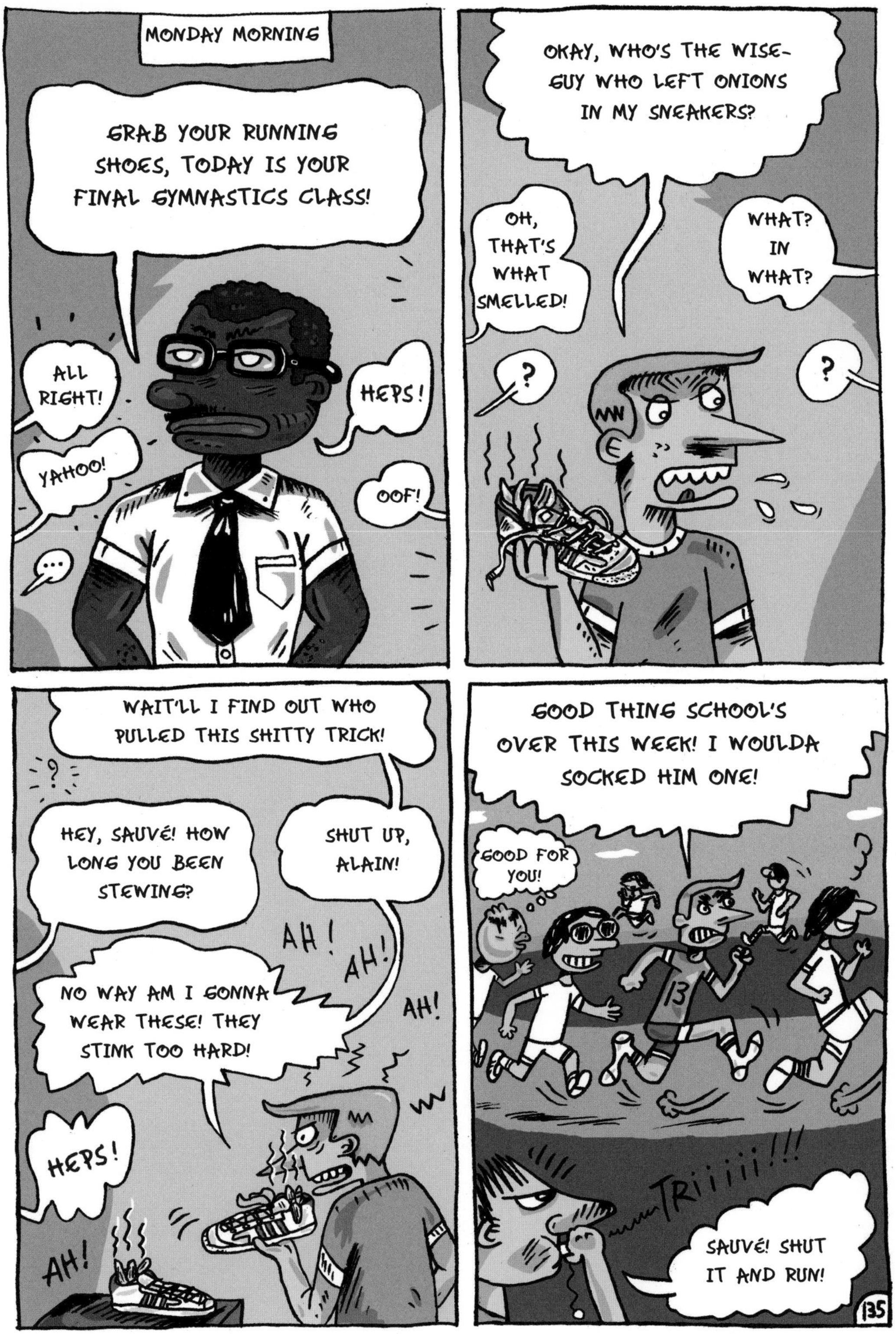
MONDAY MORNING
GRAB YOUR RUNNING SHOES, TODAY IS YOUR FINAL GYMNASTICS CLASS!
ALL RIGHT!
HEPS!
YAHOO!
OOF!
...
OKAY, WHO'S THE WISE-GUY WHO LEFT ONIONS IN MY SNEAKERS?
OH, THAT'S WHAT SMELLED!
WHAT? IN WHAT?
?
?
WAIT'LL I FIND OUT WHO PULLED THIS SHITTY TRICK!
?
HEY, SAUVÉ! HOW LONG YOU BEEN STEWING?
SHUT UP, ALAIN!
AH! AH! AH!
NO WAY AM I GONNA WEAR THESE! THEY STINK TOO HARD!
HEPS!
AH!
GOOD THING SCHOOL'S OVER THIS WEEK! I WOULDA SOCKED HIM ONE!
GOOD FOR YOU!
13
TRiiiiii!!!
SAUVÉ! SHUT IT AND RUN!
135

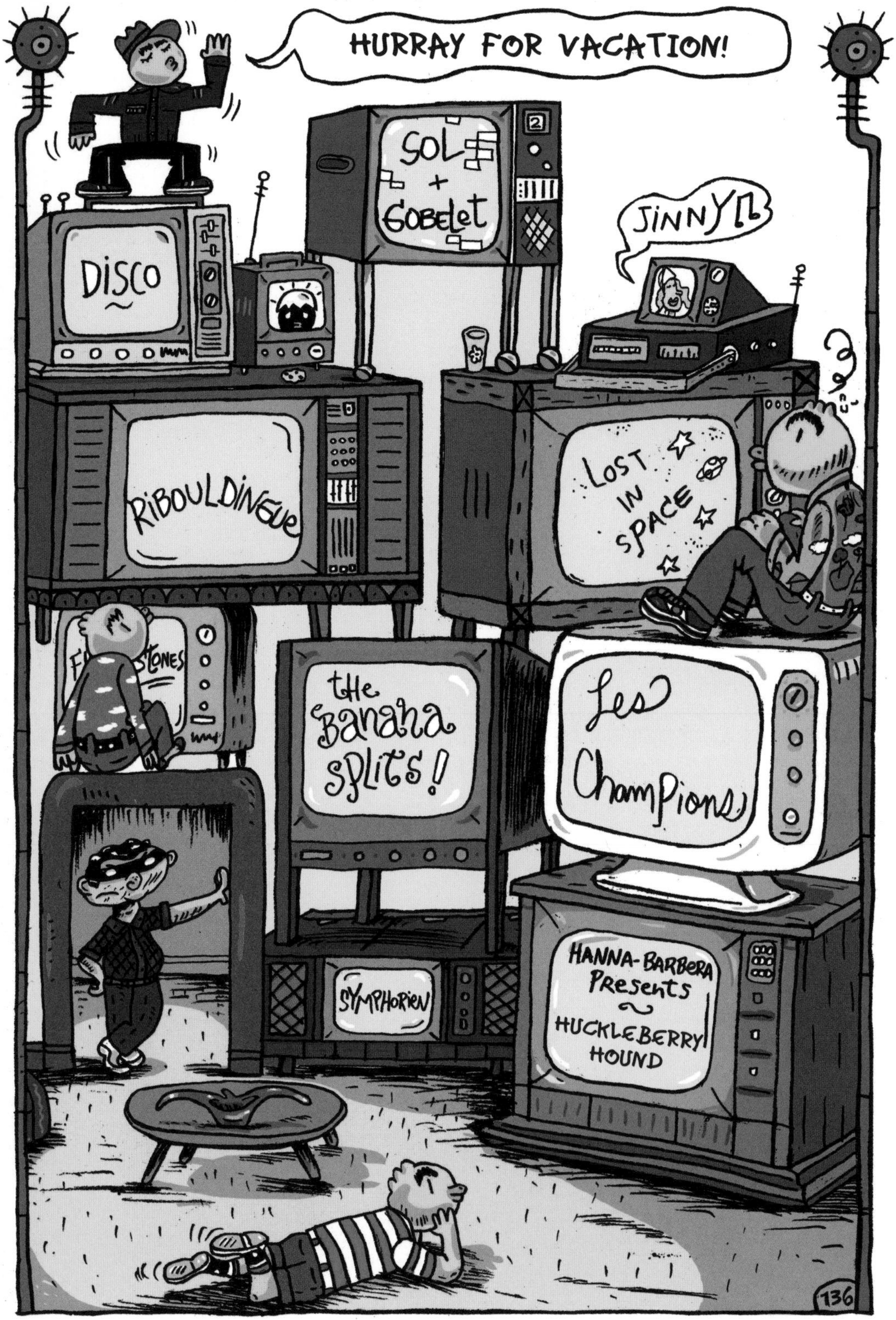
HURRAY FOR VACATION!
SOL + GOBELET
DISCO
JINNY
RIBOULDINGUE
LOST IN SPACE
the Banana splits!
Les Champions
SYMPHORIEN
HANNA-BARBERA Presents HUCKLEBERRY HOUND
136

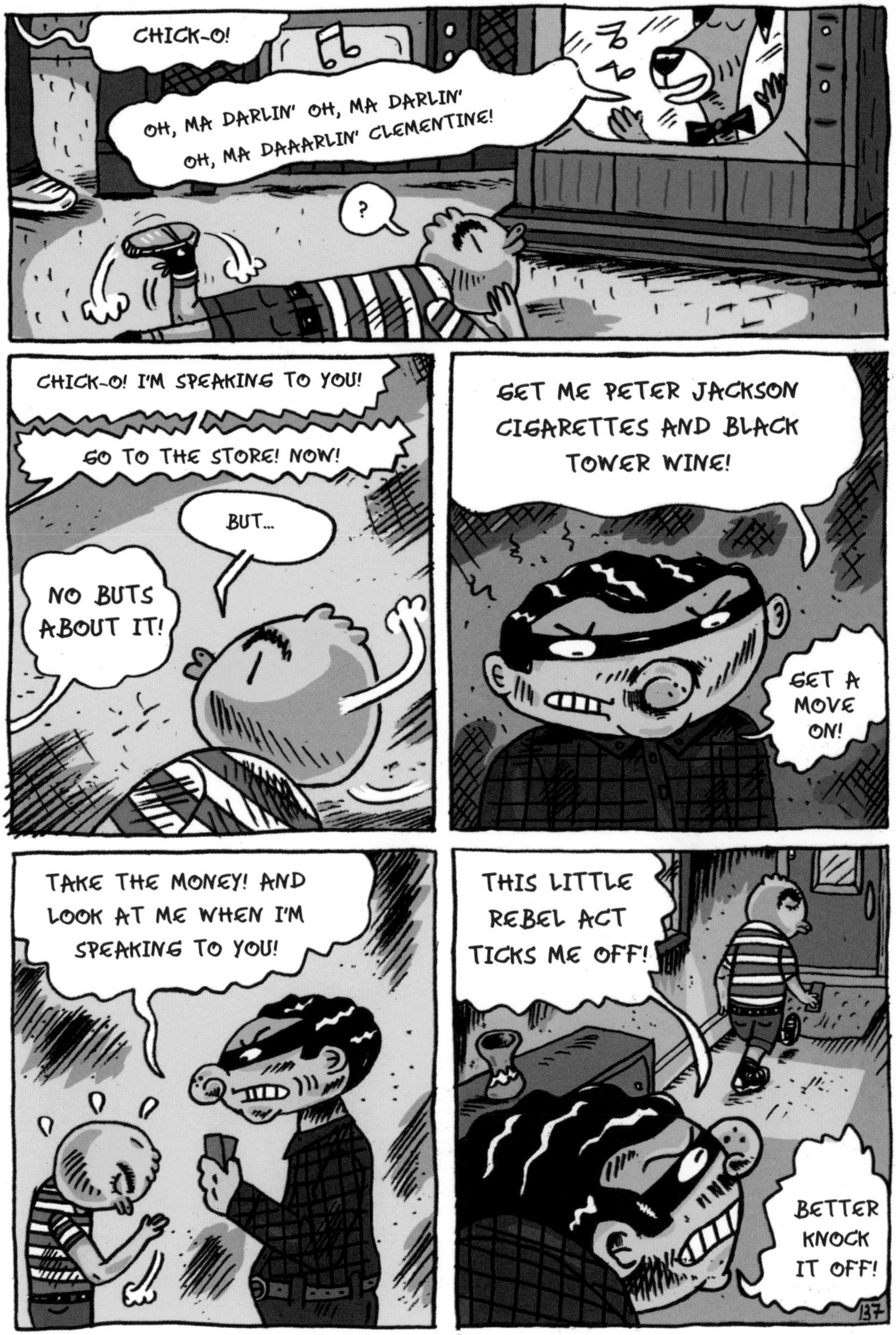
CHICK-O!
OH, MA DARLIN' OH, MA DARLIN'
OH, MA DAAARLIN' CLEMENTINE!
?
CHICK-O! I'M SPEAKING TO YOU!
GO TO THE STORE! NOW!
BUT...
NO BUTS ABOUT IT!
GET ME PETER JACKSON CIGARETTES AND BLACK TOWER WINE!
GET A MOVE ON!
TAKE THE MONEY! AND LOOK AT ME WHEN I'M SPEAKING TO YOU!
THIS LITTLE REBEL ACT TICKS ME OFF!
BETTER KNOCK IT OFF!
137

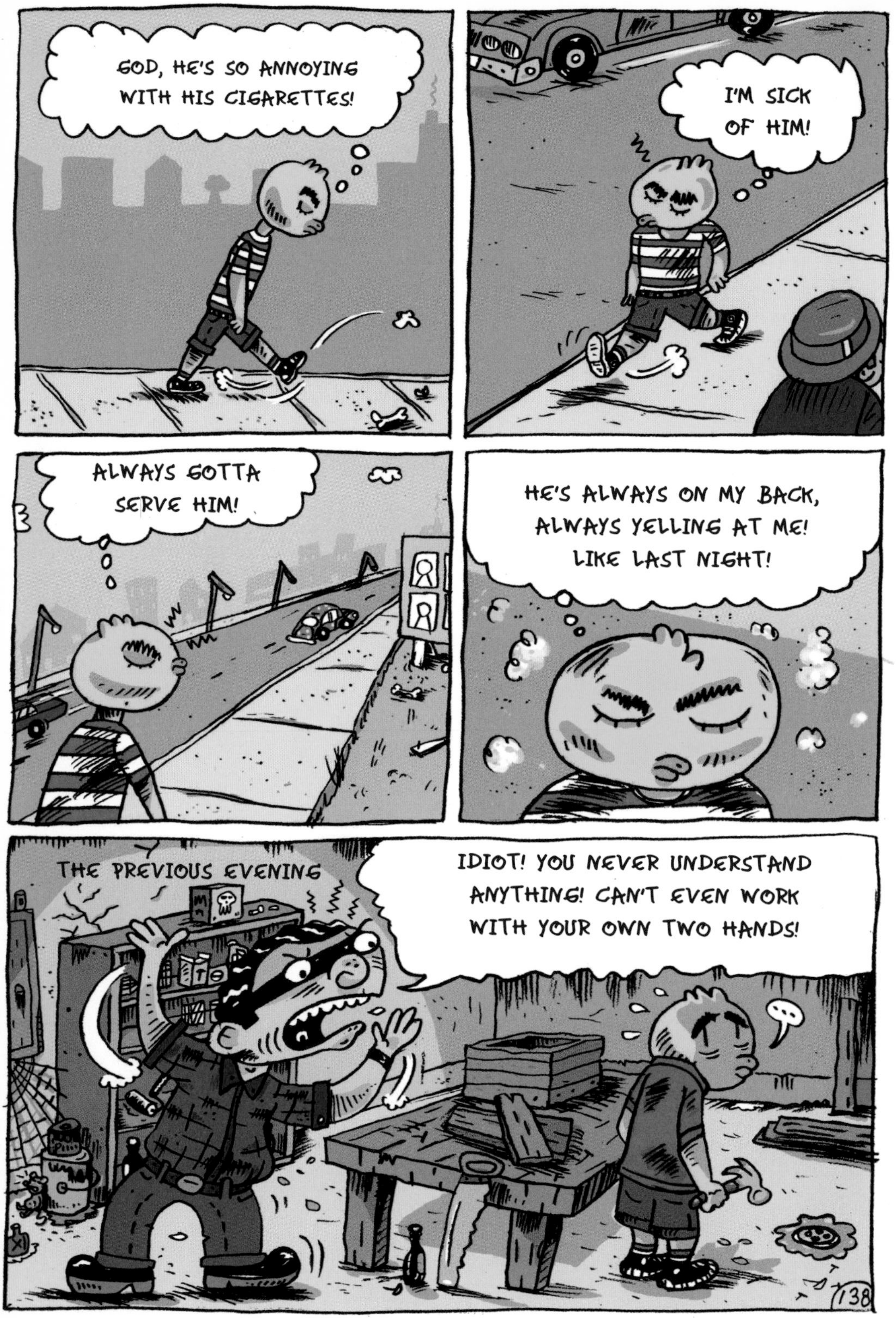
GOD, HE'S SO ANNOYING WITH HIS CIGARETTES!
I'M SICK OF HIM!
ALWAYS GOTTA SERVE HIM!
HE'S ALWAYS ON MY BACK, ALWAYS YELLING AT ME! LIKE LAST NIGHT!
THE PREVIOUS EVENING
IDIOT! YOU NEVER UNDERSTAND ANYTHING! CAN'T EVEN WORK WITH YOUR OWN TWO HANDS!
138

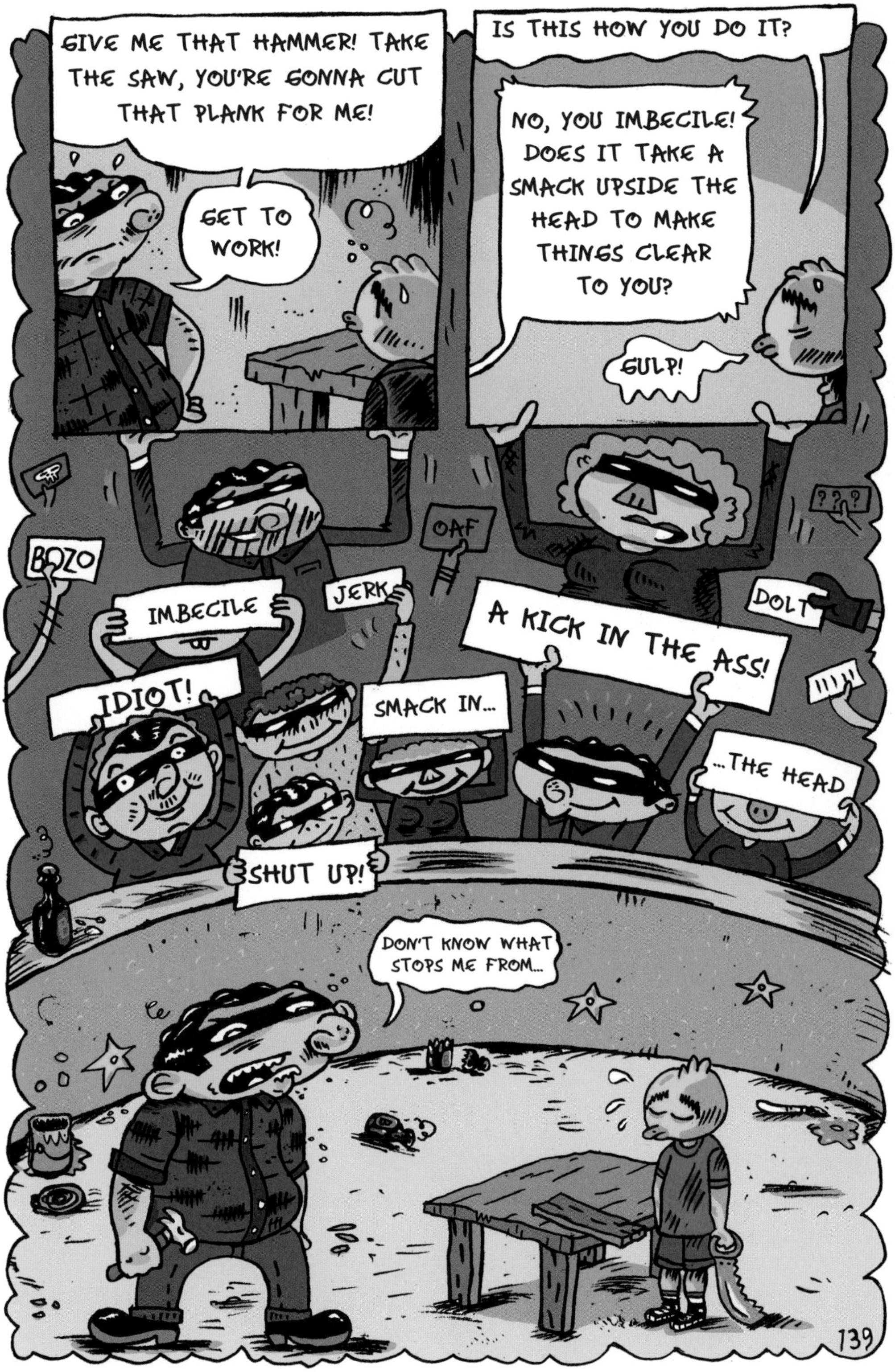
GIVE ME THAT HAMMER! TAKE THE SAW, YOU'RE GONNA CUT THAT PLANK FOR ME!
GET TO WORK!
IS THIS HOW YOU DO IT?
NO, YOU IMBECILE! DOES IT TAKE A SMACK UPSIDE THE HEAD TO MAKE THINGS CLEAR TO YOU?
GULP!
BOZO
OAF
???
IMBECILE
JERK
DOLT
A KICK IN THE ASS!
IDIOT!
SMACK IN...
...THE HEAD
SHUT UP!
DON'T KNOW WHAT STOPS ME FROM...
139

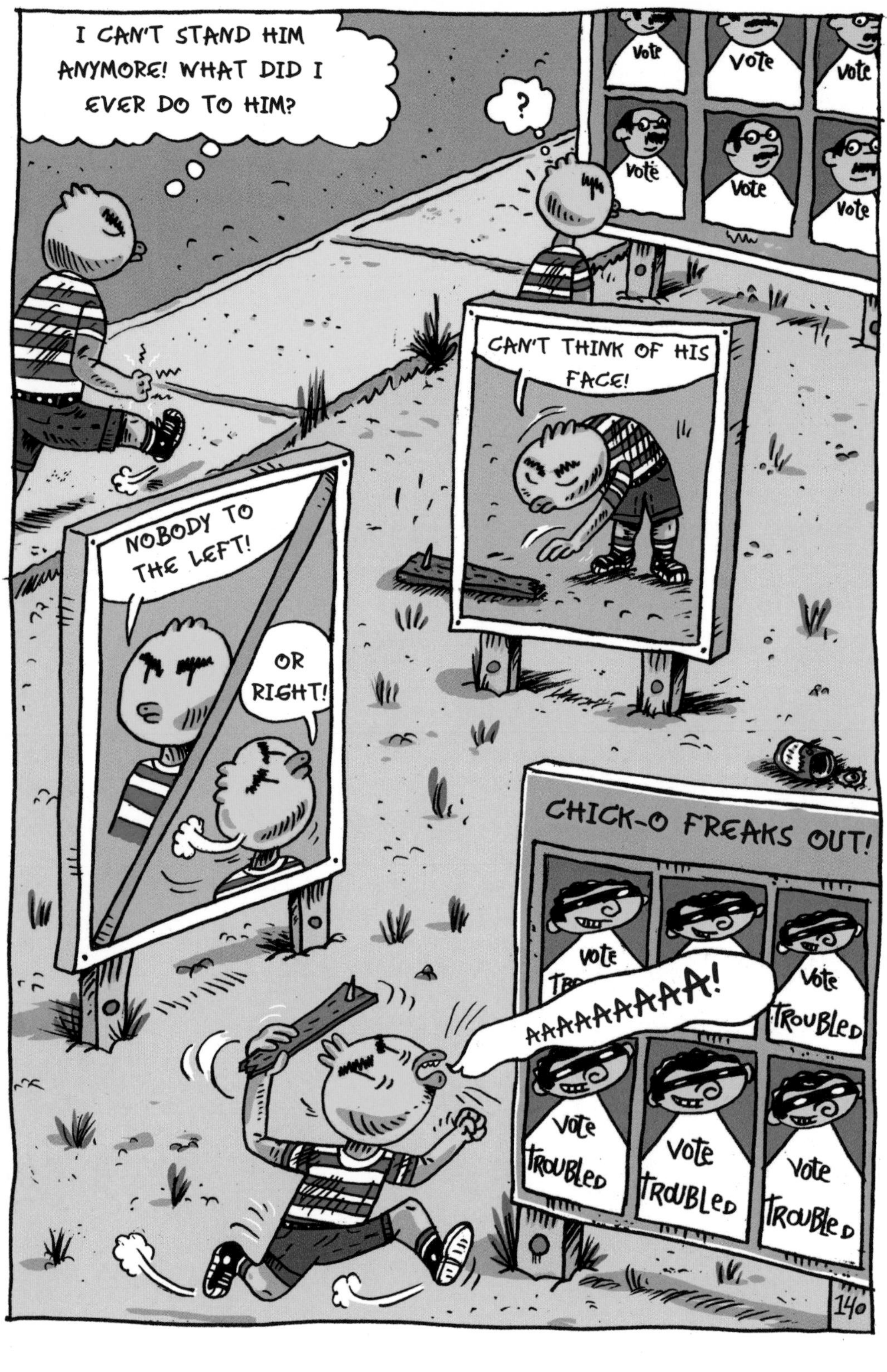
I CAN'T STAND HIM ANYMORE! WHAT DID I EVER DO TO HIM?
?
VOTE
VOTE
VOTE
VOTE
VOTE
VOTE
CAN'T THINK OF HIS FACE!
NOBODY TO THE LEFT!
OR RIGHT!
CHICK-O FREAKS OUT!
AAAAAAAAA!
VOTE TROUBLED
VOTE TROUBLED
VOTE TROUBLED
VOTE TROUBLED
140

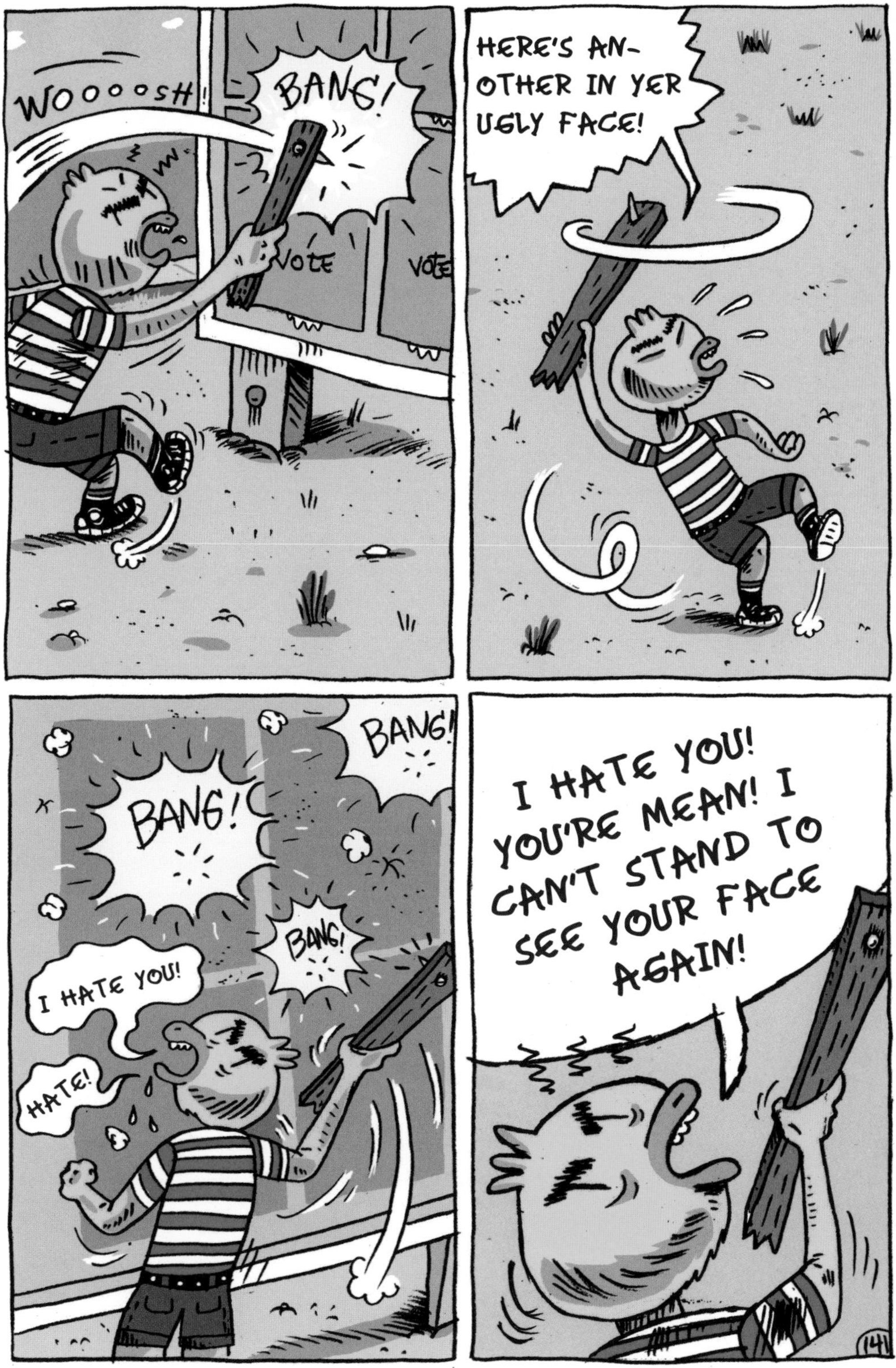
WOOOOSH!
BANG!
VOTE
VOTE
HERE'S AN-OTHER IN YER UGLY FACE!
BANG!
BANG!
BANG!
I HATE YOU!
HATE!
I HATE YOU! YOU'RE MEAN! I CAN'T STAND TO SEE YOUR FACE AGAIN!
141

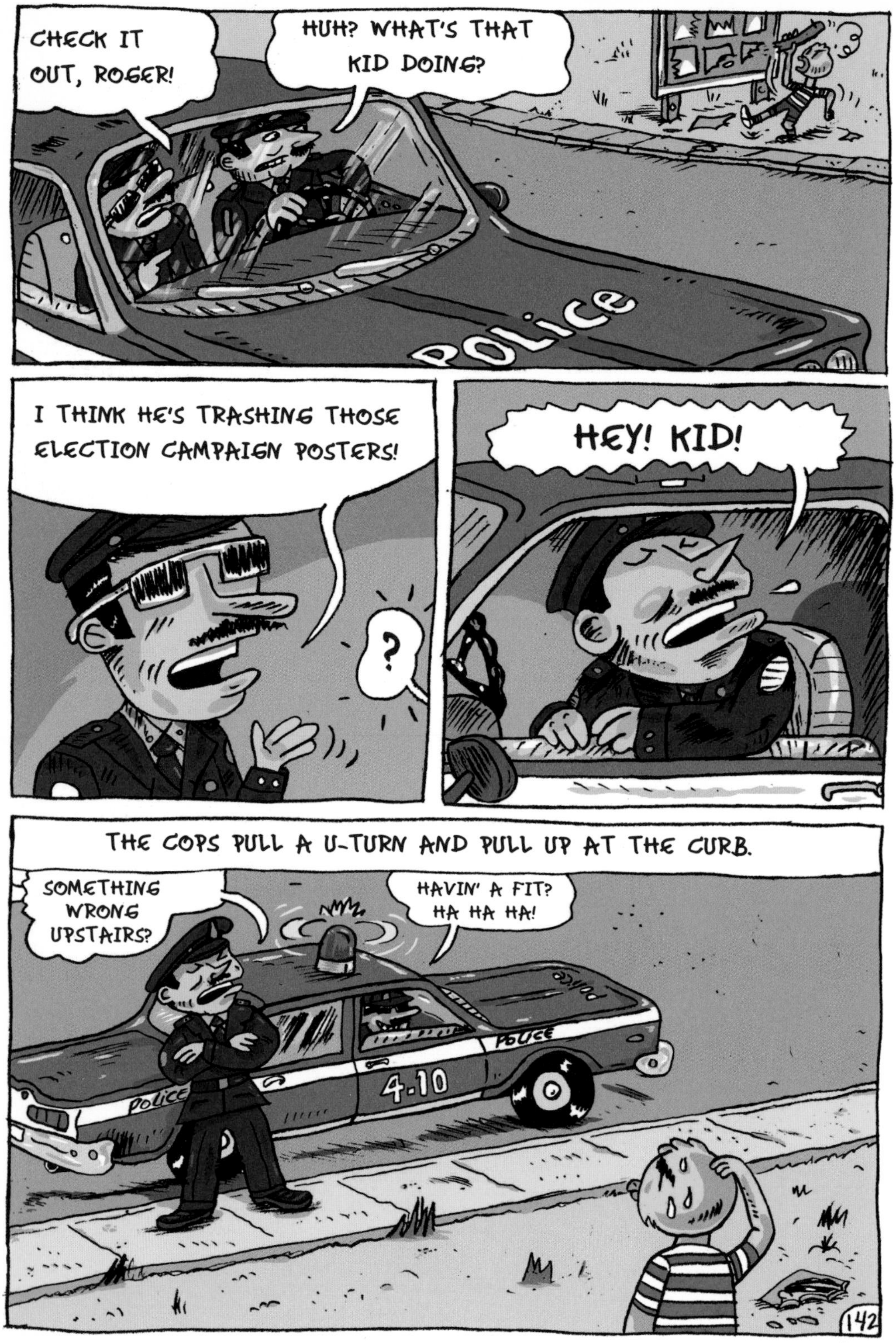
CHECK IT OUT, ROGER!
HUH? WHAT'S THAT KID DOING?
I THINK HE'S TRASHING THOSE ELECTION CAMPAIGN POSTERS!
?
HEY! KID!
POLICE
THE COPS PULL A U-TURN AND PULL UP AT THE CURB.
SOMETHING WRONG UPSTAIRS?
HAVIN' A FIT? HA HA HA!
POLICE
4-10
142

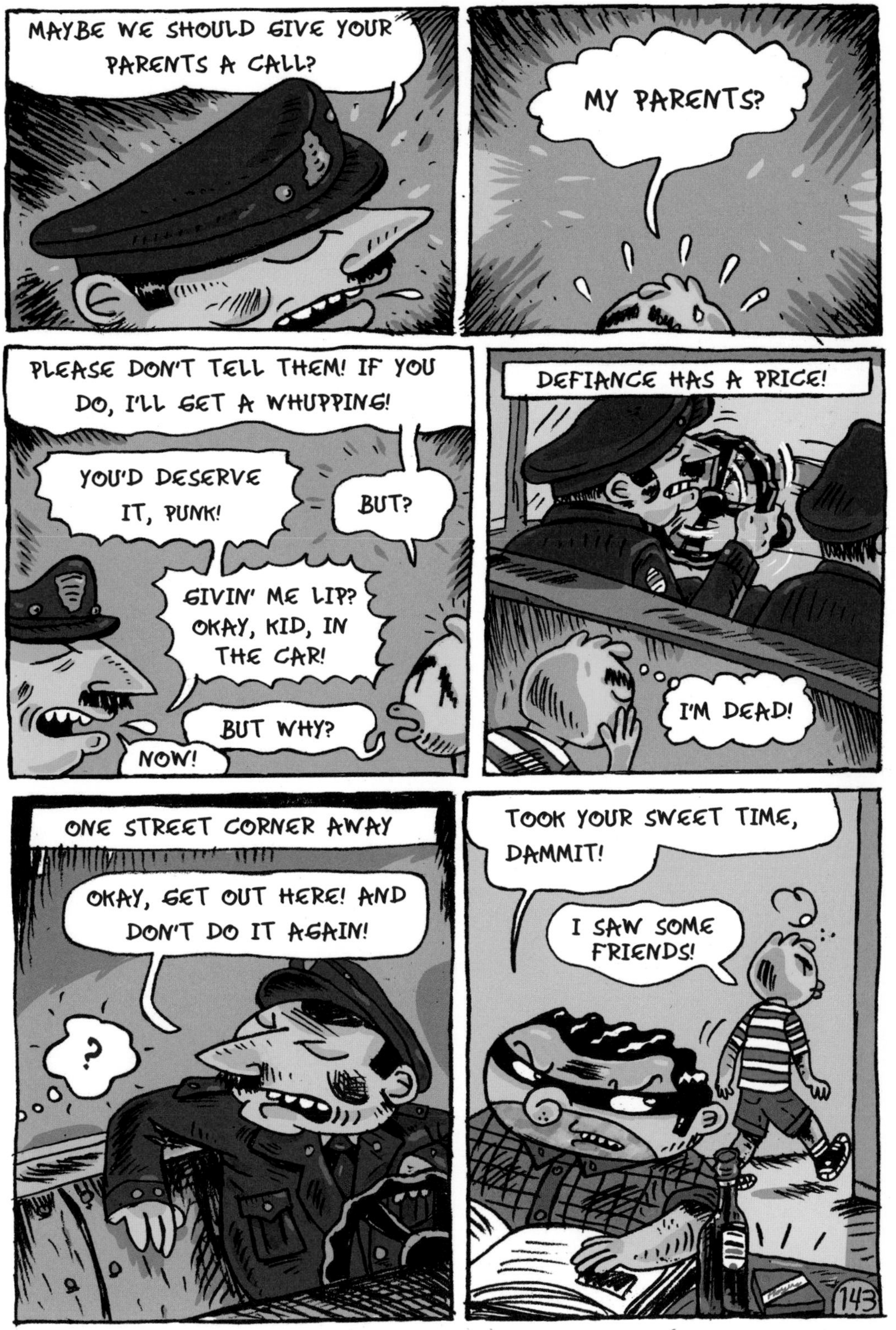
MAYBE WE SHOULD GIVE YOUR PARENTS A CALL?
MY PARENTS?
PLEASE DON'T TELL THEM! IF YOU DO, I'LL GET A WHUPPING!
YOU'D DESERVE IT, PUNK!
BUT?
GIVIN' ME LIP? OKAY, KID, IN THE CAR!
BUT WHY?
NOW!
DEFIANCE HAS A PRICE!
I'M DEAD!
ONE STREET CORNER AWAY
OKAY, GET OUT HERE! AND DON'T DO IT AGAIN!
?
TOOK YOUR SWEET TIME, DAMMIT!
I SAW SOME FRIENDS!
143

ON MR. TROUBLED'S ORDERS, CHICK-O SPENDS THE SUMMER WITH THE...

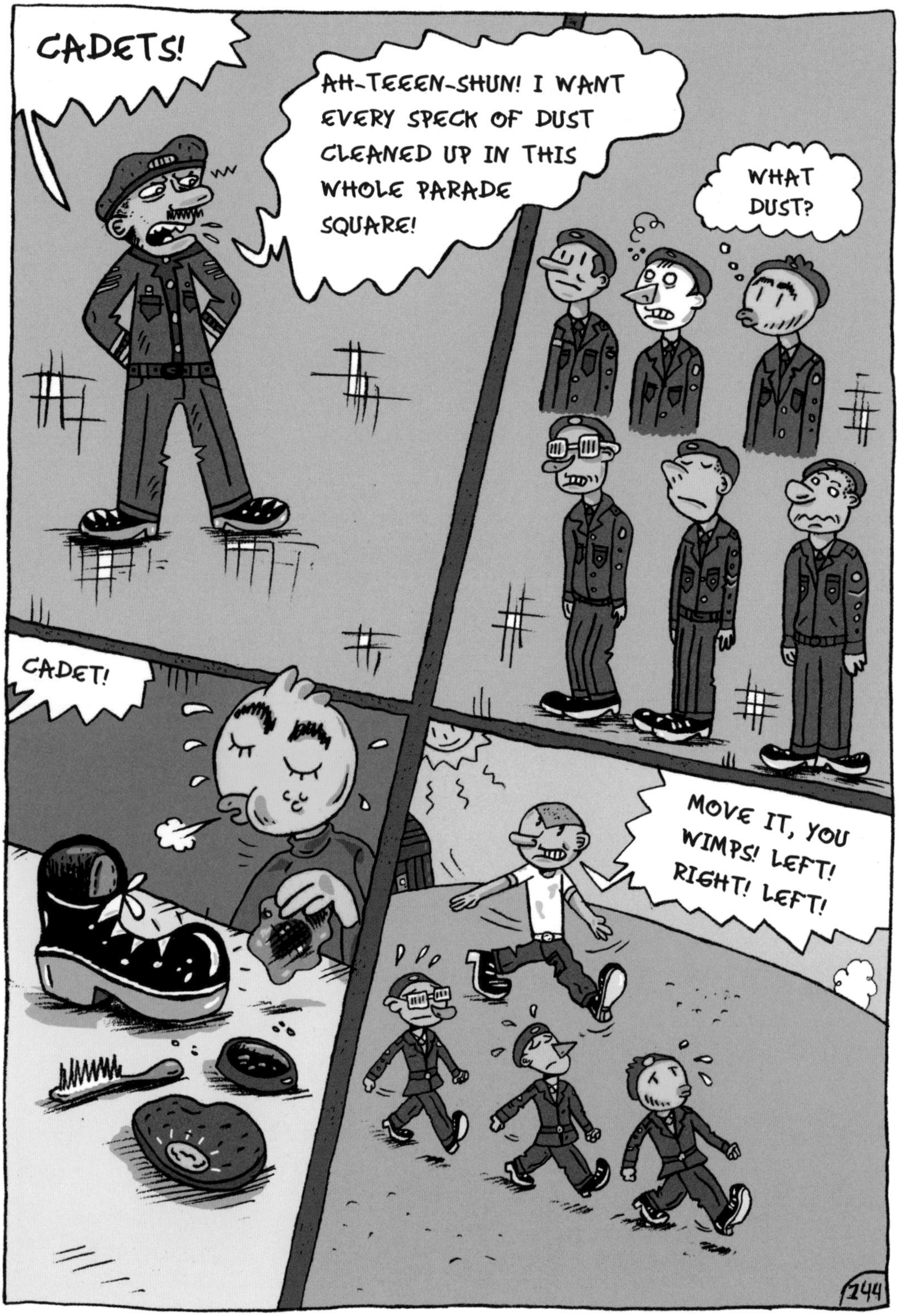
CADETS!
AH-TEEEN-SHUN! I WANT EVERY SPECK OF DUST CLEANED UP IN THIS WHOLE PARADE SQUARE!
WHAT DUST?
CADET!
MOVE IT, YOU WIMPS! LEFT! RIGHT! LEFT!
144

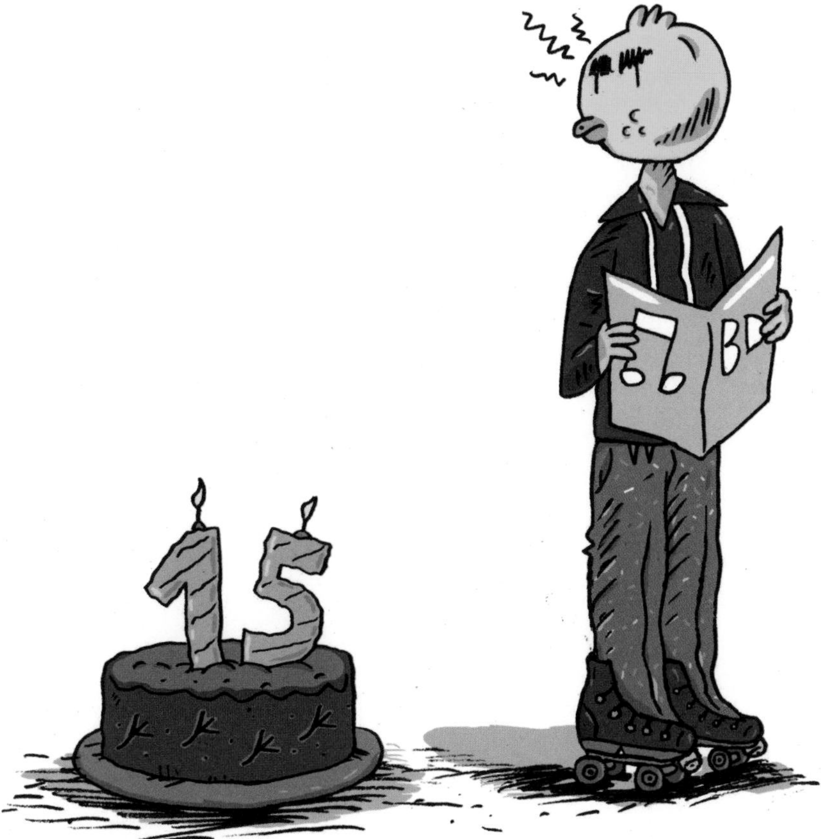
15
BD

145

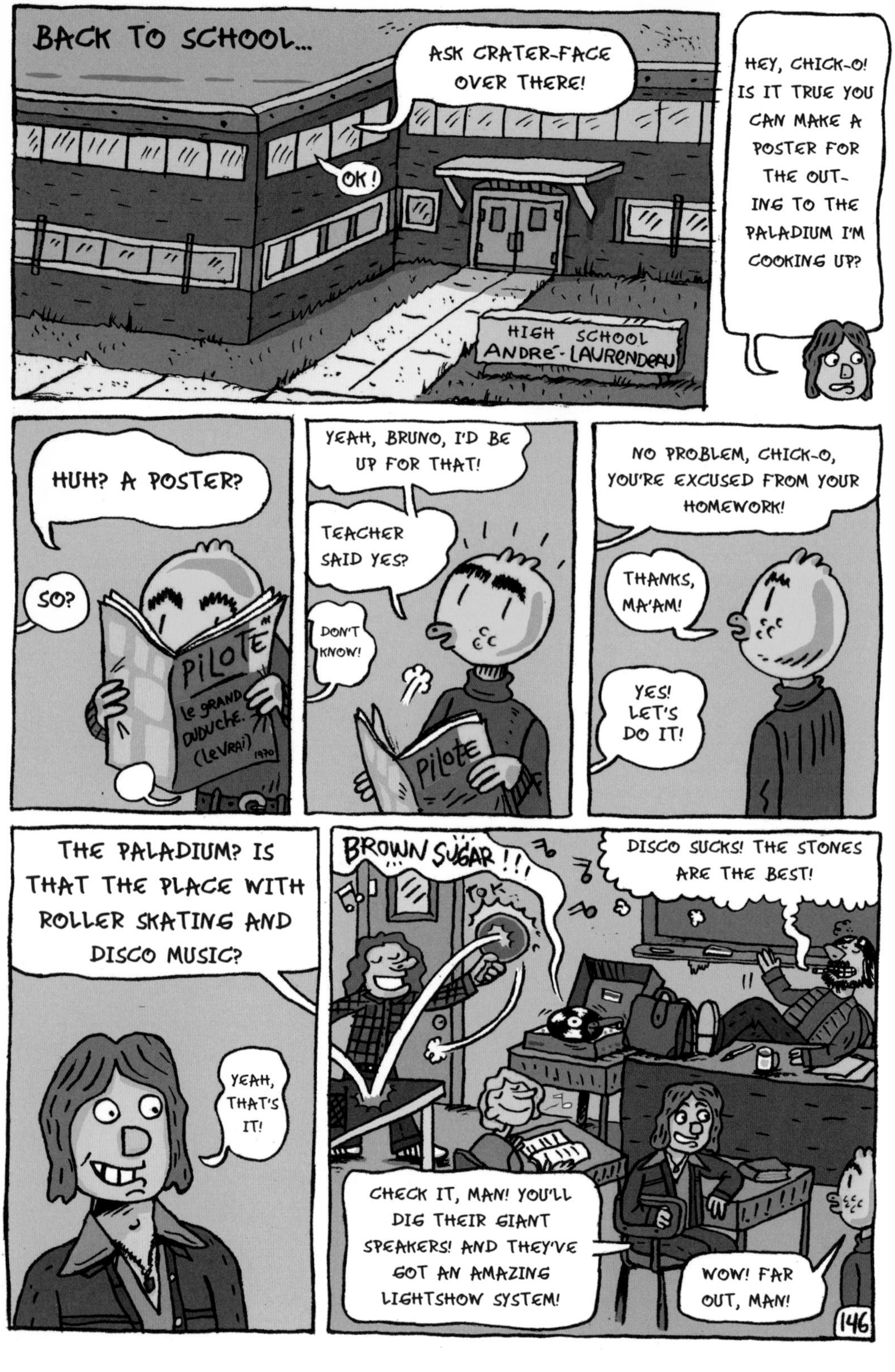
BACK TO SCHOOL...
HEY, CHICK-O! IS IT TRUE YOU CAN MAKE A POSTER FOR THE OUTING TO THE PALADIUM I'M COOKING UP?
ASK CRATER-FACE OVER THERE!
OK!
HIGH SCHOOL ANDRÉ-LAURENDEAU
HUH? A POSTER?
SO?
PILOTE
Le GRAND DUDUCHE. (Le VRAI)
1970
YEAH, BRUNO, I'D BE UP FOR THAT!
TEACHER SAID YES?
DON'T KNOW!
PILOTE
NO PROBLEM, CHICK-O, YOU'RE EXCUSED FROM YOUR HOMEWORK!
THANKS, MA'AM!
YES! LET'S DO IT!
THE PALADIUM? IS THAT THE PLACE WITH ROLLER SKATING AND DISCO MUSIC?
YEAH, THAT'S IT!
BROWN SUGAR!!!
TOK
DISCO SUCKS! THE STONES ARE THE BEST!
CHECK IT, MAN! YOU'LL DIG THEIR GIANT SPEAKERS! AND THEY'VE GOT AN AMAZING LIGHTSHOW SYSTEM!
WOW! FAR OUT, MAN!
146

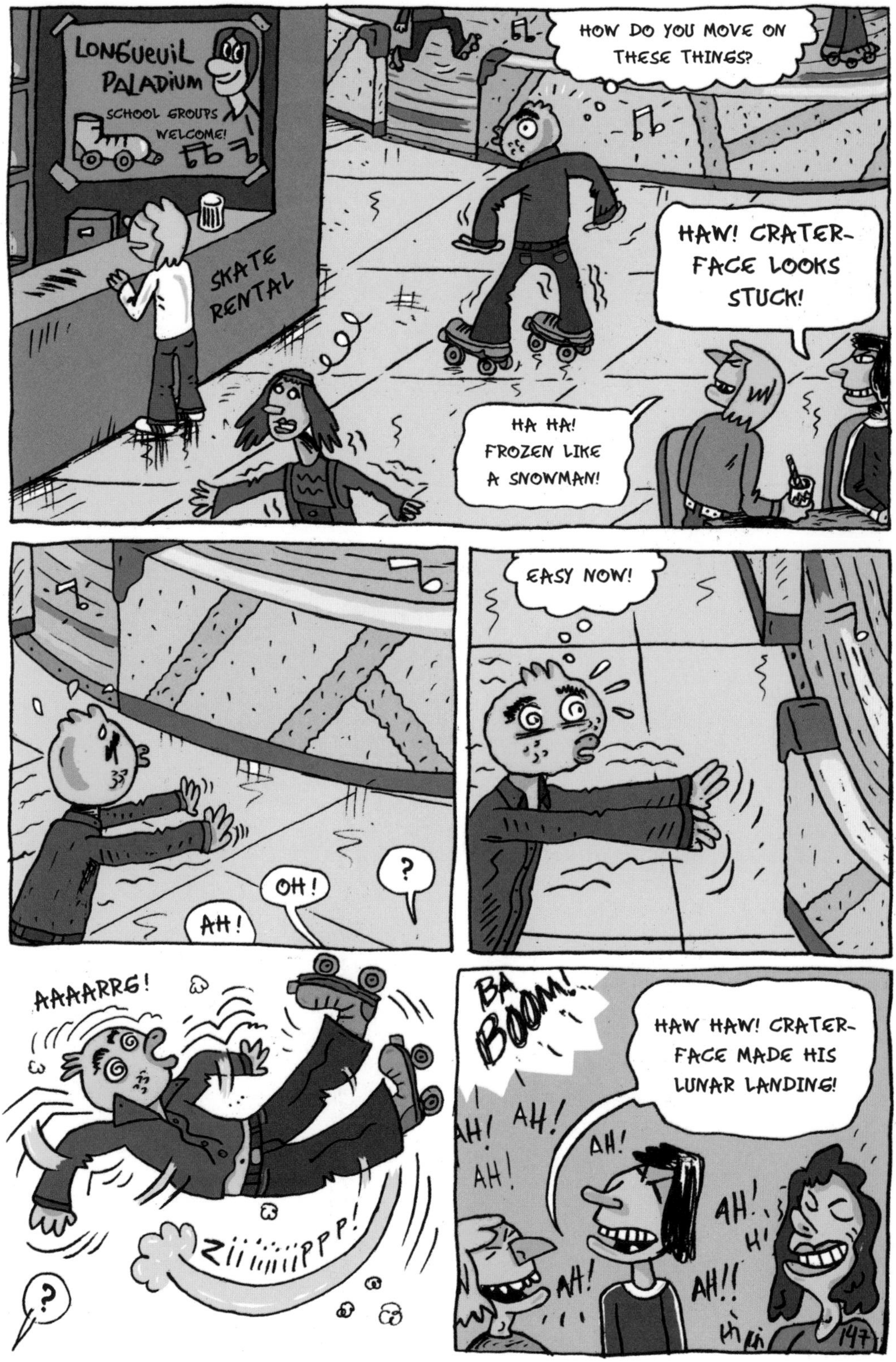
LONGUEUIL PALADIUM
SCHOOL GROUPS WELCOME!
SKATE RENTAL
HOW DO YOU MOVE ON THESE THINGS?
HAW! CRATER-FACE LOOKS STUCK!
HA HA! FROZEN LIKE A SNOWMAN!
AH!
OH!
?
EASY NOW!
AAAARRG!
ZIIIIIIIIPPP!
?
BA BOOM!
HAW HAW! CRATER-FACE MADE HIS LUNAR LANDING!
AH!
AH!
AH!
AH!
AH!
AH!
H!
AH!!
147

CHICK-O GIVES HIS FRIEND ALAIN A CALL.

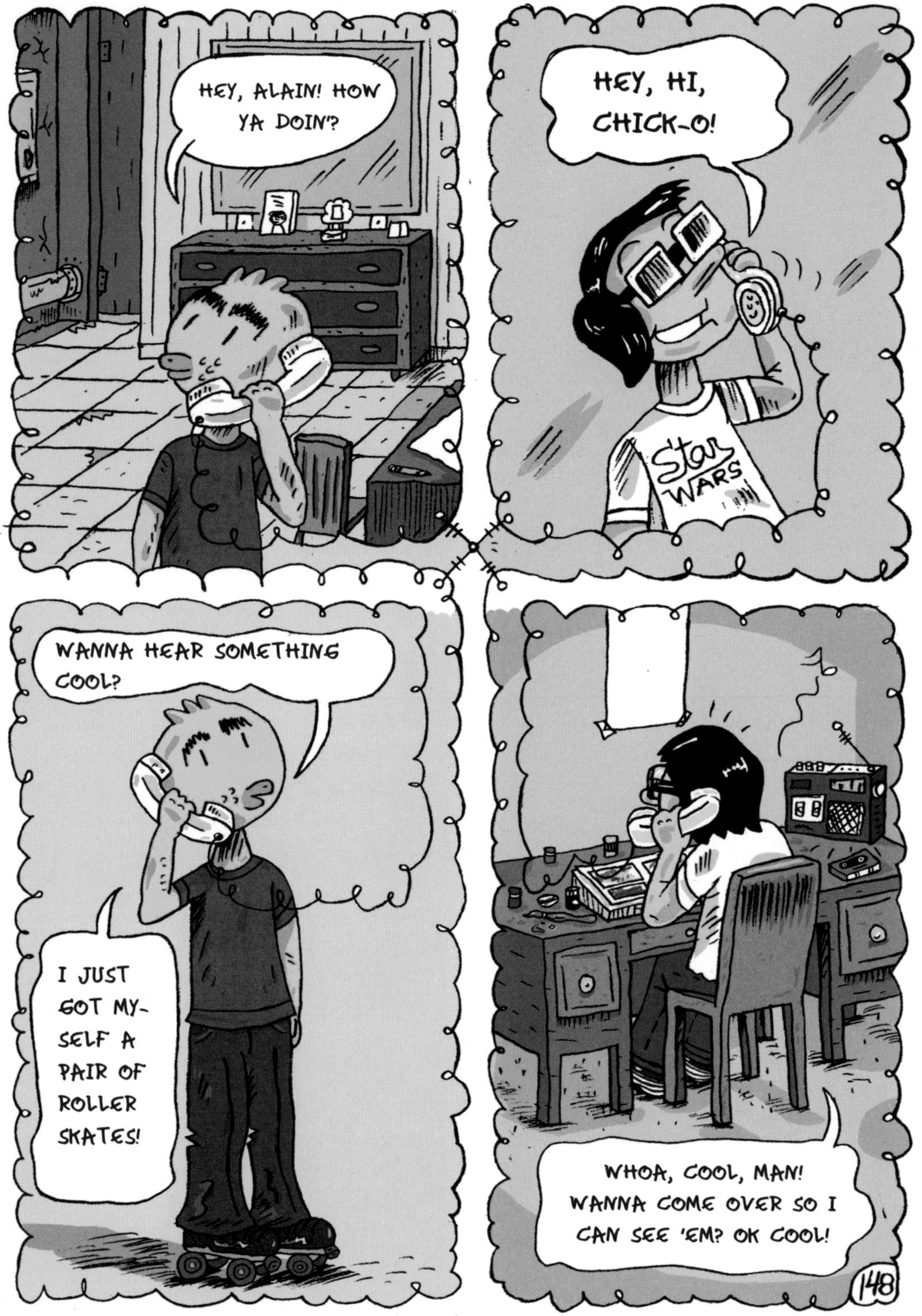
HEY, ALAIN! HOW YA DOIN'?
HEY, HI, CHICK-O!
Star WARS
WANNA HEAR SOMETHING COOL?
I JUST GOT MY-SELF A PAIR OF ROLLER SKATES!
WHOA, COOL, MAN! WANNA COME OVER SO I CAN SEE 'EM? OK COOL!
148

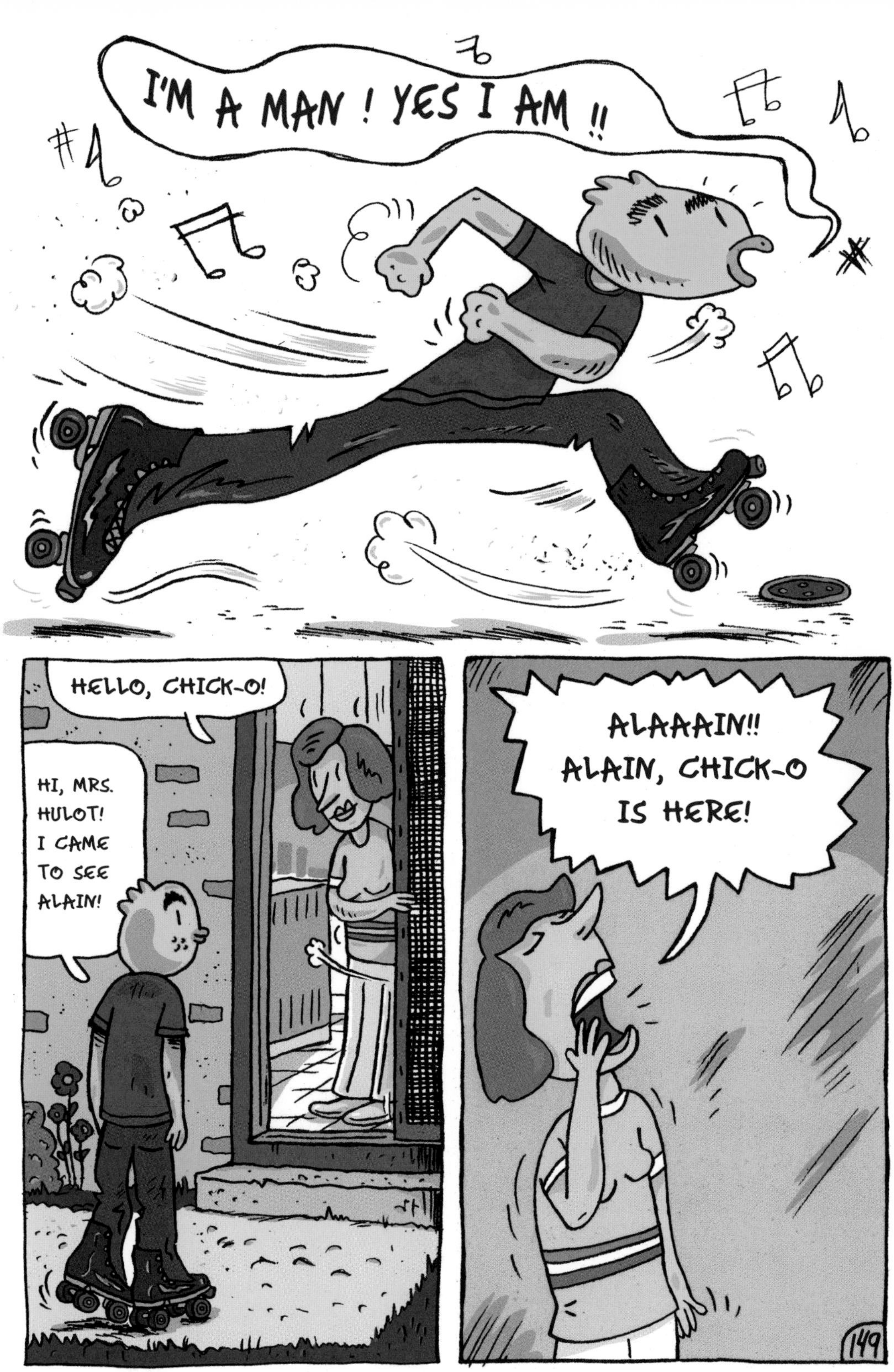

I'M A MAN ! YES I AM !!
HELLO, CHICK-O!
HI, MRS. HULOT! I CAME TO SEE ALAIN!
ALAAAIN!! ALAIN, CHICK-O IS HERE!
149

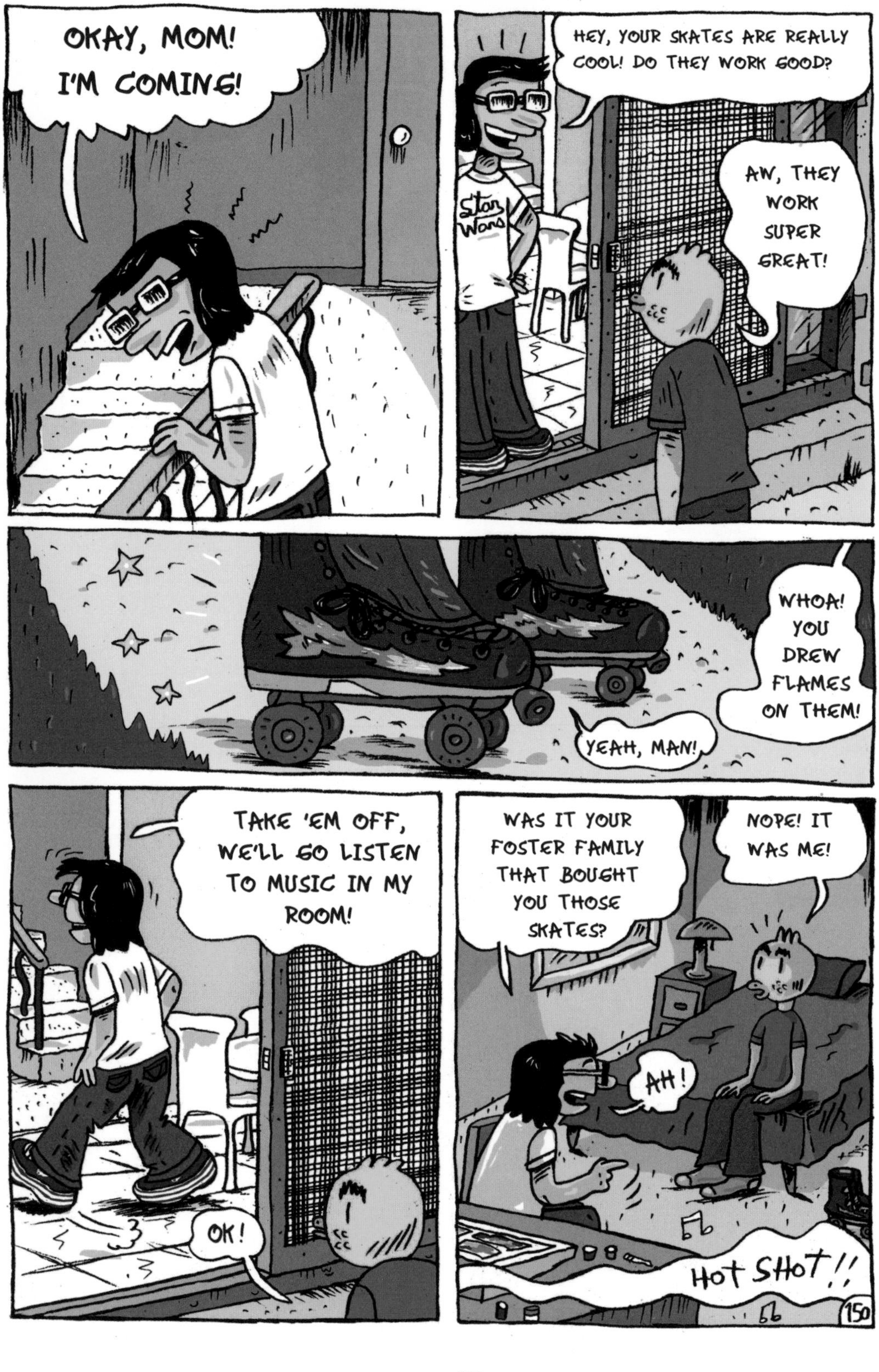
OKAY, MOM! I'M COMING!
HEY, YOUR SKATES ARE REALLY COOL! DO THEY WORK GOOD?
Star Wars
AW, THEY WORK SUPER GREAT!
WHOA! YOU DREW FLAMES ON THEM!
YEAH, MAN!
TAKE 'EM OFF, WE'LL GO LISTEN TO MUSIC IN MY ROOM!
OK!
WAS IT YOUR FOSTER FAMILY THAT BOUGHT YOU THOSE SKATES?
NOPE! IT WAS ME!
AH!
Hot SHOT!!
150

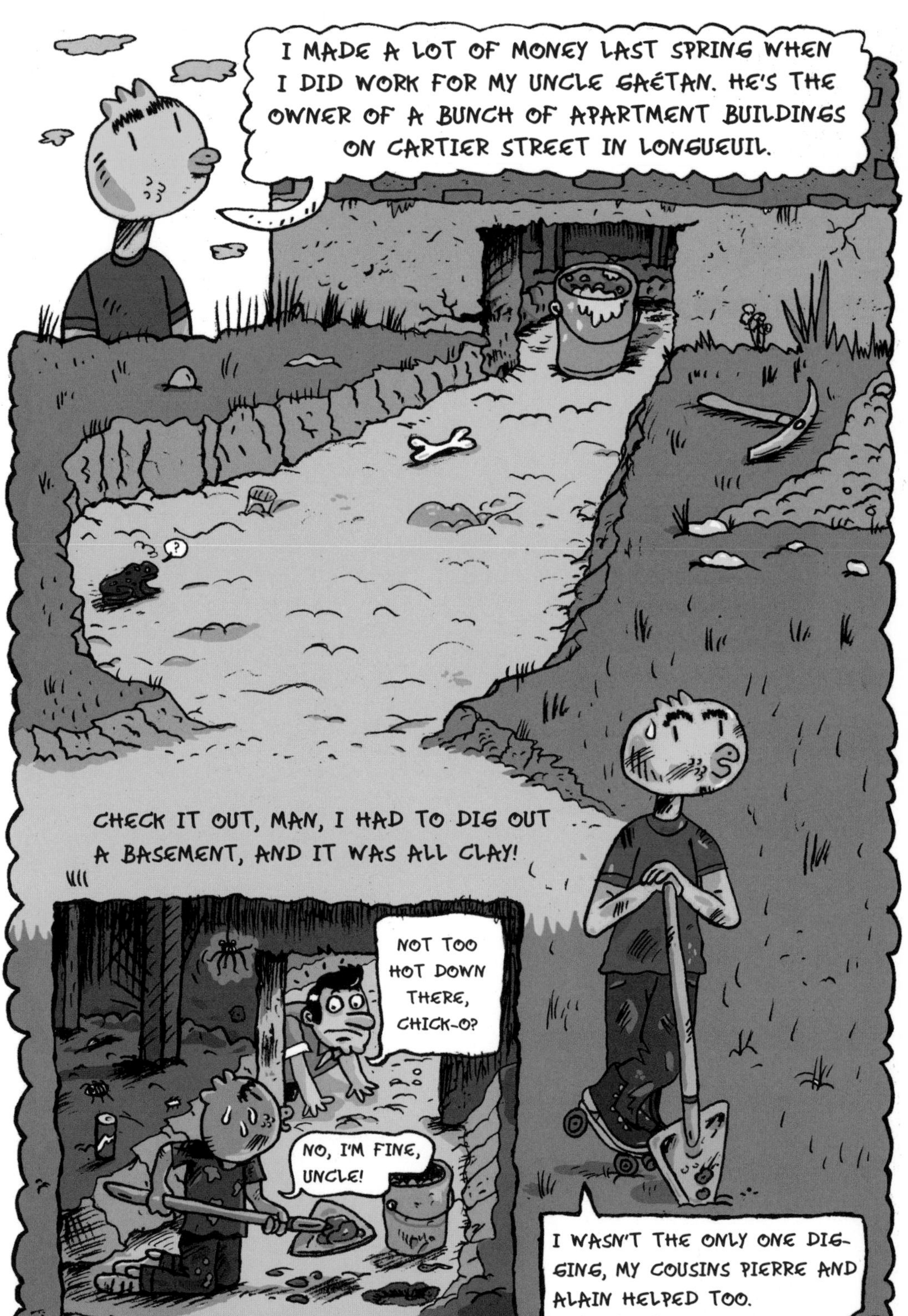

I MADE A LOT OF MONEY LAST SPRING WHEN I DID WORK FOR MY UNCLE GAÉTAN. HE'S THE OWNER OF A BUNCH OF APARTMENT BUILDINGS ON CARTIER STREET IN LONGUEUIL.
CHECK IT OUT, MAN, I HAD TO DIG OUT A BASEMENT, AND IT WAS ALL CLAY!
NOT TOO HOT DOWN THERE, CHICK-O?
NO, I'M FINE, UNCLE!
I WASN'T THE ONLY ONE DIGGING, MY COUSINS PIERRE AND ALAIN HELPED TOO.
157

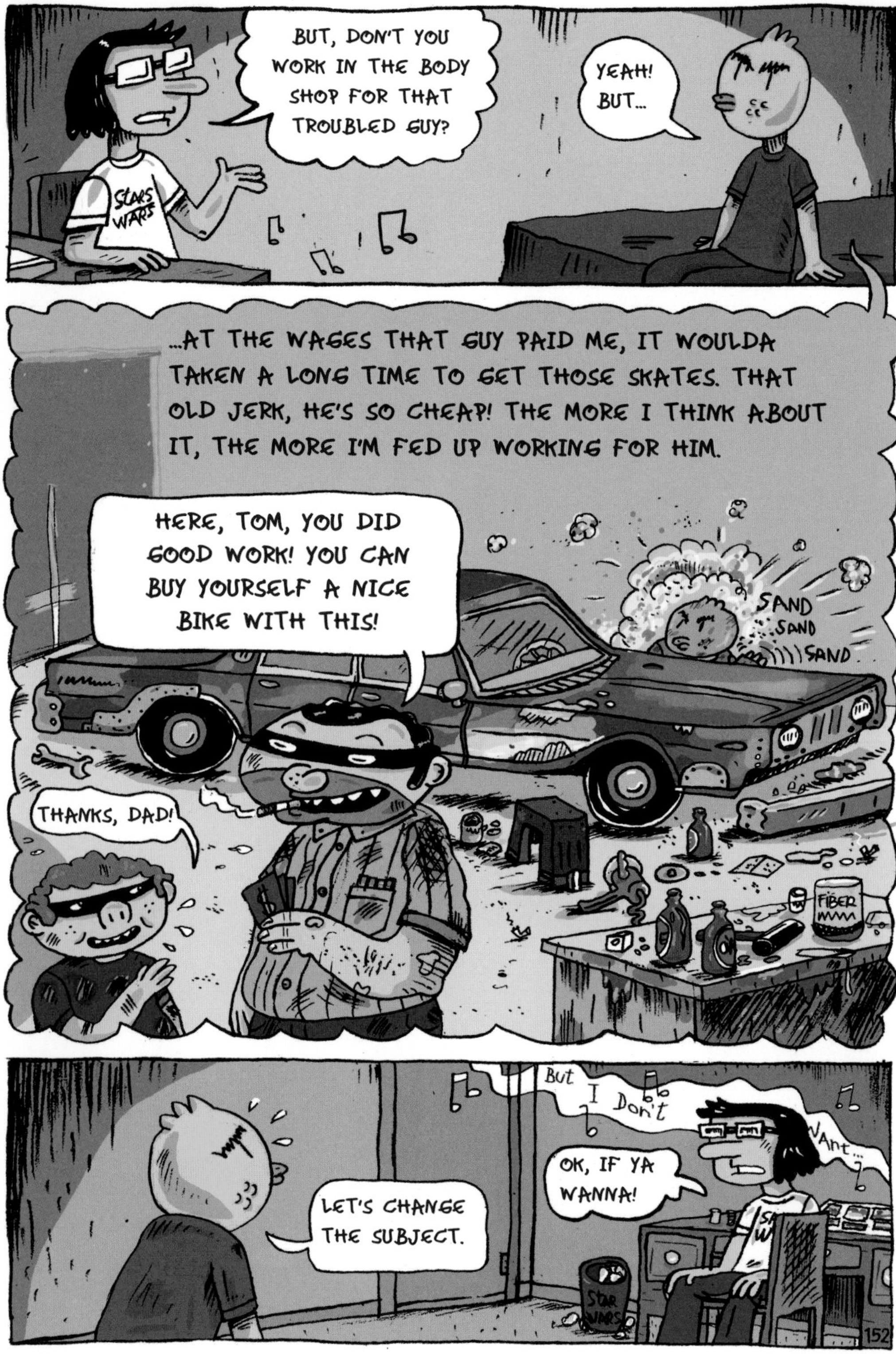
BUT, DON'T YOU WORK IN THE BODY SHOP FOR THAT TROUBLED GUY?
YEAH! BUT...
...AT THE WAGES THAT GUY PAID ME, IT WOULDA TAKEN A LONG TIME TO GET THOSE SKATES. THAT OLD JERK, HE'S SO CHEAP! THE MORE I THINK ABOUT IT, THE MORE I'M FED UP WORKING FOR HIM.
HERE, TOM, YOU DID GOOD WORK! YOU CAN BUY YOURSELF A NICE BIKE WITH THIS!
SAND SAND SAND
THANKS, DAD!
FIBER
But I Don't WAnt...
OK, IF YA WANNA!
LET'S CHANGE THE SUBJECT.
STAR WARS
152

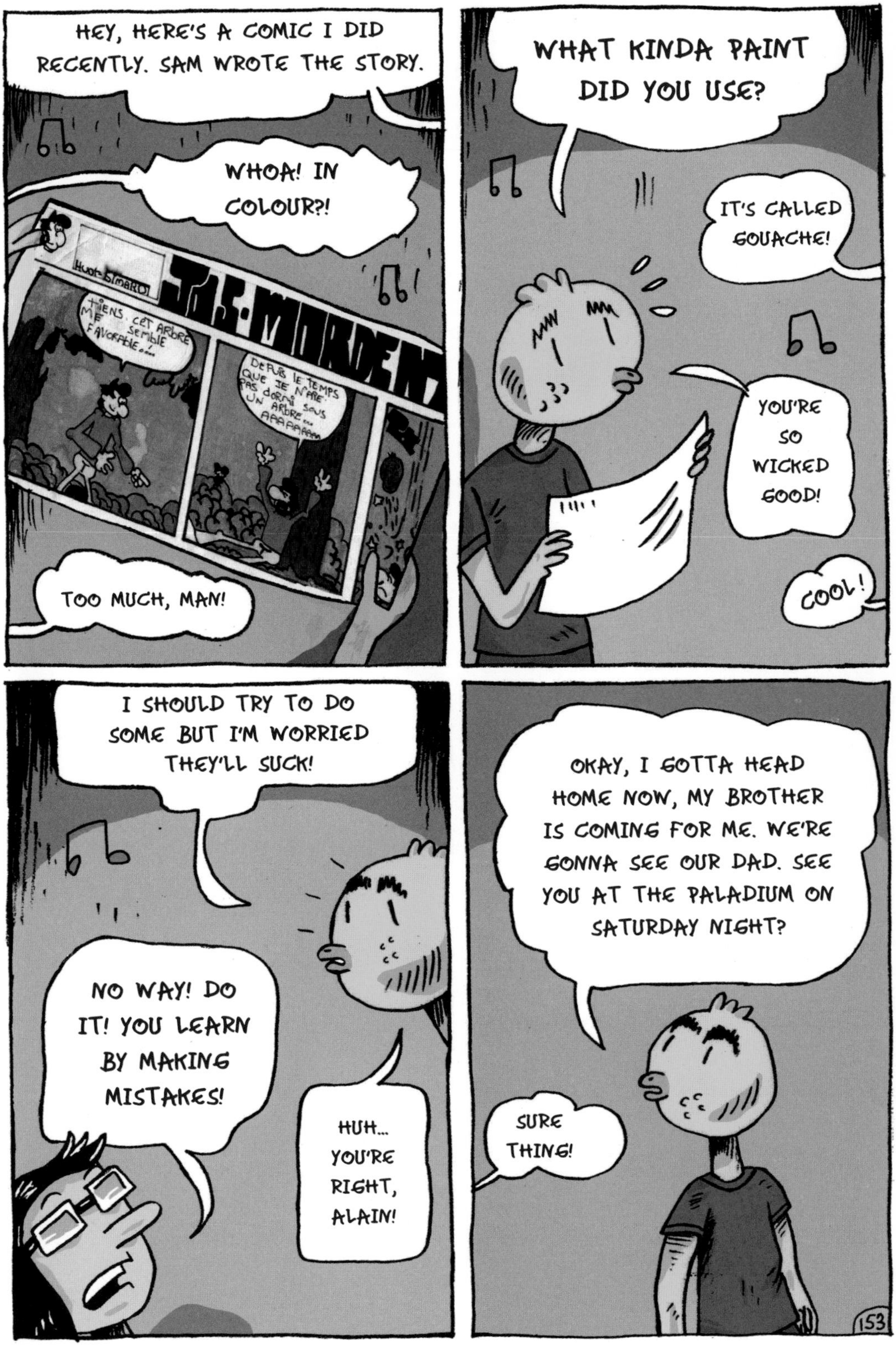
HEY, HERE'S A COMIC I DID RECENTLY. SAM WROTE THE STORY.
WHOA! IN COLOUR?!
TIENS, CET ARBRE ME SEMBLE FAVORABLE...
DEPUIS LE TEMPS QUE JE N'AIE PAS DORMI SOUS UN ARBRE... AAAAAAAA
TOO MUCH, MAN!
WHAT KINDA PAINT DID YOU USE?
IT'S CALLED GOUACHE!
YOU'RE SO WICKED GOOD!
COOL!
I SHOULD TRY TO DO SOME BUT I'M WORRIED THEY'LL SUCK!
NO WAY! DO IT! YOU LEARN BY MAKING MISTAKES!
HUH... YOU'RE RIGHT, ALAIN!
OKAY, I GOTTA HEAD HOME NOW, MY BROTHER IS COMING FOR ME. WE'RE GONNA SEE OUR DAD. SEE YOU AT THE PALADIUM ON SATURDAY NIGHT?
SURE THING!
153

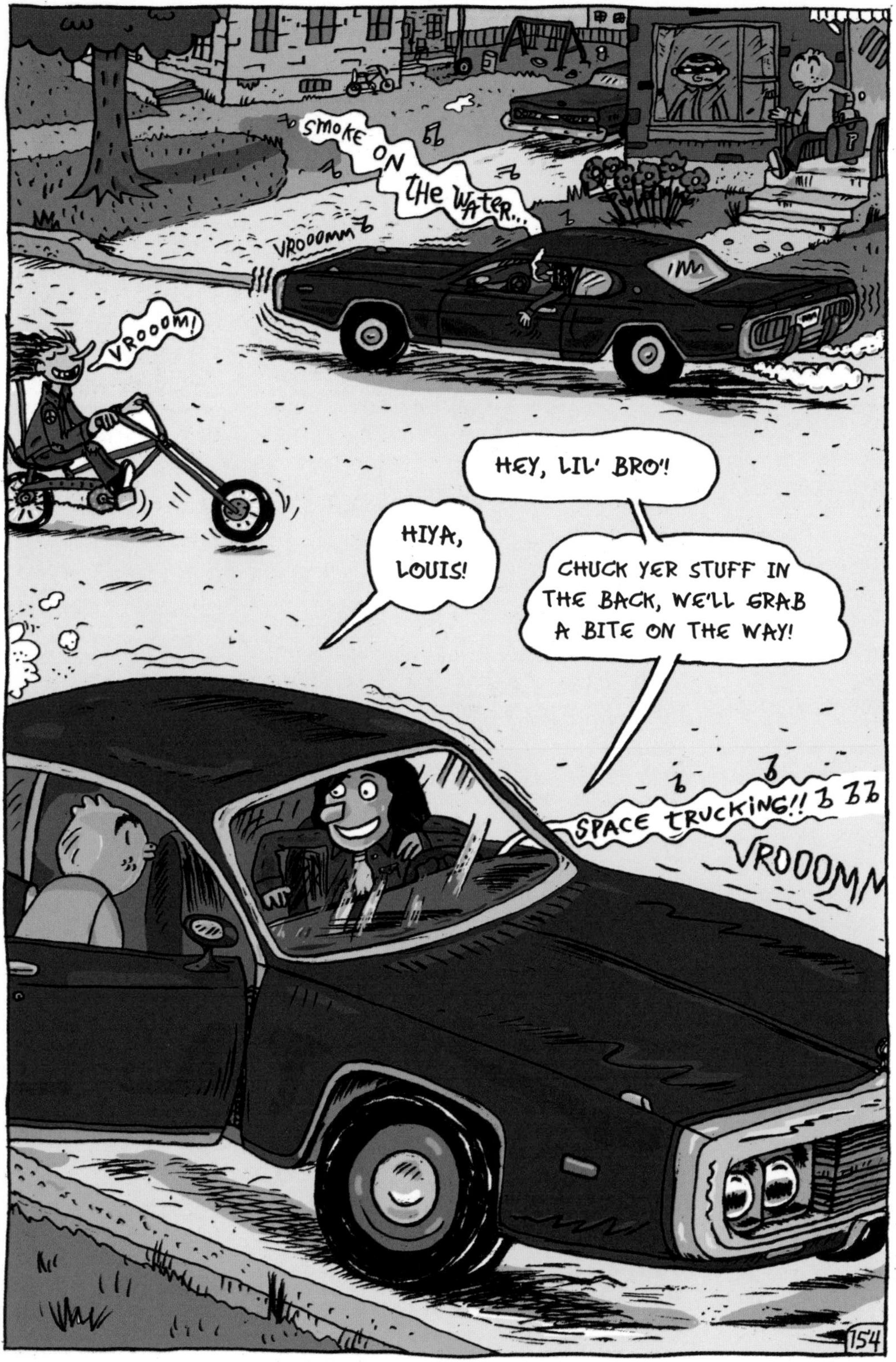
SMOKE ON THE WATER...
VROOOMM
VROOOM!
HEY, LIL' BRO'!
HIYA, LOUIS!
CHUCK YER STUFF IN THE BACK, WE'LL GRAB A BITE ON THE WAY!
SPACE TRUCKING!!
VROOOMM
154

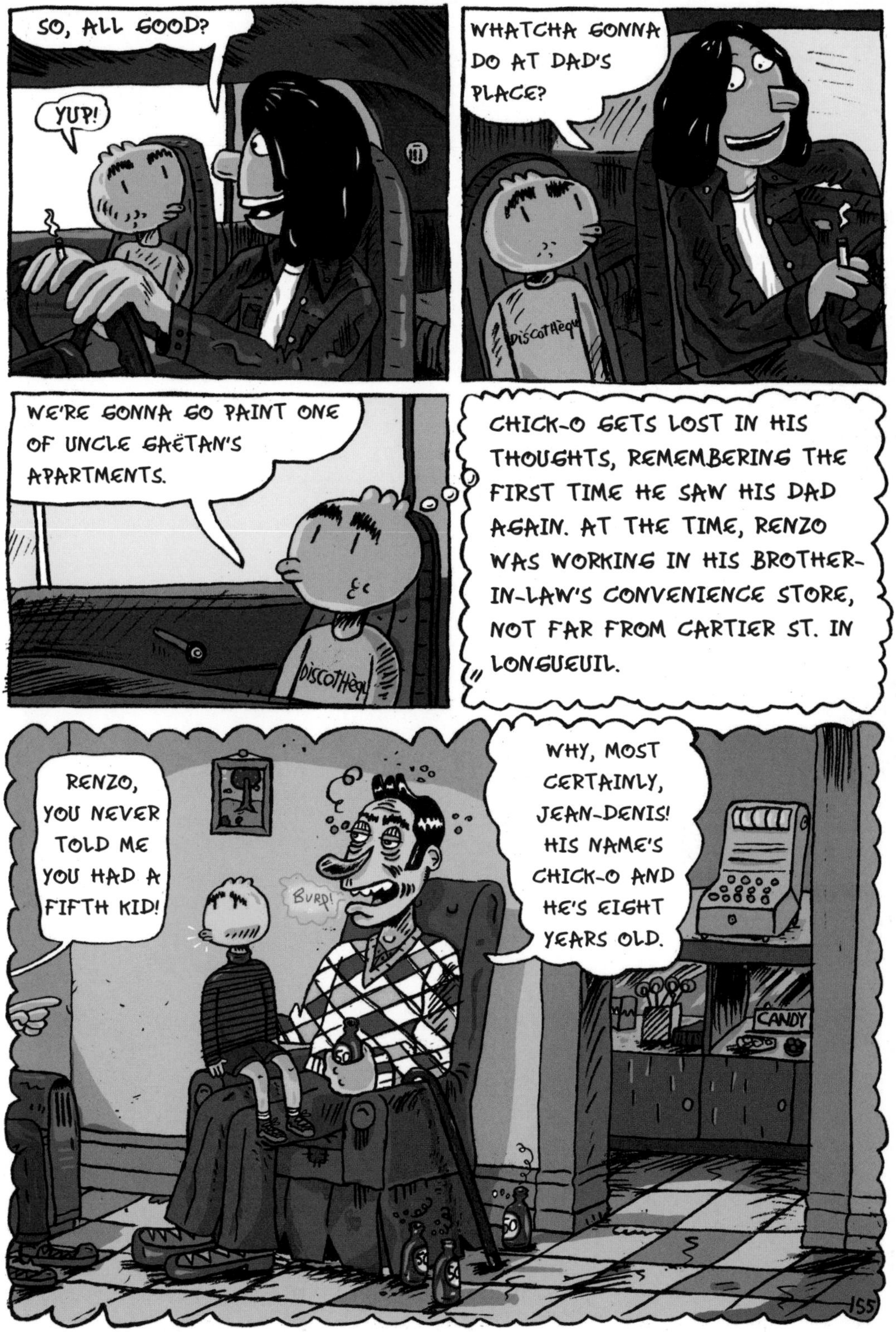
SO, ALL GOOD?
YUP!
WHATCHA GONNA DO AT DAD'S PLACE?
DISCOTHèQUE
WE'RE GONNA GO PAINT ONE OF UNCLE GAËTAN'S APARTMENTS.
CHICK-O GETS LOST IN HIS THOUGHTS, REMEMBERING THE FIRST TIME HE SAW HIS DAD AGAIN. AT THE TIME, RENZO WAS WORKING IN HIS BROTHER-IN-LAW'S CONVENIENCE STORE, NOT FAR FROM CARTIER ST. IN LONGUEUIL.
RENZO, YOU NEVER TOLD ME YOU HAD A FIFTH KID!
BURP!
WHY, MOST CERTAINLY, JEAN-DENIS! HIS NAME'S CHICK-O AND HE'S EIGHT YEARS OLD.
CANDY
155

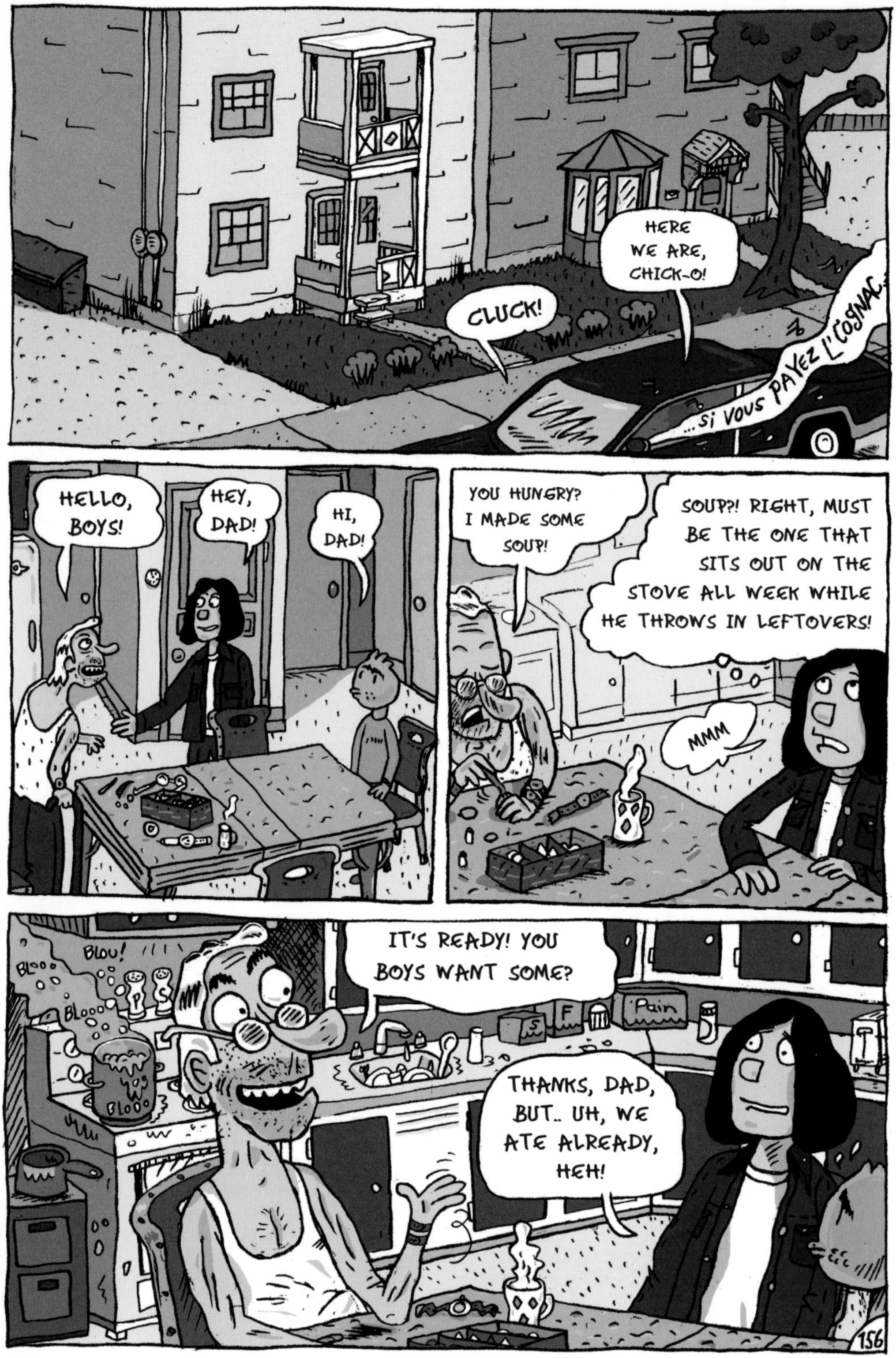
CLUCK!
HERE WE ARE, CHICK-O!
...SI VOUS PAYEZ L'COGNAC
HELLO, BOYS!
HEY, DAD!
HI, DAD!
YOU HUNGRY? I MADE SOME SOUP!
SOUP?! RIGHT, MUST BE THE ONE THAT SITS OUT ON THE STOVE ALL WEEK WHILE HE THROWS IN LEFTOVERS!
MMM
BLOU!
BLooo
BLooo
BLOoo
IT'S READY! YOU BOYS WANT SOME?
THANKS, DAD, BUT.. UH, WE ATE ALREADY, HEH!
156

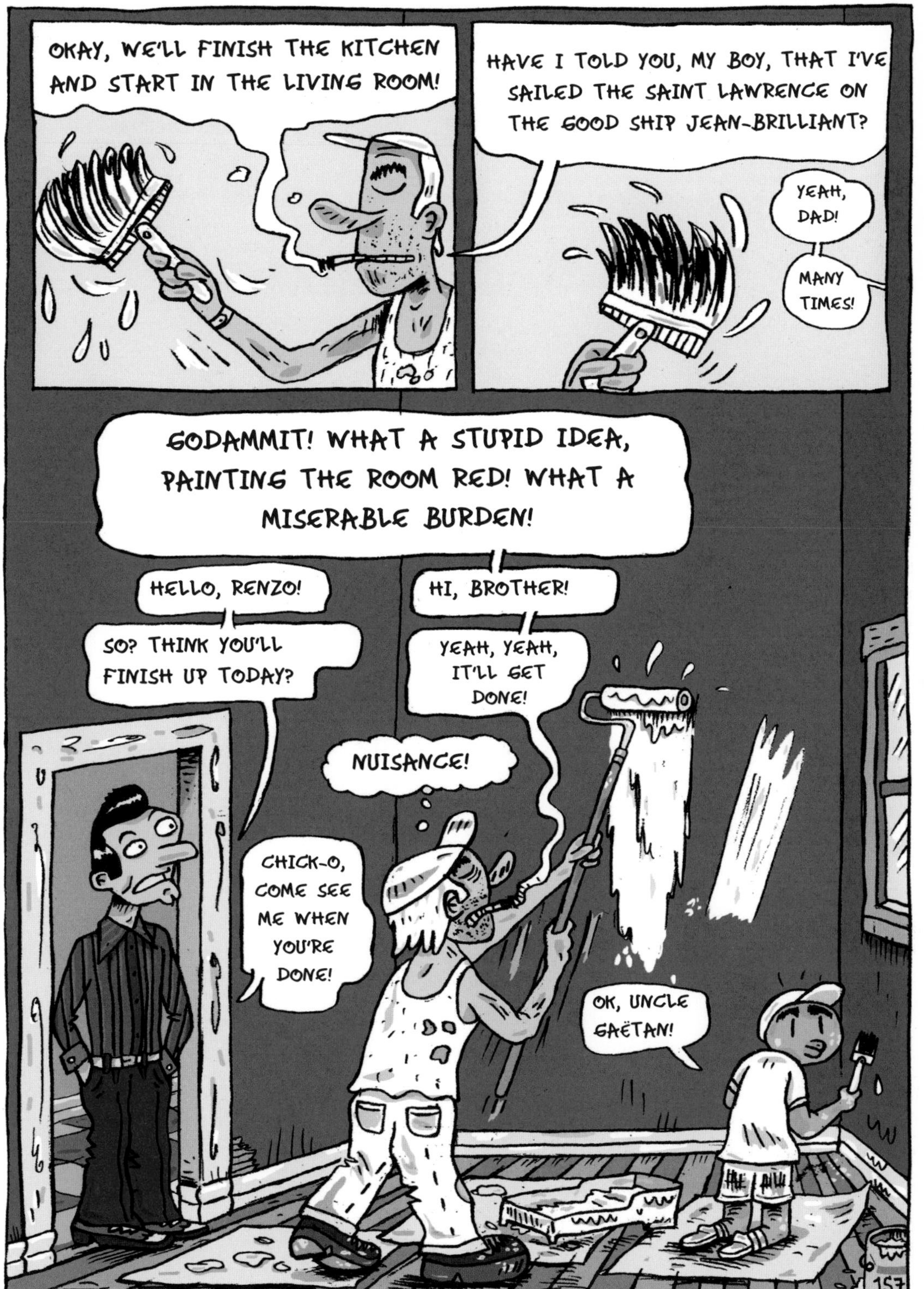
OKAY, WE'LL FINISH THE KITCHEN AND START IN THE LIVING ROOM!
HAVE I TOLD YOU, MY BOY, THAT I'VE SAILED THE SAINT LAWRENCE ON THE GOOD SHIP JEAN-BRILLIANT?
YEAH, DAD!
MANY TIMES!
GODAMMIT! WHAT A STUPID IDEA, PAINTING THE ROOM RED! WHAT A MISERABLE BURDEN!
HELLO, RENZO!
SO? THINK YOU'LL FINISH UP TODAY?
HI, BROTHER!
YEAH, YEAH, IT'LL GET DONE!
NUISANCE!
CHICK-O, COME SEE ME WHEN YOU'RE DONE!
OK, UNCLE GAËTAN!
157

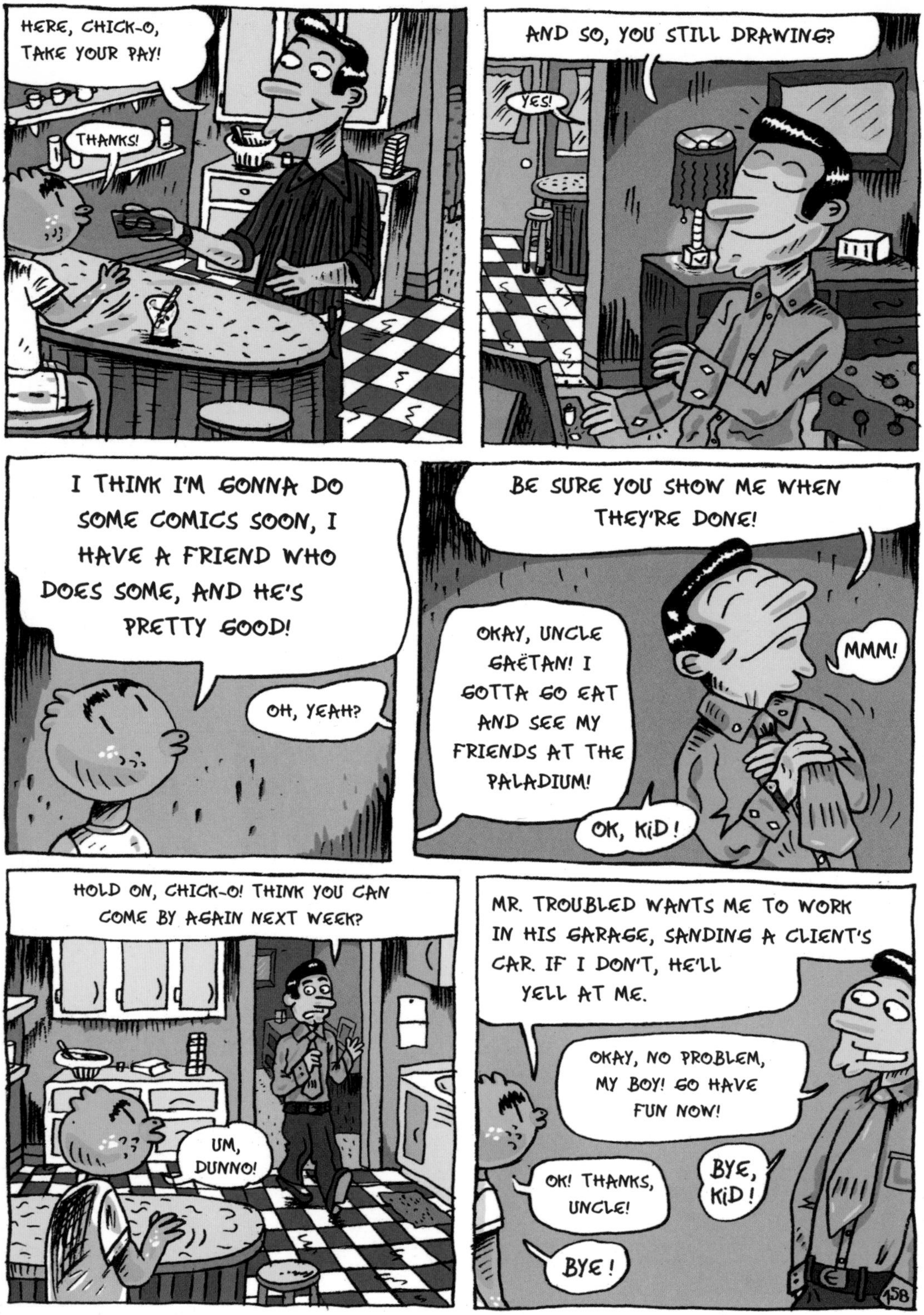

HERE, CHICK-O, TAKE YOUR PAY!
THANKS!
AND SO, YOU STILL DRAWING?
YES!
I THINK I'M GONNA DO SOME COMICS SOON, I HAVE A FRIEND WHO DOES SOME, AND HE'S PRETTY GOOD!
OH, YEAH?
BE SURE YOU SHOW ME WHEN THEY'RE DONE!
MMM!
OKAY, UNCLE GAËTAN! I GOTTA GO EAT AND SEE MY FRIENDS AT THE PALADIUM!
OK, KID!
HOLD ON, CHICK-O! THINK YOU CAN COME BY AGAIN NEXT WEEK?
UM, DUNNO!
MR. TROUBLED WANTS ME TO WORK IN HIS GARAGE, SANDING A CLIENT'S CAR. IF I DON'T, HE'LL YELL AT ME.
OKAY, NO PROBLEM, MY BOY! GO HAVE FUN NOW!
OK! THANKS, UNCLE!
BYE, KID!
BYE!
458

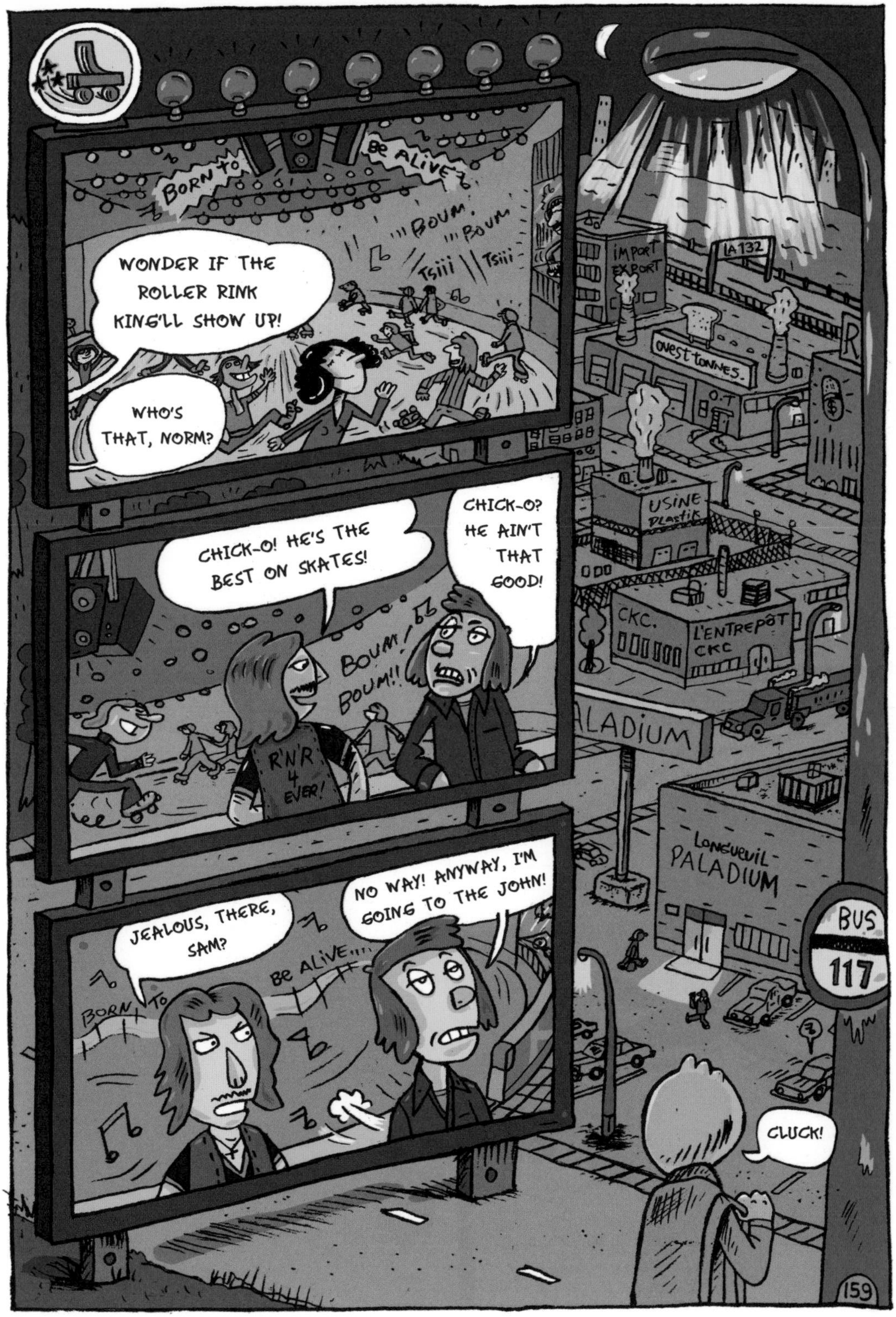

BORN TO
BE ALIVE
BOUM BOUM
TSIII TSIII
WONDER IF THE ROLLER RINK KING'LL SHOW UP!
WHO'S THAT, NORM?
CHICK-O! HE'S THE BEST ON SKATES!
CHICK-O? HE AIN'T THAT GOOD!
BOUM! BOUM!!
R'N'R 4 EVER!
JEALOUS, THERE, SAM?
NO WAY! ANYWAY, I'M GOING TO THE JOHN!
BORN TO
BE ALIVE...
IMPORT EXPORT
LA 132
OUEST TONNES
O.T.
USINE PLASTIK
CKC.
L'ENTREPÔT CKC
PALADIUM
LONGUEUIL PALADIUM
BUS 117
CLUCK!
159

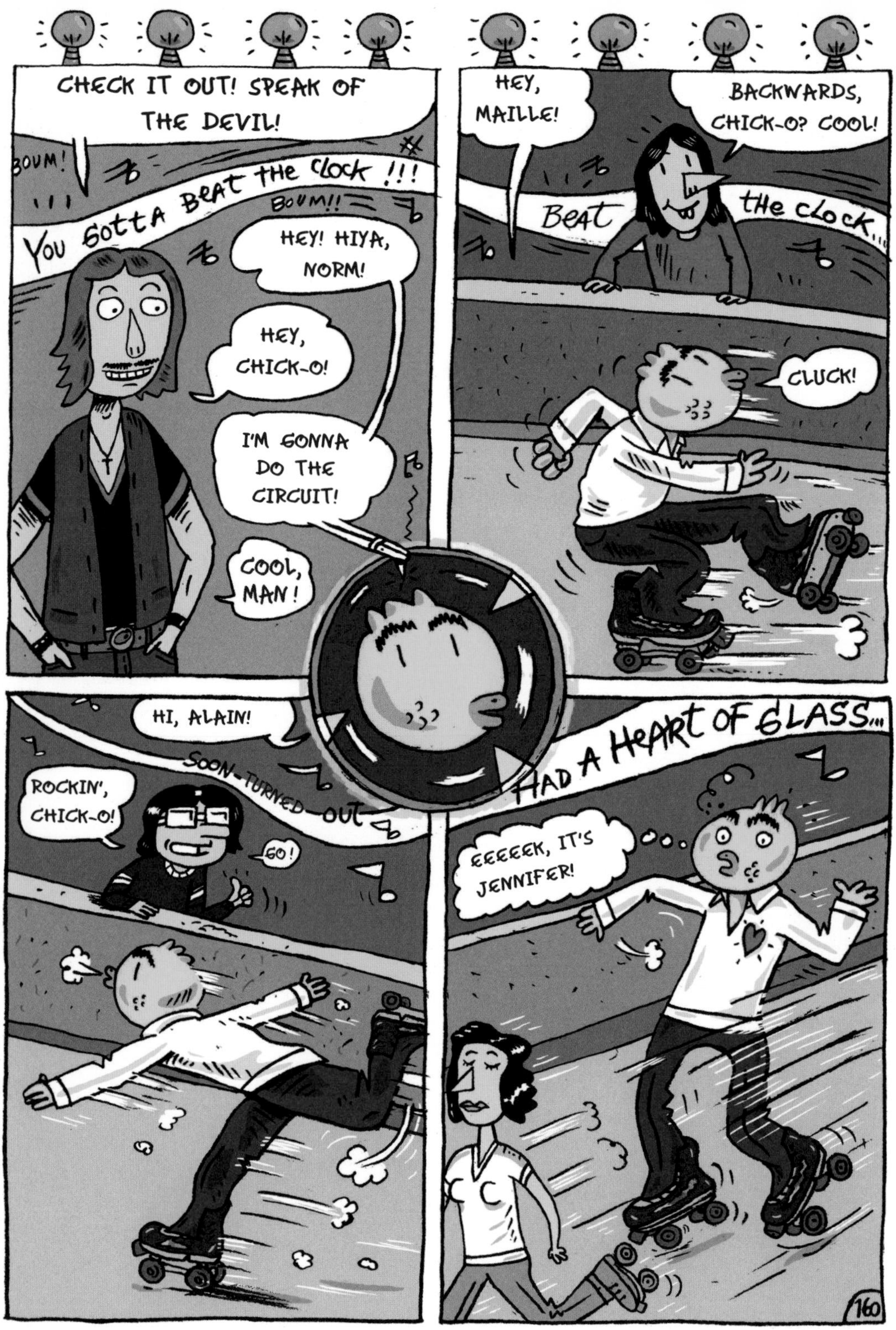
CHECK IT OUT! SPEAK OF THE DEVIL!
BOUM!
YOU GOTTA BEAT THE CLOCK!!!
BOUM!!
HEY! HIYA, NORM!
HEY, CHICK-O!
I'M GONNA DO THE CIRCUIT!
COOL, MAN!
HEY, MAILLE!
BACKWARDS, CHICK-O? COOL!
BEAT THE CLOCK...
CLUCK!
HI, ALAIN!
SOON-TURNED OUT
ROCKIN', CHICK-O!
GO!
HAD A HEART OF GLASS...
EEEEEK, IT'S JENNIFER!
160

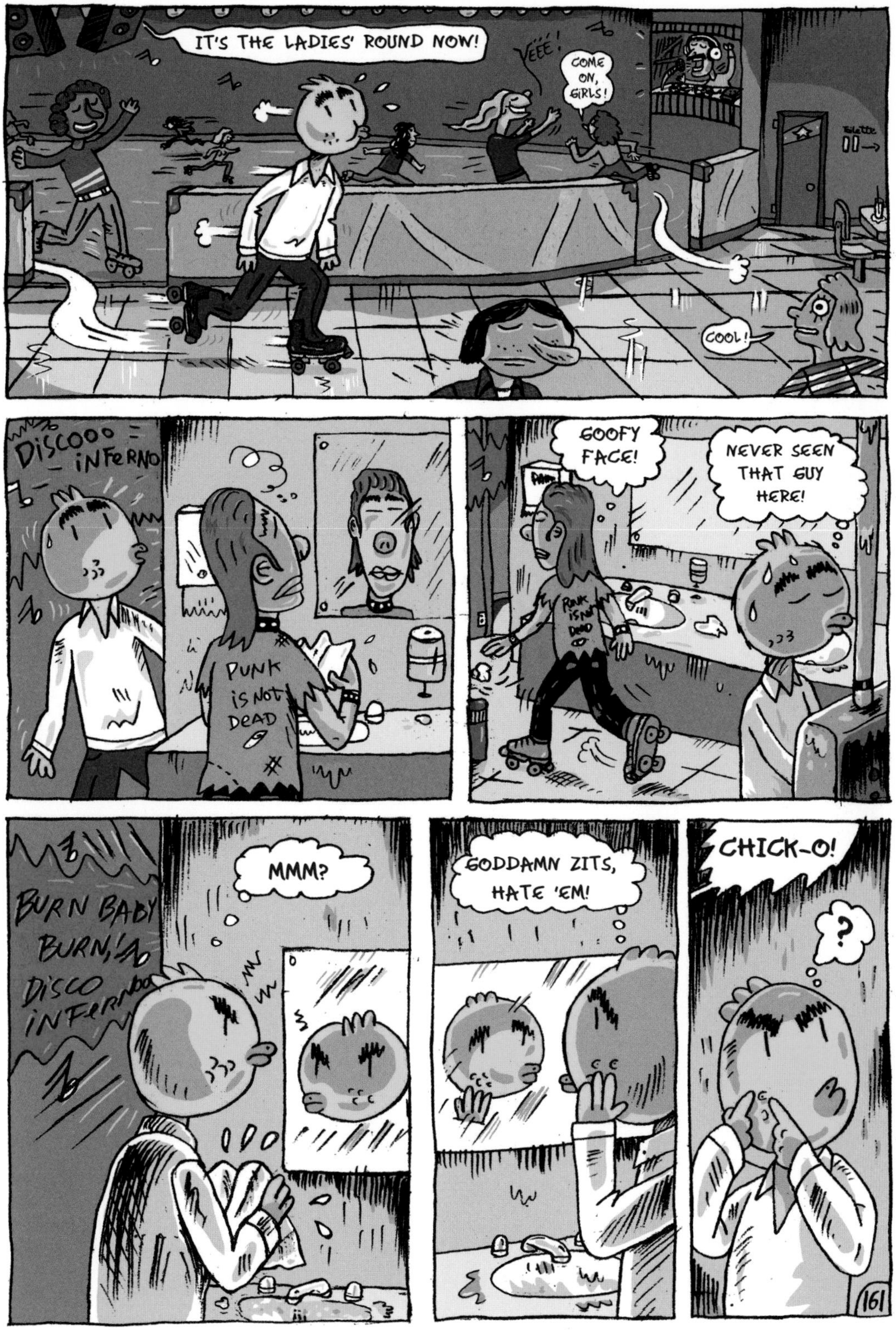
IT'S THE LADIES' ROUND NOW!
YEEE!
COME ON, GIRLS!
COOL!
DISCOOO INFERNO
PUNK IS NOT DEAD
GOOFY FACE!
NEVER SEEN THAT GUY HERE!
BURN BABY BURN, DISCO INFERNO
MMM?
GODDAMN ZITS, HATE 'EM!
CHICK-O!
?
161

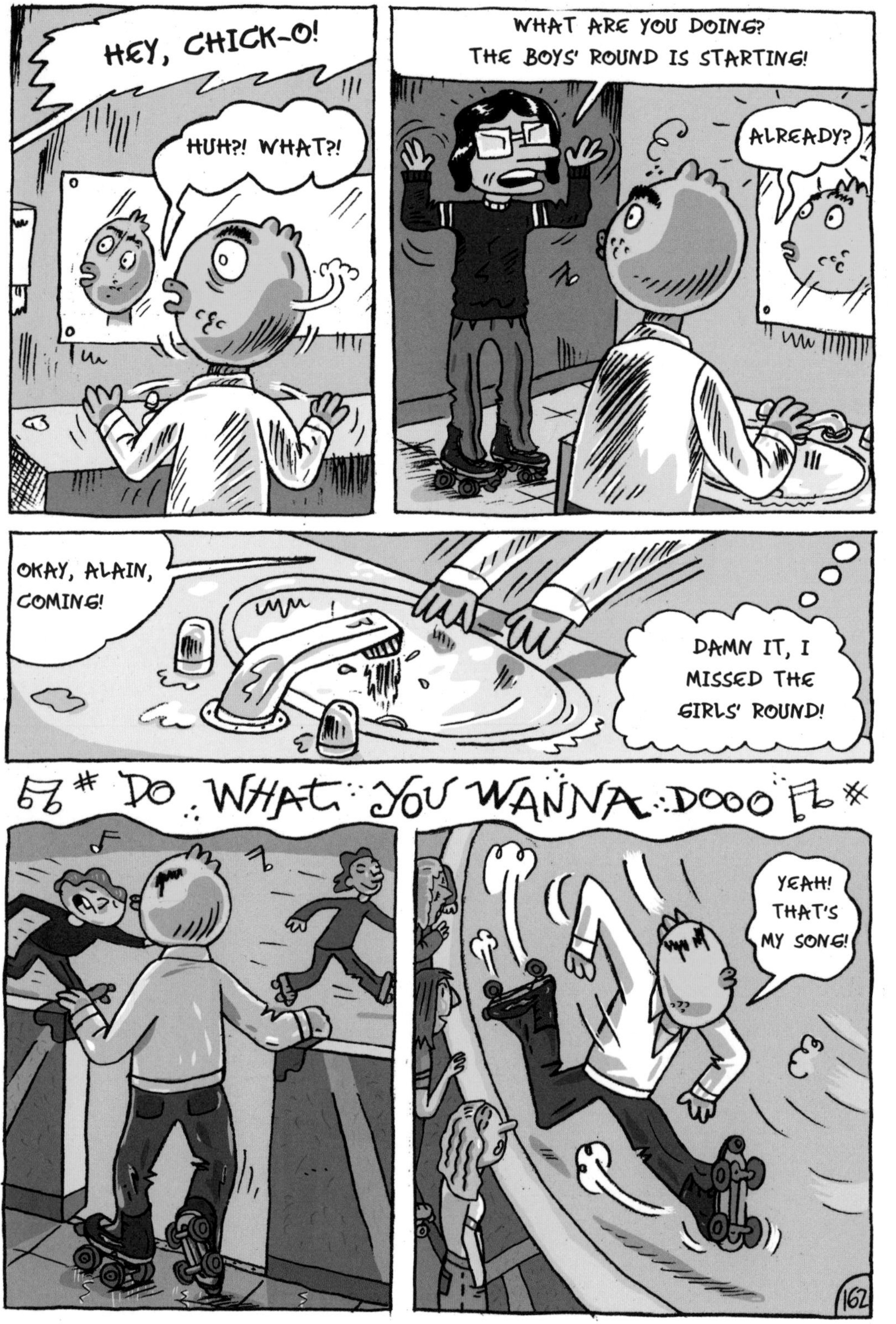
HEY, CHICK-O!
HUH?! WHAT?!
WHAT ARE YOU DOING? THE BOYS' ROUND IS STARTING!
ALREADY?
OKAY, ALAIN, COMING!
DAMN IT, I MISSED THE GIRLS' ROUND!
DO WHAT YOU WANNA DOOO
YEAH! THAT'S MY SONG!
162

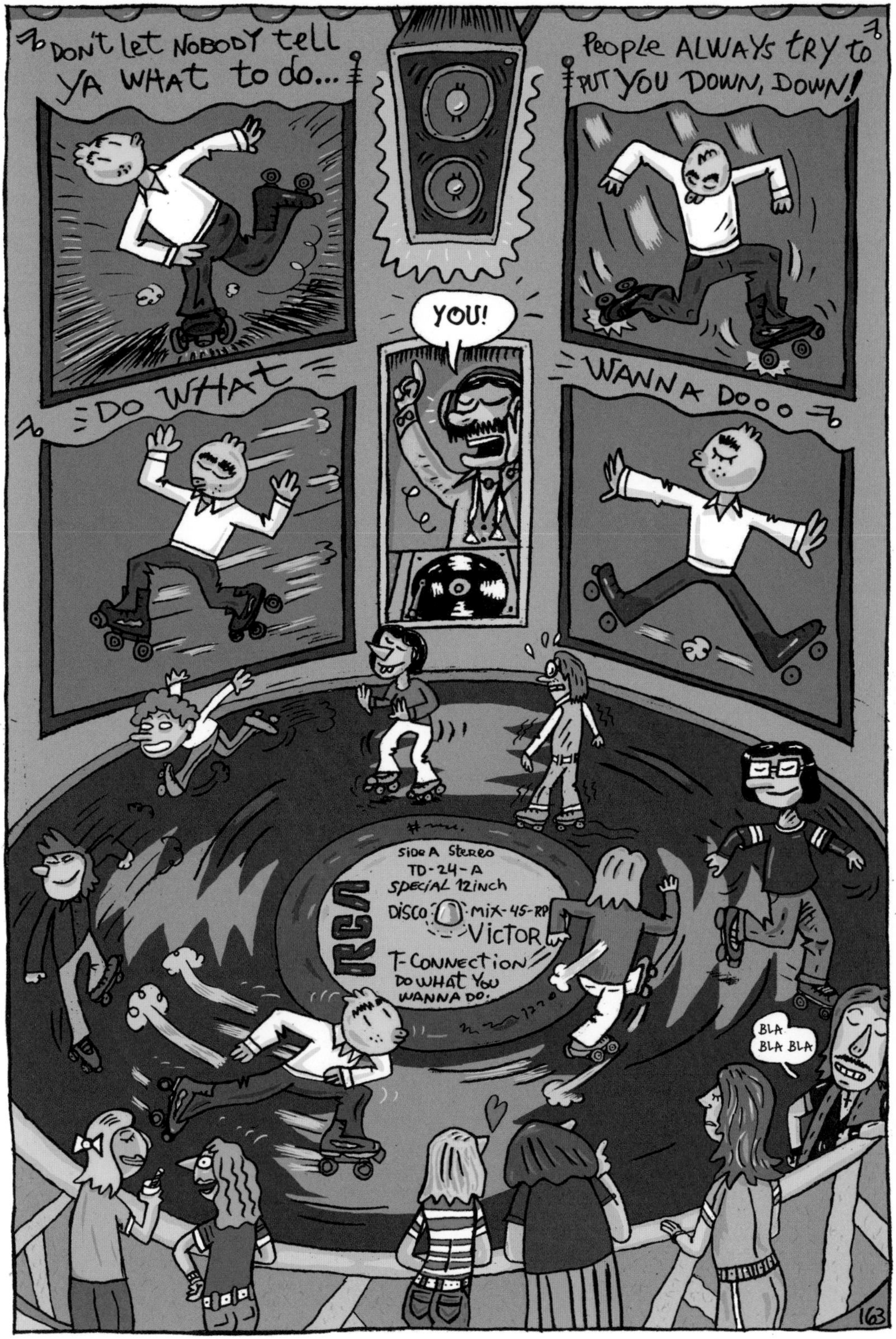
DON'T LET NOBODY TELL YA WHAT TO DO...
PEOPLE ALWAYS TRY TO PUT YOU DOWN, DOWN!
YOU!
DO WHAT
WANNA DOOO
SIDE A STEREO
TD-24-A
SPECIAL 12INCH
DISCO MIX-45-RP
RCA VICTOR
T-CONNECTION
DO WHAT YOU WANNA DO.
BLA BLA BLA
163

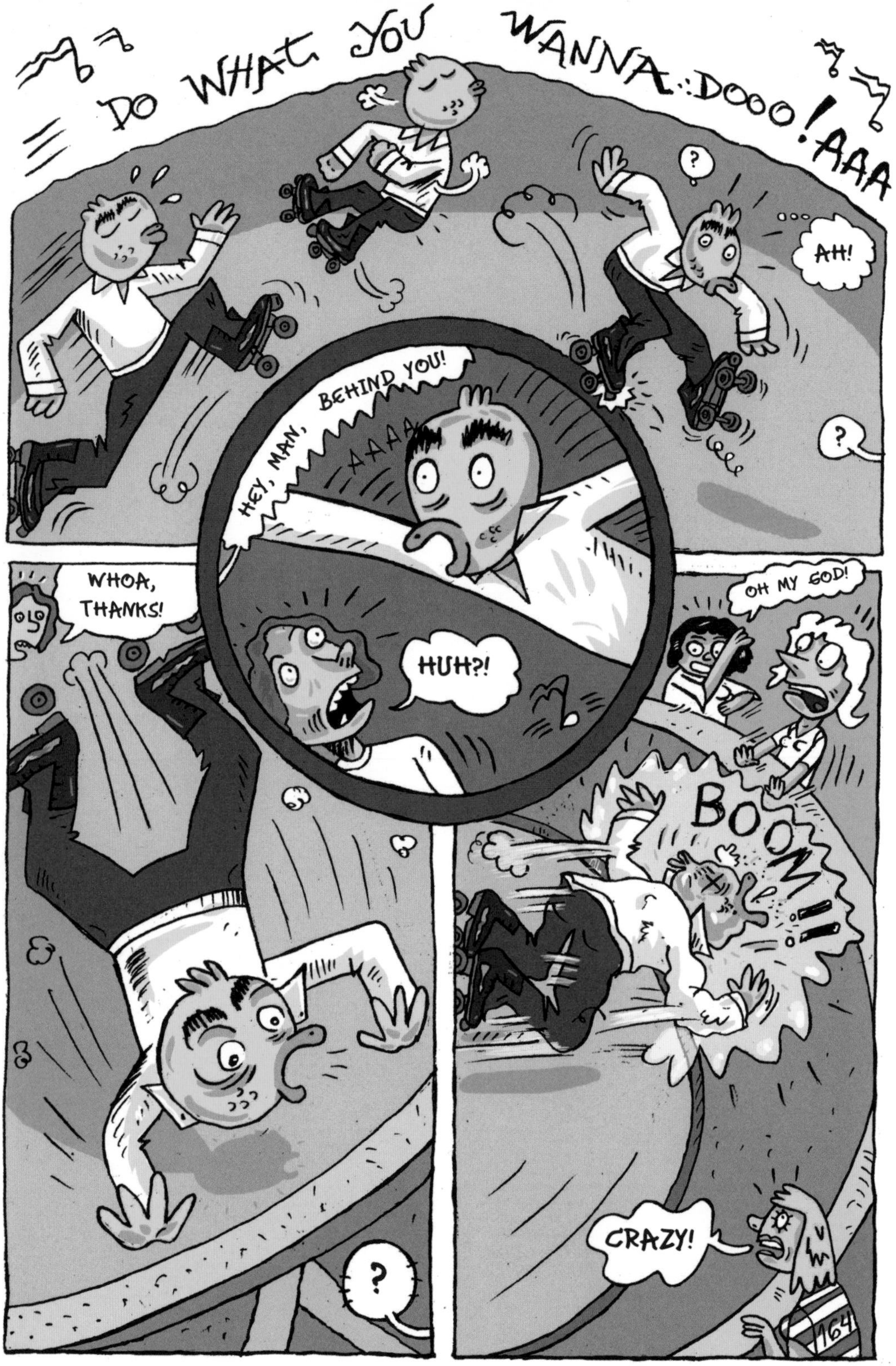
DO WHAT YOU WANNA DOOO!
AAA
AH!
?
HEY, MAN, BEHIND YOU!
AAAA
HUH?!
WHOA, THANKS!
OH MY GOD!
BOOM!!!
?
CRAZY!
164

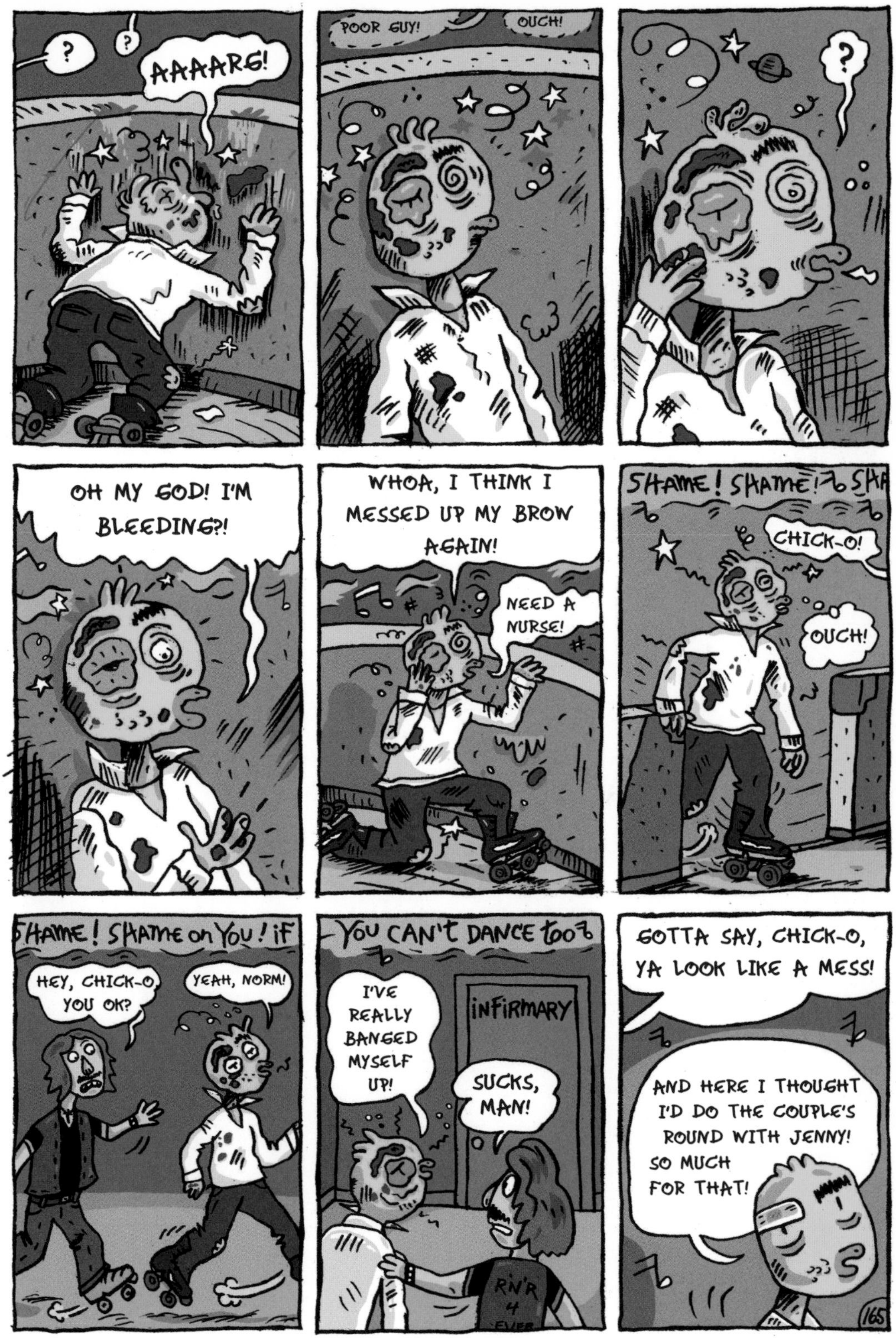
?
?
AAAARG!
POOR GUY!
OUCH!
?
OH MY GOD! I'M BLEEDING?!
WHOA, I THINK I MESSED UP MY BROW AGAIN!
NEED A NURSE!
SHAME! SHAME!
CHICK-O!
OUCH!
SHAME! SHAME ON YOU! IF
HEY, CHICK-O, YOU OK?
YEAH, NORM!
YOU CAN'T DANCE TOO
INFIRMARY
I'VE REALLY BANGED MYSELF UP!
SUCKS, MAN!
RN'R 4 EVER
GOTTA SAY, CHICK-O, YA LOOK LIKE A MESS!
AND HERE I THOUGHT I'D DO THE COUPLE'S ROUND WITH JENNY! SO MUCH FOR THAT!
165

THE EVENING ENDS AT ALAIN'S, WITH PEANUT BUTTER ON TOAST, HOT COFFEE AND FREE-FLOWING CONVERSATION.

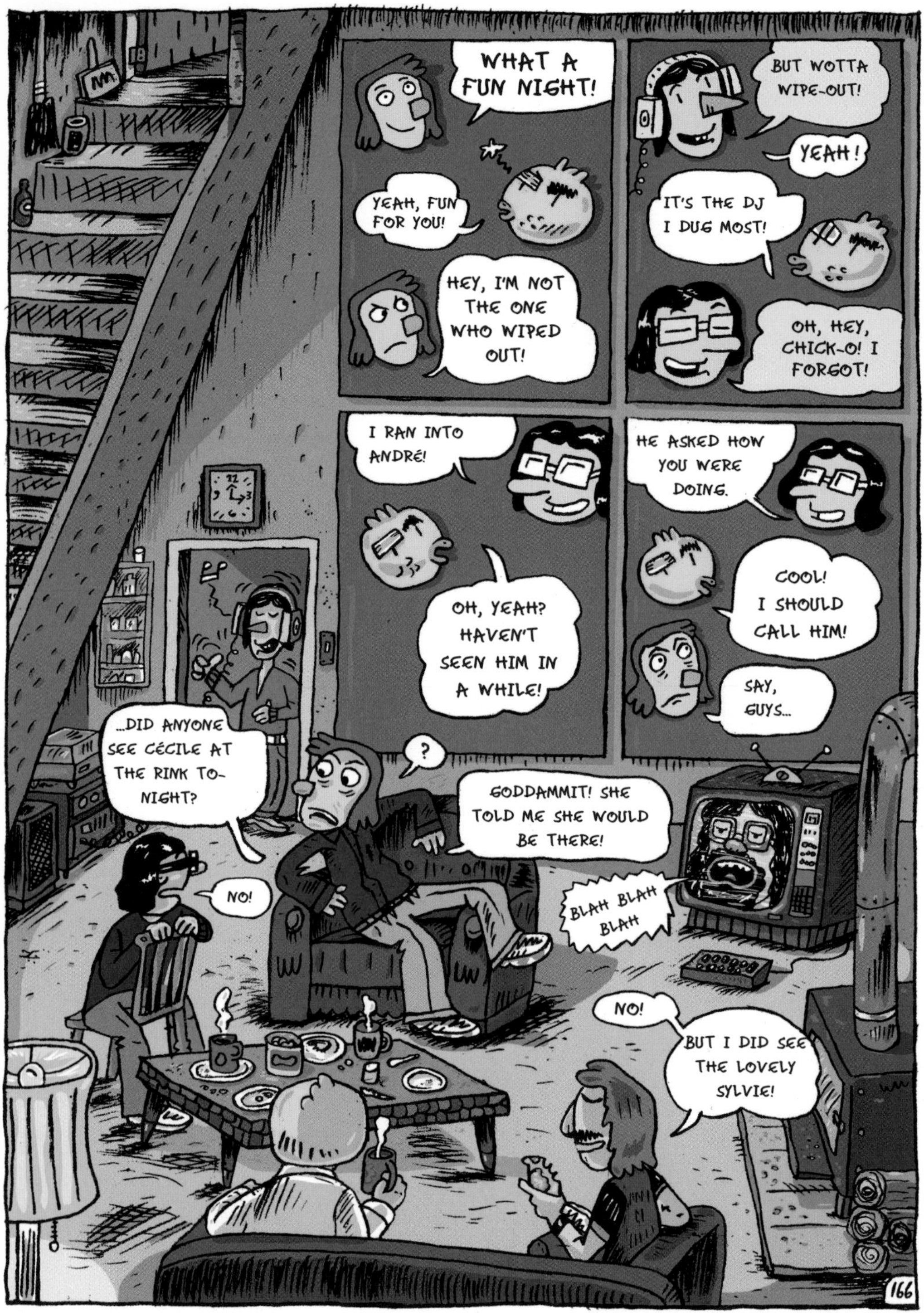
WHAT A FUN NIGHT!
YEAH, FUN FOR YOU!
HEY, I'M NOT THE ONE WHO WIPED OUT!
BUT WOTTA WIPE-OUT!
YEAH!
IT'S THE DJ I DUG MOST!
OH, HEY, CHICK-O! I FORGOT!
I RAN INTO ANDRÉ!
OH, YEAH? HAVEN'T SEEN HIM IN A WHILE!
HE ASKED HOW YOU WERE DOING.
COOL! I SHOULD CALL HIM!
SAY, GUYS...
...DID ANYONE SEE CÉCILE AT THE RINK TO-NIGHT?
?
NO!
GODDAMMIT! SHE TOLD ME SHE WOULD BE THERE!
BLAH BLAH BLAH
NO!
BUT I DID SEE THE LOVELY SYLVIE!
166

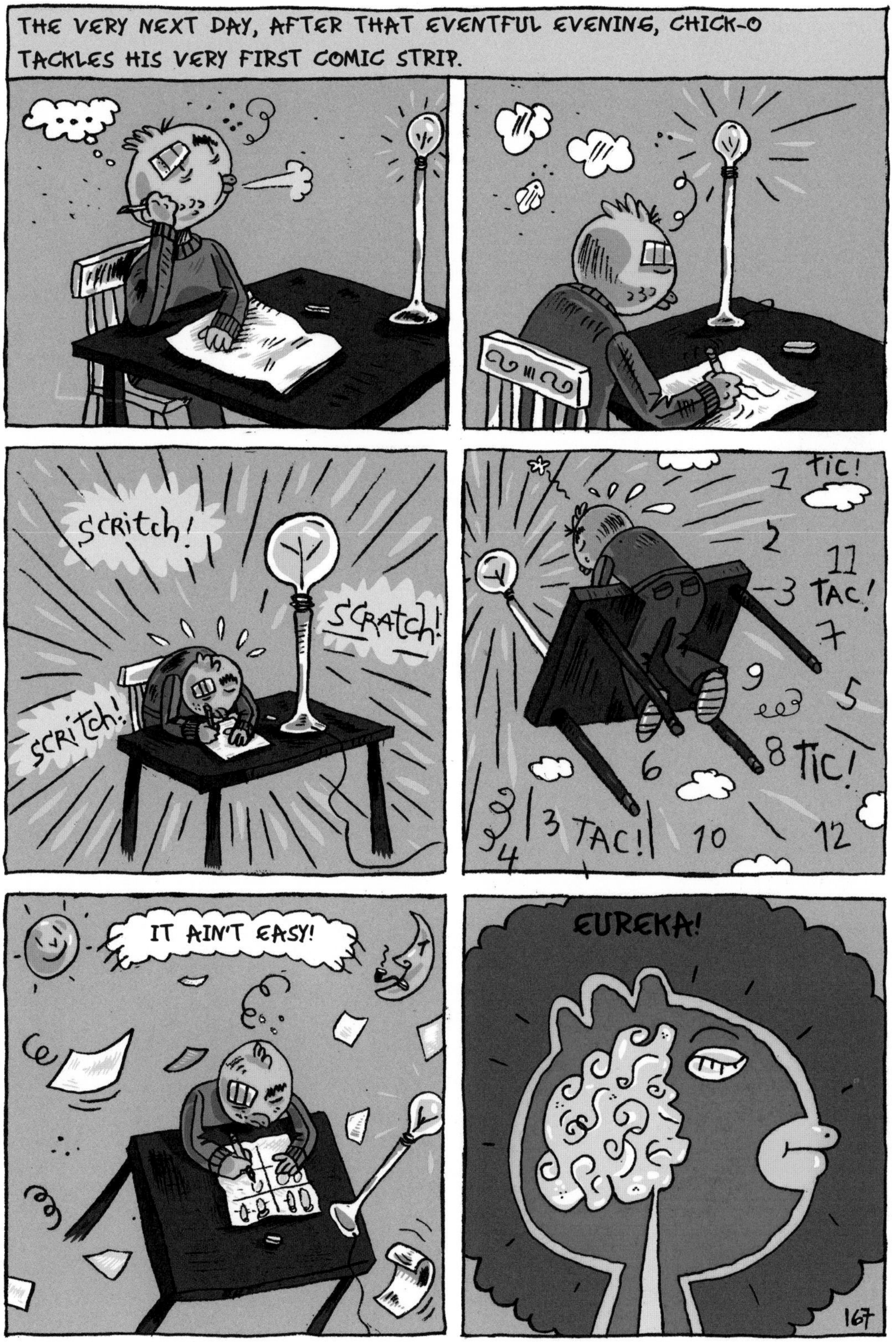
THE VERY NEXT DAY, AFTER THAT EVENTFUL EVENING, CHICK-O TACKLES HIS VERY FIRST COMIC STRIP.
SCRITCH!
SCRATCH!
SCRITCH!
TIC!
TAC!
TIC!
TAC!
IT AIN'T EASY!
EUREKA!
167

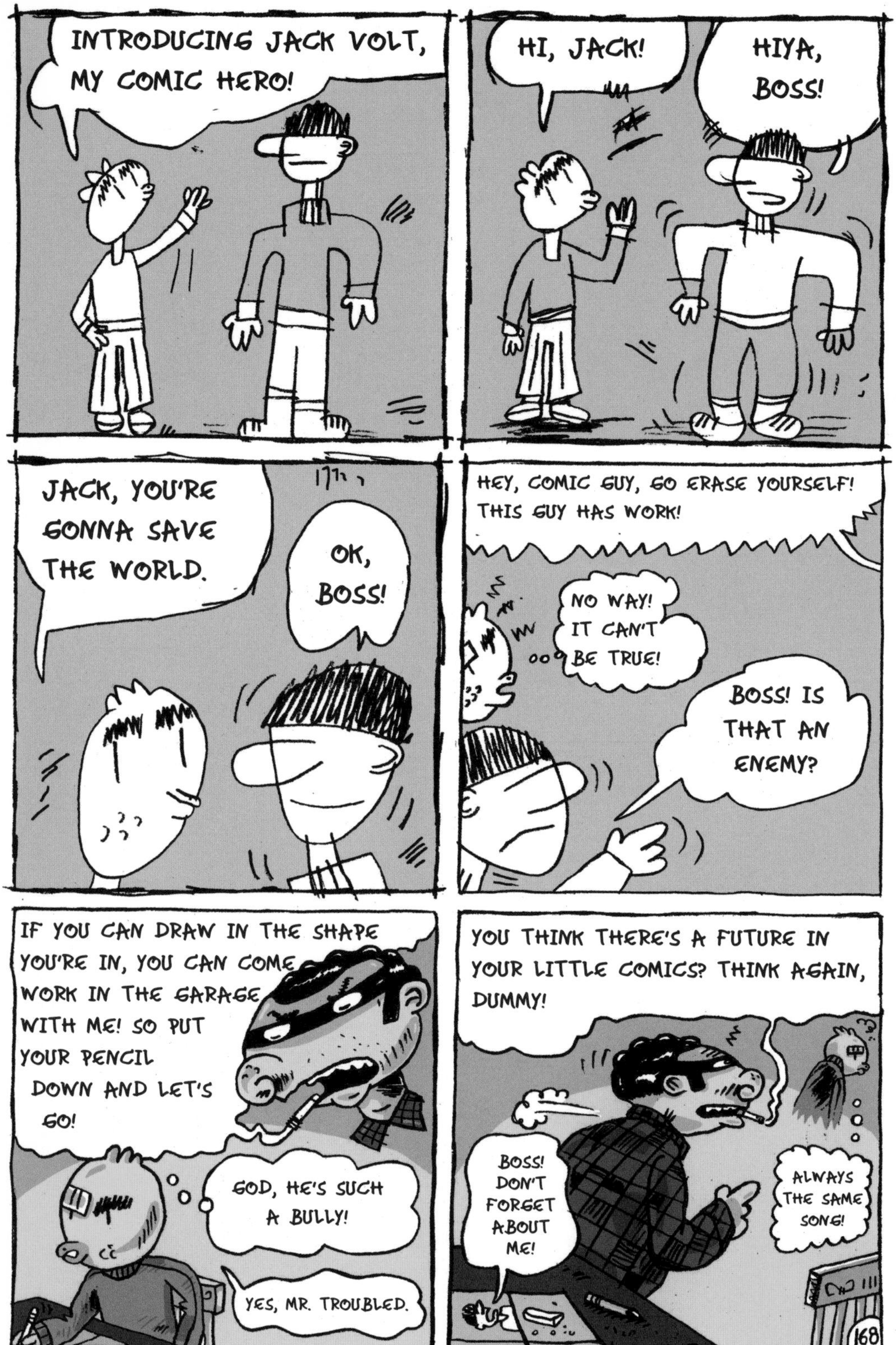
INTRODUCING JACK VOLT, MY COMIC HERO!
HI, JACK!
HIYA, BOSS!
JACK, YOU'RE GONNA SAVE THE WORLD.
OK, BOSS!
HEY, COMIC GUY, GO ERASE YOURSELF! THIS GUY HAS WORK!
NO WAY! IT CAN'T BE TRUE!
BOSS! IS THAT AN ENEMY?
IF YOU CAN DRAW IN THE SHAPE YOU'RE IN, YOU CAN COME WORK IN THE GARAGE WITH ME! SO PUT YOUR PENCIL DOWN AND LET'S GO!
GOD, HE'S SUCH A BULLY!
YES, MR. TROUBLED.
YOU THINK THERE'S A FUTURE IN YOUR LITTLE COMICS? THINK AGAIN, DUMMY!
BOSS! DON'T FORGET ABOUT ME!
ALWAYS THE SAME SONG!
168

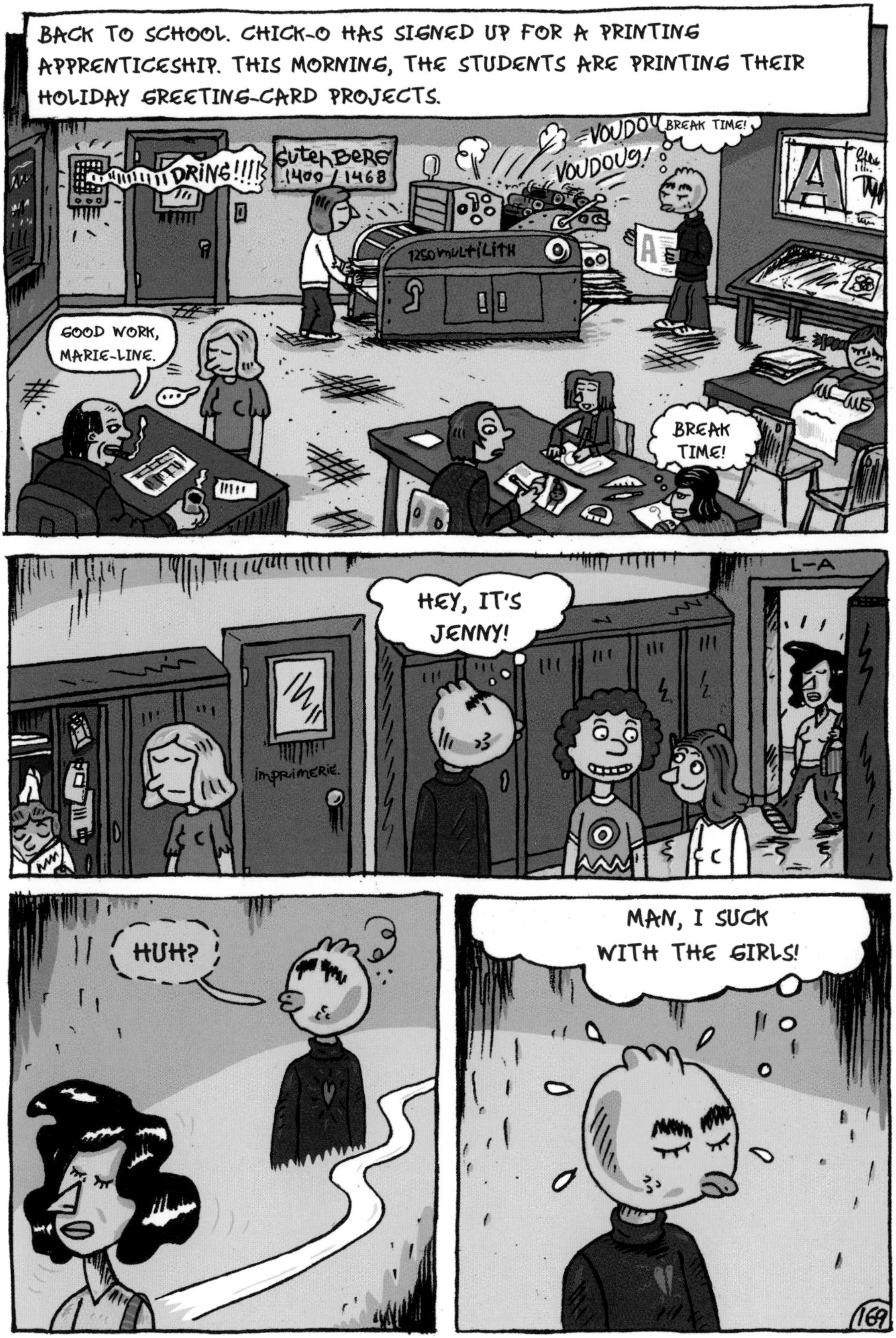
BACK TO SCHOOL. CHICK-O HAS SIGNED UP FOR A PRINTING APPRENTICESHIP. THIS MORNING, THE STUDENTS ARE PRINTING THEIR HOLIDAY GREETING-CARD PROJECTS.
DRING!!!!
GUTENBERG 1400 / 1468
VOUDOU
VOUDOUG!
BREAK TIME!
1250 MULTILITH
GOOD WORK, MARIE-LINE.
BREAK TIME!
L-A
HEY, IT'S JENNY!
IMPRIMERIE
HUH?
MAN, I SUCK WITH THE GIRLS!
169

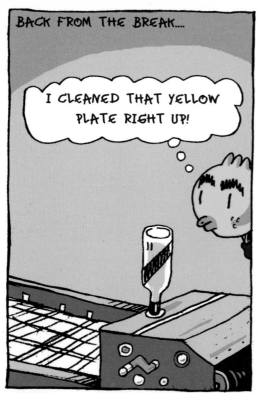

BACK FROM THE BREAK....

I CLEANED THAT YELLOW PLATE RIGHT UP!

CHICK-O! DON'T OVERDO THE INK!

YES, SIR!

THE PRINTER DOES PASSES OF YELLOW, RED, BLUE...

STOUDOUM!! STOUDOUUM! Z

Piiii

125 O'MULT

...AND FINALLY, BLACK!

WOW! EIGHT OUTTA 10?!

THANKS, SIR!

YOU DID GOOD WORK!

(170)

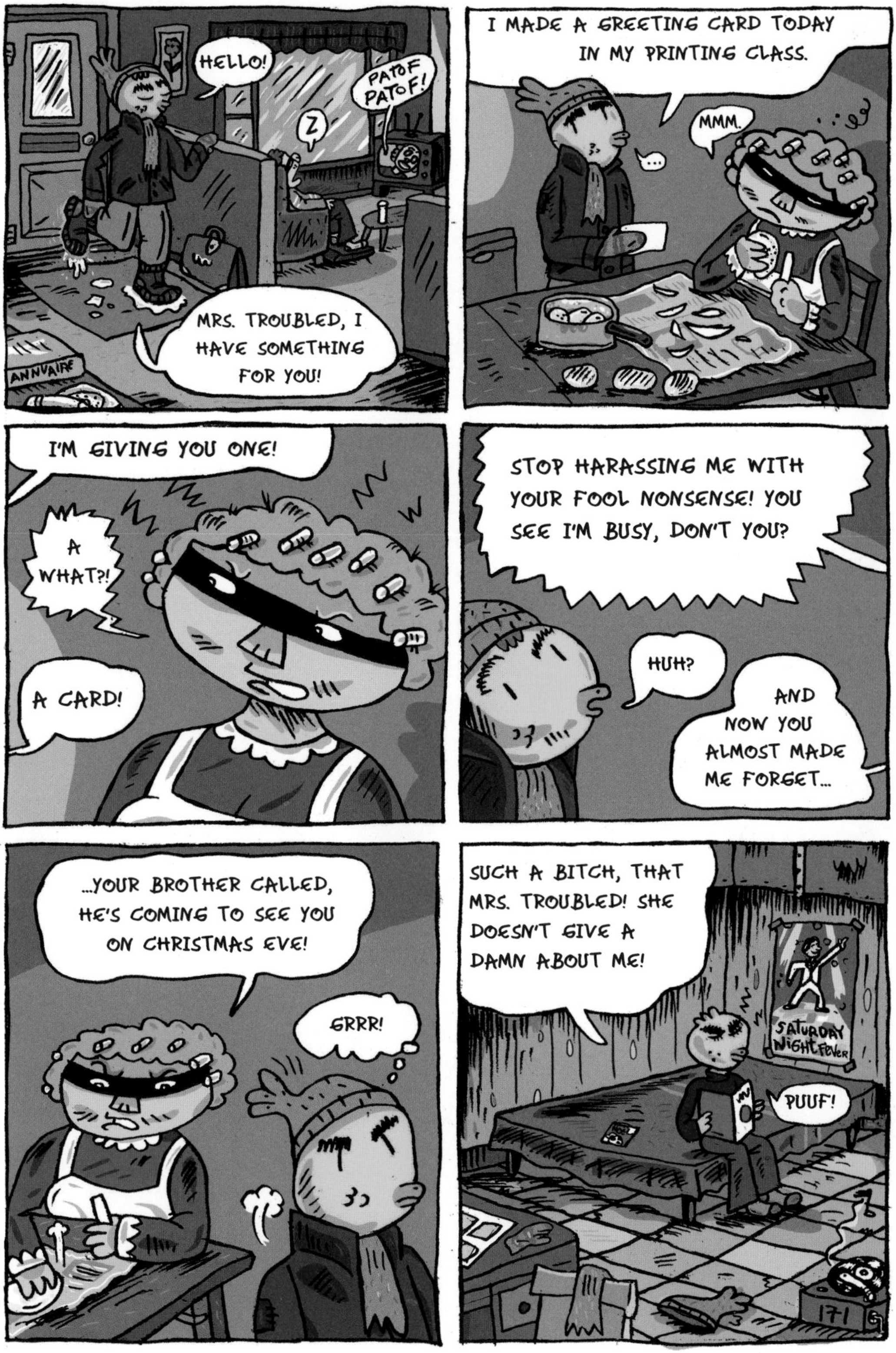
HELLO!
Z
PATOF PATOF!
ANNUAIRE
MRS. TROUBLED, I HAVE SOMETHING FOR YOU!
I MADE A GREETING CARD TODAY IN MY PRINTING CLASS.
...
MMM.
I'M GIVING YOU ONE!
A WHAT?!
A CARD!
STOP HARASSING ME WITH YOUR FOOL NONSENSE! YOU SEE I'M BUSY, DON'T YOU?
HUH?
AND NOW YOU ALMOST MADE ME FORGET...
...YOUR BROTHER CALLED, HE'S COMING TO SEE YOU ON CHRISTMAS EVE!
GRRR!
SUCH A BITCH, THAT MRS. TROUBLED! SHE DOESN'T GIVE A DAMN ABOUT ME!
SATURDAY NIGHT FEVER
PUUF!
171

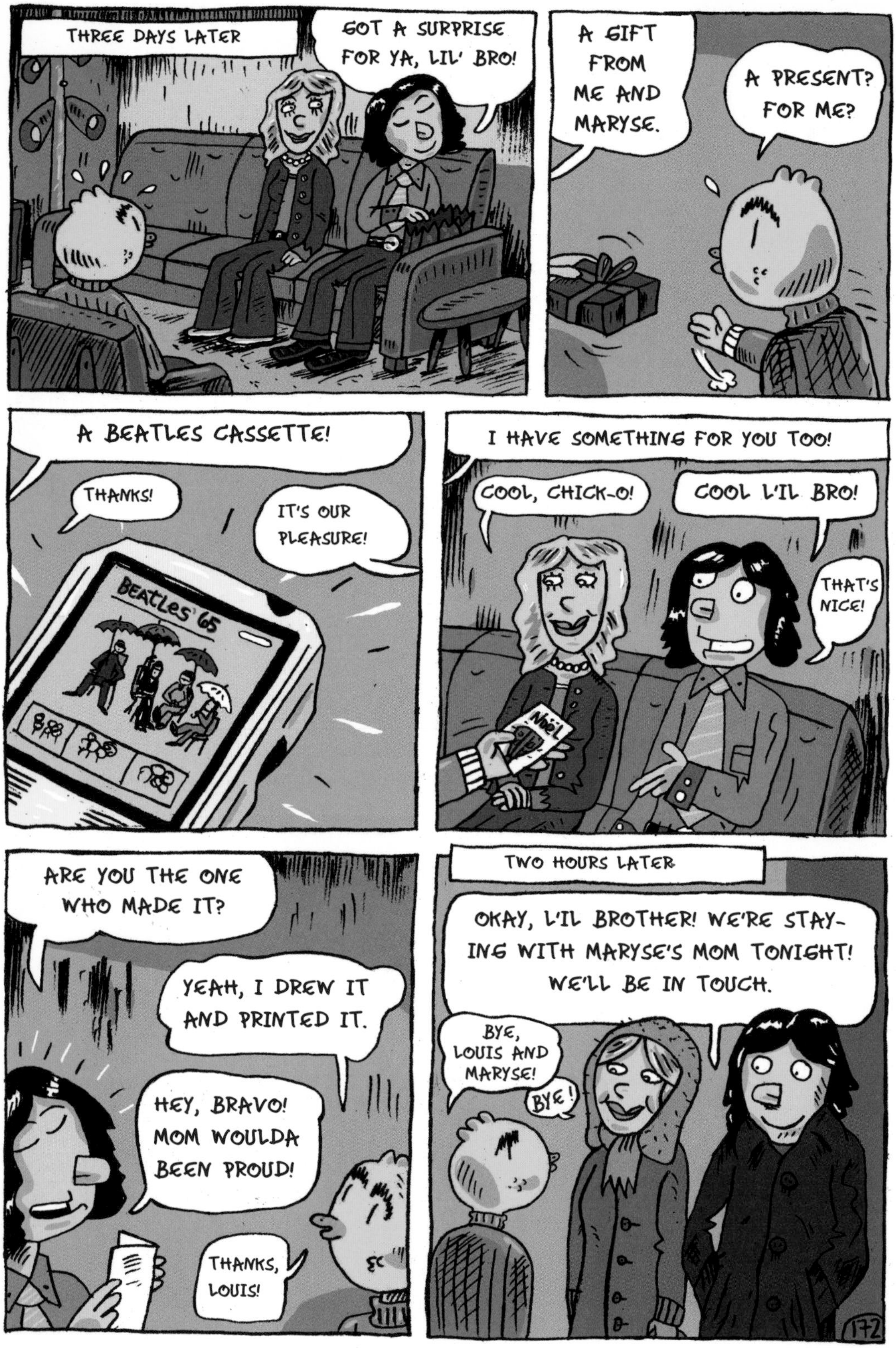
THREE DAYS LATER
GOT A SURPRISE FOR YA, LIL' BRO!
A GIFT FROM ME AND MARYSE.
A PRESENT? FOR ME?
A BEATLES CASSETTE!
THANKS!
IT'S OUR PLEASURE!
BEATLES '65
I HAVE SOMETHING FOR YOU TOO!
COOL, CHICK-O!
COOL L'IL BRO!
THAT'S NICE!
Noël
ARE YOU THE ONE WHO MADE IT?
YEAH, I DREW IT AND PRINTED IT.
HEY, BRAVO! MOM WOULDA BEEN PROUD!
THANKS, LOUIS!
TWO HOURS LATER
OKAY, L'IL BROTHER! WE'RE STAYING WITH MARYSE'S MOM TONIGHT! WE'LL BE IN TOUCH.
BYE, LOUIS AND MARYSE!
BYE!
172

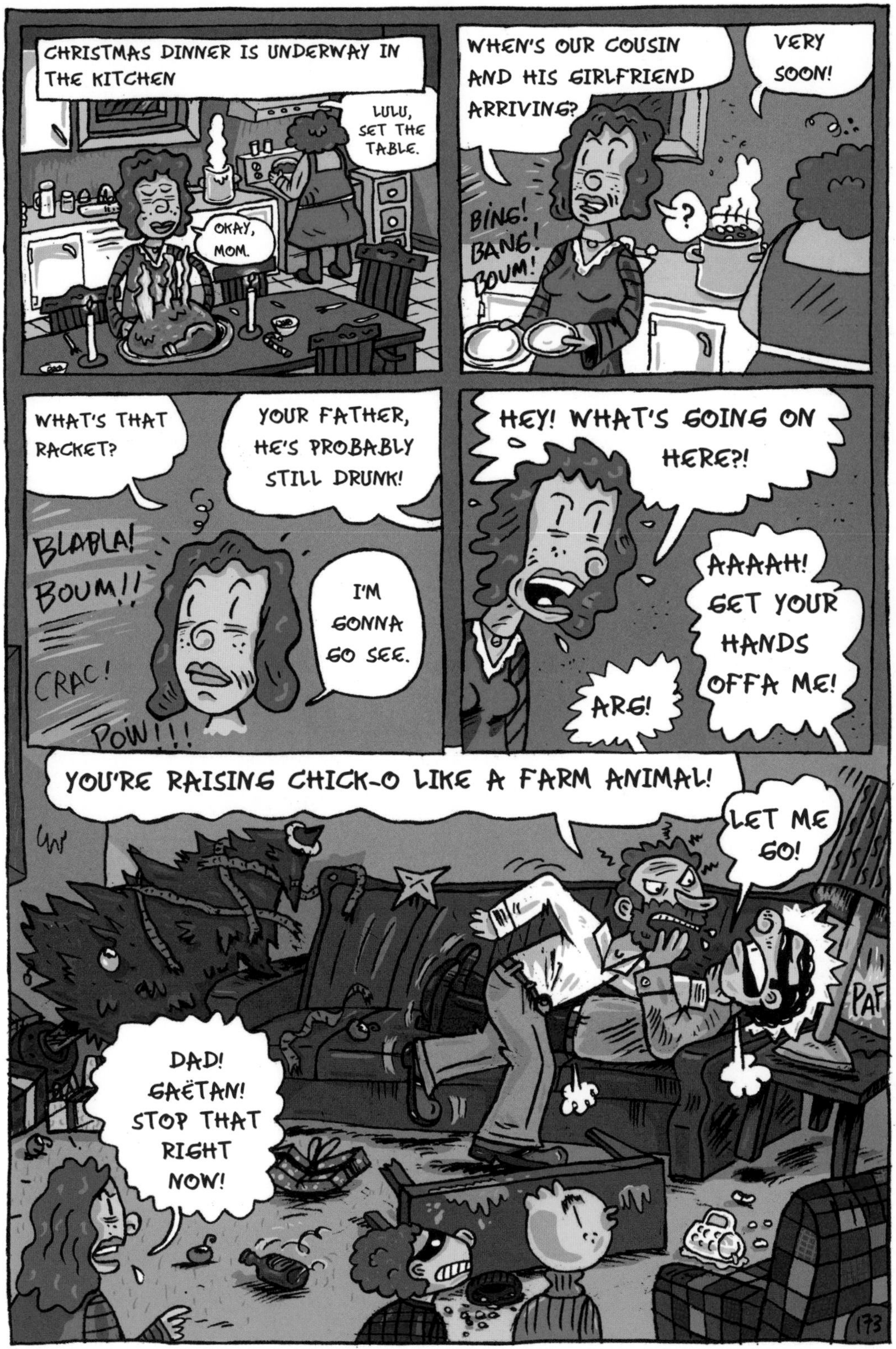
CHRISTMAS DINNER IS UNDERWAY IN THE KITCHEN
LULU, SET THE TABLE.
OKAY, MOM.
WHEN'S OUR COUSIN AND HIS GIRLFRIEND ARRIVING?
VERY SOON!
BING! BANG! BOUM!
?
WHAT'S THAT RACKET?
YOUR FATHER, HE'S PROBABLY STILL DRUNK!
BLABLA! BOUM!!
CRAC!
POW!!!
I'M GONNA GO SEE.
HEY! WHAT'S GOING ON HERE?!
AAAAH! GET YOUR HANDS OFFA ME!
ARG!
YOU'RE RAISING CHICK-O LIKE A FARM ANIMAL!
LET ME GO!
PAF
DAD! GAËTAN! STOP THAT RIGHT NOW!
173

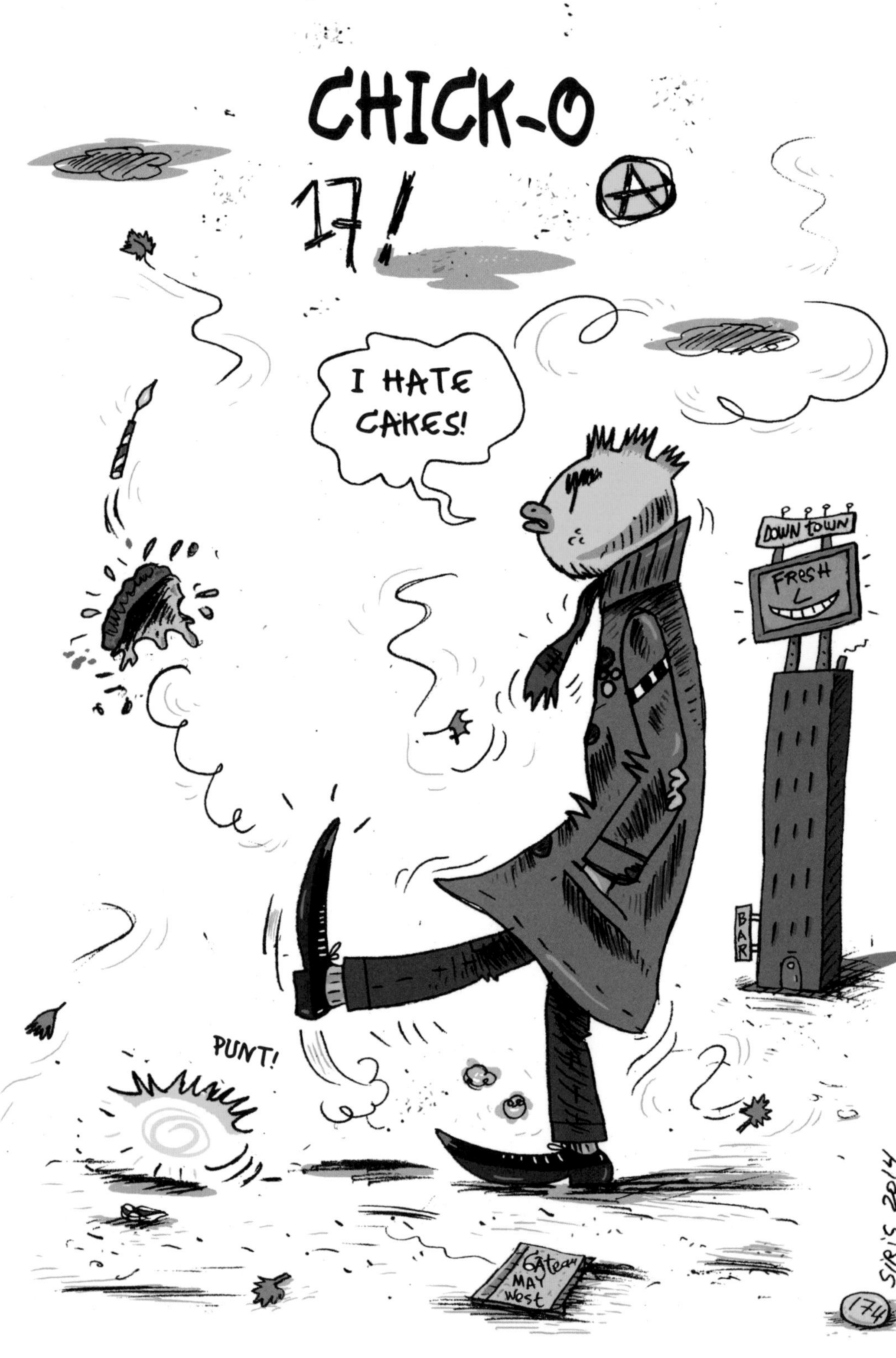
CHICK-O
17!
I HATE CAKES!
DOWN TOWN
FRESH
BAR
PUNT!
Gâteau MAY West
SIRIS 2014
174

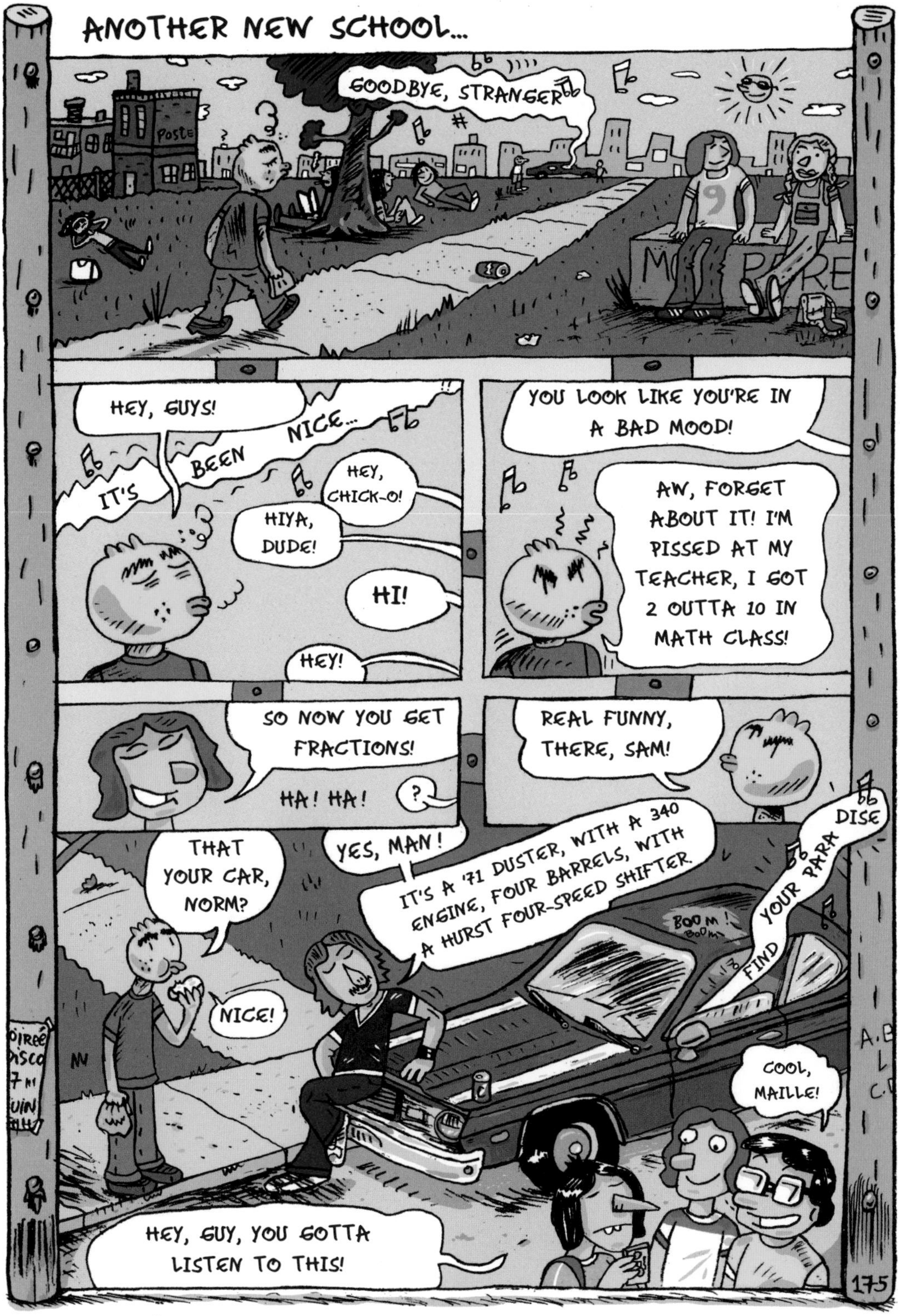
ANOTHER NEW SCHOOL...
POSTE
GOODBYE, STRANGER
MORE
HEY, GUYS!
IT'S BEEN NICE...
HEY, CHICK-O!
HIYA, DUDE!
HI!
HEY!
YOU LOOK LIKE YOU'RE IN A BAD MOOD!
AW, FORGET ABOUT IT! I'M PISSED AT MY TEACHER, I GOT 2 OUTTA 10 IN MATH CLASS!
SO NOW YOU GET FRACTIONS!
HA! HA!
?
REAL FUNNY, THERE, SAM!
THAT YOUR CAR, NORM?
YES, MAN!
IT'S A '71 DUSTER, WITH A 340 ENGINE, FOUR BARRELS, WITH A HURST FOUR-SPEED SHIFTER.
FIND YOUR PARADISE
BOOM! BOOM!
NICE!
COOL, MAILLE!
HEY, GUY, YOU GOTTA LISTEN TO THIS!
175

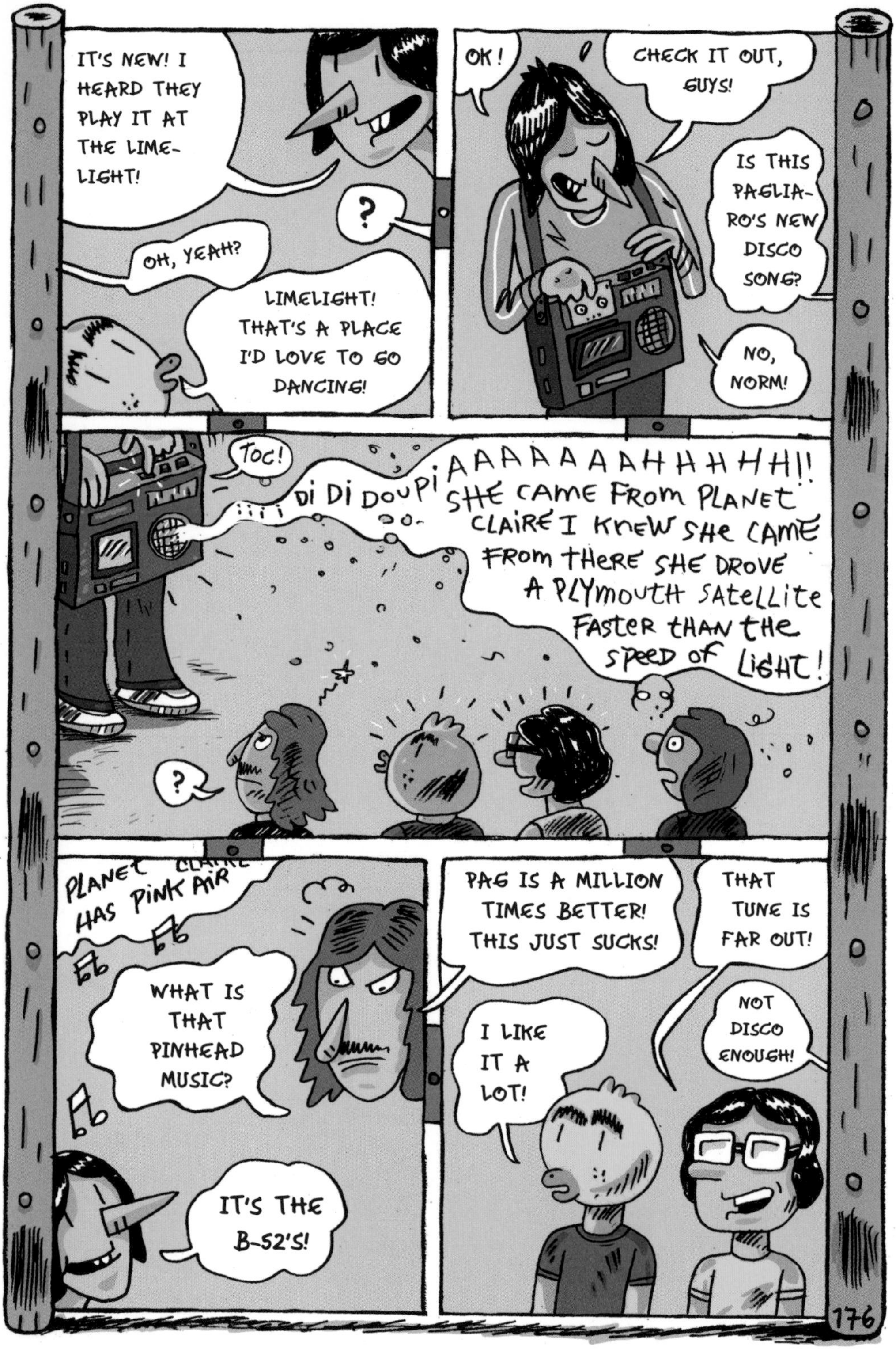

IT'S NEW! I HEARD THEY PLAY IT AT THE LIME-LIGHT!
?
OH, YEAH?
LIMELIGHT! THAT'S A PLACE I'D LOVE TO GO DANCING!
OK!
CHECK IT OUT, GUYS!
IS THIS PAGLIA-RO'S NEW DISCO SONG?
NO, NORM!
TOC!
DI DI DOUPI AAAAAAAHHHHHH!! SHE CAME FROM PLANET CLAIRE I KNEW SHE CAME FROM THERE SHE DROVE A PLYMOUTH SATELLITE FASTER THAN THE SPEED OF LIGHT!
?
PLANET CLAIRE HAS PINK AIR
WHAT IS THAT PINHEAD MUSIC?
IT'S THE B-52'S!
PAG IS A MILLION TIMES BETTER! THIS JUST SUCKS!
THAT TUNE IS FAR OUT!
I LIKE IT A LOT!
NOT DISCO ENOUGH!
176

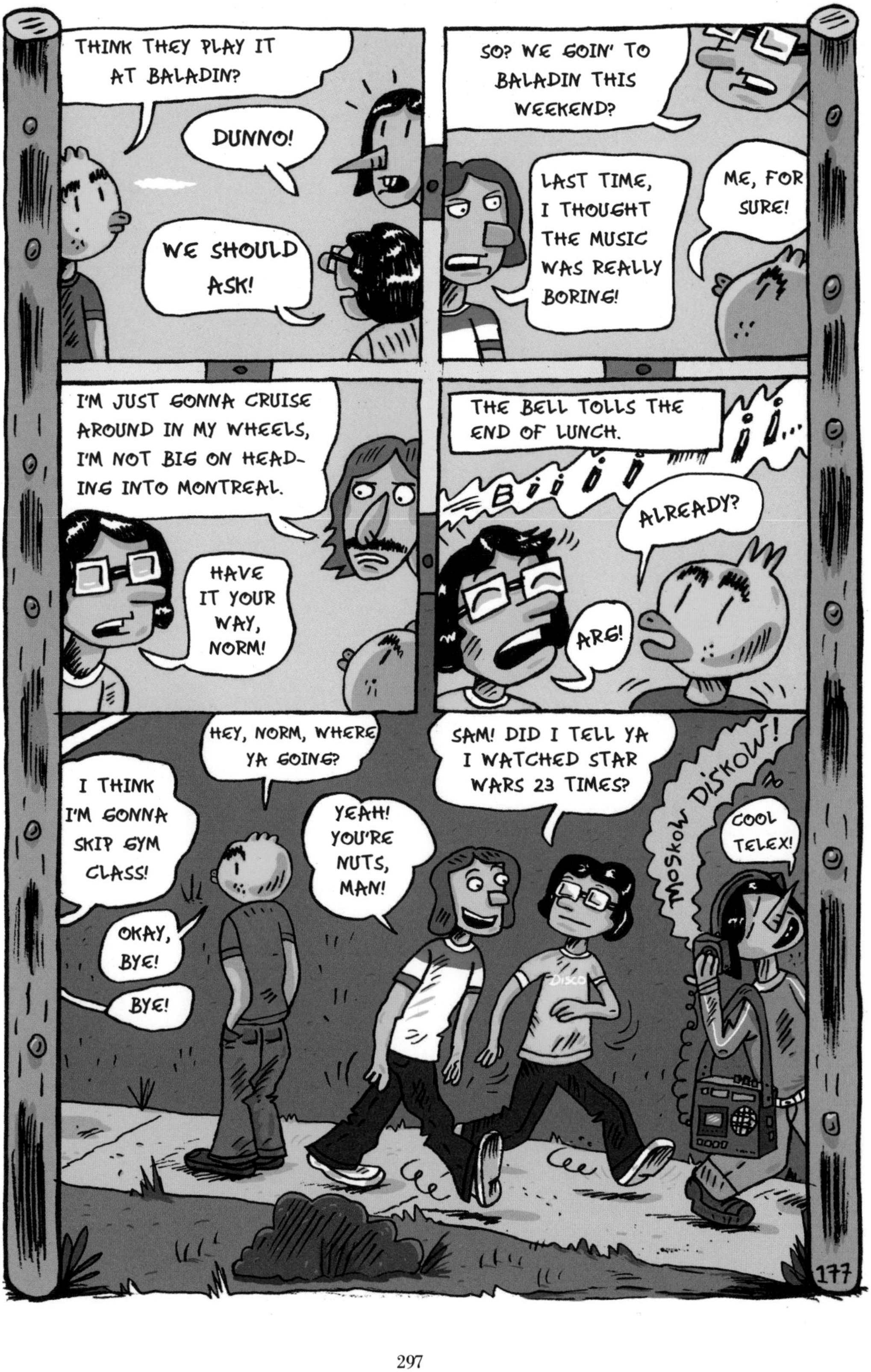
THINK THEY PLAY IT AT BALADIN?
DUNNO!
WE SHOULD ASK!
SO? WE GOIN' TO BALADIN THIS WEEKEND?
LAST TIME, I THOUGHT THE MUSIC WAS REALLY BORING!
ME, FOR SURE!
I'M JUST GONNA CRUISE AROUND IN MY WHEELS, I'M NOT BIG ON HEADING INTO MONTREAL.
HAVE IT YOUR WAY, NORM!
THE BELL TOLLS THE END OF LUNCH.
BiiiiiiiiI...
ALREADY?
ARG!
HEY, NORM, WHERE YA GOING?
I THINK I'M GONNA SKIP GYM CLASS!
YEAH! YOU'RE NUTS, MAN!
OKAY, BYE!
BYE!
SAM! DID I TELL YA I WATCHED STAR WARS 23 TIMES?
MOSKOW DISKOW!
COOL TELEX!
DISCO
177

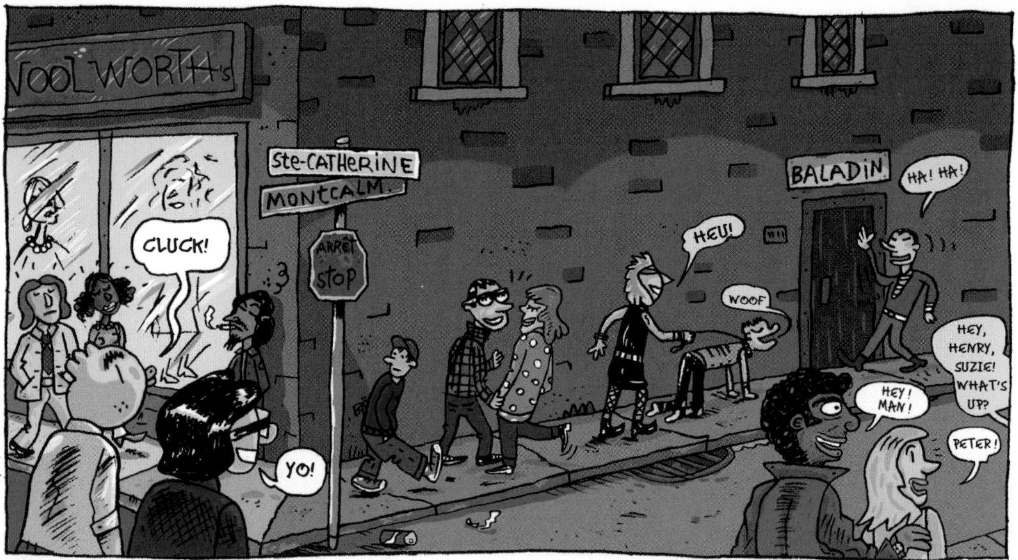
WOOLWORTH's
Ste-CATHERINE
MONTCALM
ARRÊT
STOP
BALADIN
CLUCK!
HEU!
WOOF
HA! HA!
HEY, HENRY, SUZIE! WHAT'S UP?
HEY! MAN!
PETER!
YO!

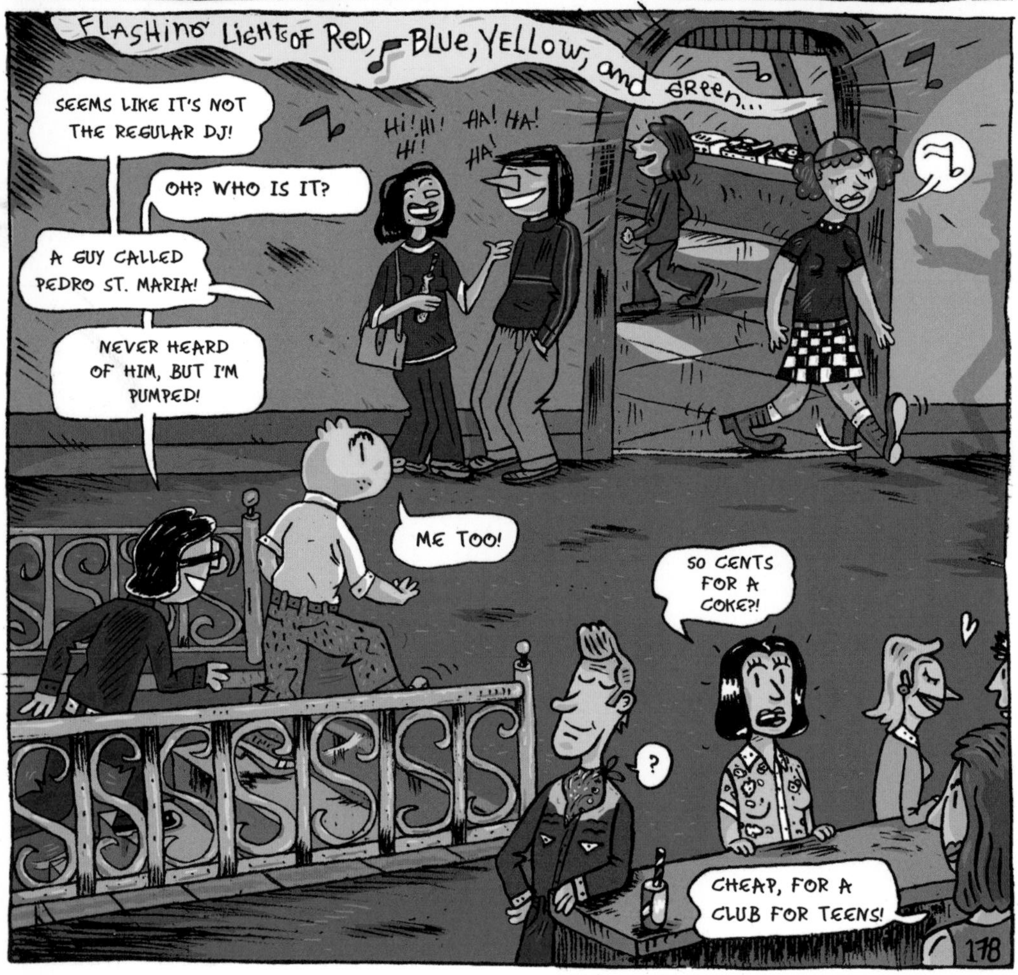
FLASHING LIGHTS OF RED, BLUE, YELLOW, AND GREEN...
SEEMS LIKE IT'S NOT THE REGULAR DJ!
OH? WHO IS IT?
A GUY CALLED PEDRO ST. MARIA!
NEVER HEARD OF HIM, BUT I'M PUMPED!
HI! HI! HI!
HA! HA! HA!
ME TOO!
50 CENTS FOR A COKE?!
?
CHEAP, FOR A CLUB FOR TEENS!
178

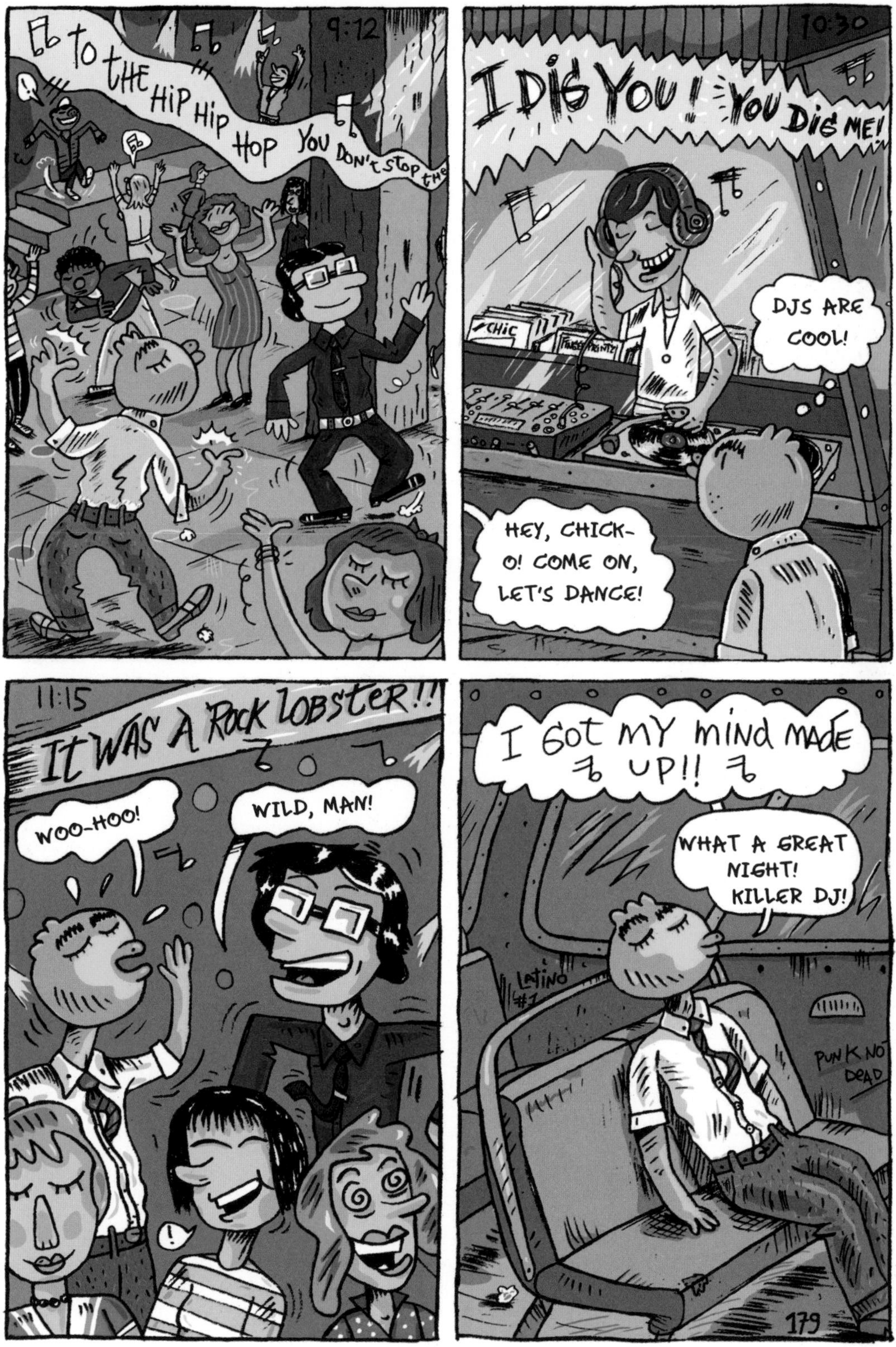
9:12
to THE HIP HIP HOP YOU DON'T STOP THE
10:30
I DIG YOU! YOU DIG ME!
CHIC
DJS ARE COOL!
HEY, CHICK-O! COME ON, LET'S DANCE!
11:15
IT WAS A ROCK LOBSTER!!
WOO-HOO!
WILD, MAN!
!
I GOT MY MIND MADE UP!!
WHAT A GREAT NIGHT! KILLER DJ!
LATINO #1
PUNK NOT DEAD
179

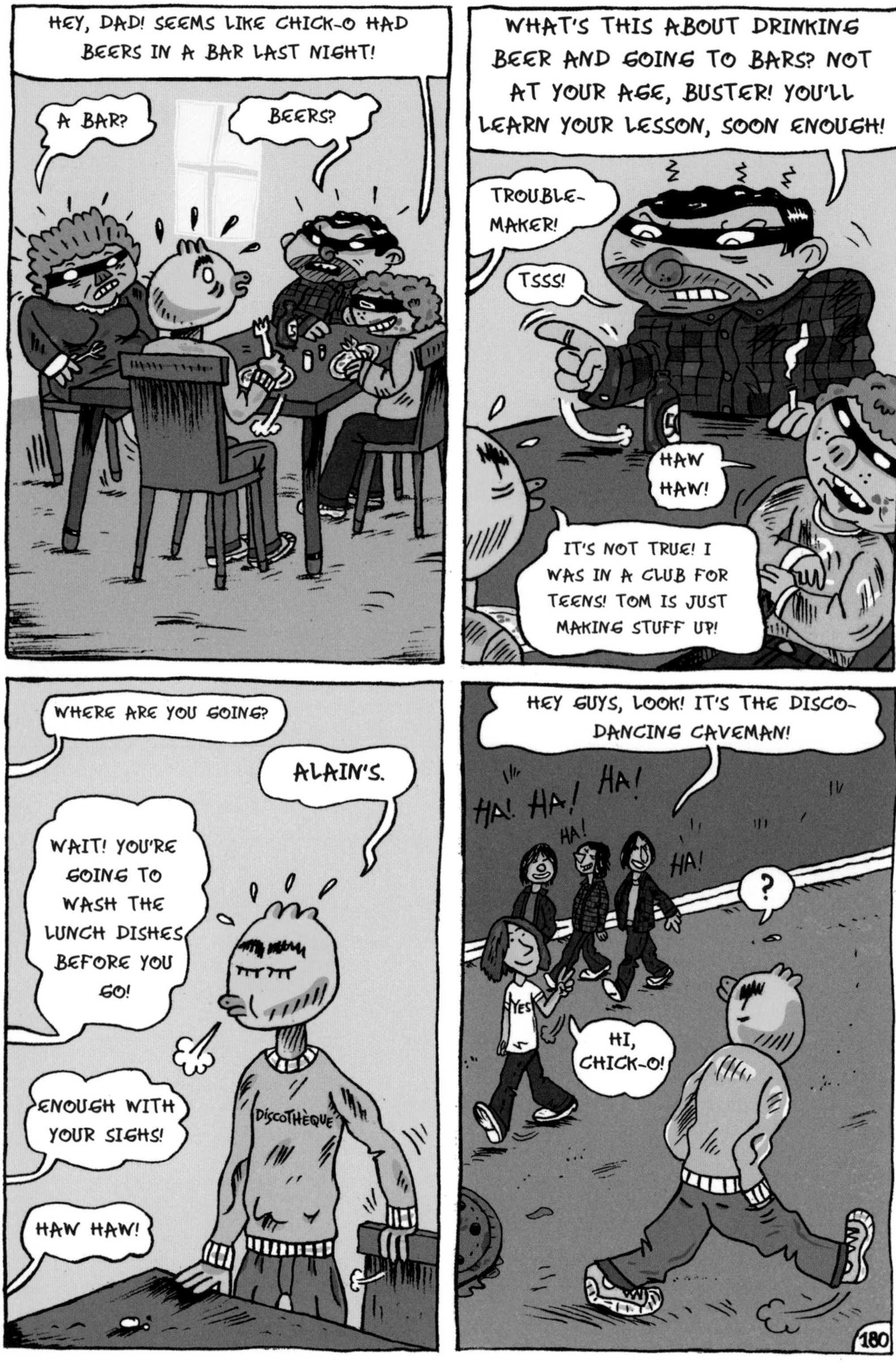
HEY, DAD! SEEMS LIKE CHICK-O HAD BEERS IN A BAR LAST NIGHT!
A BAR?
BEERS?
WHAT'S THIS ABOUT DRINKING BEER AND GOING TO BARS? NOT AT YOUR AGE, BUSTER! YOU'LL LEARN YOUR LESSON, SOON ENOUGH!
TROUBLE-MAKER!
TSSS!
HAW HAW!
IT'S NOT TRUE! I WAS IN A CLUB FOR TEENS! TOM IS JUST MAKING STUFF UP!
WHERE ARE YOU GOING?
ALAIN'S.
WAIT! YOU'RE GOING TO WASH THE LUNCH DISHES BEFORE YOU GO!
ENOUGH WITH YOUR SIGHS!
HAW HAW!
DISCOTHÈQUE
HEY GUYS, LOOK! IT'S THE DISCO-DANCING CAVEMAN!
HA! HA! HA! HA! HA!
?
YES
HI, CHICK-O!
180

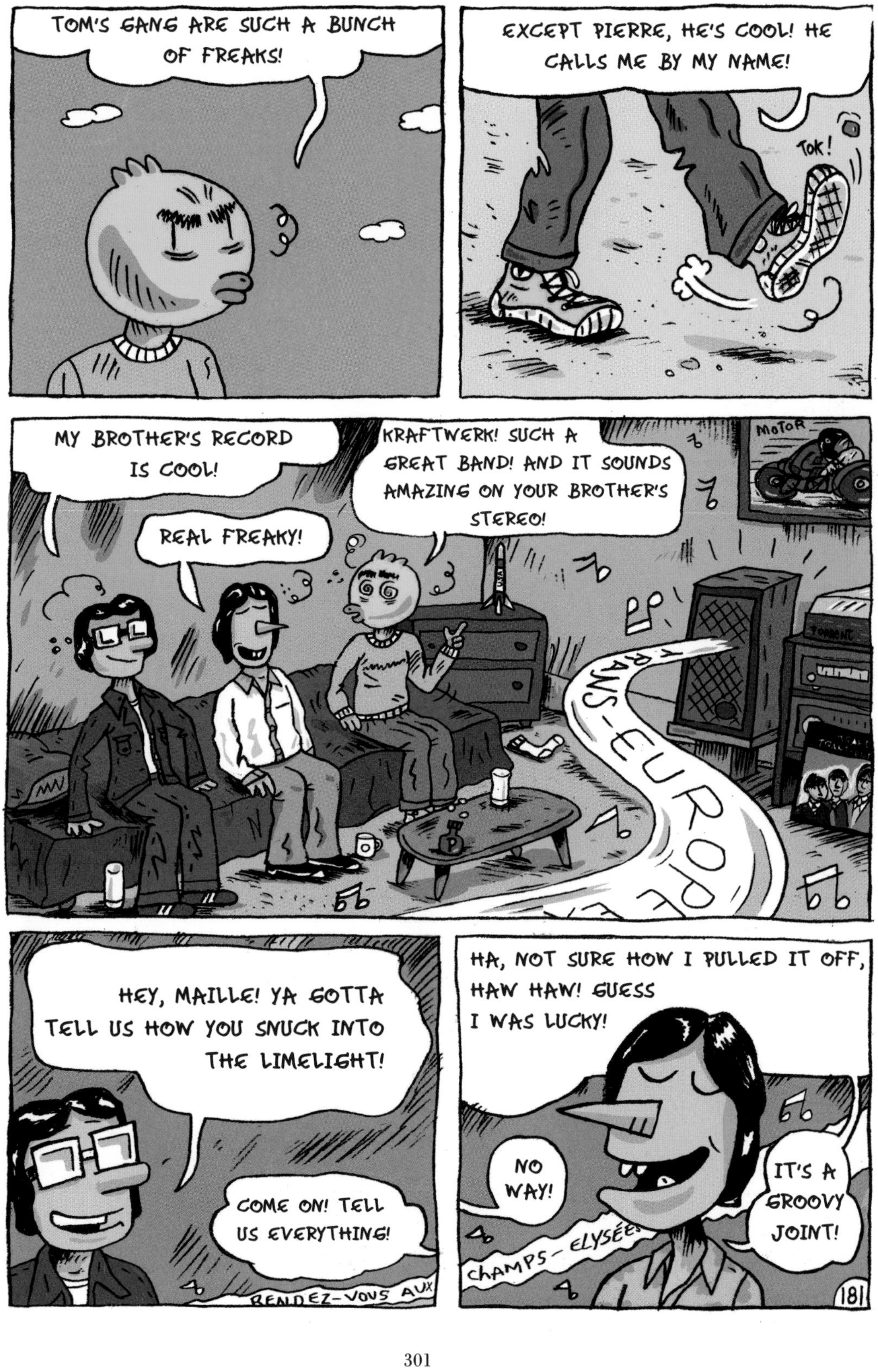
TOM'S GANG ARE SUCH A BUNCH OF FREAKS!
EXCEPT PIERRE, HE'S COOL! HE CALLS ME BY MY NAME!
TOK!
MY BROTHER'S RECORD IS COOL!
REAL FREAKY!
KRAFTWERK! SUCH A GREAT BAND! AND IT SOUNDS AMAZING ON YOUR BROTHER'S STEREO!
MOTOR
HEY, MAILLE! YA GOTTA TELL US HOW YOU SNUCK INTO THE LIMELIGHT!
COME ON! TELL US EVERYTHING!
RENDEZ-VOUS AUX
HA, NOT SURE HOW I PULLED IT OFF, HAW HAW! GUESS I WAS LUCKY!
NO WAY!
IT'S A GROOVY JOINT!
CHAMPS-ELYSÉES
181

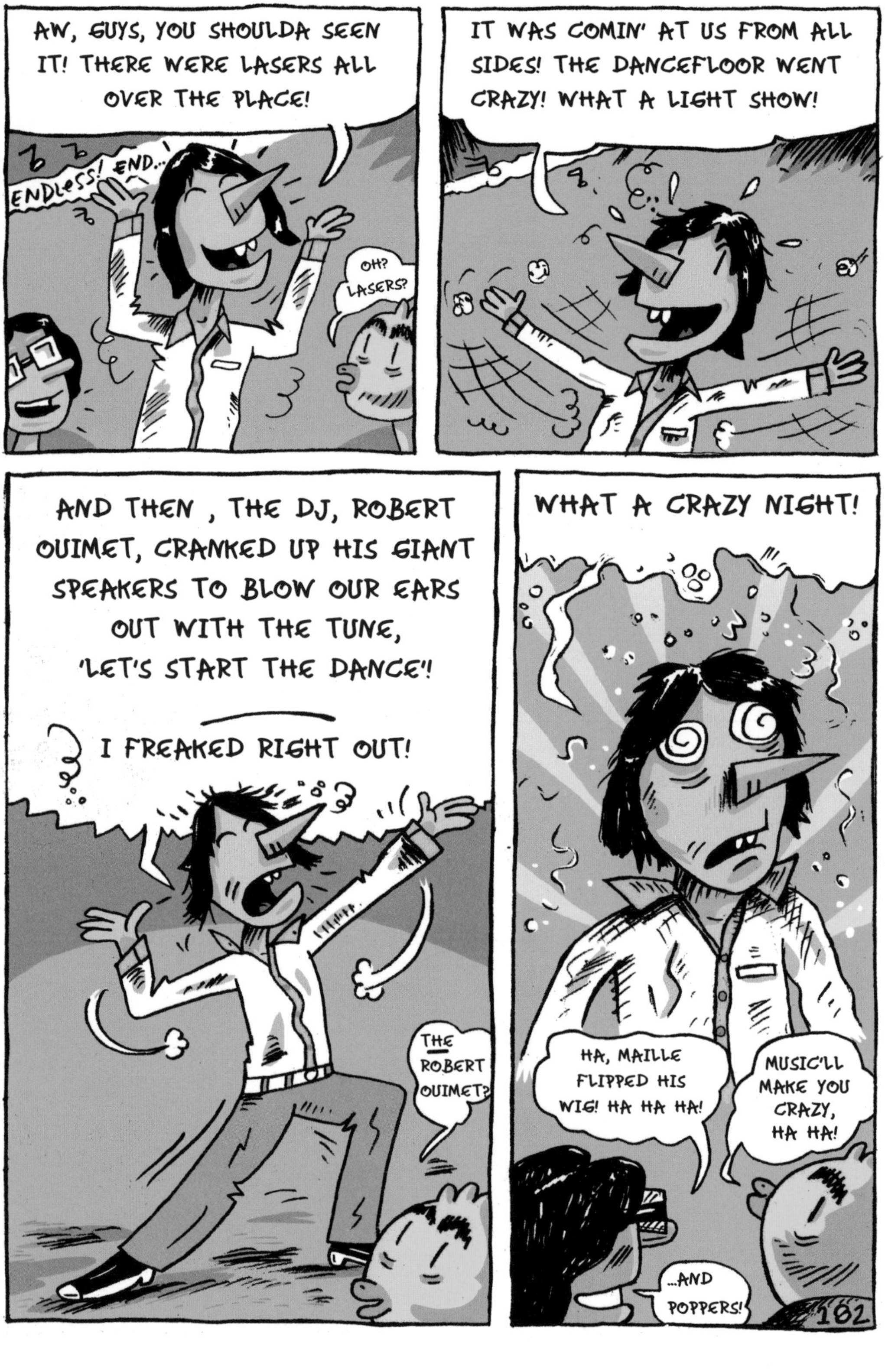
AW, GUYS, YOU SHOULDA SEEN IT! THERE WERE LASERS ALL OVER THE PLACE!
ENDLESS! END...
OH? LASERS?
IT WAS COMIN' AT US FROM ALL SIDES! THE DANCEFLOOR WENT CRAZY! WHAT A LIGHT SHOW!
AND THEN , THE DJ, ROBERT OUIMET, CRANKED UP HIS GIANT SPEAKERS TO BLOW OUR EARS OUT WITH THE TUNE, 'LET'S START THE DANCE'!
I FREAKED RIGHT OUT!
THE ROBERT OUIMET?
WHAT A CRAZY NIGHT!
HA, MAILLE FLIPPED HIS WIG! HA HA HA!
MUSIC'LL MAKE YOU CRAZY, HA HA!
...AND POPPERS!
102

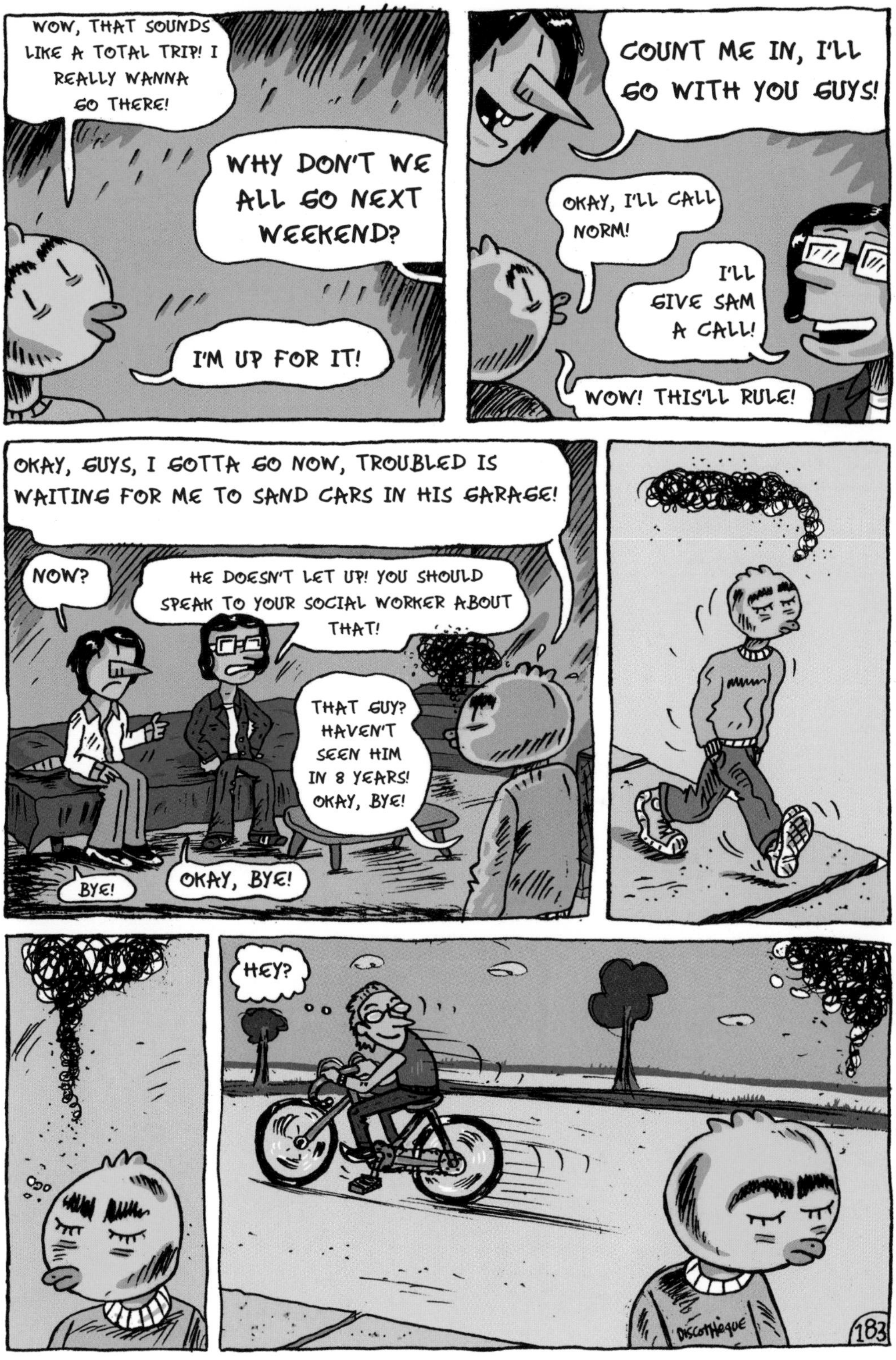
WOW, THAT SOUNDS LIKE A TOTAL TRIP! I REALLY WANNA GO THERE!
WHY DON'T WE ALL GO NEXT WEEKEND?
I'M UP FOR IT!
COUNT ME IN, I'LL GO WITH YOU GUYS!
OKAY, I'LL CALL NORM!
I'LL GIVE SAM A CALL!
WOW! THIS'LL RULE!
OKAY, GUYS, I GOTTA GO NOW, TROUBLED IS WAITING FOR ME TO SAND CARS IN HIS GARAGE!
NOW?
HE DOESN'T LET UP! YOU SHOULD SPEAK TO YOUR SOCIAL WORKER ABOUT THAT!
THAT GUY? HAVEN'T SEEN HIM IN 8 YEARS! OKAY, BYE!
BYE!
OKAY, BYE!
HEY?
DISCOTHEQUE
183

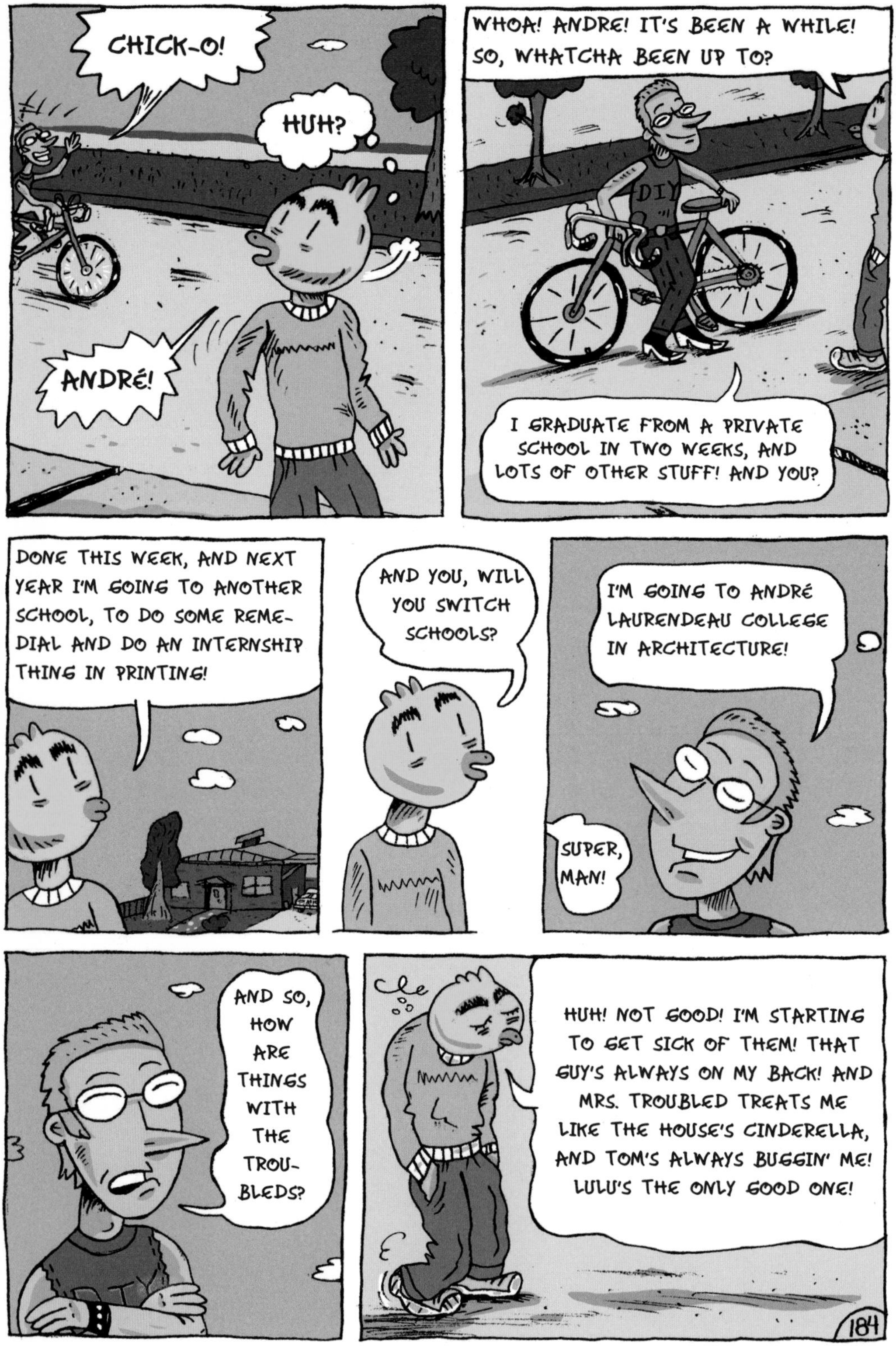
CHICK-O!
HUH?
ANDRÉ!
WHOA! ANDRE! IT'S BEEN A WHILE! SO, WHATCHA BEEN UP TO?
DIY
I GRADUATE FROM A PRIVATE SCHOOL IN TWO WEEKS, AND LOTS OF OTHER STUFF! AND YOU?
DONE THIS WEEK, AND NEXT YEAR I'M GOING TO ANOTHER SCHOOL, TO DO SOME REME-DIAL AND DO AN INTERNSHIP THING IN PRINTING!
AND YOU, WILL YOU SWITCH SCHOOLS?
I'M GOING TO ANDRÉ LAURENDEAU COLLEGE IN ARCHITECTURE!
SUPER, MAN!
AND SO, HOW ARE THINGS WITH THE TROU-BLEDS?
HUH! NOT GOOD! I'M STARTING TO GET SICK OF THEM! THAT GUY'S ALWAYS ON MY BACK! AND MRS. TROUBLED TREATS ME LIKE THE HOUSE'S CINDERELLA, AND TOM'S ALWAYS BUGGIN' ME! LULU'S THE ONLY GOOD ONE!
184

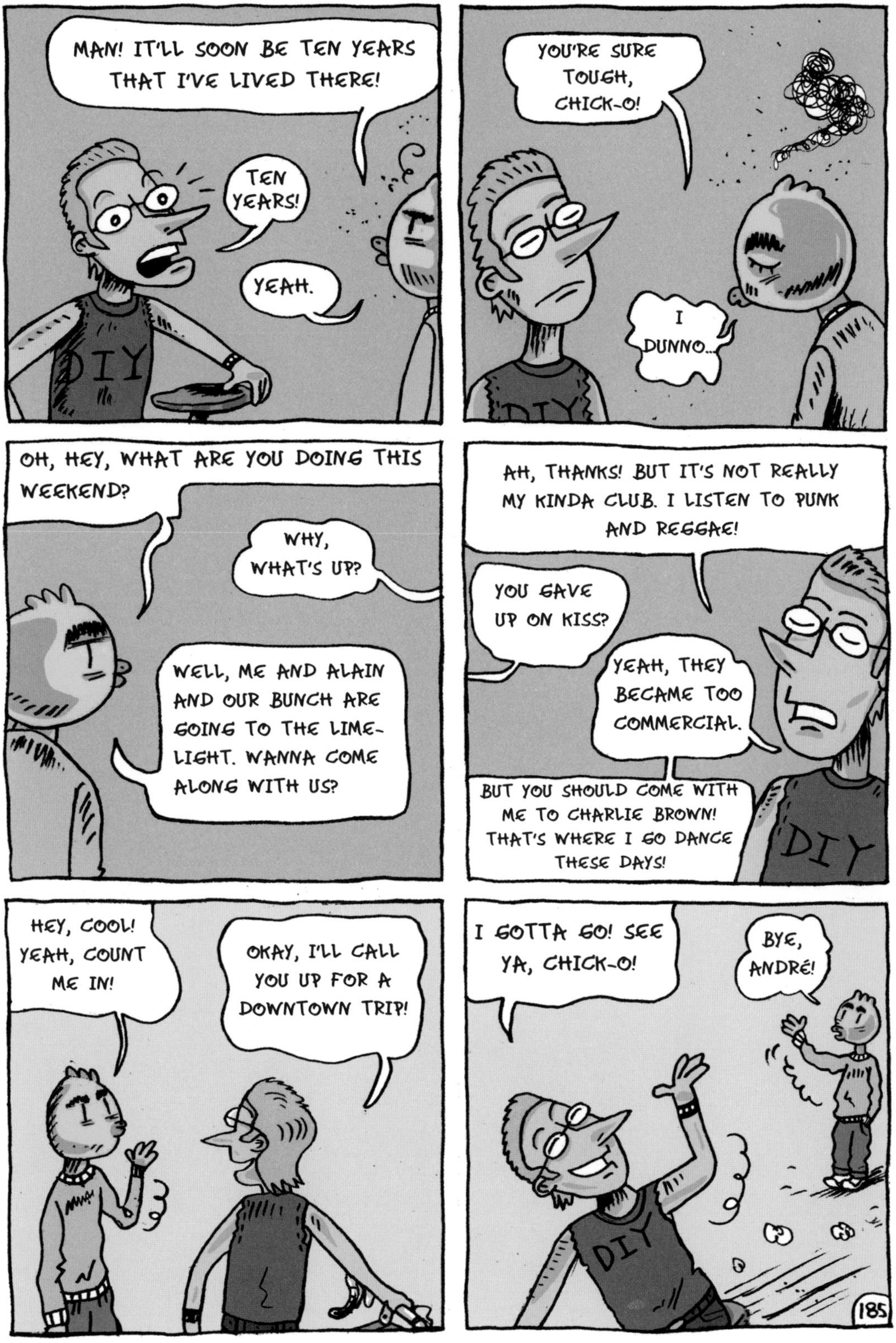
MAN! IT'LL SOON BE TEN YEARS THAT I'VE LIVED THERE!
TEN YEARS!
YEAH.
YOU'RE SURE TOUGH, CHICK-O!
I DUNNO...
OH, HEY, WHAT ARE YOU DOING THIS WEEKEND?
WHY, WHAT'S UP?
WELL, ME AND ALAIN AND OUR BUNCH ARE GOING TO THE LIME-LIGHT. WANNA COME ALONG WITH US?
AH, THANKS! BUT IT'S NOT REALLY MY KINDA CLUB. I LISTEN TO PUNK AND REGGAE!
YOU GAVE UP ON KISS?
YEAH, THEY BECAME TOO COMMERCIAL.
BUT YOU SHOULD COME WITH ME TO CHARLIE BROWN! THAT'S WHERE I GO DANCE THESE DAYS!
HEY, COOL! YEAH, COUNT ME IN!
OKAY, I'LL CALL YOU UP FOR A DOWNTOWN TRIP!
I GOTTA GO! SEE YA, CHICK-O!
BYE, ANDRÉ!
185

THE BIG NIGHT OF SUMMER 1979

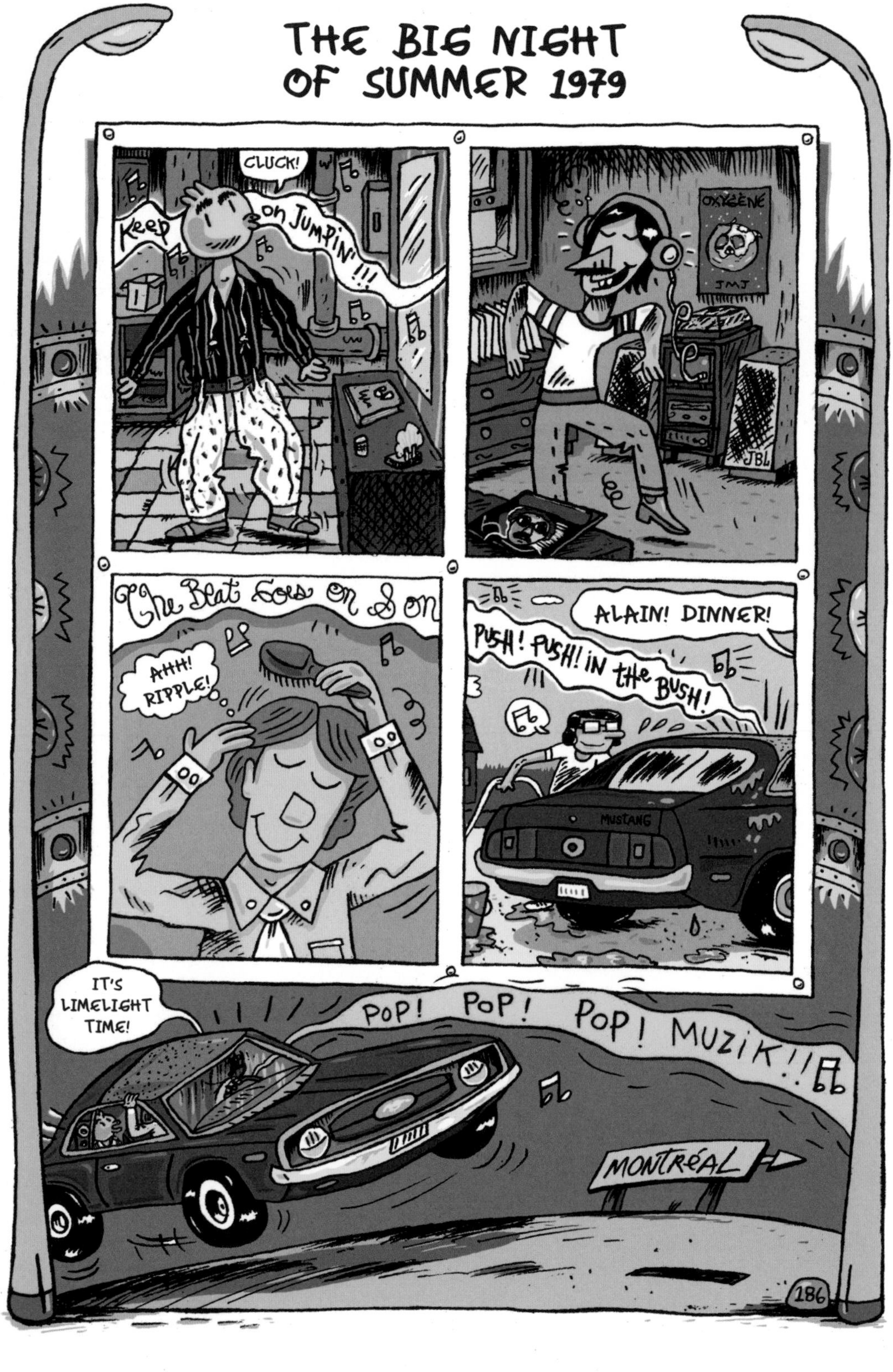
CLUCK!
Keep on Jumpin'!!!
OXYGÈNE
JMJ
JBL
The Beat Goes on & on
AHH! RIPPLE!
ALAIN! DINNER!
PUSH! PUSH! IN THE BUSH!
MUSTANG
IT'S LIMELIGHT TIME!
POP! POP! POP! MUZIK!!
MONTRÉAL
186

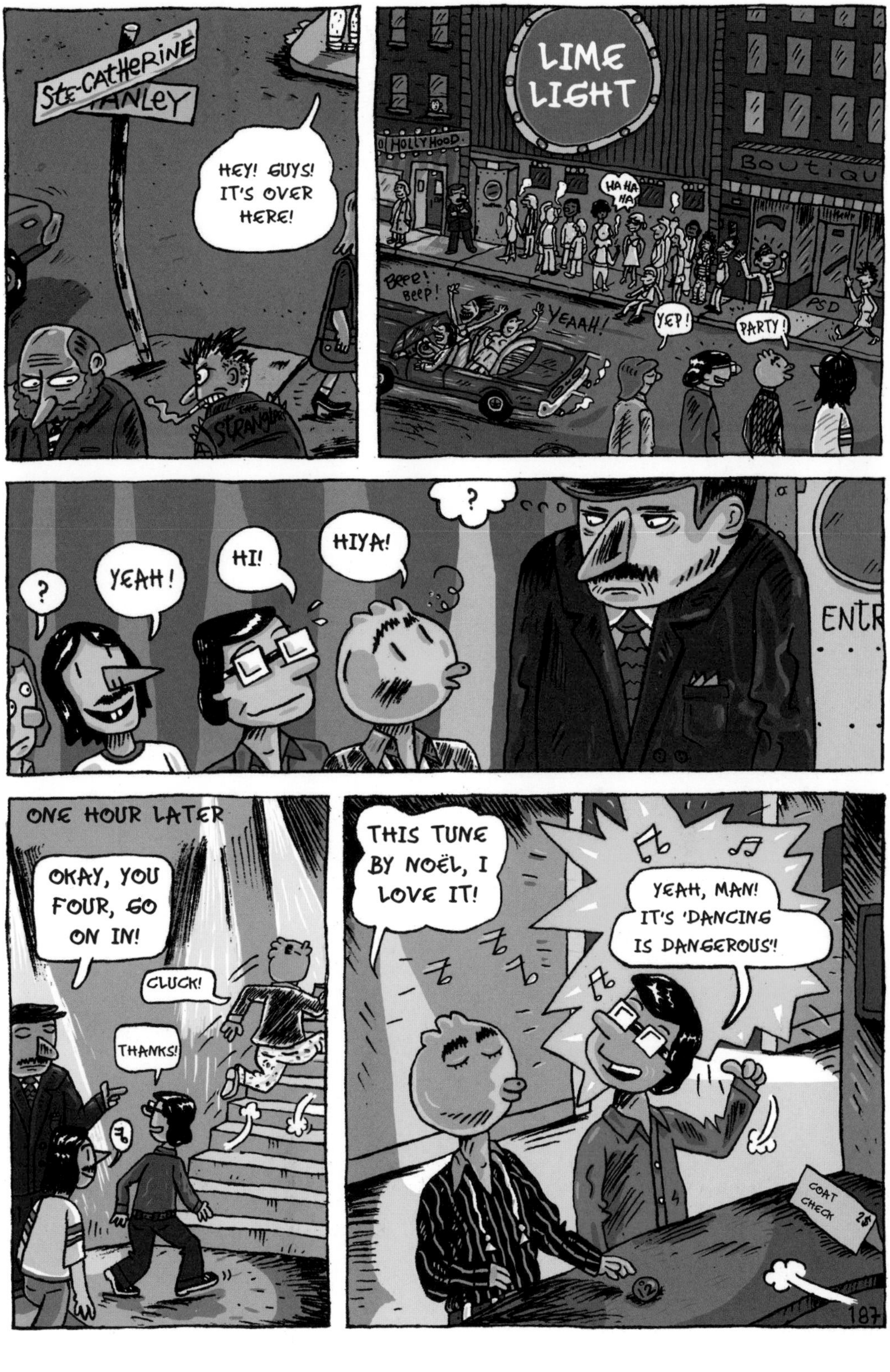
STE-CATHERINE
STANLEY
HEY! GUYS! IT'S OVER HERE!
THE STRANGLERS
LIME LIGHT
HOLLYHOOD
BOUTIQU
HA HA HA
BEEP! BEEP!
YEAAH!
YEP!
PARTY!
PSD
?
YEAH!
HI!
HIYA!
?
ENTR
ONE HOUR LATER
OKAY, YOU FOUR, GO ON IN!
CLUCK!
THANKS!
THIS TUNE BY NOËL, I LOVE IT!
YEAH, MAN! IT'S 'DANCING IS DANGEROUS'!
COAT CHECK 2$
187

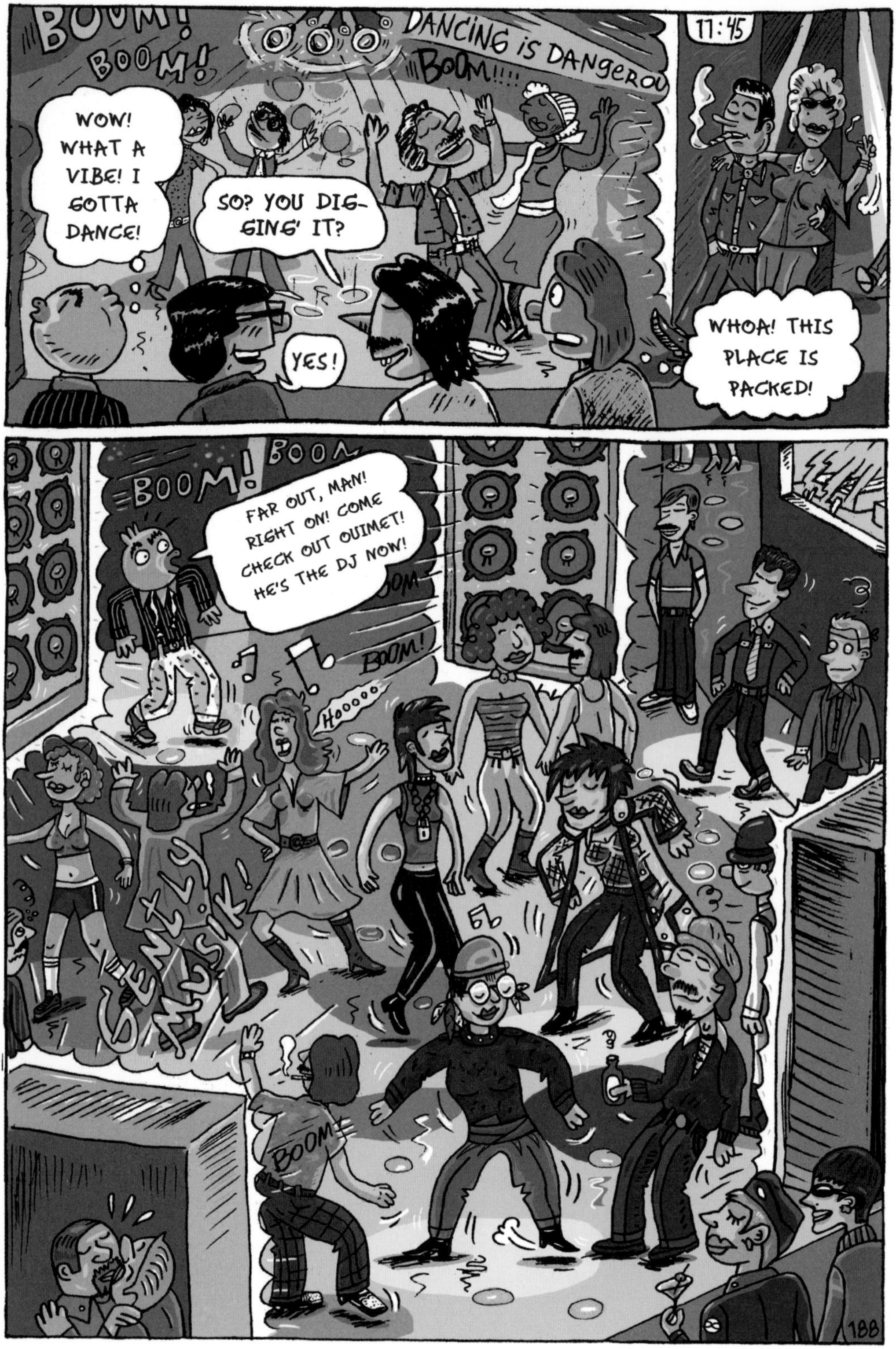

BOOM!
BOOM!
DANCING IS DANGEROU
BOOM!!!!
WOW! WHAT A VIBE! I GOTTA DANCE!
SO? YOU DIG-GING' IT?
YES!
11:45
WHOA! THIS PLACE IS PACKED!
BOOM!
BOOM
FAR OUT, MAN! RIGHT ON! COME CHECK OUT OUIMET! HE'S THE DJ NOW!
BOOM!
Hoooo
BOOM
188

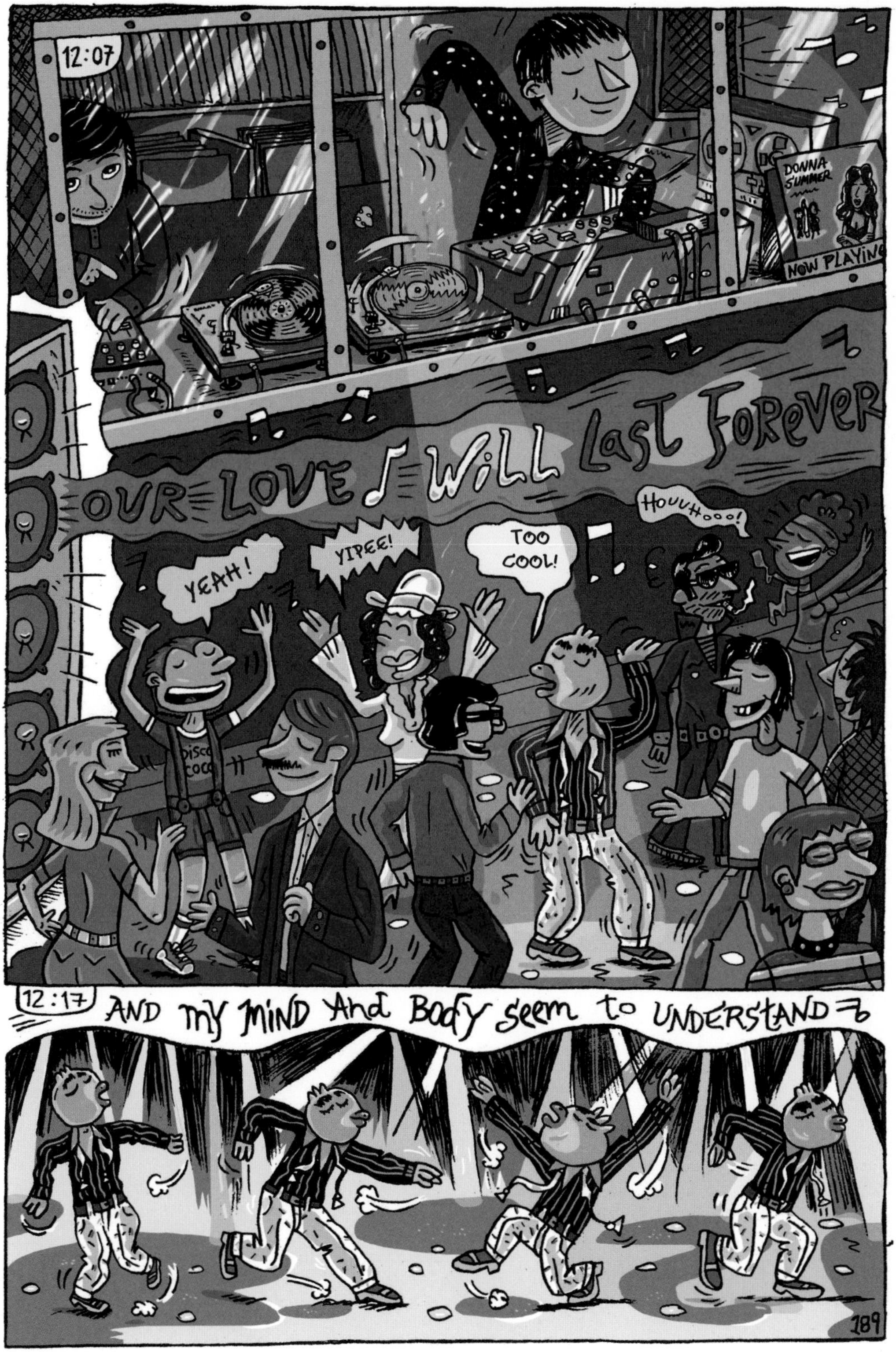
12:07
DONNA SUMMER
NOW PLAYING
OUR LOVE WILL LAST FOREVER
HOUUHOOO!
YEAH!
YIPEE!
TOO COOL!
DISCO COCO
12:17
AND MY MIND AND BODY SEEM TO UNDERSTAND
189

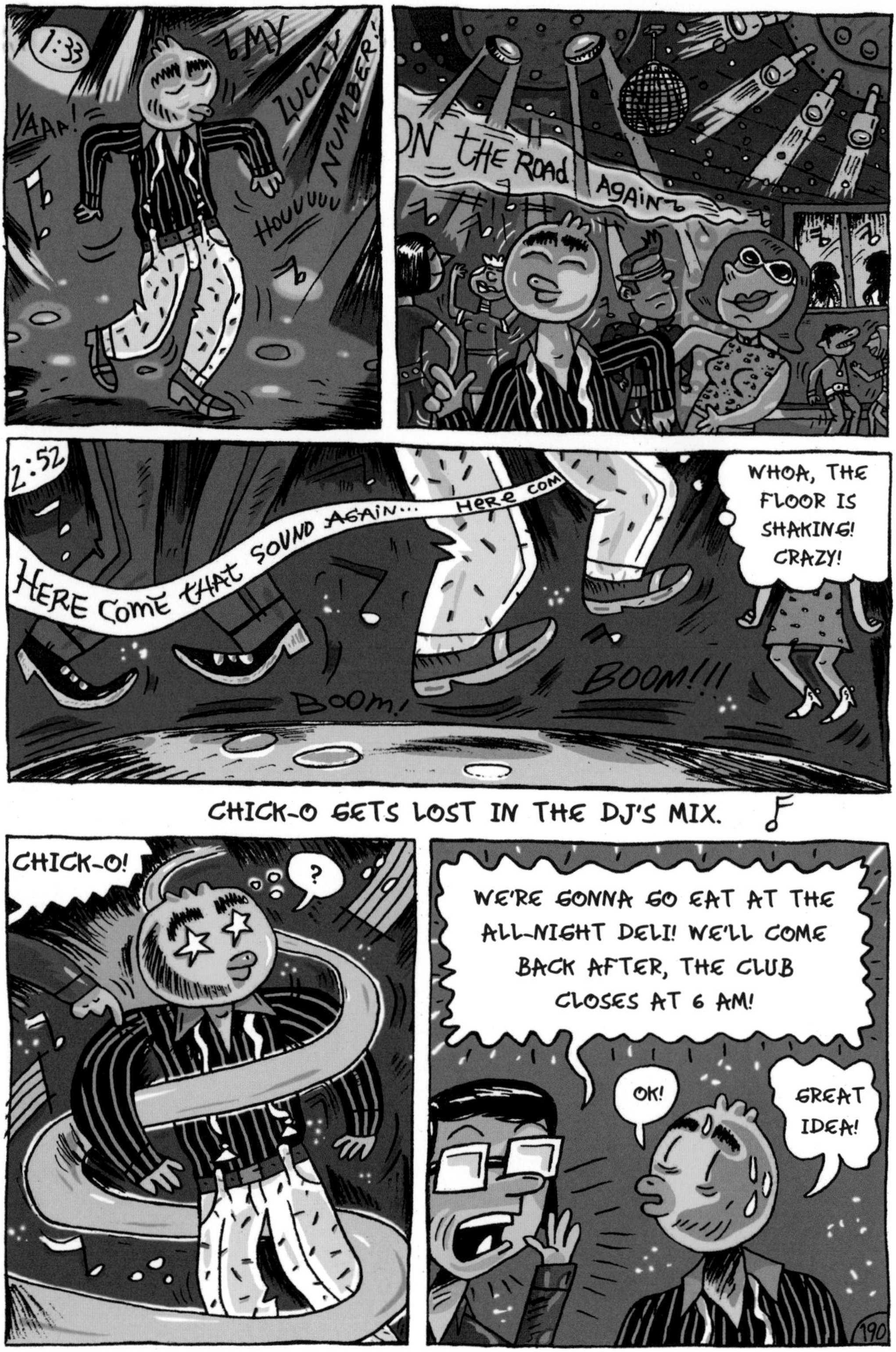
1:33
YAAA!
MY LUCKY NUMBER!
HOUUUUU
ON THE ROAD AGAIN
2:52
HERE COME THAT SOUND AGAIN... HERE COM
WHOA, THE FLOOR IS SHAKING! CRAZY!
BOOM!
BOOM!!!
CHICK-O GETS LOST IN THE DJ'S MIX.
CHICK-O!
?
WE'RE GONNA GO EAT AT THE ALL-NIGHT DELI! WE'LL COME BACK AFTER, THE CLUB CLOSES AT 6 AM!
OK!
GREAT IDEA!
190

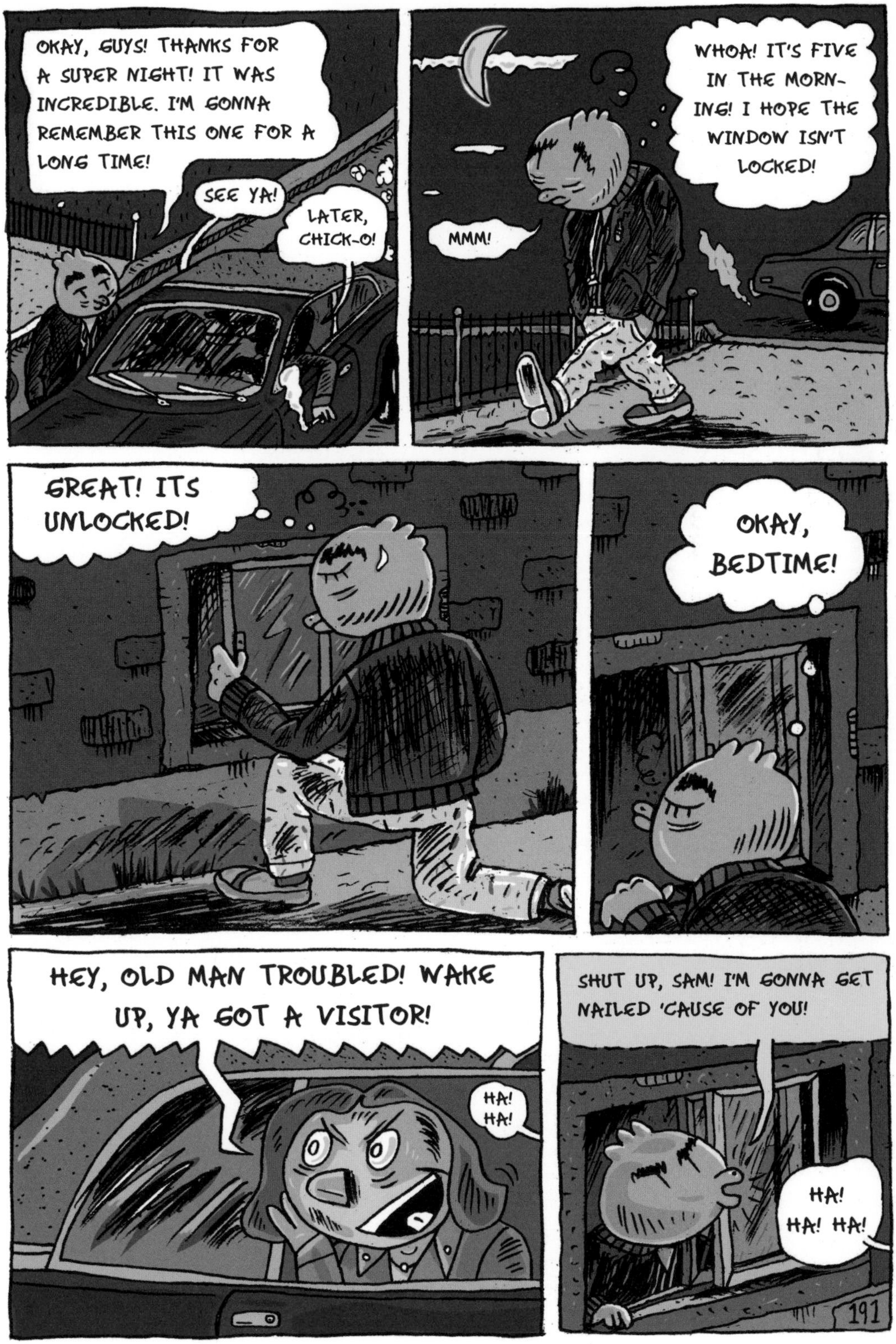
OKAY, GUYS! THANKS FOR A SUPER NIGHT! IT WAS INCREDIBLE. I'M GONNA REMEMBER THIS ONE FOR A LONG TIME!
SEE YA!
LATER, CHICK-O!
MMM!
WHOA! IT'S FIVE IN THE MORNING! I HOPE THE WINDOW ISN'T LOCKED!
GREAT! ITS UNLOCKED!
OKAY, BEDTIME!
HEY, OLD MAN TROUBLED! WAKE UP, YA GOT A VISITOR!
HA! HA!
SHUT UP, SAM! I'M GONNA GET NAILED 'CAUSE OF YOU!
HA! HA! HA!
191

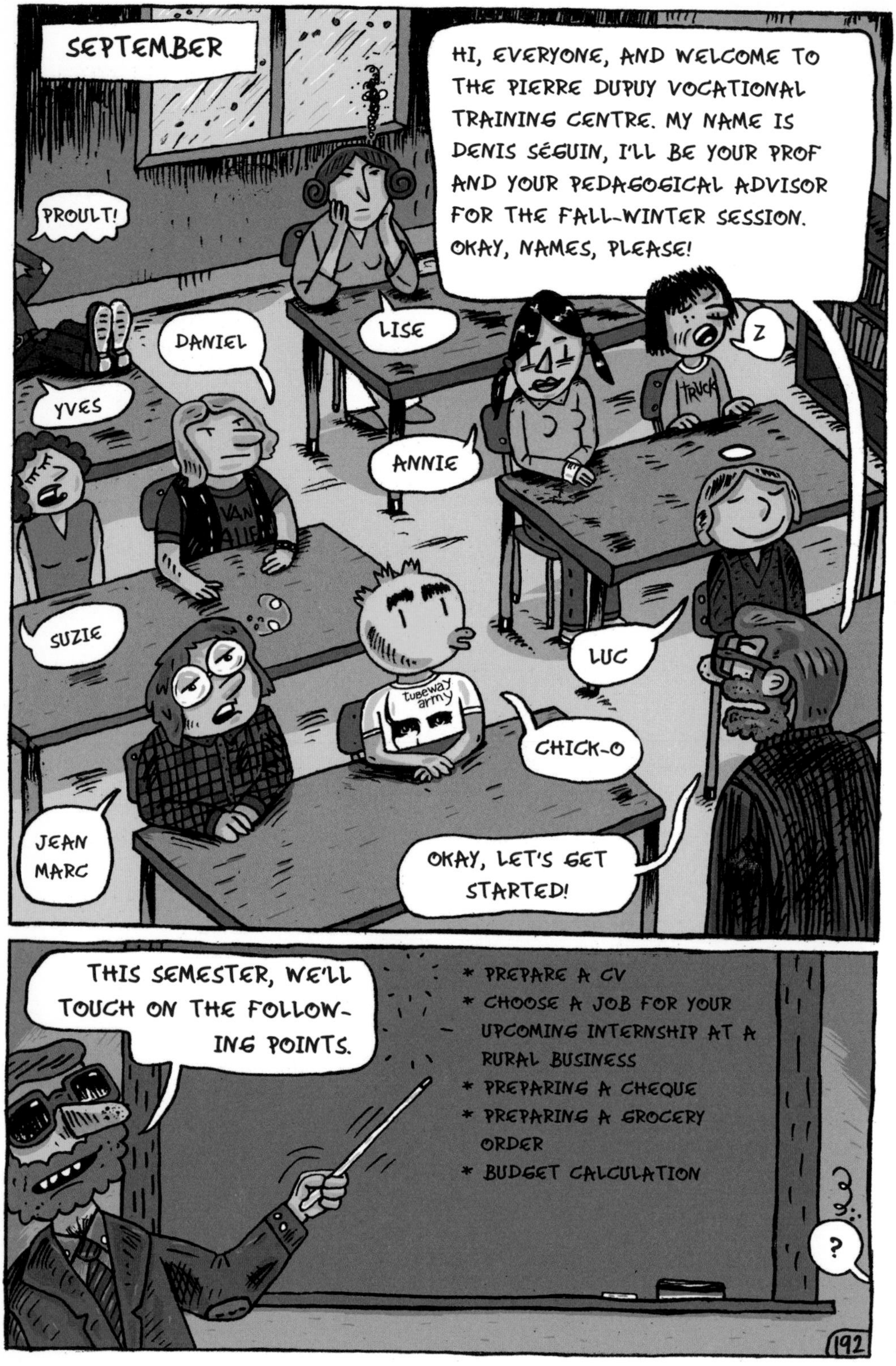
SEPTEMBER
HI, EVERYONE, AND WELCOME TO THE PIERRE DUPUY VOCATIONAL TRAINING CENTRE. MY NAME IS DENIS SÉGUIN, I'LL BE YOUR PROF AND YOUR PEDAGOGICAL ADVISOR FOR THE FALL-WINTER SESSION. OKAY, NAMES, PLEASE!
PROULT!
LISE
DANIEL
Z
YVES
ANNIE
SUZIE
LUC
CHICK-O
JEAN MARC
OKAY, LET'S GET STARTED!
VAN HALEN
TRUCK
tubeway army
THIS SEMESTER, WE'LL TOUCH ON THE FOLLOWING POINTS.
* PREPARE A CV
* CHOOSE A JOB FOR YOUR UPCOMING INTERNSHIP AT A RURAL BUSINESS
* PREPARING A CHEQUE
* PREPARING A GROCERY ORDER
* BUDGET CALCULATION
?
192

FIRST INTERNSHIP: DE MONTAGNE BREWERY IN BOUCHERVILLE

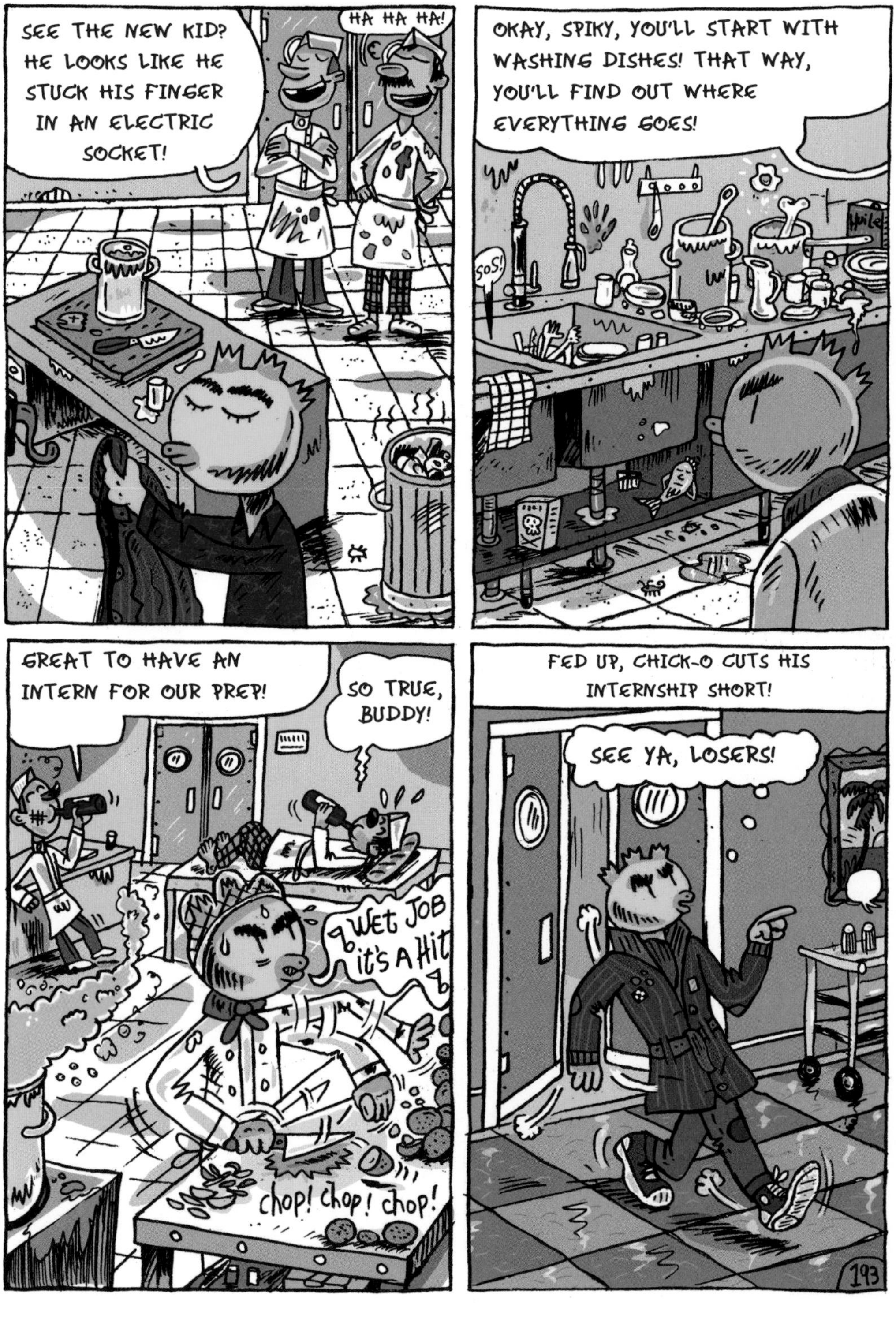
SEE THE NEW KID? HE LOOKS LIKE HE STUCK HIS FINGER IN AN ELECTRIC SOCKET!
HA HA HA!
SOS!
OKAY, SPIKY, YOU'LL START WITH WASHING DISHES! THAT WAY, YOU'LL FIND OUT WHERE EVERYTHING GOES!
GREAT TO HAVE AN INTERN FOR OUR PREP!
SO TRUE, BUDDY!
Wet JOB it's A Hit
chop! chop! chop!
FED UP, CHICK-O CUTS HIS INTERNSHIP SHORT!
SEE YA, LOSERS!
193

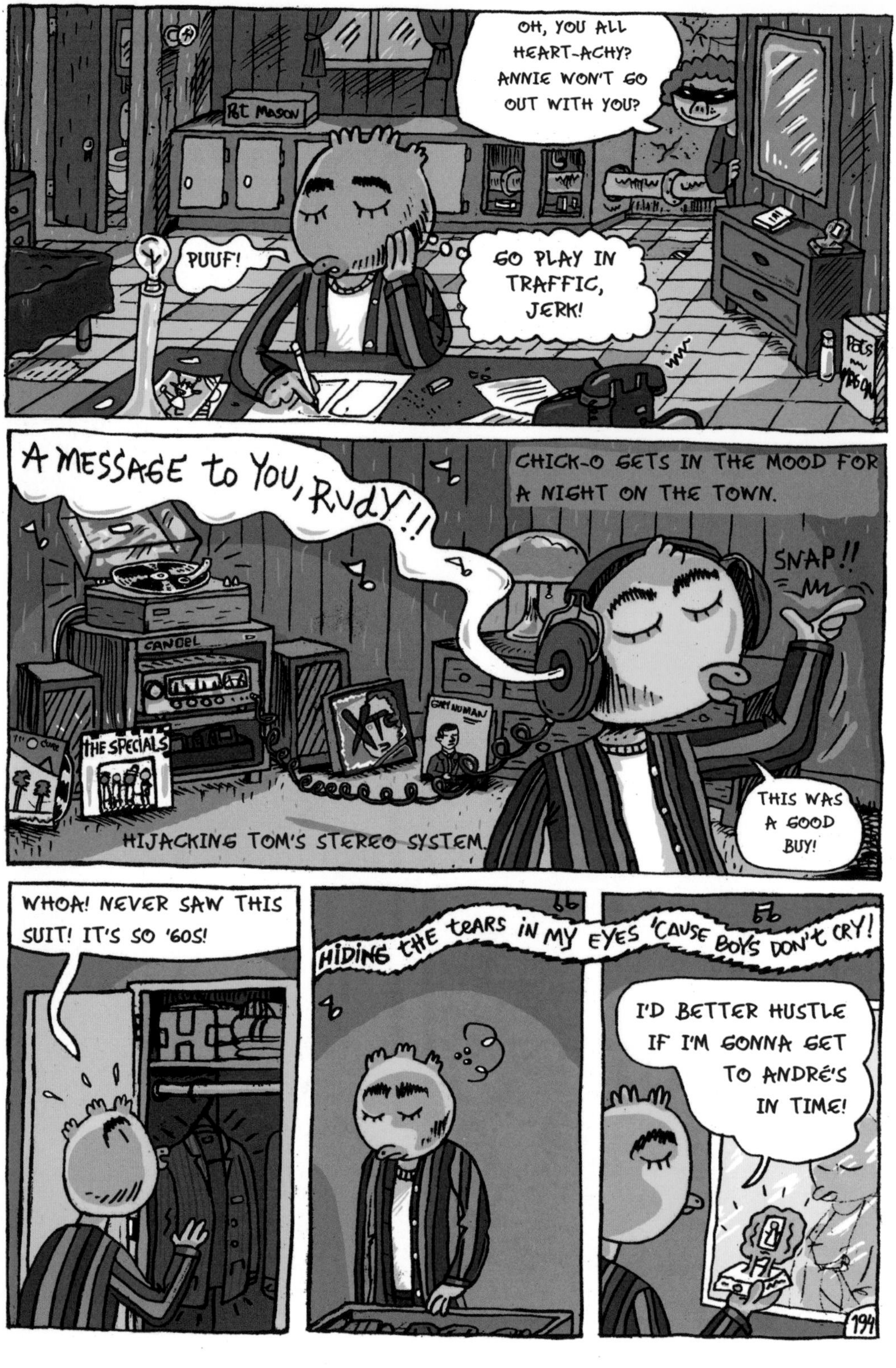
OH, YOU ALL HEART-ACHY? ANNIE WON'T GO OUT WITH YOU?
PUUF!
GO PLAY IN TRAFFIC, JERK!
A MESSAGE to YOU, RUDY!!
CHICK-O GETS IN THE MOOD FOR A NIGHT ON THE TOWN.
SNAP!!
THE SPECIALS
GARY NUMAN
HIJACKING TOM'S STEREO SYSTEM.
THIS WAS A GOOD BUY!
WHOA! NEVER SAW THIS SUIT! IT'S SO '60S!
HIDING THE TEARS IN MY EYES 'CAUSE BOYS DON'T CRY!
I'D BETTER HUSTLE IF I'M GONNA GET TO ANDRÉ'S IN TIME!
194

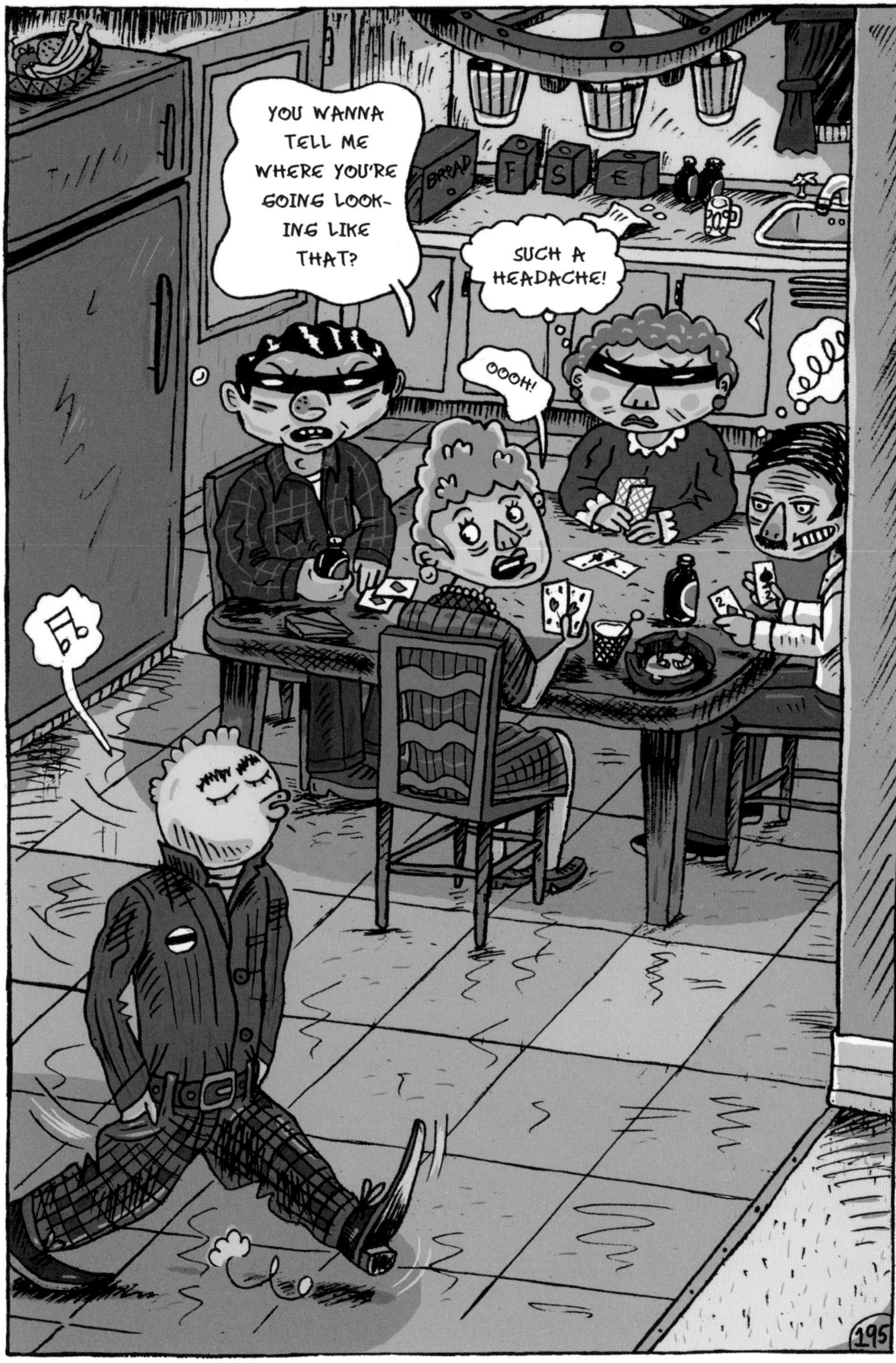
YOU WANNA TELL ME WHERE YOU'RE GOING LOOK-ING LIKE THAT?
SUCH A HEADACHE!
OOOH!
BREAD
F
S
E
195

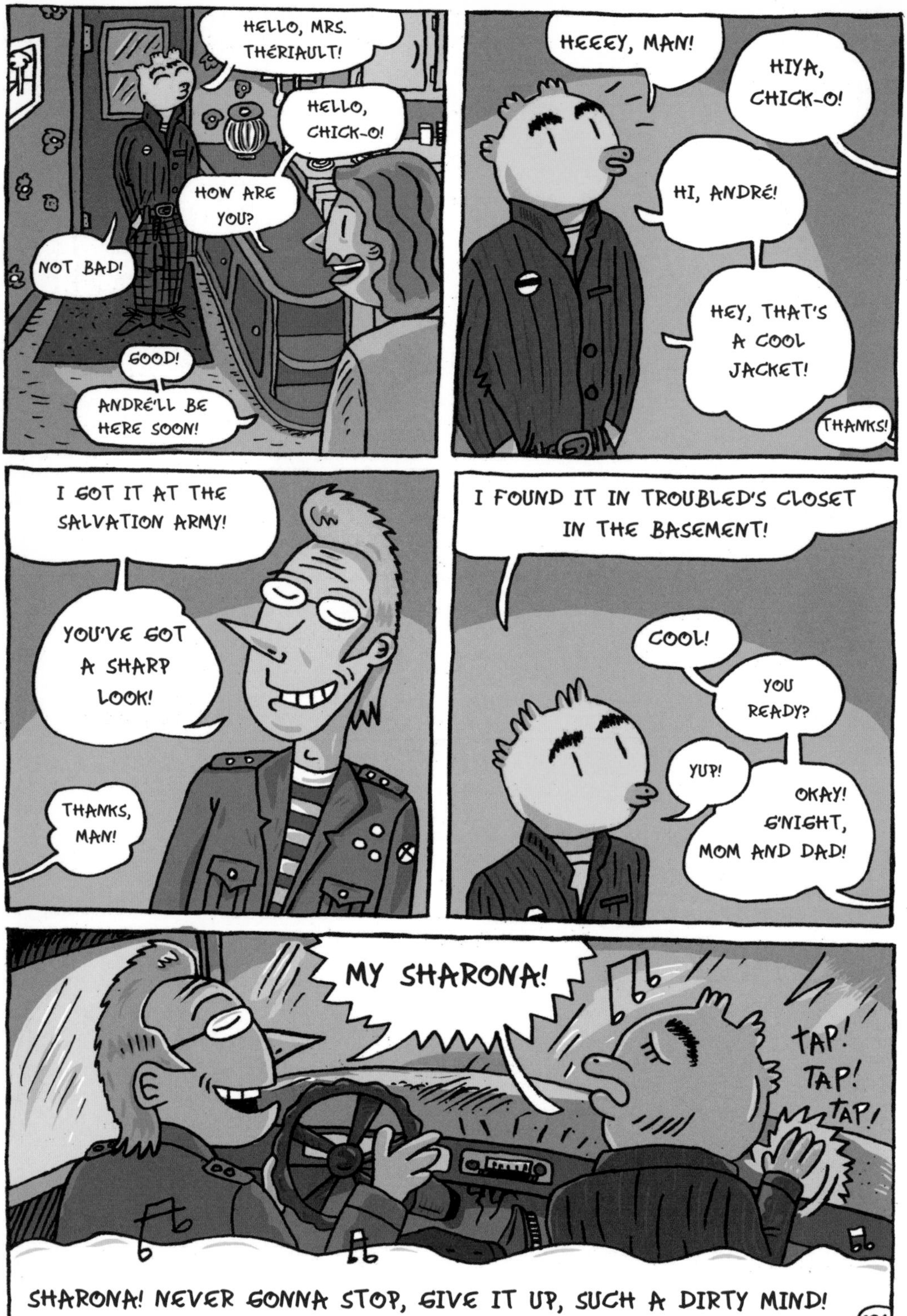
HELLO, MRS. THÉRIAULT!
HELLO, CHICK-O!
HOW ARE YOU?
NOT BAD!
GOOD!
ANDRÉ'LL BE HERE SOON!
HEEEY, MAN!
HIYA, CHICK-O!
HI, ANDRÉ!
HEY, THAT'S A COOL JACKET!
THANKS!
I GOT IT AT THE SALVATION ARMY!
YOU'VE GOT A SHARP LOOK!
THANKS, MAN!
I FOUND IT IN TROUBLED'S CLOSET IN THE BASEMENT!
COOL!
YOU READY?
YUP!
OKAY! G'NIGHT, MOM AND DAD!
MY SHARONA!
TAP! TAP! TAP!
SHARONA! NEVER GONNA STOP, GIVE IT UP, SUCH A DIRTY MIND!
196

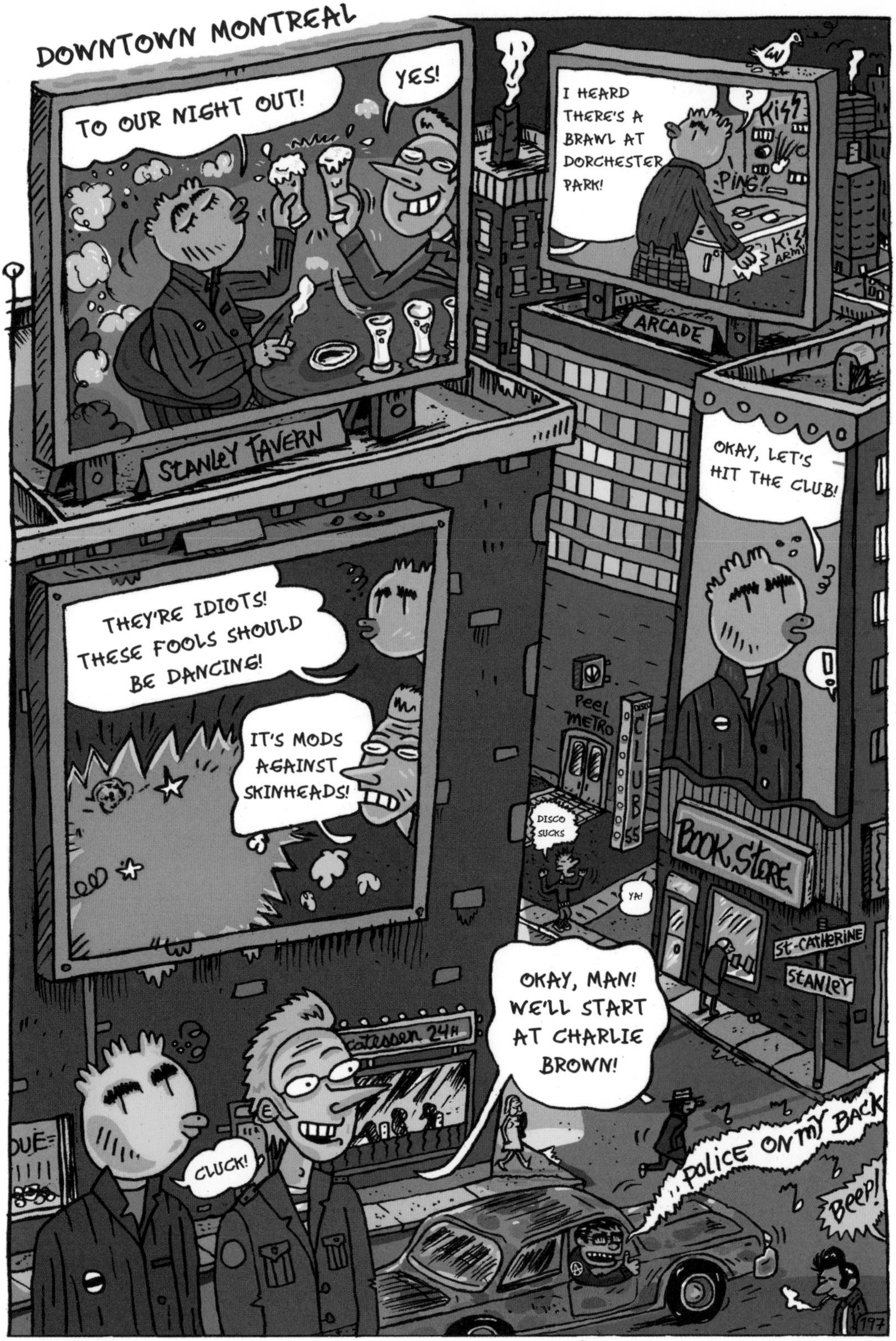
DOWNTOWN MONTREAL
TO OUR NIGHT OUT!
YES!
STANLEY TAVERN
I HEARD THERE'S A BRAWL AT DORCHESTER PARK!
?
KISS
PING!
KISS ARMY
ARCADE
OKAY, LET'S HIT THE CLUB!
THEY'RE IDIOTS! THESE FOOLS SHOULD BE DANCING!
IT'S MODS AGAINST SKINHEADS!
!
Peel METRO
DISCO CLUB 55
DISCO SUCKS
YA!
BOOK STORE
ST-CATHERINE
STANLEY
OKAY, MAN! WE'LL START AT CHARLIE BROWN!
CLUCK!
POLICE ON MY BACK
BEEP!

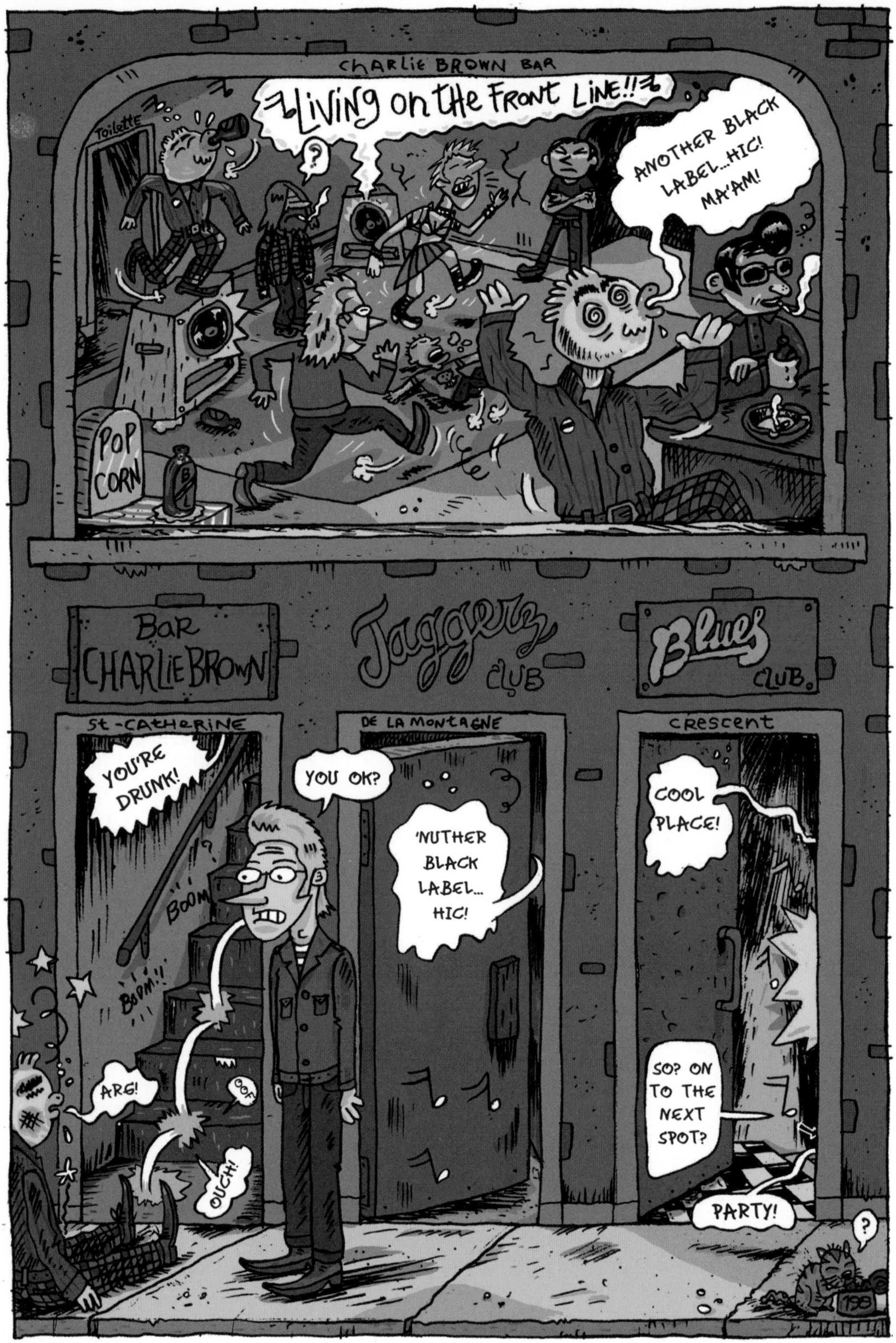
CHARLIE BROWN BAR
Toilette
LIVING ON THE FRONT LINE!!
?
ANOTHER BLACK LABEL...HIC! MA'AM!
POP CORN
BAR CHARLIE BROWN
Jaggerz CLUB
Blues CLUB
St-CATHERINE
DE LA MONTAGNE
CRESCENT
YOU'RE DRUNK!
YOU OK?
'NUTHER BLACK LABEL... HIC!
COOL PLACE!
BOOM
BADM!!
ARG!
OOF
OUCH!
SO? ON TO THE NEXT SPOT?
PARTY!
?

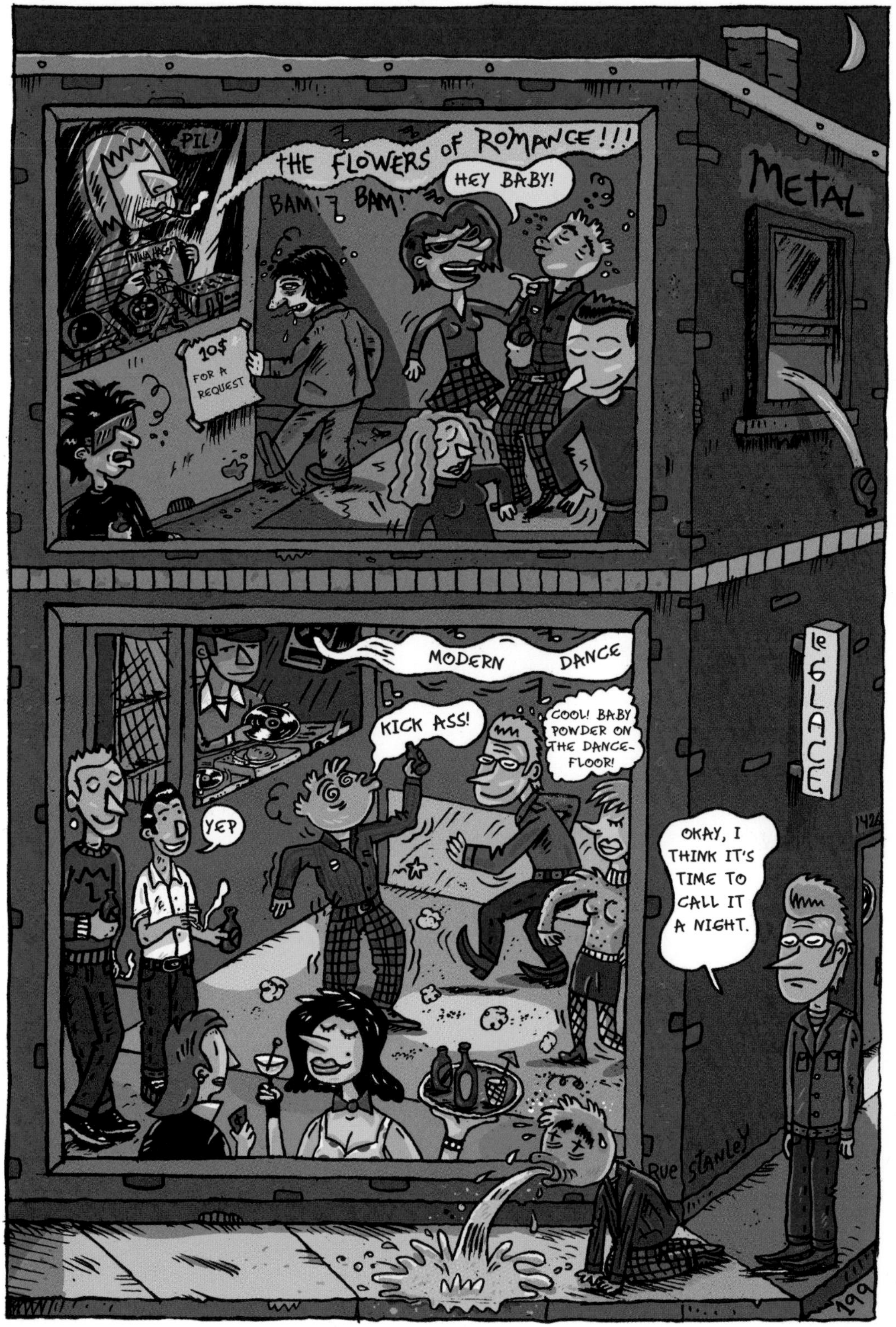
PIL!
NINA HAGEN
THE FLOWERS OF ROMANCE!!!
BAM! BAM!
HEY BABY!
METAL
10$ FOR A REQUEST
MODERN DANCE
KICK ASS!
COOL! BABY POWDER ON THE DANCE-FLOOR!
YEP
le GLACE
OKAY, I THINK IT'S TIME TO CALL IT A NIGHT.
RUE STANLEY

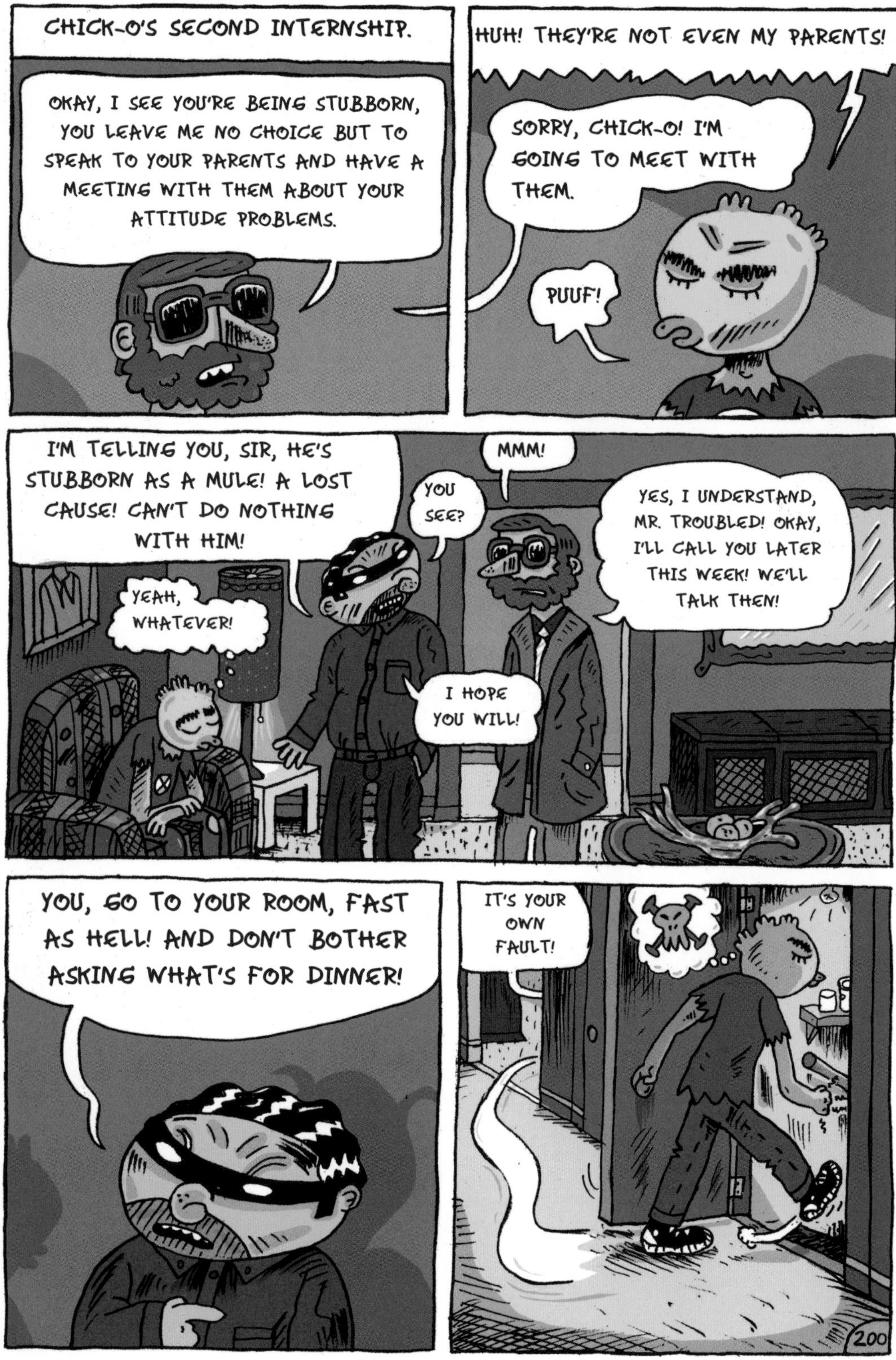
CHICK-O'S SECOND INTERNSHIP.
OKAY, I SEE YOU'RE BEING STUBBORN, YOU LEAVE ME NO CHOICE BUT TO SPEAK TO YOUR PARENTS AND HAVE A MEETING WITH THEM ABOUT YOUR ATTITUDE PROBLEMS.
HUH! THEY'RE NOT EVEN MY PARENTS!
SORRY, CHICK-O! I'M GOING TO MEET WITH THEM.
PUUF!
I'M TELLING YOU, SIR, HE'S STUBBORN AS A MULE! A LOST CAUSE! CAN'T DO NOTHING WITH HIM!
YOU SEE?
MMM!
YES, I UNDERSTAND, MR. TROUBLED! OKAY, I'LL CALL YOU LATER THIS WEEK! WE'LL TALK THEN!
YEAH, WHATEVER!
I HOPE YOU WILL!
YOU, GO TO YOUR ROOM, FAST AS HELL! AND DON'T BOTHER ASKING WHAT'S FOR DINNER!
IT'S YOUR OWN FAULT!
200

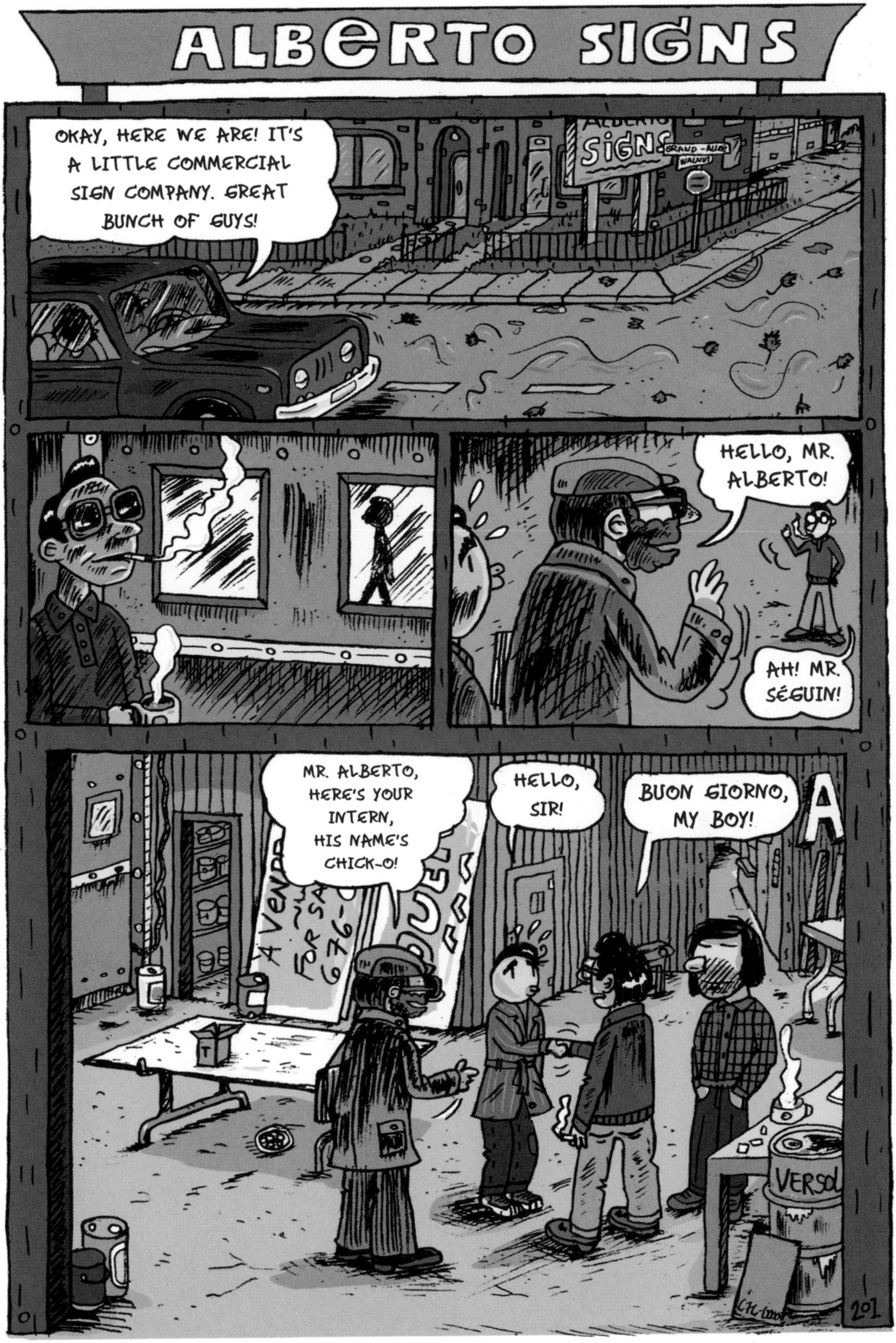
ALBERTO SIGNS
OKAY, HERE WE ARE! IT'S A LITTLE COMMERCIAL SIGN COMPANY. GREAT BUNCH OF GUYS!
HELLO, MR. ALBERTO!
AH! MR. SÉGUIN!
MR. ALBERTO, HERE'S YOUR INTERN, HIS NAME'S CHICK-O!
HELLO, SIR!
BUON GIORNO, MY BOY!
VERSOL
207

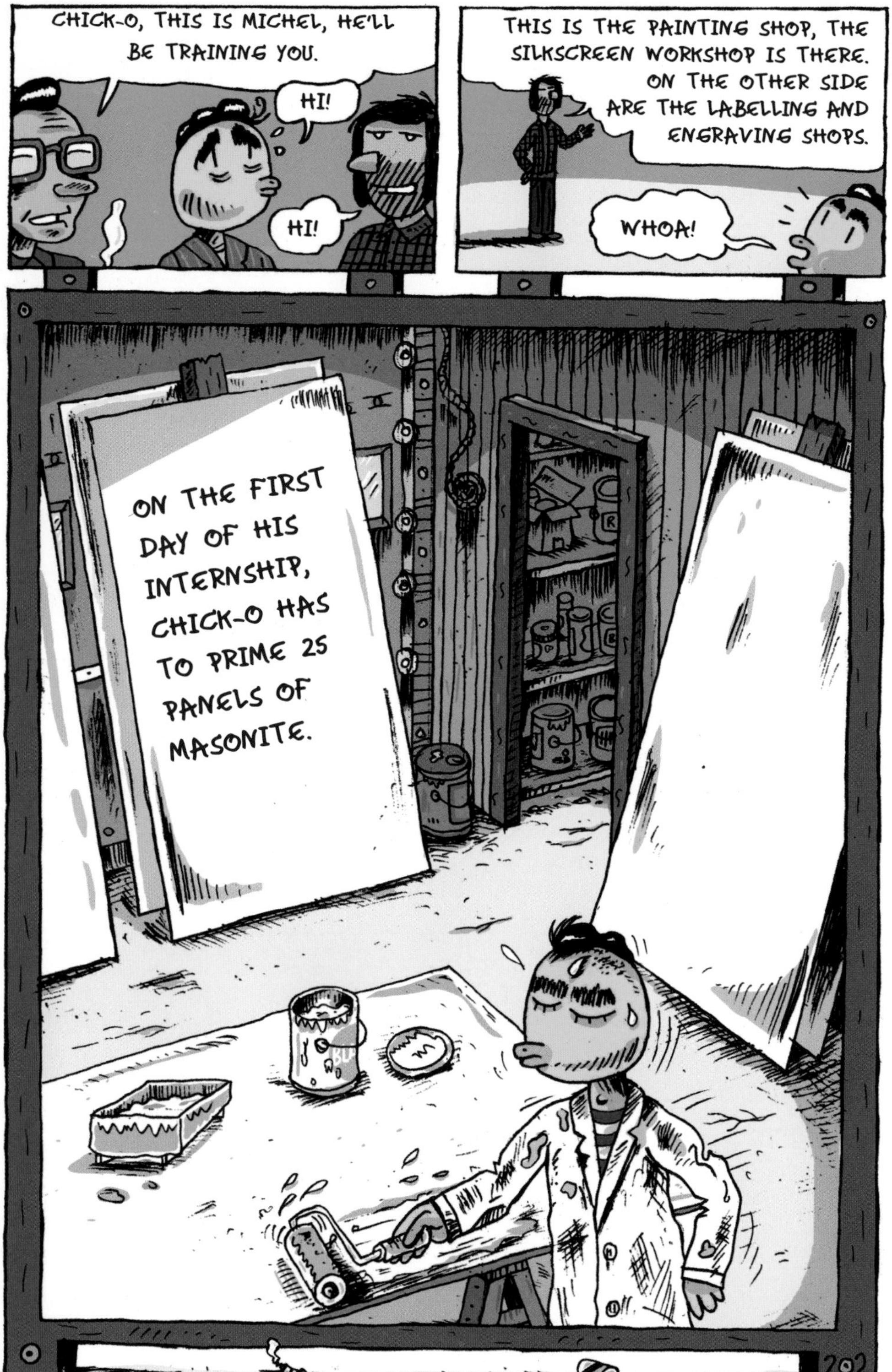
CHICK-O, THIS IS MICHEL, HE'LL BE TRAINING YOU.
HI!
HI!
THIS IS THE PAINTING SHOP, THE SILKSCREEN WORKSHOP IS THERE. ON THE OTHER SIDE ARE THE LABELLING AND ENGRAVING SHOPS.
WHOA!
ON THE FIRST DAY OF HIS INTERNSHIP, CHICK-O HAS TO PRIME 25 PANELS OF MASONITE.
202

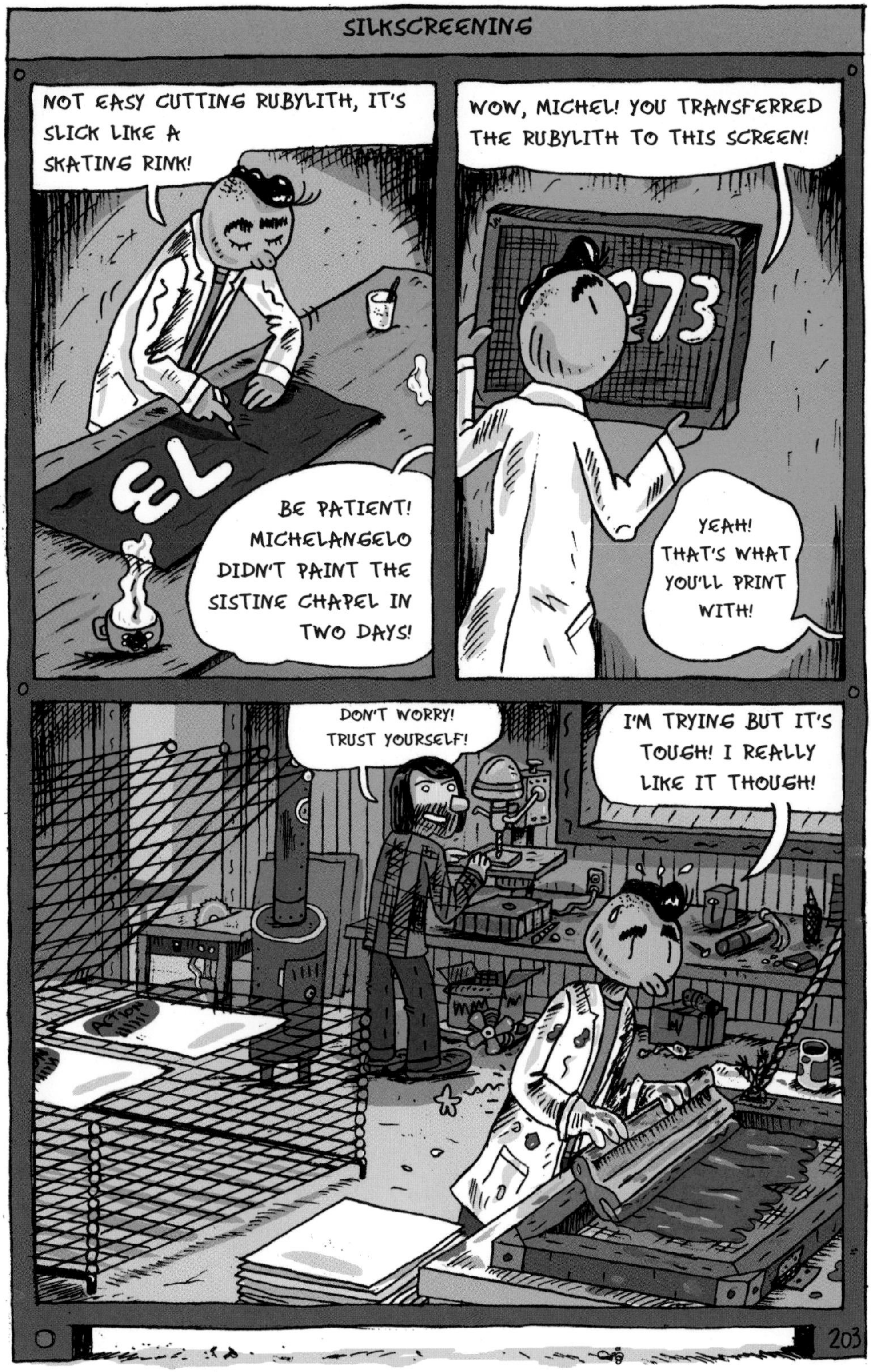
SILKSCREENING
NOT EASY CUTTING RUBYLITH, IT'S SLICK LIKE A SKATING RINK!
BE PATIENT! MICHELANGELO DIDN'T PAINT THE SISTINE CHAPEL IN TWO DAYS!
WOW, MICHEL! YOU TRANSFERRED THE RUBYLITH TO THIS SCREEN!
YEAH! THAT'S WHAT YOU'LL PRINT WITH!
DON'T WORRY! TRUST YOURSELF!
I'M TRYING BUT IT'S TOUGH! I REALLY LIKE IT THOUGH!
203

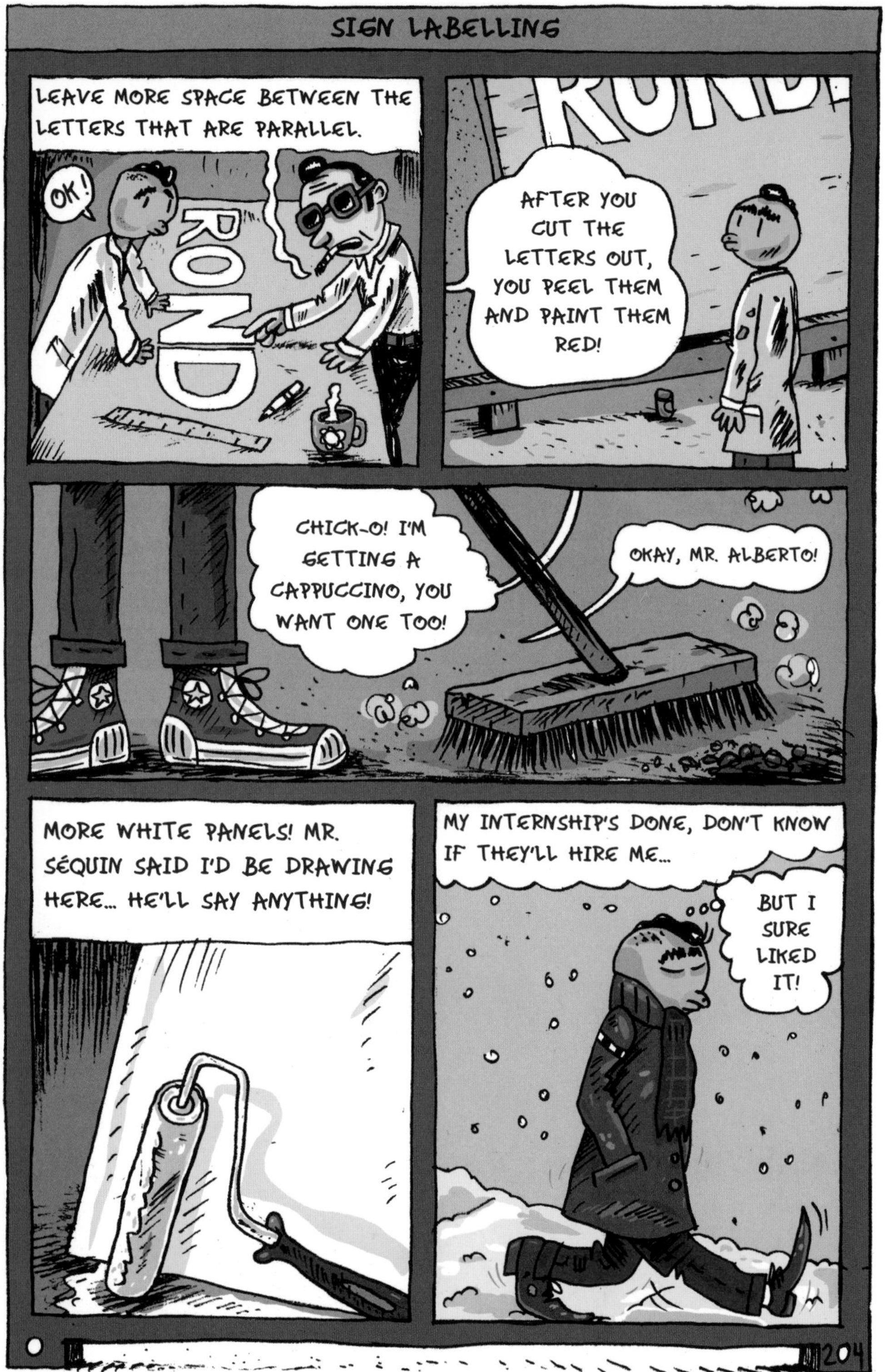
SIGN LABELLING
LEAVE MORE SPACE BETWEEN THE LETTERS THAT ARE PARALLEL.
OK!
ROND
AFTER YOU CUT THE LETTERS OUT, YOU PEEL THEM AND PAINT THEM RED!
CHICK-O! I'M GETTING A CAPPUCCINO, YOU WANT ONE TOO!
OKAY, MR. ALBERTO!
MORE WHITE PANELS! MR. SÉQUIN SAID I'D BE DRAWING HERE... HE'LL SAY ANYTHING!
MY INTERNSHIP'S DONE, DON'T KNOW IF THEY'LL HIRE ME...
BUT I SURE LIKED IT!
204

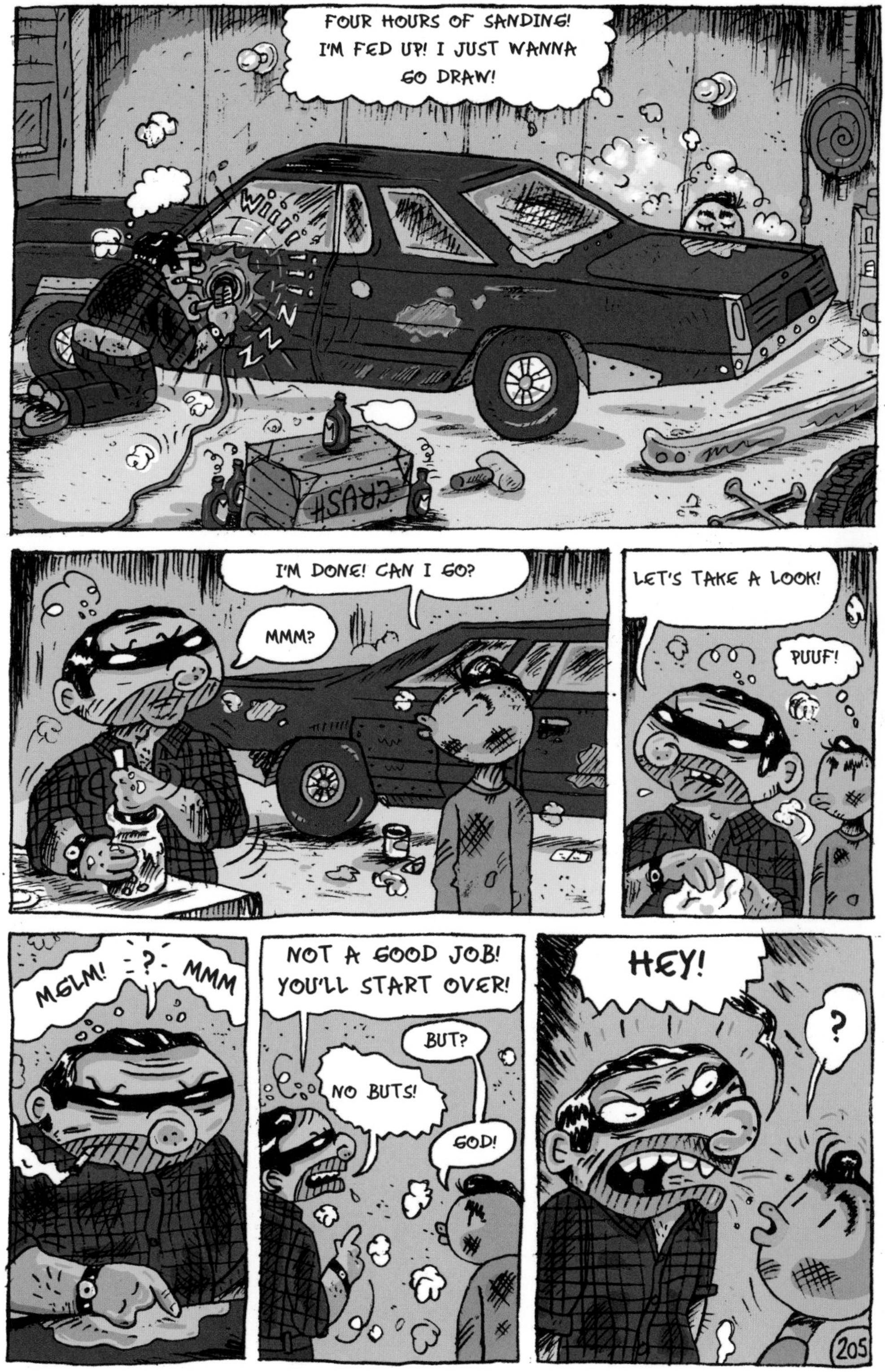

FOUR HOURS OF SANDING! I'M FED UP! I JUST WANNA GO DRAW!
WIIII!
ZZZ
CRUSH
I'M DONE! CAN I GO?
MMM?
LET'S TAKE A LOOK!
PUUF!
MELM!
?
MMM
NOT A GOOD JOB! YOU'LL START OVER!
BUT?
NO BUTS!
GOD!
HEY!
?
205

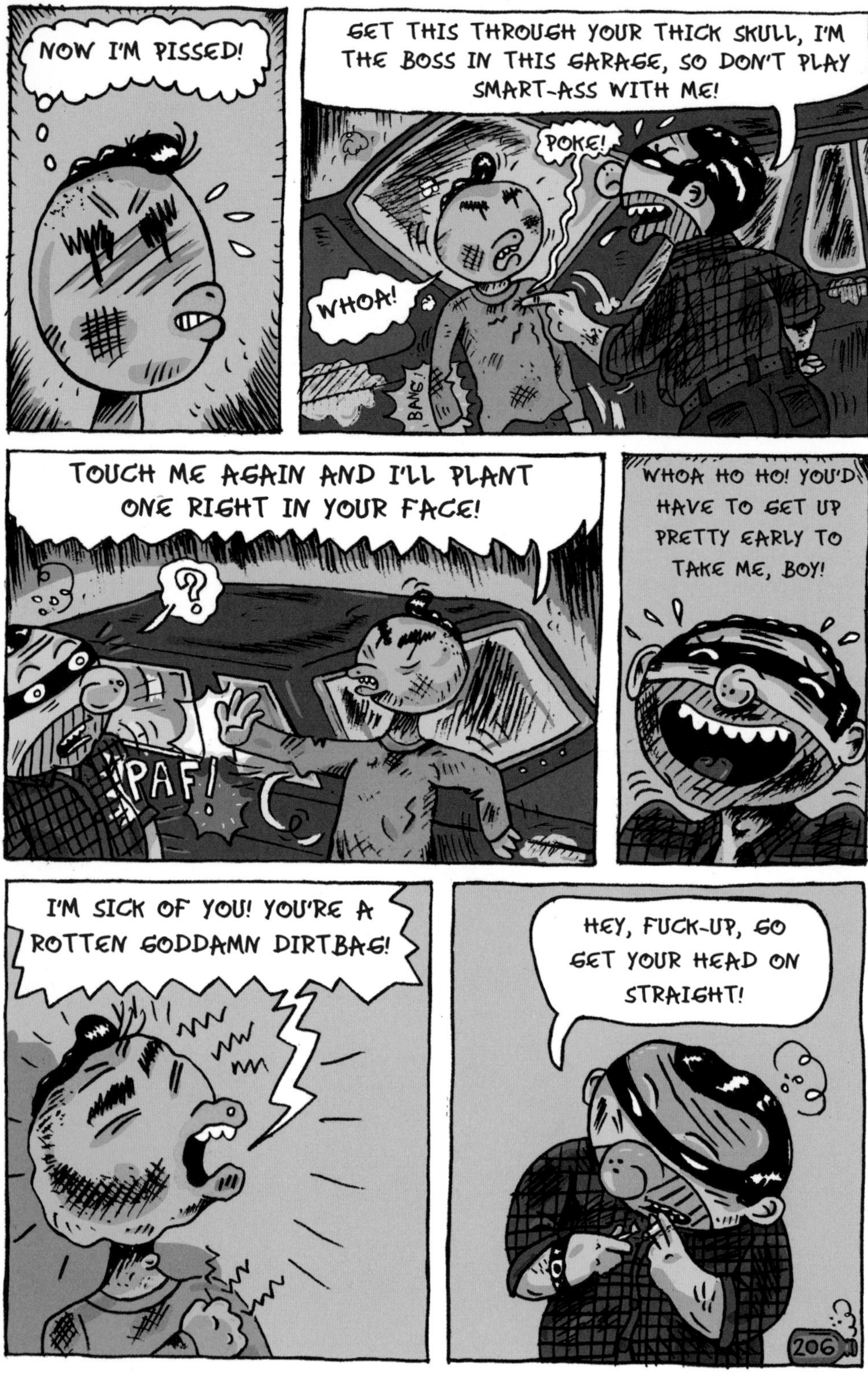
NOW I'M PISSED!
GET THIS THROUGH YOUR THICK SKULL, I'M THE BOSS IN THIS GARAGE, SO DON'T PLAY SMART-ASS WITH ME!
POKE!
WHOA!
BANG!
TOUCH ME AGAIN AND I'LL PLANT ONE RIGHT IN YOUR FACE!
?
PAF!
WHOA HO HO! YOU'D HAVE TO GET UP PRETTY EARLY TO TAKE ME, BOY!
I'M SICK OF YOU! YOU'RE A ROTTEN GODDAMN DIRTBAG!
HEY, FUCK-UP, GO GET YOUR HEAD ON STRAIGHT!
206

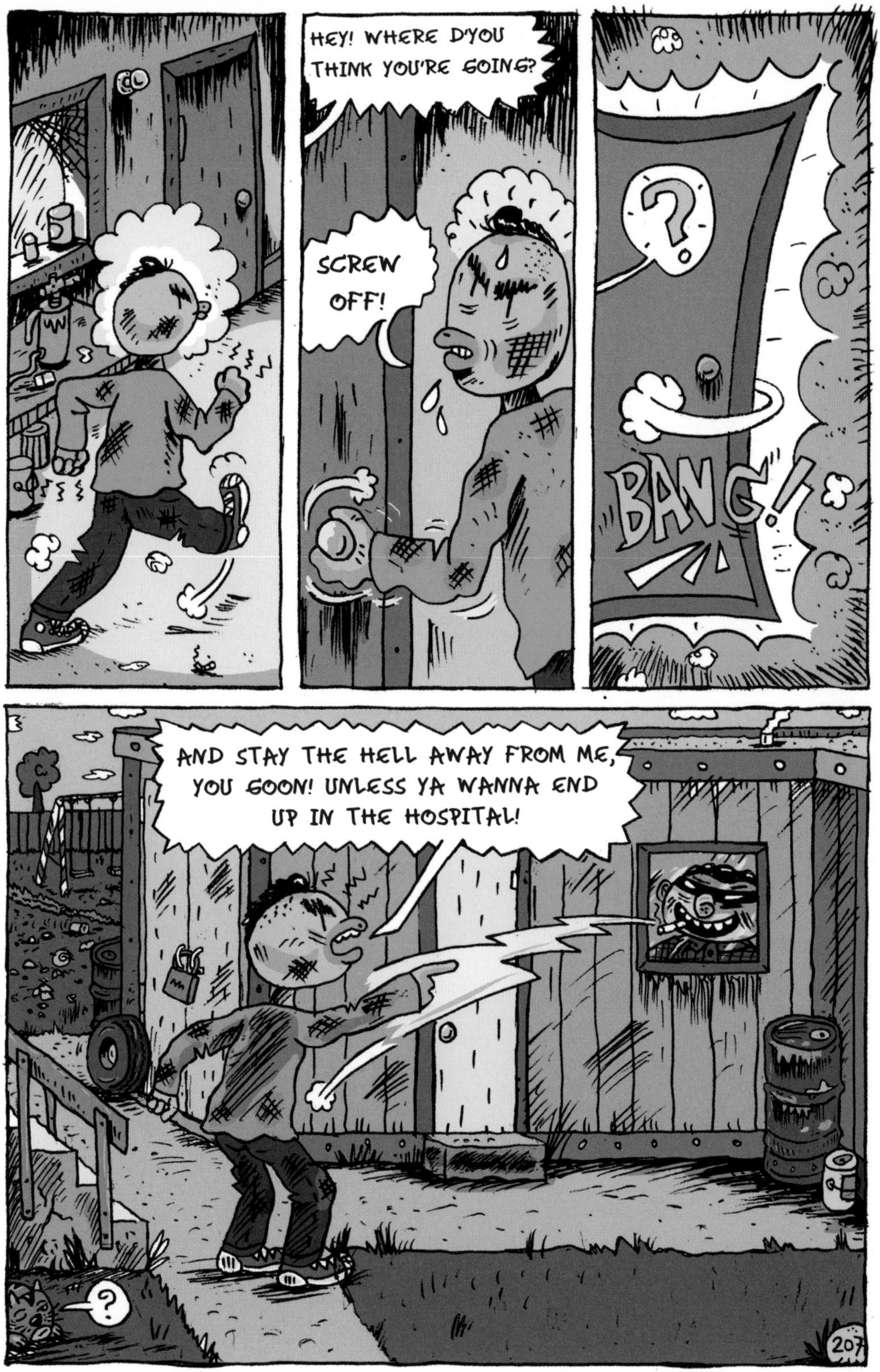
HEY! WHERE D'YOU THINK YOU'RE GOING?
SCREW OFF!
?
BANG!
AND STAY THE HELL AWAY FROM ME, YOU GOON! UNLESS YA WANNA END UP IN THE HOSPITAL!
?
207

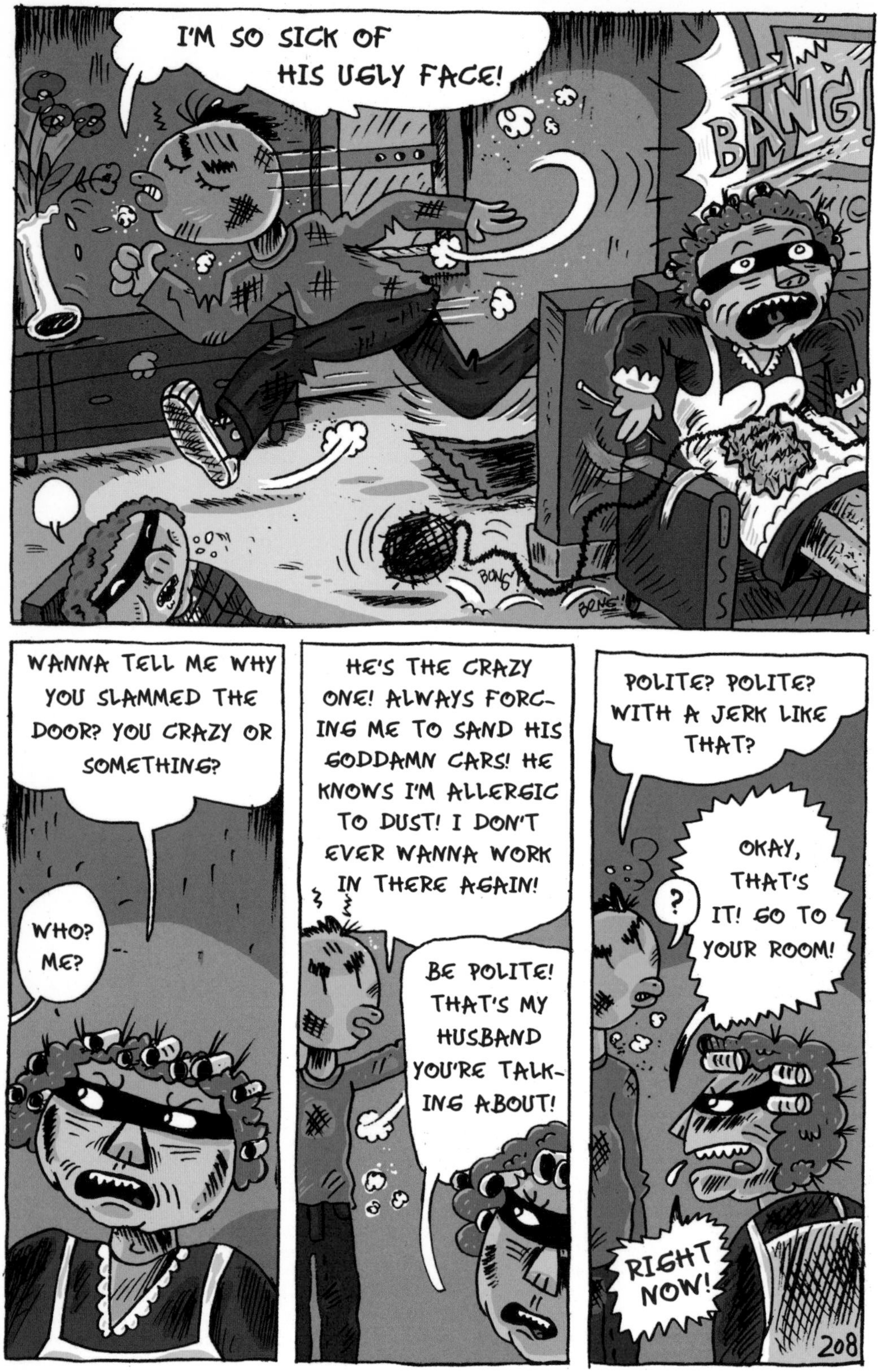
I'M SO SICK OF HIS UGLY FACE!
BANG!
BONG!
BONG!
WANNA TELL ME WHY YOU SLAMMED THE DOOR? YOU CRAZY OR SOMETHING?
WHO? ME?
HE'S THE CRAZY ONE! ALWAYS FORCING ME TO SAND HIS GODDAMN CARS! HE KNOWS I'M ALLERGIC TO DUST! I DON'T EVER WANNA WORK IN THERE AGAIN!
BE POLITE! THAT'S MY HUSBAND YOU'RE TALKING ABOUT!
POLITE? POLITE? WITH A JERK LIKE THAT?
?
OKAY, THAT'S IT! GO TO YOUR ROOM!
RIGHT NOW!
208

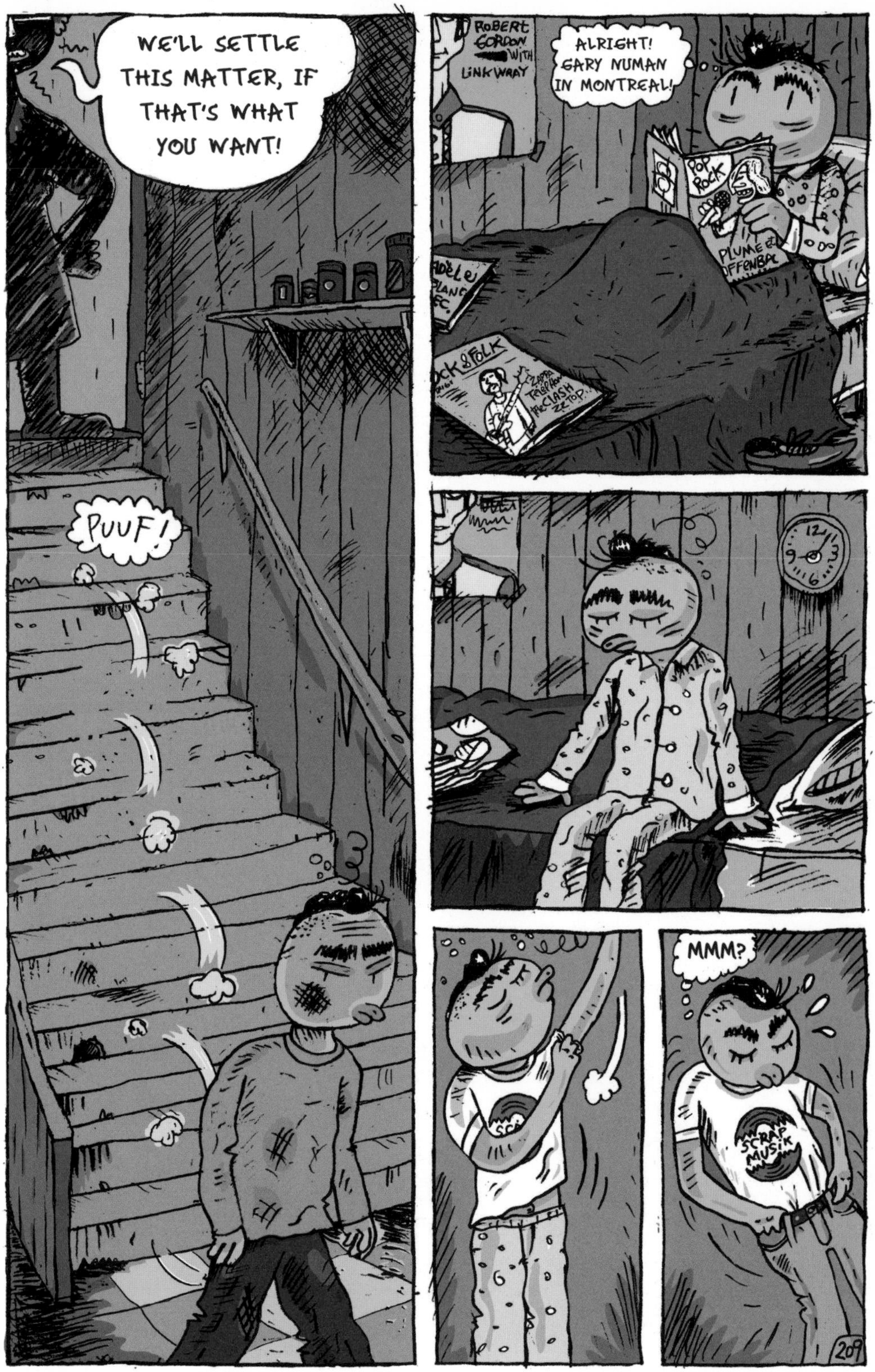
WE'LL SETTLE THIS MATTER, IF THAT'S WHAT YOU WANT!
PUUF!
ROBERT GORDON WITH LINK WRAY
ALRIGHT! GARY NUMAN IN MONTREAL!
POP ROCK
MMM?
SCRAP MUSIK
209

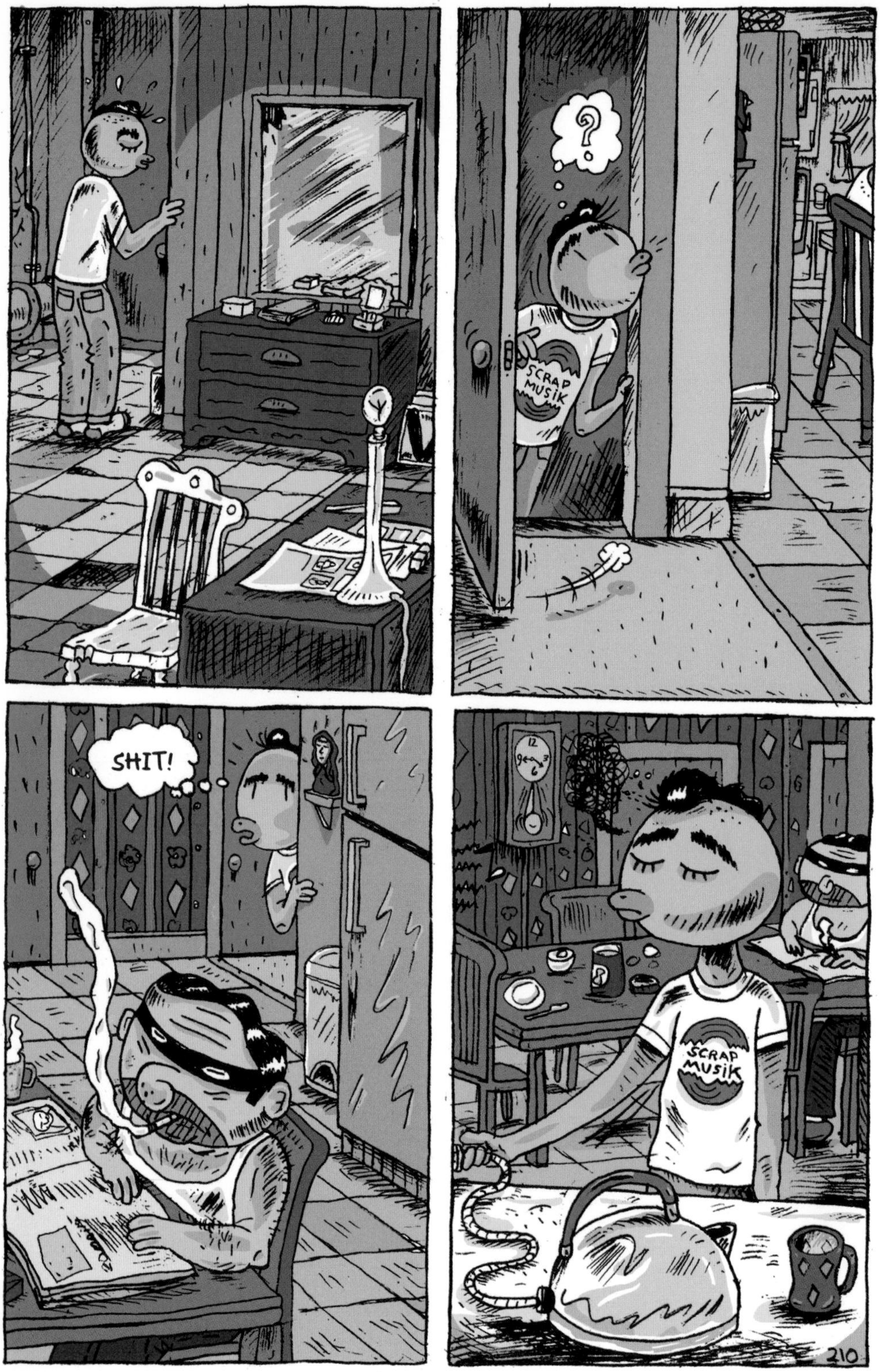
?
SCRAP MUSIK
SHIT!
12
9
3
6
SCRAP MUSIK
210

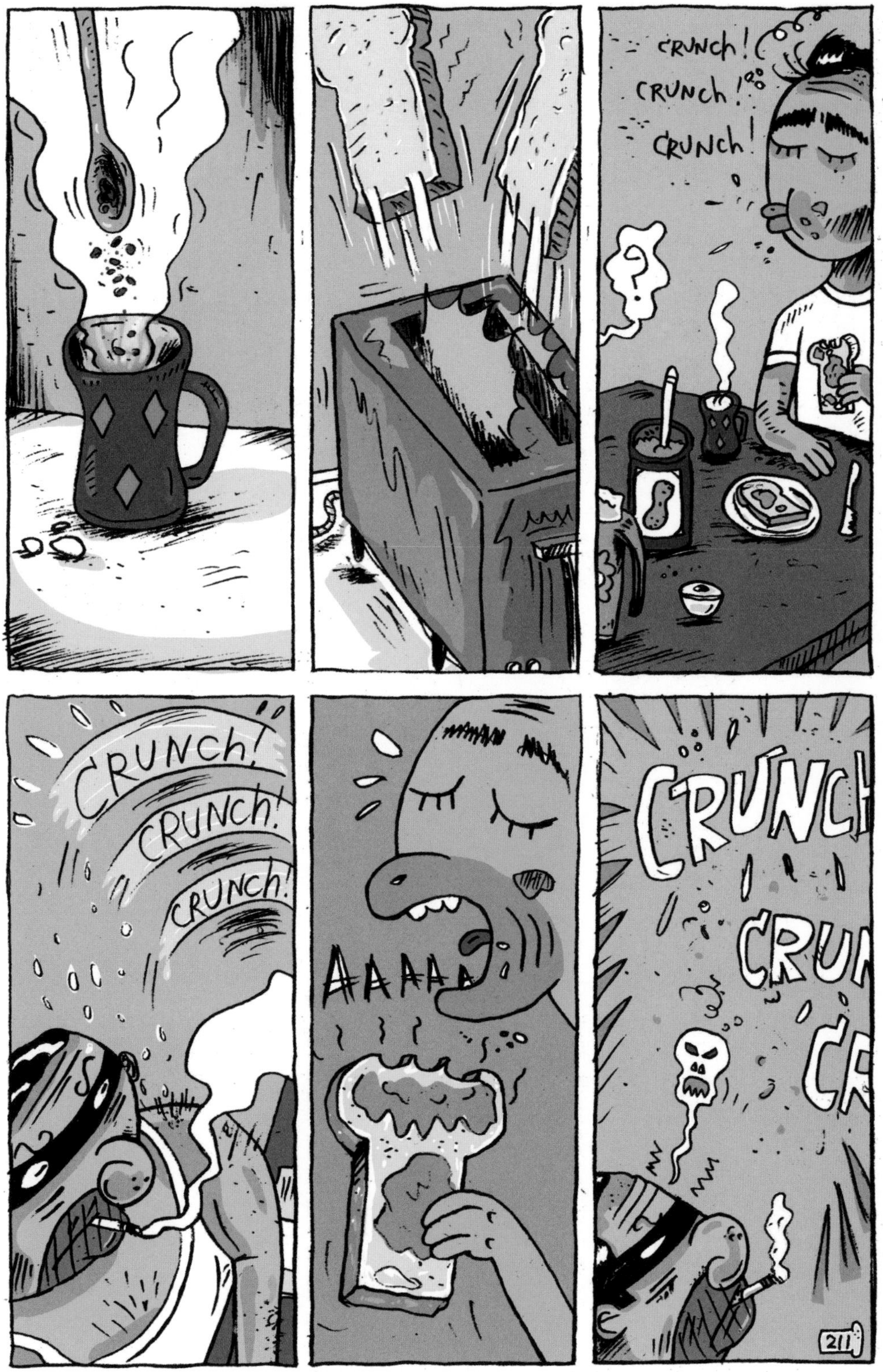
CRUNCH!
CRUNCH!
CRUNCH!
?
CRUNCH!
CRUNCH!
CRUNCH!
AAAAA
CRUNCH
CRUN
CR
211

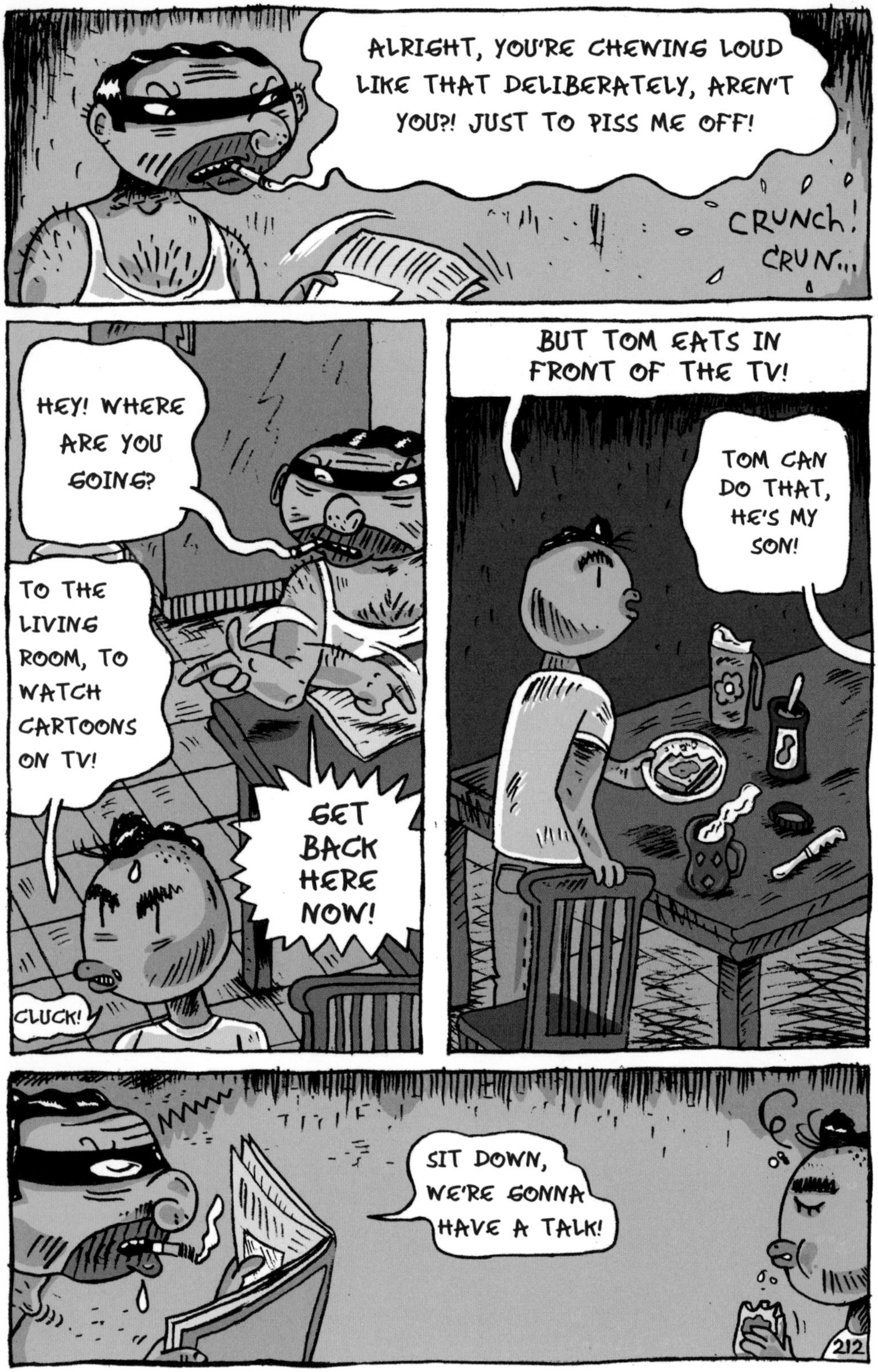
ALRIGHT, YOU'RE CHEWING LOUD LIKE THAT DELIBERATELY, AREN'T YOU?! JUST TO PISS ME OFF!
CRUNCH! CRUN...
HEY! WHERE ARE YOU GOING?
TO THE LIVING ROOM, TO WATCH CARTOONS ON TV!
GET BACK HERE NOW!
CLUCK!
BUT TOM EATS IN FRONT OF THE TV!
TOM CAN DO THAT, HE'S MY SON!
SIT DOWN, WE'RE GONNA HAVE A TALK!
212

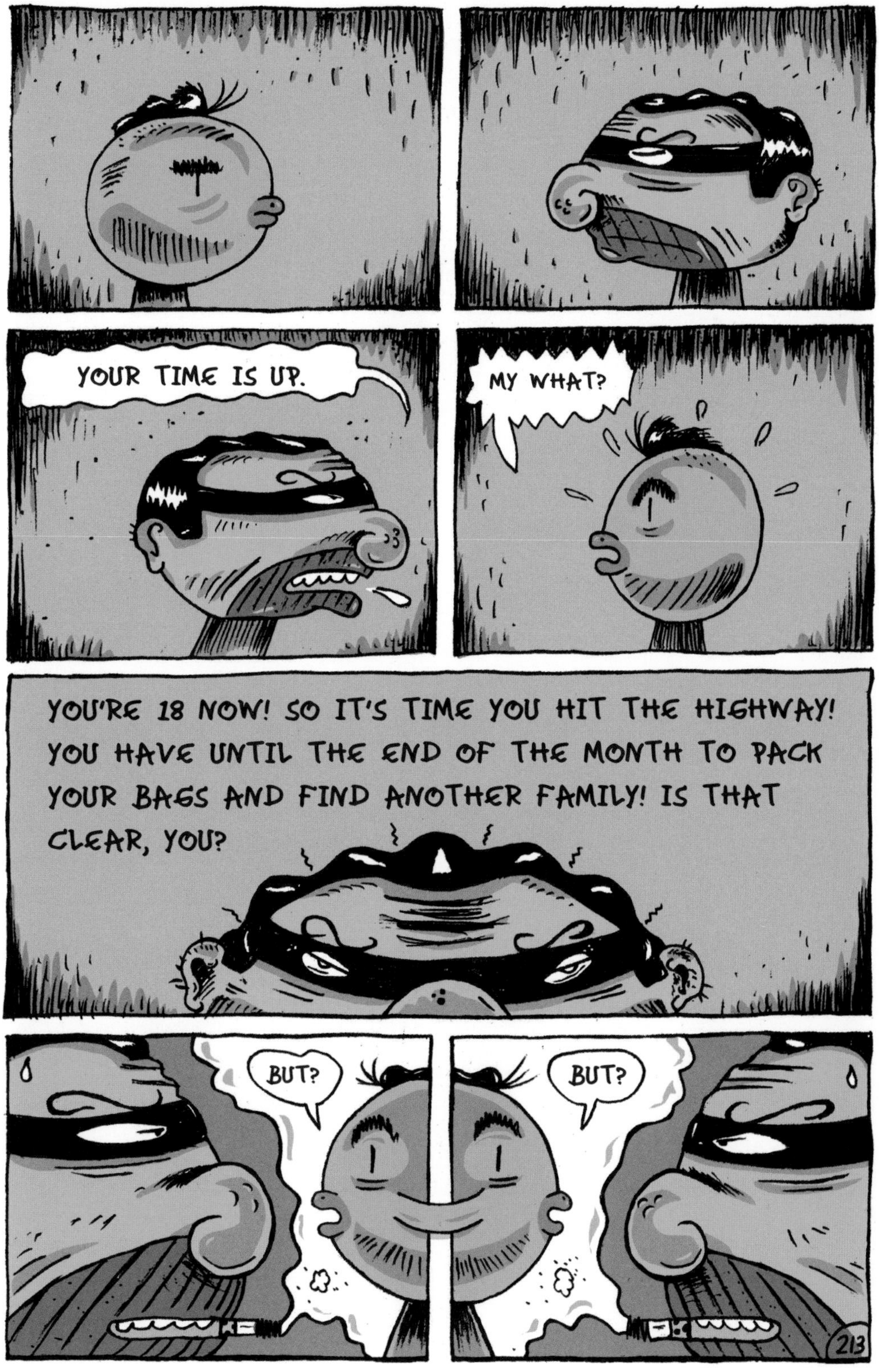
YOUR TIME IS UP.
MY WHAT?
YOU'RE 18 NOW! SO IT'S TIME YOU HIT THE HIGHWAY! YOU HAVE UNTIL THE END OF THE MONTH TO PACK YOUR BAGS AND FIND ANOTHER FAMILY! IS THAT CLEAR, YOU?
BUT?
BUT?
213

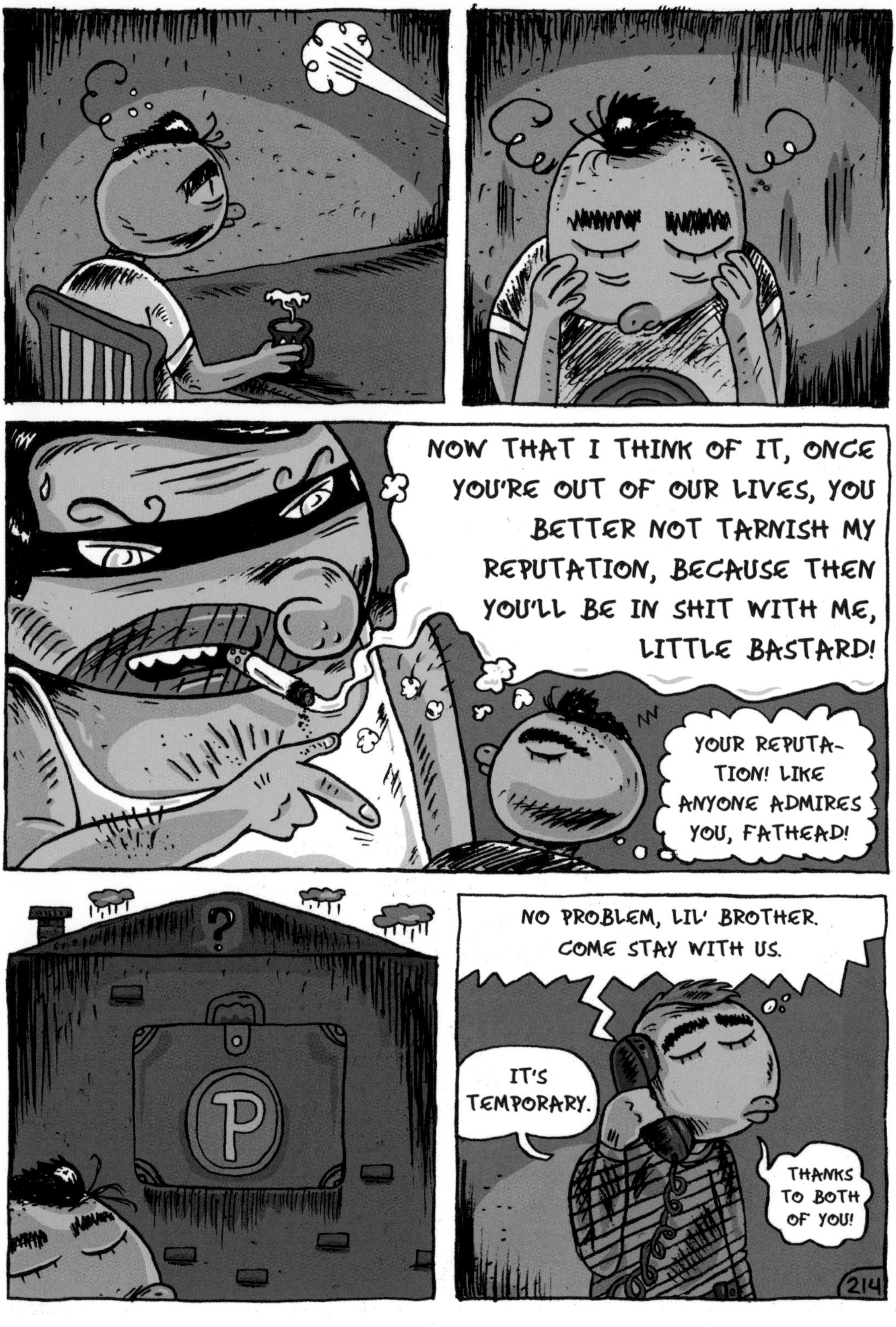
NOW THAT I THINK OF IT, ONCE YOU'RE OUT OF OUR LIVES, YOU BETTER NOT TARNISH MY REPUTATION, BECAUSE THEN YOU'LL BE IN SHIT WITH ME, LITTLE BASTARD!
YOUR REPUTA-TION! LIKE ANYONE ADMIRES YOU, FATHEAD!
P
NO PROBLEM, LIL' BROTHER. COME STAY WITH US.
IT'S TEMPORARY.
THANKS TO BOTH OF YOU!
214

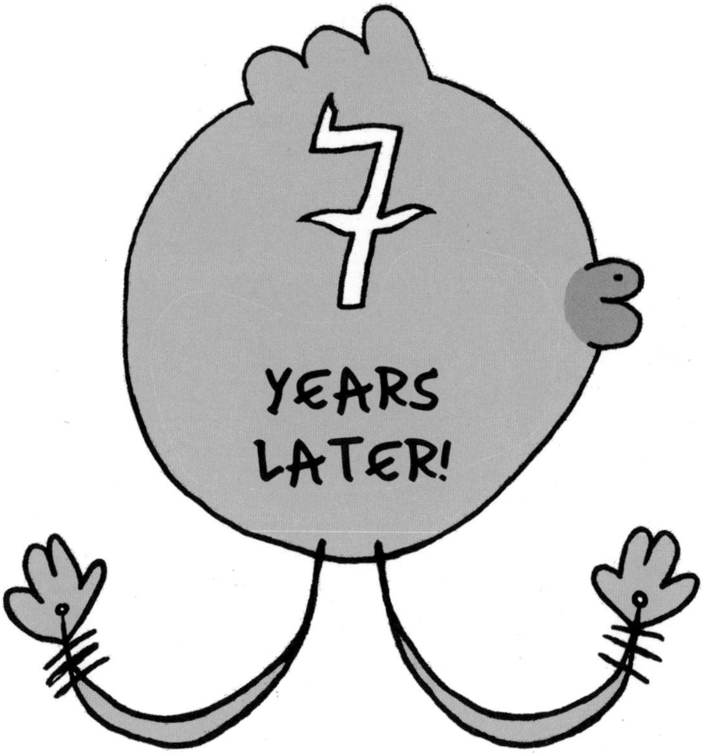
7
YEARS
LATER!

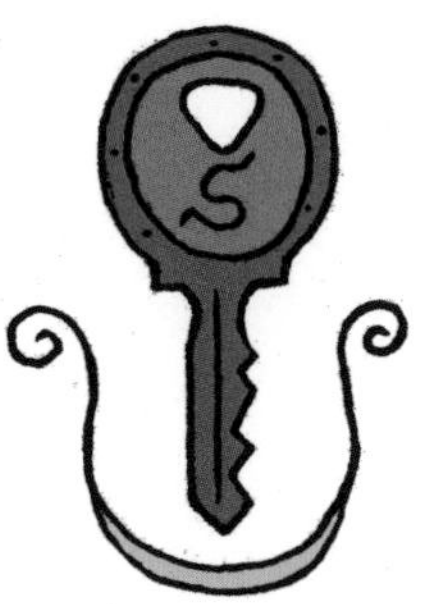

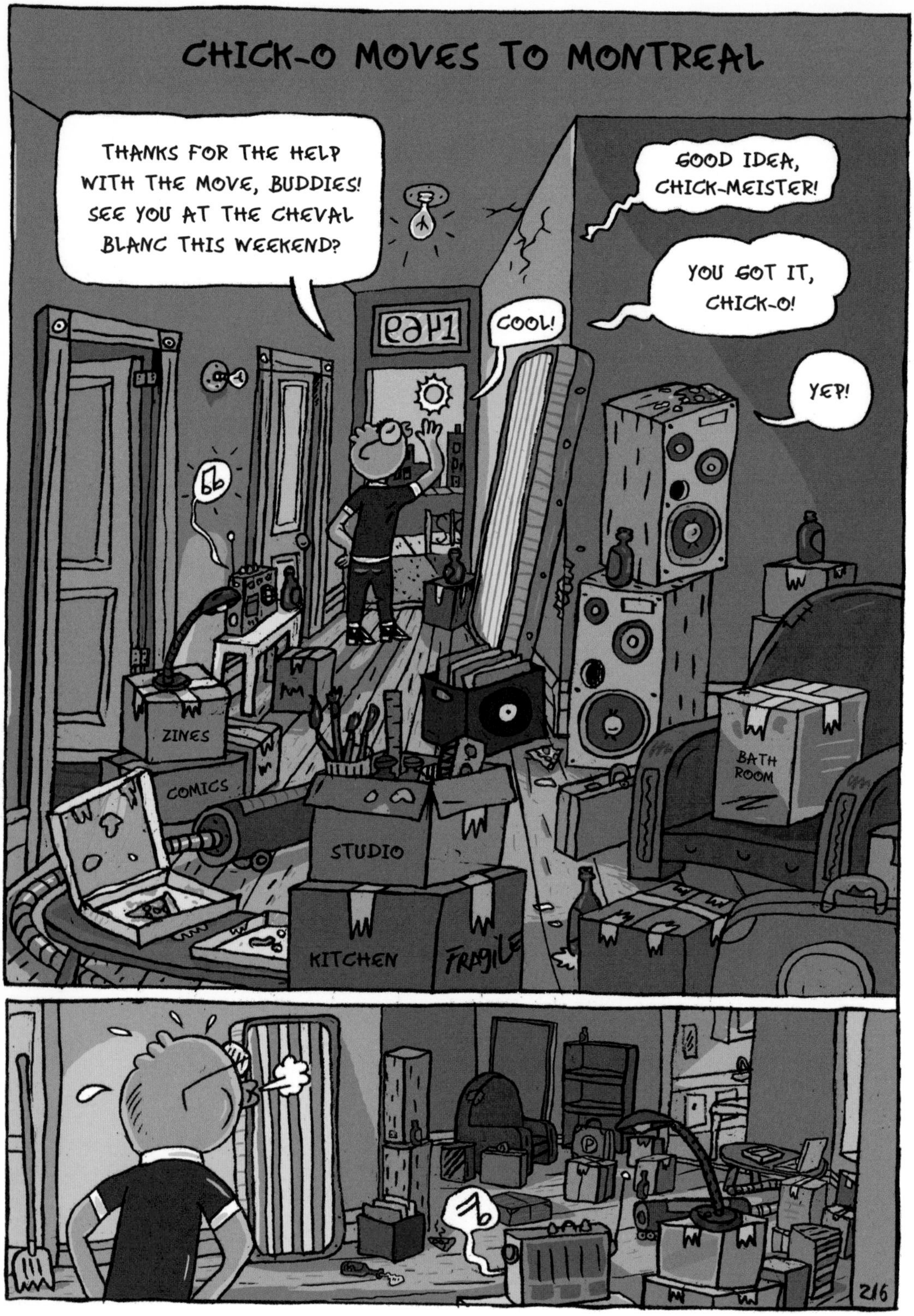
CHICK-O MOVES TO MONTREAL
THANKS FOR THE HELP WITH THE MOVE, BUDDIES! SEE YOU AT THE CHEVAL BLANC THIS WEEKEND?
GOOD IDEA, CHICK-MEISTER!
YOU GOT IT, CHICK-O!
COOL!
YEP!
ZINES
COMICS
STUDIO
KITCHEN
FRAGILE
BATH ROOM
216

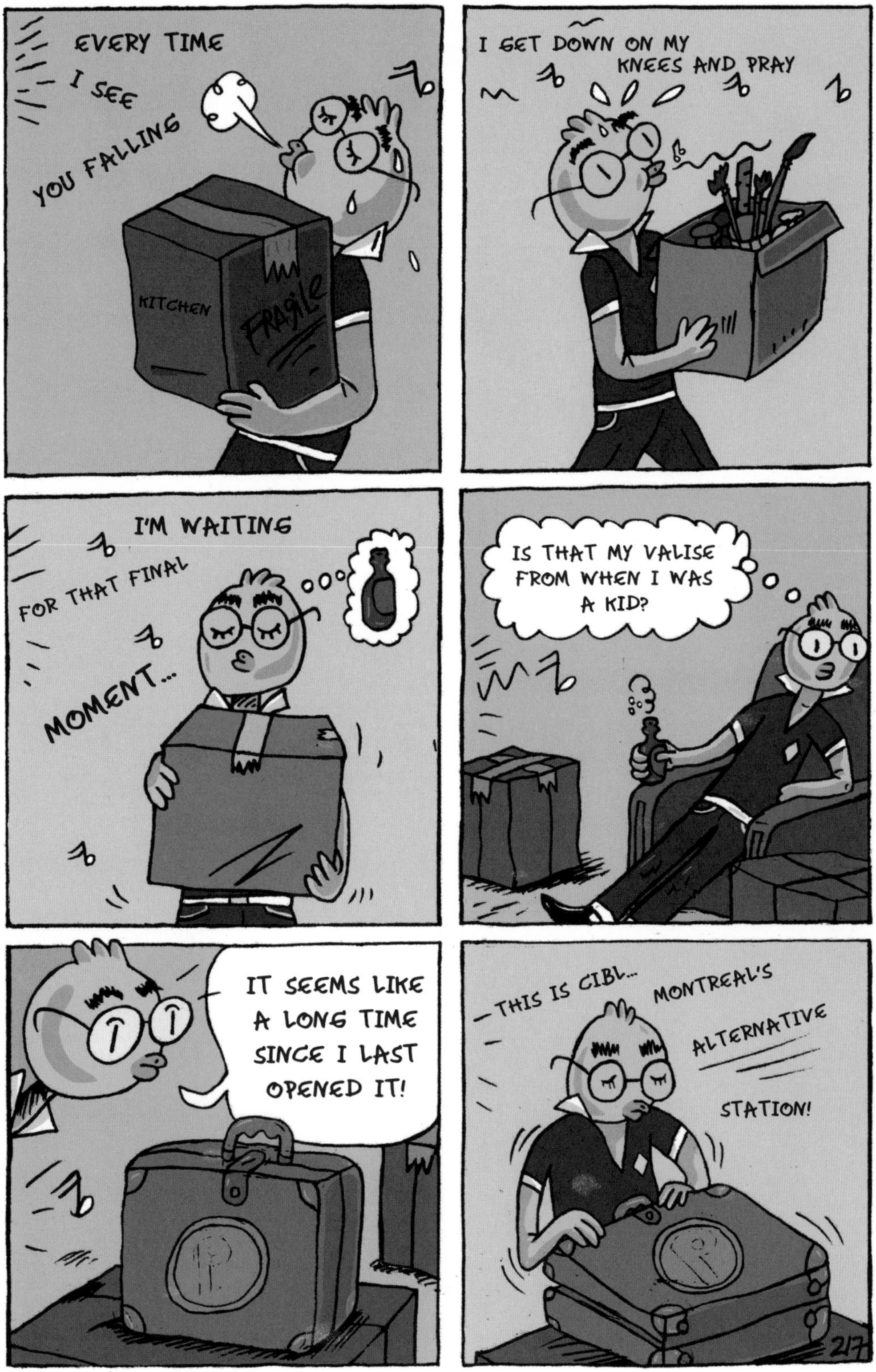

EVERY TIME
I SEE
YOU FALLING
KITCHEN
FRAGILE
I GET DOWN ON MY
KNEES AND PRAY
I'M WAITING
FOR THAT FINAL
MOMENT...
IS THAT MY VALISE FROM WHEN I WAS A KID?
IT SEEMS LIKE A LONG TIME SINCE I LAST OPENED IT!
THIS IS CIBL...
MONTREAL'S
ALTERNATIVE
STATION!
217

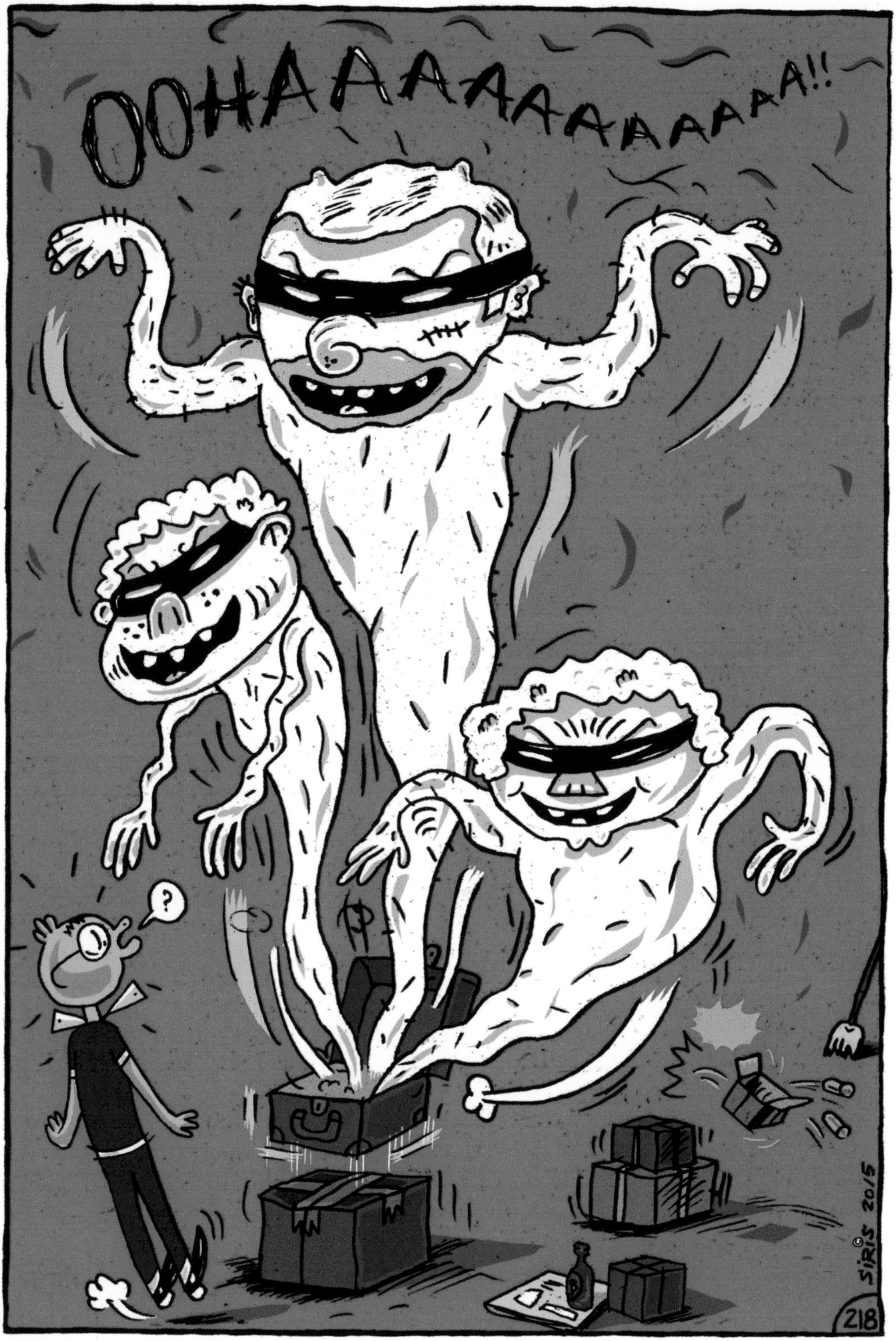
OOHAAAAAAAAAAAAA!!
?
SIRIS 2015
218

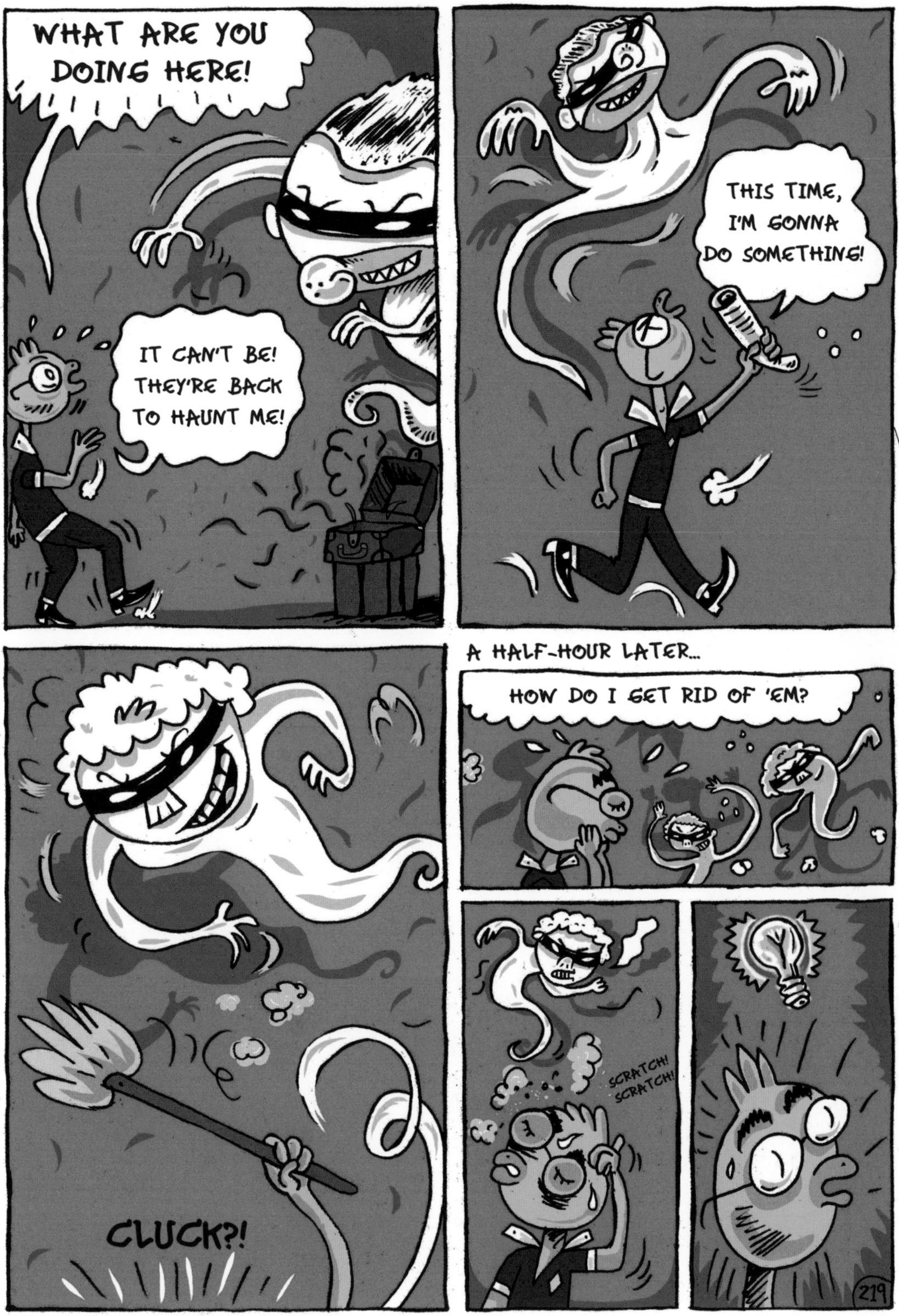
WHAT ARE YOU DOING HERE!
IT CAN'T BE! THEY'RE BACK TO HAUNT ME!
THIS TIME, I'M GONNA DO SOMETHING!
CLUCK?!
A HALF-HOUR LATER...
HOW DO I GET RID OF 'EM?
SCRATCH! SCRATCH!
219

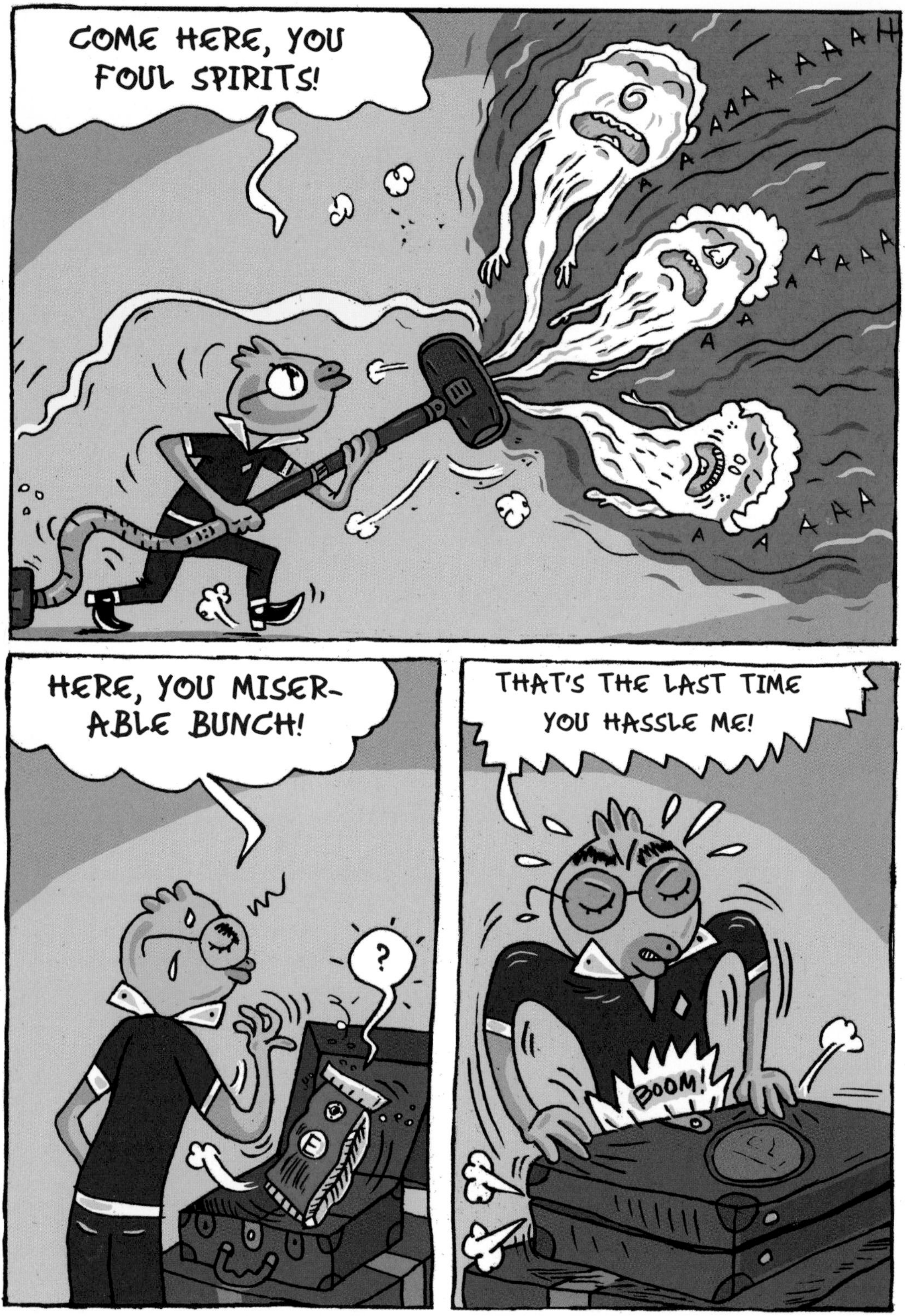
COME HERE, YOU FOUL SPIRITS!
AAAAAAAAAAAAAH
HERE, YOU MISER-ABLE BUNCH!
?
THAT'S THE LAST TIME YOU HASSLE ME!
BOOM!

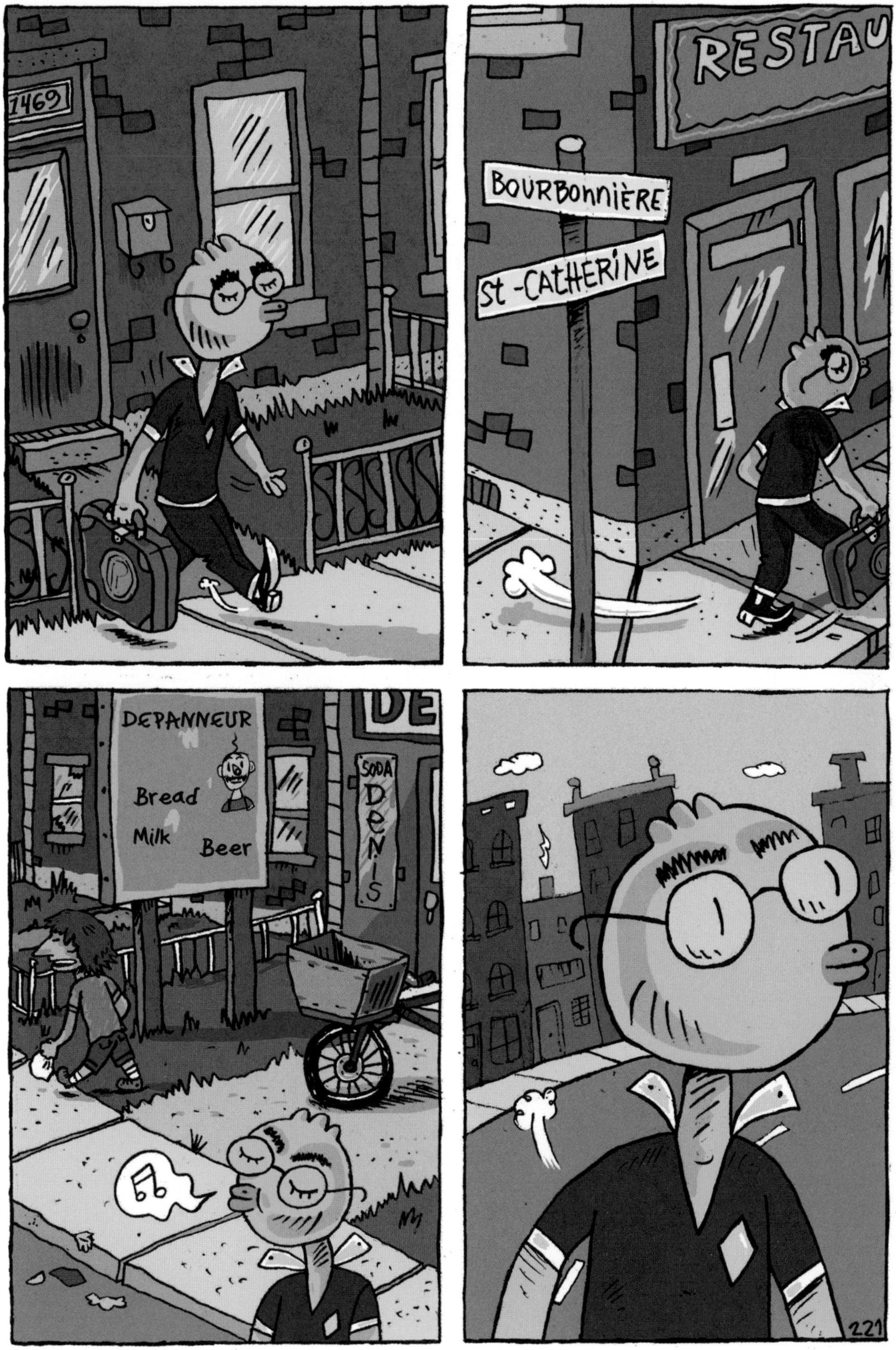
1469
RESTAU
BOURBONNIÈRE
St-CATHERINE
DEPANNEUR
Bread
Milk
Beer
SODA
DENIS
221

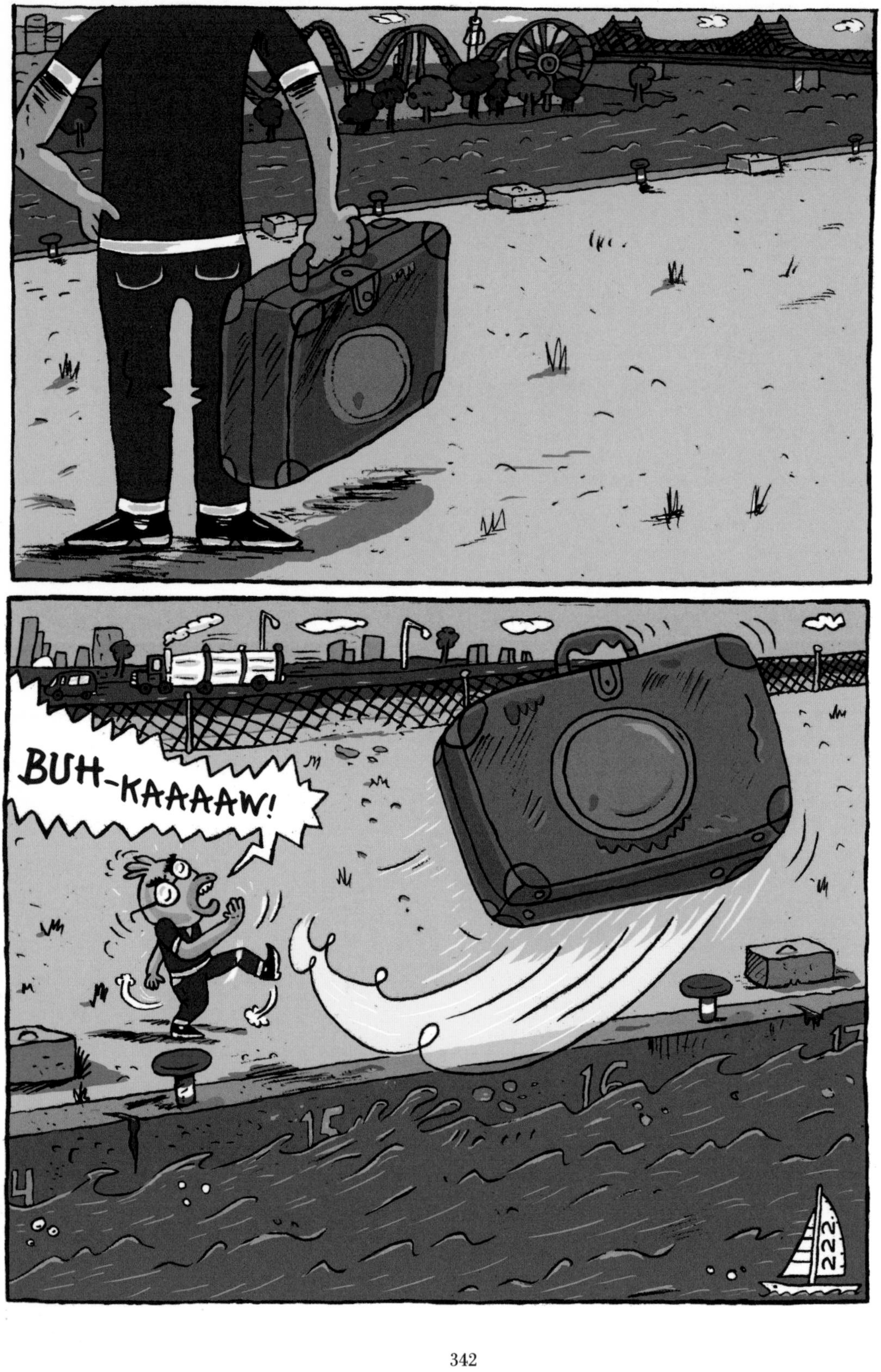
BUH-KAAAAW!

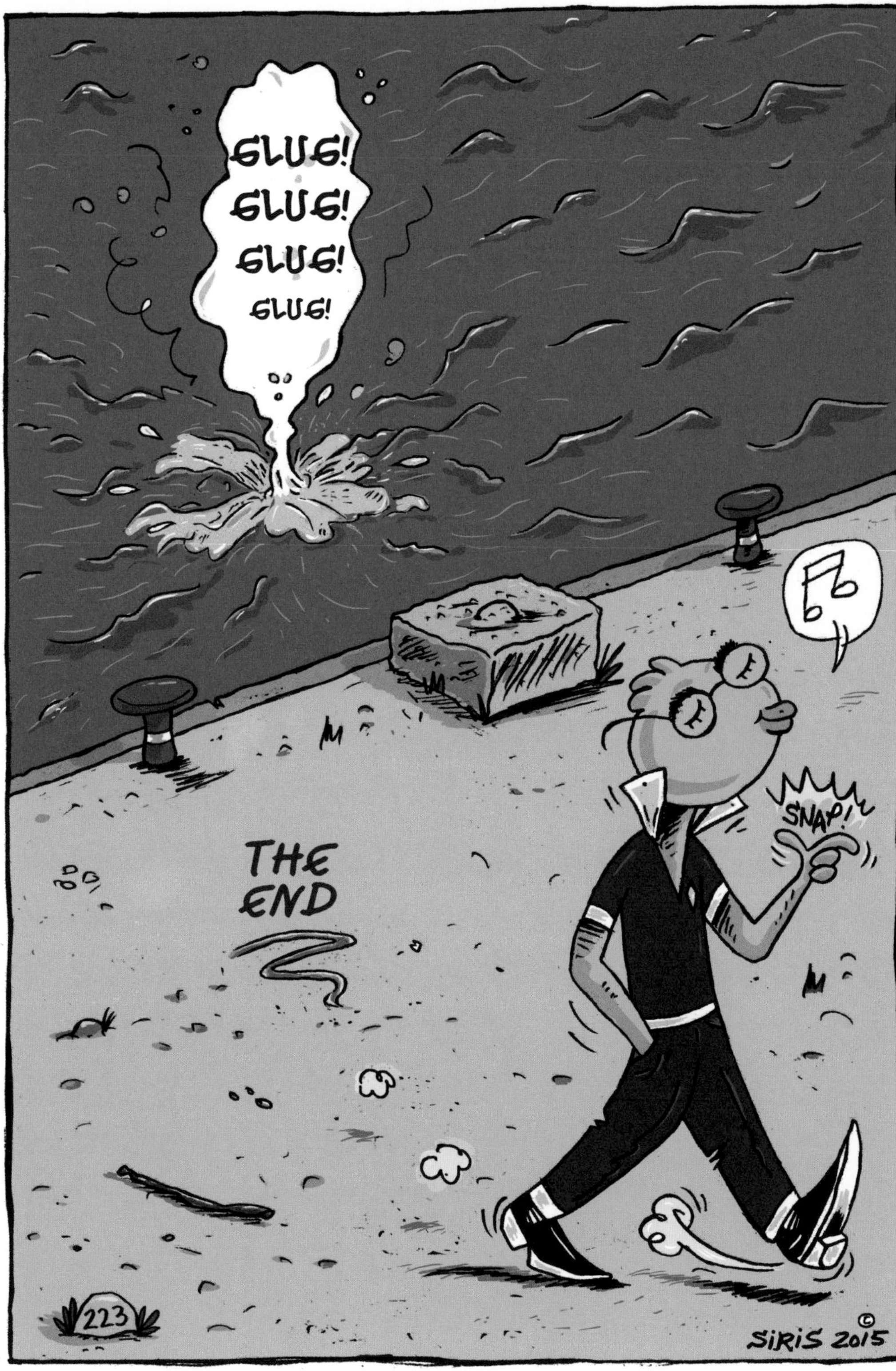
GLUG!
GLUG!
GLUG!
GLUG!
SNAP!
THE END
223
© SIRIS 2015

This book is dedicated to my late mother, Lucie Bélair.

I extend my thanks...

To Andy Brown, publisher of the English-language edition of this book. I am very grateful to him for the confidence he has placed in me.

To Frédéric and Martin at Les Éditions de la Pastèque, for the patience they afforded me while I was creating this book's original edition, *Vogue la valise*.

To the Canada Council for the Arts in 2003, and the Conseil des arts and des lettres du Québec in 2011, for their financial help.

And to all the people who supported me with their encouragement and their patience, without which I could not have finally finished the second part of *The Vagabond Valise*. This includes Line Gamache, Richard Beaulieu, Iris Boudreau, Serge Sirois, Carole Sirois, Danielle Sirois, Christine Sirois, my nephews and nieces, and all my colleagues in the world of comics! Sorry if I've forgotten names...

A special thanks to my sister Carole, who helped me tremendously with the first chapter.

I thank a hundred times all those who have bought one or two original pages from the first volume of *Vogue la valise*. I'm very grateful for this financial support, which allowed me to sit and draw without doing a thousand and one jobs. This allowed me to finish the second part of the 352-page tome that you hold in your hands. thanks to Stéphane Lemardelé and Isabelle Grenier, Nancy Saint-Onge and Denis Moisan, Michel Louis Viala and Sara Mills, Marc Bisaillon, Marc Tessier, Mario Girard and Josée Boulay, Bruno, Martin Desroches, Monique Vermandte and Marcel Gaudreau, Réal Godbout, Denis-Carl Robidoux and Stéphanie Mondor, Johanne Bérubé, Alain Réhel, Jacques Réhel, Paul Bordeleau, Sylvie Turgeon, Antonia Hendrix and Pierre Gamache, Pierre Saint-Marie and Brigitte Renaud, Danielle Sirois and Christian Aubry, Luc Grenier, Denis Bougard†, Claude Mayrand, Élaine Perron, Yves P. Pelletier, Renée Barrière and Michel de Bellefeuille, Zeb Peyrat, Gigi Perron, François Mayeux, Brigitte Martin, Luc Melanson, François Azambourg, Marie-Sophie Villeneuve, Sylvain Lemay and Rosaura Guzman Clunes, Geneviève Sirois, Hélène Deslières, Christian Quesnel, Louis Carrière, Jean-Charles Sarrazin and Nidia Sanchez, Rick Tremblay, and Bhirman Comtois.

To those whose likenesses appear in this book... thank you for accepting, you have inspired me tremendously! Marc Tessier, Sylvie Tremblay, Suzanne Labreche, Patricia Hudon, Mario Lavoie, cameo DJs "Robert Ouimet" and "Pierre St-Marie", Gino Salotti for the photo of Rob O, Dan Layer, Éric Lefebvre, the late Marc Langevin †, André Thériault, Normand Paquette, Christian Maillé and Francis Berger.

And a special thank-you to Alain Huot, for making me want to make comics!